The Bible of the Big Bands

by
Richard Grudens

Books by Richard Grudens

The Best Damn Trumpet Player
The Song Stars
The Music Men
Jukebox Saturday Night
Snootie Little Cutie-The Connie Haines Story
Jerry Vale-A Singer's Life
The Spirit of Bob Hope
Magic Moments - The Sally Bennett Story
Bing Crosby - Crooner of the Century
Chattanooga Choo-Choo - The Life and Times of the World
Famous Glenn Miller Orchestra
The Italian Crooners Bedside Companion
When Jolson was King

Published by

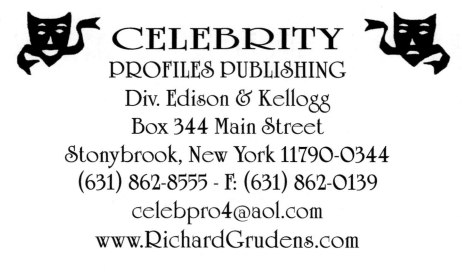

CELEBRITY
PROFILES PUBLISHING
Div. Edison & Kellogg
Box 344 Main Street
Stonybrook, New York 11790-0344
(631) 862-8555 - F: (631) 862-0139
celebpro4@aol.com
www.RichardGrudens.com

Book Design and Editing by Madeline Grudens

Library of Congress Control Number in Progress

ISBN: 978-0-9763877-5-6
Printed in the United States of America
King Printing Company Inc.
Lowell, MA 01852

INTRODUCTION

BY KATHRYN CROSBY

Well, here it is, Richard Grudens' long-awaited "Bible of the Big Bands."

Not only is he the ideal craftsman to envision and create such a project, In my mind, he's the only one.

A discussion of over forty of our twentieth century's big bands, many of its most famous musicians, thirty-eight of its greatest vocalists, their associates and arrangers, together with their predecessors, followers, and European counterparts, demands a scope which no other writer could presume to possess.

Largely as a consequence of my marriage to Bing, I was acquainted with perhaps a score of the celebrities whom you will encounter in this book, I could have recognized them on the street, and that was about it.

Richard Grudens, on the other hand, has the greatest breadth of anyone who has ever undertaken to describe the giants of our musical world. Here you will meet, in intimate detail, the leading performers of our finest era, and I trust you will enjoy the brilliant narrative as much as I did.

Read on, my friends.

Kathryn Crosby and Richard Grudens

STAR✹DUST

The Bible of the Big Bands

A Collection Of Personal Profiles Featuring Twentieth Century's Greatest Musical Stars

Bandleaders + Musicians +Vocalists + Arrangers

"A Million Nostalgic Memories Come To Life."
Frankie Laine

TABLE OF CONTENTS

Introduction By Kathryn Crosby 12

Foreword by Frankie Laine 16

PART ONE

The Big Bands - Will They Ever Return? 18

Star*Dust Song History 26

Opening Set-Richard Grudens 30

Art Hickman - Big Band Moments 33

So You Want To Lead A Band By Van Alexander 36

Themes Of The Big Bands 42

Your *Lucky Strike* Hit Parade 50

The Cotton Club Parade 53

Big Band Million Sellers 1921-1947 56

The First Gold Record 66

The Century's Best - RIAA Top Sellers 68

Authors Choice-Best Songs & Their Composers 74

WNEW Top 50 Poll 77

Great Moments In Big Band History 80

PART TWO
Remembering The Early Innovators

Paul Whiteman 88
Casa Loma 90
Jean Goldkette 90
Leo Reisman 91
Fred Waring's Pennsylvanians 92
Coon-Sanders Nighthawks 93
Vincent Lopez Speaking 93
Ted Lewis: "Is Everybody Happy?" 94
The Waltz King - Wayne King 94
The Great Fletcher Henderson 94
Gus Arnheim Cocoanut Grove Orchestra 95
Isham Jones 95
Ben Pollack - Bandleader Maker 96

The Recording Ban 262

The Street That Never Sleeps 264

Anecdotes & Fables 270

PART THREE
The Musicians and Vocalists - Person To Person

Budd Johnson - Musician's Musician. 272
Johnny Mince -The Truth About The Glenn Miller Sound 276
Lyle "Skitch" Henderson - What's In A Name? 280
Paul Tanner - Skunk Hollow To Millerland 283

The Greatest Male Vocalists
It's Make Believe Ballroom Time

with William B. Williams, Billy Eckstine,
Margaret Whiting & Dizzy Gillespie. 287
Bing Crosby - Hey, Jolson, It's Me! 293
Frank Sinatra - Secrets Of The Chairman 302
Dick Haymes - KeepinG It Simple 310
Tony Martin - What's Good About Goodbye 315
Nat "King" Cole - The Lush Life 319
Bob Eberly & Ray Eberle-Family Music 324
Tony Bennett - Another Saloon Singer 326
Jerry Vale - He Still Hears The Applause 331
Frankie Laine - Mr. Rhythm 336
Perry Como - The Barber From Canonsburg 341
Tex Beneke - Glenn's Reluctant Vocalist 344
Dean Martin - Andiamo 347
Mel Torme - The Velvet Fog 353
Johnny Mathis-The Voice Of Romance 357
Joe Williams - Every Day He Sang The Blues 362
Herb Jeffries - Arriving By Flamingo 366
Al Martino - He Has But One Heart 369
Guy Mitchell - A Crying Heart 372

Frances Langford - Where There's Hope, There's Langford 491

Lynn Roberts - Last Of The Big Band Singers 495

Dinah Washington - Time For A Name Change 499

Love & Marraige 503

More Ladies Who Sang With The Bands 505-514

Ivie Anderson • Pearl Bailey • Betty Carter • June Christy • Blossom
Dearie • Helen Humes • Carmen Mcrae • Dinah Shore • Keely Smith
Maxine Sullivan • Martha Tilton • Bea Wain • Helen Ward • Casssan-
dra Wilson • Lee Wiley

Honorable Mentions - Some More Chicks 515-520

The Canaries - The Girl Vocalists And Their Bands . . 521-535

Singing Groups Of The Big Band Era & Beyond . . . 536-556

Brox Sisters 536

Boswell Sisters 536

Andrews Sisters 537

Pied Pipers 541

Ink Spots 544

Modernaires 544

Mills Brothers 546

Lennon Sisters 549

Mcguire Sisters 553

King Sisters 553

Hi-Lo's 554

Ames Brothers 554

De Castro Sisters 555

Fontane Sisters 555

PART FOUR

Big Band Associates

John Hammond - Friend Of Jazz. 558
Mitch Miller -Major, Minor 558
Willard Alexander - Big Band Salesman 559
Sally Bennett - Big Band Hall Of Fame 562
Jack Lebo - Big Band Report 565
Al Ham - The Music Of Your Life Begins 566
John Tumpak - The Jazz Writer 567

The Broadcasters

Joe Franklin 569
Art Ford. 571
Martin Block 571
Al Jarvis 571
Peter Potter 573
Chuck Cecil 573
Al"Jazzbeaux" Collins 574
Jack Ellsworth 575
Fred Hall 576
Freddie Robbins 576
Symphony Sid 577
Dick Whittinghill 577
Jonathon Schwartz 577
Rich Conaty 578
Al Monroe 579
Chris Valenti 579
Don Kennedy. 580
Ron Della Chiesa. 581

The Big Band Ballrooms With Milt Bernhart 583-590

PART FIVE

The Song Writers - with Ervin Drake 592
The Arrangers 607-617
The Effects Of Bill Challis
The Musical Architects
> **With Berklee Music College Professor Richard Grudzinski:**
> **The Sinatra Effect-The Importance Of The Arrangers**

Nelson Riddle • Billy May • Frank De Vol • Gordon Jenkins

Billy Strayhorn • Bill Finegan • Pete Rugolo

Big Band Top Ten Picks 618

PART SIX

Big Bands Of Today (And The Active Tribute Bands)

Leading The Big Band Hall Of Fame Band In The 21st Century
   With Ben Grisafi, Musical Director 625
Mike Ficco's Long Island Jazz Orchestra 629
The Canadian Spitfire Band 630
The Pat Longo And His Hollywood Jazz Band 631
The Max Vax Orchestra And Big Band 631
Vince Giordano & The Nighthawks 631
Jerry Costanzo And His Swingtime Big Band 632

"Hey, You Must Be One Of The Newer Fellers" - *Bing To Frank In High Society*

Tony B. Babino 637
Jane Monheit 639
Michael Buble 640
Peter Cincotti 641
Julia Rich 641

Tom Postilio 643
John Primerano 644
Lou Lanza 646
Diana Krall 648
Laura Fygi • Steve Tyrell • Madeline Peyroux • Norah Jones 650-651

The European Bands Over There Then & Now 352-680
        The Max Wirz Report Including The Special: U.K.
        John Miller's China Gig 2007

Europe & England's Honorable Mentions 681-687

PART SEVEN

The Lists

Big Band Publications 688
What's In a Name - Non De Plume 691
Top Ten Big Band Favorites by Celebrities. 618

Bibliography 693

About The Author 696

Acknowledgements 697

Commemorative Frank Sinatra Stamps - 2008

Signs of the Times

FOREWORD

by Frankie Laine

Frankie Laine

For over twenty-five years Richard Grudens and I have contemplated the mercurial condition, or ups and downs if you will, of the state of the Golden Age of Music, known to most of you as the Big Band Era, along with its bandleaders, musicians and vocalists. At our first meeting backstage at what was once known as the Westbury Music Fair on Long Island, he, along with radio's legendary WNEW William B. Williams, Helen O'Connell, Warren Covington of the Pied Pipers group, Tommy Dorsey ghost band leader Buddy Morrow, and myself, spent a few hours discussing the subject between performances on stage that evening.

A few years later, during the inception of his first book, The Best Damn Trumpet Player, we worked together to present an illustrous list of shorts about many musical stars of that time. Richard would forward installment after installment as he wrote it and we would talk on the phone from my home in San Diego to his in Stony Brook, adapting, changing, even adding to each one until joint revision satisfaction was achieved.

In that landmark book I stated the following: "That starting with the Big Bands in the 1930s and continuing through today, we were blessed with the opportunity to enjoy music that creates a feeling of well being and familiarity. Not the frenetic sounds of the various types of rock, and other more modern, similar musical material, but the pure melodic sounds of some bands and the swinging jazz styles of others have provided a common bond between all peoples, no matter what their nationalities or social background.

"Time, unfortunately has robbed us of the pleasure of having most of the great performers among us physically, but their recordings survive them. One can help but wonder how, for instance, Glenn Millers's style would have evolved over the years had he not met his untimely death over the English Channel.

The Big Bands served a purpose aside from soothing our senses with their musical arrangements -they spawned such legendary singers as Doris Day, Helen Forrest, Kay Starr, Connie Haines, and Frank Sinatra, to name a few. Although severely restricted in the development of their own styles with the bands, many band singers eventually went out on their own, giving them the opportunity to be as innovative as their capabilities permitted.

Nat "King" Cole was one of the first balladeers to start his career without the aid of a Big Band background. And, not to blow my own horn, but I believe I was the first white male singer to achieve success sans a Big Band boost. Definitely not an easy road, but I've never regretted any of the hardship, as I met many kind, helpful people on the way up. Among them were Perry Como, Carl Fischer, Al Jolson, Bing Crosby, Hoagy Carmichael and Al Jarvis.

There are still a number of bands working today, some are ghosts of the original Big Bands, like Artie Shaw's - with leader Dick Johnson, and Glenn Miller's -led by the incomparable Larry O'Brien with original Miller arrangements, both appearing all over the country like "the good old days." There are the singers like Tony B. (Babino) and Michael Bublé, Natalie Cole, and Harry Connick, Jr. who have emerged, a throwback to the days of the great vocalists. And, Tony Bennett is still knocking them dead.

Although the time of the great bands, musicians, vocalists, and arrangers has passed, Richard Grudens has embarked upon a labor of love, painstakingly researching the lives of those included in this book, some who are and were personal friends of us both, which, of course, eased the way towards this monumental works.

But come - spend a few hours reminiscing about the people who will live in our hearts and, hopefully, our children's forever.

Frankie Laine
San Diego, California
December 2006

Part One

The Big Bands - Will They Ever Return?
Star Dust Song History
Opening Set - Richard Grudens
Art Hickman - Big Band Moments
So You Want to Lead A Band - by Van Alexander
Themes of The Big Bands
Your Lucky Strike Hit Parade
The Cotton Club Parade
Big Band Million Sellers - 1921-1947
The First Gold Record
The Century's Best - RIAA Top Sellers
Author's Choice - Best Songs & Their Composers
WNEW Top 50 Poll
Great Moments in Big Band History

Martin Block on his Make Believe Ballroom Program

The Big Bands

Will They Ever Return?

It was Thomas Wolfe who wisely counseled the romantics when he declared: "You can never go home again." But some people are afflicted with what is known as Joe Di Maggio Syndrome. They fantasize that someday the legendary Yankee Clipper, Joe Di Maggio, will somehow return to Yankee Stadium to smash a game-winning, walk-off home run to win a close pennant race.

Do you recall those who once believed that Dean Martin and Jerry Lewis would be reunited once again, and that the followers of Ian Fleming's 007 spy thriller movies somehow expected Sean Connery to suddenly rejuvenate his aged body and make over his face to personally embark upon yet another James Bond film to please the pleading faithful?

Despite all this fantasy, it is said that some speculate about a full and immense return of the Golden Era of the Big Bands as America's prime entertainment. Over the years the Big Bands have been reduced to the mini- proliferation of a smattering of "ghost bands," a term coined by none other than Woody Herman whose own ghost band is performing today under the baton of Frank Tiberi leading Woody's Thundering Herd.

At the height of the Big Band Era Glenn Miller was experiencing unprecedented success when he disappeared in December 1944 while flying over the English Channel to set up the American Band of the Allied Expeditionary Force in Paris for the entertainment of our fighting men. Afterwards a number of valiant attempts to continue the band were tried by former members or associates Jerry Gray, Ray Anthony, Tex Beneke, Ray McKinley, Ralph Flanagan and Buddy De Franco, not exactly in that order, all trying to keep the Glenn Miller sound alive, but they were unable to fully re-create the original, elusive, disciplined sound that Glenn worked for so long and so hard. Glenn's stern dedication and all-around talent for keeping the band together in all aspects was no longer present, nor was his skillful editing or the presence of his unique choice of arrangers.

Today, over 60 years later, Larry O'Brien remains the longtime leader of the Glenn Miller Orchestra playing mostly the original charts and touring everywhere for most of the year. The Florida-based Glenn Miller organization has also issued franchises to Glenn Miller Orchestras in Europe, Australia, and England. And, despite the fact that mostly rock and roll and similar styles of music dominate the airwaves, a handful of bands still roam the limited, but growing Big Band venues around the country.

Artie Shaw Orchestra with Helen Forrest

There are still some dwindling numbers of disc jockeys playing Big Band music during off-hour radio, like Atlanta based Big Band Jump championed by Don Kennedy, and Jack Ellsworth's Memories in Melody You can also tune in Big Band music on Music Choice, a computer generated 24 hour a day commercial-free television channel and on Sirius Satellite radio which can be installed in your car.

Legend has it that the Big Band Era began with Art Hickman's band in San Francisco about 1930, although it was Benny Goodman who officially launched the Big Band or Swing Era one night in 1935 at the Palomar Ballroom in Los Angeles. Benny and his musicians were tired of the boring dance music they were churning out night after night for dancers, consequently, on the final night of his engagement he defiantly broke out into a wild, swinging session which surprised and delighted everyone, including Palomar management. The crowd went wild and the King of Swing was crowned that night.

The Big Band Era developed from thereon as one band after another was spawned in a process when individual band members spun off successive bands by forming their own musical organizations. The immensely popular Paul Whiteman, Fletcher Henderson and Ben Pollack bands alone accounted for many spinoffs: Louis Armstrong and Coleman Hawkins off Henderson; Benny Goodman, Glenn Miller, Charlie Spivak and Jack Teagarden off Pollack: Tommy and Jimmy Dorsey and Henry Busse off Whiteman, and so on and on it continued until there was a proliferation of hundreds of Big Bands operating throughout the land.

It was clearly an uphill fight for those pioneers: "We were all struggling, "said Harry James in has last interview with me in 1982," and nobody was getting paid. Guys were jumping from one band to another. I almost gave up running my own band a number of times."

Conditions in the late thirties were just right for the formation of the Big Bands. There were dance pavilions, ballrooms, and large motion picture stages where Big Bands performed to standing room only patrons.

Big Band leaders became the great celebrities of the day, and most bands featured vocalists and sometimes added a vocal group like the Pied Pipers, Modernaires, King Sisters, Andrews Sisters, or Boswell Sisters, where within some of the vocalists developed their craft: Bing Crosby, Frank Sinatra, Dick Haymes, Perry Como, Don Cornell, Doris Day, Connie Haines, and Jo Stafford, to name just a few. The Big Bands dominated prime-time network radio whether on their own or attached to popular big-time programs. Bandleader Skinnay Ennis conducted on Bob Hope's show, John Scott Trotter on Bing Crosby's, Phil Harris on Jack Benny's. Benny Goodman, Glenn Miller, Harry James, the Dorsey's and Ozzie Nelson were featured regulars on their own programs. With network radio linking stations from New York to California, the shows were heard coast-to-coast for the first time attracting millions of new fans.

The bands would perform on live "remotes" from major hotels, immense ballrooms, movie theater stages, and endless radio studios throughout the land. Fans could now hear the Big Band sounds filter directly into their living rooms for the first time. The most popular bandleaders became featured motion picture stars complete with their bands and vocalists intact. Selected biographies of Big Band leaders drew millions to movie theaters.

After the war, for many reasons, the very popular dance pavilions began closing down. Most of them were located in amusement parks at the outskirts of just about every American town which was accessible by electric trolleys, surface railroads, or just a short walk away. With the war over, the availability of automobiles and commercial air flights radically increased, altering the way people lived and traveled. They were no longer restricted to just attending local Big Band dances at convenient, town pavilions and parks. It was also a time when street railways were being dismantled in favor of the more mobile buses and automobiles, overwhelmingly promoted by expanding oil and tire companies now back in postwar consumer production. Automobiles could transport you to the drive-in movie, where couples had more privacy, or down newly constructed interstate highways leading to other kinds of attractions held every where and anywhere.

When the advent of television arrived it kept many Big Band fans at home watching wrestling and roller derby competition and variety shows with former vaudevillians who appeared on programs like Toast of the Town emceed by newspaper columnist Ed Sullivan. The Big Band radio showcases diminished in favor of the revolutionary picture tube located in every living room....and it was free of admission charges. Remote broadcasts were silenced. Network radio was forced to reduce an array of musical programs for lack of listeners. Listeners were now watchers. There was nothing to see on radio.

Television shows featuring Howdy Doody, I Love Lucy, Molly Goldberg, Milton Berle and Arthur Godfrey and dozens of other shows erased the Big Band music of Artie Shaw, Woody Herman, Tommy Dorsey, Harry James and Benny Goodman. All the above changes contributed to the demise of the beautifully developed musical wonder we knew as the Big Band Era, giving way to an age of the great vocalists: Frank Sinatra, Perry Como, Kay Starr, Dick Haymes, Frankie Laine, Margaret Whiting, Doris Day, Billy Eckstine, Sarah Vaughan, Dinah Shore, Patti Page and Rosemary Clooney, mostly on recordings, then graduating to the television tube itself, although some of them started with the Big Bands. Eventually, the encroachment of rock and roll and Top Forty radio pressed forward with the Beatles and Elvis Presley leading the charge, which, contrary to summary predictions of the time, has lasted though today.

It's safe to say the Big Band Era was comprised of very special ingredients like those occurring in a classic painting - never to be captured again in quite the same way. You may ask, "Will there ever be another Glenn Miller, Tommy Dorsey or Benny Goodman?" I answer with "Will there ever be another Renoir, Manet or Picasso?"

The will and interest to exactly recreate any great success is one of man's eternal failings. The manner in which a successful creation evolves can never be planned or measured in advance. Frank Sinatra clones never work, and there have been hundreds, I doubt that anyone during this period could have simply created the Big Band Era phenomenon by formulating a plan: "Let's organize Benny, Glenn, Erskine, Duke, Harry and the rest of the stellar musicians on this list I have in my hand and get them started with their own musical organizations and we'll call it The Big Band Era.

Preposterous!

Although the performers of the Big Band Era along with their sidemen, vocalists, arrangers and songwriters, dominated performances of almost all popular music for some twenty-five years, it is certain that it evolved quite accidentally. Since the 1960s dedicated followers have tried over and over to proclaim a rebirth of the Big Bands. However, who will reiterate the melodious "Frenesi" with the undulating excellence that once punctuated the fastidious clarinet of Artie Shaw, or dish up the brassy, expressive trumpet of Harry James playing "You Made Me Love You?" And, who do you find to replace Glenn Miller performing his endearing masterpiece "Moonlight Serenade?"

Who would you have play "Apple Honey" or "Caledonia" ...surely not even Woody himself.

"My favorite record is the one we'll make next year!" Woody once told me, "You can't live in the past."

Preserved on records, and, although re-created and enhanced on CDs, none of the above recordings could ever sound the same musically or spiritually. You would need the original musicians in their corresponding musical mindset, require the same quality studio, mikes, instruments and equipment, good or bad. The chemical expression and ability of each of those players would have to be identical to the original. The charts may be the same, but as English writer Agatha Christie once said about a character in one of her stories, the Big Band revival fan is "...an old soldier with an unfortunate weakness for reliving the past."

It's a fact that music constantly changes. "Music today is completely different than the music of the forties," Harry james told me in the early 1980's, "You would think that people would like only the old stuff. Not so! Anyway, I don't think you can compare what you used to do with what you have to do to stay alive in this business today."

The Big Band Era is considered history now with expected, lingering aftershocks that include revival, reliving, reunion, and, of course, the written word. Along the Big Band circuit today are those Ghost Bands I mentioned earlier, each with a famous Big Bandleader name attached, a name of former greatness and fame in hopes to attract former fans and their children to their concerts. These bands tour and perform on cruise ships always adding new members and ever changing leaders.

Today, as of May, 2008, your favorite bands still tour. Among them are Harry James, Les Elgart, Hal McIntyre, Nelson Riddle, Cab Calloway, Tommy Dorsey, Les Brown, Russ Morgan, Jimmy Dorsey, Tommy Dorsey, Dick Jurgens, Gene Krupa, Woody Herman, Sammy Kaye, Artie Shaw, Count Basie, and, of course Glenn Miller.

The Big Bands were the delicious musical relics of the past who attached their indelible mark upon several generations of music lovers - both those who enjoyed dancing and those who preferred listening. Through the modern magic of compact disks with their advanced technology, the excellence of the Big Band Era's original material carries on forever, or as long as there are ears to listen. The original will never come back for it has been clearly over for some time. This book will try to offer to chronicle a portion of some of the lives and lists of the principal and even the obscure and certainly the successors to the Big Band Era.

Stardust - the Song's History

Stardust ...

... IS THE SIGNATURE STANDARD SONG OF THE BIG BAND ERA

The music of the song "Stardust" was originally composed by Hoagy Carmichael in 1927 as a jazz piece. Legend says he wrote it on a battered piano on the grounds of Indiana University in the alumnus campus hangout, the Book Nook. A friend, Stuart Gorrell suggested the name of the tune, saying: "It sounds like dust from stars coming down through the summer sky."

Lyrics were added by Mitchell Parish two years later. This landmark song has been recorded more times by more artists than any other song. It has became a slow ballad recorded by Glenn Miller, Artie Shaw, Louis Armstrong, John Coltrane, Dizzy Gillespie, and vocalists Frank Sinatra, Billie Holiday, Mel Torme', Connie Francis, Ella Fitzgerald, Willie Nelson, Harry Connick Jr., Barry Manilow, Rod Stewart, and more than a thousand others. Yes, more than a thousand, proved in the 1980's by Jim Ferguson of radio station WGSM, Huntington Station, New York. He spent more than three years searching out all the possible recordings of the tune and easily surpassed over 1500 versions. It became the ultimate feature of his morning AM radio show. The song has been translated into more than forty languages.

The best vocal version of "Stardust" belongs to Nat "King" Cole, whose recording was the last recording played on radio station WQEW, successor to WNEW, New York, before it went off the air on December 28, 1998. The best instrumental version belongs to Artie Shaw. It has sold over eight million copies.

In a contest held by WQEW-AM (1560 on the dial) for the 156 best recordings of all time among their listeners "Stardust" came in second (Nat King Cole), and third (Artie Shaw).

It is more than conjecture that "Stardust" is considered the finest love song ever written. The verse matches the melodic verse beautifully.

STAR DUST

Mitchell Parish & Hoagy Carmichael

And now the purple dusk of twilight time
Steals across the meadows of my heart
High up in the sky the little stars climb
Always reminding me that we're apart
You wandered down the lane and far away
Leaving me a song that will not die
Love is now the Stardust of yesterday
The music of the years gone by

Refrain

Sometimes I wonder why
I spend the lonely night
Dreaming of a song?
The melody haunts my reverie
And I am once again with you
When our love was new
And each kiss an inspiration
But that was long ago
Now my consolation
Is in the Stardust of a song
Beside a garden wall
When stars are bright
You are in my arms
The nightingale tells the fairy tale
Of paradise where roses grew
Tho' I dream in vain
In my heart it will remain
My Stardust melody
The memory of love's refrain.

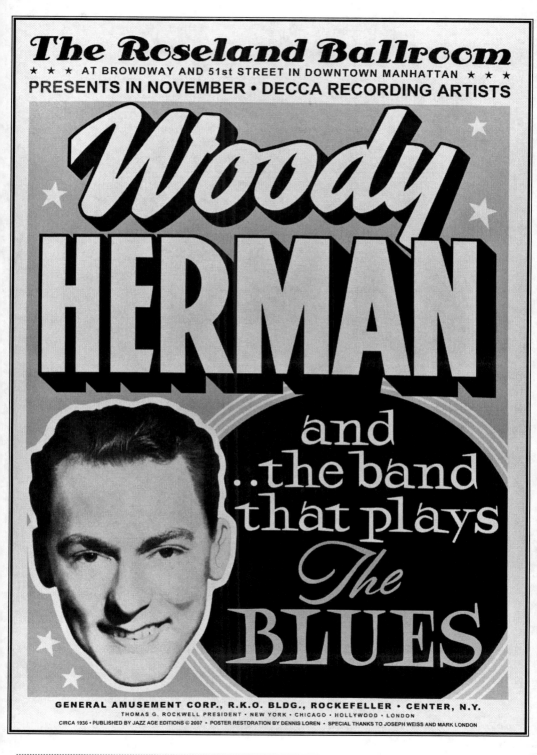

Ted Lewis Orchestra - "Is Everybody Happy?"

OPENING SET

Every kid had his heroes. To some, it was the crew of StarTreck and the Enterprise, and to others the players in Star Wars. Some found the greatness of Curie, Einstein or Edison to appreciate. I have friends, like you who had revered the demeanor of John Wayne or the excitement of "joltin" Joe Di Maggio and his New York Yankees.

My heroes were the bandleaders and vocalists of the thirties, forties, and fifties, in a time known as The Big Band Era, although some called it the The Swinging Years. There you could find, as my mother once defined, the noisy, brash new sound that she didn't necessarily appreciate because it eclipsed her own heroes, those sturdy Sigmund Romberg operettas, Al Jolson's magic and her favorite Jeanette McDonald and Nelson Eddy duets, as well as her love for the early Crosby recordings.

However, the Big Bands accomplished for me what Hopalong Cassidy and Gene Autry did for others. These musicians and vocalists instilled in me the musical satisfaction I needed. When I skipped classes at Manhattan's Food Trades High School on West 13th Street in the late forties, I traded the rolling out of puff pastry classes for the sights and sounds of Benny Goodman, Harry James, Count Basie, Glenn Miller, Woody Herman , or Gene Krupa, performing either at the Paramount, the Strand,or Roxy theaters. I was a New York kid listening to the great sounds of my time who received considerable support from New York's radio station W.N.E.W. and it's legendary disk jockey, Martin Block.

Many years had passed, and then suddenly and urgently in 1980, I realized my heroes were disappearing from the face of this earth: No, no, not their music, individual or collective, which of course is permanently preserved on records, tapes, CDs and film, but the living men and women, the flesh and blood human beings who actually performed this wonderful music for my own personal pleasure, providing me with the musical nutrition I required all my young life. So I realized then I had to make an effort to meet these heroes face-to-face, elbow to elbow, eyeball to eyeball, before it was too late and they were gone. So I earnestly initiated a search for those celebrity lions. Fortunately, I was once a magazine writer who also wrote news and sports for N.B.C. News, The Bob & Ray Radio show, as well as the early Today Show back in the early fifties. Then, as fortune would have it, I picked up a copy of a tabloid size entertainment-oriented newspaper called Long Island P.M. which was circulated to New York area hotels and restaurants.

In that particular issue, Paul Raymond, its owner and editor, advertised for writers and I answered the call submitting a query for a short article I wrote about an interesting, although little-known (but much revered) Big Band arranger Bill Challis, who was an arranger with Paul Whiteman's great King of Jazz Orchestra of the thirties, and who once arranged charts for legendary cornetist, Bix Biederbecke, bandleaders Jean Goldkette and Glenn Miller, to name a few. Bill Challis and I shared many hours together while he was working temporarily as a clerk in a building supply yard in Uniondale, Long Island during the mid 60's and we would chat away about the big band business while I, a distributor salesman, was waiting to write orders for materials and fireplace flues for his boss. Raymond accepted the piece and I was on my way. The first assignment was an interview with Broadway's Earl Wrightson and Lois Hunt at their Long Island home on the North Shore. I was elated at the assignment and Raymond was happy with the results. Although he could not pay me much, (his fledgling newspaper operated from his home) we hit it off and I traded my acceptance as his chief entertainment writer for expenses, but it didn't matter since it was a jump-start towards my goal.

The rest of the story is contained throughout these pages as my appreciation goes out to Paul Raymond, for his newspaper was the catalyst for the implementation of my otherwise impossible dream.

RICHARD GRUDENS, STONYBROOK, NEW YORK 2008

Jean Goldkette Orchestra - Bill Challis in Circle

ARRANGED
&
PLAYED
by
ART HICKMAN
AND HIS
HOTEL ST. FRANCIS
ORCHESTRA

6

ART HICKMAN
BIG BAND MOMENTS

The Very First Dance Band

There seems to be little question about the Art Hickman band being the first organized dance band formed at the foundation of the Big Band Era.

Before drummer, pianist , Hickman, dance bands were usually formed by pickup musicians who played impromptu settings without a name to the band or an organized group.

Beginning in 1913, Art Hickman organized his band to entertain the San Francisco Seals Baseball team, then brought his original six piece group of players to the St. Francis Hotel. After his engagement at the 1915 San Francisco World's Fair the demand for big band entertainment was created, especially for dancing, and the demand increased which spawned many new bands that eventually formed what has become known as the Big Band Era.

While at the St. Francis Hotel, the story goes that the great Florenz Ziegfeld was there one night and invited Hickman to play at the New York Biltmore Hotel Roof, an engagement which lasted almost a year followed by an steadier job playing for Ziegfeld during the run of his 1920 Ziegfeld Follies show on Broadway.

Hickman was invited to be the dance band at the opening of the famed Cocoanut Grove nightclub located in the Ambassador Hotel in Los Angeles. After that engagement, Hickman once again returned to the Biltmore in New York.

Hickman recorded with Columbia and The Victor Talking Machine Company.

Hickman wrote a song called "Rose Room," which was also his theme song throughout his tenure as a bandleader.

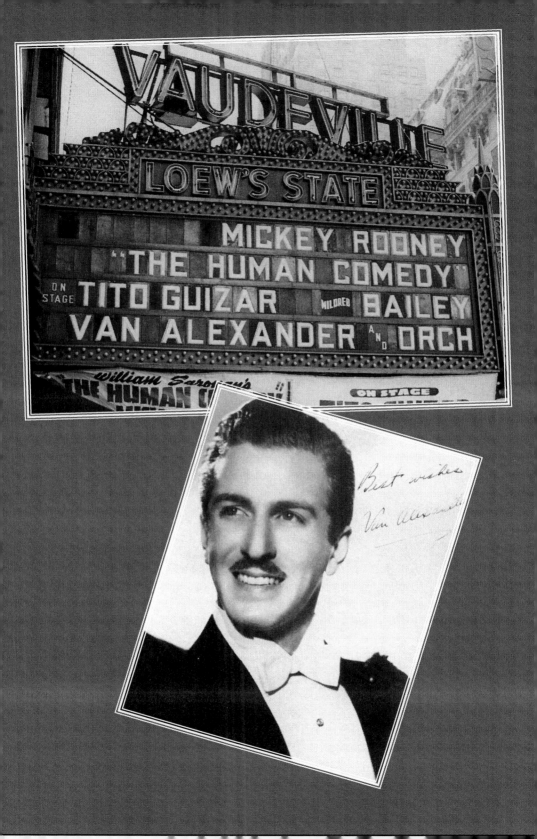

Van Alexander

So You Want To Lead A Band?

Van Alexander was one of the most enthusiastic bandleaders to ever lead a Big Band. Even now, at the age of ninety-two, because he loves the music, has become an valid contributor to this book. Considered one of the greatest arrangers of all-time, Van worked with a variety of orchestras during the Big Band Era. In 1938, with Ella Fitzgerald, Van co-authored and arranged Ella's first successful recording, "A -Tisket, A -Tasket" while she was the girl singer with Chick Webb's orchestra. That charming little tune quickly became the the nation's number one hit and is still revered today.

A TISKET, A TASKET
Words and Music by Ella Fitzgerald and Van Alexander

A-Tisket, A-Tasket,
A green and yellow basket
I bought a basket for my mommie
On the way I dropped it
I dropped it, I dropped it
Yes on the way I dropped it
A little girlie picked it up
And took it to the market
She was truckin' on down the Avenue
Without a single thing to do
She was peck, peck, peckin' all around
When she spied it on the ground
A -Tisket, A -Tasket
She took my yellow basket
And if she doesn't bring it back,
I think that I shall die
(Was it red?)
No, no, no, no,
(Was it brown?)
No, no, no, no,
(Was it blue?)
No, no, no, no
Just a little yellow basket!

That same year Van organized his first band and recorded several sides for Bluebird Records. By 1942 he was hired by bandleader Kay Kyser as an arranger even while leading his own orchestra. During the ensuing years he worked with bandleaders Tommy Tucker, Larry Clinton, Benny Goodman, Paul Whiteman, Les Brown, Bob Crosby, along with vocalists Kay Starr, Doris Day, Peggy Lee, Patty Andrews, Dinah Shore, Gordon MacRae, mostly for Capital Records. In the 1950s Van recorded several albums and went on to become a highly successful composer and arranger in the film and television industry. Television credits include I Dream of Jeannie,

Hazel, Bewitched, Donna Reed Show and Dennis the Menace Show. He worked with Connie Haines, Jane Russell, and Beryl Davis on their Bible music albums.

In Hollywood he had scored twenty-two full length feature films and hundreds of television segments which earned him three Emmy nominations. His credits include work on The Dean Martin Show, The Golddiggers Chevy Show, The Wacky World of Jonathan Winters, the Dom De Luise Specials, the 1969 Emmy Awards Show, The Guy Mitchell Show Series, and Gene Kelly's Wonderful World of Girls.

Van Alexander, August 25, 2007

"I was a big band leader from 1938 thru 1943. Those years were special because they were fraught with laughter, tears, and high hopes dashed by looming disasters. We were recording for RCA Victor on their Bluebird label and were on the air often with numerous appearances on the Fitch Bandwagon radio show, in addition to remote broadcasts from the Roseland Ballroom and clubs like the Top Hat in Union City and at Palisades Park, both in New Jersey. After our records were released and considering all the live airtime performed, we were now ready to tour the ballrooms, theaters and colleges all over the country.

"The first two years we rented a big band bus with a driver and road manager, and were signed by the most influential booking office, MCA (Music Corporation of America). Our personal agent was none other than Irving 'Swifty' Lazaar.

"The first tour would be two consecutive weeks of one-nighters throughout New England. The first night was a college date at the Copley Square Hotel in Boston. We assembled at the Forrest Hotel in New York to meet our bus. I had hired a band boy whose job it was to help load the bus with the guys luggage and instruments and, of course, our all-important music library.

"So, amid laughter, excitement and anticipation heading for out first date, we got to Boston in plenty of time to rest a bit and clean up. Suddenly I hear a nervous cry from the band boy. 'Gee Whiz!, Mr. Alexander, I think I left the first trumpet case in the lobby of the Forrest Hotel back in New York' he moaned.

"Wow! What trauma. If it had been any other music missing we could have gotten by, but without the music of the lead trumpet it would be impossible to play our arrangements. Luckily, my friend, Leighton Noble, whose orchestra was playing at the Copley Square Hotel, was available when I called him with my predicament. ' Get a few of the guys and come to my room. I've a lot of printed stock arrangements you can use. Stock arrangements are those printed and distributed free to any band and can be played on the air. Four of us rushed to his room and grabbed a batch of stocks, took them apart, and in about two hours we had enough music for our engagement. The four guys were Butch Stone, Ted Nash, Don Jacoby, and me. At the conclusion of our first evening of play the College Dean said to me: 'Mr. Alexander, when we booked your band I was afraid that it would be a loud swing band. However, I must tell you that your music tonight was perfect. The people were very happy, I could tell.'

"Well, so much for all my special arrangements. We finally retrieved the original charts, but it was a helluva way to start a first tour.

"Boston had a place called the Raymore Ballroom, a twin ballroom with two bandstands. It was 1940 and we were booked featuring vocalist Butch Stone, opposite Harry James featuring Frank Sinatra. Most of the guys in the band were frustrated baseball players, so many of us organized teams and whenever possible we would find a public field and engage another team band. In a game against Harry James band we won seven to two, but I'll always remember skinny Frank smashing three solid hits. Our Ted Nash was a terrific shortstop and Butch Stone a great catcher. That was our fun and relaxation during those periods when traveling from gig to gig while on the road."

Like most bands of the era, each featured two vocalists, a girl and boy singer. Van's first vocalists were Phyllis Kenny and David Allyn, a soldier who had won a Purple Heart.

"In 1944, as the war was ending, the Capitol Theater in New York decided to reactivate their big band stage policy after showing only films during the war. Bob Crosby had just been released from the service and they wanted him to restart the new stage show policy. Bob had no band, but being the brother of Bing he was easily signed, so my manager Joe Glaser cooked up a deal where the billing would state Bob Crosby with the Van Alexander Orchestra. Well, after four great weeks Bob and I enjoyed a great rapport and he asked me if I ever thought about going to California where I would put a new band together for him and write a lot of new arrangements. It seemed like a good idea for both my career and for moving to the coast, so I jumped at the chance.

At first, all was well. I put together a really good band that included Johnny Best, Billy May and Matty Matlock, but after about thirteen weeks, shortly after he and I had a major disagreement, Bob Crosby fired me. That was the end of my career as a big band leader. Of course, I had established a good reputation in the East, but few in California knew my of my work. At first I thought the event to be a major disaster, but it was really a blessing in disguise. Ironically, if it hadn't been for Bob Crosby I might never had come to California and developed my successful career in films and television."

Van Alexander Notices:

1962 - President of Los Angeles Chapter National Academy of Recording Arts and Sciences
1986 - Induction into the Grammy Hall of Fame for "A-Tisket , A -Tasket"
1995 - First Recipient The Irwin Kostal Award -American Society of Music Arrangers & Composers
1996 - Diamond Circle Award - Pacific Pioneer Broadcasters
1997 - Golden Bandstand Award - Big Band Academy of America
1997 - Composer and Arranger Award - Los Angeles Jazz Society
2002 - Lifetime Achievement Award - ASCAP Foundation
2005 - Ambassador Award - Society of Composers and Lyricists

SO YOU WANT TO LEAD A BAND?!

Van Alexander: "It is now the year of our Lord 2007. The long ago days of the great and popular big bands has passed. Gone are the nation's ballrooms, theaters, and opulent hotel dining rooms that once showcased stage shows with well established bands and their vocalists. Of course, there are many big bands playing out there today mostly composed of ghost bands of the great names of the past.

"However, if you feel you would still want to be a Big Band leader, the following may be of some assistance in your quest and some of the hurdles you may have to deal with on the way.

"First, you should be well-voiced in some phase of music to gain the respect of the guys (and/or gals) in your band. You should play an instrument, or at least be a singer or an arranger so that you do something besides standing in front waving your arms. Then you should choose a music style you will be playing. It may be a sweet Guy Lombardo style or a swinging Benny Goodman, or perhaps a tenor sax leader like Freddy Martin.

"Now you are going to need some 'seed' money to buy music stands with your initial or logo and uniforms for each member, and you probably will have to buy arrangements, rent rehearsal rooms and be able to meet general expenses.

"Add a good and honest manager who will promote your band's name and secure a record deal. You will, of course, require an agent to book appearances and an accountant to handle the books and payroll (Don't fool around with Uncle Sam). Be certain you are thoroughly familiar with every arrangement in your repertoire so when you tap off, the tempo is true. Counting off too slow or too fast will screw up the playing and sound of a good arrangement. And, yes!. You must have personal control and instill discipline without becoming a tyrant and you'll have the needed respect of your players.

"Well, I hope I haven't discouraged you and if you still want to lead a band, go ahead, but be careful and and say lots of prayers.

"God Bless and good luck!"

STARDUST

BIG *International* BANDS

THE WORLD'S LEADING BIG BAND SOCIETY

P.O. Box 111,
Reading, Berkshire
RG4 7DB
England

U.S.A.
2000 Richard Drive
Broomall
Pa 19008 - 2741

MAGAZINE

No. 82 February 1998

(Photo: courtesy of Audree Kenton)

A BLAST FROM THE PAST!

(left to right): Buddy Rich, Woody Herman, Willard Alexander, Benny Goodman, Count Basie,
Stan Kenton and Mel Torme.

Themes Of The Big Bands

Alexander, Van - *Alexander's Ragtime Band*

Anthony, Ray - *Young Man with a Horn*

Armstrong, Louis - *When it's Sleepy Time Down South*

Arnheim, Gus - *Sweet and Lovely*

Ballew, Smith - *Home*

Barnet, Charlie - *Redskin Rhumba & Cherokee*

Barron, Blue - *Sometimes I'm Happy*

Basie, William "Count" - *One O'Clock Jump*

Beneke, Tex - *Moonlight Serenade*

Berigan, Bunny - *I Can't Get Started*

Bernie, Ben - *Opening: Lonesome Old Town, Closing: Au Revoir*

Bradley, Will - *Think of Me*

Count Basie

Blue Barron

Nat Brandwynne - *If Stars Could Talk*

Brown, Les - *Leapfrog w/closer Sentimental Journey*

Busse, Henry - *Hot Lips, When Day is Done*

Butterfield, Billy - *Moonlight in Vermont*

Calloway, Cab - *Minnie the Moocher*

Les Brown

Carle, Frankie - *Sunrise Serenade*

Cavallaro, Carmen - *Polonaise & My Sentimental Heart*

Chester, Bob - *Sunburst & Slumber*

Clinton, Larry - *A Study in Brown & The Dipsy Doodle*

Larry Clinton

Coon-Sanders - *Nighthawk Blues*

Craig, Francis - *Near You*

Crosby, Bob - *Summertime*

Cugat, Xavier - *My Shawl*

Donohue, Al - *Lowdown Rhythm in a Top Hat*

Dorsey, Jimmy - *Contrasts*

Dorsey, Tommy - *I'm Getting Sentimental Over You*

Duchin, Eddie - *My Twilight Dream*

Al Donohue

Eddy Duchin

Duchin, Peter - *My Twilight Dream*

Elgart, Les - *Heart of My Heart*

Ellington, Edward Duke - *Take the A Train & East St.Louis Toodle-oo & Solitude*

Ennis, Robert "Skinnay" - *Got a Date with an Angel*

Ferguson, Maynard - *Unknown*

Fields, Shep - *Rippling Rhythm*

Fina, Jack - *Dream Sonata*

Fio Rita, Ted - *Rio Rita*

Flanagan, Ralph - *Singing Wind*

Garber, Jan - *My Dear*

Goldkette, Jean - *I Know That You Know*

Goodman, Benny - *Let's Dance & Goodbye*

Gray, Glen - *Smoke Rings*

Jan Gerber

Gray, Jerry - *Desert Serenade*

Grier, Jimmie - *Music in the Moonlight*

Hall, George - *Love Letters in the Sand*

Hampton, Lionel - *Flying Home*

Harris, Phil - *Rose Room*

Hawkins, Coleman - *Body & Soul & Honeysuckle Rose*

Hawkins, Erskine - *Swing Out*

Haymes, Joe - *Midnight*

Lionel Hampton

Hayton, Lennie - *Times Square Scuttle*

Heath, Ted - *Listen to My Music*

Hefti, Neal - *Coral Reef*

Heidt, Horace - *I'll Love You in My Dreams*

Henderson, Fletcher - *Christopher Columbus*

Herman, Woody - *Blue Flame & Woodchopper's Ball*

Hickman, Art - *Rose Room*

Hill, Tiny - *Angry*

Himber, Richard - *It Isn't Fair*

Hines, Earl "Fatha" - *Cavernism*

Hite, Les - *It Must Have Been a Dream*

Howard, Eddy - *Careless*

Hutton, Ina Ray - *Gotta Have Your Love*

James, Harry - *Ciribiribin*

Jenney, Jack - *City Night*

Jones, Isham - *You're Just a Dream Come True*

Jones, Spike - *Cocktails for Two*

Joy, Jimmy - *Shine on Harvest Moon*

Jurgens, Dick - *Daydreams Come True at Night*

Kassel, Art - *Hell's Bells*

Kay, Herbie - *Violets and Friends*

Horace Heidt

Woody Herman

Kaye, Sammy - *Kaye's Melody*

Kemp, Hal - *When the Summer is Gone*

Kenton, Stan - *Artistry in Rhythm*

King, Wayne - *The Waltz You Saved for Me*

Kirk, Andy - *Clouds & Until the Real Thing Comes Along*

Vincent Lopez

Krupa, Gene - *Starburst (Apurksody)*

Kyser, Kay - *Thinking of You*

Lanin, Sam - *A Smile Will Go a Long, Long Way.*

Lawrence, Elliot - *Heart to Heart*

Lewis, Ted - *When My Baby Smiles at Me*

Light, Enoch - *You Are My Lucky Star*

Lombardo, Guy - *Coquette & Auld Lang Syne*

Long, Johnny - *In a Shanty in Old Shanty Town*

Lopez, Vincent - *Nola*

Lunceford, Jimmie - *Jazznocracy*

Madriguera, Enric - *Adios*

McCoy, Clyde - *Sugar Blues*

McIntrye, Hal - *Moon Mist*

McKinley, Ray - *Howdy, Friends*

McKinney's Cotton Pickers - *If I Could Be with You One Hour Tonight*

Johnny Long

Marcellino, Muzzy - *I'll Take an Option on You*

Marterie, Ralph - *Carla*

Martin, Freddy - *Tonight We Love*

Masters, Frankie - *Scatterbrain*

May, Billy - *Lean Baby*

Miller, Glenn - *Moonlight Serenade*

Monroe, Vaughn - *Racing with the Moon*

Moreno, Buddy - *It's That Time Again*

Morgan, Russ - *Does Your Heart Beat for Me*

Vaughn Monroe

Morrow, Buddy - *Solo & Night Train*

Nelson, Ozzie - *Loyal Sons of Rutgers*

Nichols, Loring (Red) - *Parade of the Five Pennies*

Noble, Ray - *Goodnight Sweetheart & The Very Thought of You*

Norvo, Red - *Mr.   & Mrs Swing*

Olson, George - *Beyond the Blue Horizon*

Will Osborne

Russ Morgan

Osborne, Will - *Beside an Open Fireplace*

Owens, Harry - *Sweet Leilani*

Pastor, Tony - *Blossoms*

Phillips, Teddy - *Thankful*

Pollack, Ben - *Song of the Islands*

Powell, Teddy - *Blue Sentimental Mood*

Prima, Louis - *Sing, Sing, Sing & Way Down Yonder in New Orleans*

Redman, Don - *Chant of the Weed*

Reichman, Joe - *Variation in G*

Reisman, Leo - *What is this Thing Called Love*

Teddy Powell

Rey, Alvino - *Nighty Night & Blue Rey*

Rich, Buddy - *Love for Sale & West Side Story Medley*

Rich, Freddie - *I'm Always Chasing Rainbows*

Rogers, Buddy - *My Buddy*

Sauter-Finegan - *Doodle Town Fifers*

Alvino Rey

Savitt, Jan - *It's a Wonderful World & Quaker City Jazz*

Scott, Raymond - *Toy Trumpet*

Shaw, Artie - *Nightmare & Begin the Beguine*

Sissle, Noble - *Hello, Sweetheart, Hello.*

Slack, Freddy - *Strange Cargo*

Specht, Paul - *Evening Star*

Spivak, Charlie - *Stardreams*

Charlie Spivak

Dick Stabile

Stabile, Dick - *Blue Nocturne*

Steele, Blue - *Coronado Memories*

Teagarden, Jack - *I've Got a Right to Sing the Blues*

Thornhill, Claude - *Snowfall*

Trace, Al - *You Call Everybody Darlin'*

Tucker, Orrin - *Tucker, Tommy - I Love You*

Vallee, Rudy - *My Time is Your Time*

Venuti, Joe - *Last Night*

Waring, Fred - *Sleep*

Webb, Chick - *Let's Get Together*

Weeks, Anson - *I'm Sorry Dear*

Weems, Ted - *Out of the Night & Heartaches*

Jack Teagarden

Welk, Lawrence - *Bubbles in the Wine*

Whiteman, Paul - *Rhapsody in Blue*

Young, Victor - *A Ghost of a Chance*

Zentner, Si - *Up a Lazy River*

Claude Thornhill

Paul Whiteman

Your Lucky Strike Hit Parade

Tag Line "Lucky Strikes Means Fine Tobacco."
Be Happy, go Lucky,
Be Happy, go Lucky Strike
Be Happy, go lucky

Go Lucky Strike today!

A VERY POPULAR RADIO, AND THEN TV SHOW, YOUR HIT PARADE PARADED THROUGH 19 DIFFERENT ORCHESTRAS AND 52 DIFFERENT SINGERS FROM ITS 1935 RUN THROUGH 1959

NATIONAL BROADCASTING COMPANY
RCA BUILDING RADIO CITY STUDIOS NEW YORK

SAT.
22
APR.
1950

LUCKY STRIKE
PRESENTS
YOUR HIT PARADE
L.S./M.F.T.
COMPLIMENTARY TICKET—NOT TO BE SOLD

Studio Section
FLOOR
8
Doors Close
8:45PM

Some of the singers were Bea Wain, Buddy Clark, Dinah Shore, Georgia Gibbs, Martha Tilton, Ginny Simms, Dick Haymes, Johnny Mercer, Doris Day, Andy Russell, Eileen Wilson, Lanny Ross, Joan Edwards. Lawrence Tibbett, Barry Wood and Wee Bonnie Baker, Beryl Davis, and, of course, the most famous of all - Frank Sinatra. When television came in it was Dorothy Collins, Giselle McKensie, Russell Arms and Snooky Lanson.

Some of the bandleaders were: Lennie Hayton, Al Goodman, Harry Sosnik, Harry Salter, Leo Reisman, Ray Sinatra, Mark Warnow, Peter Van Steeden. Lyn Murray conducted the chorus and served as musical director.

The program showcased mostly

Dinah Shore

standard arrangements of the week's most popular recordings with an added "Lucky Strike Extra," an up and coming tune not yet in the top ten.

Gerald Nachman from Raised on Radio: Long before the onslaught of Top 40 formats, Your Hit Parade was the sole oracle of pop music trends - a kind of weekly Grammy Awards. At first, the songs were the stars: The singers, who earned a hundred dollars a show, weren't even credited. How songs were surveyed and selected was a secret highly guarded by the agency that ran the show, which insisted that its system was beyond reproach and, as announcer Andre' Baruch stated smartly each week, was the result of a tally of sheet music sales, listener requests, and jukebox selec-

Frank Sinatra and Beryl Davis

Lucky Strike Tin Ashtray - 1.5" W x 2.25"H

tions 'coast-to-coast.' In fact, it was fairly random, and allegedly 'scientific' sampling put together by hundreds of 'song scouts' across the country who talked to DJs, bandleaders, and record and sheet-music sales clerks and then reported the week's best-selling tunes. The show in turn, boosted record and jukebox sales, so the show's hits became self-perpetuating.

The show started a few years earlier when Lucky Strike

Joan Edwards

aired the Lucky Strike Dance Orchestra Show that featured popular songs on Saturday night at ten and urged their listeners to" reach for a Lucky instead of a Sweet."

Frank Sinatra joined the show and remained for two years, then returned to appear with Doris Day from 1946 through 1949. Beryl Davis, the singer from England, was chosen by Frank Sinatra to replace Doris Day, who was off to Hollywood for her first movie, *Romance on the High Seas* in which she sang "It's Magic."

Beryl Davis: "Richard, Frank was always kind to me and very supportive. He always included me, as after each show we would go out to dinner."

During the war years the show's theme was "This is Your Lucky Day," written by Ray Henderson, Buddy De-Sylvia and Lew Brown.

Be Happy-
Go Lucky!
Always
Dorothy Collins

Dorothy Collins

THE

STORMY WEATHER

Cotton Club
presents
ETHEL WATERS
GEORGE DEWEY WASHINGTON
in
COTTON CLUB
PARADE
22nd EDITION
with
DUKE ELLINGTON
AND HIS FAMOUS ORCHESTRA

Jimmie Lunceford is the new king of syncopation by acclamation of thousands of radio listeners, phonograph disc fans, patrons of theatres and dance lovers who have admired the "Harlem Express" and his streamlined rhythms!

Write, wire or phone for booking information on this attraction.

COTTON

CLUB

The Cotton Club Parade

"**Sunday Night at the Cotton Club was the night. All the big New York stars in town, no matter where they were playing, showed up.**" **Duke Ellington.**

"**The Cotton Club was an exotic jungle-like cafe. The shows had a primitive, naked quality that was supposed to make a civilized audience lose its inhibitions.**" **Lena Horne**

African- Americans were the talent, the mobsters were the owners, and white America were the patrons at this world-famous Harlem, New York City entertainment palace at Lenox Avenue and 142nd Street long before the jazz emporiums of 52nd Street came of age.

Sunday Nights were "Celebrity Nights" on which celebrities like Jimmy Durante, George Gershwin, Al Jolson, Mae West, Irving Berlin and other famous names would take a bow and perhaps perform a number or two.

The Cotton Club proliferated during the roaring 20's to the 1940s with the great bands of Fletcher Henderson, Duke Ellington, Cab Calloway, Louis Armstrong, Jimmie Lunceford, and performers Ethel Waters, Ella Fitzgerald, Adelaide Hall, Lena Horne (who performed there at the age of sixteen), Ivy Anderson, dancers Fayard and Harold Nicholas, and Bill "Bojangles" Robinson. Radio broadcasts originated weekly from the club catapulting Ellington's Orchestra to national fame.

The famed songwriting team of Harold Arlen and Ted Koehler wrote the song "Stormy Weather" and "Happiness Is Just a Thing Called Joe" for Ethel Waters and wrote songs and produced acts for the club for a number of years before going to Hollywood where Arlen composed the music for The Wizard of Oz, among many other standards.

The three Dandridge Sisters appeared at the club but only one, Dorothy, went on to stardom. Sadly, she died at the age of 42.

The Cotton Club opened a second club at 200 W. 48th Street and Broadway after riots in 1936 closed the original Harlem site. When the club closed its Broadway doors in June, 1940, Lou Walters opened the future Latin Quarter nightclub on that spot. A new Cotton Club opened its doors in Harlem once again in 1978. A West Coast branch of the club existed in Culver City, California during the late 20s and early 30s and featured many of the same New York bands and performers.

The Cotton Club still operates in Harlem today.

STARDUST

Big Band Million Sellers
1921-1947

Song(s)	Artist(s)/Band	Year
WHISPERING/JAPANESE SANDMAN	PAUL WHITEMAN	1921
WABASH BLUES	ISHAM JONES ORCHESTRA	1921
DARDANELLA	BEN SELVIN ORCHESTRA	1921
DOWN HEARTED BLUES	BESSIE SMITH	1923
IDA, SWEET AS APPLE CIDER	RED NICHOLS	1927
TIGER RAG First million seller by a vocal quartet	MILLS BROTHERS	1930
PICCOLO PETE First Novelty tune to sell a million	TED WEEMS ORCHESTRA	1929
MINNIE THE MOOCHER	CAB CALLOWAY	1931
SUGAR BLUES	CLYDE MCCOY	1936
BEI MIR BIST DU SCHON First million seller by a female group	ANDREWS SISTERS	1937
SWEET LEILANI First of Bing's 22 million sellers	BING CROSBY	1937
MARIE	TOMMY DORSEY/ JACK LEONARD	1938
BOOGIE WOOGIE	TOMMY DORSEY ORCHESTRA	1938
A-TISKET, A-TISKET Van Alexander and Ella wrote this song.	CHICK WEBB/ ELLA FITZGERALD	1938
ONE O'CLOCK JUMP Harry James' first million seller	HARRY JAMES ORCHESTRA	1938
BEGIN THE BEGUINE	ARTIE SHAW ORCHESTRA	1938
NIGHTMARE & BACK BAY SHUFFLE	ARTIE SHAW ORCHESTRA	1938
BODY AND SOUL	COLEMAN HAWKINS	1939
AT THE WOODCHOPPERS BALL	WOODY HERMAN	1939
CIRIBIRIBIN	HARRY JAMES ORCHESTRA	1939
LITTLE BROWN JUG IN THE MOOD SUNRISE SERENADE	GLENN MILLER	1939
THREE LITTLE FISHES	KAY KYSER ORCHESTRA	1939
OH, JOHNNY, OH! It also sold 1 million sheet music during World War I	ORRIN TUCKER/ BONNIEBAKER	1939
SAN ANTONIO ROSE Bing's second million seller	BOB CROSBY/BING CROSBY	1940
PENNSYLVANIA 6-5000 TUXEDO JUNCTION	GLENN MILLER	1940
SUMMIT RIDGE DRIVE FRENESI STAR DUST	ARTIE SHAW ORCHESTRA	1940
AMAPOLA	JIMMY DORSEY ORCHESTRA	1941
GREEN EYES	HELEN O'CONNELL	

Song(s)	Artist(s)/Band	Year
MARIA ELENA		
BOB EBERLY		
YOU MADE ME LOVE YOU	HARRY JAMES ORCHESTRA	1941
RACING WITH THE MOON	VAUGHN MONROE	1941
CHATTANOOGA CHOO CHOO Glenn received the very first GOLD record on February 10, 1942	GLENN MILLER, TEX BENEKE	1941
DANCING IN THE DARK This was Shaw's eighth million seller	ARTIE SHAW	1941
WHITE CHRISTMAS By 1968 it had sold over 30 million-a world selling record for a single	JOHN SCOTT TROTTER, BING CROSBY/ KEN DARBY SINGERS	1942
I HAD THE CRAZIEST DREAM	HARRY JAMES/ HELEN FORREST	1942
PRAISE THE LORD AND PASS THE AM-MUNITIION	KAY KYSER	1942
WHY DON'T YOU DO RIGHT	BENNY GOODMAN/ PEGGY LEE	1942
KALAMAZOO AMERICAN PATROL This was 8th and 9th million sellers for Miller	GLENN MILLER/ TEX BENEKE	1942
COW-COW BOOGIE This was first million hit for the new Capitol Records	FREDDIE SLACK/ ELLA MAE MORSE	1942
PAPER DOLL Unexplained colossal success sold 7 million	MILLS BROTHERS	1942
PISTOL PACKIN MAMA Bing's 7th	BING CROSBY/ ANDREWS SISTERS	1943
BESAME MUCHO Jimmy Dorsey's 4th million	JIMMY DORSEY, KITTY KALLEN, BOB EBERLY	1943
YOU'LL NEVER KNOW Dick Haymes first million seller	DICK HAYMES/ SONG SPINNERS	1943
ALL OR NOTHING AT ALL	HARRY JAMES/ FRANK SINATRA	1943
RUM AND COCA-COLA	VIC SCHOEN/ ANDREWS SISTERS	1944
ON THE SUNNY SIDE OF THE STREET	TOMMY DORSEY/ SENTIMENTALISTS	1944
DON'T FENCE ME IN	VIC SCHOEN, BING CROSBY, ANDREWS SIS-TERS	1944
OPUS NO 1	TOMMY DORSEY	1944
COCKTAILS FOR TWO	SPIKE JONES	1944
MOONLIGHT IN VERMONT First one for Margaret	BILLY BUTTERFIELD, MARGARET WHITING	1944
SENTIMENTAL JOURNEY	LES BROWN/ DORIS DAY	1945
TILL THE END OF TIME A HUBBA-HUBBA-HUBBA TEMPTATION	RUSS CASE ORCH./ PERRY COMO	1945
COTTAGE FOR SALE PRISONER OF LOVE These were 1st and 2nd million seller for Billy who performed the vocals, too.	BILLY ECKSTINE ORCHESTRA	1945
LAURA	WOODY HERMAN	1945
TAMPICO	STAN KENTON, JUNE CHRISTY	1945
ARTISTRY IN RHYTHM	STAN KENTON	1945

Song(s)	Artist(s)/Band	Year
DREAM	PAUL WESTON ORCH., PIED PIPERS	1945
SOUTH AMERICA, TAKE IT AWAY This was Bing's 4th million seller in collaboration with the Andrews girls	VIC SCHOEN ORCHESTRA, BING CROSBY, ANDREWS SISTERS	1946
TO EACH HIS OWN THE GYPSY	THE INK SPOTS	1946
SHOE FLY PIE AND APPLE PAN DOWDY	STAN KENTON, JUNE CHRISTY	1946
NEAR YOU	FRANCES CRAIG	1947
EVERYTHING I HAVE IS YOURS	BILLY ECKSTINE	1947
PEG O' MY HEART	HARMONICATS	1947
CONFESS	DORYS DAY/BUDDY CLARK	1947
MAYBE YOU'LL BE THERE First million seller for Jenkins	GORDON JENKINS, CHARLES LA VERE	1947
BALLERINA	VAUGHN MONROE	1947
MAM'SELLE	ART LUND VOCAL	1947
THAT'S MY DESIRE Frank's 1st million seller	FRANKIE LAINE	1947

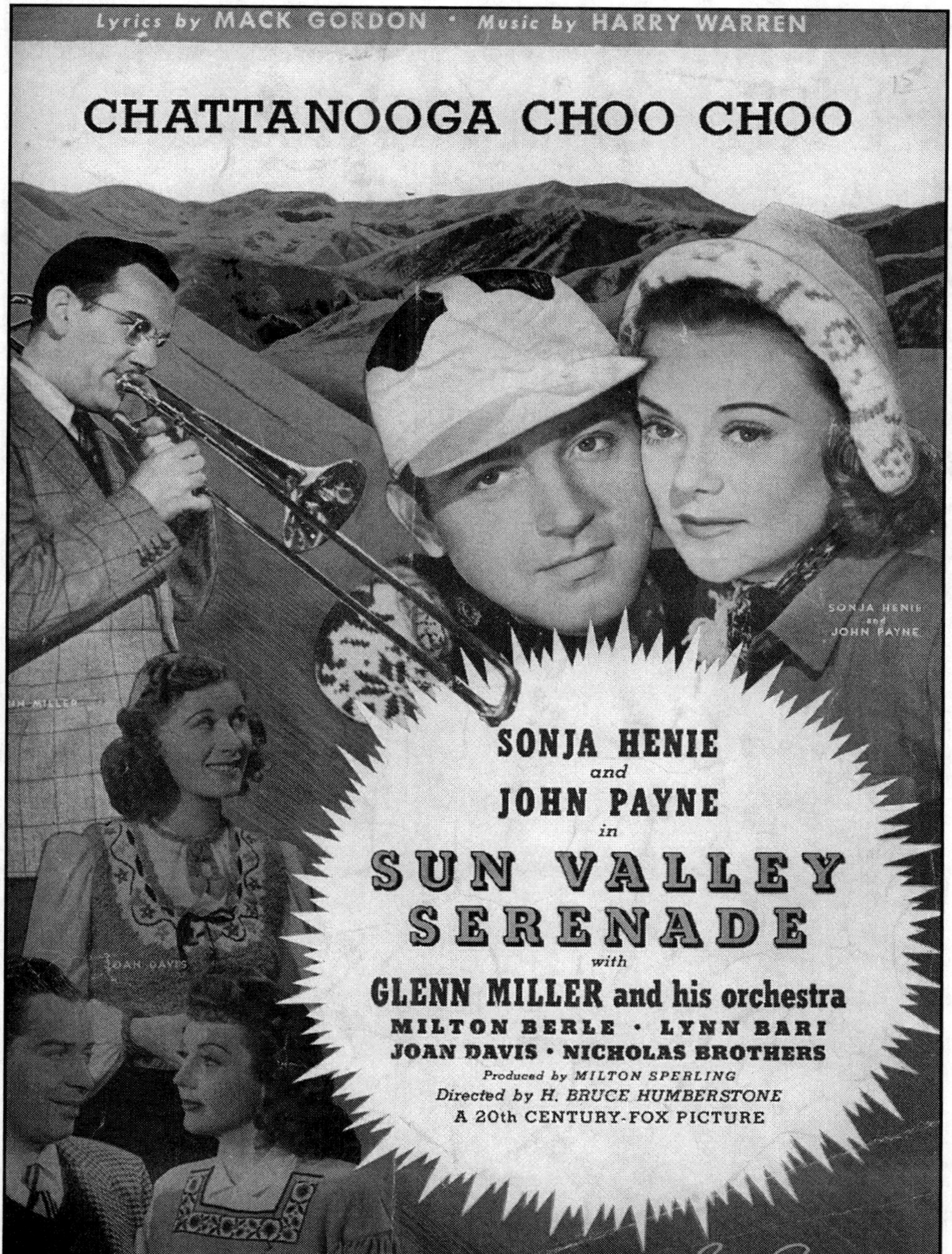

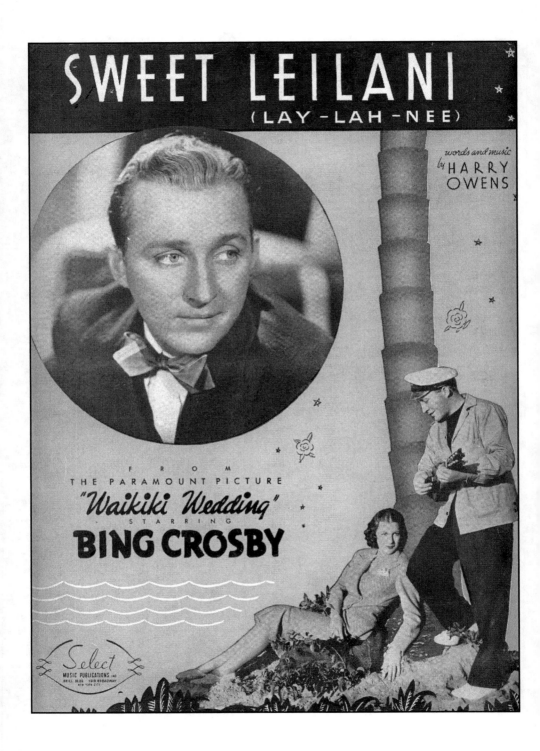

STARDUST

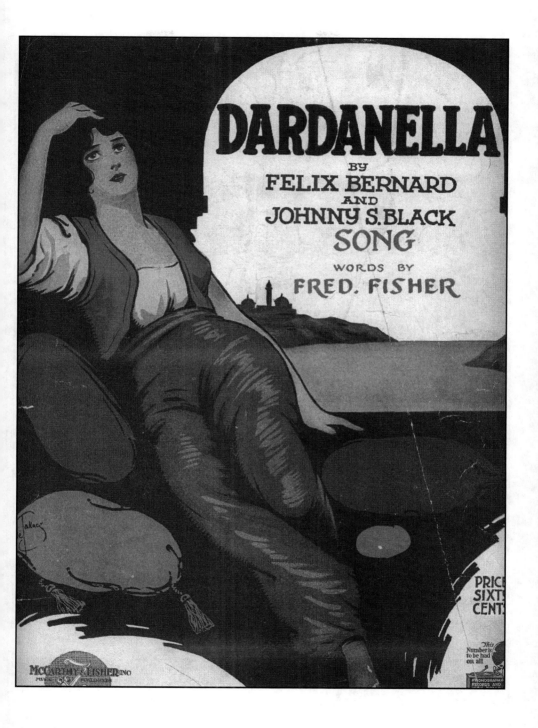

CIRIBIRIBIN
NEAPOLITAN LOVE SONG
by A PESTALOZZA

Featured by JAN GARBER
Star of the Yeast Foam Program—Over W.G.N. and N.B.C

Lyric by
Jerry Castillo

**WITH
UKELELE CHORDS
GUITAR CHORDS
AND
SPECIAL HAWAIIAN
GUITAR CHORUS**

CALUMET MUSIC CO.
201 EAST 26th STREET
CHICAGO ILLINOIS
V 210

First Gold Record

"Chattanooga Choo Choo"

February 10, 1942
Awarded on Nationwide Radio

Glenn Miller is honored with the VERY FIRST symbolic Gold Record Award.

Announcer Paul Douglas: "Glenn, I would like to present Mr. W. Wallace Early, the Manager of Record Sales for Victor and Bluebird Records."

"Thanks, Paul, it's a pleasure to be here tonight. And speaking for R.C.A. Victor, we're mighty proud of that 'Chattanooga Choo Choo' and the man who made the record, Glenn Miller. You see, it's been a long time, fifteen years in fact, that any

Paul Douglas, W. Wallace Early and Glen Miller

record sold a million copies. And 'Chattanooga Choo Choo' certainly put on steam and breezed right through that million mark by over 200,000 copies. And we decided that Glenn should get a trophy. The best one we could think of was a Gold Record of 'Chattanooga.'

"And now Glenn, it's yours, with the best wishes of R.C.A. Victor Bluebird Records," (to wild applause).

Glenn: "Thank you, Wally, that's really a wonderful present."

Paul: "I think everyone listening on the radio should know, Glenn, it is actually a recording of 'Chattanooga Choo Choo,' but it's in gold---solid gold, that is really fine."

Glenn: "That's right, Paul. And now for the boys in the band and for the whole gang, thanks a million, two hundred thousand."

Paul: "That's nicely put, Glenn, and our sponsors are mighty proud of that record, too. So now, suppose we enjoy you and the boys playing what's on that Gold Record."

The orchestra swings into "Chattanooga Choo Choo."

CHATTANOOGA CHOO CHOO

Mack Gordon & Harry Warren

Pardon me boy
Is that the Chattanooga Choo Choo
Track twenty-nine
Boy you can gimme a shine
I can afford to board a Chattanooga Choo Choo
I've got my fare
And just a trifle to spare
You leave the Pennsylvania station
'Bout a quarter to four
Read a magazine
And then you're in Baltimore
Dinner in the diner
Nothing can be finer,
Than to have your ham'n eggs in Carolina
When you hear the whistle blowin'
Eight to the bar
Then you know that Tennessee
Is not very far
Shovel all the coal in,
Got to keep it rollin'
Woo, Woo, Chattanooga there you are
There's gonna be
A certain party at the station
Satin and lace,
I used to call funny face
She's gonna cry
Until I tell her that I'll never roam
So Chattanooga Choo Choo
Won't you choo-choo me home

Billie Holiday

Paul Whiteman

THE CENTURY'S BEST

The RIAA, (Recording Industry Association of America) and the National Endowment for the Arts, determined the top selling songs of the 20th century.

We have cherry-picked out the BIG BAND ERA related winners, the year of their success coupled with the artist and recording company.

Beginning in 1920, approximately, the start of the Big Band Era.

Year	Artist	Recording	Label
1920	PAUL WHITEMAN	WHISPERING	VICTOR
1923	W.C. HANDY	ST LOUIS BLUES	OKEH
1923	BESSIE SMITH	DOWN HEARTED BLUES	COLUMBIA
1923	JELLY ROLL MORTON	KING PORTER STOMP	GENNETT
1924	ISHAM JONES	IT HAD TO BE YOU	BRUNSWICK
1928	HOAGY CARMICHAEL	STAR DUST	GENNETT
1931	CAB CALLOWAY	MINNIE THE MOOCHER	BRUNSWICK
1936	BING CROSBY	PENNIES FROM HEAVEN	DECCA
1937	COUNT BASIE	ONE O'CLOCK JUMP	DECCA
1938	LOUIS ARMSTRONG	WHEN THE SAINTS GO MARCHING IN	DECCA
1938	BENNY GOODMAN	SING, SING, SING	VICTOR
1938	ELLA FITZGERALD	A TISKET, A TISKET	DECCA
1938	ARTIE SHAW	BEGIN THE BEGUINE	BLUEBIRD
1939	BILLIE HOLIDAY	STRANGE FRUIT	COMMODORE
1939	GLENN MILLER	IN THE MOOD	BLUEBIRD
1940	COLEMAN HAWKINS	BODY AND SOUL	BLUEBIRD
1941	ANDREWS SISTERS	BOOGIE WOOGIE BUGLE BOY	DECCA
1941	DUKE ELLINGTON	TAKE THE "A" TRAIN	VICTOR
1941	BILLIE HOLIDAY	GOD BLESS THE CHILD	OKEH
1942	BING CROSBY	WHITE CHRISTMAS	DECCA
1942	ALVINO REY	DEEP IN THE HEART OF TEXAS	BLUEBIRD
1943	LENA HORNE	STORMY WEATHER	VICTOR
1943	MILLS BROTHERS	PAPER DOLL	DECCA
1945	LES BROWN	SENTIMENTAL JOURNEY	COLUMBIA
1945	DIZZY GILLESPIE	SALT PEANUTS	GUILD
1946	CHARLIE PARKER	ORINTHOLOGY	DIAL
1947	FRANCIS CRAIG	NEAR YOU	BULLET
1948	THELONIUS MONK	AROUND MIDNIGHT	BLUE NOTE
1949	VAUGHN MONROE	GHOST RIDERS IN THE SKY	RCA VICTOR

The Ballroom Operator Has His Say

Listed below are the bands that drew the best business during the past season for the ballroom operators and dance promoters represented in the accompanying article. Also listed are the orchestras that went over best with the respective ballrooms' patrons, regardless of their showing at the box office. The first three are given in each instance.

It must be pointed out, of course, that there can be no basis for any comparative values or standards, inasmuch as some ballrooms play name bands only, some alternate names with territorial favorites, while still others play only territorial and local bands.

What is significant, however, is the discrepancy noted in some cases between the good business done by a band and its reception by the ballroom's clientele. The reverse may also be noted—where a band does not figure in the best gross registered at a spot, and yet may be first in the affections of the spot's patronage.

BALLROOM	BEST BUSINESS	BEST PATRONAGE REACTION
Auditorium, Knoxville, Tenn.	Cab Calloway, Count Basie, Jimmie Lunceford	Erskine Hawkins, Jimmie Lunceford, Cab Calloway
Canadarago Park, Richfield Springs, N. Y.	Guy Lombardo, Gene Krupa, Cab Calloway	Gene Krupa, Guy Lombardo, Bob Crosby
Enna Jettick Park, Auburn, N. Y.	Mike Riley, Les Brown, Rita Rio	Les Brown, Rita Rio, Mike Riley
Fairyland Park, Kansas City, Mo.	Hal Kemp, Pinky Tomlin, Cab Calloway	Jay McShann, Ben Pollack, George Hall
Fiesta Danceteria, New York City	Ben Bernie, Gene Krupa, Shorty Allen	Jack Denny, Joe Marsala, Antonio De Vera
Joyland Casino, Lexington, Ky.	Blue Barron, Ella Fitzgerald, Ted Weems	Blue Barron, Ella Fitzgerald, Ben Bernie
King's Ballroom, Lincoln, Neb.	Henry Busse, Vincent Lopez, Hal Leonard	Vincent Lopez, Hal Leonard, Nat Towles
Meadowbrook Ballroom, Bascom, O.	Carl (Deacon) Moore, Blue Barron, Emil Velazco	Carl (Deacon) Moore, Blue Barron, Tommy Carlyn
Myrtle Beach (S. C.) Pavilion	Bill Clarke, Bob Sylvester, Freddy Johnson	Bill Clarke, Freddy Johnson, Bob Sylvester
Natatorium Park, Spokane, Wash.	Phil Harris, Eddy Duchin	Muzzy Marcellino, Phil Harris
Ocean Pier, Wildwood, N. J.	Jimmy Dorsey, Larry Clinton	Lou Breese
Pier Ballroom, Buckeye Lake, O.	Ben Bernie, Jan Garber, Carl (Deacon) Moore	Jan Garber, Ace Brigode, Russ Morgan
Pla-Mor Ballroom, Lincoln, Neb.	Paul Moorehead, Jimmy Barnett, Skippy Anderson (all tied)	Paul Moorehead, Jimmy Barnett, Ralph Slade
Saltair, Salt Lake City	Jimmy Walsh, Phil Harris, Anson Weeks	Jimmy Walsh, Phil Harris, Skinnay Ennis
Sandy Beach Park, Russells Point, O.	Artie Shaw, Blue Barron, Jan Garber	Jan Garber, Blue Barron, Glen Gray
Sherman's Caroga Lake, N. Y.	Fletcher Henderson, Ray Keating, Robertshaw	Ray Keating, Robertshaw
Starlight Ballroom, Chippewa Lake, O.	Ace Brigode, Tommy Tucker, Tiny Hill	Tommy Tucker, Ace Brigode, Tiny Hill
Summit Beach, Akron, O.	Bob Chester, Clyde McCoy, Arden Wilson	Bob Chester, Will Bradley, Clyde McCoy
Turnpike Casino, Lincoln, Neb.	Glenn Miller, Ted Lewis, Paul Whiteman	Ted Lewis, Dick Jurgens, Glenn Miller
Westwood Supper Club, Richmond, Va.	Bruce Baker, Glen Garr, Barry MacKinley	Glen Garr, Bruce Baker, Barry MacKinley

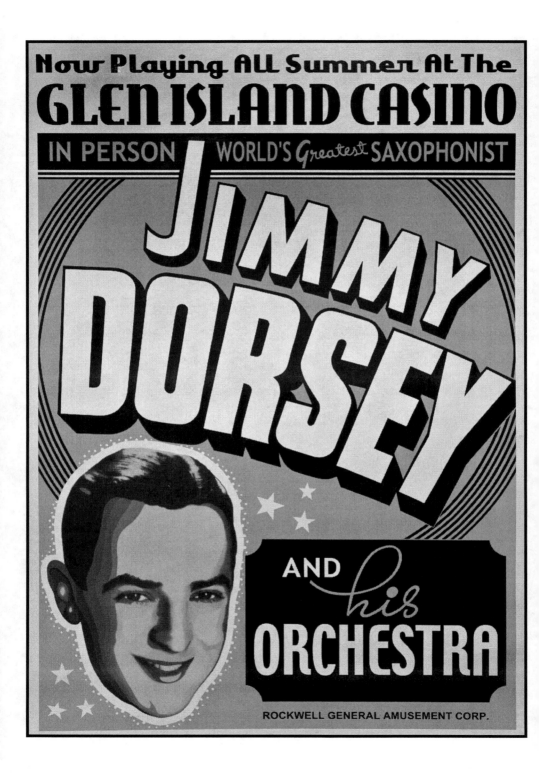

Capitol Records Building - Still In Operation Today!

Richard Grudens' Choice
Best Songs and Their Composers

Song	Year	Composers and Arrangers
w. = words, w.m. =words and music		
Ac-cent-tchu-ate the Positive	1945	w. Johnny Mercer m. Harold Arlen
Amapola	1924	w.m. Joseph Lacalle (Enlgish)
And the Angels Sing	1939	w.m. Johnny Mercer, Ziggy Elman
As Time Goes By	1931	w.m. Herman Hupfeld
A Tisket, A Tisket	1938	w.m. Van Alexander, Ella Fitzgerald
At Last	1942	w.m. Mack Gordon & Harry Warren
Begin the Beguine	1935	w.m. Cole Porter
Boogie Woogie Bugle Boy	1941	w.m. Hughie Prince, Don Raye
Chattanooga Choo Choo	1941	w. Mack Gordon m. Harry Warren
Chickery Chick	1945	w.m. Sylvia Dee, Sidney Lippman
Deep Purple	1934	w. Mitchell Parish m. Peter De Rose
Don't Be That Way	1938	w.m. Mitchell Parish, Benny Goodman, Edgar Sampson
Don't Sit Under the Apple Tree	1942	w.m. Sammy Stept, Charles Tobias, Lew Brown
Dream	1945	w.m. Johnny Mercer
Frenesi	1940	w. Alberto Dominguez m. Ray Charles
Green Eyes	1929	w. L. Wolfe Gilberto. Nilo Menendez
I Can't Get Started	1935	w. Ira Gershwin, m. Vernon Duke
I Had The Craziest Dream	1943	w. Mack Gordon, m. Harry Warren
I'll Be Seeing You	1938	w. Irving Kahal, m. Sammy Fain
I'll Never Smile Again	1940	w.m. Ruth Lowe
I'm Getting Sentimental Over You	1932	w. Ned Washington, m. George Bassman
In The Mood	1939	w.m. Andy Razaf, Joseph Garland
It Isn't Fair	1933	w. Richard Himber, m. Richard Himber, Frank Warshauer, Sylvester Sprigato
I've Got My Love to Keep Me Warm	1937	w.m. Irving Berlin
I've Got You Under My Skin	1936	w.m. Cole Porter
Jersey Bounce	1942	w. Buddy Feybe, Robert B. Wright, m. Bobby Plater, Tiny Bradshaw, Edward Johnson, Robert B. Wright
Little Brown Jug	1869	w.m. Joseph Winner
Oh, Look at Me Now	1941	w.m. John de Vries, Joe Bushkin
One O'clock Jump	1938	w.m. Wm. Count Bassie, Harry James
Maria Elena	1933	w.(Eng.) S.K. Russell, m. Glenn Miller
Moonlight Serenade	1939	w. Mitchell Parish, m. Glenn Miller
Night and Day	1932	w.m. Cole Porter
Paper Doll	1915	w.m. Johnny S. Black
Prisorer of Love	1931	w. Leo Robin, m. Russ Columbo

Song	Year	Composers and Arrangers
Rum and Coca-Cola	1945	w.(Eng.) Morey Amsterdam, m. Jeri Sullivan, Paul Baron
Sentimental Journey	1945	w.m. Bud Green, Les Brown, Ben Homer
Sing, Sing, Sing	1937	w.m. Louis Prima
Stardust	1929	w. Mitchell Parish, m. Hoagy Carmichael
String of Pearls	1942	w.m. Eddie de Lange, Jerry Gray
Stompin' At the Savoy	1936	w. Andy Razaf, m. Benny Goodman, Chick Webb, Edgar Sampson
Sunday Kind of Love	1946	w.m. Barbara Belle, Anita Leonard, Louis Prima, Stan Rhodes
Take the "A" Train	1941	w.m. Billy Strayhorn
You Made Me Love You	1913	w. Joseph McCarthy, m. James V. Monaco

Benny Goodman - "Oh' Those Bluebird Recordings Were Wonderful," with Richard Grudens - 1983

BILLIE HOLIDAY

TOWN HALL · SATURDAY, FEBRUARY 16 · 5:30 p. m.

STARDUST

WNEW 1130

AM NEW YORK RADIO PROGRAMMING

SEPTEMBER 25, 1982

The 50 GREATEST RESULTS OF THE MAKE BELIEVE BALLROOM POLL. *Voted by "You, You & Especially You!"*

1.	I CAN'T GET STARTED - BUNNY BERIGAN
2.	BEGIN THE BEGUINE - ARTIE SHAW
3.	SING, SING, SING - BENNY GOODMAN
4.	MOONLIGHT SERENADE - GLENN MILLER
5.	IN THE MOOD - GLENN MILLER
6.	I LEFT MY HEART IN SAN FRANCISCO - TONY BENNETT
7.	WHITE CHRISTMAS - BING CROSBY
8.	I'LL NEVER SMILE AGAIN - TOMMY DORSEY, FRANK SINATRA/PIED PIPERS
9.	MACK THE KNIFE - BOBBY DARIN
10.	GREEN EYES - JIMMY DORSEY, HELEN O'CONNELL, BOB EBERLY
11.	TAKE THE "A" TRAIN - EDWARD "DUKE" ELLINGTON
12.	APRIL IN PARIS - COUNT BASIE
13.	BECAUSE OF YOU - TONY BENNETT
14.	YOU BELONG TO ME - JO STAFFORD
15.	MARIE - TOMMY DORSEY - JACK LEONARD
16.	PAPER DOLL - MILLS BROTHERS
17.	A STRING OF PEARLS - GLENN MILLER
18.	CHEROKEE - CHARLIE BARNET
19.	NEW YORK, NEW YORK - FRANK SINATRA
20.	OVER THE RAINBOW - JUDY GARLAND
21.	STORMY WEATHER - LENA HORNE
22.	STARDUST - ARTIE SHAW
23.	A-TISKET, A-TASKET - CHICK WEBB, ELLA FITZGERALD
24.	THE CHRISTMAS SONG - NAT "KING" COLE
25.	SENTIMENTAL JOURNEY - LES BROWN, DORIS DAY
26.	TENDERLY - ROSEMARY CLOONEY
27.	MONA LISA - NAT "KING" COLE
28.	BODY AND SOUL - COLEMAN HAWKINS
29.	YOU MADE ME LOVE YOU - HARRY JAMES
30.	TANGERINE - JIMMY DORSEY, HELEN O'CONNELL, BOB EBERLY
31.	FRENESI - ARTIE SHAW
32.	PRISONER OF LOVE - PERRY COMO

33.	MISTY - ERROLL GARNER	
34.	ON THE SUNNY SIDE OF THE STREET - TOMMY DORSEY/CLARK SISTERS	
35.	MOONLIGHT IN VERMONT - MARGARET WHITING	
36.	I'M GETTIN' SENTIMENTAL OVER YOU - TOMMY DORSEY	
37.	ONE O'CLOCK JUMP - WILLIAM "COUNT" BASIE	
38.	MY WAY - FRANK SINATRA	
39.	I APOLOGIZE - BILLY ECKSTINE	
40.	NIGHT AND DAY - FRANK SINATRA	
41.	HOW HIGH THE MOON - LES PAUL & MARY FORD	
42.	UNFORGETTABLE - NAT COLE	
43.	HELLO DOLLY - LOUIS ARMSTRONG	
44.	TUXEDO JUNCTION - GLENN MILLER	
45.	NATURE BOY - NAT "KING" COLE	
46.	CHATTANOOGA CHOO CHOO - GLENN MILLER, TEX BENEKE	
47.	OLD CAPE COD - PATTI PAGE	
48.	LINDA - BUDDY CLARK	
49.	WOODCHOPPER'S BALL - WOODY HERMAN	
50.	TRUE LOVE - BING CROSBY & GRACE KELLY	

Martin Block

GREAT MOMENTS
IN BIG BAND HISTORY

1913 - Adelaide Hall records "Creole Love Call" with Duke Ellington in 1927 marking the first use of a voice as orchestral instrument.

1927 - Duke Ellington opens at the Cotton Club and remained for 5 years.

1929 - Duke Ellington records "East St. Louis Toodle-Oo," his first theme.

1935 - *Downbeat Magazine* proclaims that Benny goodman woke up the West Coast with his Swing style. Benny Goodman's breakthrough appearance at the immense Palomar Ballroom in Los Angeles on August 21, 1935, is the date the Swing Era began. Leading up to that day, Goodman's appearance was regularly promoted by Al Jarvis's popular radio show *Make Believe Ballroom*, which may account for the overwhelming attendance, as Jarvis virtually created a fan base before the Goodman band arrived. Fans were eager to see the band in person. "It was unbelievable, sax player Hymie Schertzer said, "They stood in front of the band by the hundreds. They knew the charts. They loved it!"

1935 - Artie Shaw performs for the benefit of Local 802, Musicians Union at the Imperial Theater with his Arthur Shaw's Swing String Ensemble composed of two violins, a cellist, guitar, string bass and drums and clarinet, fusing strings with brass, and unheard of effect at the time. Some have called that concert a milestone in jazz history, as being the first real jazz concert.

1937 - The Andrews Sisters record "Bei Mir Bist Du Schon" at Decca Records.

1938 - First Jazz Concert at Carnegie Hall with Benny Goodman, Count Basie & Harry James, and Gene Krupa. "In the best and truest sense, the joint actually was rocking." Time Magazine Review.

1939 - Harry James sold-out appearances at the New York Paramount with a surprising assist from Martin Block of WNEW Radio and his *Make Believe Ballroom* show playing "You Made Me Love You" for weeks before James' arrival.

1939 - Glenn Miller opens at the Meadowbrook in Cedar Grove, New Jersey, on March 5, his first important booking.

1940 - Discovered him singing at the Rustic Cabin near Alpine, New Jersey, Harry James hires Frank Sinatra to join the Harry James Orchestra.
1941 - Opening night at the famed Hollywood Palladium with Tommy Dorsey, Frank Sinatra, Connie Haines, and the Pied Pipers.
1942 - February 10: Presentation of the first Gold Record "Chattanooga Choo Choo" to Glenn Miller by R.C.A. Victor Bluebird Records.
1943 - Frank Sinatra makes his first appearance on Your Hit Parade on February 6th.
1944 - Glenn Miller disappears in a single engine plane while flying over the English Channel on his way to Paris to entertain servicemen and women.
1944 - Les Brown records "Sentimental Journey" with Doris Day on November 20th. Brown's first million seller.
1945 - Artie Shaw returns from his Mexican retreat with a new composition "Frenesi" that takes the country by storm.
1946 - March 25: Woody Herman performs at Carnegie Hall with Igor Stravinsky's composition "Ebony Concerto" written expressly for the Woody Herman Orchestra.
1982 - Johnny Mince tells the truth to Richard Grudens about Glenn Miller finding his famous sound: "Doubling a melody on saxophone with a clarinet an octave higher, versus the movie version which was strictly a Hollywood myth."

Benny at a Jam Session with Joe Thomas Band at New York's WOR Radio

BIG BAND
PHOTO GALLERY

Billy Butterfield

Lee Castle

Ralph Flanagan

Buddy DeFranco

Kenny Gardner

Sammy Kaye

Carmen Cavallaro

Jack Morgan

Sam Donohue

Richard Maltby

Thelonious Monk

Gray Gordon

Clyde Lucas

Frankie Masters

Bobby Byrne

Lawrence Welk

Kay Kyser

Enric Madriguera

Shep Fields

Maynard Ferguson

Ben Grisafi

Xavier Cugat

Russ Morgan

Al Donahue

McFarland Twins

Guy Lombardo Brothers

PART TWO

Remembering The Early Innovators

GET READY, GET SET, LET'S DANCE!

Proliferating throughout the Big Band Era, the musical organizations of Benny Goodman, Artie Shaw, Duke Ellington, Glenn Miller, and Tommy and Jimmy Dorsey attracted colossal crowds at America's dance pavilions, theaters and hotels. Earlier, those very same venues hosted dozens of pioneer dance bands. The unique musical congregations of Paul Whiteman, Fred Waring, Vincent Lopez, Wayne King, Casa Loma, Fletcher Henderson, Coon-Sanders, Ted Lewis, Jean Goldkette, Leo Reisman, Gus Arnheim, and Isham Jones set the stage for the dynamics that was to come.

In the grand ballrooms of New York's Waldorf-Astoria, Biltmore, Savoy, and Roosevelt hotels and at rural small-town locations like the Sunnybrook Ballroom in Pottstown, Pennsylvania, enthusiastic dancing partners could swing to all the great dance bands in the early decades of this century.

Paul Whiteman

Paul Whiteman's King of Jazz Orchestra

Paul Whiteman's 1920 landmark recordings of "Whispering" and "The Japanese Sandman" spurred national interest in jazz dance music in the days when radio was still a novelty, television far off into the future, and sound films years away. Showcased at San Francisco's Fairmont Hotel (long before Tony Bennett left his heart there) and Los Angeles' Alexandria Hotel, both songs

enjoyed unexpected, spectacular success. With their catchy, infectious phrasing, you'll find your-self whis-tling and hum-ming those tunes over and over all day long.

Billy May Orchestra, 1952 - Pennsylvania Hotel, NY

A recording contract followed as well as a long run at the Palais Royale in New York City. Paul Whiteman and his mis-named King of Jazz Orchestra was on top of the beat that people were dancing to in what is considered the beginning of the Jazz Age, even though Whiteman was hardly considered a jazzman. His world-famous orchestra employed some of the later greats of pop and jazz music including Tommy and Jimmy Dorsey; arranger and composer Ferde' Grofe; arranger Bill Challis; vocalist Bing Crosby; legendary cornetists Bix Biederbecke and Henry Busse; guitarist Eddie Lang; vocalist Mildred Bailey; violinist Joe Venuti; cornetist Loring "Red" Nichols; saxist Frankie Trumbauer; composer, pianist Hoagy Carmichael; pianist, leader and arranger Lennie Hayton; saxist, bandleader Roy Bargy; trumpeter, bandleader Bunny Berigan; trombonist and leader Jack Teagarden; trumpeter Charlie Teagarden, trumpeter Billy Butterfield, and many others, a virtual who's who of American popular music. Even the great entertainer Al Jolson was once backed by Whiteman on the original "Kraft Music Hall" radio show.

I personally enjoyed the almost daily acquaintance of Paul White-man at his NBC studio office in the early fifties. An NBC studio page, I observed him frequently while directing visitors to his office, always receiving a personal thank-you and sometimes a fatherly arm about the shoulder. At the time I did not fully realize his significant contribution to the music of the Jazz Age. Remember, it was Paul Whiteman who premiered George Gershwin's classic composition "Rhapsody in Blue" to the world at an Aeolian Hall concert, New York City's then sanctuary of classical music, on February 12, 1924, with the composer himself at the piano. Paul Whiteman's King of Jazz Orchestra with thirty-four all-stars was the biggest name and the most creative force in the music business during that period.

The Casa Loma Orchestra

The Casa-Loma Orchestra, originally named The Orange Blossom Band, began playing dance music at the Glen Island Casino in New Rochelle, New York, and the Colonnades in Manhattan's Essex House. The Casa Loma name originated when the Casa Loma Hotel in Toronto, Canada, went bankrupt and the band's manager , Jean Goldkette, sent the now-unemployed Orange Blossom Band on tour, re-naming it the Casa Loma Orchestra. Orchestra members, always outfitted in bow ties and tails, were also its board of directors, each man receiving an equal share in the profits, making it a cooperative band. It became the nation's favorite dance orchestra - not a hot band - but sweet and popular. On one 1939 Decca album alone, the group recorded composer Hoagy Carmichael's "Rockin'Chair," "Georgia On My Mind," "Riverboat Shuffle," "Little Old Lady," "Lazy River, "and of course, the ultimate standard "Stardust."

With a playing style that was considered new and different, alto-sax player Glen Gray, who eventually became the band's leader, led the Casa Loma Orchestra to great commercial success. My longtime friend Bill Challis arranged some of the organization's lasting charts, as he did earlier for the Goldkette band and later for the Whiteman band. Smoke Rings, written by H.Eugene Gifford and Ned Washington was the Casa Loma theme. This now very classy orchestra continued running strong, especially when they succeeded Ray Noble's Orchestra at the celebrated Rainbow Room up on Radio City's 65th floor, lasting until the Second World War began, when it disbanded. Some say Casa Loma initiated the swing craze by the prolific use of riffs (repeated phrases by alternate sections of the band) and an energetic approach to the unmistakable intonation of their brass and reed sections.

I recall Buddy Rich telling me that he enjoyed listening to the recordings of Casa Loma when he was at home between engagements and in the mood for "some very good music." The photo here of Casa Loma is the front -face of a promotional postcard I found recently in an outdoor memorabilia show at Cold Spring Harbor Park on Long Island.

Jean Goldkette's Prolific Orchestra's

Jean Goldkette, a former French concert pianist, led a star-filled concert-style musical group rather than a dance band, and he also managed other bands. Jimmy and Tommy Dorsey, Joe Venuti , and Bing

Crosby's favorite guitarist Eddie Lang, Bix Biederbecke and arranger Bill Challis were all Goldkette employees. When Goldkette, who also owned the Graystone Ballroom in Detroit, discontinued his short-lived band after a stunning farewell engagement in New York's Roseland, a number of his players migrated to Paul Whiteman's King of Jazz Orchestra.

Leo Reisman's Society Orchestra

Leo Reisman

In the early twenties Leo Reisman's Orchestra played strictly sweet dance music. A true society dance band, its muted brass, silky saxes, and singing violins achieved notable success. At the age of ten Reisman was handed a violin by his dad and a year later he became the leader of his grammar school band. At twelve, young Leo began plugging songs in W.T. Grant Department Stores for Houghton & Dutton Music Publishers.

After studying at the New England Conservatory of Music in Boston, he led a big band in the Egyptian Room of the Brunswick Hotel. Reisman, a busy entrepreneur, maintained and managed over 20 bands at one time, all by different names, thereby becoming a music impresario, being hailed by many as a genius of the music world.

Reisman tried to bring to Boston all he had heard in New York, especially the success of Whiteman with Gershwin's music. Leo Reisman's bright group of musicians performed for thirteen straight years in the Waldorf's prestigious Wedgewood Room (later re-named the Empire Room), employing the first female big band singers Mildred Bailey and Lee Wiley. Reisman's long list of vocalists on recordings included: a young Bing Crosby crooning "Brother Can You Spare a Dime;" Fred and Adele Astaire vocalizing Broadway's The Band Wagon on RCA's first long-playing recording score in 1931--just before Astaire's Hollywood career began; Astaire's definitive recording of Cole Porter's "Night and Day" from the movie The Gay Divorcee in 1932, and Harold Arlen's - yes, Harold Arlen's vocal on a 1933 recording of his own composition "Stormy Weather," which he composed with lyricist Ted Koehler.

Reisman's career spanned 44 years, over twenty in the recording studio alone. He was directly responsible for the careers of both Benny Goodman and Dinah Shore, among others, and was the very first to feature a black artist in his orchestra. At first resisting jazz, for him an unacceptable innovation of music, he later accepted the idea, adapting it to his personal style.

Fred Waring's Pennsylvanians

Charming and handsome Fred Waring, whom most know as a leader of Fred Waring's Pennsylvanians singing group, started his first band in 1916 with his brother Tom as vocalist. After first trying to make it as a dance band at the Colonial Theater in Richmond, Virginia in the early twenties, he later developed his singing musical-show organization instead. First, he developed a quartet of banjo players; then, further developing in radio on Detroit's WWJ, he moved his group to Philadelphia, calling them Waring's Pennsylvanians. Tom and Fred Waring would perform their own vocals on recordings like "Collegiana," becoming one of the best-known orchestras on radio from 1933 onward. He started at CBS where he adopted his signature tune, "Breezin' Along with the Breeze" but wound up at NBC in the late Thirties, appearing on "Chesterfield Time" and later "The Fred Waring Show," where I first knew him. His office secretary, Cora, once told me that it was Fred who invented the famous Waring Blender while working at the Shawnee Inn he owned on 600 acres in Pennsylvania.

Fred Waring's Pennsylvanians triumphantly performed in Paris at Des Ambassadeurs during a European tour in 1928. Variety described Waring's players as "one of the most imitated groups on radio, especially those great choral arrangements for the rocking chair crowd."

Coon-Sanders Nighthawks

Radio's Aces was the Coon-Sanders Nighthawks sobriquet, as if they needed one. Carlton Coon, drummer and vocalist, and pianist-arranger Joe Sanders led this collegian-type, partner-led dance band from Kansas City on WDAF, with rollicking rhythms and cheery greetings. True radio dance band pioneers, Coon-Sanders Nighthawks performed requests sent to the studios via a Western Union ticker installed in the studio. It was probably the first request (radio) show. Arranger Joe Sanders was the first to spread saxophone-sec-tion voicing, insert-ing a vocal into almost every selection. Coon-Sanders played jazz, calling it concert jazz. Two good-looking, person-able guys, their music was peppy, origi-nal and unique for the times, which accounted for their success. Mel Torme' first sang with Coon-Sanders Nighthawks.

"RADIO'S ACES"

The COON-SANDERS NIGHT-HAWKS

Tin Lizzies, Racoon Coats, Yellow Slickers, Hip Flasks and a New Invention Called Radio That Made Stars of Coon and Sanders and Their Music of the Jazz Age.

The ten piece group first arrived in Chicago in 1924 and scored so well at the Lincoln Tavern and Congress Hotel that, when MCA booking agency promised the popular Blackhawk Restaurant a top-flight band in 1926, Coon-Sanders got the job, broadcasting nightly over WGN, sometimes sharing the mike with Wayne King's and Ted Weems' orchestra.

Coon-Sanders Nighthawks took to the road and when they played at Angell Park Pavilion in Sun Prairie, Wisconsin in 1931, they earned thousands of new fans playing often requested songs "Ball and Chain," "What a Girl," "Georgia on My Mind," and "St.Louis Blues. "With a lengthy stay at New York's Hotel New Yorker and a recording session for RCA Victor, they returned to Chicago and played in the famed College Inn at the Hotel Sherman. That "once in a lifetime band" Coon-Sanders disbanded with the early death of young Carleton Coon in 1932. Joe Sanders tried vainly to lead his own band, mostly in the mid-west, but it simply didn't live up to the former days of Coon-Sanders.

"Vincent Lopez Speaking"

Vincent Lopez brought his piano and his well-trained musicians into focus playing his signature tune "Nola," thus becoming one of the most prolific dance bands in America during the 1920s. His famous deep-baritone introductory opening words on his WJZ radio program, "Hello, everybody. Lopez speaking," became household words and made him a national figure on radio. In 1925 his band also performed in London at the Hippodrome and the Kit-Kat Club.

Ted Lewis: "Is Everybody Happy?"

The great Ted Lewis thought himself a jazz musician, but he really wasn't. He certainly was a show business phenomenon showcasing an impressive list of sidemen: Benny Goodman, Jack Teagarden, Muggsy Spanier, Jimmy Dorsey, and Fats Waller, to mention a few. Ted's famous catchphrase "Is everybody happy?" and his theme "Me and My Shadow," as well as his enduring performance of his own composition "When My Baby Smiles at Me" while sporting an old battered top hat, were all house-hold words during the 1920s, as he and his almost-corny show band devoted enough time to the dance field to be considered an important part of it.

Ted Lewis started at Coney Island in Brooklyn, New York ,in 1916 with intentions of becoming a vaudeville act. The band went on to play in top vaudeville houses here and in Europe, especially London's Hippo-drome and the famous Kit Kat Club, and for many years up into the '60s and '70s at New York's Roseland and Latin Quarter and at Las Vegas' Desert Inn, where he had his final appearance in the Inn's famous lounge where he always drew great nostalgic crowds.

The Waltz King-Wayne King

Wayne King's Orchestra was a true dance band. His theme, "The Waltz You Saved for Me" identified this incomparable group of musicians who were featured at the Trianon Ballroom in Chi-cago in 1927 and later at Atlantic City's Steel Pier. His eight year tenure at the famous Aragon, where he was crowned "The Waltz King" popularized him nationally over network radio, featuring the vocals (and whistling skills) of Elmo Tanner, Charles Far-rell, Buddy Clark and The Barry Sisters.

The Great Fletcher Henderson

Another landmark group of fine musicians was Fletcher Hender-son's orchestra who started up in New York City at the Club Alabam in 1923, followed by a tenure beginning in 1925 at the Roseland Ballroom for the ensuing five years. Fletcher Henderson and his devoted follow-

ing of happy dancers were the talk of New York. His orchestra featured an absolute all-star group of players that included Edgar Sampson, Don Redman, Walter Johnson, Benny Carter, Rex Stewart, Sid Catlett, Louis Armstrong, Roy Eldridge, Coleman Hawkins, and other later greats to be. A virtual showcase of some of the best black jazz musicians of all time.

Some say that Henderson's style, compositions and arrangements may have been the catalyst for the formation of the Big Band Era, popularized by Benny Good-man employing his charts back in 1935. (It was Henderson who wrote and arranged "King Porter Stomp." In 1982 Benny Good-man told me that the time spent recording with Henderson's arrange-ments were his happiest years in music.

Fletcher Henderson and his jazz-flavored pioneer band, who con-centrated mostly on smooth dance tempos, toured the forty-eight states playing a variety of ballrooms, hotels, and theaters, then toured Europe twice, the first time in 1929. He disbanded shortly after World War II, when he semi-retired, concentrating on arranging for other orchestras and the Hollywood movie studios.

Gus Arnheim Cocoanut Grove Orchestra

Gus Arnheim's Cocoanut Grove Orchestra performed regularly for dancers at both the Cocoanut Grove and the Ambassador Hotel in Los Angeles. Here, bandleader Stan Kenton got his start, as did Bing Crosby and the Rhythm Boys (later featured with Paul Whiteman),vocalists Russ Columbo and Andy Russell, and sideman musician Fred Mac Murray (Yes, Fred MacMurray before those movie glory days). Arnheim's 1930s radio show from the Cocoanut Grove was two hours long and heard from "coast-to-coast," as they said in those days, describing network radio programs. Arnheim and his Orchestra appeared in the 1929 movie The Street Girl.

Isham Jones Dance Band

Another one of early dance bands was Isham Jones, who be-gan it all in 1919 when he formed a small ensemble in his hometown of Coaltown, Ohio. Jones played both piano and saxophone equally, and

even learned to play the string bass. Jones was a prolific songwriter as well. He found a home for his musical group at the College Inn, where the band remained for five years. His songs are evergreen dancing songs: "I'll See You in My Dreams," "You've Got Me Crying Again," "When My Dream Boat Comes Home," "Swinging Down the Lane," "It Had to Be You," great tunes all. Bandleader Woody Herman was both a sideman and vocalist with Isham Jones before forming his first Herd. Jones' band was very popular in Atlantic City at the famous Steel Pier, where so many bands played for the dancers of the thirties, as well as performances at New York's Lincoln Hotel and Denver's Elitch's Gardens.

After retiring because of bad health, Isham Jones returned to New York in 1936 and was featured for a while back at the Lincoln Hotel. His was a sweet ensemble of great music.

Ben Pollack, Bandleader Maker

Ben Pollack's band spawned an impressive number of important musicians who later went on to great fame as bandleaders in the Big Band Era. Try Glenn Miller, Benny Goodman, Jack and Charlie Teagarden, Charlie Spivak, Jimmy Mc-Partland, and in a later band, an unknown named Harry James. Some list! Pollack

was originally a drummer, and like his playing, a very dynamic, hard-driving man. He was a rather unhappy kind of musician, but musically excellent. His never-ending quest to form new bands, winding up as leader of a small dixieland group of players, never worked out, mostly due to his on-again, off-again interest in bandleading.

Epilogue
The reign of the early dance bands punctuated the beginning of a time that musically dominated the lives of both its participants and audiences identified as both dancers and listeners. The formation of these pioneer groups of musicians spawned new and even greater organizations that grew into a phenomenon we recognize as the dawn of the Big Band Era, that is, the birth of America's Golden Age of Music that mesmerized the next several generations of its fans. The dance bands had a great impact on America's popular culture and came to a climax beginning in the late Thirties when the Big Band explosion began to make its mark on the musical landscape.

THE BIG BANDS
MUSICAL ROYALTY

Top Row-L-R: Stan Kenton, Lawrence Welk, Les Brown, Harry James, Ray Anthony, Freddy Martin, Orrin Tucker.
Bottom Row-L-R: Sam Donahue, Woody Herman, Leroy Anthony, Jerry Gray

L-R: Buddy Rich, Woody Herman, Willard Alexander, Benny Goodman, Count Basie, Stan Kenton and Mel Torme

GLENN MILLER

HIS MUSIC KEEPS GOING
with LARRY O'BRIEN

The very mention of the name Glenn Miller conjures up visions of a brilliantly lit-up Wurlitzer jukebox and peppy jitterbugs in zoot suits swinging and hurling one another across a dance floor to the swinging sounds of "In the Mood," "Chattanooga Choo-Choo," or perhaps "Jukebox Saturday Night."

"...making one Coke last us til it's time to scram."

Major Glenn Miller disappeared on December 15, 1944, while on a wartime plane trip that was to take him across the English Channel, although neither his body or the plane has never been recovered, his music plays on to this day, some 64 years later. His music charts remain as timeless.

Since Glenn's disappearance the band has been led by a number of worthy musicians. Tex Beneke, the band's original sax player and vocalist on the numbers "Chattanooga Choo-Choo" (which earned the world's first Gold Record) and "I've Got a Gal in Kalamazoo," led the band for a while, followed by former member, drummer Ray McKinley (1956 to 1966), as well as member/saxist Peanuts Hucko; clarinetist Buddy De Franco in the

STA

seventies; then Jimmy Henderson, Larry O'Brien; and, from 1983 to 1988, Dick Gearhart; and, now in 2008, once again it's Larry O'Brien.

In 1982 I spoke with Larry O'Brien during a Glenn Miller band get- together I covered for Long Island PM Magazine with famed WNEW New York disc jockey William B. Williams and vocalists Margaret Whiting and Billy Eckstine. Present, too, was the man who booked the show, Willard Alexander, foremost head of the prestigious Willard Alexander Big Band Booking Agency:

"Larry was working at the Dunes in Las Vegas and I had my people approach him to lead the Miller band," Willard explained, "He was working for the Dorsey organization led by Sam Donahue and a house band in Vegas. I forgot who brought Larry to my attention. Anyway, we recommended him. We felt he would keep in tune, so to speak, with the Miller sound, and he looked darn good, too."

Glenn Miller with Tex Beneke

When Larry played with the Glenn Miller Orchestra while Ray McKinley was directing back in 1961, he didn't believe the band would last. "The band is not only still around, but it's flourishing," Larry said. "There are a lot of people who still love the original sound of Glenn's immortal charts."

In 1996, we got together again. Larry talked about the future of the Miller band once again, saying: "It's amazing. The applause is still tremendous today. Those tunes bring back a lot of memories. For example, we do 'That Old Black Magic' and 'People Like You and Me,' in addition to the regular stuff." But, then, like today, as Larry confirms, "In the Mood" and "Moonlight Serenade" are the top requested tunes.

"At one time I was concerned about our audience, but you know," he told mutual friend Big Band Jump Newsletter Editor Don Kennedy, "continually we're getting more and more young people at our concerts, and that gladdens my heart because they are our audience of the future. It also means that young people are opening their ears to something besides their own frenetic music."

Every Big Band buff knows the Glenn Miller story. In its heyday Glenn's was the most popular band of the late thirties and early forties, its world-famous, lyrical theme, Glenn's beautiful "Moonlight Serenade," a Big Band masterpiece. Clarinetist Johnny Mince described Glenn's success to me one afternoon during a conversation at the Three Village Inn in Stony Brook, New York in 1983. It was Johnny Mince, the catalyst, who with Glenn "discovered" the unique, elusive Glenn Miller sound.

Glenn decided to form his own band, which he did in 1937, but he struggled to keep the band going. The band finally caught on, but only after Glenn had mortgaged both his and his in-laws homes to keep the band going. Woody Herman revealed that to me in 1981 when we were discussing Glenn.

Glenn disbanded and tried again with a new manager and a new group of musicians. He chose an unusual, new clarinet player named Wilbur Schwartz, whose tone was exceptional. He found a saxophone player named Gordon "Tex" Beneke. Tex, of course , was the band's personality performer. Though he could not sing well, he nevertheless became the key vocalist on those great tunes "Jukebox Saturday Night," "I've got a Girl in Kalamazoo," and "Chattanooga Choo Choo," all accomplished with the help of the Modernaires, Chuck Goldstein, Hal Dickenson, Ralph Brewster, Bill Conway, and Dorothy Claire, or Marion Hutton.

Glenn hired vocalist Ray Eberly, Bob Eberle's brother. Bob was singing with Jimmy Dorsey and alerted Glenn to his brother's availability. Their names were spelled differently to avoid confusion.

Then, the band was booked into the famed Glen Island Casino in New Rochelle, New York. Glenn had appeared at Frank Dailey's Meadowbrook in New Jersey for a short gig before his Glen Island opening. The band was heard over the radio from the Meadowbrook, and success was just around the corner after appearances that summer at the Glen Island Casino.

Glenn recorded prolifically during that period. Bill Finegan arranged the swinging "Little Brown Jug," Kay Starr, temporarily replacing Marion Hutton, recorded "Love With a Capital You" and "Baby Me," two of Glenn's best lady vocal recordings; Tex Beneke and Al Klink recorded their tenor sax duel on "In the Mood", Joe Garland's catchy tune originally offered to Artie Shaw; Billy May wrote a great opening for "Serenade in Blue", and tunes like "Tuxedo Junction" and "Moonlight Serenade," Glenn's theme, became huge successes for the band.

Larry O'Brien - 1980

Engagements in the Cafe Rouge in the Hotel Pennsylvania with players like Ray Anthony, Johnny Best, Hal McIntyre, and Billy May increased the band's popularity. Glenn made two successful movies with the band, Sun Valley Serenade with Sonja Henie, and Orchestra Wives with Jackie Gleason and a lot of terrific Harry Warren music.

In 1942, with the war in full swing, Glenn disbanded his immensely popular band to join the Army Air Force. In a few months he formed the Glenn Miller American Band of the Allied Expeditionary Force. The all-soldier band, except for vocalist Beryl Davis, played for American fighting men and was heard on radio broadcasts from coast-to-coast and throughout Europe.

It is now 2008, more than a half-a-century later, and the Glenn Miller band itinerary remains booked far into the new Millennium. Today I spoke at length to Larry O'Brien about his life as a musician, his accidental benefactor Glenn Miller, and the destiny of today's Glenn Miller Orchestra .

Larry's introduction to the world of music occurred the day his dad, a

Larry O'Brien - 2004

craftsman who could make anything with his hands, fashioned him a pretty good homemade violin in the kitchen of their Ozone Park, Queens home. Larry was just ten.

"He placed it on the kitchen table. But, the violin was not for me. I wanted to play the trombone, especially when I heard a friend practicing on one in the rear of his dad's dry-cleaning shop. My dad obviously could not make one for me, so I had to get one. It had to wait until I got into John Adams High School where I borrowed one, while taking lessons at school."

Larry later received advanced lessons from a technically excellent

Today's Glenn Miller Orchestra in Rehearsal

teacher named Eddie Collier, an older, fellow high school alumni who was playing in Broadway shows. At sixteen, Larry won the New York Philharmonic Scholarship and "made" the prestigious All-City School Orchestra.

Larry O'Brien began his Big Band career playing a very smooth trombone in the house band at the Frontier Hotel in Las Vegas, backing various big-name acts who were performing as part of the Vegas star policy of the time. Along the road to his Glenn Miller success, he played in the bands of Buddy Morrow, Sammy Kaye, Art Mooney, Billy May, Ralph Marterie, Ray McKinley's Glenn Miller Orchestra, Urbie Green, Les Elgart, and the Tommy Dorsey Orchestra with Sam Donahue ---quite a compendium.

"I've had a checkered past, you could say."

How did Larry O'Brien capture the coveted Glenn Miller appointment.

"As far as I know, they invited me to lead the Glenn Miller band probably because of my experience with the Tommy Dorsey Orchestra and maybe conducting for Frank Sinatra, Jr., that lit up a lamp in somebody's head. So I was called and offered the job. I said, 'Yeah! I'll take

it.' and then David MacKay called me, talked further, then came out to Vegas to watch me perform, and sealed the deal. David, the son of Glenn's close friend, attorney, and executor of his estate, owned the worldwide rights to license the use of the Glenn Miller name and music book, or charts, as they are referred to in the business."

Besides his skill as a leader who drives a sparkling band, Larry O'Brien is a brilliant trombonist. His version of "Danny Boy" regularly captivates the crowd. His Dorsey breath-control style playing is dominated by those long legato phrases. His own musicians admire him greatly.

"I keep the band in an upbeat condition. Tonight's concert in Westhampton Beach will start with 'The Volga Boatman' chart. It will wake them up and get them started on an upbeat.

"It appears as though Larry O'Brien will lead the band well into the future. The purity and nostalgic value of Glenn Miller's music remains a mystery. Of all the famous Big Bands, Glenn Miller's music is the most recognizable and the most performed worldwide. Was it because he featured great soloists? No! Great vocalists? Not a chance! Then what was it? It was a composite of everything accomplished in middle-of-the-road perfection. It wasn't hot Artie Shaw or loud Charlie Barnet swing, nor was it Guy Lombardo sweet, Lawrence Welk corny, or Basie or Red Norvo jazz- influenced music.

The definitive Glenn Miller music we are talking about was the artfully arranged material by musicians like Jerry Gray, Bill Finegan, and Billy May. Their prolific charts, now preserved eternally in their 1940s style, remain timeless. More smash hits were "Pennsylvania 6-5000," "American Patrol," "Song of the Volga Boatmen," "Sun Valley Serenade," "Don't Sit Under the Apple Tree," "Blue Evening," "String of Pearls," "At Last," and countless others.

Neophyte or staunch outright fan, those Glenn Miller evergreens never fail to satisfy.

Listen, can you hear it? It's Paul Douglas on one of those radio air checks announcing from the Hotel Pennsylvania in New York on NBC:

"Ladies and Gentlemen, may I introduce Glenn Miller, bandleader, arranger, leading exponent of the swing trombone, direct from the Cafe Rouge in the Hotel Pennsylvania.

"Now, here's Glenn Miller's music!"

Microphone Left: Kevin Sheehan and Julia Rich with Nick Hilscher and the Glenn Miller Orchestra

It's Benny Goodman Day
His Real Voice was His Clarinet

The King of Swing is gone. For over fifty years Benny Goodman was the King of Swing securely anchored to his musical throne since that one night in 1935 when he almost single handedly ushered in the Big Band Era moments after his unexpected, triumphant success at Los Angeles' vast Palomar Ballroom. "I called out to the boys for one of our big Fletcher Henderson arrangements," he remembered, "and the boys seemed to get the idea." The crowd stopped dancing and rushed the bandstand.

And, indeed, it was Benny Goodman who brought needed respectability to jazz with an absolutely all-star ensemble at his milestone 1938 Carnegie Hall concert that reshaped music history and opened the doors forever to every jazz musician who followed. A generation was mesmerized by the sound of his master instrument and incomparable style.

In 1982, when Jack Ellsworth of radio station WLIM invited me to Benny Goodman Day it was, at last, my chance to talk with the King. Benny was chauffeured by limousine to North Patchogue in Central Long Island. Jack, who had interviewed Benny many years before in Providence, R.I., and maintained a relationship with him over the years, secretly confided to me that Benny absentmindedly believed Jack was once his manager, so Benny had agreed to come out to be a guest on Jack's popular Memories In Melody show. Jack would play Benny's records all day long and Benny would meet the station's advertisers, friends, and local dignitaries, and be interviewed by myself and NBC Television's Six O'clock News team. It was an absolute grand-slam for Jack who had just started up his radio station a few months before, lending a needed boost to the station's success.

So, without entourage or fanfare, without bodyguard or secretary, agent or impresario, Benny Goodman arrived in a late-model station wagon

Benny Goodman and Jack Ellsworth with Jack's son Glen

at WLIM's tiny, whitewashed building with its two, very tall and narrow, fenced-in antennas hovering above, where I greeted him along with Jack's wife, Dot, and my photographer Camille Smith. Benny's first words were: "Made it, at last." uttered in a somewhat tired, gravely voice and wry smile.

"Welcome to North Patchogue," said I, happily shaking his distinctive dead-fish, unenthusiastic hand. A lone, older fan stood anxiously on the sidelines hoping for an autograph. Benny noticed him and graciously signed his LP album, uttered a few kind words, and then walked into the building with that slow gait and quizzical grin.

Jack was on-the-air in the tiny studio. Bob Dorian, WLIM's morning man then, and later interviewer and host in his own right on tv's American Movie Classics joined us as we led Benny into Jack's office. I guided Benny to a comfortable couch situated under a large, colorful banner advertising the station's call letters near where Dot had set up a neat paper-plate deli lunch on a folding table covered with a large, disposable tablecloth. Benny grabbed a pastrami sandwich while being introduced to station personnel, valued advertisers, and local dignitaries.

By that time the NBC crew had arrived, but my photographer Camille Smith was able to hold them back until my interview with Benny was wrapped. Benny and I sat face-to-face on the couch and talked about Lionel Hampton, Teddy Wilson, and Gene Krupa, his famous sidemen of the Benny Goodman Quartet. I could sense that Benny was feeling a bit charmed with all the attention. Was this the giant who brought that wonderful swing-music into the lives of countless millions with his peerless musical ability on his clarinet? Is this the man who broke the color line in music by bringing the great jazz-pianist Teddy Wilson, and vibraphonist Lionel Hampton into an all-white band before a startled public? There was no doubt about those facts.

Our conversation then became centered around his affection for the old Bluebird series recordings that he favors over all his other work.

He recalled that it was Gene Krupa, his favorite drummer, who coined the words Swing Band one day while touring in Colorado and in response to a reporter's inquiry about the band's new style of music. "We just call it Swing!" said Krupa.

Minutes later, Jack was ready for his live interview where he and Benny played and talked about a variety of Goodman recordings. At one point while they were on live, Jack asked him: "Benny, how do you feel about a full day of your music on our station?"

"Well, if you can take it- - - so can I." Benny shot back to everyone's laughter.

And later, we asked him if there were any new mountains he wanted to climb, or if there was anything he hadn't done that he would like to do, he smiled and said: "I think I did it today. Coming here was quite a trip. I thought we'd never get here," he added, to almost instant laugh-

ter by everyone.
he was some sixty
perhaps at Montauk
of Long Island.
Later, while
Benny didn't notice
of some as they po-
very close beside
clicked a camera.
notice the reac-
rent or the daring it
to approach him,
autograph without
dignity. Some
him---but what
seemed too unlikely
very spot, at this
seated one of the
the 20th century, a
place in music his-
or two he would be
ence.
He was the
epitome of what the
represented musi-

Benny still thought
miles further out,
Point, the eastern tip

slowly sipping coffee,
the awe in the faces
litely took turns sitting
him while someone
I'm sure he did not
tions, the undercur-
must have required
or maybe ask for an
compromising their
wanted to talk with
would they say? It
that here, on this
very moment, was
great musical icons of
man who is assured a
tory, and in a moment
gone from their pres-

genuine article, the
entire radio station
cally from morning till

night every day of the year, much like the formats of hundreds of similar, dedicated radio stations throughout the country.

In an unexpected moment I sensed Benny's patience was wearing and he signaled accordingly by excusing himself and backing out the door into an anteroom in preparation for leaving. "Get me out of here," he growled, I'm tired." He clearly needed to leave after a long day. On the way out good-byes and vows were briefly exchanged as we guided him into the station wagon in the same way he arrived.

The station buzzed for days afterwards and there was a glow over Long Island. Jack Ellsworth walked taller, his enthusiasm reinforced, his purpose justified. I beam still to this day, some twenty-five years later, for as a chronicler of such individuals, it was an all-important day.

Benny Goodman passed away from us on Friday, June 13, 1986. In 1989, Benny's daughter, Rachel Goodman Edelson, who was engaged at the time writing a documentary about her father's life, wrote to me about the progress of her book and enclosed a booklet and an actual clarinet reed once used by her father. She said he used to throw them on the floor when he rehearsed in his studio at his home on East 66th Street in New York City. She had collected them. It was a welcome present, no, rather a personal link to greatness.

Benny Goodman has thrilled generations with his exciting, pulsat-

ing, uncompromising improvisations on his master instrument, the swing-ing clarinet. To sum it up, George T. Simon, author of the book The Big Bands, once wrote, "How many other Kings, musical or regal, have done as much for so many of us for so many years?"

Goodman, Krupa, Dawn Win O. W. Awards

Honored As Year's Outstanding Stars

THE 1937 ORCHESTRA WORLD ACHIEVEMENT AWARD closed on January 17, 1938, elevating Benny Goodman, orchestra leader; Gene Krupa, musician; and Dolly Dawn, orchestra vocalist into the three top ranks of selection. According to the thousands who participated in this first annual poll, Goodman, Krupa, and Dawn are the outstanding individuals in the music business for the year 1937.

Taking an early lead, the leaders maintained their position throughout the entire poll. All were selected by overwhelming majorities, ranging nearly 50% ahead of their nearest competitors.

The rise of Martha Tilton as an orchestra vocalist is amazing. Only a few months in the business, she copped second place in a field of nearly 60 vocalists.

Dorsey Strong

Equally interesting is the fact that Tommy Dorsey, more so than Benny Goodman, is regarded as a leader close to his instrument. Tommy polled second place both in the orchestra leader and musician columns.

The ACHIEVEMENT AWARD is the mark of achievement set up by THE ORCHESTRA WORLD to recognize the leader, the musician, and the vocalist who accomplished the most benefit for the music business during the year. It was not a popularity contest.

From the field of hundreds of entries the following are the 20 leaders in all three groups.

Orchestra Leader
1. BENNY GOODMAN
2. TOMMY DORSEY
3. BOB CROSBY
4. Jimmie Lunceford
5. Horace Heidt
6. Hal Kemp
7. Casa Loma
8. Bunny Berigan
9. Raymond Scott
10. Duke Ellington
11. Jimmy Dorsey
12. Art Shaw
13. Woody Herman
14. Chick Webb
15. Guy Lombardo
16. Eddy Duchin
17. Fletcher Henderson
18. Hudson-DeLange
19. Red Norvo
20. Sammy Kaye

Musician
1. GENE KRUPA
2. TOMMY DORSEY
3. HARRY JAMES
4. Benny Goodman
5. Ray Bauduc
6. Teddy Wilson
7. Lionel Hampton
8. Louis Armstrong
9. Bunny Berigan
10. Artie Shaw
11. Adrian Rollini
12. Art Tatum
13. Johnny Hodges
14. Ray McKinley

DOLLY DAWN
1937's Outstanding Vocalist

15. Bob Zerke
16. Jack Teagarden
17. "Red" Norvo
18. "Fats" Waller
19. Jimmy Dorsey
20. Coleman Hawkins.

Orchestra Vocalist
1. DOLLY DAWN
2. MARTHA TILTON
3. JACK LEONARD
4. Edythe Wright
5. Mildred Bailey
6. Ella Fitzgerald
7. Kay Weber
8. Kenny Sargent
9. Connie Boswell
10. Ivy Anderson
11. Maxine Sullivan
12. "Pee Wee" Hunt
13. Perry Como
14. Louis Armstrong
15. Billie Halliday
16. Maxine
17. Peg LaCentra
18. Maxine Grey
19. Skinny Ennis
20. Helen Ward

The contest brought selections from every part of the United States; from Canada, Mexico, Philippine Islands, Alaska, Great Britain, Australia, South Africa, India, France, Denmark, Hawaii, South America—and one coupon from Japan.

Radio Eds Vote

Included in the final returns are the selections of nearly two hundred radio editors of the United States, who were canvassed in a special sub-poll. It is interesting to note that their selections coincided with the three final selections, but were at complete variance with the rest of the leaders. Few got past Gene Krupa in selections for the musician's award. Benny Goodman and Dolly Dawn were overwhelming choices for orchestra leader and vocalist.

In recognition of their selections, Goodman, Krupa, and Dawn will be presented with plaques, commemorating their 1937 achievement. It is expected that these plaques will be awarded on radio programs featuring these artists. Plans for the presentation were being made as THE ORCHESTRA WORLD went to press.

BENNY GOODMAN
1937's Outstanding Leader

GENE KRUPA
1937's Outstanding Musician

Benny Goodman in Russia - 1962

Harry James
THE BEST DAMN TRUMPET PLAYER

A contortionist by age four, a drummer by seven, performing trumpet solos in a circus band by twelve. A star sideman, a consistent winner of Metronome and Downbeat Magazine Awards, a Number One bandleader, setting

Helen Forrest sings with Harry James

all-time attendance records for Big Bands. An excellent arranger, the composer of "Flash," "Back Beat Boogie," "Feet Draggin' Blues," "Tango Blues," and "Ultra." A hit maker, a movie maker, and a star virtuoso.

Simply a legend in his own lifetime.

The name is Harry James, perhaps the most popular bandleader ever. Harry James was born on March 15, 1916, in Albany, Georgia. His parents, Everett and Maybelle James, worked in the Haig Traveling Circus. Mom as an aerialist and dad as the conductor of the circus band.

"As a rule, everyone had to contribute and I was no exception." Harry explained.

Harry's first brush with music was as a drummer, a skill he re-

tained all his professional life. However, Harry's dad determined that success for his son would be his playing of a trumpet in the band. By ten, lessons with dad as tutor began and, as Harry recalled," with progress, I was soon doing solos with the circus band."

The circus wintered in Beaumont, Texas, where the James family settled down in 1931. Harry attended school there and took gigs with local bands Hogan Hancock, Herman Waldman, and Art Hicks. In 1935, with Hicks' in Chicago, bandleader Ben Pollack noticed Harry and invited him to join his band, giving him his first legitimate chance for national exposure, as the Pollack band commissioned air check recordings, a sixteen- inch disc that bandleaders and advertiser used to check their performances on aired radio programs so they could improve their band's future performances. Sitting in with Harry at the time were trombonist Glenn Miller, clarinetist Irving Fazola, pianist Freddie Slack, trumpeter Clarence "Shorty" Sherock, and saxist Dave Mathews. Harry would spend 1935 and 1936 with Pollack, where he met, then married the band's singer Louise Tobin. They had two sons, Tim and Jeff.

Harry was noticed by Benny Goodman's brother Irving, who heard Harry's exemplary work on a recording "Deep Elm" and advised Benny to add the young trumpeter to the band's roster, which he did Christmas week of 1936. Although Harry received like offers from Glenn Miller and Tommy Dorsey, who were forming their own organizations, Harry elected to go with Goodman. A legend was being born.

Goodman's powerhouse band was loaded with future leaders, drummer Gene Krupa, pianist Teddy Wilson, xylophonist Lionel Hampton, and pianist Jess Stacy. Sitting alongside Harry were trumpeters Ziggy Elman and Chris Griffin. This trio became the acclaimed trumpet section of the Big Band Era. Within weeks Harry elevated to first chair trumpet. His unflagging spirit and dynamic playing would propel the band to even greater prominence. There are, no doubt, readers here who may recall showing up early for the band's performances to hear Harry, Ziggy, and

Chris go through their warm-ups. Harry's exceptional works with Benny include "Ridin' High," "St.Louis Blues," and "Roll Em." Along with his magnificent work during the famed January 1938 Carnegie Hall Concert, Harry also recorded independently with members of Goodman's and Count Basie's orchestras, as well as work with Lionel Hampton, Billie Holiday, Teddy Wilson, and Red Norvo. The group used to hang out at Red Norvo and Mildred Bailey's house in Forest Hills, Queens, where they put ideas together. The Benny Goodman quartet was formed at one of the Norvo house sessions.

If you will search out a recording Harry performed with Wilson and Norvo in 1937 called "Just a Mood," a blues number you could not have heard no better trumpet playing than Harry's expressions performed on that session that day. With Gene Krupa's departure from Goodman in early 1938, Harry ran a close second to Benny as the band's main attraction. Night after night, Harry and Benny would duke it out, with Harry matching Benny note for note. With an irresistible urge to lead his own band, Harry left the comfort and security of the King of Swing's organization, borrowed $4,500.00 from Benny himself, and left him with good wishes."

February 1939 saw Harry with his spanking new band open at the Ben Franklin Hotel in Philadelphia. It was a swinging group, heavy on the brass, but, while the critics wrote good reviews, trouble lay ahead.

Swing music was diminishing. The mood of the listening public was changing. With so many excellent, established bands to compete with, Harry found many choice locations closed to his group. This meant less money playing lesser venues. By 1940, Harry was deep in debt. Even the addition of girl singer Connie Haines and a boy singer, a skinny kid named Frank Sinatra that Harry found performing in a New Jersey roadhouse, failed to move the band forward.

Sinatra went over to Dorsey. "We were all starving and his wife was pregnant and he had a chance to go with Tommy Dorsey for $ 120.00 a week. He was only making $ 75.00 a week with me and not getting it." explained to me back in 1981. "I told him, if things don't get better with us in the next six months, get me a job with Dorsey, too."

Harry went from Columbia to Variety Records, a less than suitable venture. Things got so bad that Louise recalls that some weeks Harry paid everyone but himself. Harry hung in while gradual changes were being made. He softened the brass with strings, and Dick Haymes was hired to replace Sinatra. Helen Forrest left Goodman and Harry hired her. Columbia re-signed the band. Corky Corcoran joined the band at age seventeen, remaining with Harry for over thirty years. At one point, Harry was appointed legal guardian of the very young man who sparked the sax section.

A May, 1941 recording session featured a number on the "B" side of a tune he admired ever since he heard Judy Garland's recorded version. It was called "You Made Me Love You." When it hit the markets, and with lots of help from Martin Block, a disc jockey on New York's WNEW, who was playing it frequently, it became an overnight sensation. When the band arrived in New York to play the Paramount Theater, Harry found huge crowds gathered around the theater. At last, he had achieved fame and fortune; in his own words, "When the band eats better, they just naturally play better."

Hit followed hit. "I'll Get By" (with Dick Haymes vocal), "Sleepy Lagoon," "Velvet Moon," "I've Heard That Song Before," "I Had the Craziest Dream" (the classic Helen Forrest version from the movie Springtime in the Rockies), and "I Don't Want to Walk Without You." By 1943 Helen left because Harry divorced Louise and married Betty Grable. It was known that Helen and Harry were lovers. When I interviewed Helen Forrest about the various bandleaders she performed with, Harry was the hands-down winner being her favorite leader, her best boss, and the nicest person in her musical life, along with her good friend and Autolite Radio Show singing partner, Dick Haymes.

After Helen, enter pretty Kitty Kallen with the recordings "I'm Beginning to See the Light" and "It's Been a Long, Long, Time," both very big hits for the band.

The band's reputation grew at a rapid pace, eventually reaching number one in the music polls. Harry replaced Glenn Miller on the Chesterfield Radio Show when Glenn joined the Army Air Force Band. Harry and the band went on to make twenty-two movies.

Harry and Betty had two daughters. Jointly, they were among the top money makers in the business.

As a show of contrast, Harry's obligation to the IRS in 1940 was nil, but his earnings in 1943 would elevate his payments to over $500,000.00. During the war years Harry was Columbia Record's biggest moneymaker. The recording ban of 1942-1943 surely deprived Harry of even greater heights. It may have contributed to the rise of the individual vocalists and the demise of the bands. By 1946, most of the Big Bands had folded and Harry disbanded briefly. When he came back, a new band was formed, loaded with younger, more jazz oriented musicians. The strings were gone, and he embarked upon a more progressive style of playing. As Harry stated," These talented kids make me really want to play."

The 1950s and '60s were great years of artistic achievement for Harry, with nifty arrangements from Neal Hefti and Ernie Wilkins and tunes such as "Blues for Sale," "Bangtail," "J. Walkin'," and revised renditions of Count Basie hits "Shiny Stockings," "Lester Leaps In," and "April in Paris." Much was said about Harry's taking on Basie styles, but, in fact, Harry was too much his own man to be anyone's clone.

The James band was the most active organization in the business during this period, consistently playing to sellout crowds in Las Vegas, Reno, and Lake Tahoe, and wherever they traveled. Carnegie Hall in 1964, the annual Monterey Jazz Festival in 1965, tours to Germany in 1964, England during 1970 and '71, and South America in the '80s. The band also appeared annually on Ed Sullivan's television show.

> **Joe Pardee (Harry James Scholar)**: Harry paid his people the best salaries and naturally he hired the best musicians. While never a strict disciplinarian , when the night's work began, Harry expected one-hundred percent from his players. He set personal demands of his own performance, and would stand for no-less from the other musicians The sidemen through the years reads as a Who's Who of the trade: alto-man Willie Smith, trombonist Ray Sims, alto saxman Joe Riggs, trombonist Ziggy Elmer, saxist Vido Musso, trumpeter Art DePew trombonist Ray Coniff, and pianist Jack Percival. Drumming chores were assigned to Buddy Rich, Louis Bellson, Sonny Payne, and Tony De Nicola, who would spend six years with Harry. He tells the story of when he received a new chart, and Harry would read it over just once--- never to look at it again. Not only did he remember his own part, but, everyone else's in the band, as well. Of the hundreds of charts in the band's book, Harry knew them all by number, every one memorized. Harry also had a keen ear for vocalists, beginning with Sinatra, Haymes, Buddy DeVito, Connie Haines, Helen Forrest, Kitty Kallen, and Lynn Roberts; all would grace his bandstand down through the years. Harry's long time band manager Pee Wee Monte was loyal to Harry until the end of Harry's life."

For a nationwide celebrity tour of a 1978 show The Big Broadcast of 1944, Harry chose Lynn Roberts to be the vocalist. Lynn had paid her dues early-on in her career singing with Goodman and both Dorsey brothers. After the tour Harry asked Lynn to stay on as the regular vocalist, which lasted until 1983. Harry held great praise for Lynn Roberts, and vice versa:

"Harry was my favorite," Lynn Roberts told me during an interview, "maybe because I was older. Before the 1978 tour, I had met Harry years before when I was singing with Tommy Dorsey. Harry didn't remember the meeting, but it was in 1954 at the Last Frontier Hotel in Vegas. I don't think I need to say anything about Harry's trumpet playing. He was magnificent and even in '78 he was still playing great. We'd sit on the bus and talk about his life. He'd talk about his mom and always about Betty (Grable). He adored her, even though they were divorced for years. I guess it was just one of those sad romances that just didn't seem to work. Professionally, Harry was extremely generous. He was not intimidated by anyone's talent. He loved to be surrounded by talent and gave everyone a chance to shine. He had a wonderful sense of timing and could put a show together that was perfect, for whatever was required. Harry was a showman--- not just a bandleader. We were friends, and I'm grateful for that. After he died, I recorded a tribute album (with trumpeter Mel Davis) to Harry called 'Harry, You Made Me Love You.' I think he really would have been happy with it.

"So, for whatever reason, I'm not really sure --- I felt very connected to Harry James, so I would have to say that he was my favorite bandleader."

> *Joe Pardee:* Harry blew them all away for forty-four years. By early 1983 it was clear to all that Harry was a very sick man. So many years of touring, suffering under a poor, traveling- man's diet, and incessant smoking finally wore the Maestro down. He would play his final engagement just weeks before the end. The date July 5th held great meaning for Harry. He and Betty were married on July 5, 1943. He lost Betty Grable on July 5, 1973, and ironically, Harry passed away on July 5, 1983.

"I loved Harry James," said Frank Sinatra, Harry's first boy singer, "I loved him for a long time. I shall miss him. He is not gone. The body is, but the spirit remains."

Well, the great trumpet man is gone, but the sound of his expressive trumpet continues on through his recordings. It was Ray Anthony,

HARRY JAMES
and his Chesterfield Music Makers

describing his mentor, who coined the phrase, as the best damn trumpet player, for which I named my first book in 1996. Harry's legacy of music reminds us of what we possessed in his presence.

Front Row (Center Three):
Connie Haines
Harry James
Frank Sinatra

 Artie Shaw
The "Begin The Beguine" Band Begins

What an exhilarating experience conversing with renowned bandleader Artie Shaw. Artie's depth as a thinker and reputation as a constantly analyzing musician follow him from his restless days as an outspoken bandleader right up to today. Artie Shaw was 89 years old at the time of our encounter, but spoke and interacted like he was 50.

I spent two weeks preparing for our forthcoming interview from his home in Newbury Park, California, but no form of preparation was enough.

We faced off phone to phone, and, suspicions confirmed, it was not an easy encounter, although it was at times dramatic, funny, and for certain, stimulating, somewhat like navigating through white water-- very difficult at best, but strangely gratifying.

But, hold on, I think we are getting ahead of ourselves. Let's back up to the year 1910 where Arthur Jacob Arshawsky was born in New York City, although was raised in New Haven, Connecticut from the age of eight. He played saxophone in the high school band. After some effort with the school's Peter Pan Novelty Orchestra, he joined Johnny Cavallaro's local band, where, at fifteen he was the youngest member. There he learned the many harsh lessons of a musician's life then headed to Cleveland and finally Chicago, carefully honing his playing qualities and arranging skills with Joe Cantor's Far East Orchestra, Austin Wylie's band, and Irving Aaronson's Commanders.

"Yeh, ...working every night until 3 A.M., then heading for the 'Negro district' to sit in with Earl Hines and go till daylight. One had to get away from the respectable band to play some

jazz," Artie said. Playing with and watching musicians like trumpeter Muggsy Spanier and clarinetist Frank Teschemacher influenced the young clarinetist.

"I was the kind of guy who listened to everybody, that's how I learned," he said. "Sure, it's easier when someone can show you how to do what you want to do. But the big thing is to learn - some way - just so you do learn. My home grown method of learning may be tougher - but once you do learn it my way you don't easily forget what you've learned. But, I didn't know I wanted to be a bandleader. It never entered my mind. It just happened as anything happens," Art went on. Although he swears he patterned his music after no one in particular, he also swears he remembers it all as ".....nothing but work, work, work, until from time to time I got tired and quit for awhile --which, as you know, I did a number of times when I felt I had to."

Artie Shaw returned to New York as a freelance player for CBS, appearing in concert in a clarinet-and-strings quartet that didn't really work out. He was nineteen and had to remain in New York because of an accident. A man stepped in front of his car and, as a result, died. He was forced to stay on for legal reasons. Artie Shaw knew no one at all in New York.

Trecking uptown to listen to jazz players, he met and was befriended by Willie "The Lion" Smith in Harlem. "I had never heard piano playing like that in my life." Artie joined in with Smith and went on to meet bandleader Chick Webb and a young and then-healthy kid vocalist, Billie Holiday. "There was the great Jack Teagarden and his younger brother

Charlie, Eddie Condon, Gene Krupa, Benny Goodman, Wingy Manone and the whole Chicago crowd who also had come to New York about the same time as I did to try their luck in the Big Apple."

Artie encountered the budding, legendary jazz cornetist Bix Beiderbecke, who was on the downgrade after leaving Paul Whiteman's King of Jazz Orchestra, and now a pitiful wreck of a man unable to control his drinking which was interfering with his fine cornet playing. He also met Jimmy Dorsey, who had already established himself, and would come around now and then and play in their jam sessions. Artie encountered a successful Tommy Dorsey, a flat-broke, struggling Bunny Berigan, who was trying to earn a living as a trumpet player, and a young piano player named Joe Bushkin, who later played with Tommy Dorsey.

"We hung out at Plunkett's, a hole-in-the-wall joint under the Sixth Avenue El at 53rd Street and Ninth Avenue, where I met a music conductor from CBS who got me an audition and a part-time job with Red Nichols' band. As a result, I got to play first saxophone in the CBS staff orchestra. I was only 20 years old." Artie began focusing on becoming "somebody," driving himself through hard work and a "feverish need to know about things."

PLUNKETT'S

There was a number of passwords used at Plunkett's in those days, according to Esquire's 1947 Jazzbook. In those free and easy days tabs represented more of the business than cash. There were two booths in the small back room, but they were seldom used except for a siesta or the occasional visit of an angry wife. Every day the barreled beer arrived at Plunkett's in a different truck: a florist's delivery car, a milk wagon, or even a hearse. Eddie Condon's dressing room, the icebox Tommy Dorsey talks about, was loaded to the ceiling with thousands of dollars' worth of instruments -- everybody's ---from Jimmy Dorsey's famous collection of gold saxophones to Pee Wee Russell's crud- caked clarinet, or Bix Beiderbecke's cornet in a corduroy sack, and even Joe Venuti's fiddle and Jack Teagarden's and Glenn Miller's trombones. The camaraderie at Plunkett's was something special. Why, when the Dorsey Brothers started their orchestra , Jimmy Plunkett was their manager. The bar was about ten feet long and on the shelves above it were a half-dozen nondescript beer steins. In the telephone book Plunkett's was listed as The Trombone Club.

Back to Artie Shaw:

Between gigs, Artie applied his earnings as a radio studio musician, one of those elite group of excellent instrumentalists, to finance a general education in the hope of becoming a writer. He purchased a small farm in rural Bucks County, Pennsylvania, where, for about a year, he wrote a book about Bix Biederbecke, then scrapped it because he wasn't satisfied with the results. He returned to New York: "I began working my head off in the radio and recording studios, making several hundred dollars a week playing on soap and cereal sponsored programs. Now and then there would be a recording session, a distinct improvement on the sickening advertising music I was forced to do. I also tried to go back to arranging. I dreamed up a little piece of music , a composition I entitled 'Interlude in B Flat,' drawn from ideas supplied by Mozart and Brahms - people and stuff like that.

"I played it at a swing concert with the help of two violin-playing friends, a violist, a cellist, and added guitar, string bass, and drums for the sake of rhythm, It was such a huge success that agents kept calling me." Art refers to Joe Helbeck, a nightclub owner who had invited him to participate with his then small group to perform for the benefit of Local 802 of the musician's union at the Imperial Theater. Artie called his group Arthur Shaw's Swing String Ensemble, fusing strings with brass, an unheard of effect at the time. The excellent results prompted Tommy Rockwell, head of the Rockwell-O'Keefe Booking Agency, to ask Artie to form a permanent band. Some have called that concert a milestone in jazz history, as being the first real jazz concert.

During the summer of 1935, Artie put together a regular band just after some valid efforts with Bunny Berigan's band. Artie performed on that famous original recording "I Can't Get Started" that remains a hit even today.

"The first gig with my new band...I called it Art Shaw and his Orchestra... was at the Lexington (Hotel) in New York," Art continued, "playing what we did best. I had two fellow musicians from Aaronson's days, tenor saxist Tony Pastor and Lee Castle playing trumpet. I also added a string quartet that was a different approach. Jerry Gray set this up. He was a jazz fiddle player and a very good arranger."

I reminded Art that his first band sounded much like Dixieland:

"Well, everybody sounded like everybody in those days. What's Dixieland, anyway? Maybe shades of that sound entered our brain, I don't know."

If you listen to those early 1936-37 Brunswick recordings "It Ain't Right," with Peg La Centra on vocal, "Thou Swell," "Sugarfoot Stomp," and a swinging version of "Goodnight Angel," you'll see what I mean. They were the pre-"Begin the Beguine" stardom days. The band had four strings, three brass, and only two reeds. Artie and Jerry Gray did all the arrangements. Then the "Begin the Beguine" band arrived:

"When we recorded Cole Porter's 'Begin the Beguine' in 1938, we soared, even though it was the 'B' side. That tune was nowhere and suddenly a guy named Artie Shaw comes along and makes a record of it with a totally different arrangement, and it becomes a hit. How do you figure it?" Artie said, "You seek perfection and settle for what you get."

The arrangement developed for Artie Shaw's "Begin the Beguine" transpired in Boston where they had a long engagement at the Roseland-

State Ballroom. "I asked Jerry to re-arrange ' Begin the Beguine,' a tune that the band liked to fool around with. I wanted to get the attention of the (ballroom) dancers, and it did. Jerry wrote a strong introduction for that reason. He substituted a modified 4/4 beat for the original beguine rhythm."

I told Artie that New York's WQEW radio had just conducted an annual listener's poll of the 156 best recordings of all time, and that his original version of "Begin the Beguine" came in number one.

"It was a good recording, I'm not surprised that it has stood up this long."

"And your 'Stardust' was number eight."

"Yeah, I heard that. That's fine."

"And 'Frenesi' was forty-one."

"Well, that proves my point. It's all relative, isn't it? It's like art - very subjective. I really don't follow polls - never have. I only care whether I achieved close to what I wanted to do. Everytime you go into a studio you have an idea of what you want to do. Somebody has to come out on top no matter what you do. But, what does it really mean? How do you measure that?

"You have no idea what's going to happen when you make a record. All you can do is make the best record you can . I didn't follow the idea of make success - make things what people wanted. I tried to do what I wanted and to do it as well as I could do it. Some of it worked. I call myself an eighty-percent loser."

"Most people think you are a ninety -percent winner."

"No - no, no! If I was a ninety-percent winner, I'd be a zillionaire. A ten-percent winner is very big."

After the "Begin the Beguine"(with "Indian Love Call" on the "A" side) success, the Shaw band began recording for Bluebird and included the bouncy, jazzy "Back Bay Shuffle" (which Artie still enjoys; the "ghost" band playing it quite differently today, he says), and "Nightmare," that Artie composed in his hotel room during that Boston stay, which became his eerie-like band theme.

Another kind of musician, jazz singer Billie Holiday, sang with Artie Shaw's band for the Boston engagement in Roseland-State, until she decided to quit. She was tired of the racism dished out to her mostly on Southern tours, being replaced by co-band singer Helen Forrest. Artie composed and arranged a tune especially for Billie entitled "Any Old Time" which eventually became a hit - now a standard - a tune loved by the musicians. It is magnificent, to say the least. Find the original version and listen carefully. It's pure Shaw and Holiday excellence. You will come to love the work of Artie Shaw and Billie Holiday for this recording alone. After recording the song with Billie, the record company (RCA) would not release it, citing Billie as not being commercial. "So I told Billie about that and that I had to record it with somebody else," Artie explained, "So I used Helen Forrest, and they released the record. Stupid, but true! Billie was a remarkable singer. I chose her because she was a singer I could afford at the time and the only singer that could keep up with the band. Helen Forrest was also very good. She learned a lot from Billie; she sat next to her for a while. They split up the work . I always thought that later, Helen sounded a lot like Billie...same kind of feeling."

Just before Christmas 1998, when I asked Helen Forrest about her association with Artie Shaw, she complimented Billie Holiday's singing, "I loved Billie's singing and listened to her phrasing quite a bit.And, Richard, my favorite recording with Artie was 'All The Things You Are.' Artie always made sure that I was comfortable doing my songs in my own style. After all, Artie was my first Big Band leader."

In choosing which musicians would play in his band, Artie described it to me this way: "I hired the guys who I thought could play what

Artie Shaw and His Navy Band at Pearl Harbor During World War II

I wanted to hear and what we needed from them as musicians. If they couldn't make it after they played with us for a while, you learned pretty soon who could and who couldn't handle themselves. I kept guys who I thought had potential, and weeded out the guy who couldn't blow. Les (sax player) Robinson said, 'What do you see in me', and I said, 'I heard what you are trying to do.'"

Of all his sidemen Artie respected drummer Buddy Rich and tenor sax player Georgie Auld the most. "Buddy was a difficult musician, hard to harness, but he had something to say with his percussion, and he said it well and it helped my band at the time. Georgie Auld was also a hard-headed musician who sometimes went against my musical grain. But, like

Buddy, he kept the band going with his energy and skills and became, like Buddy, a major asset."

Then my inevitable November 1939 Artie Shaw question: "Why did you give up leading and playing your band so suddenly by walking out on your band at the Cafe Rouge in New York and taking off for Mexico on an unscheduled vacation, vowing never to return to bandleading?"

"It wasn't sudden. It was a buildup of disillusionment with what I was doing. I wanted to play music, and an audience wanted me to play 'Begin the Beguine.' It gets a little old after a while. We needed a little chance to play something else once in a while. I wanted to play real music, not music just for dancers, or treat it all as a business like the bands of Guy Lombardo or Sammy Kaye were doing."

Artie had left the band in the hands of Georgie Auld, who fronted what he called Georgie Auld and His Artie Shaw Orchestra, but it only lasted three months or so without Artie, who was south of the border in Acapulco resting up, playing in local jam sessions, always thinking and planning new and exciting new ways to play and present music, and collecting Mexican-Latin style music to bring up North.

When Artie returned he brought along a tune which, when recorded, became a major hit. The title was "Frenesi."

"No one expected that great success. I didn't think - my God-- 'Frenesi' - the last thing on Earth we expected was for that to take off. It seemed about as far removed as possible from what they would call mainstream hit music in those days. But it did. "It went crazy," Artie told my colleague Fred Hall for the 1989 book Dialogues in Swing.

By this time, it seemed Artie Shaw could not escape success. His new orchestra was his finest. It had a string section and stars like Billy Butterfield on trumpet and Johnny Guarnieri on guitar and harpsichord (a new jazz instrument), Ray Coniff on trombone, Lennie Hayton on piano, and later, Hot Lips Page on trumpet, Lee Castle and Max Kaminsky on trumpet, and Georgie Auld on tenor sax. Artie's memorable "Concerto for Clarinet" was recorded during the "Frenesi" period.

"It came out of a film I was working on for Warner Brothers with Fred Astaire. I wrote the piece for Fred, who was gonna do a dance around it. So I wrote a thing called 'Concerto for Clarinet.' It was a framework kind of piece, part blues and part jazz. It was a lot like a thing I once did at a Paul Whiteman concert earlier, only less extensive."

When America entered the war in 1941, Artie Shaw joined the Navy, and as a Chief Petty Officer led a Navy band on downright dangerous tours in the South Pacific entertaining the troops: "We arrived at Pearl Harbor on Christmas Day, 1942. Our band was called Navy Band Number 501, with players like trumpeter Max Kaminsky and drummer Davy Tough. Our base was New Caledonia. We set out on a tour of the New Hebrides, the Solomon's, spots like that. We played on ships, in jungles, on airfields, and anywhere they booked us. We hopped from place to place to place - jungles mostly. Not that we had any choice. On flight decks we were lowered into the ship, just like when we played the Strand or the Paramount in New York, only the stages there were raised like a giant elevator. On battleships we played under the big guns. We had a number of close calls when the Japs decided to bomb the ships we played on. We stayed on in Australia, however, and traveled up and down that whole continent before we began to come apart. Our instruments were in bad shape, as were our bodies. It was combat fatigue, and it was impossible to go on, so we shipped back to the U.S. I was in the Oak Knoll Naval Hospital for a few months, pretty much washed up, to say the least."

For a while Artie organized another band and recorded for Musicraft Records. Mel Torme's Meltones, a young, and new group from Chicago, recorded some very nice sides including "Get Out of Town" and "What Is This Thing Called Love," and songbird Kitty Kallen recorded a splendid version of "My Heart Belongs To Daddy," which she still talks about today. Artie still wasn't happy, just always unsettled and wanting.

Artie Shaw went East and settled down for a while in Norwalk, Connecticut, after trying Hollywood and being involved making movies.

"I was at last able to write. For me, it was more important than playing a clarinet or leading a band."

Some consider Artie Shaw's small groups - his band -within-a-band groups like the pre-war Gramercy Five (named after a New York telephone exchange), who played lightweight, jazz-oriented material as an excellent approach to creative music. Some choices were "Summit Ridge Drive" (which became a million seller, named after a street on which Shaw lived at the time of the recording), "Special Delivery Stomp," "My Blue Heaven," and the breezy "The Grabtown Grapple," featuring, at different times, trumpeter Roy Eldridge, guitarist Barney Kessel, drummer Nick Fatool, trumpeter Billy Butterfield, guitarist Johnny Guarnieri, bassist Jud DeNaut, drummer Lou Fromm, bassist Morris Rayman, and pianist Dodo "The Moose" Marmarosa.

As a last musical stand, Artie Shaw resumed recording with an extension of the Gramercy Five group featuring guitarists Tal Farlow or Joe Puma and pianist Hank Jones. There were memorable sessions with this group including terrific versions of "S' Wonderful," "Little Jazz" (also a sobriquet for Roy Eldridge), "Love Walked In," "Summertime," "Lady Day" (as a tribute to Billie Holiday, who was known as Lady Day), and "Dancing On the Ceiling."

"Didn't you get some satisfaction performing that body of work with the small groups like Gramercy Five? You had people like trumpeter Billy Butterfield and guitarist Johnny Guarnieri-----"

"...and I had guys like (pianist) Dodo Marmarosa and (trumpeter) Roy Eldridge. And I had guys like (pianist) Hank Jones and (guitarist) Tal

Farlow."

"You have to be satisfied with some of those things."

"True. Satisfaction is doing it. The misery is having to keep doing the same thing year in and year out. I can't stand it. Nobody could stand it. Why should we play the same thing over and over just because it was successful? Some people put up with it, I didn't. A guy like Glenn Miller was a businessman. To me his was boring music. Very boring charts done over and over and over."

Dick Johnson who fronts the Shaw Band Today

"Well, a lot of Goodman and Miller has stood up over all these years with the public and their tribute bands enjoy immense success even today with the re-issuance of CDs and appearances on cruise ships and in Vegas and Atlantic City, and everywhere else," I argued.

"Maybe some people like that. I don't! You see, as far as I was concerned the only good white bands in those days were me and Dorsey ....and Goodman. Nobody played better than Goodman, but he had no musicality. I mean within his scope he was excellent. You see - it's not a foot race. I don't know how you can gauge who's better. It has nothing to do with better because there's no criteria. Just because you run a mile and say this guy got there quicker, so he is better. How do you say who's better, Rembrandt or Picasso? Completely, there is no such thing as a criteria by which you can say 'this is the best,' unless you define your terms. But I had to go on to make a living, pay my bills, and help my mother at the time. But you need an audience and you have to be playing for somebody. You attract an audience and they give you money and you pay your men. The audience doesn't come --you can't pay your men. That means you're out of business. See what I'm getting at."

Artie Shaw gave it all up in 1955, setting down his clarinet on the shelf forever.

We talked about his "ghost band" still operating today under the baton and clarinet of the capable Dick Johnson. "I remembered talking to band booker Willard Alexander in the mid-eighties when he was bugging you to get a ghost band going."

"Well, Dick has been doing it for some years. He's as good as good can be. But, I wouldn't like it. And, that term 'ghost band' - I hate it - I'm not a ghost. It's just a band."

"Woody Herman coined the phrase 'ghost band,' I reminded him, and "How did you find Dick Johnson?"

"Someone sent me a recording of his small group. The guy said Dick had grown up on me, and I could tell it was true from listening to the record. He's a remarkable musician. So, a few years later when Willard (Alexander) pushed me for a new band, I thought of this guy Dick Johnson."

"Have you traveled much with the new ghost band? "

"Yes, only to get it established when we first put it together. I wanted to make sure it was working right ---it takes a few weeks to shake a band down. So I went out on the road with it for a few weeks. It was with a Tony Bennett and Rosy Clooney show. That was it! I'm actually doing a concert out here at the end of the month (October 1998) at the Wilshire Theater in LA for KLON radio, although I don't really like playing for the public anymore. I'm going to put the band together, rehearse the band--stand in front of it..... and give the downbeats......that's it."

"What else are you doing. I know you have written three books besides your Trouble With Cinderella biography."

"That's what I do now. I have been working on a very long one, but I can't find any way to edit it down. I've had a broken leg for two years which is driving me crazy. That doesn't help. Editing is very difficult...writing is rewriting. Constantly. Someone once said, 'A work of art is never finished...it's abandoned.' A pretty good line....(we laugh)."

"What would you have done differently if you had to do it all over again?" I inquired suddenly and carefully.

"Well, knowing what I know now? Well....I certainly would not have done what I did. I would have kept going another year or so and I'd have been a multi-zillionaire. I would have gone with it long enough so I wouldn't have to think about money for the rest of my life."

"So what do you do every day of your life? "

"First, I get up and breathe ...devoutly! After that I do what I want to do...that's mostly writing --it's an addiction, and ...I read a lot...but, I am not a fan...I'm not interested in reading about Peggy Lee or Helen O'Connell. I read completely different material. Anyway, most of those musicians and bandleaders were not exactly brain surgeons.....I ran into that problem with Ken Burns who's doing that documentary show on jazz - and his executive producer ....Lynn Novack...who did most of the baseball show, says it's very difficult to get them to say anything....trouble with them....they don't know much...that's also the trouble with most writers... anyone can put sentences together...but what do they have to say? That's what's important. Tolstoy, who was a pretty good writer, and Dostoyevsky, they had something very important to say. That's what I read."

"You converse during interviews more than most subjects."

"I'm sure that's true. Another thing about the band business is that all musicians know is how to blow a horn. They're all Johnny one-note people. So what are you going to talk about. I mean...which way do you play a middle B? Which finger do you use?"

I explained that writers like me may approach things from a different perspective.

"Well, you're trying to identify with the public and what they like. I know what I like, and I tried to do it. 'Who's Who' ..after fifty years they ask you for an epitaph. So, I give them the first one which is 'He did the best he could with the material at hand. But, the material in my hand was not very good. But, I did the best I could.' A lot of the music that was being played was not very good. Although, some of it was very good. I never will be satisfied. You know what my new epitaph is...simplified...the new one is 'Go Away'. (We laugh loudly together.) That's how much I feel about that. I mean, what's an epitaph? You're gone...who gives a damn? Some say, 'I want to be buried at so and so, or in so and so....' who cares where you are buried. Such a stupid thing to be occupied with. I guess people have this damn awful ego problem. Me! Me! Me! The center of the Universe...in other words...people are narcissistic. Everybody is at the center of the Universe... new gods for old...in America we have 260 million Universes. No wonder we get into trouble. Pretty sad."

Artie Shaw, despite his irreverence towards others in his field and personal negative feelings of disillusionment in the way music is controlled by people other than musicians, remains an important figure in the history of the Big Band Era. I have the feeling that from the very beginning Artie Shaw wanted to be a writer, finally causing him to place his instrument aside forever in favor of his pen, his true first love. But, in retrospect, it was his talent with the music that punctuated his life's work, not his pen. Millions have thrilled to his impeccable renditions of some of the best music of the Big Band Era and beyond.

Artie Shaw retired in his prime, a major loss to music. To Artie Shaw the best was rare, and the biggest wasn't necessarily big.

Artie Shaw was big and Artie Shaw's work is rare, and he has survived on his own terms.

We lost Artie Shaw at the age of 94 on December 30, 2004

Peg La Centra with Artie

Les Brown

LES BROWN HOPE'S BAND OF RENOWN

In 1940, at the age of eight, I distinctly recall my first encounter with a Big Band. The scene was the New York World's Fair; the band was Les Brown's Band of Renown. The vocalist, a Cincinnati-born seventeen year old attractive blond beauty with freckles on her face, Doris Kappelhoff, who had recently acquired   a permanent sobriquet: Doris Day.

I remember the thrilling, full band sound at the Dancing Campus Pavilion. It forged a considerable impression. But, my Aunt Irene urged me on to the other sights and, glancing back over my shoulder as the rich sounds diminished, I was drawn further and further away from the music I would come to enjoy for a lifetime.

LES BROWN

HOT CLARINET and DIRECTOR, OWN BAND

USES CONN CLARINET EXCLUSIVELY

Some 57 years later, in 1997, world-famous bandleader Les Brown and I shared a priceless conversation at his comfortable California home. We talked about his early experiences in music, including those World's Fair days, and about our mutually favorite group of musicians -- Bob Hope's longtime (over fifty years) employees -- Les Brown and His Band of Renown.

Les Brown had always wanted to lead a band. Even at 87 years old, Les was still an active bandleader working four or five "gigs" a month. His band is listed in the Guinness Book of Records as the longest running Big Band in history. He had just returned from

London, England, where he, bandleader Ray Anthony, and bandleader, arranger Billy May were honored as special guests of the BBC Big Band Legends in Concert held at famous Ronnie Scott's in Birmingham, England.

Les' early life in Reinerton, Pennsylvania, was a happy one living with a baker-father who always led a local brass band, playing mostly John Philip Sousa marches. He fiercely encouraged and fostered his talented son's aspirations in music.

"Encourage me! Are you kidding? He forced me stay in the bake shop and practice. He did not encourage me; he was my boss and practically forced me to play, which probably explains why I have always been too easy with my own band members over the years."

Les' dad lived to the age of ninety-two, fortunately able to enjoy his three sons' successes in music, including, of course, Warren and Stumpy.

Before college, Les attended the Ithaca Conservatory of Music where he learned demanding arranging skills. He wound up at Duke University in North Carolina in 1936, initiating his career as the bandleader of a twelve-man group of undergraduates (his scholarship obligation) called the Duke Blue Devils Band. The band lasted for a year, after some limited traveling, performing at both Playland Casino in Rye, New York, and Budd Lake, New Jersey.

"We weren't bad for a college band, but we didn't make much money in those days, so we broke up. Anyway, the parents wanted their sons back in school."

For a short period Les arranged for the Isham Jones , Larry Clinton, and Red Nichols bands. "It was sort of a year-off thing. I worked freelance before I reorganized a new band of my own again."

In 1938 Les returned to Budd Lake to lead a local band. "I met my wife Clare at Budd Lake that year. We got married, and we stayed married, and that was that."

Searching for future recording artists, Ely Oberstein, the head of RCA Victor, realizing Les' talent, lured him into forming a Big Band, then promptly booked him into the Edison Hotel in New York for three months: "I received a hundred dollars a week, which was quite a bit of money. Joe Glaser, who was also Louis Armstrong's manager, took us on. He got us booked into the Arcadia in New York and into the 1939-1940 World's Fair in Flushing Meadow (New York)."

"Those were our developing years with the band, Richard," Les continued, "It was where we started it all. Doris Day had just joined us. The audiences really loved her. She not only sang well, but had a good voice on recordings, which made her an additional asset."

Another 'Sentimental Journey'

LES BROWN
AND HIS BAND OF RENOWN

1955

ALSO ON
CAPITOL RECORDS
FEATURING
THESE GREAT
STARS...

JO ANN GREER

BUTCH STONE

STUMPY BROWN

RAY SIMS

ANNUAL SUMMER TOUR

June 30 - BLUE MOON CLUB - Tulsa, Okla.
July 1 - TRIG BALLROOM - Wichita, Kans.
2 - TURNPIKE BALLROOM
Lincoln, Neb.
3 - STARLINE BALLROOM
Carroll, Iowa
4 - VAL-AIR BALLROOM
Des Moines, Iowa
5 - RIVIERA BALLROOM
Lake Geneva, Wis.
6 - WESTLAKE TERRACE
Indianapolis, Ind.
7 - MESKER MEMORIAL
Evansville, Ind.
8 - JOYLAND PARK - Lexington, Ken.
9 - CASTLE FARM - Cincinnati, Ohio
10 - MEYERS LAKE - Canton, Ohio
11 - WALDAMEER PARK - Erie, Pa.
12 - IDORA PARK - Youngstown, Ohio
13 - CHIPPEWA LAKE
Chippewa Lake, Ohio
14 - WESTVIEW PARK - Pittsburgh, Pa.
15 - SUNSET PARK - Carrolltown, Pa.
16 - JACKIE GLEASON SHOW
16 - 21 BASIN ST. - New York
22 - HUNT'S BALLROOM - Wildwood, N.J.
23 - HERSHEY'S PARK - Hershey, Pa.
24 - PLEASURE BEACH
Bridgeport, Conn.
25 - NEW PAVILLION - Lykens, Pa.
26 - CRYSTAL BEACH PARK
Crystal Beach, Ontario
27 - STORK CLUB - Port Stanley, Ontario
28 - KENWICK - Sarnia, Ontario
29 - BUCKEYE LAKE PARK
Buckeye Lake, Ohio

30 - JEFFERSON BEACH - Detroit, Mich.
31 - CRYSTAL BEACH - Vermillion, Ohio
Aug. 1 - UPTOWN THEATRE - Cleveland, Ohio
2 - CENTENNIAL TERRACE
Sylvania, Ohio
3 - FRUITPORT PAVILLION
Fruitport, Mich.
4 - TERRACE GARDENS - Rochester, Ind.
5 - LES-BUZZ BALLROOM
Spring Valley, Ill.
6 - CRYSTAL PALACE - Coloma, Mich.
7 - GEORGE DEVINE BALLROOM
Milwaukee, Wis.
8 - DELEVAN GARDENS
Lake Delevan, Wis.
9 -
10 - 14 - BLUE NOTE - Chicago, Ill.
16 - AVALON BALLROOM
La Crosse, Wis.
17 - ROOF GARDEN - Arnolds Park, Ia.
18 - ARKOTA BALLROOM
Sioux Falls, S.D.
19 - VAL-AIR BALLROOM
Des Moines, Ia.
20 - ARMAR BALLROOM - Marion, Ia.
21 - SHORE ACRES - Sioux City, Ia.
22 - KATO BALLROOM - Mankato, Minn.
23 - COBBLESTONE - Storm Lake, Ia.
24 - ELECTRIC PARK - Waterloo, Ia.
25 - COLISEUM - Davenport, Ia.
26 - PEONY PARK - Omaha, Neb.
27 - PLA-MOR - Kansas City, Mo.
28 - MEADOW ACRES - Topeka, Kans.
29 - AMER. LEGION - Hutchison, Kans.
30 - AUDITORIUM - Holdredge, Neb.
31 - ELITCH'S - Denver, Col.
Sept. 2 - 5 - LAGOON - Salt Lake City, Utah

LET'S MEET IN YOUR TOWN!

BOOKED EXCLUSIVELY BY
ASSOCIATED BOOKING CORP.

DAVE   DON   RONNY

DORIS DAY

"Richard, people ask me why I left the Bob Crosby band to go with Les Brown. It's an old, old story. Bob actually told Les about me. I was very young then and my work with the band had to do with a commercial they had on a radio show, but they became agency contract-bound to feature a girl called Bonnie King on the commercial. They were stuck with this girl even though they didn't like it. So they tried to locate other work for me. I didn't know Les Brown or even much about his band either. They

Doris Day

spoke to him and asked him to come to the Strand Theater in New York where I was appearing with Bob Crosby.

"Well, he did just that. He came right backstage and said, 'I want you to sing with my band, I loved what you did in there.' My mother and I were invited to hear his band, and we loved it. I met all the guys and they were great. Bob Crosby told me that Les was going to be a big success and that it would be a wonderful thing for me to do. So that's how I did it, and was I happy that I did. I adored every minute of it and I love him and all the guys. They're all still my buddies, and one of them, Ted Nash (sax player), moved here with his wife because they were coming up to visit me all the time and fell in love with Carmel (California).

"Enough of that! See," she added, "I told you it was a long dull story, right?"

"Not really, Doris. Readers will want to know it right from your heart - directly from you to them," I explained.

"I also have to say -- Les was, and still is, a marvelous man, and, despite his youth at the time, was a strong father figure for me. He was also a first-class musician. He played the clarinet and did his own arrangements. Unlike Glenn Miller, Benny Goodman and Tommy Dorsey, Les' band sound was staccato, amplified by his theme, 'Leap Frog,' and he had wonderful arrangements full of twists and surprises."

LES BROWN

"Our first engagement with Doris," he continued, "was at Mike Todd's Theater Cafe in Chicago in 1940. Gypsy Rose Lee was the headliner and we did two twenty-minute dance sets with Doris singing four or five songs. Her pay was seventy-five dollars a week. By the time she left me in 1946, it had risen to five hundred. I'd say that next to Frank Sinatra, Doris was the best in the business on selling a lyric."

DORIS DAY
"We had great bus trips. Sometimes they were a little bit long. We also were able to get jobs at a hotel or a theater. That kept us in one place at least a week, mostly two, sometimes three. The bus trips were the most fun. I adored them because of the guys; they were the greatest and all we did was laugh as we traveled from place to place."

I asked Doris about some of the locations she appeared at with the band:

"The Glen Island Casino in New Rochelle (New York) was a wonderful place to work and we adored it. We really loved the classy Hotel Pennsylvania in New York, and the College Inn at the (Hotel) Sherman in Chicago was another favorite place along with the (Hollywood) Palladium in Los Angeles. Les loved working the Palladium, and he still does."

LES BROWN
"Why did we call Doris Doh-Doh.? ...I guess that was because it was D for Doris and D for Day.....and just for affectionate fun," said Les," I don't know, we just did. She was the band's kid sister. She made a big hit with a song called 'Sentimental Journey.' One of my arranger's, Ben Homer, and I wrote the melody. I got lyricist Bud Green of 'Once in a While' fame to put it into words. Once I heard Do-Do sing it, I knew for sure we had a hit on our hands."

Doris Day had first performed "Sentimental Journey" in the Cafe Rouge at the Hotel Pennsylvania in New York, where the band was appearing. The song became a symbol for homesick servicemen. The recording still rates high on recent polls of the most popular recordings of all time.

DORIS DAY
"'Sentimental Journey' was a World War II song and the first time I sang it at rehearsal I knew it was going to be a smash hit. And, of course it was! The guys that were in the service, especially overseas, went ape over it, and it became a huge hit for us. When we first played in New York, Les wouldn't play it over the air because he didn't want another band to get a hold of it and record it before he could."

LES BROWN
"And right about then, after Doh-Doh left us the first time, we did

an entire summer at Log Cabin Farms in Armonk,New York, from July 4th until Labor Day, and we had a radio wire every night...and every afternoon, too. The band was just building and the radio exposure did it for us and we went big from there. The boys really enjoyed that summer, living in local houses, and having a chance to play baseball, tennis, and lots of swimming."

The band's first real hit, "Joltin' Joe DiMaggio," with a vocal by Betty Bonney, who succeeded Doris for a while, occurred in 1941. Fifty years later, the recording enjoyed a revival during the anniversary of the unbroken, record-setting 56 game hitting streak that DiMaggio established with the New York Yankees baseball team.

Les claims that Doris was inadvertently responsible for his long-time association with show business legend Bob Hope:

"Someone took Doris' 'Sentimental Journey' recording to Bob Hope, when Bob was sort of looking for a new singer for his radio show. When he heard the recording, he decided to hire the band, but that did not include Doris. He had Frances Langford singing and was reluctant to let her go because of their long association. It's ironic, though, because he hired Doris a year later, but had to pay her more because in the meantime 'Sentimental Journey' made a star out of her."

"After Doris left the band, how did you manage to get her to come back?"

"Well, I'll let Doris tell you that story."

DORIS DAY

"After I had my baby (Terry), I was singing again at WLW in Cincinnati, doing the late show - called Moon River. It was just me and a fabulous organist. I sang three beautiful ballads every night and we were on at midnight, of all hours. WLW was a 50,000 watt station so it went everywhere. Les was traveling in automobiles with the band and they had the radio on and heard me -' That's Do-Do!', he said, screaming aloud in the car, and he now realized that I had started to sing again after having Terry. That's how he tracked me down and convinced me to return and it was the best thing I ever did in my life. I loved the band. It was a great, swinging band and I loved the musicians. We just had a great time and Les was a dreamboat."

My favorite Doris Day/Les Brown recording is "My Dreams Are Getting Better All the Time." "Well, that was my arrangement," Les said, "I doubled up the tempo on that recording because the song was kinda dull sounding. Doris is so sweet on that tune." The recording of "You Won't Be Satisfied" is another Doris Day unforgettable:

YOU WON'T BE SATISFIED
FREDDY JAMES & LARRY STOCK

Oh, you won't be satisfied until you break my heart,
You're never satisfied until the teardrops start,
I tried to shower you with love and kisses,
But all I ever get from you is naggin' n' braggin'
My poor heart is saggin'.
The way you toss my heart around's a cryin' shame,
I bet you wouldn't like it if I did the same,
You're only happy tearin' all my dreams apart,
Oh, you won't be satisfied until you break my heart

Les Brown has had subsequent lady singers in the band over the years:"Lucy Ann Polk was different than Doris. Eileen Wilson and Jo Ann Greer also did very well with us. They each had their own style, I would say."

The recordings of "Bizet Has His Day" and "Mexican Hat Dance" have also been early Les Brown successes. In 1958 the band won the Downbeat Magazine "Best Dance Band" poll for the fifth consecutive year and was voted The Favorite Band of 1958 in Billboard's poll of the nation's disc jockeys. The Les Brown Band always had the best reputation of any band around:

"I ran a tight ship," Les declared, "The band was clean with no drinking, no drugs, or hard language while working. I didn't discipline the fellows too much, you know, I was opposite to what Glenn Miller was- he was too tough and I was too easy. Maybe that's why all the musicians stayed on so long. (He chuckles). Life in my band was a little too easy, now that I think about it. The truth was that over time all the guys began thinking alike and phrasing alike, so we had a smooth, steady sound."

Another reason for Les Brown's great success was the presence of former Paul Whiteman and Kay Kyser arranger Van Alexander:

"Les and I both got married in same year, 1938. When my band broke up, I had a guy in the band named Butch Stone. I did a thing (arrangement) with Butch called "A Good Man is Hard to Find," and, when the band broke up I allowed Butch to take the arrangement to Larry Clinton's Band and then to Jack Teagarden and finally to Les' Band, where he still performs that song right up to today. It was a smash everywhere he went. Les was the only one that recorded it, and it sold a half-million records. And, Rich, the point of the story," he chuckles aloud, "is that...... I never got paid a dime for it." We both laughed.

Butch Stone, who first joined Les in 1944, remains with the band today. Although he no longer plays his baritone sax, Butch handles the novelty number vocals "My Feet's Too Big, "Robin Hood," and, of course, "A Good Man is Hard to Find!" Remember the silly novelty recording "Frim Fram Sauce" by Butch? "They're just words made up by songwriters," explained Les, "They're just nonsense words for novelty songs.

The selection process when joining Les' band was simple. "We usually knew a little about them beforehand, you know - from reputation, or having heard them with another band," said Les, "As I explained earlier, we looked carefully into their reputation-- if they were clean with drugs, and not drinking too much liquor. I wouldn't hire any guy who had a bad reputation, no matter how well he played."

The band was actually called the Milk Shake Band, a sobriquet leveled on them by bandleader Stan Kenton, and first revealed by Big Band author George Simon: "Stan wryly opined, 'You know - my guys make it on weed... Woody's (Herman) band makes it on booze, and Les Brown's band makes it on milkshakes.'"

Although an arranger, Les' greatest instrumental hit "I've Got My Love to Keep Me Warm" was actually arranged just perfectly by another arranger in the band, Skip Martin. "Over the years it has been our second best selling record - next to 'Sentimental Journey' with Doris.

"Funny thing about that recording, Richard," Les further explained, "We recorded that song in 1943, or about then....then one night in '48, we played it on one of Hope's radio shows. We received a great reaction and Columbia Records wired us to come back into the studio to record it the next day, because they thought it was a great arrangement. They had forgotten that we actually recorded it back three years, but for some crazy reason they never released it. I wired them back to look into their files. They did. They released it. It became a hit."

That Irving Berlin composition along with Artie Shaw's "Frenesi," Stan Kenton's "Artistry in Rhythm," and Glenn's immortal gem "Moonlight Serenade" are my four favorite instrumental recordings of the era.

"Well, Les," I said, "We have a mutual friend in Bob Hope. I have written about him for many years and you have traveled and played for him for much longer- especially on those USO Christmas shows. How did you manage the risky traveling during those wartime days?"

"Oh, it was very rewarding. We were entertaining the troops. They were a great audience. It was wonderful doing it. My band members got to see parts of the world they wouldn't otherwise have seen. We had people fighting one another to go on those tours. Everyone who went was enthusiastic. They would say, 'If so and so can't make it, I'll go, just let me know. '"

Les spent eighteen continuous years overseas with Bob Hope and his USO troupe between each December 15 and December 30th, becoming an important part of the legendary Bob Hope Christmas Tours.

"Bob always brought along the greatest talents and prettiest girls for the GIs to enjoy. He took a lot of criticism from some folks. The GIs liked it, so it was okay with Bob. And he was never afraid of the possible danger we faced in those days. Once, when we flew into Tokyo during the Korean War, I got the news that the Chinese crossed the Yalu River

Bob Hope and Author

immediately after we
left. So I called Bob to tell him, 'Hey, the Chinese have come across,' He said, 'You're kiddin'!'

I said, 'No, I'm not kiddin,' Bob, that's not a joking matter. We could have been killed.' As usual, Bob laughed. Bob is number one in radio, television, films, everything. We have never had a written contract between us all those years. As far as I'm concerned, he's number one - a prince."

BOB HOPE

"Once, when we were headed for Iceland, I learned that a second plane had to turn back to Prestwick to pick up a drummer from Les' band who had dallied too long in the snack bar. After the plane was back in the air again, the drummer remembered the sax player wasn't on board, so the plane had to turn back and make a second landing. The pilot insisted that another nose count be made before the plane took off again. 'That won't be necessary,' Les said. 'Get out your instruments, fellows, and strike a chord. I'll know then if anyone's missing!' I love, and will always appreciate my friend Les Brown."

"Richard, the best band I've ever had was my 1954-55 group. The personnel was outstanding. We had Abe Most. After I found him, I gave up playing the clarinet myself.

We had Tony Rizzi on guitar; Don Paladino on first trumpet; my brother Stumpy playing bass trombone; Don Fagerquist played some wonderful things on trumpet; Jack Sperling was a genius on drums; Butch Stone on vocal and on baritone; Dick Noel played trombone; Ray Sims also managed a great trombone - he was a good soloist, - it was my best band, Richard. This is the group who made the album "Concert at the Palladium" . It was my best band and that album was the best thing we have ever done. The Palladium was by far the best place we ever played in--ever."

ABE MOST

Clarinetist Abe Most first joined the Les Brown Band in 1939 when Les stepped into Kelley's Stable nightclub on New York's famed 52nd Street where Abe was playing with a small group. Typical of Les Brown, he simply invited Abe to join his band:

"He didn't say I would be taking his spot, but before I knew it, I was. I took all of the solos except sometimes on 'Sentimental Journey' when the crowd expected him to solo and Doris (Day) to sing. The band was a harmonious group of nice people including those in management, like Don Kramer, the manager, who always treated me very well. I don't remember ever having an argument about money or anything. It always felt like home. My many years with the band were interrupted just a few times (once playing for one year with Tommy Dorsey in 1946, just after re-turning from war service), but I always returned and finally stayed for over twenty-two continuous years starting in 1950. I even took a few tours with the first Bob Hope USO traveling shows.

Today, (late 1980's) I play various venues, usually highlighting my own group with the music of Benny Goodman in the form of a tribute or salute. I still play, and as long as my health holds up, even though I am seventy-eight, I will continue to play.

We talked about his Les' brothers:

Curious, I asked, "Why do they call your brother Clyde Stumpy?"

"Well, he's only five feet tall. Does that answer your question? All kidding aside, he prefers the name Stumpy, and hardly uses Clyde. He is the band's manager and keeps us all well-organized. Les' two younger brothers, Warren and Stumpy, both learned the trombone, later participat-ing in their brother's band. Stumpy, who provided me with lots of assis-tance and photographs for this chapter, told me he joined the band at the age of eighteen, after graduating from the New York Military Academy. "He came out to the coast to try out for the band at my father's firm suggestion, and he's been with us ever since," said Les.

"Since we don't travel too much, we are able to keep the same players. Today we mostly do private parties for affluent people who followed us when they, and we, were young. Successful in their own life, they can now afford these parties." The band plays only about four gigs a month these days.

"Leap Frog," a composition written by Joe Garland, once a tenor sax player for Louis Armstrong and who also composed "In The Mood," Glenn Miller's signature recording, is the band's longtime theme. "But we don't always play it at these recent parties. We sometimes play it at the end of an evening, after dinner. And we keep it down until they have had enough to drink and they've finished their speeches, and then -- let it go."

DORIS DAY

"I used to see Les quite often, as a matter of fact. In the '90s we did a fundraiser up here for the animals (Doris Day Pet Foundation, Carmel, California) and he brought his whole band up and it was a swinging night. It was really wonderful of him to do that. He always enjoyed coming to Carmel, and he and his wife Clare used to come up a lot. I haven't seen him lately, but you never know when he will pop in. We always talk about the good old days and the fun we had and how we laughed a lot. The

Les Brown and Doris Day

memories...Richard...of those long ago days are still fresh in my heart liked it happened yesterday. Isn't that something?"

Les Brown has accomplished it all, as they say. A guest conductor of the Los Angeles Philharmonic and the United States Air Force Band, he has been the musical director for the television shows of Bob Hope, Steve Allen, Dean Martin, Jackie Cooper, Mel Torme', and many

Hollywood Palace Shows, as well as Marineland Specials on PBS. Two Presidents have had Les Brown personally direct their Inaugural Ball, and Frank Sinatra engaged Les to perform for the Queen Elizabeth II Gala in 1984. His new CD, "Live at the Hollywood Palladium" is doing quite well. Like our mutual friend Bob Hope, Les Brown was also a true American institution.

Max Wirz (Top Left) Les Brown (R)
Ray Anthony (Bottom)

DUKE ELLINGTON

Billy Strayhorn and Duke Ellington

Edward Duke Ellington
Ellingtonia Means Belief in the Music

It's 1999....

Here, we will try to acknowledge the genius of Duke Ellington, through the eyes of his sister , Ruth Ellington; nephew Michael James; Big Band Academy President Milt Bernhart, blues vocalist Joe Williams; vocalist Herb Jeffries, and drummer Louis Bellson.

Edward Kennedy Duke Ellington has been designated the patron saint of Berklee Music School in Boston, and is invariably adored by a great number of musicians throughout the world. Duke's only sibling, his sister, Ruth Ellington James, thought all had been written about her loving brother, but, by repeating accounts of his life over and over again for the benefit of the new citizens of the world, accounts of his life and career become an appreciative celebration in itself.

The formidable Duke Ellington Band and its body of work had, over many years, survived the demise of the Big Band Era - the inroads of bebop, the rock and roll invasion, the death or desertion of its own stars and colleagues, and its own internal problems- successfully spanning the entire period of jazz. If you add it up, it counts approximately 50 years of nonstop bandleading, 800 musicians filtering through the band, over 10,000 recordings, 20,000 gigs, some 2,000 compositions, and millions of miles traveled to bring his unique category of music to fans all over the world. As an unofficial ambassador, Duke toured the world in the 1960s, sponsored by the United States Department of State.

Miles Davis, the famed trumpet player, once said of Duke Ellington: " I think all the musicians in jazz should get together on one certain day and get down on their knees to thank Duke."

In late 1998, I spoke to vocalist Herb Jeffries, the last surviving member of the 1930s-1940s orchestra, about his former boss. Herb's outstanding 1940 Ellington recording "Flamingo," arranged by Billy Strayhorn, sold millions. It's in the top ten of my all-time personal favorites. You never get tired of listening to that version of "Flamingo."

Herb said exactly this: " It was one of the highlights of my life singing with the great genius of Duke Ellington. Historically, down the road a hundred years or so, it may someday be compared to having played alongside Mozart or Beethoven- yesterday's great composers. I believe Ellington will go down as one of America's great composers. Music was everything to him. He was in love with music, more than anything in the world."

Duke and Connie Haines Signing Autographs

Milt Bernhart, the outstanding trombonist of the innovative 1940's "Artistry In Rhythm" Band of Stan Kenton, and the trombone soloist in Frank Sinatra's "I've Got You Under My Skin," had something to say about Duke Ellington's music when we discussed the subject just a few months ago:

"While it was once dance bands, it is now big band concert music the people sit down and listen to, just like they do with symphony orchestras. With Artie Shaw, Stan Kenton, and Duke Ellington, the idea was never to play dance music. Duke Ellington made it clear that if he were in an auditorium, the music probably would be in broken tempos and not in a steady pulse from beginning to end, because that was only designed for dancing.

" Musically, Duke Ellington is our proudest possession, "Milt declared, "he was ahead of his time. And the great part of it was that he didn't fight anything. He never fought---he just continued. He didn't make offensive statements, where others did, so when history draws the past, the name that will be always there will be Ellington, where others may be forgotten."

So, shall we consider Ellington the bandleader, Ellington the piano playing musician, or Ellington the composer? Let's see!

Early 1920s and 1930s musicians who became bandleaders grew

out of the few bands around, so one band's intonation was not notably different from the other. There were only a few who dared to be totally unconventional. Artie Shaw tried to be one; Tommy Dorsey another, but the most outstanding was Edward Kennedy Duke Ellington. His music was certainly different from any other emerging band. You can always distinguish Duke's recordings from others without much doubt. His uniqueness was the use of precision playing instruments that seemed to

Duke Ellington - Chicago 1932

talk, even when the reeds were wailing high and low. Some say it's because Duke relied on showcasing the talents of individual players, rather than composing charts at random and training his musicians to use them. He wrote music solely for his individual players. He actually tamed his musicians otherwise demeanor by waiting them out, never bothered by their off-stage, sometimes unruly actions. In the New Yorker Magazine, Whitney Balliett once wrote: "...he wrote for them, they played for him!"

Duke Ellington: "When we're all working together a guy may have an idea and he plays it on his horn. Another guy may add to it and make something out of it. Someone may play a riff and ask, 'How do you like this?' The trumpets may try something together and say, 'Listen to this.' There may be a difference of opinion of what kind of mute to use. Someone may advocate extending a note or cutting it off. The sax section may want to put an additional smear on it," said the maestro about his amazing group of musicians, and further, "We write to fit the tonal personalities of the individual instrumentalists who have the responsibility of interpreting our works. "This also afforded Duke an opportunity to hear and review his every newly- written composition instantly.

"The biggest thing I do in music is listen," said Ellington. "While I'm playing I also listen ahead to what I will be playing. It may be thirty-two, or just one, or an eighth of a bar ahead but, if you're going to try to play good jazz, you've got to have a plan of what's going to happen."

In the mid- thirties it seemed like the whole country was caught up with something later identified as the Big Band Era. But, Ellington had already been playing that kind of music for almost ten years. Because the Duke's band was composed of all black players, they were not accepted in most of the fancy ballrooms and restaurants like those that featured the white swing bands of Benny Goodman, Artie Shaw, or Tommy Dorsey, although each of these leaders gradually began featuring black players and singers in their own group. However, Ellington was playing the best interracial clubs and was being reviewed and written about by important reviewers, being unanimously well received.

When Duke was asked about the racial problem, he merely stated," I took the energy it takes to pout, and wrote some blues." And, Oh! What blues he wrote.

"There was always something different happening every night when the Duke was playing because he gave his players a great deal of freedom, freedom to learn about tempos, blending, and endurance," said his one-time drummer Louis Bellson.

Ellington didn't play the hits of the day, unless it was a hit he created or unless it originated through or was composed by his own personnel. He was fearless in his quest to take unpopular musical positions. Sideman Juan Tizol's composition "Caravan" is an example. Juan wrote it and plays lead in every Ellington recording of the piece. "Caravan" is a stunning example of players in a band being featured for what they do best - from violin solo to drums - trumpet to clarinet - each piece expressing an individual flavor, breaking like a wave on the shore of the musical stage.

Edward Kennedy Ellington was born just before the turn-of-the-century of hardworking parents James Edward and Daisy Kennedy Ellington, who fostered love and affection on their son and his younger sister, Ruth Dorothea Ellington. The nickname Duke began in high school , bestowed on him by a friend, Edgar McEntree, suiting his aristocratic bearing. His father provided comfortably for the family, creating income first as a butler to a prominent doctor and later as a caterer, including serving food at White House occasions and at embassies in Washington. "He raised our family like he was a millionaire," Duke declared in his book

Music Is My Mistress. His mother instilled religion within the family, and always praised the children, fostering dignity and poise, and providing security and a powerful belief conveyed to them that they were specially blessed.

"When I was a child, my mother told me I was blessed, and I have always taken her word for it. Being born of ---or reincarnated from ---royalty is nothing like being blessed. Royalty is inherited from another human being, blessedness from God."

Duke took occasional piano lessons, later playing piano at church, but received motivating inspiration from observing eighteen year old Harvey Brooks playing a swinging piano in Philadelphia. So impressed, he said : "Brooks was swinging, and he had a tremendous left hand, and when I got home I had a real yearning to play. "Suddenly, jazz and ragtime music attracted his interest. In Washington, his first band, The Duke's Serenaders, was formed. Soon, Harlem's musical influence reached his senses, so he invaded New York and Tin Pan Alley as an optimistic, charming, and hungry young musician. Here he hired James "Bubber" Miley, a musician who played an exceptional muted and growl-ing-sounding trumpet. Duke Ellington had found a catalyst in Miley and began replacing players, transforming the band into a jazz band. The growling brass became an Ellington imprint.

The early Ellington evergreens "East St. Louis Toodle-Oo," "Black and Tan Fantasy," "Creole Love Call," "Black Beauty," and "Old Man Blues," largely composed with Miley, followed. Then the Cotton Club gig came along:

"The job called for a band of at least eleven pieces and we had been using only six," Ellington recalled, "At the time, I was playing a vaudeville show in Philadelphia. The audition was set for noon, but by the time I had scraped up eleven men it was past two o'clock. We played for them and got the job. The reason for that was the boss, Harry Block, didn't get there till late either and didn't hear the others who were audition-ing earlier. That's a classic example of being at the right place at the right time with the right thing before the right people."

On December 4, 1927, a date important to jazz, Duke Ellington opened at the Cotton Club. The five year engagement as leader of the Cotton Club Orchestra was a productive time for Ellington, earning him a national reputation and financial stability. He recorded 200 sides during his tenure under the guidance of his agent, Irving Mills. The orchestra's exotic, jungle-like sound was an original attempt to apply his own rules, a technique developing his own harmonic spin. He utilized instruments differently, notably in "Mood Indigo," having the trombone working the high notes and the clarinet the low notes, the reverse of the accepted way. This introduced blends of musical color never accomplished before. The vaguely menacing number "The Mooch" fit neatly into this new wave of Ellington creations for the club's reviews. Duke Ellington's credo: ".... find the logical way, and when you find it, avoid it. Let your inner self break through and guide you. Don't try to be anyone else but yourself," counciled the African American composer Will Marion Cook to the young, believing, emerging bandleader.

What followed was a lifetime of scraping, finagling, and suffering to keep his orchestra going year after year after year.

The occasion of Ellington's departure from the Cotton Club established him, alongside Louis Armstrong, as one of the two foremost figures in jazz. Dodging racial discrimination by sleeping the band in private railroad cars while on tour because hotels would not admit them, being forced to take freight elevators, and being kept from eating in some restaurants, Ellington always managed to solve the problems and keep going, his dignity and stylish projection prevailing over the more prevalent discrimination.

The great hits "Sophisticated Lady," "Caravan," "It Don't Mean a Thing (If It Ain't Got That Swing)," and "Solitude," launched during his triumphant European tour of 1933, continued his experimentation with special musical elements and forms. Later, imaginative recordings like "Ko Ko," one of the magnificent ensemble pieces with swiftly changing instrumental voices, and the striking plunger solo by Tricky Sam Nanton join forces to create a masterpiece. Then Cootie Williams original "Concerto for Cootie," later renamed "Do Nuthin' Till You Hear From Me" showcased Williams, just as Ben Webster is showcased on "Never No Lament" which was re-titled "Don't Get Around Much Anymore." It added yet another standard to the book. Influences from other cultures, picturing distant and exotic places, were incorporated into his jazz repertory. The name had changed too. It was now Duke Ellington and His Famous Orchestra.

Inspired by various moods, Duke Ellington composed his best music. "The memory of things gone is important to jazz," he said. And his son Mercer once told me that his dad always wrote what he felt. "The happy tunes were written in happy times and the sad songs were composed when he felt sad. Isn't that sort of natural?"

The indispensable arranger and composer Billy Strayhorn entered Duke Ellington's life in 1939. He was twenty-four and stayed for 30 years. The two were a collaborative team that grew closer and closer over the years, much like the association Stan Kenton and Pete Rugolo experienced.

The year 1943 brought the Ellington Orchestra to Carnegie Hall where they performed the hour-long "Black, Brown and Beige" to a standing-room only crowd. A symbolic, historical sort of piece, it was then his most ambitious composition. Ellington had reached his personal zenith and continued composing concert pieces.

World War II's end spelled disaster for the Big Bands. Bebop, folk singing trends, big-name vocalists, and the inflated salaries required for musicians forced bandleaders to disband. Many dance pavilions closed in deference to a more mobile population who headed for the road instead. Television had arrived, taking center stage. Radio was entering an eclipse. Times were changing for Duke Ellington. His star players were deserting to form their own combos. A crisis indeed had arrived for everyone. But, he never ever disbanded his orchestra, even though he lost some of its important players through illness and death and some through fluctuation of personnel. Even though income for the band was low, Duke Ellington paid his men with royalty checks he received for his compositions.

While Ellington recuperated in England from an operation performed in the United States, the band's sidemen performed in small groups on their own until their boss returned. He kept the band together: "I like to keep a band so I can write and hear the (newly composed or arranged) music the next day," he said, "The only way you can do that is to pay the band and keep it on tap fifty-two weeks a year. By little twists and turns we manage to stay in business and make a musical profit. And a musical profit can put you way ahead of a financial loss." It was the music above everything for Ellington.

Maestro Arturo Toscanini commissioned Duke Ellington to compose a piece for the NBC Symphony, and it was performed in 1951. I was present during that NBC radio broadcast. The tickets I was commissioned to distribute, as co-manager of the NBC Ticket Division, were printed on a gold embossed soft oilcloth so the rustling of the program did not disturb the Maestro during the performance. The composition was entitled" Harlem." It was a miniature piece, set off by a bass simulating footsteps, and very well received by an appreciative audience and critics alike.

On New Year's Day 1999, Ruth Ellington and I had a revealing conversation about her celebrated brother: "He was practically a grown man when I was born and always a saint. Ever, overly protective of me at all times, I was his little doll. He was like a father and mother to me, especially after our parents passing while I was attending college. Every day, going to school, he kept me locked up in the car in an effort to protect me. I meet people today who remember me in those early days, and through my years in college. They would say, 'I remember you when Duke kept you locked like a baby in the car. He felt so responsible...' they would say," she laughs -- reminiscing, "...and he was always sensitive to moods." Duke was almost seventeen years older than his only sister.

"Duke was the kind of person who never acknowledged his greatness to himself," Ruth Ellington continued, "He just went on his own way of living, never thinking of himself as great... in any way whatever. He loved our mother, Daisy, more than anyone in life. Next to God, he valued his family the most; that's why he spent the last ten years of his life writing music giving thanks to God. He was a brother sent from Heaven, because he was perfect.

"He took good care of me then...and he still takes care of me today through royalties from his work." Ruth was still operating Tempo Music Publishers on Park Avenue in New York, publishing mainly the music of her brother, among other material. Ruth had two sons, Stephen and Michael James, who managed the business with their mom, as well as their own Stephen James Productions. As a youngster Michael learned trumpet, and was fortunately coached by band member Clark Terry.

"We traveled around the country and in Europe with our uncle during the summers when we were kids, helping valet and performing chores for the band."

Upon Duke Ellington's passing, after the funeral, Ruth presided over the get-together of friends, acquaintances and well wishers of the family. That elegant and gracious lady made sure everyone had enough to eat and drink and someone to talk to in this otherwise dark hour. "It was exactly the way Duke would have planned it, had he been there," said author Don George, who co-wrote "I'm Beginning to See the Light" with Duke Ellington, "He loved to see people having a good time."

On January 21, 1999, legendary blues vocalist Joe Williams talked to me about Duke Ellington: "Well, I was always in awe of Duke. He had a rare musical gift that was so varied. And, Oh, man! He was such a spiritual person. His concepts ---he always said he was only a messenger boy (He laughs deeply). And, he did what made him happy. He'd say wonderful things like, 'I'm not going to let you or anybody else let me lose my pretty ways.'

"We worked together several times," Joe went on , "Once at a celebration for (Billy) Strayhorn---(Metropolitan Opera star) Leontyne Price and Lena Horne were also there. And in Detroit, right after I left the Basie band, Duke and I --- we worked together for a week in a show. I think it was 1972. I didn't sing with the band; I was a separate attraction. Talk about Duke being self-effacing---I brought along a piano player named Ellis Larkins, and Duke called me into his dressing room after the first show and said rather sternly, 'Obviously you didn't read the fine print in the contract.' So, I said, 'What's that?' and he said, 'Your piano player--- while playing at no time is your piano player to use his left hand.'"

We both broke out in laughter, Joe's rich in his deep, deep basso.

"He was love, Richard. At his funeral services his drummer Sonny Greer was crying, you know, and he said ever so proudly, 'Joe, the Duke was my man!'

"Duke had elegance, grace, and style, Richard," Joe said with passion, "No matter where I have performed in the world, I would say, to myself, 'Wow! God! --- he was here first.' Duke's music was religious, but he called it sacred. Sacred music, Richard, sacred."

"My uncle's status was built on his achievement as an original musician," nephew Michael James, whose godfather was Billy Strayhorn, commented during our long conversation about his beloved uncle. "He created something new, through personal expression, and formed a new environment for musical instruments."

At the time, some musicians and composers employed European instruments and ideas to maintain American musical styles. "Duke understood that jazz - the new musical language - meaning (Sidney) Bechet and (Louis) Armstrong and the vocabulary they were bringing forth, so the sixteen piece bandstand could be turned into the new American art form." Michael said. Inadvertently, Duke had discovered a new idiom built upon jazz rhythms and harmonies.

Impresario Sol Hurok once approached Duke Ellington: "You're a great artist. I want to present you the way you should be presented, properly on the concert stages of the world. But I don't want you to play any nightclubs or dance halls. You will play strictly concerts."

"Duke was flattered by the prospect," Michael said, "but he enjoyed playing various styles and venues; a dance one night, a concert here and there, perhaps a night club the following night. He liked the diversity, to be in touch with the entire range of musical experiences. So he declined Hurok's invitation."

Ellington's "stable of stars" was important to him. They refreshed his mind and were given a backdrop they could find no other place, enabling them to be individual stars, not merely members of an ensemble as in most bands. Paul Gonsalves, who had played with Basie and Ellington, said, "You know, the difference is, Basie is a piano player with a band, but Duke is a composer. And what kept him in Duke's band is "that Duke is always coming up with something new. It kept me stimulated." In other bands, once a musician learned the "book," they would get tired of it. The musicians held Duke Ellington in great respect because they couldn't do what he did, creating new and exciting charts for them to play almost daily.

At one point Michael and I tried to pinpoint Duke's best period with his band: "On the whole," Michael suggested, "the band that Duke Ellington had, particularly in the mid-fifties - - up to the early sixties with Clark Terry, Paul Gonsalves and all those guys like Louis Bellson, and Johnny Hodges returning, might have been Duke's best because they could do it all. Even Johnny Hodges and Ray Nance could handle the early style of "growling" trumpets to demonstrate the old stuff of the twenties and thirties."

About the lady vocalists in the band: "The most associated with Duke was Ivie Anderson ('Stormy Weather')," said Michael, "Jazzwise, the best will be Betty Roche. Her 1952 version of 'Take the 'A' Train' is best.

Classical things best belong to Kay Davis. Joya Sherill was best on swing things, and the sweet sounding Marie (Maria) Ellington Cole (Mrs. Nat King Cole, no relation to the Duke)."

Duke always handled his fame well, never high, never faltering. He could step outside himself, at the same time. He said, "'You know, we have been liked longer that most people who only enjoy that 15 minutes of fame they talk about. Our fame has been in overtime, having lasted for a long time.'"

"Love you madly," the Duke would always say.

Critics are wonderful ....
They're just one satin-doll after another.
thanks!
Love You Madly

ARVELL SHAW
And the Louis Armstrong All-Stars Legacy

When his hero, Louis Armstrong, came through St. Louis, Missouri, to play at the Plantation Club back in 1946, Lady Luck was there in full regalia for 22-year old resident Arvell Shaw. Luckily, Louis's bass player suddenly had to rush home to Philadelphia where his wife was giving birth, creating a need for a replacement bass player to fill the engagement. Armstrong telephoned the union, asking for the best local bass player. Guess who got the job?

Arvell Shaw was born in St. Louis in 1923 and had what he calls

Louis Armstrong and His All Stars - Earl Hines - Piano, Jack Teagarden - Trombone, Barney Bigard - Clarinet, Cozy Cole - Drums, Louis, Arvell Shaw - Bass, Velma Middleton - Vocalist

an average childhood. His dad was a Protestant minister who had affection for Louis Armstrong records, especially those Hot Five and Hot Seven's recordings, so Arvell was well exposed to Armstrong's magic. Arvell was playing tuba in a local band for Fate Narable, a former bandmate of Armstrong who had played with him on the river boats going to and from Alton, Illinois and St. Louis. Fate told many stories of the old days.

"It was my ambition to play someday with such a great musician as Louis Armstrong."

During the Second World War, armed services representatives

Louis Armstrong

visited the all black high schools to recruit black musicians. With the armed forces then integrated, they needed to fill the newly-created bands for troop entertainment. Arvell joined the Navy and stayed for 3 years serving in the Pacific. He learned to play the bass fiddle in the Navy band.

It's interesting to note that Louis Armstrong received a similar career break when he was just seventeen. His own hero, New Orleans trombonist and bandleader, Edward Kid Ory, who had heard about Armstrong's reputation as a cornetist, called on him to replace cornetist King (Joseph) Oliver who had left Kid Ory's Brown Skinned Babies band to go to Chicago on his own. Later, in 1922, Armstrong would join the famous Oliver band, which acted as a catalyst for the development of jazz players. Armstrong's reputation had by the time had spread throughout the jazz world, although it's well to point out that earlier Oliver was both teacher and mentor to Armstrong.

Much later, in 1984, photographer Camille Smith and I were shoehorned in at Sonny's Place on Merrick Road in Seaford, Long Island to interview Arvell Shaw who had lived just a few miles away from this former jazz showcase, a tiny storefront nightclub where the owner, Sonny Meyerowitz, lost his shirt every night in a business that was for him strictly a labor of love. If you glanced up at the framed photos on the wall above the bar and tables you would have seen Count Basie, Louis Armstrong, and others who had once graced this now hallowed hall. Arvell Shaw was a cuddly bear of a man who embraced his giant bass as a mother envelopes a troubled child. He wore a crisp gray beard and played with a gentle rocking motion believing

Oil Painting By Richard Grudens

every note and every word, loving his work as Armstrong had surely loved his.

After playing awhile with Armstrong's big band and just after making the movie, A Song is Born, with Danny Kaye, Benny Goodman, Tommy Dorsey and Lionel Hampton, Arvell returned home, but Joe Glaser, Louis' longtime manager, who had disbanded the big band, (many big name bands were closing down at the time) promptly called and asked Arvell if he would be interested in joining Louis Armstrong's newly formed small group at a gig in Billy Berg's nightclub in Los Angeles.

"Is the pope Catholic?" He replied to Glaser in the affirmative.

"When I got to Berg's I went up close to the marquee and read: 'Louis Armstrong's All Stars, with Jack Teagarden, Barney Bigard, then below that, Big Sid Catlett, Dick Cary,' and way down at the bottom 'Arvell Shaw', and I began to shake. It was an exciting moment for me."

"So I presume that was the beginning of the Louis Armstrong All-Stars?" said I.

"Yes, it was. And it lasted twenty-five odd years until Louis died in 1971 shortly after completing a two-week engagement a the Waldorf-Astoria in New York. The All-Stars, originally an idea of New York promoter, Ernie Anderson brought the greatest commercial success to Louis Armstrong and his group making him the best-known jazz musician in the world at the time. Arvell left the group for a while in early 1958. Over the years much of the personnel changed for one reason or another. Armstrong also had confessed that he preferred Joe Glaser to choose the musicians that were to play in the group so no one would be offended by Armstrong's personal choices. That way he kept his friends as friends.

VOL. 19—No. 20   CHICAGO, OCTOBER 8, 1952

ARMSTRONG AND JENKINS, that unlikely pair who turned out to be a perfect team for best-selling records, are seen here at a party thrown jointly for Satchmo and Gordie during their joint engagement at the Paramount theatre. Decca records and the *Pittsburgh Courier* combined to throw the shindig.

Louis with Gordon Jenkins

After Louis, he toured colleges, played in Broadway's Bubblin' Brown Sugar, and joined the band in the show Ain't' Misbehavin'.At the time of our interview Arvell had just come off tours that included gigs in Germany and England, where, he said, jazz is more widely accepted as the art form. "It's no big deal for seven to eight thousand people to attend a show. Jazz draws the big crowds overseas. It's a shame." he lamented, "...jazz is the most played music in the world today...but not in the U.S. One of the most important art forms of the 20th Century is jazz and it's generally ignored by its own people. It's inexcusable," he went on passionately, "that great musicians have to travel thousands of miles and live away from home to make a living-and rock artists play only about three chords and they're making millions. It's a sick scene that I hope will change."

Of course, all that has changed dramatically since 1984. Jazz patronage is up in the new millennium. Now the Grammy wins and other signs of interest are more prevalent. New York and L.A. clubs and music halls regularly feature jazz ensembles and tributes to departed fellow-musicians, with leading artists, including Arvell Shaw who named his group 'The Louis Armstrong Legacy Band' in tribute to his old boss.

During that Germany tour which included pianist Teddy Wilson, vibraphonist Red Norvo, guitarist Tal Farlow, tenor sax artist Buddy Tate, trumpeter Billy Butterfield, and clarinetist Johnny Mince, Teddy Wilson became ill: "We were in a restaurant when Teddy got up to go to the bathroom and he suddenly just collapsed. He turned gray and couldn't breath. We figured he had a heart attack so we called the ambulance. They thought he had bleeding ulcers because he was loosing blood for so long. Then, after tests were taken, they said he had cancer. He remained in the hospital for three weeks and they flew him to Boston. (Teddy passed on in 1986 from that illness.) Johnny Mince and I went on to England with Johnny Guarnieri (pianist), Barrett Deems (drums), Ed Hubble (trombonist), and Keith Smith, an English trumpet who sounds so much like Louis you can't tell them apart., The group was named The Hundred Years of American Dixieland Jazz Band.

And, like his old boss, Arvell Shaw began to sing. It started when he was appearing in Oslo. Norway when one of the musicians bet he wouldn't sing during his featured spot. "So I went out and announced to ten thousand people at this concert that I would like to sing. I looked back at Louis and he rolled up his eyes and he looked like he was thinking, 'this cat is crazy', and I sang "St James Infirmary," the only song I knew all the lyrics to and the house came down. I began singing seriously about two years ago and the people liked it so I said, maybe I have something there." After that he sang at every performance. His solo rendition of "Yesterdays" was terrific. But, he's a better bassist.

Although Armstrong was a very innovative and excellent musician, (as Teddy Wilson once told me, "He had balance and tone. Harmonic sense. Excitement. Technical skill. Originality.)" he considered himself mainly an entertainer. Jazz aficionados saw him as an important jazz musician, but he preferred all around entertaining, not just exclusively performing jazz material. Projecting his personality was important to him as was singing and recording with people like Bing Crosby and Ella Fitzgerald.

The change for Armstrong, from virtuoso jazz performer to singer and entertainer, happened after an eighteen month European tour that ended for him with a split lip in 1935. Some say it was musical deterioration, others swear he could play just as good, but he simply choose the vaudeville style of performing much to the dismay of jazz purists. Following in Armstrong's footsteps, Arvell Shaw had arrived at a similar crossroads: To be just a musician, or a homogeneous entertainer?

Over those many years, Armstrong would always take care of his protégé: "He had no children of his own, and he wouldn't show me any affection openly. But, if things would go wrong for me, he would say 'Leave him alone!' or 'Give him this or that', and 'Let him do this or that.''

When former bandleader Earl "Fatha" Hines replaced All-Star Dick Cary at the piano, young Arvell found another friend and mentor: "Earl was great because he really believed in helping young musicians and would spend time and give them a chance. He took me under his wings, helped me, and taught me about all aspects of show business. You Know, he did a lot for Sarah Vaughan and Billy Eckstine back in the old days."

Arvell said that Armstrong loved making movies. "Did you catch the scene in High Society when Bing Crosby introduces us All-Stars (Trummy Young-trombone, Ed Hall-clarinet, Billy Kyle-piano, Barrett Deems-drums, Arvell, and Louis) in the song scene "Now you Has Jazz?"

Of course I had, the whole world has. Arvell and the other members of the group took their licks on a specialty solo while Bing and Louis vocalized and Louis wrapped the number up in a stunning finish with Bing. It was the best Crosby/ Armstrong jazz duet ever.

So Arvell and his close association with perhaps the greatest jazz musician of the century had helped him carve out a niche of his own in the world of music he loved so well. But instead of struggling as a just a studio or pickup musician, he had established an élite group of his own, although the marketplace was different then and the tours scant in comparison to those past glory days.

"To survive, you must change and grow constantly, Arvell pointed out. "It's always been true, but I don't discard anything if it's good. I still listen and learn most every time out. You cannot become stagnant or you will die. Woody Herman taught me that. I'm sixty (actually seventy-one in 1995) now and I will always keep on learning and working. I'll keep going till I die. I'll never find myself pacing the floor looking for something or other to do. My music keeps me young and keeps me happy. The older you get, the more effort it takes. (chuckling) But it still keeps you alive and the musical adrenaline cooking."

Up to November of 1995 Arvell Shaw was still at it, performing jazz concerts with his All-Stars at the Adams Playhouse at Hofstra University in Hempstead, Long Island, for the benefit of P.L.U.S.. Group homes for Autistic Adults. This is his twelfth year at the project which was started by his late wife, Madeleine, for the original benefit of his only child and other deserving people.

The last time I spent with Arvell Shaw was in early 2002, at Five Towns College on Long Island where he performed. Backstage, we talked for a while. He was almost totally blind from glaucoma, but never-theless put on a great performance.

Arvell Shaw suffered a heart attack and passed away in December of 2002. He was seventy-eight.

With a Little Instruction From Richard

Volcano Of Energy

LIONEL HAMPTON: An interview:

One of his early idols was jazz great Louis Armstrong: "Louis had come to L.A. without his regular backup band and so he asked us if we would back him in a recording session. Louis spotted a set of vibes (in the studio) and asked if I knew how to play them, which I did, since I knew the basic keyboard. (It was actu-

ally a vibraharp NBC used to use as it's identification signal chime during station breaks.) That was the first known time jazz had been played on the vibes."

Lionel Hampton and Louis Armstrong recorded Eubie Blake's immortal "Memories Of You" that day, and a young jazz buff named John Hammond heard it and rushed to L.A. to hear it live at the Paradise Club where Hamp was playing. The next evening, a hot August night in 1936, while Hamp was leading his band at the Paradise Club, a place where sailors bought a 25 cents pitcher of beer while they awaited a bus trip return to San Pedro and Long Beach bases in California, John Hammond and Benny Goodman dropped by and sparked a historic 3 1/2 hour jam session before Benny and Lionel were ever introduced to each other, and it nearly tore off the roof. "I guess it was a little bit of nerve and a little luck thrown in for good measure." Lionel said.

"We were playing," he recalled while we and WGSM radio's disc jockey, Bruce Herbert, munching on Burger King Whoppers, conversed and rambled on with him for an hour before show time in a dressing room trailer behind the new , but incomplete, Harry Chapin Amphitheater in Huntington Long Island's Hecksher Park back in 1984. "then, the next thing I knew there was Benny on stage during a break playing his clarinet. I looked over my shoulder and there was Gene Krupa banging away and Teddy Wilson smilin' at the piano. What a sound...it was unbelievable to me .....I joined in with my vibes....and that was the beginning of the Benny Goodman Quartet." The very next day they recorded the legendary "Moonglow" and "Dinah."

Lionel Hampton and Richard Grudens

John Hammond had welded them together. "Benny enjoyed it so much he asked me to join his group. "It's amazing too, that Benny's ingenious coupling of Teddy Wilson and Lionel was inadvertently brave, even courageous, since black musicians simply didn't play then in white bands. But Benny was more concerned about the quality of the music than the racial issues he might have created. He didn't give a damn about the racial issue. "The people accepted us and did not seem to resent our playing together. But some of Benny's friends didn't like (or accept) it." Lionel said. They stuck together however, for four memorable years.

Lionel Hampton was the most outstanding vibraphonist of the jazz age, although he was originally a drummer. He was a volcano of energy who could carry thousands of people into a state of ecstasy by his sheer playing power and showmanship. He loved a big band behind him---trumpets, saxes, playing almost without consideration for intonation, blend, or any kind of precision. All of that simply added to his own firepower.

Hamp humbly credited all his success to God, who he says "Gave me the talent," but it was his wife, Gladys, who gave him the inspiration which drove him all his career. She managed his business affairs and was his eyes, ears and the human power behind him. (He married her on Armistice Day in Yuma, Arizona, on his way to join Goodman in New York.)

It's a remarkable thing to see and feel the enthusiasm that Lionel Hampton generated at a performance. When I noticed him pause for a momentary prayer just before going on stage, I inquired about it:

"I always keep the faith---studied Bible through my grandmother--Mama Louvenia, I loved her so---she read me the psalms, so it's always in my mind. I give grace to the Lord every time I play on the bandstand."

He once wrote a piece entitled "The King David Suite" while on a trip to Jerusalem where he visited King David's tomb: "The music came to me in the tomb---I was inspired to write that work. I feel that God has a hand in everything we do. He puts all my ideas together and they always work."

Lionel always enjoyed working live concerts and going from one city to another, unlike many other musicians who love the music but hate the monotonous traveling: "We always have a wonderful gathering everywhere we play and we meet old friends, just like you and Bruce here. It makes you tick. It gets you to meet with the people who admire your work. You got to let the people see you work---you got to do it---you're in the profession and you have to be out where you can test your skills to see if they are working or not, and if you are playing the right thing. The people react to it and then you know if you're on the right track."

While we spoke I verified the legendary story of how he discovered two great jazz singers in a single day: "A little girl named Ruth Jones who worked in the powder room of a club (Garrett's Bar in Chicago) , where I was playing, and sometimes worked for Walter Fuller's Quintet, came out and sang for me and I hired her on the spot. I instantly changed her name to Dinah Washington , but she didn't care what I called her so long as I gave her a job with my band. Another fellow auditioned on the same day later on after the matinee, and I hired him on the spot, too. His name was Joe Williams." Joe was a doorman at the Regal Theater, and wound up staying with Hamp for a year or so, and Dinah for about the same, then they moved on. It was Lionel who introduced the perennial and extraordinary Quincy Jones to the world of music. It was, also, with a Hampton band that Nat King Cole first achieved fame as a vocalist. And you can add the names of Betty Carter and Aretha Franklin as Hampton discoveries, too.

Further Hampton band graduates include Clark Terry, Fats Navarro, Charlie Mingus, Wes Montgomery, Art Farmer, Dexter Gordon, and Illinois Jacquet. Hamp was a man of tremendous zest, who lived and breathed music, whose vitality was contagious, and who loved his fellow beings. No complaints. Just enthusiasm and accommodation. He seemed comfortable with tributes and celebrations of his music and his celebrity status. In 1983 he was honored at the Kennedy Center in Washington and at the White House, where he's been many times before. A friend and supporter of then President Reagan, a Special Events Director for President Ford, he was also the first black to lead his orchestra at a Presidential Inaugural Ball---Harry Truman's back in 1949---- and has played for seven Presidential Inaugurations since. He's been an Ambassador of Music to the United Nations, a Human Rights Commissioner in New York City, honored at a Lionel Hampton Day under the L' Arch de Triomphe in Paris, France, and possesses numerous Doctorates at many Universities across the U.S., and has established the Lionel Hampton Jazz Endowment Fund across U.S. campuses.

"My music has certainly taken me a long way from Holy Rosary Academy back in Kenosha, Wisconsin," he reminisced. "I learned from strict Catholic Dominican Sisters, you know. That's why I'm so disciplined. That's why I work so hard."

Well, since he recorded his classic theme song, "Flying Home" in 1942, shortly after he left Goodman to form his own group, the band always included a version of that recording in every concert, usually at the opening. (The original recording included sidemen Dexter Gordon and Illinois Jacquet. That night, while out front, I actually heard someone say in a whisper, as if Lionel could actually hear him over the band's great vibration, "Play like Hell, Lionel, Play like Hell."

Over the years, Lionel Hampton endowed scholarships and lectures against drugs , when he played at high schools. He fulfilled his annual obligation to teach and perform at the Lionel Hampton School of Music at the University of Idaho. He toured tirelessly. He kept his band full of men who are young, and acted and played accordingly. "I play with young cats...I got lots of good guys."

You had to know him to fully understand it all. When he was home in his high-rise overlooking Lincoln Center, you could find him quietly playing Thelonious Monk's "Round Midnight" on the vibes sometimes at three in the morning. Then he would look up and declare to any visitor or friend: "We got a helluva band. The best in the Country."

It was truly astounding that at eighty-six he was performing live at the Blue Note, then recorded a session that sold 25,000 recordings in the first two weeks of release and wound up with a Grammy nomination, then promptly signed a contract with Mojazz, the jazz division of Motown.

Honestly, Lionel Hampton was accepting limited international bookings through the late nineties. Volcano of Energy was the right description. In August of 2002, the year after fire destroyed most of his personal belongings in his New York City apartment high above Lincoln Center, Lionel Hampton passed on. Nobody will ever forget Hamp. He was music personified.

WOODY HERMAN

Relegated To The Cellar

You'd think an intimate conversation with vintage, creative jazz-artist, Woody Herman, would be held at a nostalgic reunion or memorial jazz concert. Not this time: The playlands of Eastern Long Island was the setting.

At 5 P.M. one early Summer evening in 1981, Long Island PM Magazine Editor Paul Raymond called me to say that he heard Herman was to be performing a one-nighter out in the Hamptons in-spot Le Mans Disco. That's all I had to hear!

Photographer Gus Young and I, with cold sandwiches and two cokes in a brown bag, drove out to Southampton in my 1969 Mercedes to the junction of Sunrise Highway and Hampton Road to see if we could find one Woody Herman. At that precise spot, we found what looked like a converted bowling alley. It was Le' Mans all right, and it was barely an hour before performance time. There was Woody's band bus parked at the far end of the lot. We could not find Woody anywhere on the premises, and time was growing short. If we didn't talk to Woody now, we would have to wait until the show was over, and then, just maybe, he'd have no time for an interview and the trip wasted.

We explored the club as the band tuned up. The entire place featured auto-orientated decor. Tables were a tire above half an axle covered with glass, and seats were cut-off-parts of actual buses, cars, or anything that normally moved on the ground with wheels had been converted to the nightclub's furniture, and was named after the famous racetrack in LeMans, France.

Richard Grudens and Woody Herman, Southampton, NY -1982

With time running low, our search ended suddenly when we ran smack into Woodrow Charles Herman leaving the Men's Room where he must have been all along. We quickly corralled him. He was cordial and willing, but needed to get to rehearsal, so we hastily found a couple of seats in the nearby 'Quiet Zone' and began our conversation with this very friendly midwesterner:

"It feels like I'm meeting a legend, and it feels good," I began as Gus Young set up his camera.

"That's because I've lasted longer that I should've. The only reason I'm a legend is because I am still alive and kicking," he said, chuckling, "I'm too old to retire and as long as I have reasonable health, I'll continue to work.

"I love the music but I hate the travel," responded my hero to the inevitable retirement question which I put away early. You sometimes detest those annoying inquiries you must put to these living icons, but how else can you get the needed answers.

Although Woody spoke in that pleasant drawl, and his age was

Woody Herman Orchestra

beginning to show in his ever familiar face (he was 67 at the time), you knew he was unmistakably that lovable pint-sized giant whose Band That Played The Blues1930's skyrocket ride is still legendary in and out of jazz circles. His renditions of "Caledonia" and "Apple Honey" alone would have been enough for anyone. But Woody will not dwell on the past even though he acknowledged it was important to his career. "Caledonia" and "Apple Honey" is simply history to Woody. His favorite record was unexpectedly "The one I'll make next year" . He grinned and looked over to the bandstand which was now in full swing rehearsal.

"It's very boring to play the same old music. But, there are things that I'm proud of that were very good for the time. I'm interested to prove to anyone who cares to listen that I know where my roots are and that I am responsible for everything I've ever played. I never copped out and said the record producer made me do this or that. And I enjoy the music business or I couldn't do it for all these years. If everything remained the same and I had to play only the old things, I'd've thrown in the towel a long time ago."

And to my amazement, Woody disclosed his favorite instrument was not the clarinet, but rather the sax. "I feel I'm a better sax player, but when I was a young man it was important to play the American hot instrument of the day, and that was the clarinet."

At the age of just nine, Woody was already a vaudeville trouper, being billed as The Boy Wonder of the Clarinet when playing with local bands around Milwaukee, including Isham Jones. The boys first big hit was the "Woodchopper's Ball" in 1939, which is now an all-time jazz standard.

But, even after all this time, Woody is still riled up about booking agencies of yesterday and the record executives of today who run the music business: He recalled how he and Glenn Miller would sit in the outer offices of booking agencies waiting to get to the inner offices:

"They'd throw a dart at a map like they did 100 years ago and that's where you went. And it's still the same now. Today in Southampton and tomorrow in Colum-bus, ..no kidding. The record industry today is also ran by accountants who have no knowledge of music and they don't want any," he revealed, "it's just a business with no feelings and they are evidently success-ful- - so they must be right. They have re-lieved themselves of the responsibility of having creative people a long time ago."

It cost about $25,000.00 a week to keep the Herman band on the road at that time. And that means 6 bookings out of 7 days. Payroll has to be met, plus the bus, hotel bills, commissions, and other expenses. That is an average amount for band of this size. If the band had well-known side-men, instead of young players, it would be even more. Add a vocalist and it gets bigger. Booking agencies say you break even the first four nights. If someone requests the band specifically, then the profit goes up, and maybe that's a seventh day, too.

For a moment or two we discussed comparisons of yesterday's and today's music; (1981) There's Billy Joel, Rush, Pink Floyd, and oth-ers, versus the Big Bands of the past : "Well there is a lot of material that has quality and there is a lot of garbage. But there was a lot of garbage 45 years ago. My music was not accepted by the mature person, they said it was noise. My records were bought by kids and their parents rel-egated them to the cellar with their phonograph."

As of that day in 1981, Woody had been clearly out of the cel-lar for 44 years and was still part of the scene. The crowds continue to come--some are young and some are older. His sixteen players sitting on the bandstand a hundred feet away were very young, the average being 25, very much like Larry O'Brien's Glenn Miller Orchestra of today.

"I consider myself a coach---a coach can be old, but not the players," he quipped, "you need energy to play." You couldn't help but notice Woody's slumped-forward shoulders and pale face. He seemed older than his years, like someone carrying great weight around, but you couldn't tell it by his enthusiasm. "Music constantly changes and that's one gratifying thing about the whole scene. It's completely different from the music of the forties."

Woody Herman is, of course, responsible for the success of many jazz greats including sax man Stan Getz and vibraphonist Terry Gibbs who were once band members. They still were getting together at annual

Under the direction of Igor Stravinsky - Woody rehearses for the Carnegie Hall Premier of Ebony Concerto - written by Stravinsky

reunions at Woody's home in the Hollywood Hills and at various festivals. In 1977, almost everyone from his past bands and herds showed up for his 40th anniversary performance at Carnegie Hall, "and they all played. Zoot Sims, The Candoli Brothers, Pete and Conte...Chubby Jackson, Don Lamond--- they all came out. Then a few months ago we did the Monterey Jazz Festival and Getz was there and I had him do one of our charts."

Woody never arranged his charts, but he claims to be a very good editor. He kinda prides himself on his ability to make a young player give a better performance than he would ordinarily by rubbing off some of the Herman experience on him. That, I think, kept him musically sharpened and in tune with the continuous growth of music on a day-by-day basis, which explains his joy at staying in the business.

"Over 80 percent of my year is spent visiting high schools and colleges. What we do there," he went on, "is hold seminars with clinic sessions where our young men are utilized by players as teachers---so I learn from youth, being around them so much---it's a different environment so you are open to learning where most people my age are not."

Woody wouldn't let us go without telling us to tell you about his revered experience recording with Igor Stravinsky some years back. Stravinsky , then considered to be the World's greatest living composer, wrote a piece entitled "Ebony Concerto" just for the his band. Woody called it the high point of his career with demure pride.

Woody admitted he has a lot of miles on him and reminded me that he has spent 44 years as a jazzman and the same amount of years married to the same woman.

"Which is a record for a jazz musician," he touted as we shook hands and exchanged goodbyes then watched him amble over to the bandstand, charts in hand, ready to play and lead his youthful troupe of players.

For a few years, before he passed on in 1986, Woody was harassed with overwhelming IRS claims which forced him to forfeit his home, which he bought from Humphrey Bogart and Lauren Bacall. His daughter, Ingrid Herman Reese, started a fund within the jazz community who rallied to help him out of his financial dilemmas. They said he owed the government 1.5 million, but they would never offer him a justifiable settlement.

The following year the Woody Herman "ghost band" hit the road. The phrase "ghost band" originated from Woody Herman's own lips, as if he knew.

THE KID DRUMMER FROM REDBANK
THE BAND WAS LIKE SOME GREAT LOCOMOTIVE

Count Basie Orchestra - 1941

On a bitter cold evening in February of 1982, I set out to meet Count William James Basie, the enduring piano player from Red Bank, New Jersey, who led the longest-running jazz institution at the even older Northstage Theater in Glen Cove, New York where he was appearing with his band for a one-nighter. Bill Basie was ailing and had even ordered a mechanical wheelchair, but that didn't stop him from performing. When I spoke to him by telephone at his hotel just a few days before, he asked us not to bring any cameras. We couldn't help but wonder, ...why?

The Northstage stage entrance was dark, the stage door decrepit, and the backstage facilities bleak, cold, and bare. It was hard to believe the great Count Basie was to use these facilities this night. We waited around, talking to band member Freddie Green , the veteran Basie guitarist who has been with him since 1937, the acknowledged true pulse of the band.

When Basie and his party arrived, cold winds blew in behind them further chilling the backstage corridor the old steam radiators could not adequately heat. We slipped into the warmest dressing room. Catherine , Basie's wife of over 40 years, was literally holding him steady. He held a cane for added support. He look wasted, physically diminished, but cheerful and even enthusiastic, still his life and vitality was indeed waning. Now we understood why the 'no cameras' request. He had a severe case of arthritis of the spine and had had a 1976 heart attack, but it was pancreatic cancer that was to end his life a few short years later.

Basie, his valet and myself sipped some Chablis and talked about the Count's great career. At one point we had to excuse the

Count Basie

women, while we helped Bill change from street clothes to stage clothes. Basie placed his hands across my shoulders as he attempted to stand up receiving added assistance from his valet until we finally got him dressed for the performance. Friends and acquaintances showed up, popped in their heads for a handshake or a glass of Chablis that the theater manager furnished . The manager also handed Basie a fistful of cash which Basie waved over his head like the winner in a crap game, then pocketed it with a grin.

We began the taped interview talking about myriad Basie personnel, a who's who of jazz artists who played or vocalized with him over many years: Lester Young, Illinois Jacquet, Harry "Sweets" Edison, Clark Terry, Jo Jones, Roy Eldridge, Benny Carter, Buddy Tate, Stan Getz, Buddy De Franco, Lucky Thompson, and singers Billie Holiday, Jimmy Rushing, Helen Humes, and Joe Williams. I chided him about his three-note signature, the beguiling, "Plink, Plank, Plink" piano ending and he simply smiled and explained that it was, "A trademark, you know, just like Bing's bub-bub-boo-in', but our band is like some great locomotive- then it ends quiet-like, you know."

And when I asked him why he keeps on turning out for those grueling one night stands, he simply replied, "Got to eat---just like you---got to pay my rent and go to the super market, you know!" And about his accession to the status of "Count," he confirmed that it was a radio announcer in Kansas City, deciding that he was on a par with "Duke" Ellington, and "King of Swing" Benny Goodman, who dubbed him accordingly.

As almost any longtime Basie fan can tell you, his great fantasy as a young leader was "To go on the road touring everywhere". It was his great fortune to put the talent and fantasy together in a career that lasted longer than most people's entire lives.

L-R Nat King Cole, Count Basie, Ella Fitzgerald and Joe Williams

Basie spoke endearingly about his one time, magical vocalist, Billie Holiday, who spent one year or so with the band early-on (he was 34 and she was 25) and concluded with: "She and I kinda almost started up together--you know," lowering his voice to escape his wife Catherine's listening range, but didn't quite make it. Catherine delivered an understanding and knowing smile and the wry comment: "Well, I don't know about that!" as Bill Basie turned quickly away. The only recordings Billie made with Basie were those rare radio broadcast air checks performed at the Savoy Hotel just before she went over to Artie Shaw.

I asked if he ever played any other instrument besides his beloved piano. Basie said that he liked the drums and once auditioned with the original Dixieland Band," but they asked for the sticks back.". ... and when I asked him who his mentor or hero was, Fats Waller was the notable figure: "I used to watch him in the first row play organ for the silent movies and fell in love with his music right away."

'Do you prefer the work you do today, maybe those dynamic Neal Hefti arrangements, or the hard-swinging stuff, or do you think it was the early band that was your favorite?' to the answer: "I liked the first band (it made him immortal), but the new band (since 1952) made me some money. "And what's your favorite piece? "Why, 'One O'Clock Jump,' of course----- you kiddin, don't you know that?" Of course, I did.

And "April In Paris"? "It's nice too," he said.

Over the years Basie perfected his light, swinging style with a beat that is always there, and, unlike most bands, he placed an emphasis on simple, hummable riffs which appeal to everyone because the music can be easily understood: "Is your playing really pretty much the same as it was a long time ago?" "Sure! There is no other way." his voice rising emphatically. I left Bill and Catherine to the adoring crowd, now building up inside the theater. After this session and one later at the Jones Beach summer theater, the Basie's were headed for their Bahamas retreat.

If there was a Pulitzer for music, Basie deserves it more than anyone. He employed more worthy musicians, he changed the direction of the sounds of jazz by allowing his players to use the devices they employed best with their instruments in a undisciplined manner, unlike Ellington who worked his stricter arrangements around his players. Those offbeat accents and jarring dissonance's blew away many recording sessions and concerts than you could count. Call it jazz or call it great influential jazz music: it is more magnificent than you could describe. America should be grateful for its music royalty in Basie.

Count William Basie told me he wants to be remembered : "Just as I am right now...sittin' in front of a piano." I was a very humble human in the presence of William "Count" Basie, the kid from Redbank.

The Fabulous Dorsey Brothers

The battling Dorsey brothers, Jimmy and Tommy, grew up in Shenandoah, Pennsylvania. Their coal miner father quit to become a music teacher and to lead a small, local band. He handed Jimmy a

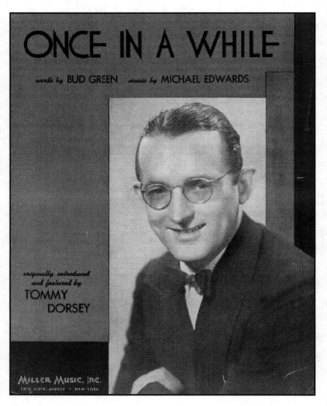

saxophone and Tommy a trombone and taught them to play. A disciplinarian, he kept them late at practice sessions. Jimmy was a year older than the dominant Tommy. The boys constantly argued. Jimmy had a more "take-it-easy" attitude, but when provoked, his temper was the equal of Tommy's. As their music education progressed, their father brought them into the band, thereby saving the salaries of two players. While still teenagers, the brothers left home to form the Dorsey Wild Canaries and were booked into long stays in various Baltimore hotels and ballrooms.

In those early years, before the big time, before Helen O'Connell and Bob Eberly, and well before Frank Sinatra and Connie Haines, Jimmy and Tommy Dorsey became studio musicians. Together or singularly, they appeared in the top bands of the thirties, including those of Red Nichols, Jean Goldkette, Victor Young, and Paul Whiteman's King of Jazz Orchestra with trombonist Jack Teagarden, Bing Crosby, cornet legend Bix Beiderbecke, Henry Busse, pianist/ arranger Lennie Hayton, and arranger Bill Challis.

In the Spring of 1934, the boys formed the Dorsey Brothers Orchestra and hired a fellow musician named Glenn Miller to arrange and

Tommy and Jimmy Dorsey

play trombone, and Bing Crosby's brother, Bob to sing. The band worked just fine, but the brothers were constantly engulfed in an adversarial relationship, to say the least, most arguments, which often became violent, were about music. Glenn Miller reluctantly took on the task of peacemaker to help keep them separated.

The boy's hangout in those days was Plunkett's saloon on 53rd Street in New York City. All the city musicians (Artie Shaw and Bix Beiderbecke among them) could make their radio dates on time from that strategic location. It was a great pickup spot for studios hiring musicians. From that group they formed their first orchestra, recruiting members of other bands who were out-of-work for the moment.

The band first signed with Okeh Records and, later, Decca Records, performing regularly at New York and New Jersey hotel ballrooms. They were booked into the famed Glen Island Casino in New Rochelle, New York, staying for a long engagement. Glenn left the band partly because he could not stand the constant bickering. The arguments persisted, climaxing one night when the boys flew at each other while on the bandstand. Tommy grew violent and stormed off leaving Jimmy to carry on alone. What had been building for years finally happened, and it came as no surprise. The breakup lasted for a long eighteen years, during which time each managed to become a legend of the Big Band Era with equally successful musical organizations.

JIMMY DORSEY

Jimmy's initial dilemma was filling Tommy's chair in the trombone section. Jimmy remembered a very young sixteen year old Bobby Byrne, who he had once heard. He sent for, auditioned and hired him. The other musicians were skeptical, but after listening their doubts were dispelled. Jimmy added vocalist Bob Eberly and drummer Ray McKinley to beef up the rhythm section. Tutti Camarata came aboard as trumpeter and arranger.

Jimmy was well-liked by his musicians, and although he retained the infamous Dorsey temper, he kept it well under control. His fine musicianship complemented the rich, lush sound he brought forth from his saxophone. He was a true master of the sax. Jimmy's personal life never captured headlines. He preferred to keep his non-music life private. He once courted vocalist Mary Ann McCall, and it was rumored that he would marry her, but it never occurred.

His orchestra now stabilized, Jimmy appeared on the radio series The Kraft Music Hall for over a year, which curtailed the band's recording output. He added vocalist Kay Weber, then, near the end of the series, replaced her with vocalist Martha Tilton, who did not fit in well and was replaced by a seasoned performer in June Richmond. Martha, of course,

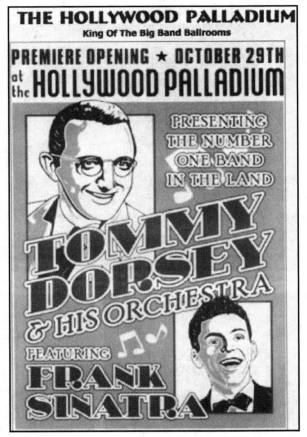

went on to star with Benny Goodman.

Evolving from a 'sweet band' to one that combined swing and sweet sounds, and, after a few hit recordings with Bob Eberly on the vocal with perfect singles like "Maria Elena," Jimmy hired precocious Helen O'Connell as his definitive girl singer who recorded some sweet duets with Eberly.

HELEN O'CONNELL

"We had a unique group with Jimmy, who was a wonderful person-

Helen O'Connell and Bob Eberly with
The Jimmy Dorsey Orhcestra

--never the boss. But, if any-body made trouble, I don't care how well he played, he didn't keep him very long." Helen told author Fred Hall in 1991.

In 1943, Helen left to get married and raise a family, so Jimmy brought in pretty Kitty Kallen, who had graduated from Jack Teagarden's band, and teamed her with Bob Eberly to record the admirable hit "Besame Mucho," utilizing the same formula as the Eberly-O'Connell duets. With World War II in force, Bob joined the army in December, 1944. No vocalist attained the success with Jimmy that Bob had, and his loss was a negative blow to the band.

Kitty Kallen departed shortly thereafter, again diminishing the success the band had enjoyed with Helen, Bob, and Kitty. With vocalists fortunes on the rise, the Big Bands were losing their draw. At the end of the war, veterans returned from military life with images of jobs, marriage, and homes. This left little time for personal entertainment, attendance at night clubs and dance halls. In December 1946, eight of the top bands folded due to lack of bookings. Jimmy struggled on with his band for a few more years. By 1950, television was flickering brightly in living rooms featuring wrestling, Ed Sullivan's variety show, and Roller Derby action, capturing an important share of entertainment time. New automobiles found their way onto the nation's newly constructed highways. Times were changing for the Big Bands. Jimmy Dorsey inevitably gave up his band in 1950.

TOMMY DORSEY

After the breakup at the Glen Island Casino, in contrast to Jimmy's slow rise to stardom, Tommy promptly contacted an old friend, Joe Haymes. Haymes was leading a hotel-style band with less than great success, so Tommy hired twelve of Haymes' musicians and formed the Tommy Dorsey Orchestra. Tommy wasted little time in whipping his band into top shape. A driven man who demanded the best from himself and expected the same from his players, his temperament was explosive, yet he possessed a tender side and was caring towards those men who were as dedicated to the music as was he.

Tommy Dorsey Orchestra - 1941

A recording deal with RCA Victor Records produced the recording "On Treasure Island," with vocalist Edythe Wright, soon reaching number one on the charts. Tommy constantly changed band personnel. He brought in classy Jack Leonard to handle the vocals, drummer Davey Tough and clarinet/saxist Bud Freeman . Trombonist Axel Stordahl was signed, eventually becoming the band's arranger. He hired Bunny Berigan for the trumpet section and produced "Marie" with Leonard doing the vocal and Berigan creating a timeless solo for this hit recording. The release of the "Song of India" catapulted Tommy Dorsey into a top rated band leader and from then on amassed over two-hundred records in both the sweet and swing category.

Although famous as a bandleader, it must be realized that Tommy was a superb trombone player and in all respects, the equal of contemporary Jack Teagarden. Just listen carefully to his original recording of "I'm Getting Sentimental Over You" or "Once In a While" to appreciate the extent of his talent.

The years 1935 through 1938 were flourishing years for Tommy Dorsey, although his personal life did not mirror his public

The Dorsey Brothers Orchestra Rehearsing at NBC

success. Experiencing ongoing marital troubles, a divorce became inevitable. Then, Edythe Wright and Jack Leonard left the band; drummer Davey Tough was replaced with Buddy Rich, and Ziggy Elman joined the trumpet section. Tommy hit pay dirt when he managed to hire Frank Sinatra away from Harry James in the spring of 1940, and a very young Connie Haines, who had also sung with James, had also joined him. Frank, Connie, the Pied Pipers singing group (including Jo Stafford) immediately clicked with the million seller "I'll Never Smile Again."

JO STAFFORD

Jo Stafford remembered Frank Sinatra when he first joined the band and the Pipers, "As he came up to the mike, I just thought, Hmmm - kinda thin. But by the end of eight bars I was thinking, "This is the greatest sound I've ever heard,' But he had more. Call it talent. You knew he couldn't do a number badly," Jo told me back in 1999.

The Sinatra tenure with the band were glory days for both Sinatra and Dorsey. Sinatra became The Voice and Tommy, The Sentimental Gentleman of Swing. The list of musicians were outstanding. Among them clarinetists Johnny Mince and Buddy De Franco; arrangers Deane Kinkaid and Sy Oliver; pianist Joe Bushkin; trombonists Nelson Riddle and Earle Hagen.

The band turned out a remarkable string of hits; "Snootie Little Cutie" and "Let's Get Away From It All," "Oh,Look At Me Now;" "There Are

Such Things," "Street of Dreams," "Everything Happens to Me," "East of the Sun" (with that great Bunny Berigan solo), "Will You Still Be Mine," (Connie Haines is perfection phrasing this one, the first recording that Tommy allowed her to sing in her own key), "On the Sunny Side of the Street," "Yes, Indeed," "Deep Night," all these recordings were made with Sinatra, Connie Haines, and the Pipers with Jo Stafford, alone or collectively. "Boogie Woogie," "Song of India," and "Opus No. 1 "were great instrumentals, too.

In 1940, the opulent Hollywood Palladium opened, and the Dorsey band, being the most popular dance band in the nation at the time, was chosen to appear as its star attraction on opening night.

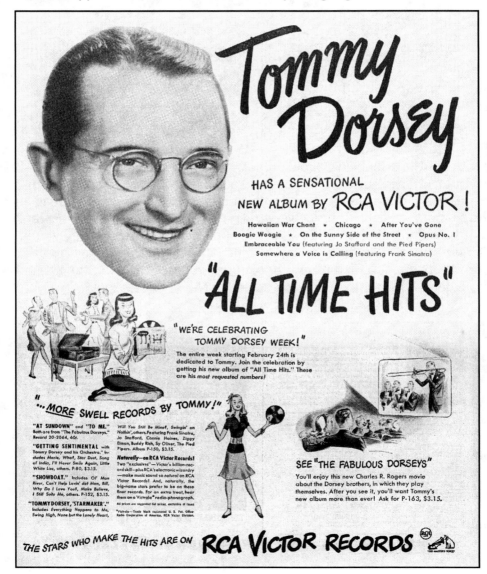

Opening at Palladium in Hollywood

CONNIE HAINES

"It was wonderful, and you could feel the excitement. Actress Dorothy Lamour cut the big red satin ribbon, revealing a mountain of orchids. The place was packed. The dance floor was filled --- they had room to swing and sway together," according to Connie Haines in her forthcoming biography Snootie Little Cutie. "We spent eight exciting weeks there each year."

World War II caused drastic problems for the Big Band business. Gasoline and tires were rationed, curtailing travel for the touring bands. The draft claimed many of their players. Buddy Rich and Ziggy Elman were soon wearing uniforms. In late 1942, Sinatra decided to go it alone. However, the business man in Tommy Dorsey surfaced when he negotiated a percentage of Frank's future earnings in exchange for letting him out of his contract. The rich baritone of Dick Haymes replaced Sinatra and the band struggled on until the end of the war.

DICK HAYMES

"The actual Tiffany's of the orchestra world in those days was

Tommy Dorsey's orchestra," Dick Haymes told author Fred Hall in 1978, "because he gave you a showcase. He was a star maker. He carried the arrangers --- Axel Stordahl, Paul Weston, and Sy Oliver; I mean we had the cream of everything --- this huge, wonderful orchestra. Tommy would say, 'Okay, here's your spot --- do your song,' I learned great lessons in performing as well as sing-ing and breath control with Tommy."

Dick sang with the band for its nine week appear-ance at the Hol-lywood Palla-dium that year. His own ver-sion of "Maria Elena" rivaled Bob Eberly's performed a year or so ear-lier with Jimmy Dorsey.

Tommy Dorsey was now entering a phase of his life where he became quite a business man. His band booking busi-ness Tomdor

Tommy Dorsey, Frank Sinatra, Connie Haines and the Pied Pipers with Jo Stafford

Enterprises was thriving, and he began a music magazine titled The Bandstand to compete with Metronome and Downbeat. Unfortunately, only six issues were printed before it folded, a distinct financial loss for Tommy Dorsey the businessman. Undaunted, he demanded more money for his band's performances at the Hollywood Palladium and didn't receive it. Searching for another ballroom, he purchased the Casino Gardens in nearby Ocean Park, California. Bandleader Harry James and his brother Jimmy were also partners in the deal. Evidently the brothers were able to work together in an enterprise where the sparks didn't fly. Casino Gardens proved to be a moneymaker, competing with the Palladium for the services of all the other important name bands, but Tommy found himself stretched between the band and his other ventures, so the band suffered. He took on an added position as director of popular music for Mutual Radio. By 1946, bookings for the major bands slowed to a mere trickle, and in December, Tommy and seven other top bands quit.

Tommy Dorsey took a breather from the bandstand and devoted time between his record companies, his new job, and his almost defunct booking agency, to get married again, this time to actress Pat Dane. In 1948 he reformed the band and claimed that he would revitalize the Big Band business. His named carried some weight, but he struggled until 1950, when he and brother Jimmy buried their differences to form the Dorsey Brothers Orchestra, their first collaboration since the infamous breakup.

Tommy assumed the role of leader of this new enterprise and Jimmy seemed content to simply take a seat in the saxophone section. The band was known as The Dorsey Brothers Orchestra or The Tommy Dorsey Orchestra, featuring Jimmy Dorsey. Both were used depending on the booking. Appearances were widely spaced, but the boys were back in business and working peacefully with one-another. In 1955, Jackie Gleason, a big fan of the Dorseys, asked them to appear on television as a summer replacement for his popular CBS show, which they did for two seasons.

LYNN ROBERTS

"I was seventeen when I joined the band," Dorsey vocalist Lynn Roberts said when I talked with her in January, 1999: "When I first saw him in the coffee shop of a hotel in Fayetteville, North Carolina, he appeared larger than life. He had a very gruff voice and was terribly intimidating. I had no arrangements of my own, so I had to sing the things that were already in the book, written for someone else---most of them not in my key. In spite of all that, he was pleased with my work. I learned to sing by listening to T.D. --- as we called him. Listening to him play was an education, like going to music school every night for four hours. He was a musician who knew the lyrics to the songs he played. He thought about them while he was playing and that, in my opinion, is the reason that so many singers latched on to his incredible phrasing. Tommy was my mentor---my teacher---he taught me how to sing. Thank you, Tommy Dorsey. Jimmy Dorsey joined T.D. in 1953, so that was how I came to work with both of them. He was a sweet, almost shy guy. And - - yes, - they did fight."

Times were good for the band once again, but Tommy was in-volved in a divorce with his third wife Jane, a one time Copacabana showgirl. This weighed heavily on Tommy, and on November 26, 1956, after a very heavy meal, Tommy took some sleeping pills and went to bed. During the night he became ill, vomited, suffocated on his regurgitated food and died while he was asleep.

LYNN ROBERTS

"When Tommy suddenly died in 1956, we were appearing at the Cafe Rouge'," Lynn Roberts said, "It was our day off and we all learned of his tragic death on the TV or in the morning paper. He was only fifty-one years old. I often wonder how the music busi-ness would have been different had Tommy lived. We, the fabulous Dorsey Brothers Band, were doing better than ever. We had a five day a week radio show on NBC plus lots of book-ings into the following year. Tommy was a wonderful business man and a great trombonist. I still miss him."

Tommy Gives Lynn a Hair Cut

ROBERT MELVIN - Dorsey Scholar and Big Band writer:

"Jimmy was badly shaken by his brother's death but rallied and took over as leader of the orchestra and tried to carry on. This was not to be and Jimmy fell ill and died of cancer a few short months later.

"In six months, two luminaries of the Big Band Era passed away. As a final starburst for the Dorseys, a recording of "So Rare" recorded earlier, became a hit record in March 1957. Both bands have been active as ghost bands and perform to this day. The Jimmy and Tommy Dorsey Orchestras are surely playing somewhere on Earth today. A fitting tribute to the musical excellence of the Dorsey Brothers."

Tommy Dorsey with Hoagy Carmichael - Collaborating - 1939

Stan Kenton
Sweet Sound of Thundering Music

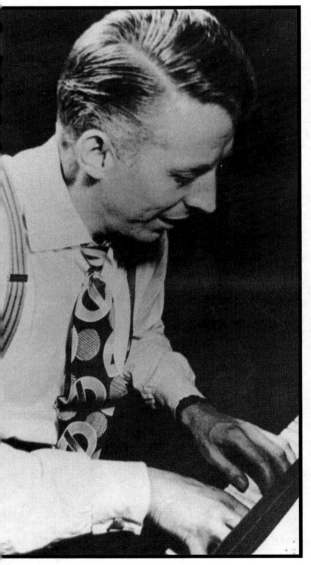

My one connection to the Stan Kenton Band besides a recent working relationship for this piece with his wife Audree Coke Kenton who has been an absolute Godsend, was a friendship I shared with bass player Eddie Safranski at the NBC studios in New York back in the 1950s.

"I never knew anyone who ever worked with Stan who didn't like him and enjoy working in his band," I recall him saying.

If you listen mindfully to the January, 1945 recording of Pete Rugolo's arrangement of Stanley's composition "Artistry In Rhythm," as I have hundreds of times, the romantic, smooth flowing Kenton piano, the punctuating brass, the thumping drums, the flowing saxes, all signature material associated with Kenton, may move you to become a Stan Kenton fan, if you are not already one. Then perhaps you might want to explore the fluent saxophone and rhythm classic "Opus in Pastels" In any case, to remain a Kenton aficionado you have to move musically forward as Stan Kenton always did directly into the future of the exciting and thrilling music he dreamed would someday permeate the airwaves and concert halls, not merely sounds played to accommodate dancers who pervaded the ballrooms and dance halls. That, he once mused "Is a musical horse of a different color." With each successive recording the Kenton mystique always moved on, always changed and growing, always different.

Stan Kenton's music was, at times, rejected by critics, even when he was leading the popularity charts. Despite their cries, he found himself playing the best venues, the premier classical concert halls and colleges. A virtual lifetime of effort affirmed his steady rise to success, thanks to showcasing a totally revolutionary repertoire, including recognizing and fostering the brilliant arrangements of Pete Rugolo.

Stan Kenton's early credo:

"With high regard and respect for each other's individuality...a group of personalities can make music wide in scope...from tender, soft sounds to screaming, crashing dissonance. "This is an orchestra," Stanley Kenton declared upon the release of his 1952 Capitol LP "This Is An Orchestra!"

Two years later he deliv-
ered a statement for the opening
of the Festival of Modern American Jazz, at Carnegie Hall, New
York on October 9, 1954:

"In spite of the hazards to
which jazz has been subjected in
its growth, we now can celebrate
its victory. No longer does it have
to suffer from an obligation to
Tin Pan Alley. Nor does it have
to function in other forms. It has
served its apprenticeship and is
blossoming into maturity independently."

Stanley Newcomb Ken-
ton was born in Wichita, Kansas,
on December 15, 1911, a date
earlier in question, but verified by
birth certificate obtained by The

Stan Kenton and Vocalist Anita O'day

Network, a long-running Stan Kenton Newsletter of which Anthony Agosti-
nelli is editor.

Young Stanley learned piano and developed arrangements for various dance bands during the 1930's, forming his first musical group. On Memorial Day, 1940, his became the resident band at the Rendez-vous Ballroom located on a narrow peninsula in Balboa, California. His music created immediate excitement, earning him a coveted booking into the famed Hollywood Palladium in 1942, a spot reserved for then really big-name bands. Engagements at New York City's Roseland, and Frank Dailey's Meadowbrook on the Pompton Turnpike in New Jersey, followed.

His first recordings, commercial and thus unrewarding to Kenton, were cut with Decca. When composer/vocalist Johnny Mercer and former record store owner Glenn Wallichs formed Capitol Records in 1943, they signed him, allowing him musical carte-blanche. Then, fortunately (some say unfortunately), comedian Bob Hope hired him to replace Skinnay Ennis' orchestra on Bob's very popular network radio show, attaining for Stanley and his band important exposure and personal prestige, as they traveled to countless military bases around the country in nerve-wracking flights in every kind of weather to bring entertainment to U.S. servicemen, even though Stanley later regretted accepting the job because it diluted his musical idealism. The recording sessions with Capitol lasted through 1947 and have all been reissued by Mosaic Records, which includes previously unissued masters.

In 1953 Stan Kenton and the band, with vocalist June Christy, flew to Europe in an Air Force plane, leaving Westover, Massachusetts on September 25th and played a gig the very same night in the Azores and the following night in Tripoli, both shows for the U.S. Army. They opened their official tour in Frankfurt, Germany on September 28th and went on to further bookings in Denmark, Sweden, Belgium, Holland, France, Switzerland, Austria and Italy. What a terrific tour that was for the band, its popularity flying higher than ever before.

On Saturday, October 9, 1954, Stanley arrived at the very realization of his dream, that was leading the Festival of Modern American Jazz at Carnegie Hall in New York, performing with his fresh and innovative orchestra and showcasing pianist Art Tatum and his Trio; saxophonist Charlie Ventura; trumpeter Shorty Rogers; drummer Shelley Manne; guitarist/ arranger Johnny Smith; premier trombonist Milt Bernhart; Cuban bongo drummer Candido; new stars saxophonist Lee Konitz and trombonist Frank Rosolino, and veteran trumpeters Conte Candoli and Maynard Ferguson, earning all of them well-deserving accolades in the press. It was his second trip to the revered of all venues and all music, Carnegie Hall.

For Stan Kenton and his band of musicians, it was certainly a night to remember. It was centuries away from the embryonic days at the Rendezvous. He was now the champion of modern music, his arrangements then being practiced in music classes at major universities all over the world, for instruction at dance studios; for modern dance sequences on television; for motion picture sound tracks - and for the repertoire of the Sadler Wells Ballet Company. The early, difficult years that once made things seem hopeless were eventually conquered with perseverance and hard work.

The Kenton sound became synonymous with strength in music. A lively, enthusiastic conductor, urging his musicians on with every crescendo, Stan Kenton, triumphantly lifting and thrusting his arms forward with sheer joy, as he propels the music onward with great artistic conviction, with every musician equally enthralled. "There was only one place on earth that was joy and happiness to Stan Kenton, and that was fronting has musicians on the bandstand," according to band trombonist Milt Bernhart.

AUDREE COKE KENTON

Audree Coke Kenton, a public relations specialist, was married to Stan Kenton from 1975 until he passed away in 1979. She still works very hard every day to keep the Kenton music legend alive through the efforts of the American Jazz Institute, first formed in 1997 under the direction of Mark Masters. This venerable jazz organization, based in Pasadena, California, celebrates with annual festivals in Redondo Beach, just a few miles from the Rendezvous Ballroom in Balboa, where Stan Kenton started, and twenty years after he played his last engagement. Audree sits on the Institute's Board of Directors.

On an exceptionally cool afternoon in September of 1998, Audree Kenton and I sat down to talk about her legendary husband:

"We have just done a jazz concert in Pasadena, California, Richard, made up largely of Kenton Band alumni, through the American Jazz Institute. I am pleased to report that we had a sold-out house. I am also happy to say with certainty that the Kenton name still pulls."

One week the group will present the Neophonic Orchestra, which Stanley led in the mid-60s, and the next week it will be the Mellophonium Years (1960-63). Perhaps they will be followed by a Milestones Concert featuring the chestnuts "Eager Beaver," "Intermission Riff," "Peanut Vendor," and so forth, eventually covering the work of all the orchestras he created and named for the sounds that inspired them: Chronologically, Artistry in Rhythm, Progressive Jazz, Innovations in Modern Music, New Concepts of Artistry in Rhythm, and the Neophonic Orchestra.

Stan Kenton always wanted his band to be an instrumental band performing only concerts, rather than a dance band, "But," as Audree explained, "At one time there was only a market for dance bands. He started writing music for dancing, but then he discovered the dancers were standing in front of the bandstand anyway - not moving - not dancing, so he concentrated more on the listening aspect --- concert music. Stanley's music was different from what the critics were used to hearing at that time, so they panned it, labeling it empty and pretentious.

"In 1941, when I first met Stanley I was working for a newspaper. At the time I was married to Jimmy Lyons (outstanding jazz DJ and founder of the Monterey Jazz Festival), and Stanley was married to his first wife Violet Peters, a wonderful woman and a dear friend of mine. The four of us hung out together. Jimmy and Stanley walked the streets of Balboa soliciting funds from merchants to string radio lines into the ballroom so the broadcasts could be made over the Mutual Broadcasting System."

Jimmy got Stanley his first air time for the band when he hosted the first remotes of the broadcasts from Balboa on the Mutual Broadcasting System. In 1949 Stanley began having serious marital problems with Violet. "She was sick and tired of being left alone at home with their daughter, Leslie, while Stanley was continuously on tour. So he took some time off hoping to patch things up. He remained restlessly at home for about a year or so but he just couldn't deal with that quiet and uneventful kind of life. He had to get back to the music, and so the marriage just disintegrated. He later married Ann Richards, a singer with the band. They had two children; Dana, who is now forty-two, very tall, strongly resembling her father, and a son named Lance.

"Much later, in 1971, when he was developing Creative World Records, what he needed- and what he hired me for - was public relations. Public relations turned into marketing, publicity and advertising.... and eventually marriage in 1975, I'm happy to say. By the time Stanley passed away I was his personal manager. Even then, after forty years, his whole life was still music."

"I understand that some writers and critics have characterized the personality of Stan Kenton as a 'bundle-of-nerves' type," I said.

"I can't agree. I'd say he was more an intense person, always dedicated to creating new jazz sounds in music. He looked deep within himself for those sounds. He was a great arranger and a good conductor.

"In creating that revolutionary music, Pete Rugolo and Stanley were so close --- as collaborators --- to one another that they would forget who had written what. They were so busy in those days, especially while doing the one-nighters, and they would have an idea and write six or eight bars and Stanley would say to Pete, 'What do you think of that?' and then they had to locate a piano, which wasn't always easy, to write those ideas down before they forgot them."

Unlike Woody Herman and some other bandleaders, Stan Kenton loved the traveling aspect of leading a band. "Stanley enjoyed traveling from one city to another, bringing his music to far-flung places. Playing the concert halls of America was part of his true dream, Richard."

To Kenton , traveling meant independence. Grounded in the studio he felt at the mercy of directors and producers. "When we are on the road we play our music the way we think it should be played, and we've absolute freedom," he once told Don Kennedy of Big Band Jump, "I think if I had to punch the same time clock every day and go to work the same way and eat the same food every day, I think I'd probably die of boredom."

Then, there were the popular and constructive clinics the band conducted on college campuses during each Summer:

"We did clinics heavily for about the last ten years of his life," Audree went on, "I think we did the first clinics at the University of Indiana, the University of Michigan and in Denver, in the late 60s. And then it got to the point where we did six or seven week-long clinics each year during the summer months. Stanley really enjoyed teaching and coaching youngsters.

Audree Kenton manages Stan Kenton's estate and is one that states there will be no "ghost" band and that his name may not be used to front any nostalgia band.

Just before arranger Pete Rugolo joined the band, Stan Kenton had recorded their then number one hit "And Her Tears Flowed Like Wine" in May of 1944. The vocal was performed by sparkling song star Anita O'Day, becoming her signature song and a first real hit for Kenton. "Funny thing about that recording, Richard," Anita told me in 1997, while interviewing her for my book The Song Stars, "the first take had no Kenton piano accompaniment

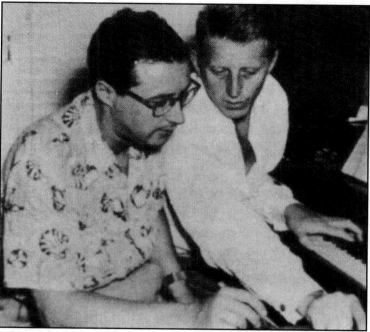

L: Pete Rugolo - R: Stan Kenton

and was the original release. The second release on a 1952 LP featured the second take with Stanley at the piano. I love the second take with Stanley at the piano the best."

But Anita wasn't really happy in the Kenton organization. I spoke to her about it in Febuary of 1999: " I couldn't stand that upbeat, so I left after a year. I said,'I'll get you a singer, and I gave them June Christy, and I went on to sing with swing bands. We were playing at the Chicago Theater and across the street there was a place called Three Deuces, a restaurant that had a Big Band playing at lunchtime. ` So I went there, and after watching the singer, a little light-bulb went off in my head. I went backstage and I said to the singer - 'What's your name?', and she says

'Shirley Luster,' and I said 'How'd you like to be rich and famous?' and she said, 'What do you mean?' I said, 'Come across the street and meet Stan Kenton, and please take the job. I've been there a year and I just gotta change.' She said,'I'll be over.' And she came over - -- they liked her--- and that was that!"

In May of 1945 Kenton recorded another milestone, "Tampico," June Christy' first-ever vocal recording. A followup recording for June was the popular "Shoo Fly Pie and Apple Pan Dowdy" recorded in 1946. June, a pretty blonde who sounded a lot like her predecessor, Anita O'Day, married band member, tenor saxist Bob Cooper and remained married to him for the rest of her life. Her given name, as Anita said, was Shirley Luster, but Stanley thought it sounded like a shampoo and asked her to change it.

1946 brought forth the Artistry In Rhythm album that characterized the band forever as the Artistry In Rhythm Band.

PETE RUGOLO - ARRANGER

It is November 1998. I am speaking to arranger Pete Rugolo from his California home. It was Rugolo, a modernist, progressive, and innovative arranger who, with Kenton, was able to create that revolutionary Kenton intonation. Kenton liked Pete Rugolo's work so well that he asked him to rearrange the band's theme "Artistry In Rhythm," when he first engaged this young arranger to help develop special arrangements for the band.

Born in Sicily, Italy, Pete Rugolo and his family arrived in this country in 1921, when he was five years old. " My dad was an out-of-work stone mason, so he immigrated here to work in my uncle's shop as a shoemaker. He got his own place in Santa Rosa (California) where my grandfather lived. I went to school there and then attended San Francisco State College and later received my Master's studying with Darius Milhaud."

Milhaud, a French composer, developed polytonality - a simultaneous use of different keys.

"It was 1945 when I first joined the Kenton band. I first met him at the Golden Gate Theater in San Francisco. I was still in the Army and leading an Army band. Stan had a record that just came out, and I loved that style a lot and started to write like the recording. One day I went backstage to see him and brought five arrangements with me. He was very nice --- and he said he would try them out, and I said for him to return them to me if he couldn't use them, as I copied them out myself and had no other copies. He got a really big kick out of that. I didn't hear from him for a month or so. Then, one day at the barracks I got an exciting call over the P.A .---'Stan Kenton calling Pete Rugolo' - much excited, I went to the post telephone and talked to him and he said he tried the arrangements, telling the band, 'that the kid from San Francisco left me.' After trying them out he said, 'My God! You do write like me, and you're even much more modern.' I was so excited."

By that time Stan Kenton was performing regularly at the Hollywood Palladium and Rugolo brought several more arrangements to him, "...and he loved them," Pete continued, " he said 'when you get out of the Army the (arranging) job is yours. ' It was all like a fairy story to me...but, that's exactly how it happened.

"When I became discharged, I contacted Stan---he was now playing the Meadowbrook in New Jersey---and he sent me the money and I went there and stayed with the band 'til he disbanded it in late '49."

"You radically changed the musical course of the Kenton band," I noted.

"Yes...I created ---what they called progressive jazz. I promptly rearranged "Artistry in Rhythm" at his request, and, over the course of my tenure, a couple of hundred other pieces."

Pete Rugolo actually arranged about 95% of all the band's albums up through 1950.

"I added all kinds of dissonance and incorporated some of Darius Milhaud's modernistic ideas into jazz using 5/4 material which was never used before," Pete went on to say, " I began writing compositions - more like concert pieces, for the tours. Stan really liked them.

"With Stan, well, when we were on tour, he wanted you to come over to the dance hall every night to check the arrangements. During the last set of the evening, he liked to step off the bandstand to talk to the people---the dancers, and he would leave me to play the piano, you know, taking his spot in front of the band for that short time. I was a pretty good piano player, although I played much differently than he did - I was more of a light piano player - like Teddy Wilson ---he played more like Earl Hines' style, which he preferred. But, I finally gave it up. I had no time to play anymore when I started writing an awful lot. At first we got bad reviews because the critics didn't understand that kind of music. It wasn't a swing band like Woody Herman's or Benny Goodman's, you know. The people enjoyed Stan's early work too, like "Eager Beaver" and that sort of thing."

"Pete, I said,"this relationship reminds me of the Duke Ellington - Billy Strayhorn association---busy, prolific bandleader, and almost exclusive arranger, working hand in hand - a very close relationship."

"Exactly. Like Ellington, Stan stopped writing because we were doing one-nighters and he was just too busy. We had a radio show going, too. We would get together and discuss things --- we'd sit at the piano and he had a few ideas about a tune or something and we would kind of write out a menu, and he would say, ' Let"s start off with a bass the first twelve bars.' It was actually like a menu. We would flesh it all out. And we wrote quite a few tunes together, in a sort of collaboration. I was such a fan of his and we were always good friends, too. Stan was an amazing guy. He looked so good in front of the band."

Their first album together was called "Artistry in Rhythm" in which Pete wrote eleven of the twelve selections. In the various album selections Rugolo projected the progressive influences of Stravinsky during "Artistry in Percussion;" Debussy in "Willow Weep for Me;" and Ravel in "Artistry in Bolero."

When Kenton gave up that band in 1949, Pete Rugolo migrated to Capitol Records for two years where he expanded his repertoire with the Capitol contract stable artists of the time: June Christy, Nat King Cole, Miles Davis, and Dizzy Gillespie, as well as many other developing bebop artists.

Later on in 1958, Pete Rugolo with Milt Bernhart and others, produced an album of music under the Stan Kenton name with Stanley at the piano and undoubtedly as a consultant. The album was called "Lush Interlude" and brought Pete Rugolo back to writing and leading, overcoming a recent hiatus.

MILT BERNHART
1947 Kenton Band Supreme Trombonist

Milt Bernhart played a stellar trombone with Stan Kenton beginning with the "Artistry in Rhythm" band, performing on the original recording of the Kenton classic. I talked with him recently while he was stuffing envelopes to remind members to pay their dues to the The Big Band Academy of America, an institute founded 15 years ago by Big Band historian,and author Leo Walker. Milt was currently President.

"I joined Stan when I came out of the Army. I loved the sound of the band and always wanted to play with him. I was only twenty. Stan was a great front man who could face any audience, because he was very friendly. There were no formula charts like (Glenn) Miller or (Benny) Goodman."

Milt, an alumnus of Benny Goodman and other bands, felt musically secure in the Kenton organization: "I found Stan, in comparison to other famous band leaders I worked for, to be more considerate and easy to communicate with, and he was one who spoke his mind, but he allowed each member of the band to be themselves. And there was no pretense even though he allowed a pretentious title for his band--- obviously someone other than Stan thought of the phrase "Artistry In Rhythm," but it was one of the few instances where he got into the business of so-called 'packaging.'"

Milt considered himself fortunate to be with Kenton. "His plan was that he wanted to explore music - always to be different --- just like Artie Shaw--- always moving forward. I knew that his music was going to come first, above everything, and it was going to be of a high standard, with music that could end up meaning something. I thought, 'If I could get on that band, it would be the best thing for me'. But, because he didn't perform exclusively as a commercial dance band, he struggled financially. He never complained right down to the bitter end. His dream was to be a concert master, not a dance band leader. That would have bored him silly."

"Perhaps his fate was likened to Artie Shaw's," I said. It was just a month ago when Artie Shaw told me the very same thing about his own career, saying, "I could have been a zillionaire if I had stayed with my early success of the Begin the Beguine Band, instead of forging ahead with innovative and new material that was unaccepted at the time."

"Well, for sure, if Stan went completely commercial, and, that perhaps he would've been a millionaire may be going beyond reality. It's always been a mystery why some commercial music enterprises connect and others don't. Generally, if you are aiming to please the public, you are aiming down. Stan, from day one, couldn't do that. For him, it would have been out of the question." The musical goals of Kenton and Shaw paralleled. As true artists, both sacrificed their financial and celebrity future to play what they created, not what the bookers dictated and the public demanded of them. Milt Bernhart concurred.

As with Shaw, playing exclusively in concert halls was Kenton's goal. Stan Kenton and his 1950s Innovations in Modern Music Orchestra, a thirty-nine piece (including 16 strings) group, played only new material, omitting early hits of the band or other accepted standards. "It was thrilling to be part of that group of musicians," Milt told me, "A lot of new music was played. People listened to things they had never heard before. We played only the major concert halls coast-to-coast, like the Academy of Music in Philadelphia, the Civic Opera in Chicago, the Hollywood Bowl several times, Symphony Hall in Boston and Carnegie Hall in New York. And it didn't matter to him if there was only half a house or just a few in the audience, it would not have changed anything. His feeling of uplift coming from deep down into the soul is as real as anybody's ever was."

The first time Milt played in Carnegie Hall at the 1954 Festival of Modern American Jazz with Kenton, he said, "It was a thrilling night for all of us who played at Carnegie - especially with Stan---something to which I'm sure every musician aspires."

Stan Kenton personally chose each band musician. "When he was selecting who would play for the band --- if there was an opening---an applicant would have to actually sit in and try out. Nobody ever got hired without playing first," Milt went on, "because that would be foolhardy. But afterwards, he would ask certain people in the band, whose opinion he respected, if they thought this person was going to work out. He would always take a consensus. And it mattered to him, as he tried very hard to make life in his band a democracy."

Because the Kenton Band had no sponsor, Stan quickly ran out of money and was forced to return to the dance hall tours in order to meet expenses. "So," Milt continued, "(drummer) Shelley Manne, (trumpeters) Maynard Ferguson and Shorty Rogers, and I all left, preferring not to play music for dancers, which meant too much weary traveling, one night stands, and playing the same charts over and over. A performer can get stale playing the same music all the time and lose interest, and then what?"

But Stan never begged any musician to stay. He felt he'd always find replacements: "He wished us good luck and with no hard feelings ever, mind you. He understood. He never gave up his dream. That's why I respected him so much. I never knew any musician who worked for Stan who didn't adore him. Why, even during dance band dates, Stan would make an announcement that there would be a mini-concert, so anybody who wanted to hear his special brand of music would gather around the bandstand just to listen. It was fun for the musicians and the listeners as well. The selection "Collaboration," arranged by Rugolo, was a great favorite."

Stan Kenton's music was always exciting, especially for the musicians themselves: "Even Billy May will tell you today," Milt continued, "that it was just a job playing with Glenn Miller, and if it's just a job, what have you? Miller made no pretense, and he did very well at it, but if you looked very closely at the members in his band, they appear as if they were asleep. He made them smile, and they played, but musicians certainly didn't have the time of their life playing in bands like Glenn Miller's. That wasn't the case with Stan. The problem here is money versus art. There has never been a real meeting of the two. Benny Goodman played what he wanted to, but he always made sure it was music the dancers could dance to. All these bands, except Kenton, made money pleasing the dancers. When Kenton played it was unlikely you were going to hear his greatest hits. If Stan could keep the band going, and keep people coming, and somehow pay the expenses every week, including the expenses of traveling, it made us all very happy, but it certainly was very difficult."

STAN KENTON - On the future of his music:

"Well, I think nostalgia is certainly the worst commercial commodity in every way. People, somehow, are always looking back and I think there's a psychological problem there. I think they feel they've made it through one part of their life, and they're afraid of today and tomorrow, they want to go back and relive the past again."

Audree and the rest of us lost Stanley Newcomb Kenton in 1979, but we will never lose the legacy of his original and extraordinary music.

Kenton Performing - Photo William Gottlieb

RAY ANTHONY

NOT ALWAYS IN THE
FOOTSTEPS OF TRADITION

Raymond Antonini of Bentleyville, Pa. came by his music naturally: "My dad taught me when I was five years old. He started me on the trumpet, so I'm from a musical family."

Ray Anthony, as he is known, began in the Antonini Family Orchestra, comprised of a sister, two brothers and dad. "Then I started and played in my own band when I was just fourteen. The other players were in their twenties and thirties. I was way ahead of my time."

During high school, Ray played trumpet with local bands and quickly rose to featured trumpeter with Al Donohue's orchestra in Boston. By eighteen he joined with Jimmy Dorsey and then became a member of the distinguished Glenn Miller Orchestra.

"I guess you had to play pretty good to land a job with Glenn Miller," I said to him during our conversation at radio station WLIM in New York where he was a guest of veteran Big Band radio jock Jack Ellsworth.

"I was a lot better than I even knew myself because... yes, you're right, Glenn Miller is not going to hire you because of your looks, or anything else except what you can do on your instrument. He was the number one band and asked me to audition for him while I was with Donohue's band. I guess he heard of me, so I thought I must be pretty good."

"Then why did you leave the band so quickly afterwards?"

"He fired me."

"He what?" I was really surprised. With a wry grin and a shake of the right shoulder: "He fired me."

"Why?"

Well, that's hard to say. I don't think I was a bad guy, but I was obviously cocky...it might have been plain enthusiasm, you know, me being so young--- and so excited to be there that I did things that didn't fall into line and I did other things like auditioning for Benny Goodman and Artie Shaw just for the kick of doing it."

Andy Prior and Ray Anthony

"Guess Glenn might have resented that," I said.

"Well that might have been a kick for me, but he obviously didn't like it---and that actually only crossed my mind in the last so many years....that it was one of the dumb things I did as a kid. But, he re-hired me a few months later because my influence in the brass section was a strong one." I later learned that he was let go by Miller after a New York engagement at the Cafe Rouge, mostly to save money and was rehired again in Cleveland when the band came through and Miller realized he was a better player than his replacement, Ralph Brewster.

"It's known that he admired your energy and enthusiasm and that you remained as a member of the band for a few years."

"Yes, but he fired me again," laughing out loud now, "Glenn was a disciplinarian whether it was in your playing, your mannerisms, or what you wore on the bandstand. He wanted and expected the best. He offered the people his best and I had a great respect for him. He was also like (bandleader) Lawrence Welk, tight with a buck although he paid me enough, and his featured players like Beneke too, but other players weren't so happy." I then remembered Woody Herman telling me about Glenn's great financial losses on the long, rocky road to eventual success. Perhaps that was the reason he was so frugal, he had lots of practice.

"I guess you were satisfied playing in that band with his kind of music because you emulated him in your future band when you got out of the Navy after the war."

"True, his music was the most accepted by the American GIs so when I started up my new band in Cleveland, I restyled it for that reason." I believe that when Ralph Flanagan started the parade of Glenn Miller mimics, Ray fell in line and, like other imitators, made good money touring many of the country's top spots, then went on to record for Capitol and built and promoted a good swinging band, featuring his own gutsy, low-registering horn.

Ray was also influenced earlier by his idols Harry James and

Louis Armstrong: "Harry was the best damned trumpet player ever. He played sweet, pretty, fast, hot, high or low--everything that is possible to do on the horn. He was the one of the best players of all time. "He said all that with strong emotion. "And Louis....what can you say....he influenced every trumpet player including me and Harry James."

Richard Grudens and Ray Anthony

"I know Harry James is a friend, but did you ever tell him that?"

Pause and reflection: "I don't know if I have---or not. But we talk about other things. You don't talk about that. And , as far as a jazz influence is concerned, Roy Eldridge stands alone as my teacher."

In those postwar years Ray was one of the fastest-rising new dance bands, despite the fact that the overall band business was in decline. When he was performing on the Nevada circuit for twenty years, (1960's to 1980's) he had a small group show called the Bookend Revue with two female vocalist/dancers that played the lounges of Las Vegas and Lake Tahoe, then traveled to Acapulco and Honolulu where he appeared at the Royal Hawaiian Hotel.

Ray also pioneered his craft by offering original music themes for some television shows in the 1960s. His best-selling recordings of "Dragnet" and "Peter Gunn" themes are nothing short of sensational. From 1950 through 1954, Ray Anthony was voted Number One Band in all the trade magazine polls, and during the same period was the most played instrumental recording artist on radio. The seventies saw Ray with his show Directions 71 which combined the best sounds of the big bands with current stylings. He was always an innovator with vision.

In the mid-eighties Ray returned to touring going from venues in Texas to Hackensack, New Jersey: "The jobs are where they are and you have to go to them, that's always been true. That's where the people will be able to see you and get to know you. It's great to play to different crowds."

Well, this band leader, movie star, television performer, and occasional stage actor, and entrepreneur is still a pretty busy guy these days. He is concentrating on those record sales from his mail-order company, leading his band on weekends here and there, and still releasing albums, including two featuring the Glenn Miller sound on song titles never recorded before.

Though active, Ray Anthony is leading a relatively quiet life lately. He's a nine-to-fiver doing mail order and his whole social life is centered around tennis and hanging out with friend, Hugh Hefner at the Playboy Mansion. "We always have dinner and sometimes watch old movies. A bunch of old guys hang out with us---including my friend Jerry Vale as we get a little older we kind of find comfort in the friendship of people we've known for many years."

Syndicated radio's Big Band Jump director and commentator Don Kennedy, once asked Ray how he felt about getting older: "Getting old starts in your mind. You have to get old in your mind before your body'll get old. At least in my case, and in a lot of cases, if your mind gets old, your body's gonna follow. I don't think much about it, but I'm so busy that it's not of importance to me. I do need glasses to read...and I sometimes get forgetful....In fact, who are you, anyway?"

Ray Anthony will keep going 'til he drops.

BUDDY RICH

GRANDSTANDING DRUM WONDERBOY

my Dorsey Orchestra with Buddy Rich

Upon casual inquiry, everyone who is anyone counseled against pursuing an interview with big band music bad boy, Buddy Rich . They said it wouldn't work. Big Band writer and broadcaster, Don Kennedy, of Big Band Jump radio fame said: I once did a quickie (interview) but didn't get nearly anywhere; he was most difficult (with me) ...maybe a (another) clash of personalities." Buddy clashed with many and often.

Tony Bennett actually shook his head and shrugged his shoulders about such a possibility: "He's a tough one. He doesn't like it. Buddy keeps to himself in his band bus." A large Band bus is parked outside the theater where he 'lives' during tours. He almost never uses backstage theater dressing rooms.

They said he was arrogant, sharp -tongued, downright nasty. But Mel Torme was his friend, and Mel Torme talked with him often and they got along well. Two opposites.

However, one lucky night after a lovely conversation with the enchanting and sweet Sarah Vaughan between shows, we spotted Buddy Rich's band bus out of view in a rear parking lot behind the theater. It was a bitter 10 degree Winter evening and very windy in the lot. The bus appeared like a spaceship just waiting to aspire upwards into the firmament. With steam rising from above the craft, photographer Camille Smith and I wandered over and simply rapped on the door a few times. A young man opened the door and asked what we wanted. We explained our circumstances and produced our card. He nodded for us to wait and flipped the door closed (we thought we could hear the theme from the Twilight Zone riding the bitter winds) , but in a moment Buddy Rich appeared in the doorway perky and fresh from a shower and wrapped in a terry- cloth robe and a New York Yankees baseball cap. He posed the same question, and we replied accordingly. "All right -----" he held his finger high like a teacher to a truant student and said " I'll give you two minutes."

We were admitted.

Brooklyn born, all-time ace drummer, Bernard Rich talked his head off that cold winter evening, which we now know was a rarity, so I thought it best to print it just the way I asked it and he answered it. Talking came easy to Buddy Rich. He's played with them all, beginning with his first recording as back-up drummer on the Andrew Sisters evergreen, Bie Mir Bist Du Shon. As you will be able to determine from the next few pages, Buddy was bright, witty, and very, very smart. His acid wit was always in evidence:

RG: Buddy, people in the trade say you are the busiest and most traveled band leader on the scene today. We recently talked to Woody Herman who says he hates the traveling, but loves the music.

BR: Well, if I didn't like it, I wouldn't do it. I like to enjoy my life. I certainly prefer this to getting in a car and driving up and down expressways going to an office all day---the traffic is insanity---to me this is an absolutely normal way of life---it's perfect. I see the whole world, man! (pause) Who could do better than that?

RG: How have you been feeling since your illness? (His 1983 bypass operation).

BR: I never think about it. I never really think about it.

RG: People say, of course they'll always talk, that you drive yourself hard, you play (the drums) hard, and you work even harder.

BR: ....and I live hard! I also hold a black belt in martial arts. I'm in good shape. I don't think I drive myself hard. I do what my body tells me to do and I never go any farther than what my body says.

RG: Recently I talked to Johnny Mince. You remember Johnny from the Dorsey days (an excellent clarinetist profiled in this book) I asked him about your altercations with Frank Sinatra where you would throw things at each other, but.....what interests me (I had to talk fast, as this made him uncomfortable) is how you got back together again. What happened there?

When did it end?

BR: The next day! You see, when you're twenty-two years old and you're both striving for a certain amount of recognition, after all I was a sideman in the band and he was the singer, we both wanted to be recognized and both trying to do something, you have ego problems. Then you grow up and realize that ego is bullshit. It's what you do and be recognized for that counts. You have to become friends. You just can't carry on a vendetta---it's insanity. We're friends, of course we're friends. We've been friends for years.

RG: Is that legendary story true about you sending up a fan to ask Frank (Sinatra) for a number of autographs and he told Frank that he would trade in for of his for one of Bob Eberly (singer with Jimmy Dorsey who made those wonderful duet recordings with Helen O'Connell).

BR: That's the most bullshit story that ever was told. It never happened. My mind doesn't work in that area, and I like to think of myself as a fairly witty person. I don't have to go around doing bad moves and bad numbers on people. I'd rather do it with my so-called brain than have to resort to childish bullshit things. So that story, I must have heard it a million times in the last thirty years, and to sit and deny it only makes it more feasible, so I don't talk about it at all.......so I just finished doing five minutes on it. (to loud laughter from Buddy, Camille, and myself.)

RG: Buddy, it is true that you taught yourself to play the drums?

BR: I don't know if I've ever taught myself. I've never taken a lesson, if that's what you mean. You can't teach yourself something unless you know it first. So I think I just did it. I had a natural ability, I guess.

RG: Whom do you look up to in your own field?

BR: From the time I was able to recognize the talents of various drummers from the early thirties until the present day, I've been impressed with everybody that has ever played. Everybody you listen to leaves some kind of mark on your brain and on your ear and there are things you dislike and things you love. I happen to be a lucky guy because I came up at the time where there were fifty great drummers. Besides Krupa there was Chick Webb, Jo Jones, and I could go on with names like Sid Catlett, Davey Tough, Spencer O'Neil, and people you probably never heard of each of whom impressed me, of course! And I was friends with all those guys.

RG: I guess you played a lot with Krupa in the past.

BR: Gene and I did tours with Jazz at the Philharmonic for six years.

RG: Was that the (Norman) Granz thing?

BR: Yeah, Norman Granz.

RG: Who books all your work now, Willard?

BR: Yes, Willard Alexander and his agency in New York.

RG: Dizzy Gillespie told me, not too long ago, that everything he does he wants to extend further. Like an architect who designs and builds a building and adds on to it. He extends his work and his work grows, so someday he can be looked to as somebody who always improved in his work. Do you have any comment on that? Is that your way too?

BR: You see, it would be a very biased comment because I'm such a fan of Diz. For him to say that is only a natural extension of how he feels about life. His playing--when you are as great as Diz---you're never satisfied with your playing. You try to improve upon it all the time. That's what makes him the greatest jazz trumpet in music. That's what he means--you're just creating---you never stop.

RG: We were just talking to Tony Bennett a few days ago, and he says when he gets in front of an audience his emotions rise and he becomes another person when he is on stage. He thinks that's why people are attracted to him. And that's why they come to see him perform. Now, when you're on stage you are Buddy Rich the performer, and here you are Buddy Rich the man. Do you feel any kind of high or emotion when you are on stage?

BR: When I'm on stage. I'm Buddy Rich --the Buddy Rich.

RG: Are you saying you're the same on or off?

BR: I involve myself in my playing and I involve myself with my band and become one with the audience. It isn't a separate thing. There's an energy level when people listen and understand what you're doing and you become one thing---the energy goes from them to us---from us to them. I don't feel any difference when I'm around people who give me the same kind of energy feeling That is on the stage or off. There's an emotional impact somewhere.

RG: Buddy, someday there will be somebody like me who will write the history of this kind of music---maybe twenty-five years down the road. How will you want the world to see Buddy Rich of these days?

BR: As I am!

RG: Tell me what that is.

BR: Well, I'm a million things. Tell me what you are! You can't---you see. To be able to say what you are---you are many things to many different people. You just got through saying that Tony Bennett feels he's a different person when he's on stage---another personality. I too, have many personalities. I'm funny. I'm arrogant. I'm sad. I'm angry. I'm all the emotions that you can have in a body. I am, so to say, what kind of a guy are you?---well, I'm the same kind of guy you are. You're unhappy when something sad happens and happy when you feel good, and you're good when you feel happy. You're in love, out of love. You eat and don't eat, and all the things you are---you are. That's you. That's what I am. I don't say who I am. It's what I am. I'm a whole lot of things. People misunderstand me. They think, 'Well this guy, you can't talk to him. He's this and he's that.' O.K. That's the personality he sees. That's how he'll remember me. No matter what I do he'll remember me as being an arrogant S.O.B. "Who does he think he is?'

Somebody else will see me as a fairly sensitive man who understands a whole lot of things and though others will fight about it. 'He's not really like that,'....and so....who are you?

RG: Changing subjects--Benny Goodman recently told me he thinks the music's are merging---crossing over --that people are dancing again. Any comment? What's happening to the music business?

BR: How the hell do I know? (laughing mischievously)

RG: You're in the business. You are supposed to know these things. (I was scolding him/chiding him.)

BR: Well, anything that Benny Goodman says has some basis of truth because to me he's the greatest thing that ever happened to jazz. From the beginning since I heard his band in 1936,. I remember vividly the first time I heard it, up until that time I used to listen to the radio to the old Casa Loma, Glen Gray Band and I thought that was the hottest thing that ever happened until I heard Goodman's band. And I went WHOA! I was 16 years old then...what the hell's that all about? I mean it was another thing entirely. I grew on Benny's music and I am a great fan of his. I love him---he's nuts---but I love him.

RG: Of all the recordings done by all the big bands, including your own, which one do you rate the best?

BR: None.

RG: What does that mean?

Buddy Rich and Tommy Dorsey

BR: The kinds of things I listen to you would not think somebody like me would listen to. I like the old Jackie Gleason things with Bobby Hackett on the trumpet. I am a great fan of good singers--Sinatra, Torme, Bennett, Jack Jones, Eckstine--people like that. So, instead of listening to every hot jazz group that comes along, I'm selective about that. But, I happen to like, and this is not a step back, this is not nostalgia, this is music to my ears, instead of the junk screaming and yelling to loud guitars---the only way to get back to reality is to listen to someone where a guy wrote a lyric about something besides having sex with some broad. He wrote about love and there was a story for 32 bars and a musical concept and arrangements and loveliness. So that's what I listen to. It's not your

Richard Grudens and Buddy Rich

favorite recording---it's your overall favorite music. All good music is my favorite. I hate bad stuff.

RG: And our last question Mr. Rich is---simple and silly though it may seem, but they draw you out. Who is your favorite musician, living or not living, in this business as we know it?

BR: That's an impossible question to answer because there are so many great artists you just can't pick out. I often get asked,' What is the perfect all star band?' There will never be an all-star band until you put every star that ever played together. You can't say one thing about one guy because there's, also, that other guy that you love. So you can't say who's your favorite because there are too many of them---like the great Count Basie band, Ellington's band, Woody's old bands, Goodman.... it's just impossible to say. I love Stan Getz (musing) and I love Coleman Hawkins, Lester Young, and Ben Webster. So you can't insult the other giants. So all of them are my favorites.

EPILOGUE

Well, we did it! And afterwards, Buddy said, "I told you five minutes and I've given you forty minutes. How the hell did I do that?"

For the first time I realized that all along he was trying to justify all of that to us. That some people have type-cast him as the heavy. But he was explaining that he really was a mis-understood guy with an un-deserved negative reputation, but with a brisk personality that has been mistaken for gruffness and arrogance. Why even some of our inquiries involved that question. He was informing us he was an O.K. kind of guy after all, and that it was okay to get together and talk. He was blunt and definite, and it was difficult to argue with his rational philosophy, his kindnesses to fellow performers, and the personal praise of his own heroes. Some peers said he was too demanding and a mercurial leader, expecting excellence from other musicians with respect to timing and execution. Some were intimidated by those sharp criticisms, but all agreed his musical performances were beyond reproach.

Buddy Rich's performances occupied the extremes of American entertainment---and his musical approach was indeed a reflection of his personality. He was aggressive one moment and sentimental the next. The latter was how we visualized him that day.

A brain tumor took Rich away at the age of 69. He was brave in the face of this illness right up to the end.

It was said that a nurse, upon administering medication, asked Buddy if he was allergic to anything. His answer: Yeh! Country music."

Mel Tormé and Buddy Rich - Good Friends!

Chic Webb and Ella Fitzgerald

ᗝne ᗝf ᔕhe ᕼreat ᖴour

TEDDY WILSON
WITH BENNY
GENE
& LIONEL

August,1981: When I think of the great piano players of the Big Band Era, Teddy Wilson always prevails in my mind as the most accomplished, the most easy to listen to and the most mysterious. Some of the best music ever made has to be those outstanding sides Billie Holiday recorded with Teddy Wilson's very fine orchestra during 1939, the one and only year he led his own band. "Our band only lasted a year or so. We were too tame. Everybody then expected a black band to be more

Lionel, Teddy , Benny and Gene

exiting. We made some great recordings. We had Ben Webster, Doc Cheatham, J.C. Heard and played a lot at the Famous Door nightclub on 52nd Street," said Teddy.

    Teddy Wilson learned to play the piano while in grade school and developed his style with a dance band in high school, where he, also, played oboe and clarinet. He went on to classical musical training for a year at Taladega College in Alabama. He was a disciplined student mostly owing to the fact

Teddy Wilson

that both his parents were teachers at Samuel Houston College, when he was a child. Talladega spawned his life-long love of classical music, but jazz remained his first love and in the summer of 1929 he migrated to Detroit where he began his career with the Speed Webb band. He then moved on to Toledo and Chicago with the Milton Senior Band.

It was John Hammond, the most enthusiastic and influential jazz buff around in those days, who discovered Teddy: "He helped me a great deal---perhaps more than anyone, except the players themselves." Teddy and I were talking about old times and old music at MacArthur Airport in Ronkonkoma, Long Island, where he was preparing to perform for the local Arts Council summer evening jazz concert. We were sitting in his Cadillac---me in the back and he and his secretary up front-- articulating his life and times. The interview was held in the car because it was so windy near the airfield that words were inaudible and you had to shout to be heard.

Teddy was really a shy celebrity, almost unwilling to talk too much or expand on topics affecting his life, and peculiarly, unwilling to talk about his old friend and fellow musician, Benny Goodman. I didn't know why, but Budd Johnson later told me that Teddy felt that everyone was more interested in Benny Goodman , when they spoke to him, so he simply refused to honor any questions that included Benny Goodman in order not to be totally eclipsed by his former leader. It's a bit ironic because Benny Goodman once called Teddy Wilson, "the greatest musician irrespective of instrument." Actually, Teddy only played with Goodman for three years, but is most remembered for that time and exposure, although they later had a few reunions including one at the Brussels World Fair in 1958 and the famous Goodman Russian tour in 1962. And then there was the Benny Goodman Story movie where Teddy portrayed himself.

Richard Grudens and Teddy Wilson at LI MacArthur Airport

When I reminded him of his influence on piano players who followed him, like Art Tatum, The McPartlands, Mel Powell, and Joe Bushkin, his reply was simple: "Well, I am pleased and flattered, but they are really their own people. After all, I played in the tradition of Earl Hines, Fats Waller and Fletcher Henderson. They helped me, you know!" His typically humble rationale.

"Every day playing is my favorite day. I loved playing with the old quartet (Goodman quartet with Lionel Hampton and Gene Krupa). I enjoyed playing with Mel Torme at Carnegie Hall in 1980. (Mel and Friends--A George Wein weekend with George Shearing, Gerry Mulligan, Woody Herman and others.)

Teddy also taught at Juilliard and the Metropolitan Music Schools in Manhattan in the forties and fifties. I particularly remembered a Saturday afternoon weekly radio program on CBS when I was a kid when he played beautifully for half-an-hour . It consisted mostly of a delicately swinging piano and some delightful non-flashy classics. I always wondered if anyone kept the transcriptions. They would make a great album.

Teddy never expected to become a world-class musician when he started out: "I always wanted to play and I arrange all my own music. I was lucky as I got a good start with Benny in Chicago on a radio show for Elgin watches." That was the only time he mentioned Benny Goodman during our half-hour interview.

"I like my life better now. I do better in small groups. I could be featured better that way. It is less on the nerves with more time for practicing... than running a big band."

I wondered, as I wonder about all those musicians who, as Woody Herman said, have lots of miles on them, why they travel so much at that time of their life:

"It's the money. The one night stands pay well. It's hard to say no, and the folks get a chance to see and hear you."

At this time of his life, Teddy does mostly freelance work alone and in a trio composed of him and his two sons. "I do a lot of what we're doing tonight...like an all-star group."

It turns out Teddy Wilson had cancer at the time of the interview, and the hospital visit a few weeks before in upstate Syracuse, New York was for treatment, but didn't want his condition known. He continued to tour throughout the world either as a soloist or with his trio, his career ending only a few months before his death in New Britain, Connecticut on July 31, 1986. He was 73. Teddy Wilson proved that jazz could be both elegant and exciting, and entertained us for the greater part of this century. I was honored by my short friendship of this self-effacing giant of jazz.

RED NORVO
Father of His Instrument

In 1992, singer Frankie Laine introduced me to jazz pioneer Red Norvo. Since then Red and I have held many conversations from his cozy, tree-lined home on Alta Avenue in Santa Monica, California. Those conversations centered mostly around his music, especially his unique choice of instrument, the vibraharp, (also called the vibraphone, although Red doesn't like that word) and allegories depicting the career of his first wife Mildred Bailey, the very first girl Big Band singer.

In what may have been our final conversation held from a convalescent home in Santa Monica, Red Norvo and I continued talking about his career as a dedicated professional musician. Unfortunately, Red had serious, ongoing problems with his hearing, among other medical difficulties, and although his recall of the old days remains sharp enough, he found it exceedingly difficult to accurately hear me; thus, he was unable to respond adequately, which forced conversations to an early conclusion. His voice has changed from a natural deep resonance to a higher pitch. Earlier, when talking from his home, his specially equipped telephone allowed him to listen more easily than the convalescent home phone. Ironically, it was Red Norvo's ultra- sensitive ear for subtle jazz that catapulted him to worldwide fame as a magnificent mallet musician.

Red Norvo, one of the gentle giants of jazz, celebrated his ninety-first birthday on March 31, 1999, the day I completed writing this chapter. I tried to reach his daughter Portia that day for an update only to find that red was suddenly confined to a hospital. A bleak birthday.

Red (Joseph Kenneth Norville) Norvo was born on March 31, 1908, in Beardstown, Illinois, a small town built along the Illinois River. His dad played piano while a working dispatcher for the Chicago, Burlington, & Quincy Railroad. His mother, a former trumpet player, was determined to teach her children music. When Kenneth was six, he took just twelve piano lessons: "My teacher found out I was memorizing my lessons by ear. My brother Howard would play and I would listen. She nailed me." Red gave up studying music for a while.

Then, while on daily excursion trips aboard touring riverboats, young Norvo observed a number of great jazzmen including jazz-trumpeter Louis Armstrong, cornetist Bix Beiderbecke, and saxophonist Frankie Trumbauer. That experience influenced him back on to the road to music.

"One year, a flood levee broke in town and flooded our house. We went to Rolla, Missouri for a while. I liked to listen to a marimba player in a pit band at the theater in that town. He let me try the thing out. I did pretty good. I liked playing it. When I got back to Beardstown, it bugged me and I thought about playing (the marimba) .So my father let me work on a railroad gang for the summer and sell my pony so I could buy an instrument."

Red Norvo

Norvo learned himself to play his brand-new, three-octave xylophone, that he purchased from a mail-order catalog, playing solo at high school dances. "I could play anything once I heard it. I learned stuff from some of those old Edison recordings. I learned harmony later. Then I went to Chicago to find work."

Norvo sought work with the traveling Chautauqua circuit, touring with a marimba octet, but, uncertain and embarrassed, he wouldn't go because he realized he couldn't read music. Back in Beardstown, his family decided he would

attend the University of Illinois the following fall, his mother urging him to try working the Chautauqua tour for the summer, just for experience. The group was called the Colle-
gians.

"I learned a lot on that tour. I worked with the other players and also took a lot of solos. I tried school again, but I split to go back on tour. We went out west to Seattle and places like that. I used to play a thing called 'Xylophone Rag.' I first heard about jazz music then."

Red Norvo with Louis Armstrong

Improving his play-ing skills and discovering jazz sounds, Norvo was booked as a solo into the Oriental The-ater in Chicago. At the time, Chicago flourished with ma-rimba and xylophone players performing on vaudeville stages. Constantly listening to recordings of Red Nichols, Earl Hines, Frankie Trumbauer, and Louis Armstrong, Norvo carefully honed his playing skills. In vaudeville he acquired the sobri-quet "Red" because of his red hair and ruddy completion, and the name Norvo by an ever-erring announcer who could never remember his name. Variety, the show business chronicle, "picked it up and it stuck, so I kept it Norvo," Red explained," It was easier."

"People liked to watch me perform. I would look at them...they would look back at me. I got to be quite an entertainer in vaudeville. That was about 1929."

Joining a band at the Eagle Ballroom, Norvo became its leader, adding jazz numbers, then emigrated to Minneapolis where he led a band at the Marigold Ballroom and worked on the staff of a radio station. The break came when conductor, composer Victor Young, needed a xylophon-ist for his NBC radio show. Norvo filled the bill perfectly.

"I also worked part time between shows with Ben Bernie's orches-tra at the College Inn (in the Sherman Hotel) in Chicago. Paul Whiteman showed up one night. He was drunk. I didn't know who he was at first. If I had known he was there, I would've been too nervous to play. Anyway, he hired me for NBC and got me to play xylophone, marimba and vi-brapharp. But, they wanted me to play vibes just for effect, not as playing an instrument. I also got on a show with (bandleader) Wingy (Manone) for a couple of afternoons every week. That's when I met Mildred (Bailey). She was singing for Whiteman. We liked each other right away. We started working together in Chicago as an act. Mildred was hot tempered, but we got along anyway." Mildred was the sister of Bing Crosby's singing partner in the Rhythm Boys, Al Rinker. She helped them get started.

THE VIBRAPHONE

Used mainly for novelty effect, "Mallet instruments were a novel accouterment of percussionists in the 1920's," according to Leonard Feather in his Book of Jazz. Norvo's instrument was the xylophone, a sort of hydrated vibraphone. Its keys were wood instead of metal; there was little resonance, and the only way to give the impression of sustaining a note was to use a halftone tremolo or hit the same note repeatedly.

A marimba is a fuller-sounding variant in the xylophone family, fitted with resonance tubes beneath each key. The vibraphone, like the xylophone, is an instrument with a sustaining pedal, resonating tubes under the keys, and small rotating fans, placed beneath the keys and operated electrically.

"To me, the vibraharp is a peculiar instrument because it tends to take on the characteristics of the people who play it. And it's peculiar because vibraharpists are a pretty warm fraternity. Guitarists are also like that. Certain people pick certain instruments, and vibraharpists in general are gentle, quiet people. Trumpet players and drummers, on the other hand, can be pretty argumentative. But the main thing is to play the right instrument," Red Norvo told Whitney Balliett in the 1970s for his book Portraits in Jazz.

When the Paul Whiteman band headed East, Red Norvo took along his xylophone and his new wife, Mildred. "We got married when we were on tour upstate in New York."

BENNY GOODMAN:

"When Red finished his routine, he would grab the bars off his instrument and throw them on the floor like he was angry. But, it was only a joke with him. The audience ate that up."

The Norvo's remained with the Whiteman band for a year or so. "That's when I made 'Rockin' Chair' with Mildred and Matty Malneck's band. She became known as the Rockin' Chair Lady." At this time the Norvo's lived on Pilgrim Circle in Forest Hills, Queens, New York.

Mildred Bailey

"We had jam sessions at our house. (pianist) Teddy Wilson, Benny (Goodman), (jazz violinist) Joe Venuti, (trumpeter) Bunny Berigan, and (blues vocalist) Bessie Smith - they'd come over just for fun. That's where the Benny Goodman trio was born, you know - but before (Gene) Krupa went with him. (Jazz producer and "angel" John Hammond added Krupa to make the trio, along with Teddy Wilson). Mildred loved to cook - and could she eat. She developed diabetes. She was supposed to be on a diet. She loved Bessie Smith. They got along just fine. Red Nichols lived just across the street. When I finally got my union card, me and Charlie Barnet would share a band--- actually my first band. One time he would lead and the next time I led - depends on who booked the job first. When Charlie led for a full week at the Apollo (theater in Harlem), it turns out we were the first white band to play there. How about that!"

After that engagement, Red Norvo signed up to play in Bar Harbor, Maine. "I led a band and had Dave Barbour on guitar, Chris Griffin on trumpet, and (arranger/composer) Eddie Sauter. I had Fletcher Henderson charts. But the people up there were not used to our wild music, so they wouldn't pay us. Our little group finally gave up trying gigs in Maine. It got so bad that Mildred had to come up to pick me up. We were out of food and money by this time. It was a good, but trying experience. We had to bum food from farmers. Maine wasn't hospitable to musicians who played jazz in those days."

With an entirely new band, Red Norvo opened at the Famous Door on 52nd Street in New York. "It went just fine. We had a trumpet, clarinet, tenor sax, guitar, bass and xylophone. We had no drums or piano - that was different. We played riffs things, swinging things. We were a sensation. We played my 'Dance of the Octopus' and things like 'Gramercy Square' and Bix's 'In a Mist.' I expanded my group and played the New York City circuit of hotels."

With Eddie Sauter as the group's arranger, Red Norvo was booked into what turned out to be a very successful run at New York's Commodore Hotel, after an engagement at the Versailles, an East Side club, that didn't work out. "When the boss asked us to play a rhumba, the boys didn't know how," Red said, "He shooed us out fast. We were very uncomfortable jazz musicians."

The same, happy group toured New England that fall and opened up in Syracuse, New York, for three weeks, then back to Chicago at the Blackhawk again, but this time for several months.

"That was from 1936 to 1938. Mildred came out to join us. We were called 'Mr. and Mrs. Swing.' "I love their recorded version of "Smoke Dreams" that Eddie Sauter arranged for them.

Some believe that Mildred's appearances with the band helped it commercially, since she was well-known in the area from her Whiteman band-singing days. When Mildred contracted diabetes, the band returned to the New York Commodore Hotel for a while, then disbanded. The Norvo's sold their Forest Hills home for a Manhattan apartment, although they also owned a country place in Kent Cliffs, New York where they took occasional refuge from the big city.

The years of 1939, '40, and '41 were pivotal years for the Red Norvo group of players, who were ever-changing. It was a time for him to give up trying to maintain a big band. Small groups became the trademark for the remainder of his career.

Back on Fifty-second Street in 1942,'43 and '44 Red tried a small group, enjoying great success there and on limited East coast tours; "But the army draft grabbed too many players and I wound up playing xylophone in the Benny Goodman Quartet in 1945, doing what Lionel Hampton used to do. But I couldn't work it out with some of the passages," Norvo told me, "so I grabbed a vibraphone in a rehearsal studio, and Teddy Wilson suggested that we should mix vibraphone and clarinet with piano--and it worked out just fine." That began Red's career as strictly a vibraphone (vibraharp) player. During a special New York concert with Goodman, Red played a very delicate, sensitive solo on George Gershwin's "The Man I Love" with his first working vibraphone.

Besides working with Goodman, Red recorded with two stalwarts of bebop, Charlie "Yardbird" Parker and John Birks "Dizzy" Gillespie, fitting in with them perfectly in an all-star sextet led by Red himself.

Then: "Mildred and I got divorced. We both wanted children, but Mildred couldn't have any, so we parted - and we stayed friends till the day she died," he told me during one of our long phone conversations. He and Mildred had arranged several separations before deciding on divorce. After Red married Eve Rogers, the sister of trumpeter Shorty Rogers, they often visited Mildred on her small farm in Stormville, New York, with their two children whom Mildred adored. Mildred died on December 12, 1951, in an upstate New York hospital remaining friends with Red Norvo until the end. She was only forty-four.

From Goodman, Red joined with Woody Herman in the original First Herd, finally settling down in his long time home in Santa Monica, California. With guitarist Tal Farlow and bassist Red Kelly, Red performed for a while in Honolulu, "where the trio really got its start - without piano and drums - a very unusual deal that worked out good." Bassist Charlie Mingus soon replaced Kelly. "Funny, but Mingus was a mailman when I found him and asked him to join up with me. He gave up the music business - but I brought him back in. He had a temper like Mildred that we had to keep under control."

The trio prospered for a number of years with a few personnel changes, rehearsals taking place at the Alta Avenue, Santa Monica living room. "Everybody contributed, so it was good," Red said.

During this time the Deagan Company, who manufactured his instrument, amplified his vibes by installing a crystal mike in each resonator tube, allowing him to play with a lighter touch and even closer to the keyboard with his mallets than ever before.

While appearing in Las Vegas during the late 1950's, Frank Sinatra took a liking to Norvo's compact jazz group that first consisted of a trio, then expanded into a quintet. He enjoyed the singing freedom Red Norvo's small group offered and eventually invited him to tour with him to Australia.

"We had worked together in Vegas --- at the Sands --- and then at the Fontainebleau in Florida, and also in Atlantic City before -- and after---we went to Australia," explained Red, "The Capitol recordings taken during that tour have just been (recently) released for the first time. Heard they are number four on the charts (1997). Isn't that sumthin'?"

FRANK SINATRA:

"The higher up you get in this business the more opportunity you have to work with the people you want. Red is a man I have tremendous respect for, musically and personally. I've always wanted to work with his band."

The Australian tour remains a classic. Listening to the tracks you can tell that Sinatra was very comfortable in this jazz setting, particularly on "Just One of Those Things," "I Get a Kick Out of You," and "I've Got You Under My Skin," Cole Porter songs all, including an album finish with a stunning "Night and Day."Unfortunately, Red and Frank never recorded a studio album together. Red, however, was the perfect backup for a loose Sinatra.

Tragedy struck Red Norvo in the early 1970's with the death of his son, Kevin, and of his wife, Eve, just two years later. "I didn't play for two years. I wouldn't play records or the radio. I just went fishing. But, I went back to playing and realized I never should have stopped. So I went back to work." During that period Red experienced medical problems with hearing disorders and underwent an operation.

Touring once again, and playing with various groups for as much as eight months at a time, Red Norvo was back on the music scene. It was a renaissance to him.

A delicate, but sophisticated musician, Kenneth "Red" (Norville) Norvo has performed on his discriminating mallet instrument with virtually every important jazz musician of the age beginning in the late 1920s right up to the '80s.

Talking with his daughter Portia in March, 1999 she was hopeful that Red may come home again. "We bring him home on weekends for a few hours each day so he doesn't become too homesick. We have to return him to the home for special care, especially at night, for care we can't give him. We tried various nurses at home, but none worked out for us."

Not as well-known as his contemporaries, except in jazz circles, Red Norvo was nevertheless one of the best bandleaders and musicians of the Big Band Era.

While talking with jazz singer Anita O'Day in March of 1999, she simply extolled Red Norvo as a great musician and a very nice man. "I liked swinging with him," she said, "He could sure handle those vibes."

We lost Red Norvo in April 1999.

Charlie Barnet

During the Big Band Era Charlie Barnet led the blackest white band of them all as he broke all house records at Harlem's famed Apollo Theater and paved the way for African-American artists to participate in the Big Bands.

Charlie's wealthy parents had hoped he would become a lawyer.

By the age of 16, however, Charlie was already leading his own band. He became well known within jazz circles after his important gig at the New York Paramount Hotel.

Barnet played with the Red Norvo Octet that included Teddy Wilson and Artie Shaw. Artie Shaw and Barnet were among the first bands to employ black players. He featured Lena Horne and later Roy Eldridge, Oscar Pettiford, among others.

Barnet's big hits was "Cherokee" and "Redskin Rhumba" played with his great stable of musicians: clarinet player Buddy De Franco, pianist Dodo Marmarosa, guitarist Barney Kessel, drummer Cliff Leeman, Clark Terry, and vocalists Lena Horne, Frances Wayne and Kay Starr. Kay told me that Barnet's hard-driving band with George Seravo arrangements practically destroyed her voice trying to sing above those powerhouse musicians. She had to be completely retrained to sing without pain or strain.

It was well-known that Charlie Barnet lived the jazz life to the fullest. His biography, Those Swinging Years unveils his bouts with hard-drinking and drug habits and his visits to houses of ill repute in detail, if you care to read about that side of his life.

Charlie Barnet was a a wild personality and his band followed the leader. He was married six times and played a excellent tenor sax. In 1944 "Skyliner" became a substantial hit for the band and he regained his popularity of earlier years.

A close friend of Count Basie, when the Palomar burned down and destroyed Barnet's charts, the great Count graciously lent his charts to him.

All the ladies and most jazz fans loved Charlie Barnet, one of the Big Band Era's best leaders.

GUY LOMBARDO

Season's Greetings from GUY LOMBARDO and his 'ROYAL CANADIANS'

GUY LOMBARDO

Born in 1902, Guy Lombardo was originally from London, Ontario, Canada. Guy went on to become the most popular bandleader in America selling at least 100 million records with his big band ensemble he named the Royal Canadians. The tag line was "The Sweetest Music This Side of Heaven." Between 1929 and 1952 there wasn't a year that a Lombardo recording didn't make the charts, with 21 recordings reaching # 1. Guy's brother Carmen was the band's sax player and vocalist. Guy's addiction to a specific, non-changing musical style labeled the band as a non-innovative group of musicians. His signature song, the Scottish anthem "Auld Lang Syne" that herald's in each successive New Year, is still played worldwide at the celebration of the New Year.

The Lombardo legacy of song includes "Seems Like Old Times," "Boo, Hoo," "Coquette," "Enjoy Yourself "(It's later than you think.), "Everywhere You Go," and "You're Driving Me Crazy." The band also played for more Presidential Inaugural Balls than any other band of its time. Brothers Victor Lombardo and Lebert Lombardo also played with the band. Guy's Jones Beach Theatre productions on Long Island in the 1960s are legendary music history.

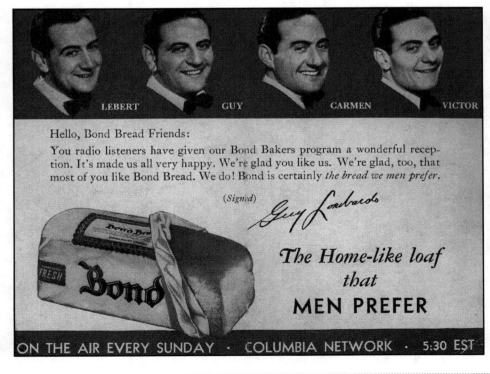

LEBERT   GUY   CARMEN   VICTOR

Hello, Bond Bread Friends:
You radio listeners have given our Bond Bakers program a wonderful reception. It's made us all very happy. We're glad you like us. We're glad, too, that most of you like Bond Bread. We do! Bond is certainly *the bread we men prefer*.

(Signed)

Guy Lombardo

The Home-like loaf that
MEN PREFER

ON THE AIR EVERY SUNDAY · COLUMBIA NETWORK · 5:30 EST

Keely Smith (R)

LOUIS PRIMA

I have always associated Louis Prima with bouncy, staccato jazz singing, delivering that truly original Italian "Godfather style" throaty voicing on favorites like "Angelina," (his mom's name) "Just a Gigolo," "Civilization," and "That Old Black Magic," performed with comedy antics, while fronting his own band in New York theaters and night clubs during the 1930s through the 1970s. Aside from that prolific talent, few realize that Louis (pronounced Louie) was the composer of the great jazz anthem "Sing, Sing, Sing" the jazz explosion composition that rocked Carnegie Hall when Benny Goodman, Harry James, Gene Krupa, and Count Basie performed it live back in 1938 during the very first jazz concert performed in that hallowed hall. The song was originally intended for Bing Crosby and named "Sing, Bing, Sing." Louis and Bing were friends and co-performers and shared a love for horse racing, Louis appearing in Bing's 1936 film Rhythm On the Range.

Born in New Orleans of Sicilian parents on December 7, 1910, Louis soaked up the music of the city he would always love, a city full of a mixture of many jazz cultures. First a violin player, then, inspired by local jazz musicians, a quality trumpeter, he eventually rose to became a main attraction on New York's famed 52nd Street. By the late

Louis with Gia Prima and Frank Sinatra

1920s Louis had started a few musical groups then moved to Cleveland, then to Chicago, and finally in the 1930s to New York City, performing as Louis Prima & His New Orleans Gang. Four years later, in February of 1935, he became the sensational first opening act at the Famous Door on 52nd Street billed as the New Orleans Five and turned that venue into the hottest club in town. His showmanship soon began drawing crowds of faithful fans who became as interested in his comedy as his fine jazz musicianship.

What a good year for jazz musicians with Basie at Loew's State, Tommy Dorsey at the Commodore Hotel, Casa Loma at the New Yorker, Chick Webb at the Savoy, Cab Calloway at the Cotton Club, and Louis Prima and pianist Art Tatum at the Famous Door.

"I got lucky early," Louis would often say, "and I let the crowd know I was solid Italian and from New Orleans."

Throughout the 1940s, Louis continued to be a sensation with his jivy singing and Sicilian slang and some very fractured, but lovable

English material. Of all the great New Orleans trumpet players, like Louis Armstrong, Louis delivered his personal and exclusive comedy, breaking up an audience, which, by now, had become endeared to him. He brought fun onto the dance floor with his wild antics.

As George Simon noted in his book The Big Bands: "Prima's success is both a healthy and a happy phenomenon. Louis just goes out there and has a helluva good time, acting like a natural showman, kidding around, poking fun at folks out front, at guys in his band, and, most of all, at himself."

It is interesting to realize that in the early years Louis Prima became the first entertainer, as both bandleader and vocalist, to introduce and record Italian songs to the American public.

As everyone knows, Louis was an accomplished, first-class musician with a feeling for jazz, better than most trumpeters of his day. He knew how to run and manage a band, and, like Glenn Miller, how to be commercially successful. Many noted sidemen appeared with him over the years; Pee Wee Russell, Nappy Lamare, Claude Thornhill, George Van Epps, and Ray Boudac. Louis collaborated composing the million selling Claude Thornhill/Fran Warren recording "Sunday Kind of Love."

Gia Prima

Louis appeared in a number of films, including, Rhythm On the Range, Manhattan Merry-Go-Round, Start Cheering, and You Can't Have Everything.

Sam Butera joined him in the 1950s and became the band's featured sax player. Gradually moving on to Las Vegas venues, Louis performed his previously popular "I Ain't Got Nobody" (more fractured English) and "Just a Gigolo" exuberant medley scoring well in the hot spots with his then new wife, vocalist Keely Smith, and Sam Butera and The Witnesses.

"Vegas was the best spot in the early years," Louis said, "but then it got too big and you got lost with all the other acts. But I ran my act regularly at the Sands, the Sahara, the Desert Inn, and the Hilton."

Louis Prima capped his memorable and terrific career performing a voice-over in a 1967 Walt Disney film Jungle Book playing the part of King Louie, an orangutan, singing "I Wanna Be Like You."

Louis' act was sometimes so wild, the audience didn't always know what to expect. A great musician and very talented musical comedian, Louis' final performances were to be at the Tropicana in 1975.

Louis' wife and performing partner was lovely Gia Maione Prima, whom Louis discovered one day in 1962 working at a Howard Johnson's in Toms River, New Jersey. This, not long after his split with band vocalist Keely Smith, whom Louis had to replace in the band. Although Gia was trained in classical voice, she possesses that same husky timbre that complimented Louis' own unique singing sound. After an audition at the Latin Casino, arranged by her uncle who owned a night club in New Jersey, and knew Rolly Dee who worked with Louis, she handily landed the job as the band's new vocalist. Louis thought she was just perfect for the job. "That was on Mother's Day in 1962. As fate would have it, Louis and I were married a year later." said Gia, "It was meant to be."

She first performed with Louis at New York's Basin Street where she totally captured the hearts of the press and her audience who included Peggy Lee, Ella Fitzgerald, and Jackie Gleason, all who sat up front and enthusiastically cheered her on.

Speaking to Gia Prima at her home on the New Jersey shore, not far from a favorite Louis Prima venue, Atlantic City, we talked about her career with Louis and just how happy her days were with her amazing husband.

Never intimidated by Louis Prima's fame when she first joined the band, unknown to him, Gia had grown to admire him from afar. Her dad was a Prima fan and Gia heard and had enjoyed his recordings from her earliest recollection:

"After my dad took me to see his idol Louis Prima in a live performance when I was just a little kid, I became attached to Louis Prima in every way. When I was fourteen, I met him face to face and secured a coveted prize - his autograph, which I have always cherished. When I won that audition, I realized I would be working with my one and only idol, ever. It was, for me, a Cinderella story come true.

When Gia was on stage she was always comfortable, always feeling the barrier of protection the stage offers:

"In that way it's different than with one on one relationships, otherwise I am generally shy with people."

When Louis and Gia decided to marry Gia's parents were concerned about the difference in age between fifty-two year old Louis and twenty-one year old Gia, but she reassured them citing Louis' ageless drive, youthful stamina, and sterling disposition, setting him apart from other possible suitors. Anyway, she had loved him for her entire life in fantasy and now it was a treasured reality. The age problem would make no difference. She loved him, and he, her. That 's all she needed.

Gia and Louis Prima worked successfully together up through 1975 when Louis became ill following a brain operation and lapsed into a coma in which state he remained for three years, Gia always at his bedside. Louis passed on in 1978, leaving Gia, Louis, Jr. and Lena to carry on his legacy. Gia is now sixty-plus years young, and carefully maintains and manages the legacy and business of her husband with help from her good friend Ron Cannatella, author and broadcaster.

Louis in the Kitchen

Good news. Today, Both Louis and Lena work to carry on the Prima tradition.

JACK TEAGARDEN

Jack Weldon Teagarden's uniquely developed style was widely imitated during his tenure with the big bands. Born in Texas in 1907, Jack Teagarden learned the trombone without any help whatsoever. Arriving in New York in 1927 at the age of twenty-two, Jack began his recording career, then advanced on to play in Paul Whiteman's famous King of Jazz Orchestra beginning in 1933. After leaving Whiteman, Jack led his own band from 1939 to 1947, finally joining up with Louis Armstrong's All-Stars and remaining for four years, only to reform his band once again continuing on until his passing.

Jack Teagarden was also an outstanding jazz singer. His engag-

ing Southern drawl fell somewhere between Louis Armstrong and Bing Crosby, who were both his friends and his playing and singing partners. Jack's demeanor and appearance, tall and handsome with a square jaw, open face and wide eyes he kept narrowed, occasionally made people take him for Jack Dempsey, the prize fighter. Some thought he was part American Indian, but his parents had come from Germany back in the late 1700's. His brother Charlie, a trumpeter, who also played with Whiteman, Jimmy and Tommy Dorsey, and Bob Crosby, was somewhat

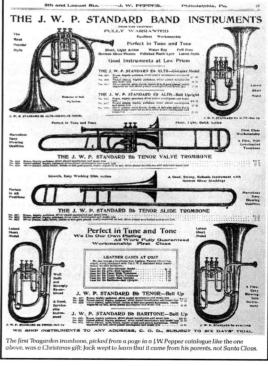

The first Teagarden trombone, picked from a page in a J.W. Pepper catalogue like the one above, was a Christmas gift; Jack wept to learn that it came from his parents, not Santa Claus.

smaller. Jack became known as Big T and Charlie as Little T.

Jack's singing, a distillation of his sentimental playing form, was delivered in a light baritone combined with a Southern drawl, a kind of "lay-me-down-to sleep" style especially when he gathered friends around, first playing tunes like "I've Got a Right to Sing the Blues," then vocalizing on it with accompaniment from sidemen.

People liked Jack because he never displayed any conceit and never got on anybody's nerves.

According to Louis Armstrong's bass player Arvell Shaw, my friend of 15 years: "I liked to listen to Jack sing. He would do songs like "Stars Fell On Alabama," "After You've Gone," "Basin Street Blues," and his best, "A Hundred Years from Today." Jack was very much like Louis and Bing...."He always liked to sing the songs he played well and I would back him up on my big bass," Arvell Shaw said. Since the loss of Teagarden and Armstrong, Arvell began singing during gigs which started in Oslo, Norway, when one of the musicians bet he wouldn't sing during his featured spot: "I sang 'St. James Infirmary,' the only song I knew the lyrics to. I thought of Jack a lot that night, and Louis rolled up his eyes at me."

In the movie Birth of the Blues with Bing in 1941, Jack Teagarden was at his sterling best as both player and jazz vocalist. He collaborated with Mary Martin and Bing Crosby singing Johnny Mercer's "The Waiter and the Porter and The Upstairs Maid."

Jack Teagarden retained his full playing and singing powers until the end of his life in his beloved New Orleans in 1964.

...AND MORE BANDS YOU KNOW

LARRY ELGART

Over the years Larry Elgart has played his great alto and soprano sax in the bands of Tommy Dorsey, Charlie Spivak, and Woody Herman- and all at the age of sixteen. Larry, with his brother Les, managed their band in the 1950s. Larry was the genius, the mixer, the editor and the manager. He imbued the band with much spirit. It was the "Elgart Touch."

Larry's classic solo of Harlem Nocturne is a joy to listen to. In 1953 it was he and Charlie Albertine who composed the American Bandstand Theme, "Bandstand Boogie," for Dick Clark's Philadelphia TV show.

In the 1980s Larry's comeback masterpiece album Hooked On Swing rode the charts for 47 weeks, selling 2 million copies, totally re-inventing his career. The album consisted of a concept of composite themes and old medleys of many of the Big Bands, but with the added touch of Elgart magic. His Manhattan Swing Orchestra brought old timers back to the record stores.

At Jack Ellsworth's anniversary party in Patchogue, New York I spent the evening on the bandstand introducing singers and their song with Larry in the chair playing his sax.

These days, Larry lives in Longboat Key,Florida. He is known as the Ambassador of Swing. That's because his album is acknowledged to be the best-selling album of swing music ever. His second, Hooked on

Swing II wrapped up the miracle and did just as well.

FRANKIE CARLE

Started his career with Mal Hallett's band from New England with members Gene Krupa and Jack Tea-garden. He credits his mother for his success, "She made me practice two to three hours a day ----even at lunch time and after school, for a total of sixteen years." Horace Heidt featured Frankie with top billing for four years and even suggested that he form his own band. "My first theater date with my own band was in April, the same year I opened at the Pennsylvania Hotel playing my top hit 'Sunrise Serenade' which I wrote.

Richard Grudens with Larry Elgart

"A fellow named Bill Lackenbaugh asked me to write something different, so I composed 'Sunrise Serenade' for him to publish. He became my lifelong friend. You see, no publisher in New York, including Jack Mills of Mills Music, wanted it because it was different."

His song, that became his famous theme, was originally introduced by the Casa Loma Orchestra at New York's Waldorf Astoria Hotel. You can find it on the original 78, with "Moonlight Serenade" on the "A" side. "So many people have recorded that tune of mine, even from foreign countries. Why, even Ray Charles recorded it," Frankie said with pride.

Frankie Carle's piano has been a musical institution for many years. "I'm going to play until the man upstairs says it's time to quit. I still get mail every day, even more than I did when I had my band going. I still practice an hour or so each day, because I like to keep playing to keep my ear tuned."

Frankie Carle was well over 90 and living in Phoenix, Arizona., when we had talked to him in 1998.

KEN PATTERSON'S PITTSBURGH MUSICIANS

An old friend Ken Patterson brought me up-to-speed on a group of musicians he circulates with in his Pittsburgh, Pennsylvania neighborhood. "Pittsburgh has contributed many musicians to the Big Bands, such as Billy May, Earl "Fatha" Hines, Dodo Marmarosa, and Billy Eckstine." How about this roster of Big Band alumni: Bob Boswell, acoustic bass with Louis Jordan; Bob Cardillo played piano with Ina Ray Hutton; Ray Crummie did his piano tricks with Ray Anthony's Navy band. Danny Conn blew trumpet with Clyde McCoy, Hal McIntyre, and Claude Thornhill; Dave LaRocca, acoustic bass with Woody Herman and Buddy Rich; and Vince Lascheid hammered his ivories with Tex Beneke; Joe Negri strummed guitar with Shep Fields; Dave Pew blew trumpet with Raymond Scott and Henry Busse's orchestras, and Rodger Ryan played drums with Woody's Herds. All these guys were still active in radio and TV and with local symphonies. And Dave Pew's wife sang with some band's as Marcy Lynn.

"With the exception of a 100 piece symphony orchestra, there is nothing to compare to the enormous precision of a 17 piece Big Band," according to Ken, "We are fortunate to have lived through that wonderful time." Benny Goodman labeled today's music "amplified" junk."

Ken documents the fact that Dakota Staton, who recorded with George Shearing and Van Alexander, was, along with famed Duke Ellington arranger and composer Billy Strayhorn, Pittsburgh alumni. So were Roy Eldridge and Erroll Garner. Henry Mancini, Billy May, and Mary Lou Williams were more treasure troves of musical talent from one city. Amazing.

Song writers Jay Livingston ("Golden Earrings"), Oscar Levant ("Blame it on My Youth"), Nancy Hamilton ("How High the Moon"), Henry Mancini ("Moon River"), Leo Robbin ("Thanks for the Memory"),were Pittsburgh-ers too. What was in the water of that vast industrial city of Pennsylvania? The list goes on with more musicians and even the great Maxine Sullivan, a true singing legend. Those coal stoves always kept them warmed up. Thanks Ken.

BILLY MAY

As I was writing this piece, I learned from Stan Kenton trombonist and then Big Band Academy President Milt Bernhart that Billy May was in the hospital. We had talked with Billy for my book, The Music Men, but mostly concerning his arranging career. Billy May also led a terrific Big Band. He's the guy that arranged "Cherokee" for Charlie Barnet, and that beautiful opening that I love so much for Glenn Miller's recording of "Serenade in Blue." For those two gems alone, Billy would deserve honors in the Big Band Hall of Fame.

Billy's band turned out the massive Time-Life re-creation's of Big Band recording's, utilizing original arrangements, and leading the band itself. Billy May organized his first band in 1952, late for Big Bands. Earlier, he spent a lot of time with Charlie Barnet. "I worked for Charlie for two years. That was in 1939 in New York. On the day Roosevelt was elected President, I joined Glenn Miller. I was in the trumpet section, but I also played solos that Glenn asked me to do. I did lots of arranging for him, too, with Jerry Gray and Bill Finegan."

After two years on the road, Billy tired of bandleading, and the band, financed by Ray Anthony, was turned over to Sam Donohue. Billy May settled in Hollywood and worked for films and television, where he was in great demand. His work with Frank Sinatra is legendary and was crucial to the ultimate success of Sinatra.

GENE KRUPA

The Gene Krupa story began in Chicago on January 15, 1909. The youngest of nine children reared in the Polish section of town, Gene attended Catholic school and worked in a music store on weekends, arousing his early interest in music.

His second job was in a dance hall where he gained his first experience playing saxophone in a junior band called The Frivolians; he soon developed an interest in playing drums. Like a plot in a movie, the drummer called in sick one night and Gene took over. At St. Joseph's College, a preparatory seminary in Indiana, Gene was encouraged by a priest, a professor of music who liked jazz. Instead of becoming a priest, Gene turned to music, and sought the help of percussion instructor Roy Knapp, who helped him improve his playing.

Impressed with other jazz musicians of the era, Gene Krupa gathered momentum: "I learned from Zutty Singleton and Baby Dodds, who taught me the difference between starting a roll or sequence of beats with the left or right hand and how the tone and inflection changed entirely when you shifted hands."

Taking a hint from what he heard, Gene worked out on tom-toms to get them in tune and learned when to implement them. "I punched holes in them with an ice-pick," he said.

Gene worked the local bands, making his first recording in 1927, impressing those who hired him so much that they acknowledged it marked the arrival of a new force in jazz drumming. Gene emigrated to New York City and found work in Broadway pit-bands, where George Gershwin applauded his percussion efforts in two of his musicals, Girl Crazy and Strike Up the Band.

Working in Red Nichols' Five Pennies band, Gene played in recording sessions alongside jazz artists Jack Teagarden, Benny Goodman, Jimmy Dorsey and Glenn Miller. Trekking uptown, Gene would jam with drummers Chick Webb and Big Sid Catlett in Harlem jazz clubs.

His most important career move was joining up with Benny Goodman, replacing Stan King. At Red Norvo's house in Forest Hills, Queens, Goodman, Krupa, Bessie Smith, Red's wife, Mildred Bailey, and neighbor Red Nichols would all get together and play. This was where Benny got the idea for his small groups. In both the small and large Goodman bands, Gene contributed heavily with his personality, good-looks, drive and exuberance, becoming a super star under the Goodman umbrella of success.

The immensely successful Benny Goodman Carnegie Hall concert in 1938 was the highlight of Gene's career. Gene formed his own band after leaving Benny, making his debut in Atlantic City in 1938 on the Steel Pier.

Anita O'Day, who recorded regularly when she sang with Krupa, told me in early 1999 that her happiest and best years with a band was with Gene Krupa:

"He allowed me to sing things my way. Gene was a groovy guy

and didn't like flat ballads or heavy upbeat things. He was smooth as jazz." Anita's recorded some hip ballads like "Skylark," swing things like "Stompin' At the Savoy," and with Roy Eldridge, a tune called "Let Me Off Uptown," the band's biggest hit and biggest moment.

Anita, one of the best jazz vocalists ever, sang at New York's Lincoln Center in June, 1999, appearing with the Manhattan Transfer singing group, among others.

Gene Krupa was one of the brightest and most popular personalities of the Big Band Era, enjoying fame as a movie star, appearing in The Glenn Miller Story and The Benny Goodman Story as himself. After spending some time in jail for minor drug-related problems, he continued on to become one of the most beloved bandleaders. Actor Sal Mineo played the role of Gene Krupa in the 1959 movie Drum Crazy, the Gene Krupa Story. We lost Gene Krupa in 1973.

SAMMY KAYE - The Swing and Sway Band

In 1945, the top three Billboard artists were Number 1 - Bing Crosby with 1,428 votes, Number 2 - Sammy Kaye with 855 votes, Number 3 - Harry James with 785 votes. Frank Sinatra came in 4th with 731 votes. In 1946 Sammy Kaye was Number 4, and was back in the Number 3 spot once again in 1947. In the later world of music , that would be equal to a Madonna, Beatles, Rolling Stones, or Elvis Presley. No easy task for a Big Band in any era.

Did you know that Sammy Kaye had more hit records than any other Big Band in history? Well, neither did I until I contacted Robert De Mars and Timothy Pierce of West Palm Beach, Florida, who are keeping the Sammy Kaye legacy of music going through The Sammy Kaye & Big Band Archives. Remember his beloved renditions of "My Blue Heaven," "Sometimes I'm Happy," "Carolina Moon," "Stardust," "On the Street of Regret," "Chicery Chick," "I'm a Big Girl Now," "I Left My Heart At the Stage Door Canteen," "The Old Lamp Lighter," "Harbor Lights," "Laughing On The Inside," "It Isn't Fair" (sung by Don Cornell), and his ensemble hit, Bobby Troup's "Daddy," plus too many more to list here.

The fact is, jazz fans not withstanding, that Sammy Kaye was the number one band from 1945 to 1949. Kaye's was a "sweet band" - a gentle, rhythmic, danceable Big Band. Sammy could play the clarinet, violin, trumpet, saxophone, banjo and guitar. He led a dance band in college called Sammy's Hot Peppers, circa 1932. His later band was compared to Guy Lombardo's, and earned him gigs at New York's Essex House and the Commodore Hotel, providing plenty of visibility for the band. Appearances at the Paramount Theater followed, then a national tour, which broke cross-country records wherever they played. The band broke attendance records at Frank Dailey's Meadowbrook in the days of their hit recordings of "Rosalie" and "Love Walked In."

Influenced by the Kay Kyser and Gus Arnheim Bands, Sammy Kaye featured song titles at the start of each record. On the Old Gold Program, The Chesterfield Supper Club radio show, and So You Want To Lead a Band show, Sammy devised a novel innovation. He would allow eager members of the audience the chance to become the bandleader. At the conclusion of each session, Sammy would autograph the participants baton and present it as a gift to the "leader" of the moment. The show graduated to television in the 1950s, paving the way for Lawrence Welk's great success.

Among some other tunes, Sammy Kaye composed the wartime hit "Remember Pearl Harbor" and "Kaye's Melody." And, remember his excellent vocalist, Nancy Norman? Some of her hits were "Walkin' With My Baby," "As Time Goes By," "There Goes That Song Again," "I'll Buy That Dream," "Chickery Chick," "Gotta Be This or That," and "There Will Never Be Another You," a treasure trove of wonderful, listenable recordings performed as well as any lady vocalist of the era.

Over the years of the Big Band Era, millions listened and danced to Sammy Kaye's Swing and Sway Orchestra. Were you one of them?

BILL ELLIOT

One of the more recent bands around is the Bill Elliot Swing Orchestra from California with featured singer Amy Weston, Paul Weston and Jo Stafford's lovely daughter. Bill performed his charts in England at Pontin's as a guest of Chris Dean and his Syd Lawrence band. Bill's music has been featured in the films Independence Day, Nixon, Dick Tracy, and Sticks, as well as work on the TV show Northern Exposure. His band played in the Disney films Aladdin and That Darn Cat. Michael Feinstein has sung with the band. On Catalina Island, Bill Elliot and his band has played the famed Avalon Ballroom.

KAY KYSER

Some of you may remember the Ol' Professor Kay Kyser and his "Kollege of Musical Knowledge" radio program. It was a mixture of musi-

Kay Kyser

cal trivia and some great swing music and novelty tunes set in rhythm by vocalists Harry Babbitt, Ginny Simms, and Merwyn Bogue, known as Ish Kabibble, who sang most of the comedy songs.

Their top recordings were "Three Little Fishes," "Two Sleepy People," "Praise the Lord and Pass the Ammunition," "Why Don't We Do This More Often," and "Jingle, Jangle, Jingle." Kay toured the USO camps and traveled to the Pacific war theater to entertain the troops. He appeared in two significant films Stage Door Canteen and Thousands Cheer.

The bands last two hits were one of my favorites, "Slow Boat To China," and "The Woody Woodpecker Song" both in the late forties. Kay Kyser , whose real name was James King Kern Kyser, retired in the early fifties, when he felt he was no longer wanted by the public and also needed to quit because of adverse health.

RAY McKINLEY

Famed drummer and bandleader Ray McKinley began his career in the Dallas area of Texas and joined with Smith Ballew's Orchestra until he met with Glenn Miller in 1929 and they joined up with the Dorsey Brothers. Glenn went to Ray Noble and Ray remained with Ballew. Ray was also a very good singer. "You Came a Long Way from St. Louis" and "Beat Me Daddy Eight to the Bar" were his big hits. He joined the Army Air Force Band that was formed by Glenn. When Glenn disappeared over the English

Channel in December, 1944, Ray assumed leadership of the band. Upon his military discharge, Ray formed his own band with the help arranger Eddie Sauter writing his material. In 1956, Ray reassumed leadership of the Glenn Miller Orchestra and remained until 1966 when Buddy De Franco took over leadership.

BUDDY MORROW

I had the good fortune to spend an evening backstage at a Buddy Morrow Big Band concert when he was leading the Tommy Dorsey Or-

Buddy Morrow with Richard Grudens

chestra back in the late eighties. He still does just that. Buddy (original name Moe Zudicoff) first gained prominence playing his outstanding trombone with Paul Whiteman, Tommy Dorsey, Artie Shaw and Jimmy Dorsey.

Buddy got his first chance at leading when Jimmy took sick and asked him to fill in. His recording of "Night Train" was a sensation, selling over a million copies. I would have to rate Buddy's playing with Tommy himself, and currently with Larry O'Brien who has been fronting the Glenn Miller Orchestra for many years.

Buddy insists the band retain the authentic sound and style of the late Tommy Dorsey Orchestra, even on tunes Tommy never played.

LORING "RED" NICHOLS

"Red" Nichols band goes back to the twenties and thirties and was greatly influenced by the cornet playing of Bix Beidebecke. Nichols father was a music teacher and taught him to play and become an excellent sight reader.

When he recorded with Bruns-

Red Nichols

COURTESY OF
FREDERICK BROTHERS
MUSIC CORP.

wick, he named his musicians "Red" Nichols and his Five Pennies, even though the band was larger. In his band you could find Jack Teagarden, Joe Venuti, Eddie Lang, Gene Krupa and Jimmy Dorsey, to name a few big names.

During the Depression, Nichols worked the Broadway shows. A movie was made of his life and starred Danny Kaye.

HORACE HEIDT

Horace Heidt was a pianist and Big Band leader. His band, Horace Heidt and his Musical Knights were national celebrities in the thirties due to his years of appearances on radio and television. He has a star on the Hollywood Walk of Fame.

Heidt's musical recordings were very successful with his number one hit, "Gone with the Wind," and "The Man with the Violin" that came in at number two.

His radio show was named Pot O' Gold and was the basis of the motion picture that starred Hiedt, Jimmy Stewart and Paulette Goddard.

Horace Heidt

Big Band Photo Gallery

Bob Crosby

Bobby Hackett

Count Basie

Tommy Dorsey

Tommy Tucker

Ozzie Nelson

Johnny McAfee

Abe Lyman

Ted Weems

Ted Heath

Clyde McCoy

Art Mooney

Woody Herman

Pee Wee Hunt and
Kenny Sargent

Les Elgart

Tony Pastor

Jimmy Dorsey

Jan Garber

Guy Lombardo

Corky Corcoran

Henry Busse

Eddy Duchin

Richard Himber

Phil Harris

Harry James

Buddy Rogers

Johnny Green

x

JACK LEBO'S SOUR NOTES

Jack Lebo

An Alphabetical List Of All Known Bands
1920 to 1990

A

Aaronson, Irving
Abbey, Leon
Abernathy, Shuffle
Agnew, Charlie
Alexander, Tommy
Alexander, Van
Allen, Bob
Ambrose, Bert
Anderson, Lew
Anthony, Ray
Armstrong, Louis
Arden, Harold
Arnheim, Gus
Arthur, Zinn
Ash, Paul
Auld, Georgie
Ayres, Mitchell

B

Back, Will
Baker, Ken
Ballew, Smith
Barnes, Walter
Barnet, Charlie
Barron, Blue
Barron, Tony
Bartha, Alex
Bartley, Ronnie
Basie, William (Count)
Bauduc, Ray
Baum, Charlie
Baxter, Les
Bechet, Sidney

Beckner, Denny
Beecher, Little John
Belasco, Leon
Belloc, Dan
Beneke, Tex
Bettencourt, Frank
Berigan, Bunny
Bernabei, Memo
Bernie, Ben
Bestor, Don
Biagini, Henry
Bishop. Billy
Blaine, Jerry
Bleyer, Archie
Block, Bert
Bothwell, Johnny
Boulanger, Charlie
Bradley, Will
Bradshaw, Tiny
Brandwynne, Nat
Breese, Lou
Bregman, Buddy
Brigode, Ace
Bring, Lou
Britton, Milt and Frank
Brooks, Randy
Brown, Les
Bryant, Willie
Burke, Sonny
Burtnett, Earl
Busse, Henry
Butterfield, Billy
Byers, Verne
Byrne, Bobby

C

Cabot, Chuck
Calame, Bob
Calloway, Cab
Campo, Pupi
Carle, Frankie
Carlyle, Russ
Carter, Benny
Casa Loma,
Castle, Lee
Catron, Johnny
Cato's Vagabonds
Cavallaro, Carmen
Cayler, Joy
Chester, Bob
Childs, Reggie
Claridge, Gay
Clarke, Buddy
Clayton, Del
Clifford, Bill
Clinton, Larry
Coakley, Tom
Coburn, Jolly
Coleman, Emil
Columbo, Russ
Cooley, Spade
Coon-Sanders
Cooper, Al (Savoy Sultans)
Corbiscello, Tony
Courtney, Del
Coy, Gene
Craig, Francis
Crawford, Jack
Crosby, Bob
Cross, Bob
Cugat, Xavier
Cummins, Bernie
Cutler, Ben

D

Dailey, Frank
Daly, Duke

Davis, Johnny
Davis, Meyer
Day, Bobby
Dean, Peter
DeLange, Eddie
Denny, Jack
Deutsch, Emery
De Vol, Frank
Donahue, Al
Donohue, Sam
Dorsey, Jimmy
Dorsey, Tommy
Dowell, Saxie
Duchin, Eddy
Duchin, Peter
Dukoff, Bobby
Dunham, Sonny

E

Eberle, Ray
Eckstine, Billy
Elgart, Larry
Elgart , Les
Ellington, Edward (Duke)
Ellis, Seger
Elliott, Bill
Elliottt Brothers
Elman,Ziggy
Ennis, Skinnay
Everette, Jack

F

Farmer, Willie
Featherstone, Jimmy
Felton, Happy
Ferguson, Danny
Ferguson, Maynard
Fielding, Jerry
Fields, Shep
Fina, Jack
Fio Rita, Ted
Fisk, Charlie

Flanagan, Ralph
Fomeen, Basil
Foster, Chuck
Funk, Larry

G Garber, Jan
Gasparre, Dick
Gee, George
Gerun, Tom
Gillespie, John (Dizzy
Giordano, Vince
Glasser, Don
Goldkette, Jean
Goodman, Benny
Cooley, Spade
Gordon, Claude
Gordon, Gray
Grady, Eddie
Gray, Glen (Casa Loma)
Gray, Jerry
Grayson. Hal
Greco, Leo
Green, Johnny
Grier, Jimmie
Grisafi, Ben

H

Hackett, Bobby
Hall, George
Hallett, Mal
Halstead,Henry
Hamp, Johnny
Hampton, Lionel
Handy, W.C.
Harris, Gene
Harris, Ken
Harris, Phil
Harpa, Daryl
Hawkins, Coleman
Hawkins, Erskine
Hayes, Edgar
Hayes, Sherman

Haymes, Joe
Hayton, Lennie
Heath, Ted
Hecksher, Ernie
Hefti, Neal
Heidt, Horace
Henderson, Fletcher
Henderson, Skitch
Herbeck, Ray
Herman, Lenny
Herman, Woody
Hickman, Art
Hill, Teddy
Hill, Tiny
Himber, Richard
Hines, Earl (Fatha)
Hite, Les
Hoagland, Everett
Hoff, Carl
Hopkins, Claude
Howard, Eddy
Hudson, Dean
Hudson, Will
Hudson-DeLange
Hunt, Pee Wee
Hutton, Ina Ray
Hylton, Jack

J

Jacquet, Illinois
James, Harry
Jaros, Joe
Jarrett, Art
Jenny, Jack
Jerome, Henry
Johnson, Arnold
Johnson, Buddy
Jones, Isham
Jones, Quincy
Jones, Spike
Jordan, Louis
Joy, Jimmy
Jurgens, Dick

K

Kahn, Roger
Kardos, Gene
Kassel, Art
Katz, Al
Kavelin, Al
Kay, Herbie
Kaye, Johnnie
Kaye, Sammy
Kayser, Joe
Kemp, Hal
Kemper, Ronnie
Kenton, Stan
Kenney, Mart
King, Al
King, Henry
King, Pee Wee
King, Wayne
Kirby, John
Kirk, Andy
Kirk, Bob
Kisley, Steve
Knapp, Orville
Kruegere, Bennie
Krupa, Gene
Kyser, Kay

L

Laine, Buddy
Landry, Art
Lane, Eddie
Lanin, Lester
LaSalle, Dick
Lawrence, Elliot
Leonard, Harlan
Lewis, Ted
Light, Enoch
Little, Little jack
Lombardo, Guy
Long, Johnny
Longo, Pat

Lopez, Vincent
Love, Preston
Lown, Bert
Lucas, Clyde
Lunceford, Jimmie
Lyman, Abe

M

Machito
Madriguera, Enric
Maltby, Richard
Marcellino, Muzzy
Marterie, Ralph
Marshard, Jack
Martin, Freddy
Martin, Paul
Marx, Chico
Masters, Frankie
Maxted, Billy
May, Billy
Mayhew, Nye
McDonald, Billy
McFarland Twins
McIntyre, Hal
McIntyre, Lani
McKinley, Ray
McKinney's Cotton Pickers
McCoy, Clyde
McCune, Bill
McGrane, Don
McKay, Marion
McShann, Jay
McGhee, Johnny
McPartland, Jimmy
Meroff, Benny
Messner, Johnny
Millinder, Lucky
Miller Brothers
Miller, Glenn
Miller, Herb
Miller, John
Miller, Ray
Mooney, Art

Monroe, Vaughn
Morgan, Russ
Moreno, Buddy
Morrow, Buddy
Moten, Benny
Mozian, Roger King
Mundy, Jimmy
Mulligan, Gerry
Murphy, Spud
Musso, Vido

N

Nagel, Freddy
Napoleon, Phil
Neighbors, Paul
Nelson, Ozzie
Nestico, Sammy
Newman, Ruby
Nichols, Red
Noble, Leighton
Noble, Ray
Norvo, Red

O

O'Hare, Husk
Ohman, Phil
Oliver, King
Oliver, Sy
Olney Big Band
Olsen, George
Osborne, Will
Owens, Harry

P

Page, Walter
Palmer, Jimmy
Pannell, Bill
Pancho
Panico, Louis
Pastor, Tony
Paul, Eddie
Paxton, George

Pearl, Ray
Peeper, Leo
Pendarvis, Paul
Perkins, Red
Phillips, Richard
Phillips, Teddy
Pollack, Ben
Pontrelli, Pete
Powell, Teddy
Prado, Perez
Prima, Louis
Pruden, Hal
Puente, Tito

R

Rae, Jackie
Raeburn, Boyd
Rank, George
Rapp, Barney
Ravazza, Carl
Redman, Don
Reed, Tommy
Regis, Billy
Reichman, Joe
Reid, Don
Reisman, Leo
Rey, Alvino
Reynolds, Tommy
Ricardel, Joe
Rich, Buddy
Rich, Freddie
Richards, Bernie
Richards, Dick
Richards, Johnny
Riddle, Nelson
Riley and Farley
Riley, Mike
Rio, Rita
Robison, Willard
Rodriguez, Tito
Rogers, Buddy
Rogers, Dick
Rogers, Shorty

Romanelli, Luigi
Rose, Vincent
Rudy, Ernie
Russell, Jack
Russell, Luis
Russo, Danny

S

Salvador, ,Sal
Sands, Carl
Sateriale, Freddie
Sauter-Finegan
Savitt, Jan
Saylor, Sonny
Scott, Raymond
Sedlor, Jimmy
Selvin, Ben
Senter, Boyd
Six Fat Dutchmen
Shand, Terry
Shaw, Artie
Shaw, Milt
Sheldon, Harvey
Sherock, Shorty
Sherwood, Bobby
Shilkret, Jack
Sissle, Noble
Slack, Freddy
Smith, Beasely
Smith, Carl
Sonn, Larry
Sosnick, Harry
Spanier, Muggsy
Specht, Paul
Spitalny, Phil
Spitfire Band
Spivak, Charlie
Stabile, Dick
Straeter, Ted
Steele, Blue
Stern, Harold
Stolzenberg, Ray
Stone, Eddie

Stone, Justin
Stone, Lew
Straeter, Ted
Straight, Charlie
Strong, Benny
Strong, Bob
Sunset Royal Serenaders
Swanson, Billy

T

Teagarden, Jack
Terry, Dan
Thal, Pierson
Thompson, Hank
Thornhill, Claude
Trace, Al
Tremaine, Paul
Trumbauer, Frankie
Tucker. Orrin
Tucker, Tommy

V

Van, Garwood
Vallee, Rudy
Ventura, Charlie
Venuti, Joe
Vincent, Lee

W

Wald, Jerry
Waldman, Herman
Waller, Fats
Waples, Buddy
Waring, Fred
Watkins, Sammy
Webb, Chick
Weeks, Anson
Weems, Ted
Welk, Lawrence
West, Alvy
Whiteman, Paul
Wickman, Dick

Wiedoft, Herb
Wilber, Bob
Wilde, Ran
Wilfahrt, John "Whoopee"
Williams. Billy
Williams, Cootie
Williams, Gene
Williams, Griff
Wills, Bob
Wilson, Teddy
Willson, Meredith

Wood, Barry
Wylie, Austin

Yankovic, Frank
Young, Victor

Zentner, Si
Zurke, Bob

Billy Eckstine - Metronome Magazine - Singer of the Year 1949

GREAT MUSICAL REPUTATIONS ARE BUILT WITH SELMER

STAN GETZ

COLEMAN HAWKINS

PAUL DESMOND

BENNY CARTER

Positive proof—
You'll play better with a Selmer

We don't say that playing a Selmer will make you an overnight sensation. But it will do more for your talent, technique, and reputation than any other horn. No question about it. That's why so many top-drawer sax stars—actually more than 80% of them—play Selmer. Never has there been a sax with such superb intonation, such vibrant tone, and carrying power; nor one so easy to handle and so comfortable to play. Try the new Mark VI as soon as you can—see if you don't agree: You'll play better with a Selmer!

FREE color folder describing 19 features of the Selmer (Paris) Mark VI Saxophone that you find in no other make. Mail this coupon now.

Selmer Elkhart, Indiana—Dept. C-41

Name_____

Address_____

City_____Zone____State_____

Melody Maker

July 27, 1963 — Friday 6d

SINATRA—HE'S KING, SAYS BING

Why he signed for Frank's disc label

By RAY COLEMAN

BING CROSBY told me from his Hollywood home this week why he had made the shock decision to sign with Frank Sinatra's Reprise record label.

"Let's face it—Sinatra is a king," said Bing. "He is a very sharp operator, a keen record chief, and has a keen appreciation of what the public wants.

"I'm happy to be associated with him after all these years. I hope our partnership will work out as a mutual benefit."

Crosby, aged 59, has been singing for 40 years and his disc sales are estimated to be around 200 million.

There has always been an atmosphere of intense rivalry between Sinatra and Crosby.

At 3 am on the MM's press day, after two days of chasing Bing around offices, cars, golf clubs and other places, I finally contacted him at his home.

It was 7 pm in Hollywood and Bing had just finished a four-hour game of golf. Told the time in Britain, he quipped: "A case of 'when the blue of the night meets the gold of the day' then?"

Many plans

Asked why he decided to sign with Reprise, Crosby replied: "Purely because it is a sensible thing for me to do. Frank is very progressive. He has so many plans for the company and really does know what he is doing.

How long did Bing plan to carry on singing? What about his recent statement that he planned to "ease up"?

"I'll sing for as long as the pipes hold out," Bing replied. "Of course, that can't be long—a few years yet. I guess I've been taking things steadier for some time now, you know.

"Right now I'm in line for four TV shows,

Sinatra—'proud moment'

Crosby—'How's Holliday?'

'I'd like to record with Duke'

a couple of films—they keep me busy most of the time.

Did he plan to team up with Sinatra on record?

"It's early to say," Bing answered. "Guess so—they tell me we're doing a Christmas album together and the A&R men over there are working out a whole host of ideas. I am very pleased about the set-up.

"Nelson Riddle, who is with Frank, has a very fertile musical brain. He gives a singer wonderful backings—some of the best in the business.

Suggestion

"The chemistry is there to dispense some wonderful music."

Crosby said he looked forward, too, to the prospect of working with some of Reprise's jazz signings—including Duke Ellington. "That'd be good," he remarked.

He reacted promptly to a suggestion that in joining Sinatra he had teamed up with a rival.

"He's no rival of mine.

"I've known him for 25 years. I've recorded with many artists—the Boswell Sisters, Rosie Clooney, Louis Armstrong, the Mills Brothers. Nobody's rivals in this business."

Admiration

Asked if Sinatra had approached him personally to sign a disc contract, Crosby replied: "No. His representative called me. I haven't seen Frank about it yet but hope to discuss things with him soon."

Sinatra said in Hollywood that the capture of Crosby was "a proud moment for the whole organisation."

Crosby added: "Frank knows this business and Reprise is going places. I have respect and admiration for his work as a record chief."

BEFORE HANGING UP, BING SAID: "GIVE MY BEST REGARDS TO MICHAEL HOLLIDAY—HOW'S HE DOING?"

THEY'RE COMING!

RUSHING TO TOUR WITH BASIE BAND

THE famous combination of Count Basie and singer Jimmy Rushing is being revived for British fans.

Rushing has been added to the Basie-Sarah Vaughan package which opens a three-week British tour at Southend Odeon on September 7.

Agent Harold Davison told the MM this week: "Rushing will be featured with the Basie Band. Sarah will be bringing her own regular backing group, the Kirk Stewart Trio, but I hope she will also do a number or two with Basie.

"There have been a number of personnel changes in the Basie band since its last visit.

BEAT CRAZY—that's Britain
centre pages

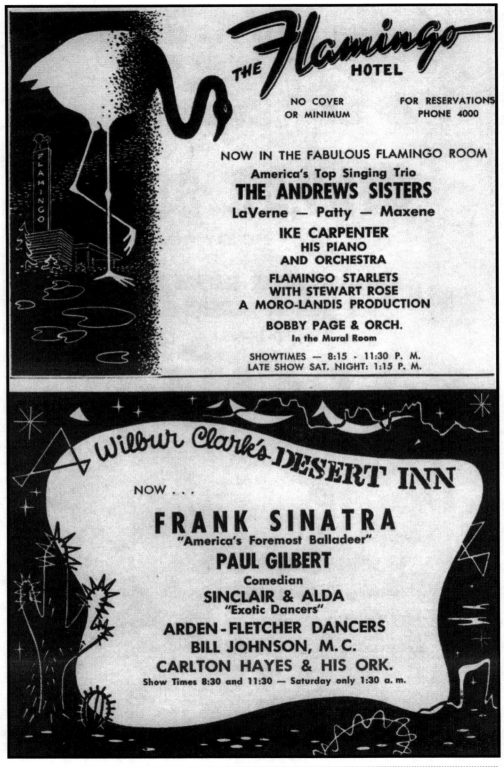

The Recording Ban
Downbeat Magazine
August 1, 1942

THE RECORDING BAN IS ON...

No new commercial instrumentals to be waxed and released for public consumption.

DID THE BAN HELP wind down THE BIG BAND ERA? Was it the straw that broke the camel's back? The Big Bands were already fighting the effects of World War II break up of their bands.

IN AUGUST OF 1942, ALL RECORDING STOPPED

because the musicians union banned all of its members from participating in recording.

Union President James Petrillo claimed that making and issuing recordings was ruining the jobs of sixty percent of the American Federation Musicians membership.

At the time all the country's radio stations, recording firms, transcription firms, radio networks and even small radio stations were affected adversely by the union ban.

Over 50% of all radio stations depended on the playing of records to exist. Without them they would likely go out of business. Angry, they jointly appealed to the Justice Department , stating," This it is a matter in the public interest which demands thorough investigation." It never happened.

Small stations simply played old records, whereas, the larger stations needed constantly new releases. However, New York's WNEW said: "With twenty thousand records in our collection, we aren't too worried about the extra twelve a week that are coming out now."

The terms were that when a musician fails to work for thirty days, he should be guaranteed work for the rest of the year, a condition rejected by the recording companies.

Of course, vocalists were allowed to record a capella utilizing vocal groups or choruses behind them, which led to the rise of the vocalists after the slow demise of the Big Bands, stealing the spotlight once dominated by the bands.

The ban ended in September, 1943 when Decca Records agreed to pay the AFM union recording royalties. Capital Records acquiesced and signed with the union one month later. Columbia and Victor finally relented in November, 1944.

Before the AFM ban ASCAP and BMI wanted more money from radio networks to use their members songs. The networks said "no" so all ASCAP songs were banned from airplay and remote. At first BMI suffered greatly as they did not have the stable of great composers like Gershwin, Porter, Mercer, Rodgers and Hart, Arlen, Kern and Berlin, as had ASCAP. The loss in song quality, inspiration , and energy on live broadcasts was damaging. The problem was eventually worked out, but then the Petrillo recording ban followed. Another devastating event that helped the demise of the Big Band Era.

James Petrillo

52^{nd St}

is no more, that is, to what it once was. It is gone like all the old music venues of the era... directly into music history....

STARDUST

Basie's Big Band at the Famous Door in 1938 with Walter Page, Jo Jones, Freddie Green, Count Basie, Bennie Morton, Buck Clayton, Herschel Evans, Dan Minor, Ed Lewis, Dicky Wells, Earle Warren, Harry Edison, Jack Washington, and Lester Young

The Street That Never Sleeps

Variety's Abel Green Dubbed
52nd Street "America's Montmartre"

In the world's musical grottos like Bourbon Street, Beale Street, Sunset Boulevard, Pigalle, U.K.s West End, among other noted places the smells and sounds of extemporaneous music and excitement prevailed over many, many years. In New York it was the same on the street that never slept, 52nd Street.

In this inauspicious block in the center of Manhattan, 52nd street between Fifth and Sixth Avenues, there was a special street that housed America's music and its musicians. It was Harlem moved downtown.

It was the digs of the great artists: Bessie Smith, Art Tatum, Billie Holiday, Dizzy Gillespie, Fats Waller, Teddy Wilson, Charlie Parker, Billy Eckstine, Sarah Vaughan, Count Basie, Roy Eldridge, Maxine Sullivan, Charlie Barnet, Buddy Rich, Woody Herman, Louis Prima and an endless list of unforgettables.

What were some of the locales? The Famous Door, Onyx Club, Jack & Charlie's 21 Club, Yacht Club, Three Deuces, Kelly's Stable, Toots Shor, and Leon and Eddie's.

Composer, arranger Alec Wilder: "52nd Street was total friendship. It was the last time than an American street gave you a feeling of security and warmth and the excitement of musical friendship."

The street was composed of brownstone row houses that had been converted to speakeasies and clubs. The 21 Club was converted into a woody, 18th century style English tavern. Taxi drivers named it the Street. It started as the downtown home of great African-American entertainers in the early thirties(then called Negroes) jazz. It has been said that the appearance of William "Count" Basie in 1938 earned the street the reputation as the jumping-off place for jazz in New York. Almost every big name in show business were patrons. It had already become the home of Billie Holiday, (a very strong Sinatra influence,) Teddy Wilson and Maxine Sullivan.

John Birks "Dizzy" Gillespie: The Street had it's own thing---an identity, but the real groundwork for the music was done in Harlem. The music gave the Street its identity, nothing else. I jammed at almost every club with Ella, or at Kelly's with Coleman Hawkins, and Benny Carter-also at Kelly's. We only got paid scale, which was enough, I guess for the time. The place was filled with characters you could only imagine, but mostly the greatest musicians and singers that you ever heard. 52nd St. gave us

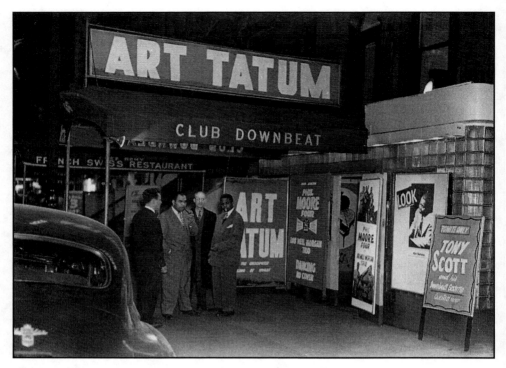

the rooms and the audiences. That's all we ever needed."

52nd street is no more, that is, to what it once was. It is gone like all the old music venues of the era directly into music history, and men-

Owner Charles Delaunay and the Andrews Sisters at the Famous Door

tioned in books like 52nd St. by Arnold Shaw.

From it's birth in the Prohibition-era where musicians jammed or a drink or for fun, to its place as the center of jazz music with clubs lining both sides of the street where black and white musicians played to filled clubs, to its decline when the Street became a place of clip joints and cheap burlesque-style entertainment.

ANECDOTES AND FABLES OF THE BIG BANDS

BENNY GOODMAN:

It seems Benny walked into a rehearsal of his band, glanced up at the trumpet section and asked one his players who the new trumpet man was.

"That's your brother, Irving."

"Well," Benny said,"Pass the word up to him to stop chewing gum."

Benny Goodman telephoned big band writer George Simon and told him that he was embarrassed when he called his house: "I can never remember your wife's name. What is her name, Bob?"

Benny Goodman came in to work with the band, when one of the members complained to him that he was cold there in the studio. Benny said, "I be right back," and he soon returned wearing a sweater.

And in the same studio, Goodman walked over a girl sitting at the end of the stage, saying: "Miss, you are not allowed in this studio unless you are a musician." The girl replied, "Daddy, I'm your daughter, Rachel." "Oh! Sorry, Hon."

WINGY MANONE

Wingy Manone, a Bing Crosby insider crony, was a cornet player who had only one arm, his left, and never learned to read music, but wanted to play in Benny Goodman's band. Benny promised that if Wingy ever learned to read notes he would give him a chance to blow his horn in the brass section of the band.

Well, Wingy learned and wired Goodman and asked for the train fare to New York. Goodman sent the money and Wingy boarded a train from L.A. to New York to join the Goodman band.

Bing Crosby: "Wingy took his place in the brass section and at the rehearsal they put the third cornet part in front of Wingy and Benny gave the downbeat. Of course the spots meant nothing to Wingy and he was lost after the opening bar or two. Benny came over to him and said, 'I thought you learned to read,' and Wingy replied, 'I did. But man, it's amazing how rusty you can get on those long, cross country train trips.'"

LAWRENCE WELK

When Lawrence Welk introduced Duke Ellington's most famous tune after being handed a list to read from, he simply said in his own Welkian way, "Our next selection is "Take a Train.""

ARTIE SHAW

When Artie Shaw and Benny Goodman both played in radio studios before their own successful bands were formed, Shaw always had a book with him to read between rehearsal time. Goodman always called Artie J.B., which was a puzzle to Artie. After several weeks Artie asked Benny why: "What does J.B. stand for?" Benny smiled and revealed "George Bernard, of course."

VAUGHN MONROE

At a rehearsal, bandleader Vaughn Monroe was conducting without enthusiasm and without air conditioning on a very hot day. Hymie Schertzer asked Andy Ferretti (in the trumpet section up against the wall with windows) if he'd open a window. Andy replied: "If I could open the window I would have jumped out an hour ago."

TOMMY DORSEY

Tommy was visiting at songwriter Johnny Mercer's birthday party. Later in the evening the band played Happy Birthday and Tommy sent a birthday cake to to celebrate. When Mercer cut into the cake, it was filled with lead sheets of his flop songs. Mercer and his wife Ginger were in hysterics.

Part Three

The Musicians and Vocalists - Person To Person
The Greatest Male Vocalists
It's Make Believe Ballroom Time
Even More Guy Singers
Big Band Guy Singers and Their Affiliations
The Ladies Who Sang With The Bands
In the Beginning
The Greatest Female Vocalists
Love & Marriage
More Ladies Who Sang With The Bands
Honorable Mentions
The Canaries
Singing Groups of the Big Band Era & Beyond

BUDD JOHNSON

In 1982, in the rural Long Island hamlet of East Norwich, the prolific songwriter Burt Bacharach owned an old wayside restaurant known as Rothman's Steak House. Alongside, he had built a modern, quality New York Hotel style inn which was the setting for one of the most inspiring interviews I have ever conducted.

Richard and Budd at Rothman's Steak House in East Norwich

The subject was Budd Johnson, one of the most exciting and original musicians of the Big Band Era. A catalytic figure in the modern jazz movement, the inspirational legacy of this man, a sterling saxophonist, who passed on from us in October,1985 at the age of 73, transcended jazz styles. As a player and arranger, his ability to create can be heard on the recordings of many bands for whom he worked so hard, including those of Earl Hines, Count Basie and Dizzy Gillespie, (he worked in the first bebop recording session with Dizzy and Coleman Hawkins) and in the output of many small groups he either led or simply inspired. On each performance Budd drives with the kind of old-fashioned strength and imagination of tenor playing that he helped establish while a bandsman with Earl Hines and Billy Eckstine in the early days, even though he was in his seventies. "I mostly played the reeds---all of them. But I best like arranging now," he said.

Billy Eckstine specifically told me that: "I think the success of my band was mainly due to the arrangements of Budd Johnson." Billy gave up his band because it was too much work and too expensive to operate and he wearied of the racism. "The entire band had to use the rear door, everywhere we performed."

Budd was the quintessential team player. vv He was really a leader, but you'd never know it. He arranged much of what he played, but you'd never know that either.

We sat and talked for hours over a very unpretentious lunch. It was the answer to the question I've heard so many times: "Who is this Budd Johnson?" And when he talked about his grandson, his warmth and humanity brightened him. I learned so much about him of which so little is written. His affection for the music and feelings for his fellow players surpassed his need to talk about himself.

Reaching back, Budd talked about how early jazz musicians consistently worked hard to improve their playing. He claimed, unlike many printed stories to the contrary by various critics, the early bands were well disciplined despite lack of formal training of some musicians and lack of money to buy the best instruments available. "The dedication to the early jazz movement was not planned," he explained. "it just developed." Most bands had a good nucleus--the majority of the players having been together for many years so they sound as one. "Everybody's breathing alike and thinking alike." he said, "It's a musical coup to get all the right guys together. That is why I tried to choose players whom I feel shared a stylistic kinship and expression." Then he would arrange accordingly to highlight their individuality.

Once, Neal Hefti left the Basie organization and traveled to California to work for the movies. When he returned to New York, Budd met him in Birdland one night and Hefti complained: "Damn--I can't for the life of me get the sound out of the same arrangements I did with Basie--in my own band---we just don't sound right...." Budd reminded him that after playing twenty-five years together Basie's men all know each move everybody's gonna make, "So it comes out better."

Budd told me the little known tale about the time Ben Webster came up to his hotel room while they were on tour and asked Budd to teach him saxophone. Ben was a piano player for the band. Budd went to work on Ben teaching him scales first and had Ben work on a song "Singing The Blues," which was a favorite of Webster's. In about eight months Ben began playing saxophone instead of piano. The rest is history, Ben Webster became one of the great tenor saxophonists.

Budd Johnson's best work of record is the fine material he accomplished while with the Basie Band, but he is really best-known for his key role as saxophonist/arranger with the Earl Hines Band of the thirties. But you have to step even a little further back to when he began being taught piano and basic music by the daughter of Booker T. Washington. This was soon after his first music lessons taught to him by his father, who played the organ and cornet. Along the way he developed an interest in playing the tenor sax, much like Webster, subsequently serving with many early bands up through the thirties including performing with Louis Armstrong and Fletcher Henderson. He has played and arranged for Woody Herman, Don Redman, and Buddy Rich, and was the musical director for Billy Eckstine's Orchestra. He has played with Sy Oliver, Cab Calloway, Benny Goodman, and the Tommy Dorsey Bands. He has toured the world with many groups and bands along the way.

"I haven't reached the highlight of my career, though," he said thoughtfully, and believing, "I want to sit down---take the time it needs--- to write a serious piece. I want to complete a jazz symphony and try to sell it to a record company. You can beat the pavement to death trying to find a recording company to give you a date!"

Budd Johnson has played and arranged for so many bands, you couldn't possibly mention them all. But, again, you'd never know it. He was a kind of cornerstone along with a handful of others who quietly helped develop all the jazz products everyone only talks about.

After spending an afternoon with him you realize he had such a clear understanding of his abilities that he never had to show his ego. He was never a public figure, he was strictly a musician's musician.

izzy Gillespie, Richard and Billy Eckstine

JOHN HENRY MUENZENBERGER
And The Truth About the Glenn Miller Sound

Once upon a time, in the days when Frank Sinatra began crooning soft tunes for Tommy Dorsey, and
Glenn Miller sat in the third row playing the trombone for Ray Noble, there
emerged an immensely talented and
happy clarinet player named John
Henry Muenzenberger, who hailed
from Chicago way and settled in Glen
Head,New York. Everyone knew him
as Johnny Mince. (changed when
a fan wrote to Downbeat Magazine
saying he liked Benny Goodman,
Artie Shaw, and that other guy in Ray

with Author Richard Grudens at the Three Village
Inn - 1983

Noble's band.) "Hell, I wasn't gonna take a chance on that happening
again!"

Johnny was one of the Swing Era's sturdiest and most stellar
players whose only goal in life was to play in a good band with the best
musicians---and he has played with the best of them.

He began his career at the age of seventeen in New York with the
Joe Haymes band which later became the Buddy Rogers band. Johnny's
friend, Glenn Miller, who was managing the band for the Englishman,
Ray Noble, signed him and Pee Wee Erwin into the organization after
Buddy quit to join J.Arthur Rank in Hollywood and Noble took over. Glenn
was also the band's arranger in those days. Players like Ziggy Elman,
Buddy DeFranco, Davey Tough, Bunny Berigan, and Buddy Rich, along
with arrangers Paul Weston, Axel Stordahl, and Sy Oliver were in the
band. It was at the beginning of the Big Band Era and one of the best
and most talented grass-root organizations.

Inadvertently Johnny became the catalyst for the original Glenn
Miller sound. As we enjoyed a solid three hour lunch, at the famed Three
Village Inn in old Stonybrook one Tuesday afternoon in 1981, he told me
the true story, different from the silly Hollywood version portrayed in the
Glenn Miller Story where they portray a trumpet player bumping his lip
and a clarinet player taking his spot in the band thereby creating a reversal of instruments.

"The truth is that we were rehearsing with Ray Noble's band at the
Rainbow Room on the 65th floor in Radio City. Trumpet player, Pee Wee
Erwin called in sick , so Glenn asked me to play the trumpet part with the
clarinet. 'I want to see what it sounds like,' said Glenn. He had been try-

ing this 'sound' idea for years, but he didn't think to use the clarinet on top--playing a double with the tenor below. Pee Wee's playing had a wonderful high register that would play those very high notes with the saxophone voice underneath him. As it turned out, I don't think we went through the first eight bars and everyone knew that was the sound that Glenn Miller had been searching for all those years. It was written all over his face. That was the beginning of the famous Glenn Miller sound that punctuated his success as the most popular band of the era."

Still retaining traces of an early, midwestern drawl, John recounted another legendary tale: "One night up in that same Rainbow Room with Noble, before we got on the stand, several of us were warming up---Glenn comes up and says he had written a tune (a lesson composed for his teacher) and asked us to go over it. It was a beautiful thing and Glenn asked up to come down to Broadway the next day to record it. So we met in one of those studios on 49th street, and for just 25 cents recorded Glenn's immortal tune, "Moonlight Serenade." Little did we know.... and I wonder what value that little plastic disc would hold today."

The next time you hear a Glenn Miller recording, I hope you will now think of Johnny Mince, who helped give birth to that wonderful sound that distinguished itself during the Big Band Era.

John was full of endless anecdotes about the Big Band glory days: "When Frank Sinatra was coming with the(Tommy Dorsey) band," he related vigorously, "we were ready to go on a one-nighter, and Tommy says, 'C'mere John."

He took me across the street and they had it on the jukebox-- that thing he did with Harry James-- All Or Nothing At All ---yeah, that was it! I says, 'Boy this guy is good!'" his voice rising.. "But my first impression meeting Frank, he was such a skinny, beat-up looking guy, compared to Jack Leonard (who was the singer who had just left the band) who had lots of class and was good-looking compared to Sinatra."

Johnny's association with Tommy Dorsey was another accidental fluke. He ran into Tommy on Broadway the day he returned from Chicago out of a job, and he says: 'What are you doing in New York ?' (the Buddy Rogers band had broken up a few days earlier in Chicago) and John told him what had happened. "Great! "says Dorsey, you're taking Jimmy's (Dorsey) place tonight."

"Holy God!" John had said. "I'm taking my idol's place tonight."

John ran back to his hotel and gave his room mate a pair of new shoes for an extra tux he owned---and it didn't fit right --but he didn't care. He only knew he was playing in Tommy Dorsey's band that night. (He stayed on for six years until 1941). He was a brilliant and most reliable member of the band, and contributed many well-structured fluent solos, adding a distinctive color to the band, the reed counterpart to Tommy's trombone. Get a copy of his 1938 version of "Chinatown, My Chinatown" and you'll see what I mean.

Unlike many players of his time, Johnny Mince did not become a leader, although he led small groups later on. "I had no ambition to be-come a bandleader. I was having too much fun. I ducked it!" He felt his freedom and a determination to become an excellent sideman was all the ambition he could handle.

Glenn and John were good friends, and when Glenn approached him about joining his newly formed band one night at Hurley's Bar, on Sixth Avenue at the foot of Rockefeller Center's NB C Studios, he and Pee Wee turned him down. "I didn't want to take a chance on being out of work again." He felt Glenn would have made a great leader and had everything going right for him, but he also knew Glenn had tried many times before to form a band and failed. (It was Woody Herman who told me that Glenn mortgaged his own and his in-laws home to finance previ-ous attempts.) Glenn offered Johnny 50%, but he was earning $175.00 a week and did not want to jeopardize that. Today, those shares would have made him rich. Even after Glenn's plane disappeared in 1944 over the English Channel , the Glenn Miller Band has played almost uninter-rupted for all these years right up to today, under it's current leader, Larry O'Brien. (Just a few months ago Larry and the Band, with new singer, Frank Sinatra-like, Tom Postilio, had just returned from an eight months European tour.)

Well, we rolled through one story after another, every one a gem. He recounted the legendary battles between Sinatra and Rich while they played with Dorsey, relating how Dorsey would physically restrain Sina-tra, and he would hold back Rich after one of their confrontations. He revealed yarns about his twenty year stint (1946-66) with his mercurial boss, Arthur Godfrey, during both his radio and television days. (That followed an army discharge with five battlestars, and a stint with Irving Berlin's This is The Army Tour for the U.S.O.).

In 1984, before heading South to retire in Florida, Johnny had been active with many jazz festivals including the Nice (France) festival with promoter George Wein, the Dick Gibson parties in Colorado, many Newport Jazz Festivals, the Sacramento, California festival, the Odessa and Midland Jazz Festivals in Texas, and with time to spare, a short tour with Louis Armstrong. John's truly at his best when playing his beloved clarinet, although like Woody Herman, also played a mean sax. He was highly regarded as one of the best clarinet players of the swing era along with Benny Goodman, Woody Herman, and Artie Shaw, but never nearly as well-known. Maybe now you know him just a little bit better.

Trying to call Johnny at his Boca Raton, Florida, for an update on his career, I sadly learned from his wife, Betty, that he passed from us in December of 1984. Fortunately, John's son, Jay, a popular educator on Long Island, was able to obtain photos of his dad for use in this book. The photos taken of us both by a bartender in the Sand Bar Room at The Three Village Inn were lost or misplaced. Anyway, I like these photos much better. It portrays Johnny Mince with his beloved instrument at two stages of his life.

Tommy Dorsey Orchestra, 1938 - L-R Front: Freddy Stulce, Skeets Herfurt, Johnny Mince, Jack Leonard; Back Row: Pee-Wee Irwin, Andy Feretti, Joe Bauer, Tommy Dorsey and Walter Mercurio

Skitch Henderson - Five Towns College - May 2005

M. Grudens Photos

SKITCH HENDERSON

Born in England in 1918, Lyle Russell Cedric Henderson rose from a roadhouse piano player in Montana and Minnesota during the 1930s to become conductor of the prestigious New York Pops. He was a composer, conductor, bandleader, arranger, pianist, jazz expert, and was the musical conductor on NBCs Tonight Show with Johnny Carson and the Today Show. The New York Pops is the largest independent professional symphonic pops orchestra to play in Carnegie Hall and tour the world.

On May 7, 2005, it was my privilege to attend a special tribute to this man at Five Towns Music College in Dix Hills, New York, where he was conferred Honorary Doctor of Music Degrees along with the late Cy Coleman and prolific songwriter Johnny Mercer. It was a joy meeting up with him once again and I handed him a copy of my book Bing Crosby-Crooner of the Century. We had lunch together along with my wife Madeline, composer/songwriter Ervin Drake and his wife, Edith, record producer Cy Leslie, and Five Towns President Stanley Cohen.

Skitch and Richard - 2005 - Five Towns College - M. Grudens Photo

I had known Skitch Henderson back at NBC where he was on the music staff and was quite a cutup with the ladies. By that time he had worked in Hollywood with the stars of MGM and toured with Mickey Rooney and Judy Garland. He worked with Bing Crosby whom he met at the home of Bob and Dolores Hope. He was Dolores' piano accompanist at the time.

"It was Bing Crosby who named me 'Skitch' because I was called the sketch kid because of the way I would quickly sketch out a new score in a new key." Bing said: "Skitch, if you're going to compete, get your name straightened out. People always forget Christian names but they never forget nicknames."

And to Henderson it was sage advice. Skitch stuck and he even changed his passport. Skitch played on Bob Hope's Pepsodent Show, and later at NBC as Musical Director for Frank Sinatra's Lucky Strike Show and on The Philco Hour with Bing Crosby.

At Five Towns, when he was introduced, he played a touching, soft melody on the piano: "I was rooming with Fritz Loewe at the time and he played a little tune that was fetching and sweet." Skitch played the tune slowly. It was a variation of the theme that eventually turned out to be the song "I Could Have Danced All Night."

It became, of course, the famous tune from the Broadway show My Fair Lady. It was a touching tribute and a memorable vignette by a master that I shall never forget.

You can find a CD of the Pops with Skitch Henderson anywhere music is sold. A recently reissued CD covering many phases of music from New York Pops, Go to the Movies to Magical Moments from Great Musicals.

Bottom Row: Guy Lombado, Vaughn Monroe, Skitch Henderson and Top: Woody Herman, Boyd Raeburn - FIVE OF A KIND

Skitch Henderson was awarded the James Smithson Bicentennial Medal in recognition of his contributions to American culture and New York City's prestigious Handel Medallion.

Skitch Henderson was music.

Skitch Henderson passed on in November of 2005. The music world and all of us will miss him.

PAUL TANNER
SKUNK HOLLOW TO MILLERLAND

During the summer of 1938, Glenn Miller found a skinny, stammering kid named Paul Tanner playing trombone in the Swing Club, in Atlantic City one night after completing his own performance. When Paul learned that Glenn was in the house, he mustered up enough courage to approach Glenn for an opinion of his playing. The two became engrossed in conversation that led to Paul being invited by Glenn to join his band right there on the spot.

One of six boys, Paul Tanner came from Skunk Hollow, Kentucky. The family moved to Wilmington, Delaware, where his dad was superintendent of a state reformatory for boys. Aided by a few trombone playing inmates, Paul Tanner mastered the trombone by the time he completed high school. He otherwise moved very slowly. Glenn facetiously named him Lightnin'. Paul had been playing part-time with Marty Caruso's band after short innings with Frank Dailey's famed Meadowbrook Ballroom band in New Jersey.

"The guys in Caruso's band liked my playing, so they chipped in and hired me for $15.00 a week out of their own pocket. I was ambitious, but pretty scared. When I finally got up the nerve to talk to Glenn that night, I stammered like mad.

"I said: 'If you like my p-playing, would you give me a recommendation?' But, he had other ideas for me, saying, ' How soon can you pack up and go with me and my band?' And I said, 'This is all I've got,' pointing to my trombone. 'I'm ready right now.' And so I went with the band. It lasted four glorious years that moved me to say one day, that when I was with the Glenn Miller Orchestra, every night was like New Year's Eve."

An accomplished upper register player when Paul first joined the band, Glenn decided to assign him only lower register parts because he wanted more of an all-around player rather than a specialist. Paul Tanner listened to Glenn who turned out to be right."

In an interview with L.A. Jazz Scene Magazine writer John Tumpak, Paul Tanner explained: "One of the first things I learned about Glenn was that he was willing to work brutally hard to achieve perfection. He was an extremely knowledgeable musician, an astute businessman, a great organizer, a chronic workaholic, and extremely patriotic.

June Allyson with Paul

He made me an even better player. And, he was a very fine and underrated trombone player himself.

"He had good tone, a respectable upper range, and was very consistent. He could also arrange and was a very good editor. I remember him spending hours on an entire score to achieve the sound standard he wanted. A good example is how he rewrote Joe Garland's 'In the Mood' to turn it into a huge hit. And take ' Slip Horn Jive' for example. It was he and I playing the trombone solos. If there were problems in the saxophone section, something Glenn didn't understand about brass, he would simply rearrange the chart, but, if there was a note missed on a trombone, he understood and tolerated that. He understood if you missed a note, but if you came in wrong, he didn't understand that, and guys were fired for too much of that. When it came to reed problems on other brass, he never understood that, either. To Glenn there was mistakes, and there were mistakes.

At Carnegie Hall on October 6, 1939, Paul remembers the band being a little tense. It was a place they had always heard about. For all of them in the band, it was extremely prestigious to be invited to appear on the revered stage, which musicians of the time regarded with great awe.

"Jerry Gray wrote the arrangement of 'Tuxedo Junction.' Glenn was a very smart musician and he always seemed to know exactly what he wanted. There was never any communication problem unless someone tried to cross him. Then you were off to the guillotine. As far as explaining things musically, this was never a problem. Speaking about how the band would advance, listen to something as simple as 'Tuxedo Junction.' If I remember it right, we took the arrangement that was given to us, then we rehearsed all night long, like six or seven hours, just to put that thing finally into shape."

"Those great recordings that the orchestra performed was headed by one man, Glenn Miller! He was the head man, and nothing went on that he didn't O.K. He ran the whole thing and that was that. Maybe that's why it all worked so well and has lasted so long. There was only one leader and it was not a case of too many cooks, if you know what I mean!

"I learned a lot from Glenn's playing and so did the other fellows. But, Glenn cut back his playing because he didn't want to be compared to Tommy and feel competitive. It was easier to cut back and let the guys in the band do their job."

According to Paul, after "Chattanooga," the band was swinging more for several reasons. One, Glenn wasn't quite so worried about money like he was before his great success. Glenn became more relaxed:

Paul Tanner: "And, very frankly, we all knew that we were going into the service. It wasn't like today when kids don't know, and they have it hanging over them. We all knew. There was no question. If you could walk around, you were going in. We lost the fear of losing our jobs, and so the band started to swing more, and it was a beautiful thing. Some of the very latest records that we made actually swing much more than the band that was on the way to becoming so famous. So, eight days after 'Chattanooga,' we recorded a great swinging version of 'Don't Sit Under the Apple Tree.'"

At the Hotel Pennsylvania, Paul tells about the afternoon shows for teenagers in the Cafe Rouge. The people were charged twenty-five to get in. The kids would just sit down and milk a coke or perhaps dance. Glenn was happy to support the special attention during those appearances, but the waiters were not happy. Glenn would give away one radio-phonograph, along with a stack of records, to a military base, and apparently not just Glenn Miller records. And, Paul went on, "Glenn paid for the prize out of his own pocket."

Big Band Jump Newsletter once asked Paul Tanner if he thought the ability to play music is principally genetic. "As a music professor, I've heard that often, but I am not convinced of it because there were six brothers in our family, three of them were able to play professionally and three couldn't. The three that played professionally practiced a lot. It's a situation of a work ethic, and we got nothing but encouragement at home, but I think a couple of the brothers who didn't play professionally wanted to start at the top and didn't want to build up muscles and all that sort of thing, but I don't know if genes have anything to do with it."

When Glenn's band played their last performance on September 27, 1942, at the Central Theater in Passaic, New Jersey, just before Glenn joined the U.S. Army to organize a military big band, the mood was weepy. Marion Hutton choked up and had to leave the stage. The Modernaires could not complete their number, and some kids in the crowd were actually sobbing. Realizing the futility of continuing, Glenn had the curtain brought down. Said Paul, "It was the end of an era."

Paul Tanner filled the years following playing with Charlie Spivak, and spent some time in the Army, working G.I. radio shows, films, and playing trombone on those big band wartime "V" discs, recorded exclusively for the troops entertainment in war zones overseas. After the war he played for a while with Les Brown's Band, eventually reuniting with fellow Miller alumni Tex Beneke and his band for six additional, happy years. The University of California at Los Angeles drew Paul Tanner into its fold and within seven years his BA degree earned him a teaching position as Professor of Music. Over the years he obtained his Masters and PhD. degrees. After teaching music to over seventy-five thousand students, writing 20 books on music theory and the trombone, and traveling as trombone soloist with the UCLA Concert Band in the off times, Paul Tanner retired from it all in 1981, after quite a marvelous musical life. When he retired, his students showcased a rare, but sizable party at the college that included an appearance of the entire Tex Beneke big band and some familiar Glenn Miller alumnus and friends.

Paul Tanner has performed as a side man with Henry Mancini, Nelson Riddle, Neal Hefti, and Pete Rugolo, and in 1975 was a founder of the World Jazz Association.

Today, Paul Tanner regularly hits the cruise ship circuit, along with performers like the perennial Beryl Davis, another alumni of the great, world famous Glenn Miller Orchestra.

Always a trombone player first, Paul Tanner is a much loved gracious professor, second. And, for the record, Paul's favorite Glenn Miller tunes were their version of "Rhapsody in Blue," "Serenade in Blue," and "Spring Will Be a Little Late This Year."

"Richard, those are the kind of tunes I prefer."

Glenn Miller's Trombone Section: L-R Paul Tanner, Jimmy Priddy, Frank D'Anolfo, and Glenn Miller

IT'S MAKE BELIEVE BALLROOM TIME

Put all your cares away.

All The Bands Are Here To Bring Good Cheer Your Way with Margaret Whiting, Billy Eckstine, Dizzy Gillespie and William B. Williams. When Long Island's Westbury Music Fair announced that veteran radio disk jockey, William B. Williams, who hosted WNEW's quintessential music radio show, The Make Believe Ballroom, was going to emcee a nos-

talgic one-nighter with singers Billy Eckstine, Margaret Whiting, and the exciting Glenn Miller Orchestra with Larry O'Brien, I promptly called William B., as he was affectionately known, at the Third Avenue studio and suggested a feature interview with cast and guests backstage just before the show for Long Island P.M. Magazine. He liked the idea and after clearing it with Westbury co-owner Lee Guber we organized our interview cards and packed up our camera.

William B. had carried the torch some 30 years for the show, the keystone of the station's early success and once hosted by legendary radio salesman Martin Block. In-between, Jerry Marshall grabbed the helm in 1954 and William B. took over in 1963.

So, on November 5, 1983, photographer Camille Smith and I headed West from the hamlet of St. James on old Route 25A to the beautiful, in-the-round, 2,800 seat theater originally built on Westbury's Brush Hollow Road as a summer stock tent in 1956, thirty feet below ground level. It was converted to a permanent building in 1966 with comedian Jack Benny and Wayne Newton as headliners.

William B. was a genuine institution. I greatly admired his ability behind the microphone, and his intimate knowledge of the music business. He was a confidant and trusted friend of Frank Sinatra, and was responsible for creating the Sinatra sobriquet, Chairman of the Board . William B. or Willie B., as he liked being called, signed on every day at 10 A.M. with the droll greeting, "Hello World!". He was a professional in every sense of the word, admired and respected by the entire industry. WNEW, New York, was the flagship station for the Big Band Era and concurrently the musical home of Bing Crosby, Perry Como, Mel Torme, Nat "King" Cole, Tony Bennett, Kay Starr, the Andrews Sisters, Lena Horne, Ella Fitzgerald, and others in the same genre.

Richard with William B. Williams

William B. personally knew all the performers whose recordings he played on the show. They would frequently visit with him and exchange topics of the day while he was on the air spinning their recordings.

"Bill, I know you enjoy doing the show, but how do you keep the patter going day after day and keep it fresh, interesting and lively?" William B. was backstage with his son, Jeff, a pleasant young man all of 18 who was just visiting his dad at the theater.

"I think if somebody awakened me out of a truly deep sleep at 3 in the morning and put an on-air sign in front of me, I'd probably start talking automatically," drawled William B.

"There's a beauty to radio, in that the imagination comes into play. If I put on an old Miller, Sinatra, or Artie Shaw recording, people can close their eyes and take themselves back to a time when they first heard that recording. There is great therapy involved in getting out of stressful situations by listening to music associated with nicer days." He articulates beautifully.

"The show was Westbury co-owner Lee Guber's idea, "he went on, "wanting to bring the show live to its thousands of fans. He felt they would make a good audience for the Big Bands and the singers--like Billy (Eckstine) and Margaret (Whiting)." William B. retained an impressive appearance with his silvery hair, good looks, and great stage presence.

We stepped into the rear dressing room where he introduced me to Billy Eckstine, one of those heroes I was telling you about whom I've admired over the years with his definitive renditions of "Caravan," "I

Apologize," and "Everything I have Is Yours." But a little-known Eckstine ballad that I favored over all the others, entitled, "Sitting By The Window," was a wonderfully sad song that tugged at you, especially if you were a young man in love. I recalled it to Billy:

"The truth is, I was handed a lead sheet by a cabby one night after a show at the Copa. I figured it would be one of those June, moon, spoon things I would end up tossing, but I was wrong. An amateur wrote it and I ended up recording it and it went on to become a hit song for me. Haven't heard it much in the last thirty years." It was an Eckstine natural. It's now 1995 and I still can't locate a copy of it except for the sheet music.

While "B.", (William B. simply called Eckstine 'B') and William B., were recording and shooting the scene, jazzman John Birks "Dizzy" Gillespie ambled in to the surprise of everyone. He and Eckstine, of course, played together and were actually weaned in the Earl Hines Band of the early 40's, and later in "B's" own, short-lived band with fellow musicians Budd Johnson, Miles Davis, Charlie 'Yardbird" Parker, Art Blakey, Fats Navarro and Gene Ammons. That conglomeration of talent was directly responsible for the birth of Be-Bop, the forerunner of what's now referred to as modern, cool jazz.

"Well, well ! It's the infamous John Birks Gillespie, wanted in 50 states." declared Wm. B. in those syrupy tones.

"And they haven't caught up to me yet." Dizzy retorted, laughing deeply and simultaneously greeting one and all, then flopping down on a convenient couch, nesting his overcoat and fedora over the top as though he came to stay.

"B, what about that thing you were telling me about... something about a rock-and-roll wife." Wm.B. was plying Eckstine.

"Oh, yeah!. I did one take on a thing called ' Condemned to Life With a Rock and Roll Wife' and, John, "he recalled to Diz, "my momma wouldn't even buy it." Laughing,Gillespie almost fell off the couch.   Mr. B. and Dizzy began swapping old buddy war stories. There was one about a girl Dizzy met in New Orleans at the King Of The Zulu's Parade, who said she came from a little town called Waycross, Georgia, and tantalizingly said to Dizzy: "Don't you remember me?" flaunting herself. "When I hear about any kind of happening's in Waycross, Georgia, and girls are mentioned, man, I know that's a line, "interrupted my photographer Camille Smith with some authority, unable to ignore what he was hearing.

"Then you don't know what you're talkin' about." Mr. B. growled back at Smith.

"We were there many times. Isn't that right, John?" he said, looking at Dizzy. (Very few called Dizzy, John.) Then all three set to loudly challenging one another, contesting each others half-truths and bravados, and boasting of youthful deeds now recalled to discussion by aging comrades. The laughter became contagious and William B. and I could not help but share their joy. I wished I could've grasped their special language, but it was impossible.

There was something going on here that defied definition. Camille understood it all right, but later could not impart a clue of it into my northern brain. It was indeed rhetoric articulated by three mature black men, in a few spontaneous moments, that I failed to interpret. Here were two absolutely genuine icons of the jazz age, whose mark on music history is surely written in stone, simply being themselves.

Before our session was over, I asked Dizzy to recount his infamous bent trumpet story:

"Well, it was the result of an accident with an earlier trumpet. I threw a party for my wife back in the early 1950's and when I laid the trumpet down to get somethin' to eat, someone had stepped on it and bent it 90 degrees up. I didn't get too upset, though. (now B was laughing). It was a revelation of a sort. When I played it, I found that shape allowed the sound to reach my ear more quickly than before. It offered a better awareness of where the beat was, so now I bend all my trumpets." (Dizzy's trumpets are made custom for him with the upswept bell.) He put his finger to his lips and blew out his cheeks, then collapsed in laughter. "That's my other trademark!"

Dizzy is so well respected in the industry, (he even garnered one of those Kennedy Center, Presidential medals the same night Katherine Hepburn received hers.) mostly for his humanity, but also for his excellent skill and vision. Buddy Rich once told me he was Dizzy's number one fan:

"When you are as great as Diz---you're never satisfied with your playing. You try to improve upon it all the time. That's what makes him the greatest jazz trumpet in music. Like an architect you build and extend your work--that's what Diz means---you keep creating-- - you never stop."

MARGARET WHITING

The dressing rooms became gradually crowded the way they always do at such gatherings with well-wishers and staff , so Camille and I wandered out and across the corridor and into my favorite singer's dressing room and caught her primping in the mirror while trying on strings of pearls: "Hi Maggie," I said, to Margaret Whiting, "You look great! I am always pleased to see you." I said to a solid kiss on the cheek.

Margaret's 1948 recording of "A Tree In the Meadow" was one of the longest running song hits played on the Make Believe Ballroom. She was only a teenager when she recorded it, and I was only a teenager when I played it to death on my new Admiral three-speed radio-phonograph. She sings lyrics like she believes every word, as Frank Sinatra does. That's her success.

"Are you re-creating some of the great songs you've recorded on the show tonight?"

"Oh, Yes! I just came in from Midland, Texas, to do this show for Willie B., whom I love. I will do some of my father's songs---- 'My Ideal,' and 'Till We Meet Again,' and some songs from my new album, *Speak Low*, and I am also doing 'Moonlight In Vermont.'" (a song that placed high on the all-time WNEW public poll taken in 1986.) Maggie Whiting, daughter of Richard Whiting, the great song writer, grew up in a house where world-famous people like Al Jolson, Johnny Mercer, Judy Garland, Eddie Cantor, George Ger-

Margaret Whiting

shwin, Harold Arlen, and Jerome Kern were regular Saturday afternoon visitors.

"Growing up, I never knew anyone who wasn't famous," she recalled. Johnny Mercer, who was a close friend of her dad's, encouraged her and helped her make her first recording at Capitol Records. When her father died in 1938, Johnny Mercer became a sort of surrogate father to the very young Margaret. Under Johnny Mercer's guidance, she began recording and her first big hit was "That Old Black Magic" in 1942.

"But, what's going on here?" I asked."Isn't our music supposed to be dead? Isn't rock and roll today's message?"

"It's a resurgence, we are enjoying a resurgence." she replied, when I was touring for the last five years with 4 Girls 4, (an act with vocalists Helen O'Connell, Fran Warren, and Kay Starr) everyone was starving for our kind of music and we always sold out. People could have a choice. We could have gone on forever." At one point Rosemary Clooney and Rosemarie were members of that troupe. "We just got tired of all that traveling all those years."

Margaret and I have exchanged many letters and notes over the years. I always send copies of articles I've written where she is a subject, (like the Bob Hope USO tours which I often write about and in which she regularly participates or is mentioned,) or it may be a congratulatory note when she appears in Manhattan at the Algonquin Oak Room, Michael's Pub, or Freddy's Supper Club.

I held back the entrance runway curtain for Margaret when she was cued onstage and watched her perform for the faithful.

I was to work once again with William B. Williams a year after this occasion in 1984 doing the same gig but this time with my friend, Frankie Laine; perky, frisky, Helen O'Connell, and teddy bear, Buddy Morrow who was leading the Tommy Dorsey ghost band . William B. was already beginning to feel the pain cancer began dealing him.

After William B. passed on in 1986, I received this note from Maggie: "...remember our meeting at West-bury a few seasons ago with William B.? God, I miss him---as a friend---but, most of all, I miss him on the air. WNEW just isn't the same any more. I know they're trying,

Richard and Margaret at Westbury Music Fair - 1984

but when Willie died and they let Bob Jones and Jim Lowe go, the whole kind of programming they used to do is just gone. "It got worse. WNEW. went off the air December 2, 1992. The great voice was stilled.

In August of 2006, Margaret Whiting and I got back together at an annual Al Jolson event. I had called her because Jan Hernstat , President of The International Al Jolson Society, want-ed to present her with copies of the radio broadcasts she per-formed with Al Jolson that she hadn't heard since the 1940s.

21 Years Later Richard and Margaret Whiting - 2005 - Jolson Festival
Photo Madeline Grudens

I proudly in-troduced Margaret to an appreciative crowd. Our bond was kept clearly intact all these years. Margaret Whiting is truly one of the best voices of the Big Band Era and beyond.

THE VOCALISTS

BRAD PHILLIPS
WINS
SMARTY PANTS PATCH
PARTY

RECENT BIG PROMOTION between WINS' Brad Phillips and name singers brought a flock of stars to the Castleholm restaurant in Manhattan to be briefed on the tie-ins for the *Singing Battle Royal* of which Brad is moderator. L. to r. are Alan Dean, Tommy Edwards, Gene Williams, Johnny Hartman, Dick Haymes, Brad Phillips, Eddie Fisher, Danny Winchell, Stuart Foster, Richard Hayes, Steve Lawrence, Danny Davis, Tony Bennett, Johnny Parker, Art Lund, Larry Douglas, Ricky Vallo, Al Martino, Rusty Draper, Danny Sutton and Jimmy Saunders.

When you hear a real hep-cat
Take a chorus in A flat,
That's the rhythm on the river,
You know what that means,
He comes from New Orleans!

BING CROSBY
"Hey Jolson, Its Me"

It is accepted in the world of music and elsewhere that prolific crooner Bing Crosby was the very first Big Band male vocalist. Similarly, Mildred Bailey is widely recognized as the very first Big Band female voice . And, as Mildred's husband, Red Norvo, once testified to me,earlier innovators Bessie Smith and Ethel Waters influenced her career. Fittingly, Bing acknowledges his obligation to dynamic pre-Big Band song-belter, and easily the World's Greatest Entertainer, Al Jolson.

Bing Crosby's singing methods juxtaposed Jolson's except that Crosby embraced the new-fangled electric microphone, directly and confidentially delivering his rich baritone voice into this new contraption, whereas Jolson's larynx was the only microphone he knew. Both were productive singers, Jolson beginning as an interpreter of Minstrel songs a la Stephen Foster style of the time and Crosby first recorded with Columbia singing selections "I'm Comin' Virginia" (arranged by the great Bill Challis), "Side by Side," "My Blue Heaven," and other pseudo-jazz softies with Paul Whiteman's Orchestra.

Harry Lillis "Bing" Crosby came to light in Tacoma, Washington, on May 3, 1903. Some, including Bing himself, always thought he was born on May 2, 1904 (because of lost records), but Ken Twiss (late President of the former Bing Crosby Historical Society), myself, and many other Crosby aficionados have since unmistakably proven to the world Bing's correct and verified birth date of May 3, 1903.

Bing was first a drummer. Yes, a drummer! I witnessed Bing's drumming in the 1940 film Rhythm on the River. He tapped drum and cymbal rhythmically to the title song while vocalizing and marching around a pawn shop with a few other musicians including Wingy Manone and Harry Barris:

> When you hear a real hep-cat
> Take a chorus in A flat,
> That's the rhythm on the river,
> You know what that means,
> He comes from New Orleans!

The sobriquet "Bing" was acquired from a comic strip called the Bingville Bugle which he enjoyed so much and was likened to as a child of seven. In school he enjoyed the art of diction and phrasing, techniques he mastered in elocution contests. A busy and hard working kid, Bing

Crosby's happiest job was as a prop assistant in the Auditorium, Spokane's big opera house. It's here his favorite singer, Al Jolson, performed while touring in the Broadway shows Sinbad and Bombo.

"Later, when I got to know and work with Al, he didn't remember me, the lop-eared lad named Crosby who watched his every move, but I remembered him vividly," Bing recalled in his 1953 autobiography, Call Me Lucky, "You could never forget Al Jolson. He was absolutely electric! When he stepped onto the stage and started to sing, young and old were immediately captured by him. He was irresistible."

Crosby organized a quartet who joined a band called the Juicy Seven, playing drums and singing. While a student at Gonzaga University he ran away, hitchhiking to California, but was driven back by hunger, not unlike his hero, Al Jolson. Returning to school, he nervously sang his first solo, "For Me and My Gal," with the band. Al Rinker, singer Mildred (Rinker) Bailey's brother, invited Bing to join in his band. He was excited by Bing's drum playing and vocal ability. The group was called the Musicaladers. They began playing at high school dances. When singing "For Me and My Gal" with the aid of a megaphone, he started his signature "ba-boo-ing" when he forgot some words. Bing once told his mother that he'd rather sing than eat.

After a few local restaurant gigs, Mildred invited her brother and Bing to come to Los Angeles to try their luck performing in speakeasies. It was Crosby and Rinker, two boys with a piano playing first at the Lafayette Cafe in Sacramento with Al at the piano and Bing scat singing while tapping a cymbal. In April 1926, the boys were hired to sing at the Metropolitan Theater in a variety show at sixty-five dollars each weekly. Variety dubbed them a success in an unsuccessful show. The amiable, easy-going Bing was a hit.

In 1926 Bing Crosby and Al Rinker began unleashing jazz rhythms into their act with enthusiasm and tricky harmonies. Then, the big break: Paul Whiteman and his King of Jazz orchestra arrived in LA. His emissaries were sent to evaluate their act. The audition earned them a contract at $ 150 a week for five years.

In Chicago: "I want to introduce two young fellas who have joined our band," Whiteman declared from center stage, "I picked them up

A Letter From Kathryn Crosby - *Something Special About Bing*

Dear Richard,

I have nothing of moment to add about Bing. As usual you've hit the nail on the head about him, and I'm just an observer, without your research or expertise.

But now that I think of it, I might mention one small thing of which only a member of Bing's immediate family might be aware: He sang all day long -- snatches of opera, foreign favorites, the latest rock numbers, even medleys of radio commercials.

At our home in Las Cruces, Baja California, Bing woke his friend Dr. Sullivan one morning with a fortissimo rendition of YOU CAN TRUST YOUR CAR TO THE MAN WHO WEARS THE STAR.

"If you want to appoint me your agent," Sullivan mused, "I'll bet I can get you some bread for that sort of work."

"Oh, I dunno, Bill," the assassin of sleep replied. "I hear they got their own fella."

And off he strode into the dawn, roaring out TOREADOR EN GARDE...

And how I miss him! And what I'd give to hear him saluting the sunrise with CIELITO LINDO just one more time!

Best Wishes,
Kathryn Crosby

Kathryn Grandstaff Crosby is a fine person and a singer in her own right. If you manage to find yourself a copy of Bing and Other Things, a book she authored in 1967, depicting her life before and after her marriage to Bing, you will get to know her a little and discover her unique qualities and understand why Bing became a lucky, happier and wiser man the day he married her in 1957. An actress, registered nurse, wife, mother, she was also a teacher, a dress designer model, and an author. She remembers Bing's first words to her, "Howdy, Tex," he drawled, "What's your rush?" She was hurrying a load of petticoats to Paramount's wardrobe department.

Twenty short years later, after a wonder life with Bing and their three children, Harry, Nathaniel, and Mary Frances, she, and we, lost Bing.

In her second book, *My Life With Bing*, Kathryn fervently noted: "His music lives, his films live, the gentle humor that he displayed is a touching living wondrous thing. His eyes will never dim and his beauty will never diminish."...

Early Bing

in an ice cream parlor in a little town called Walla Walla, and I brought them to you. They were too good for Walla Walla. Meet----Crosby and Rinker." They were simply excellent, and like the early fledgling Jolson, encores were demanded from the crowd. In New York, at the Paramount in 1927, they added Harry Barris to the act at the suggestion of Matty Malneck, a songwriter and Whiteman reed musician. Later, the trio performed twice a day for a year without Whiteman (who went touring in England) on the Keith-Albee-Orpheum vaudeville circuit. They partied excessively and got into some minor trouble with the law along the way. When Whiteman returned, they all went to Hollywood and made the film The King of Jazz. Bing, Harry, and Al, the Rhythm Boys, sang the landmark number "So the Bluebirds and the Blackbirds Got Together" (including a Bing solo), "A Bench in the Park" and "Happy Feet" with the Brox Sisters. Crosby earnings climbed to $ 400.00 a week working for Whiteman at the Cocoanut Grove nightclub. It was there Bing met his future wife, Dixie Lee.

Guitarist Eddie Lang and jazz violinist Joe Venuti joined with Whiteman and became close friends with Bing. After leaving the Whiteman organization, the Rhythm Boys reformed and successfully plied their act at the Montmarte Cafe. In-between gigs Bing acquired small parts in movie shorts. His good looks and geniality won over many new fans. Shortly thereafter, Bing recorded "I Surrender, Dear", his first hit in a Sennett film followed closely by "Just One More Chance," a Brunswick label solo, which led to a CBS radio contract. And, notably for the newly independent trio, they recorded Harry Warren's "Three Little Words" with Duke Ellington and his famous Cotton Club Orchestra.

On November 23, 1931, Bing

L to R: Al Rinker, Bing Crosby and Harry Barris

Louis Armstrong and Bing Crosby

recorded his lovely gem," Where the Blue of the Night Meets the Gold of the Day," his lifetime signature vocal, which he co-wrote.

Bing Crosby was now busy climbing music's golden ladder. By 1946, Bing had evolved as America's most important crooner, to be later followed by his emulators Frank Sinatra, Perry Como, Frankie Laine, Tony Bennett, Pat Boone, Jerry Vale and Dean Martin who all did pretty well.

Along the way Bing amassed a long list of sturdy standards: 'I Surrender Dear," "Please," "I Found a Million Dollar Baby," "Melancholy Baby," "Pennies from Heaven," "I'm Through with Love," "Sweet and Lovely," "June in January," "I've Got the World on a String," "Sweet Leilani," and in 1942, Irving Berlin's now world-famous standard, "White Christmas" the landmark Crosby recording. Of course, there were hundreds of hits. What's your favorite? I've listened to those Crosby recordings for an entire lifetime. They satisfy. That's why my personal encounter with Bing Crosby at NBC's New York studios in 1952 left me so breathless. I was just a kid in an NBC Studio Page uniform, but I realized the existence of his musical legacy even then.

After careful consideration, I determined my favorite Crosby film song to be Cole Porter's anti rock-and-roll song "Now You Has Jazz," performed with Louis Armstrong and his All-Stars in the acclaimed film High Society. A mature, jazz oriented Bing loosely flings his arms and breezes through this hip tune supported by Satchmo and his great musicians which included my friend Arvell Shaw, Louis' longtime bass player. Louis and Bing genuinely liked one another, another reason the song was performed so well.

My favorite Crosby singles in no particular order are "Shine," with the Mills Brothers; the 1932 version of "Please," "South America - Take It Away," with my pal Patty Andrews and her sisters; and "Swinging on a Star" from the film Going My Way. Of the roughly 657,000 hours I've been on this earth, I calculate 25,725 combined hours have been logged listening to Bing Crosby.

Bing performed in many films beyond all those early Mack Sennett shorts. First, a starring role in The Big Broadcast; then Going Hollywood; Mississippi; Rhythm on the Range; Pennies from Heaven, Waikiki Wedding; Rhythm on the River; all those seven wonderful Road pictures with my friend Bob Hope and sarong-sporting Dorothy Lamour. We cannot forget Holiday Inn ; Going My Way (his Academy Award Best Actor winning role); The Bells of St. Mary's; Blue Skies; Welcome Stranger (I loved that charming film in which Bing sings "My Heart Is a Hobo" to Barry Fitzgerald); Riding High; Little Boy Lost; and White Christmas with Rosemary Clooney and Danny Kaye. And, of course, High Society with Grace Kelly, Frank Sinatra, and you know who. Bing told disk jock Jack Ellsworth in 1976 that his own personal favorites were "My Isle of Golden Dreams" and "There's a Cabin in the Pines."

Bing Crosby recorded mostly in the morning and usually in one take, according to Patty Andrews, because, as she explained to me: "Bing

Bing and the Andrews Sisters

believed his voice possessed a husky quality early in the morning--- on an empty stomach. I guess he used to vocalize in the car on the way to the studio," she revealed, "and he always wore his golf clothes." Bing was an avid fisherman, hunter, golfer, and baseball fan. (Bing owned 20% of the Pittsburgh Pirates in 1947 and 10% of the Los Angeles Rams Football team in 1949).

Would there have been a Crosby without an earlier Jolson? Jolson was the very first pop singer, but too early for the Big Band Era, although he was the catalyst for it and all future singing. Did he pave the road for Crosby's successful journey? Scholars of the genre' say yes! Bing, himself, says yes! I absolutely agree!

Would there have been a Sinatra without a Crosby? Hard to say. According to Sinatra: "Crosby was my hero, the father of my career." Frankie Laine told me he consciously imitated Bing perfectly during Frank's marathon dancing days, and Tony Bennett admitted to me he was influenced "by Bing's casual way with a ballad. He enhanced my interest in singing." Pat Boone and Dean Martin have acknowledged they copied Bing's style too, as did Elvis with "Love Me Tender" and "Can't Help Falling in Love with You." Then, to conclude, Jolson and Crosby combined were indeed the foundation of popular singing.

The song production combination of Al Jolson and Bing Crosby cannot be overstated. Both voices will surely be heard far into the 21st century when the world may be listening to God knows what kind of music.

Bing: "Al, you are indefatigable. If I'd let you, you'd sing all night."

Al: "You're no slouch, Bing. Never seen you nappin' over a song, you dog!"

Decca's Al Kapp, Rehearsing Al Jolson and Bing Crosby

FRANK SINATRA
Secrets of the Chairman

For over half a century Frank Sinatra sang his heart out while the world listened. In my diligent search for the most prolific recording artist of our lifetime, I turned every stone but could not make the needed connection. I turned to Susan Reynolds of Scoop Marketing in Los Angeles who represented Frank Sinatra in those days. Regretfully, Susan was duty-bound to deny us the access we coveted, although she honestly tried.vv

At the time, Frank was on a kind of health-hiatus, and, realizing no book about singers is much of a book without him, we proceeded without the benefit of a direct interview. Instead, we talked to those who knew and worked with him over the years, thus compiling a composite of anecdotes and facts from previous interviews and declarations.

Almost everyone knows the Frank Sinatra story. Presented on film and a subject

with Harry James

of many books authorized and unauthorized, Frank's turbulent life has been a virtual open book. My friend, best-known and best-loved disc jockey William B. Williams, long time host of the Make Believe Ballroom radio program on New York's WNEW, was a great friend of Frank Sinatra. It was William B. (as he was affectionately known) who coined the Sinatra sobriquet Chairman of the Board, which Frank, himself admitted he always tried to live up to. In 1984, William B., who consistently said, "I don't care how a record sells, just how it sounds," held a rare interview with Frank, and sent me a treasured copy of the tape which began:

Hello, World! This is William B. and I'd like to introduce you to Francis Albert Sinatra, a practically unknown singer. Say something, Francis. Don't be shy!"

"Hello, (he chuckles) World, this is Francis Albert Sinatra. You know, Willy B., about 40 years ago I started at WNEW, and do you know what I got paid - - zilch-- but ---they gave me thirty-five cents in carfare to get back to New Jersey. Well, I'm back again for those of you who ever wondered what happened to me. I know they're still paying the same kind of bread which may explain why William B. has been able to keep his job here."

A little before that, in 1935, a guy named Major Bowes hosted a show called The Amateur Hour where many talented performers got their start. One night the Major introduced a new group:

"Good evening friends, we start the dizzy spin of the wheel of fortune - around and round she goes and where she stops nobody knows," he said in his gravely eloquence, "Now, first four youngsters in kinda nice suits - The Hoboken Four. They seem so happy, I guess, and they seem to make everybody else happy (gentle laughter from the audience). Tell me, where do you work in Hoboken?"

"I'm Frank, Major. We're looking for jobs. How about it! (more appreciative laughter from the audience to Frank's charming boldness) everyone that's ever heard us - liked us. We think we're pretty good."

"All right, what do you want to sing -or dance - or whatever it is you do?"

"We're gonna sing 'Shine' and then we're gonna dance."

"All right! Let's have it!", the Major announced, "... here's The Hoboken Four." They closely emulated a Bing Crosby-Mills Brothers version of the then popular song.

It was a very slim-looking Frank Sinatra's first public appearance into the world of performing that would last some 62 musically eventful years. The Hoboken Four toured with the Amateur Hour Show, earning seventy-five dollars a week.

Frank Sinatra at Capitol Records

"We were getting paid, we were no longer amateurs," said Frank.

Let's jump ahead some 10 years to 1945 where and when some things have changed. Frank was singing to thousands of screaming bobby soxers at New York's Paramount Theater with the great bands of Harry James and, later, Tommy Dorsey. Were you one of those screaming youngsters?

In 1981, while interviewing Johnny Mince, Tommy Dorsey's clarinet player, he talked about first seeing Sinatra: "We were ready to go on a one-nighter, and Tommy says, 'C-mere John.' He took me across the street - and they had it on the jukebox- that thing he did with Harry James -" All or Nothing at All." I say, 'Boy this guy is good!' his voice rising. But my first impression meeting Frank... he was such a skinny, beat-up looking guy, compared to Jack Leonard (the singer who just left) who had lots of class and was good-looking. Of course, Frank sure turned out to be a great one."

During my interview with Harry James in 1981, he said exactly this: "At that time Frank considered himself the greatest vocalist in the business. Get that! No one ever heard of him. He never had a hit record. He looks like a wet rag. But he tells me he's the greatest. He believed. And you know what, he was right." Shortly, even after Tommy Dorsey, Frank was now out on his own as a single and the

with Nat King Cole and Jack Benny

screams and carrying on continued wherever he appeared. "Time after time, I tell myself that I'm so lucky to be loving you..." Frank's way of embracing a microphone, with a new approach to putting over a song, completely won over a fast-growing female audience. He copied Bing Crosby and he absorbed Billie Holiday's way of bending a tune.

With both Harry James and Tommy Dorsey, Frank was the boy singer and Connie Haines was the girl singer; "I was just eighteen, and I remember the police escorting Frank

with Connie Haines

and me across the street from the Paramount Theater over to the Astor Hotel, through the lobby into the drugstore just to get a hamburger, "Connie and I have frequent conversations about the "history of our kind of music," as she succinctly sets it. "We could not get away from the screaming kids even to eat." Connie remembered some early enthusiasm three years before when they both sang with Harry James. "Richard, it was something about the way he'd hang on to that microphone. Something in his singing that reached out to the audience - like he was saying, 'I'm giving this to you with everything I've got; what have you got to give me?' I guess they came backstage afterwards to tell him.

"Frank and I didn't always get along in those days, but Frank showed his true colors one night - even though we were feuding while we sang songs like 'Let's Get Away from It All,' ' Oh, Look at Me Now,' and

'Snootie Little Cutie' - when my dress caught fire because someone had tossed a lit cigarette down from the balcony and it got snared in my dress netting. Tommy was still vamping, not aware of what was happening. Frank reacted quickly, throwing his suit jacket over me and flinging me to the ground, snuffing out the flames - probably saving my life."

When Sinatra joined up with Tommy Dorsey, Jo Stafford was the lead, and only female singer of the Pied Pipers singing group: "Frank made a special effort to get a good blend with the Pipers. Most solo singers usually don't fit too well into a group, but Frank never stopped working at it and, of course, as you know, he blended beautifully with us. He was meticulous about his phrasing and dynamics. He worked very hard so that his vibrato would match ours. And he was always conscientious about learning his parts. The first song I ever heard him sing was 'Stardust.' I thought, wow, this guy is destined for great success as a singer."

Gene Lees, in his book Singers and the Song, records Frank Sinatra as the best singer he had ever heard and one of the best singers in popular music history. "Sinatra learned breath control from Tommy Dorsey's technique of slowly and deliberately releasing air to support long lyrical melodic lines and was indeed instructive to Sinatra. Dorsey would use this control to tie the end of one phrase into the start of the next. Sinatra learned to do the same."

Sinatra's first recordings with Columbia Records exposed the public to a band singer who no longer sang songs to which you could only dance. Axel Stordahl from Tommy Dorsey days was his arranger, helped too, by George Siravo. Frank was just twenty-six and Stordahl about the same. They produced some classic Sinatra sides together, with music that had some imagination and gutty arrangements. Remember "Dream," "The Girl That I Marry," "Put Your Dreams Away," "Day by Day?"

At the close of the 1940's Frank Sinatra's career changed. He rebelled against Columbia's chief musical architect Mitch Miller, who was producing his own kind of music which bothered Sinatra and which he thought demeaned his skills as a singer.

Rosemary Clooney loved Frank Sinatra. Manie Sachs, A&R man at Columbia and later one of my friends at NBC, answered Sinatra's request for a girl singer by suggesting Rosemary. Frank said OK. "We did two sides of that first date together, but later on we did some other things. That first session was the thrill of my life because I had always been such a Sinatra fan. I loved him when I was in high school, and it was great working with him. He kept up the quality in every recording date."

By 1952, Frank Sinatra was without a movie contract, recording contract, or management. Because of those late 1940's forty-five to fifty shows a week, which meant 100 songs a day, the great voice tired, his personal life tumbling into a shambles. But, he promptly started on the road back to even greater success, propelled by his acting-only role in the movie From Here To Eternity, his move from Columbia to Johnny Mercer's Capitol Records, and his union with master arranger Nelson Riddle. Nelson taught Frank how to "swing." Their first album together was, what else, Swing Easy, followed by Songs for Young Lovers (Nelson and George Siravo) and In the Wee Small Hours of the Morning, literally restarting his career. He proceeded to record over twenty albums from 1953 to 1961, all hits. The songs: "Just One of Those Things," "My Funny Valentine," " A Foggy Day," "Last Night When We Were Young," "This Love of Mine," which he co-wote, "What Is This Thing Called Love?"

"I first met Frank Sinatra when he was with Tommy Dorsey," said Duke Ellington in 1973, "They all came down one night at the College Inn at the Sherman Hotel in Chicago where we were playing, about the time he was ready to split the Dorsey gig. I could tell that by the way Tommy said good night to him. He was young, crispy-crunch fresh, and the girls were squealing then. He was easy to get along with, and there were no hassles about his music. Every song he sings is understandable and, most of all, believable, which is the ultimate in theater. And I must repeat and emphasize my admiration for him as a nonconformist. When he played the Paramount the chicks were screaming. He was an individualist, nobody told him what to do or say."

Nancy Sinatra: "In 1961 my father asked Morris Ostin, who was with Verve Records, to head up his own label, Reprise," said daughter, Nancy. "It was very important for Dad to have his own recording company."

According to Frank himself, "I always like to choose my own songs

for an album.....to keep all the songs in the same genre'- swing, love songs, etc. Once I decide what type of music I want, I make up a list of song titles, and my associates - arrangers- suggest songs. When we actually get down to where arrangements have to be done, I go through the list again and pick out eight to ten songs and go with them. "The first Reprise selections: "A Foggy Day," "A Fine Romance," "Be Careful, It's My Heart."

When I talked with legend- ary jazz vibraphonist Red Norvo, he championed Frank as a great singer : "We worked together in Vegas and then at the Fon- tainebleau in Florida and also in Atlantic City. We also went to Australia. I was used to handling singers in my various bands (Red Norvo was married to the first regular Big Band girl singer Mildred Bailey), so Frank was never a problem to me. When we first worked together, I had a trio, which was too small, so I told him we needed a drummer and sax, and he said OK. We made a couple of movies: Kings Go Forth , where I wrote some of the music, and Oceans 11, a kinda funny movie where Frank plays a bank robber in Vegas. Our Capitol recordings of the late sixties are just being issued now. Heard they are number four on the charts. Isn't that sumthin'?"

Frank Sinatra continued his singing activities until he announced re- tirement in 1971. There were loud signals when Frank poured out albums like Cycles, A Man Alone, and the closer My Way , in the late sixties. He returned gradually doing some concerts into 1973 and producing an album, Old Blue Eyes Is Back, arranged by Gordon Jenkins and Don Costa. The songs: "Send in the Clowns," "You Will Be My Music." Frank toured trium- phantly with Woody Herman in 1974 and spawned the album The Main Event. The songs: "The Lady Is a Tramp," "I Get a Kick Out of You, "Au- tumn in New York," "My Kind of Town," and Sinatra's signature Paul Anka piece "My Way."

1975 produced a series of appearances at the Uris Theater in New York and then London with the great band of Count Basie which included the presence of the divine Sarah Vaughan.

In the eighties, Quincy Jones' talents became linked to Frank Sinatra's musical life, beginning with the album L.A. is My Lady. "Frank is remarkable. When we recorded at A & M's studios in New York, I called the orchestra for three hours before. We rehearsed and set the balance. Frank came in at seven o'clock and so help me God, at eight-twenty he went home We had done four songs."

The songs: "Stormy Weather," "How Do You Keep the Music Playing," "After You've Gone."

My favorite Sinatra recording is an early swinging gem, "Sweet Lorraine," a perfect blend of voice and instrument. It features jazz all-stars Nat "King" Cole on piano, Johnny Hodges on alto sax, Charlie Shavers on trumpet, Coleman Hawkins on tenor sax, and Eddie Safranki on bass. Amazing group. A perfect recording.

Frank Sinatra made many films, but didn't sing in all of them. We'll leave that for film writers to ponder.

Once, appearing with William B. Williams at WNEW on the Make Believe Ballroom Show, Frank had a speaking part: "Hi there, my name is Francis Albert Sinatra and I've got news for you. Here is your host, William B. Williams."

"Name dropper!" William B. answered tongue-in-cheek, "A question, Francis, that is somewhat philosophic. I know how keenly you feel about your family and your two granddaughters. The legacy that you leave them, is there any particular way you want to be remembered as a man...as a performer...as an American...as a human being?"

"Well, Willy, I realize it's a broad question, but I can narrow it by saying that I'd like to be remembered as a man who was as honest as he knew how to be in his life and as honest as he knew how to be in his work...and a man who gave as much energy in what he did every day as anybody else ever did. I'd like to be remembered as a decent father, as a fair husband, and as a great granddad...wonderful grandpop. And I'd like to be remembered as a good friend to my friends.

"I think the only addendum I would add is ...as a man who enjoyed."

"Ah! That's true. I didn't want to get into that because, you know, there's an old 14th century Spanish adage....'living well is the best revenge'...If that applied to anybody, it must apply to me." Frank Sinatra has always, and mostly anonymously, worked for the benefit of those in need. Helen O'Connell told me that Frank secretly paid all the medical bills for fellow singer Bob Eberly. It was also said they actually had never met.

William B. once told me about Frank's great work that gathered millions for Sloan-Kettering Memorial Cancer Hospital in New York. At the 67th Street outpatient entrance between York and 1st Avenues of that hospital there is a plaque on the wall that states This Wing of Sloan-Kettering is Through the Efforts of Frank Sinatra.

Frank and Barbara Sinatra also worked hard for Barbara Sinatra Children's Center at Eisenhower Center, Rancho Mirage, California. Profits from their book, The Sinatra Celebrity Cookbook by Barbara, Frank & Friends, supported that project.

DICK HAYMES
Keeping It Simple

When Helen Forrest and I wrapped up her chapter, "Voice of the Big Bands," featured in my book about all the girl singers, we promised one another to meet once again in honor of her favorite baritone and one time singing partner, Dick Haymes, recognized as one of the most potent baritones of all time, to prepare a suitable chapter about him for this book about the men singers, The Music Men. Helen's enthusiasm for the Song Stars book truly gratified me. "I loved the treatment of all the singers. Let's feature my friend Dick Haymes in your next book," she wrote, "I'll help you----and don't forget Don Cornell." We kept that promise on the afternoon of September 17, 1997.

Helen, recuperating from a nasty cold that had developed into a mild case of pneumonia, sipped on a tall glass of fresh orange juice while we exchanged pieces of substantive information about Dick Haymes' life and career.

Richard Benjamin Haymes arrived on Earth on a family-owned cattle ranch in Buenos Aires, Argentina , on September 13, 1918, and emigrated to the United States when he was two. He traveled throughout Europe with his mother, a famous musical-comedy soloist and singing teacher, and mining- engineer father (who hailed from Scotland). Dick lived in Europe for five years, speaking fluent French and Spanish. Attending Loyola College to be educated by Jesuit priests in Montreal, Canada, he again furthered his education in Switzerland. "This accounted for his cultured behavior, his gentlemanly bearing, and his obvious class," Helen said, "Dick Haymes was a man of class. No one would ever deny that fact."

Starting out as a songwriter with his brother Bob, Dick inadvertently wandered into singing after persuading the manager of a New Jersey summer resort to give him a job as the boy singer with the local band at the weekly pay of twenty-five dollars. Later, as a vocalist for Johnny Johnston, and later with Bunny Berigan, Dick eventually formed his own band he called The Katzenjammers.

Then Dick decided to hitchhike to New York to sell some of the songs he had written. He approached bandleader Harry James, who, it turned out, needed a singer more than a songwriter and, talk about good timing, hired Dick as the band's boy singer after hearing him demonstrate one of his songs at the Nola Studios where Harry was rehearsing. Frank Sinatra was about to leave the band, and Dick, walking in a long shadow, followed him into the bands of both Harry James and Tommy Dorsey. Dick's recording of "I'll Get By" was a best-seller with James, where he was hailed as a fine singer who, week by week, improved his phrasing, shading, intonation, and reputation. In May of 1942, Dick joined Benny Goodman where he scored once more as a fine and sensitive vocalist with the songs "Serenade in Blue" and "Idaho." In August of the same year Dick joined up with Tommy Dorsey just when the band left for California. MGM had signed Tommy and the gang for the film DuBarry Was a Lady and Dick also sang with the band during its nine week appearance at the Hollywood Palladium. But, the era of Big Band singers was winding down, and, for Dick, that either meant going solo as a vocalist or back to song writing.

"The experience with Harry was great because he had a new band and it was a new experience for him as well," reported Dick to author Fred Hall, "But, with Tommy - well Tommy's (Dorsey) band was the actual Tiffany of the orchestra world in those days - because he gave you a showcase. He was a star- maker because he said, 'Okay, here's your spot - do your song,' and he had arrangers like Sy Oliver, Paul Weston, and Axel Stordahl. I learned lessons in performing as well as singing and breath control. We had the cream of ev- erything - - this big, huge, wonderful orchestra. I lasted just two short years."

It was Helen O'Connell who told me that it was she

with Connie Haines (Left) and Helen Forrest

who introduced Dick Haymes to her then manager Bill Burton. At the time, Dick was on the ropes career-wise, having sent his wife, actress Joanne Dru, and their son Skipper to New York to live in a furnished room, while Dick, remaining in a Hollywood hotel, tried to find suitable work, but was finding it difficult to sell his songs or skills as a soloist.

On Helen's word, Burton telephoned Dick and sent him funds to pay his hotel bill and carfare to come to New York. Burton also moved Joanne and Skipper into an apartment, all before there had even been a signed contract: "He's that kind of guy," Dick said admiringly.

Burton's management proved to be a good move. Dick was quickly re- employed. First, a spot at New York's La Martinique on 57th Street, then a Decca recording contract and a NBC radio show, Here's To Romance, followed by a screen test that led to movie appearances with 20th Century Fox studios where he rose to stardom very quickly.

As a result of Burton's efforts, Dick Haymes began enjoying great popularity due to the success of the films State Fair , Diamond Horseshoe and The Shocking Miss Pilgrim. "I loved doing Billy Rose's Diamond Horseshoe-- great tunes "It was just a fun movie, and one of my pets." The songs "The More I See You" and "I Wish I Knew" were beautifully sung in that film by Dick. The tunes "For You, For Me, Forever More" and "Aren't You Kinda Glad We Did" were from The Shocking Miss Pilgrim, which also starred Betty Grable. State Fair produced the hit "That's For Me." "That was a one and only original score for motion pictures that Rodgers and Hammerstein wrote. I was pretty lucky with that one." Dick

reported.

The weekly Autolite Radio Show days began Dick's long association with Helen Forrest: "They were days of joy for all of us who got along so well," said Helen, "Our guests, like Judy Garland, enjoyed the company of Dick and Gordon Jenkins." The thirty- minute show was a Saturday night affair and achieved a number one spot in the ratings. "It was terrific fun. Dick was terrific and made work fun," Helen went on, "We'd each do a number, then a third number together, then some sort of specialty number Gordon would write, often with Matt Dennis and Tom Adair. Each week we had a different theme. With Four Hits and a Miss and Gordon's choir, we made wonderful music together. We got a marvelous sound from all the voices."

During the tenure of the Autolite show they shared from 1944 until 1948, Dick Haymes and Helen Forrest became very close, welding together a lifelong friendship: "When I became nervous before facing an audience - I would actually begin to shake inside - but Dick would always seek to distract me. He would talk about anything that came into his head. He would make me laugh so hard sometimes that I almost forgot my fear," Helen said, "But, I always recovered once I was out there and Gordie (musical director Gordon Jenkins) struck up my cue. I'd smile when glancing sideways towards the wings at Dick who grinned with satisfaction as my fears subsided. Fortunately, the audience never realized what was going on. Helen says her happiest moments were rooted in the Autolite radio days. "We came alive when we came on the radio every week," she recalled, "There will never be another musical era like those days in the history of popular music. That was it."

The show was heavily promoted. Dick and Helen toured extensively to expand the show's popularity. "The songs 'It Had to Be You,' ' I'm Always Chasing Rainbows,' ' Long Ago and Far Away," and our favorite duet of the time, 'I'll Buy That Dream,' were some of the successful numbers we promoted at theaters in so many cities. 'It Had To Be You' and 'I'll Buy That Dream' each sold more than a million copies," Helen recalled, "I always wore bright colored dresses with ribbons in my hair. I felt so feminine around Dick Haymes. He always made me feel accepted. We genuinely liked and respected one another.

By that time Dick and Helen shared the same manager, Bill Burton. "I think in retrospect that more aggressive management would have propelled Dick even further - like in the movies- as Frank was pushed. Bill Burton was a good manager, but Sinatra's people were tougher, as was Frank himself. Dick was less aggressive, always feeling the stress of facing live audiences, but he had a richer voice and was handsomer. The ladies genuinely loved him. They would write him letters and call him up. When he left the studio, they would always be waiting for him - hoping for a chance to see him up close or get an autograph. It would be difficult for him to avoid them.

Helen Forrest and I reminisced about our favorite Dick Haymes recording, "Little White Lies."

"'Little White Lies' was Dick's best. It was a last minute thing…an accident, Richard. Four Hits and a Miss was our backup singing group and Gordie and Dick put it all together right there in the studio- on the spot while we were there - because they had some recording time left over. Well, it sold well over two million, and it's funny, but Dick never really liked that song, although I did. I never met anyone who didn't like the voice of Dick Haymes," Helen declared.

When Dick sang "Little White Lies," "It Might As Well Be Spring," or "The More I See You," you can be sure no one else could mark those songs as their own, but Dick Haymes. Tony Bennett has "I Left My Heart in San Francisco." Sinatra owns "My Way," among others. Bing's is "White Christmas," and Nat "King" Cole has "Stardust," all master interpreters indelibly marking song after song.

For Helen Forrest, myself, and a great many others, Dick Haymes was certainly a superior singer among singers.

You can read more details about Dick Haymes in Ruth Prigozy's brilliant book The Life of Dick Haymes - No More Little White Lies.

TONY MARTIN

WHAT'S GOOD ABOUT GOODBYE

On a very hot summer day on July 8, 1998, Tony Martin and I sat down to talk about his phenomenal career at the very cool Regency Hotel in New York. Tony had just flown in from his Los Angeles home to appear at Carnegie Hall the following Tuesday night along with a company of fellow MGM musical stars celebrating their tenure with the Culver City dream factory in a fitting tribute. Performers scheduled were June Allyson, Betty Garrett, Dolores Gray, Betty Comden, Adolph Green, Julie Wilson, Celeste Holm, Mickey Rooney, Cyd Charisse, Ann Miller, Leslie Caron, Arlene Dahl, Gloria De Haven, Roddy McDowell, Van Johnson, Donald O'Connor, and Kathryn Grayson. The host would be cabaret singer favorite Michael Feinstein.

"I started out my professional life as an Oakland (California) newsboy with my given name Alvin Morris, and learned to play tenor sax. When I became good enough I joined a band," Tony said proudly with the tonation of a forty year old - clear, rich and succinct. Tony worked in a number of Big Bands including the Bob Crosby, Ray McKinley, and the Glenn Miller Army Air Force Band: "I actually learned to sing by mistake. I was playing in the band and the regular singer took sick." Infamous columnist Walter Winchell, who had a popular radio show in those days called The Magic Carpet featuring name bands, heard about Tony's singing. "I got up and did a song - you know - took a shot at it - and Winchell wanted to know 'who was that singer?' - and it was me!"

Tony's first big band recording was with Ray Noble. "I Hadn't Anyone Till You" became a very popular song...I was always lucky with good songs," Tony said, "I also worked in the Anson Weeks band in those days. I sang on Anson's night off - I knew him pretty well - I replaced the sax player and didn't sing regularly."

Tony claims that luck had a lot to do with his success. "Again, I joined a band led by Tom Guerin, the same day as Woody Herman did - and we worked Sunday nights. We were the only band on because the big hotels were closed on Sunday - you know - no dancing - but we worked the Bell Tavern in San Francisco and the program went down to LA and was heard at a party held at L.B. Mayer's (Metro-Goldwyn-Mayer film studio boss) house in Malibu and they heard me sing "Poor Butterfly," which was a very popular song then. Now that was the kind of luck I was experiencing at the time." Tony was quickly located by an agent sent by Mayer and was invited to do a screen test. That led to Tony's first films, Sing, Baby, Sing and Follow the Fleet in 1936 with Fred Astaire and two other hopefuls, Lucille Ball and Betty Grable.

"Where did the name Tony Martin come from?"

"Well, after the screen test, the people there said there were too many Morris' at Universal. There were (actors) Chester Morris and Wayne Morris, and I was Alvin Morris. They were concerned about the three of us possibly being cast in the same movie. So I took the name from band leader Freddy Martin who was playing at the Cocoanut Grove nightclub in 1936. I was out on a date and the girl I was dancing with suggested that Martin would work best for me and I thought that was pretty good - I liked it. Anthony - which, of course, becomes Tony, came from a fellow I knew in Maryland who liked to gamble on houseboats, so I took that name, which I thought was an exciting name and put them together. So it was Tony Martin!"

"When people talk about you they invariably recall your role as Pepe LaMoco, the movie character you played in Casbah," I said, "It was a very popular movie with some great songs by Harold Arlen. That movie certainly impressed me."

"Oh, yeh! Well, I experience the same thing...when I'm in a restaurant or if I'm shopping in a store.....and it's a good feeling. It was a

good movie with Yvonne DeCarlo, who was a very good dancer, and Peter Lorre. We filmed it mostly on the backlots at Universal - and we also went to Algiers for a couple of scenes." (Tony enthusiastically sings out a capella - "Love-love- hoo-ray for love.......It was writ-ten in the star-r-r-s........ What's go-o-od ab-out good-bye-e-e...," portions of three of the movies top songs - "Hooray for Love," "It was Written In the Stars," and "What's Good About Goodbye?"

"It

"Harold Arlen and Leo Robin wrote a great score and it was Arlen's last movie score - and he interpreted each of the songs by singing them to me....for me. We'd sit at the piano and we'd sing each song- first him - then I would take a turn. Harold was articulate, a fantastic dresser- a very nice man who always wore a flower on his lapel. I recorded 14 of his songs. I love best "For Every Man There's a Woman."

About Tony's favorites: "My theme - 'I'll See You in My Dreams' - I have always liked that song. It's my sentimental favorite. My financial favorite....(he chuckles with a tilt of his head) .... is 'Begin the Beguine' and, also, 'There's no Tomorrow' - (a song borrowed from the Italian classic "O Sole Mio") - they are my best moneymakers."   "There's No Tomorrow" is a song completely owned by Tony Martin. Another of Tony's evergreens is his 1951 recording of "I Get Ideas," thought salacious at the time, as most pop songs then did not contain sexual innuendo. Nevertheless, that song, taken from the 1932 Argentine "Tango Adios Muchachos," is one of his best. And, who could forget his version of "Kiss of Fire" in 1952, another song taken from a classic, Villoldo's 1913 Tango El Choclo, or "Stranger in Paradise" in 1954 from the Broadway hit Kismet. Sorry if

I overlooked those earlier hits "To Each His Own" and "Tonight We Love." Tony did especially well with many songs adapted from the classics.

At this point I handed Tony a tattered copy of Song Hits Magazine from 1940 that I picked up a few days earlier at a collectibles show. Tony's photo was on the cover and some of the songs he was associated with were featured inside.

"Where the hell did you get that?" Tony mused, "That goes back a ways - but, you know, I remember it like it was yesterday." Tony Martin was the subject of many a magazine article or celebrity book during those days; his good looks targeted him for romantic stories linked to big-time movie stars including Lana Turner. But, Tony was always considered to be a "good guy," being one of Hollywood's nicest people. And he is still one of the nicest people in Hollywood where he has been happily married to dancer Cyd Charisse for over 55 years. Cyd, of course, worked with the supreme dancer Fred Astaire in two memorable 1950's films, The Bandwagon and Silk Stockings, and also starred in the timeless movie Brigadoon, all were terrific motion pictures and her best work ever. Tony and Cyd are so well suited to one another. Together they wrote an autobiography, The Two Of Us, in 1976.

Tony Martin and Cyd Charisse

Tony's performance the night after our interview at Carnegie Hall was absolutely amazing, belying his age, with a voice as hearty as when he serenaded his lovely costars in those romantic movies over 50 years ago. His brief vocal salutes to some of his songs during our interview the day before were apparently precursors to the events that would follow the next evening. Tony was almost overcome by the crowd's enthusiasm and affection, "This was the most thrilling moment of my life."

The Whole Music Thing Was Natural

In his autobiography, Music Is My Mistress, Duke Ellington described Nathaniel Adams Cole's relationship with his then popular band singer, Marie Ellington:

".....she was so pretty that Nat Cole took one look at her, scooped her up, carried her off to the preacher, married her, and took her home to his beautiful Beverly Hills love- nest, where she listened to his love songs for the rest of his life."

with Oscar Moore

Recounting this charming fable to Maria Cole a few years ago while we talked at her Massachusetts home, Maria smiled: "Well, it's partly true. We met at the Zanzibar Club right after I had just been fired from the Ellington Band .... because they found out (she chuckles) I was trying to get a job as a single (she grins), and we fell in love with one-another. But, Nat was married, and in those days you waited for an interlocutory degree in California. So it all took time."

Maria speaks so clearly and warmly. Marie adopted Maria over Marie because she liked the way it blended with Cole. "It sounded more lyrical."

Together they reared five children, three of their own and two adopted. First came Carol, who is Maria's niece, adopted when Maria's sister died. "Then Natalie was born, then nine years later we adopted our son Nat Kelly Cole, so-named in honor of St. Patrick's Day, which was

Maria Cole

also Nat's birthday. Then came our identical twins three years later ; Casey, named after our good friend (New York Yankees great manager) Casey Stengel, and Timolin, named after our very dear friend composer Johnny Burke's own little girl." Maria simply fell in love with the name Timolin.

We reminisced a lot about Nat King Cole and about his phenomenal success rising first while backing jazz song star Billie Holiday on the piano as she performed her repertoire at Kelly's Stable nightclub in New York, to commercial success with his own jazz ensemble, The King Cole Trio, then ascension in a prolific career as a world-class soloist, producing an enviable list of standards to his credit.

"Nat had no particular favorite," Maria said, "although mine is 'Our Love Is Here to Stay.' For Nat, the favorite was whatever was most popular at the moment. He loved every song he ever recorded."

We journeyed back to 1939, in Los Angeles, when Nat led his King Cole Trio, with Oscar Moore on guitar and Wesley Prince on bass. "Well, Nat's great piano influence was Earl Hines," Maria recalled, "and so he loved playing piano and singing with the trio, but no particular singer influenced his singing career."

With compact, syncopated backup chords and clean, spare, melodic phrases, Nat emphasized the piano as a solo, rather than a rhythm-style instrument in his arrangements. His playing complimented his singing - both completely being under his own control.

The vocals started accidentally while performing at various club dates. "Singing came very natural to Nat. There's a vast difference, if you listen to Nat with the trio ....with the kind of exaggerated Southern accent style compared to how polished he becomes through the years. It's fantastic." Nat had an uncanny ability to sit at the piano and sing with little effort. It was no problem for him at all. "He was a musician first," Maria declared proudly, "and he never had a problem with breath control. Once Metropolitan Opera impresario Rudolph Bing, who was a fan of Nat's said - - - and I remember distinctly, Richard, exactly what he told Nat. 'Nat, come over and teach my artists some of your breathing techniques.' It was just a trick thing with Nat, I guess."

No less than Bing Crosby once added in his two cents about Nat Cole.

"I like to think of Nat Cole as a real strolling player - never pressing,never seeking for obvious effect, singing like he wanted no applause, cared little whether anyone was listening or not - singing because he liked to sing, because he liked the song. This fellow creates a wonderful mood anytime he works."

My initial interest in the King Cole Trio arrived with the recordings" It's Only a Paper Moon" and "Route 66," songs that perfectly suited his style.

Some accounts maintain that Nat Cole did not choose most of his material, and that he did not like to record the so-called rinky-dink songs "Nature Boy" (accompanied by his friend Frank DeVol), "Mona Lisa" (arranged by master arranger Nelson Riddle), "Ramblin' Rose," or "Lazy, Hazy, Days of Summer," but none of that is true according to Maria. "He enjoyed all those songs very much. They were all hits. It wasn't a matter of liking a song - he picked them ...he was smart...he could select good and commercially successful material. As a matter of fact, Nat did choose most of the songs he recorded."

I handed Maria New York radio station WQEW's Listeners' Choice Countdown Poll results for 1996, documenting Nat with the number two all-time winner among 156 recorded hits of the last 50 years: his stirring recording of "Stardust."

"Richard, to me, no one has done 'Stardust' like Nat." In the movie My Favorite Year Nat opens cold with Hoagy's (Carmichael) song "Stardust." "Just get that movie--rent it --- and listen to the way he sings that wonderful song. So crisp and clear. I can't explain it to you ---you must listen for yourself." Nat also sang the rarely performed introduction to the verse. Hoagy Carmichael also said it was his favorite version.

Composer, arranger Billy Strayhorn's masterpiece "Lush Life," a very complex song shunned by most singers became another Nat King Cole achievement. "As everyone knows," Maria said, "it's a very difficult song to sing." But, Nat Cole clearly owns the definitive version of that song which Strayhorn had shelved for over ten years until he found Cole to record it for him to Pete Rugolo's fine arrangement.

"Handful of Stars" was another deep-rooted Cole classic. He managed that song as well as any crooner of his day. Nat's work with arranger Nelson Riddle, was exemplary as was his work with arrangers Gordon Jenkins and Ralph Carmichael.

"Christmas Song" is, of course, the song most identified with Nat: "I was visiting my friend, Bob Wells' home in Taluca Lake for a work session," said the song's co-author Mel Torme' , I noticed a poem, written in pencil, resting on the piano music board; Chestnuts roasting on an open fire, Jack Frost nipping at your nose, Yuletide carols being sung by a choir, And folks dressed up like Eskimos.

"When Bob appeared, I asked him about the poem. 'I thought I'd write something to cool myself off this very hot day.'

"You know,' I said, "this just might make a song.' We sat down at the piano, and wrote "The Christmas Song" in forty-five minutes - - honest!"

Mel Torme' eventually took the song to Nat Cole, who fell in love with the tune. His recording was released in the late fall of 1946.

I was telling Maria that Kathryn Crosby revealed to me that Bing sang all day long when at home. He would vocalize radio commercials, the latest rock numbers and opera arias, as well as ditties, while in the shower or strolling in the garden.

"Nat never did that, isn't that funny?" Recalled Maria, "He would sometimes stretch his vocal chords, you know that thing that singers do to clear their voice. We had a separate playhouse on our property where he would sometime rehearse."

Like many black performers in the fifties and early sixties, Nat Cole experienced the cruelty of bigotry, especially during the early days working Las Vegas nightspots. Black performers were paid less and kept out of the main hotels, except when they performed. They lived in separate quarters on the outskirts of town. "I didn't go to Vegas with Nat - when he first started there - because of the bigotry. He never subjected me to that. The only reason to discuss the bigotry that existed at the time is because he really did live through it. It's a shame he didn't live to see it change for black performers, as it is today."

Nat Cole's television show in 1957 was unfortunately short-lived. "...although Nat had lots of support," Maria said. "His many friends, like Frankie Laine, and a roster of great talent, appeared regularly on his show, but, he gave it up on his own because he said, ' Madison Avenue is afraid of the dark,' a well-known classic line used at the time." Frankie Laine and Maria Cole have been great friends ever since those days. When Nat Cole passed away in 1965, Maria gave Frankie a money clip that was owned by Nat, as a remembrance of his friendship with her husband.

In 1992, the Society of Singers in Los Angeles announced the first posthumous award in establishing the Nat King Cole Scholarship under the auspices of the National Foundation of Advancement in the Arts. As Society president Ginny Mancini said, "It was forty-five years ago between my daily rehearsals as one of Mel Torme's Mel-Tones that Bob Wells and

Mel put the finishing touches on an inspired collaboration of melody and lyric that was to become a part of the tapestry of Americana. That was the birth of 'The Christmas Song.'"

Each year, high school seniors having demonstrated exceptional vocal artistry will have an opportunity to participate in a national competition judged by professionals in the field, with the possibility of pursuing a meaningful (singing) career.

"It was my privilege to know him and experience first hand the incredible musicianship of Nat King Cole. It is an honor for me and the singers we represent to pay this tribute in keeping with his legacy."

The tributes to Nat King Cole have punctuated the years since his passing, his stature always growing. One was held at Carnegie Hall in a two day July 1977 celebration. Guest artists included the talents of Ruth Brown, Julius La Rosa, Mark Murphy, John Pizzarelli, Freddy Cole, Abbey Lincoln, Jon Hendricks, Jonathan Schwartz, and others who are happy to pay homage to one of the best singers ever.

When Nat Cole died, our mutual friend William B. Williams told Maria he would play a Nat King Cole record every day as long as he was on the air. And he did! "Nat was the kind of person who didn't have just one good friend - he had lots of friends - but he was not a person to hang out with this one or that one when he was off. All the guys loved him. Sure, he was on the road most of the time, but he was a wonderful husband and he loved all the phases of his life. For him the whole music thing was natural. He was a guy who went along with the program, a man who kept everything inward except his songs. He loved whatever he was doing, whenever he was doing it. He loved his career - he loved the music."

Gordon Jenkins with Nat King Cole at Capitol Records

Bob Eberly and Ray Eberle
Family Music

Both handsome, romantic baritones, the Eberle/Eberly brothers sang with the top bands of the era. Bob vocalized with Jimmy Dorsey, notably on those very successful Tutti Camarata arranged duets with Helen O'Connell, "Tangerine," "Green Eyes," and with Kitty Kallen "Besame' Mucho."

Bob spelled his name ending in a Y, whereas Ray ended his with an E, in order to distinguish one brother from another. The correct family spelling was Eberle. Helen O'Connell had a crush on Bob,. As Margaret Whiting, recalled to me,

"He was so nice to her on those band bus trips. He taught her how to comfortably sleep on a bus - he would bring her a blanket - or some pillows." Margaret toured with Helen for a while in the 1980's with Four Girls Four act that included Rosemary Clooney and Rosemarie, and alternately Kay Starr.

"He sort of took care of me," Helen told me some time ago. "If Bob had gone off as a single, I wonder how successful he would have been? Would he have been as successful as Sinatra or Haymes?"

"Bob Eberly was bigger than all of us," said Dick Haymes to writer and broadcaster Fred Hall in his book Dialogues In Swing, "you know, with Jimmy Dorsey. I mean, when he was singing "Amapola" and "Green Eyes" and "The Breeze and I" and all those things with Jimmy (Dorsey), with Helen O'Connell, he was the hottest thing...of course, he was one of the nice people in the world." As most of you now know, the Eberly/Eberle's and most other vocalists of the time received only $25.00 per record date. Imagine, that for his terrific recording "Maria Elena," in my top ten list of the best recordings ever, Bob received only $25.00. Isn't that hard to believe? But, as Connie Haines told me,"That was the deal, and you were growing and being showcased, and so that's all you got."

Ray Eberle sang with Glenn Miller. His quality hits, "Blue Evening," "At Last," "Serenade in Blue," and "A Nightingale Sang in Barkley Square," alone are enough to immortalize him. "Blue Rain" and "Elmer's Tune" were pretty good, too! Some say that Glenn never gave Ray enough romantic material to sing compared to what Jimmy Dorsey allowed Bob. Ray was hired by Glenn when Glenn ran into Bob one day and asked," Do you have any brothers who sing like you?" You know the rest. Ray sang for a while with Gene Krupa after leaving Glenn Miller. Most say that Bob had the better voice, but I think I would vote for Ray as an equal. However, thank God for them both.

The Eberle's helped made the Big Band Era more listenable. There is a footnote to this story: Another brother, Walter, was also a singer but never sang with a big name band.

They're in the Army Now!

TONY BENNETT
The other Saloon Singer
"HE'S FRISKY AND FRESH"

Tony Bennett credits songwriters for his success.
"It's not whether a song is new or old that makes it great..it's whether it's good or bad that makes them live or die."

Tony never gets tired of singing the strains of Irving Berlin, Cole Porter, Harold Arlen, George Gershwin, or Harry Warren. He has a sort

with Harold Arlen

of instinct for selecting the songs that suit him. In the case of his immensely popular gem, "I Left My Heart In San Francisco," he recalls that while rehearsing it with his piano accompanist, Ralph Sharon, in a Hot Springs hotel bar before he introduced it at the Fairmont Hotel in San Francisco:

"A bartender was listening and, after we finished rehearsal, he told me he would enthusiastically buy a copy if we ever recorded it. That was the first tip-off that we had a hit in the making. Right up to today, it's my biggest request--- it gets the best reaction, and San Francisco is really a beautiful city---it's a musical city---and I love to sing about it!" Tony doesn't seem to sing anything but the finest songs, although some argue that that song is considered too sentimental and weak, but it brings in the faithful and will probably be the song with which he will always be identified, happily or unhappily.

In 1983, Tony and I had a long conversation backstage at one of his appearances while Sarah Vaughan was singing on-stage and he was slated to follow. Tony is an excellent subject because he is eternally spirited about his music and his good luck, unlike the early struggles of his counterpart Frankie Laine who was not discovered and greatly appreciated when he was past thirty. Tony makes an art out of feelings: "I conjure up emotion much

like impressionist artists who work with light. Feelings are the opposite of coldness...I try to sing in a natural key...choosing strong lyrics with meaning... then I inject my own feelings into it."

It's more than just feelings that drives Tony Bennett. Ever since he won an Arthur Godfrey Talent Scouts Contest (coming in second to Rosemary Clooney) Tony's career has always expanded upwards, helped along by a battery of million sellers, namely "Because Of You," "Rags to Riches," "Blue Velvet," (his mother's and Ella Fitzgerald's favorite), "Cold, Cold Heart," "Boulevard Of Broken Dreams," "I Left My Heart In San Francisco," and all those evergreens he has recorded during his long career.

Bob Hope once told me that it was he that changed Tony's stage name, Joe Bari, back to Tony Bennett (his real name is Anthony Dominick Benedetto) because Bari sounded phony. He had invited Tony to join his show at the New York Paramount after hearing him sing at New York's Village Barn where he was appearing with Pearl Bailey. "Right there and then he announced what would be my new name and told me I was going on tour with him all over the U.S.---it was just great."

Tony considers his audiences mature and civilized, drawing a comparison to the sixties, seventies and eighties when rock & roll artists audiences were not. He also maintains he never really experienced a serious lull in his career: "I've always enjoyed long lines around the block where I opened, even during the Beatles invasion." We agreed that the rock and roll artists, in order to sustain a future for themselves that is consistent, must cross- over and satisfy new audiences with new product because those audiences mature and change too.

"Look at the Linda Ronstadt ballad albums," (arranged by Nelson Riddle), he pointed out. "It's a great album that has left her rock and roll albums in the dust...and it made the Top Ten.

"With me, every show is my last show. When I had to record what record execs wanted back in the fifties, I did it and I luckily succeeded. But now I choose my own tunes to record. I got some of those record executives angry when I wouldn't record some of the garbage they were peddling, so they called me a fanatic and a troublemaker. I consider it a compliment. They were forcing artists to take a dive. Remember, they're accountants and marketing guys, they didn't know anything about the product. When I come out to sing, I change and emotionalize and begin to feel the audience out there, and my songs come across more person-alized--more sensitive---more dramatic---and I love it." Tony has matured into a more disciplined performer who communicates with his audience and never really ever sings a song the same way twice.

As a young man, Tony was trained to be a commercial artist at Manhattan's School of Industrial Arts, but he says "I always had to sing, it was something in my genes...my Italian heritage---I have spent my whole life studying and thinking about singing...my whole family sang too!" The school's choral director influenced him in those days. He joined the cho-rus to learn his craft, and, after singing with military bands while serving in the armed forces in Europe, came home and entered the American Theater Wing professional school under it's director Miriam Spier. While studying, he rounded out a livelihood by playing club dates around Manhattan and even served as an elevator operator at the Park Sheraton Hotel to makes ends meet. The win on Talent Scouts led to a contract on a fifteen-minute, five-nights a week, radio show with Rosemary and even-tually on Jan Murray's TV show, Songs For Sale.

Sinatra has said he owes his phrasing & breathing techniques to Tommy Dorsey's trombone playing, and Tony acknowledges that for him it was the instruction of both Art Tatum's piano and Mildred Bailey's jazz-voice. Sarah Vaughan described Tony Bennett to me one day as "....frisky and fresh. You've got to look at the movements in his face when he sings," she proclaimed. Sinatra always praised him : "He's my man, this cat, the greatest singer in the world today, Tony Bennett."

In 1978, Tony released two albums, one entitled Tony Bennett and Bill Evans-Together Again and Tony Bennett Sings More Great Rodgers and Hart, both reaching fair success. In 1986 it was The Art Of Excel-lence album. "Listen to this," he said from (his dressing room in Atlantic City when the album came out and I called him to offer congratulations, "It's number one...and it's wonderful...and to think it's in front of the Rolling Stones and the great Bruce Springsteen. It's full circle for me". It was a good album containing an amazing duet with Ray Charles on James

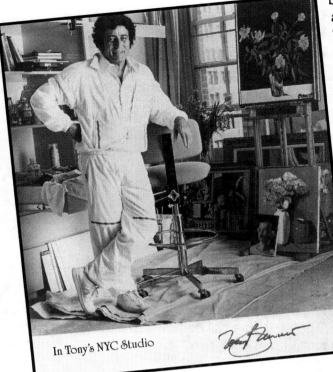

In Tony's NYC Studio

Taylor's Everybody's Got The Blues and a number called "City Of Angels" which was written by Fred Astaire, plus my favorite of the album, an almost forgotten song from Irving Berlin's, Annie Get Your Gun, "I Got Lost In His Arms." In 1993, he recorded an interesting album entitled, Perfectly Frank, which is a tribute to Frank Sinatra, but in the Bennett mold, and he won an Emmy for it. One Time Magazine critic said, "Moral: there are no definitive versions of great songs, only definitive singers." In 1994, he won an Emmy again, this time for a new album, Steppin' Out, which is a collection of Fred Astaire tunes.

"The thrill of performing hasn't changed in years. I learn something every day. I've never gotten bored yet and I don't think I ever will. It's funny...I mean I know it's hard to believe, but in my own mind, no matter what anybody else thinks, I feel I'm just starting out. I know now what I shouldn't do. And so, I feel as if I finally know what I can do and should do." He shakes his head and offers his famous, wide grin.

It is amazing that this senior citizen appeared regularly on MTV along with such artists as the perennial Eric Clapton and female icon, Mariah Carey. "He's cool." say much younger fans. In 1995 he made numerous appearances including benefits for the Society Of Singers, and "unplugged" appearances on MTV Television and at Southampton College.

Tony is also another kind of artist--a landscape and portrait painter. He signs his works, Benedetto and sells them all over the world for big bucks. Like many artists, he has painted a worthy portrait of himself. I saw some of his pieces one evening of cityscapes and landscapes. Portraits are fairly new to his work. From information gathered that evening with Tony, I was able to write a piece for an art magazine about his art alone.

Well, with his two new Grammy's to add to his others and his album total topping 90, he still walks on stage under Bob Hope's original advice: "Come out smiling, show the people you like them."

"To this day, I still follow that rule. Some performers say they don't care if the audience likes them or not. With that philosophy, they should stay home and do it."

In his living room in mid-Manhattan, there is a Hirschfeld cartoon on the wall: The caption reads, A group of America's Great Artists.

"There's Ella, Bing Crosby, Nat King Cole, Fred Astaire, Judy Garland, and I'm smack in the middle of that group. I can't believe it, but it's true."

Yes, it's true, all right, and at his age, he looks and feels great. Besides MTV, at the Grammy's, singing on the Mall in Washington, D. C. on July 4th, you can find him anywhere the music is happening. He is more in focus now than he ever was. He appreciates his life, he is kind, and makes you feel good, whether friend or fan.

"When you first start painting, and it doesn't work out, you're devastated. But you keep painting. Then you're not bothered by your mistakes. You just say, 'The next time will be better.' That's what happens in life. That's why I wouldn't change anything: Because I made mistakes, but those mistakes taught me how to live, and boy, am I living."

Well, Tony Bennett, now just past eighty, sang with the Today Show Christmas Show at Rockefeller Center on November 27, 2007. Just like that little rabbit and his batteries, Tony Bennett keeps going and going.

JERRY VALE
He Still Hears the Applause

I had always wanted to interview Jerry Vale. Like Perry Como, who is his hero, Jerry is one of those calm, pleasant and romantic singers who consistently command a legion of admirers. After many years of scuttled opportunities, Jerry and I finally got together recently on a beautiful fall Sunday evening backstage during a gig on Long Island, where he was appearing for a one-night stand costarring with comedian Dom De Luise.

Jerry arrived at 6:15 PM and had to be on stage at 7:00. We squeezed 30 minutes from that tight schedule, took some photos, and helped him get ready for his appearance. Although still in pain with a knee that recently underwent arthroscopic surgery, he sprinted carefully down the ramp to center stage at exactly seven, introduced with a fanfare and medley of his standards. I watched him for a while from the wings, his white shocks of hair highlighting his persona. A gratified audience was enthralled. Jerry was very uncomfortable because of his knee pain, but you couldn't tell, "You have to go on no matter what,"he said moments earlier, "All seasoned troopers know that. My knee hurts like mad, but I performed last night and I will do it again tonight."

Genero Louis Vitaliano was born in 1930 in the Bronx where his beloved Yankees play baseball (He and former manager Joe Torre are good friends, as were Mickey Mantle, Yogi Berra, Bobby Murcer, and

Jerry with Richard and Paul Mann - Jerry's Musical Director

manager
Casey Stengel.)Jerry worked at shoe-shining on the sidewalks of the
Bronx at age twelve. Evander Childs High School days found him labor-
ing in a fluorescent light factory after school, while frequently entering
singing contests until he won one that earned him a spot at the local Club
Del Rio.

"I always wanted to become a singer after listening to Perry Como
and Frank Sinatra, singing along with their records. Then, a friend of
mine was going up to the club to see a friend and he asked me to go with
him. When we walked in they were having a singing contest - and the
announcer said, 'Anybody else want to sing?' ...and with that my friend literally pushed me out on stage and said, 'Here he is -Jerry Como. I sang
"Far Away Places" and won the contest, so the guy offered me a job."
Jerry remained performing at the Club Del Rio for over a year, receiving
ten dollars a night.

"When I heard the applause, Jerry said with that signature grin, I
knew I wanted to make singing my life's work."

Jerry later performed at the Stardust Ballroom in the Bronx with a
fourteen piece band. He sang almost nothing but love songs.

"I like songs that tell a story, have a pretty melody, nice lyrics, and
are sentimental."

When singer Guy Mitchell, who was among the stable of singing stars under the direction of Mitch Miller, artists and repertoire man at
CBS/Columbia , who also guided the singing careers of Rosemary Clooney, Tony Bennett, Johnny Ray, Patti Page, Frankie Laine, and others,
introduced Jerry Vale to Miller, he also became one of that illustrious,
industrious, prolific group who flooded the era with a great batch of great,
memorable recordings.   Jerry's first recorded hit, "Two Purple Shadows,"
was followed by "Pretend You Don't See Her" (with Percy Faith's Orchestra) and "You Don't Know Me," still three of his favorites with audiences.

Those growing times found him perfecting his craft at choice venues all over the U.S.: The Copacabana in New York, Diplomat Hotel in Hollywood, Frontier Hotel in Las Vegas, and Century Plaza in L.A. Jerry has been acclaimed in Melbourne, Australia; The Philippines; Italy, and South Africa. He was a frequent television guest on The Tonight Show and had his own program entitled Jerry Vale's World, performed in Las Vegas back in the seventies.

Identified with numbers like "Non Dimenticar," "Arriverderci Roma," "Come Back to Sorrento," and "Anema E Core," Jerry says, "My music is like a romantic trip to Italy. They are such rich gems."

In early September I had visited Jack Ellsworth at radio station WLIM on Long Island while he was on the air with his daily show Memories in Melody . We were talking Jerry Vale and other singers. Jack's most requested Jerry Vale numbers over a long period of time are "Till the End of Time" and "Pretend You Don't See Her." "Wow," Jerry said, "I would have thought 'Ciao Ciao Bambina' or 'I Have But One Heart.' ..or even 'Because You're Mine' would have been the choices. They are my most requested. I guess it's different choices in different places."

I was telling Jerry how it was that Bing Crosby always sang around the house, according to what Kathryn revealed to me, "In the garden, or even in the shower, singing commercials or even the latest rock tunes," she said ever so proudly.

"Interesting, but I never do that," Jerry said, "I sing only during rehearsals or at engagements...never at home or when I'm alone." These days he enjoys doing benefits and sometimes working in tandem with fellow singers besides his regular schedule of performances. Recently, in Tampa, Florida, Frankie Laine told me he sang at a concert with Jerry, Don Cornell, Anna Maria Alberghetti, and Julie La Rosa. "That was for the Fiesta Italiano, "Jerry clarified," with all Italian-American performers."

Jerry's favorite of his own work is "Mala Femmina." "I sing better on that than I have ever sang in my life. I like the song and I seem to do it well." Perry Como's recording of "Song of Songs" is one of his favorites of the competition. Jerry is very vocal about all the other singers, always praising them. "Barbra Streisand's recording of 'Why Did I Choose You' is my favorite female recording. It's a beautiful song that not many are familiar with. One of her best records, I believe."

I called off some singer's names to get Jerry Vale's take on other singers: Frank Sinatra: "The best! What else can you say about Sinatra? There is only one Sinatra - and he was a good friend."

Frankie Laine: "Frank was a great artist who gave something new to the business when he made it. I mean, he sang a song like nobody ever did."

Perry Como: "Well, you know -- Como -- beautiful voice -- beautiful man--nobody ever came close to him as far as his outlook on life and the way he treated his family and his friends. He was just a beautiful guy."

Nat Cole: "I knew Nat Cole. I had gotten to know him fairly well when I was working in Las Vegas. I also met him up in Canada while I was on tour. He was such a nice man and a very great talent."

Julius La Rosa: "I love Julius La Rosa. He's been a dear friend for many, many years, and he is one of the best singer's around. He's got the best feel of any singer. I mean, he can sing anything. He does jazz and he does it well."

William B. Williams (of WNEW, New York radio fame) : "He was the best and one of the first guys to play a Jerry Vale record. I always loved his Make Believe Ballroom show."

Mel Torme': "Mel was one of the greatest artists of all time. Here's a man who wrote arrangements, conducted an orchestra, composed songs, play the drums like nobody - and sing beautifully as well. Who else do you know who could do all that?"

Dick Haymes: "I loved Dick Haymes, too. Nobody sang low notes like Dick Haymes. He had a good quality in his voice and when he hit those low notes it was a pleasure to listen to. A deep baritone, but he could also sing those high notes. He had quite a bit of success. All those people you mention - all those guys - Como, Sinatra, Dick Haymes, Frankie Laine- were all great. I look at it this way. I don't pick any one of them as my favorite-

Jerry and Rita Vale with Richard

because I think they are all terrific."

That's just what Buddy Rich once said to me when I asked him to name an all-star band. "They're all giants. So how can you insult all the other giants by picking just some of them. So all of them are my favorites."

Jerry admits that if he had the chance to do it over again, the one thing he would change is to have studied music more thoroughly: "I started out playing the bass for a while, but I never studied music - just played by ear.' I'm sorry now that I didn't really study music a lot more - I would know more about theory - I would have better timing -I would feel a lot more comfortable. For my own piece of mind, not that I have any problems, I wish I had studied more for those reasons."

Of course, a few short years later, Jerry and I got together and produced the book Jerry Vale- A Singer's Life, his definitive biography. We worked together selling the book at Jerry's personal appearances for a while. He

Robert Incagliato - Richard's Assistant and Long Time Fan of Jerry

would always sign them for his fans. Jerry is officially retired now and living in Palm Desert, California with his wife, Rita, who is still cooking up those fine Italian dishes for over 50 years. We talk and see one another as often as possible when he comes East.

Mr. Rhythm

Frank Paul Lo Vecchio Takes to the Mike

with Richard Grudens

It's difficult for me to believe that my friend of over 25 years, Frankie Laine, almost gave up on his struggling singing career, actually taking out two-and- a- half years to work at a defense plant where he earned a steady sixty-eight dollars a week. Then with a few bucks in his pocket, he returned to the fray to try again but promising himself to quit if he did not succeed on his next bid.

But, of course, he probably never would have stopped , no matter what he may have said at the time. I think I know Frank pretty well now, and his determination and dedication to his craft were always unwavering, good times and bad, to say the least. The admirable way Frank has conducted his personal and professional life in every respect since his very first success in 1946 at that infamous Hollywood hangout on Vine Street, Billy Berg's, I'm sure, with dedication and his exemplary motivation, he would have hung on until his career turned itself around:

"I was invited to sit in one night and I came away with good luck for a change by singing "Old Rocking Chair's Got Me." My luck turned, because a guy in the audience got very excited about the way I sang it, and turned out to be the song's composer, Hoagy Carmichael, (also the composer of our featured song of the Big Band Era, "Stardust") who convinced Billy to give me a job at seventy-five dollars a week."

Frank was the first he-man singer.... other than country-western singers--- who the blue-collar guys could identify with, but he really had a difficult time and some bad luck along the way.

"Earlier," he went on, "my friend, bandleader Jean Goldkette, got me a job at NBC, but England decided to declare war on Germany that day and my job went out the window. Hell, I was already 26 years old then. I hung around Ted Weems' band while my pal Perry Como was his singer. Perry recommended me for his replacement when he was leaving, but Weems didn't accept it (Frank sang "Never In A Million Years" at his audition, which turned out to be prophetic) so Perry got me a job with his old boss, bandleader Freddie Carlone. That lasted just a few weeks because my jazz style didn't match his sweet Guy Lombardo type of band."

with Mitch Miller

Frank's style was very innovative, which was why he had such difficulty with early acceptance. He would bend notes and sing about the chordal context of a note rather than to sing the note directly, and he stressed each rhythmic downbeat, which was different than the smooth balladeer of his time.

When he sang at Cleveland's College Inn in 1940, Frank introduced an unknown, starving singer, June Hart, who he really thought was terrific and needed a break. They actually hired her to replace him. More bad luck while helping someone, but that's Frank. However, she sang a ballad entitled "That's My Desire," which Frank liked very much, but forgot about for six years.

"And how about the time I was ready to sing a benefit at the Congress Hotel in Chicago when suddenly Roy Eldridge showed up and decided to go into 'Body and Soul.' Who'd dare interrupt that for a punk kid nobody knew?"

Fortunately, he decided to try out his terrific version of "That's My Desire," with head thrown back, eyes closed and mike in hand later at Billy Berg's. It

Frankie Laine

October 8, 1990

Dear Richard:

Have your letter of September 19th. I used to imitate Bing perfectly during Marathon Dancing Days expecially "Straight From The Shoulder" and "Soon".

I was tony Bennet's influence. Percy Faith once told him to stop trying to sound like me.

I'm sure your article will be very good. Please send me a copy.

Cordially

Frank.. Laine

lat-

with Helen O'Connell

brought down the house and began his climb up the ladder to success. Then he began recording those he-man hits one after another, first with Mercury and then Columbia: "That's My Desire," then "Lucky Old Sun," "Jezebel," "Mule Train," "Shine," "High Noon," "Cry Of The Wild Goose," "Moonlight Gambler," and "Rawhide" .... all memorable ---all number-one smash hits, and to prove his bona fide affinity to country music, how about his definitive interpretation of Hank Williams' "Your Cheatin' Heart."

But, as good as they were, I prefer Frank's inspiring, early rendition of "We'll Be Together Again," (which he wrote with his lifelong friend, Carl Fischer) and the inspirational, "I Believe," written by our mutual friend Ervin Drake, and Frank's own personal favorite and actually an expression of his definition of life.

I first saw Frankie Laine at the New York Paramount in 1947. He was on the in-person show with Ray McKinley and comedian, Billy De-Wolfe, during the run of the movie, "Golden Earrings". My first meeting with Frank was in 1983 backstage at New York's Westbury Music Fair .He was appearing with his discovery, and now old friend, song-star Helen O'Connell, Buddy Morrow, who was fronting the Tommy Dorsey ghost band.) and William B. Williams, of New York's WNEW and it's famous radio show, Make Believe Ballroom. We hit it off like old friends at a reunion. After a few minutes together, we rounded up Helen O'Connell from the ladies dressing room and cleared up how he first discovered Helen:

"Well, Jimmy Dorsey's secretary, Nita Moore, and I were having breakfast and she told me that Jimmy was looking for a girl singer." Helen was nodding in agreement. "It happened that I saw Helen the night before singing at the Village Barn down on Eighth Street and I told Nita about her and Jimmy went to see her that night, and that's how he got Helen O'Connell." Helen was standing right next to me and Frank when he related that story with Helen nodding approval, then snuggling up and planting a kiss on Frank's blushing cheek.

Frank recounted his phenomenal success when appearing in England where was so revered. On opening night at the Palladium, August 18, 1952, he broke the attendance record previously held by Judy Garland and Danny Kaye. He was sold out for the entire length of his two week stay, and even the standing room only places, which were sold the day of each show, sold out the fastest ever in the theater's history. The crowds milled outside the Palladium before each show. Nan and Frank were thrilled to death. It was so much more than they expected so far from home. It was then that he received a phone call from Mitch Miller, his Columbia Records producer, telling him his recording of "Mule Train" and "High Noon" were released in the states and were a smash. Carl Fischer improvised an arrangement from what he remembered of "Mule Train" and the next evening they slipped the song into the act. The audience went wild.

Frank moved on to Glasgow, Scotland, opening at the Empire Theater to an incredible reception. A crowd of over five-thousand gathered outside their hotel, and would not go away until Frank stepped out on the balcony and sang a few bars of "Rock Of Gibraltar," a song that went over big in Britain.

Frank went on to Italy to sing "Jezebel" to a screaming crowd everywhere he traveled in his parents place of birth. Appearances in Milan, Venice, Florence, and Rome, where crowds topped each previous performance, were equally exciting for the traveling performer from America. He and Nan were genuinely overwhelmed at all the attention given them overseas. In France, where he renewed his friendship with singer, Edith Piaf, known to the world as The Little Sparrow, Frankie and Nan were followed by crowds of fans everywhere they visited. "Jezebel" had been a big hit in France.

Frank returned to Europe over and over to even greater successes. He has recorded hundreds of titles over the years, and his international record sales exceeded the one-hundred million mark long ago.

In his book That Lucky Old Son, Frank recalls that special feeling, corny though he thought it was, on returning a success to New York, where he once felt the lowest point of his career. "I promised myself that I wouldn't come back to New York unless I could do so on a white horse." He couldn't forget the nights sleeping in Central Park and the days that dragged by for him without food.

"That's why I made it a point to treat myself to one very special evening during my first run at the Paramount. I spent it alone. I donned a custom made suit and a camel's hair overcoat and headed for Central Park.

There, I sought out the dilapidated bench that had once been my bed. I sat down and ate a candy bar and thought about the time when penny candy bars were all I could afford to eat. In one of my pockets sat a loaded wallet, in the other a key to one of the most comfortable hotel suites in New York. After a while I hailed a taxi and drove to the heart of Times Square, where my name was in big, beautiful lights and they were paying me $ 2,500 a week to do what I loved best." Frank hopes that everybody, at least once in their lives, know such a moment for themselves.

In 1985, while I was penning a monthly column called "Jazz and Jazzmen" for Long Island P.M. Magazine, Frank fell ill with a quadruple-by-pass heart operation. I let the readers know and encouraged them to write letters to Frank at his San Diego home that overlooked the harbor. He was so grateful.

Frank had a remarkable recovery and by the time 1990 rolled around, he had completed his fifth year since the surgery, but in April of 1990 he had to have a triple bypass. In 1991, however, Frank was having some throat troubles and took a year off. His good wife of then 42 years, the former movie actress, Nan Grey, had troubles with her vision which by way of two operations, was fully restored to 20/20.

A few years later, with Nan gone: "Nan's special way of touching my life will remain in my heart forever and lets me go on to do my work. I believe," he says so sincerely, "God is everywhere. You don't have to go to church to find him."

Frank had one of the biggest hearts in show business and one of the smallest egos. We lost a great human being in 2007 when we lost Frankie Laine. He was ninety-four. He has just finished the notes for the introduction of this book, Stardust.

Frank's last words in his own book are: "Like the song says ...the music never ends."

That's the best legacy Frankie Laine has left us.

with Bing Crosby

PERRY COMO

THE BARBER
FROM CANONSBURG

Perry Como and I go way back to the days of good old radio. He was working his durable pipes on a fifteen-minute N B C show three nights a week in studio 6-A, Rockefeller Center. I was a young studio page wearing one of those classy blue uniforms with a yellow braid over one shoulder and a monogrammed lapel pin the shape of a microphone on the other. Perry and I would always exchange a few words before the show about, of course, the show, and how many people might show up for the performance. That studio was also the weekly home of The Bell Telephone Hour, a weekly one hour program of classical and semi-classical music where outstanding vocalists like Ezio Pinza and Marion Anderson performed.

Perry always acquired inspiration from the imposing abilities of those greats. His popular program was called the Chesterfield Supper Club. It later made a successful transition to television, unlike many other radio shows.

In those days, Perry was crooning his tremendous hits "Till The End Of Time," "A Hubba-Hubba-Hubba," "Because," "Some Enchanted Evening," "When You Were Sweet Sixteen," and "Temptation." He had come a long way from those barber shop days in the small coal-mining town of Canonsburg, Pa. where, on May 18, 1912, he was born to Italian immigrant parents of 12 other children.

At the age of 14 he actually owned his own Barber shop where customers always got their money's worth. Besides shaving and grooming them, he entertained by singing popular tunes. Then, in 1933, one of the musicians who was also Perry's customer and a member of the popular Freddie Carlone Band, carried an offer to him from Carlone for 28 dollars a week singing and traveling with the band. Perry happily accepted and was on his way.

"I remember when Perry sang (later) for Ted Weems." Frankie Laine said to me when we were talking about his own career, "Perry was always

Perry Como Goes To NBC; New Show To Have Variety Format

New York — Perry Como has been signed to a firm 12-year contract with the National Broadcasting Co. in one of the largest financial deals in the history of television. The deal was closed by Thomas A. McAvity, vice president of NBC television, and Thomas G. Rockwell, president of General Artists Corp., Como's agents.

The 42-year-old singer, whose current CBS thrice-weekly show has been the highest rated 15-minute stanza for the last three years, will conclude his current CBS program for Chesterfield July 1.

The onetime barber and band singer, whose fabulous rise in the last decade has made him one of the great stars of show business, started at CBS in 1943 with a sustaining across-the-board show, earning less than $100 a week. His present annual income has been estimated at one million dollars. He acquired the Chesterfield backing in 1944 and has been sponsored by them ever since.

The new NBC show, tentatively set for a Saturday night slot emanating from New York, will be an hour-long variety format, retaining the name *The Perry Como Show*. It will have its premiere in October and will have three sponsors. The exact premiere date, time slot, and sponsorship will be announced shortly.

Downbeat, May 1945

a kind guy and got me a tryout with Freddy Carlone, just when I needed employment the most, but I didn't last but a few weeks...my music and Carlone's music clashed." Perry and Frank had remained lifelong friends.

Perry traveled with the Weems Band during the following years, perfecting his mellow vocal style. During the war years the band had a hard time keeping together, so Perry returned to Pennsylvania and resumed barbering. Encouraged by his childhood sweetheart, Roselle Belline, his wife for over 60 years, Perry answered an offer from CBS to star in his own radio show. He returned to the music business and signed his first recording contract with RCA and released his first record, "Long Ago and Far Away." He remained with RCA for over 40 years, their longest running association with any performer, after all, he amassed an enviable list of hits, 42 of them in the Top 10 between 1944 and 1958, second only to Bing Crosby.

It was "Don't Let The Stars Get In Your Eyes," "A Bushel and a Peck," "Papa Loves Mombo," "Catch A Falling Star," and "Wanted" during the fifties.

Perry tried the movies but the big screen did not adequately project his personality, so he turned to television in 1955 and became the stunning star of a very high quality, hour-long variety show that lasted eight years. At the end of each show, Perry would sit in a cardigan perched upon a stool next to a music stand and a red rose, and just sing. His relaxed informality became a part of nearly every listening household. The tunes "Hot Diggity," "Round and Round," "Magic Moments," and "Delaware" were spun by musical director Mitchell Ayres and offered by Perry from the heart with the help of the Fontane Sisters. One segment of the show featured requests: The girls would sing, "Letters, we get letters, we get stacks and stacks of letters. Dear

Perry, would you be so kind; to fill a request and sing the song I like best?" And, of course, Perry would answer the request for a thrilled listener.

Then came rock and roll and things changed. Perry reminded us that in 1970 it was Richard Rodgers who said: "This is the era of mediocrity . The kids can't play their instruments they don't know anything about music, they buy a $3 dollar guitar and go in the bathroom and make a record and it sells nine million."

"It's crazy, but it's true," said Perry. "For years, singers like Vic Damone, Steve Lawrence, and many others were unable to get recording contracts. Now, people like Tony Bennett are reinventing our kind of music, and thank God for radio and 'Music Of Your Life' stations all over the country who still play our stuff."

In June of 1970, for the first time in 25 years, Perry Como appeared live, and it was at The International Hotel in Las Vegas. Later that year, "It's Impossible" became his twentieth gold disc. The songs, "Seattle" and "And I Love You" were also great 1970s hits for Perry. At the age of sixty (he always looked like he was 35) he began a world tour. His 40 Greatest Hits was a million-seller in the United Kingdom, and did very well in Japan and Italy too. His annual TV Christmas Show became an American institution.

In 1982, Perry played sellout concerts in Manila and Japan, and starred in a TV special from Paris for ABC, with Angie Dickinson as his guest.

Mickey Glass had been Perry Como's manager and overall business guardian for over fifty years and ran Perry's career from an office on Northern Boulevard in Great Neck, Long Island, with the help of longtime secretary, Vera Hamilton.

"Perry doesn't like hectic things, but, he likes the audience. They're his friends out there," Vera told me, "and Perry is a genuinely nice guy."

When I spoke to Perry Como in 1992, about Bing Crosby and those singers who followed him, a story that I had just completed for a California magazine, Perry said, "Bing was one of my idols in those early years. I used to imitate the Bing and Russ Columbo styles which were the most popular of that time of my career."

Perry had said he missed those days in New York and the many friends he made there over the years. Although he spent most of his life in Sands Point, Long Island, he retired to his longtime West Palm Beach, Florida, vacation home, where he regularly played golf, and said "The only hair I cut now is for my grandchildren.....but, they're terrible tippers," and grinned.

with his hero Bing Crosby

TEX BENEKE
Glenn's Reluctant Vocalist

It was a genuine thrill talking with Gordon Tex Beneke. The Texas drawl is ever so familiar. The sound of this man's voice enriched the personality of the great Glenn Miller Band, especially when voicing "Chattanooga Choo-Choo," "I've Got a Gal in Kalamazoo," "Jukebox Saturday Night," "Don't Sit Under the Apple Tree," among other memorable Glenn Miller evergreens. True, he's not what you would define as a bona fide vocalist and he did not desire to become a singer, but Glenn drafted him, and Tex went along with it. "'You sure can play the tenor (sax), all right Texas,' he said to me, 'but we need you for some vocals too,'" Tex Beneke told me just before Christmas 1997, "At first I wasn't sure what he meant."

Tex Beneke wasn't feeling well that day. He had been facing some health problems lately, the discomfort restricting his activities. I found him snuggled up at home with his wife, Sandi, but we had a long conversation about his favorite subject, the vastly celebrated Glenn Miller band and his own inimitable contributions to that legendary musical organization.

On various Miller recordings you could hear Glenn or the Modernaires singing group vamp with words as Tex , whistling, worked himself down from the sax section to the front of the bandstand where he would take up the vocal:

"Hi there Tex, what'cha say?" Paula Kelly and the Modernaires would sing, "Step aside partner, it's my day. Bend an ear and listen to my version," and the Modernaires continued, "of a really solid Tennessee excursion," and you know the rest. It's the opening lines to the very first Gold Record, the immortal "Chattanooga Choo Choo." Oh, how wonderful it is to hear that 1939 recording spin on the old turntable time after time after time. I never get tired of playing it. So many of us feel the same way.

Gordon Beneke was born in Fort Worth, Texas in 1914. Playing sax since he was nine, he began in local bands. Gordon joined the Ben Young Band and toured from Texas to Ohio. "In Detroit, I got a call from a guy by the name of Glenn Miller. I didn't know who he was at the time. He was starting a new band, and Gene Krupa recommended me because he had heard me in Young's band one night when he was scouting local bands for personnel for his band. Glenn wanted to know if I were interested. He offered me $ 50.00 a week, the same as everybody would be making to start, and would build on from there. I hesitated and asked him for $ 52.50 so I could be the highest paid member. Dead silence--- Glenn was frugal, you know --- 'O.K.,' he said,' but you'll have to prove yourself .'" Gordon drove his 1936 Plymouth for twenty-four hours through the snow to his first rehearsal. "When it came time for me to take a vo-

TEX BENEKE

6/01/98

Hi, Richard:

Thank you so very much for sending me a copy of "THE MUSIC MEN" - - - Sorry I haven't gotten back to you long before now, but I've been feeling so lousy the past few months, I just haven't been able to correspond with anyone! The guy who said "THESE ARE THE GOLDEN YEARS" had ROCKS in his head! Afraid I'm now going thru all the infirmities of my age-bracket . . and can't do anything about it!!

What I've read so far, Richard, is great and I'll try to get the questionaire off to you soon as possible. It's a kick reading about so many of my personal friends of long ago. Certainly brings back many wonderful memories!

Gotta go now, Richard (time for my pills) but will try to do better next time.

Sincerely,

Tex

cal on a song called "Doin' the Jive" - - - Glenn vamped 'Hi, there, Tex, what'cha say?' That's when the whole business of calling me Tex began. I guess he liked that Texas drawl. Now only people from my old home town ever call me Gordon."

After a favorable beginning at the Glen Island Casino in New Rochelle, New York, The Glenn Miller band went off on a national tour. "We were all young and didn't mind traveling," Tex said, "People would come from hundreds of miles away to hear us play. We'd perform at theaters, barns, parks, dance halls, and (dance) pavilions. We didn't know we were making history. We were just enjoying ourselves and making a living."

Tex Beneke quickly became a valuable commercial personality for Glenn's band. Glenn never missed an opportunity to feature Tex playing and vocalizing on specialty tunes. Tex was always cast into the spotlight and the public loved him. He found it difficult to learn lyrics but could learn anything on the sax if he heard it just once.

"It's ironic, Richard," Tex continued, "I really didn't like most of those tunes I sang including "Chattanooga Choo-Choo." All I was interested in was playing my sax. Of course, I had to go along with the vocal in order to be accepted. I had to do what Glenn wanted. That was part of the deal. Finally he put me doing parts with the Modernaires vocal group.

Jack Lebo Interviewing Tex

"He first thought "Chatta-nooga Choo Choo" was a dud and would not get off the ground: "But every time we played and sang it the roof would come off the place. I really didn't care about singing. All I considered myself to be was a poor man's Johnny Mercer. I always steered clear of it until I have to sing on some of the jobs when I'm leading my own orchestra. The folks want to hear those favorites, you know. I had to keep some of those arrangements to please the folks, especially the one's that made it big."

The movie Sun Valley Serenade , featuring "Chattanooga Choo Choo," "It Happened in Sun Valley" with Tex and the Modernaires, and "I Know Why" (And so do you) and "In the Mood," catapulted the Glenn Miller Band and Tex Beneke into the big time. It was their first film that starred internationally famous ice skating star Sonja Henie, John Payne, Lynn Bari, comedian Milton Berle, the amazing dancing of the Nicholas Brothers with Dorothy Dandridge, and Glenn's entire band. The second film, Orchestra Wives, with George Montgomery, Cesar Romero, and comedian Jackie Gleason featured the Mack Gordon and Harry Warren score, the biggest Miller hits ever, "At Last," "Serenade in Blue" and Tex Beneke singing "I've Got a Gal in Kalamazoo."

As is well-known, after Glenn disappeared over the English Channel in 1944, Tex took over the band. "I was asked by Mrs. (Helen) Miller if I would front the band in 1946. We broke the record at the Hollywood Palladium in 1947. We had 6,750 people dancing on opening night. The Miller name was just magic. I kept the job until 1950, when I decided to form my own band. I called it the Tex Beneke Orchestra. We played to capacity audiences everywhere. In New York, we played the Paramount, the Pennsylvania Hotel and lots of shows at Disney-land in California. We called our show The Music Made Famous By Glenn Miller right into the 1980's." Tex and his band had played right up to recently. Patty An-drews was a frequent guest as were some of the original Miller personnel includ-ing vocalist Ray Eberle and current versions of the Modernaires singing group. "I always found it comfortable singing with Tex and his guys," Patty Andrews told me.

"Today, (early 1990's) Richard, we do engagements mostly at private parties and sometimes at the Elk's Club or at night clubs and theaters. Looking back - all I can ever think about - that special place in my heart --is that the Glenn Miller Orchestra itself was the highlight of my career. Just to be able to work with a man like Glenn,, somebody who knew exactly what he wanted and worked hard enough to get it. He was a fine arranger, a good lead trombone player, and an excellent person, someone to look up to always. He also made a singer out of me - that was something in itself."

No if, ands, or buts, elite musician Tex Beneke was an important singing, non-singer of the Big Band Era and terrific bandleader, too.

DEAN MARTIN
Andiamo

FOR DEAN MARTIN

NOTHING WAS EVER A BIG DEAL...ESPECIALLY FAME

with Jerry Vale

When I was a young man working as a studio page at NBC in New York, I volunteered on the very first Dean Martin and Jerry Lewis Telethon in studio 6B on March 15, 1952. My job was greeting and logging in the talent and recording their time in and out. Many great celebrities performed for charity that historic 24 hours including Nat "King" Cole, Jackie Gleason, Ezio Pinza, Yul Brynner, Mel Torme, Ella Fitzgerald, Frank Sinatra, Milton Berle, Eddie Fisher [in a U.S. Army uniform], Perry Como, Cab Calloway - the list goes on.

And, I learned a lot about Dean Martin from Lee Hale, fellow member of the Society of Singers, who was associated with Dean for nine years on The Dean Martin Television Show , both as musical director and rehearsal stand-in for Dean.

LEE HALE

Dean Martin was unique, one of a kind. Tall, dark and handsome. Dean was a man's man and a lady's desire, and could sing as well as any singer of his day. According to every comedian he ever worked with, including former partner Jerry Lewis, Dean was the world's best straight man.

Dean Martin hit the big time when he teamed up with Jerry Lewis while performing in East coast night clubs during the mid-1940s.

"I was supposed to be the singing half and Jerry the comic," Dean said,"and we both did a lot of both."

Lee Hale, Orson Wells, Dean Martin and Producer Greg Garrison

The boys began their ascent in show business. Their routines were almost always ad-libs. The onstage antics has audiences howling. Fans began to expect the unexpected. Soon they completed a flock of hit movies for Paramount, and their appearances on NBC's Colgate Comedy Hour pushed them to the top of the coveted Neilson ratings.

Through all this, Dean was the anything goes kinda guy, while Jerry wanted to take charge, even produce, consequently reducing Dean's responsibilities. One day, and for no particular reason Dean could remember, the easy going Italian Crooner simply walked away.

"Everybody thought that was a big mistake on my part, "Dean said, "after all, Jerry was supposed to be the funny one and I was just the straight man." Afterwards, Dean sashayed his way through a couple of forgettable MGM movies. It seemed the public assumed his career was over. But Dean knew better. Booked as a solo act in the best Las Vegas showrooms, he found a prop that would establish his image from then on: a glass of scotch liquor. Vegas audiences, both male and female, found him lovable. I was just one of the guys," he would always say. That glass of scotch was mostly water. Some accused him of being a drunk, but Dean always replied, "I would remind those people that I couldn't possibly do all the things I was doing if I were soused." Concluding, NBC would not pay him millions if he were a drunk. They would've canceled the show if he showed up drunk even once, no matter how big a star. There was only apple juice in that glass. I know. I was there.

Some funny guest spots on a couple of TV specials led NBC to offer him a weekly hour of his own. It was the time, you know, when variety shows were the staple of prime time television. But Dean wasn't sure he'd like fronting a weekly show. Many of his co-performers had tried and failed (including

Jerry), and besides, "Why would I want to waste six or seven days a week rehearsing. I had better things to do -like play golf - watch the soaps, or maybe a movie or two," Dean pointed out. So he told NBC they could have him only if he didn't have to rehearse all week and if he could come in just one day a week, and that day had to be Sunday; and if they would pay him a lot of money.

To his total surprise, NBC said, "Yes!" There was trouble at first. The bookings were fashioned around circus type acts and Dean played Ed Sullivan: "And now, I'd like to present..."

Then maybe he'd sing a chorus of "That's Amore," "Pennies From Heaven" or "Memories are Made of This," depending on how he felt that day. After the first show, performed with a multitude of pals including Frank Sinatra and Diahann Carroll, the ratings plummeted. The show's producer was fired and its director, Greg Garrison, assumed both jobs. With ideas on

with Dom DeLuise

how to boost the ratings, he hired me as a special material writer and musical director. We had to find a way to use Dean more and keep the one-day-a-week schedule.

It was discovered that the less Dean knew about the show, the more it became spontaneous and funny. Greg always kept the tape rolling, even the goofs, because Dean made his mistakes appear to be well-rehearsed. His experience with Jerry gave him an endless supply of one-liners and stock routines that could endlessly get him out of any awkward situation.

With Dean's easy-going manner and his fine singing voice, the ratings began to rise. Our experiment worked. Dean would arrive around noon Sunday for a snappy music run through with Les Brown and his band. In his dressing room Dean would watch Greg and I go through his sketches and songs on a television monitor. Later, the audience filed into Burbank Studio # 4 and the taping began. It took an hour to tape the show. Before the band finished playing the closing theme, our star was out of the studio and into his sports car.

For nine long years Dean Martin never balked at anything we threw at him - and sometimes those things were outrageous. Remember the time we had him him slide down a pole and go straight through the floor, or when he leaped up on his piano and it collapsed under him? Dean made my job easy. No matter what song we gave him, or what surprise guest appeared, he always performed with enthusiasm and excellence.

Oh, Yes! I remember that Dean Martin personally chose his one ballad performed in the middle of the show - you know, the one he'd sing with Ken Lane at the piano. You may remember those ubiquitous cue cards on which he greatly depended, or the girls pushing him this way or that. Dean would stare at me offstage as I cued his entrances. Every time he came out on the studio stage, he'd look around for me, "I owe my life to you out there," he once confided to me. His struggles with the cue cards added charm to the show.

What great fun we had, and what I'd give to bring back those glorious days.

Dean was born Dino Crocetti in Steubenville, Ohio, on June 7, 1917. His father, Guy, owned a barber shop. Dean would sing at picnics and local dance halls and tried honest work in that limited steel community, shining shoes, pumping gas, boxing (until he broke his nose), and as a blackjack dealer in one of the city's gambling operations, being a fast guy with a deck of cards.

Dino, as he was known, enjoyed listening to Bing Crosby's recordings and thought he too could sing in that laid back kind of style if he tried. He began singing in bars and clubs run by friends where he learned to handle and ply an audience. In 1939, he joined up with Ernie McKay's band. Ernie altered Dino's name to Dino Martini. His pay? Forty dollars a week. He later joined Sammy Watkins band in Cleveland, that led to a four year contract. It was Sammy who suggested the stage name of Dean Martin.

One night Dean found himself looking into the pretty eyes of Betty McDonald. They began dating, married and had a baby. The little family moved to New York where Dean was engaged as a replacement for Frank Sinatra, but did not do as well as Frank had, abruptly ending that gig. He shuttled from contract to contract, finally sending Betty and their now two children back home while he remained to find new work. He teamed up, as singers did in those days, with a comic or other act, and one day in New York was booked with a kid named Joey Levitch, the son of a husband and wife vaudeville team. He called himself Jerry Lewis. After the engagement they went their separate ways only to run into one another a year later, in 1945.

Jerry was having a hard time staying on the bill where he was booked to perform his single comedy act. He talked to Dean's agent about following Dean with antics: When Dean was singing, Jerry, dressed as a waiter, dropped a tray of dishes. Jerry would ad-lib and perform antics that would include working the audience. They did pretty well. Jerry suggested they team up, but Dean decided against it, preferring his own independence.

Soon they were both out of work. However, Jerry had a booking at The 500 Club in Atlantic City, but bombed out. He placed a hasty call to Dean's agent in New York and begged Dean to join him. The agent worked a deal for both of them to perform as a single act. It worked: As Dean attempted to sing, Jerry, as the inept waiter, dropped drinks and dishes off his tray. Taunting Dean and throwing steaks at him, taking over the drums in the band, drowning out Dean's songs, spritzing him with seltzer water, and creating havoc, almost destroying the club, Dean would laugh, but continued singing as Jerry romped through his hijinks. Before long, now in demand, the pair rocked New York nightclubs and prevailed as the hottest act of 1948. All this was followed by television appearances on the Ed Sullivan Show and Texaco Star Theater and engagements in Los Angeles and Miami. By this time Betty[with their now three kids] filed for divorce, as a normal life for her and Dean became impossible as he was never home. Dean soon met Jeannie Biegger, a pretty blonde model, while performing in Miami and married her a month after his divorce from Betty became final.

After a few movies and a milk-warm try at an NBC radio show of their own, the pair garnered a coveted, regular spot as rotating guests on the Çolgate Comedy Hour television show and simultaneously signed with top-rated agency, MCA, to manage their contract bookings and financial affairs. They sprinted through 16 films between 1949 and 1956 and appeared in person for the last time in 1956 at the Copacabana New York. Over time, Dean felt exploited by Jerry, who dominated their professional relationship and diminished Dean's contributions to the act.

Many insiders figured that Dean Martin would not make it on his own without the presence of Jerry Lewis. However, as you know, after a slow start, which began in Las Vegas, Dean was immensely successful with his nine yearlong television show and went on to make over thirty additional films without Jerry Lewis, and costarred with John Wayne, Frank Sinatra, and Bing Crosby. His pivotal role in The Young Lions in 1958, Rio Bravo in 1959, and the Sons of Katie Elder in 1965 were straight dramatic performances, devoid of any singing or comedy and he held his own quite nicely. Dean spoofed through a couple of Matt Helm private eye films in the 1960s.

Appearing in the film, Budd Shulberg's Some Came Running with his future blood brother, and fellow Italian Crooner, Frank Sinatra, helped establish the famous "Rat Pack" composed of Frank, Dean, Sammy Davis, Jr., comedian Joey Bishop and British actor Peter Lawford.

Dean joined Frank Sinatra at Frank's Reprise Records where he recorded "Everybody Loves Somebody" suggested and written by his future piano accompanist Ken Lane.

Ironically, Dean's success on a Hollywood Palace television show was a replacement for the ailing two-hour ABC Jerry Lewis Show. The Palace led to the NBC series The Dean Martin Show that ran for nine years, followed by Friar Club Television Roasts, Vegas dates, movies, TV specials, and lots of golf...Yes! Golf.

Romance followed romance. Jeannie divorced Dean in 1972. Dean tried marriage once more with Kathy Hawn.

A memorable event occurred on Jerry Lewis' 1976 Muscular Dystrophy Telethon. Frank Sinatra came on and sang his songs, and then informed Jerry he had a friend that, well "...loves what you do every year and would like to come out." Upon that declaration, Dean Martin meandered out and embraced Jerry Lewis. It had been twenty years. It was an emotional and genuine greeting. Jerry chirped, "Ya working?" that broke up everyone. Dean sang with Frank and blew Jerry a final kiss and left. The audience was enthralled. Jerry was enthralled.

On a last ditched, final tour with Frank and Sammy, Dean bolted, flew back home and checked into a hospital. Liza Minelli took Dean's spot for the tour's remainder. Dean's health deteriorated over a short period and Jeannie returned to his side. His voice became weak. His spirit diminished.

Dean recorded over 600 songs, hosted 275 Dean Martin television shows and performed as a guest on 200 more. Dean starred in 50 films and performed on over 100 radio shows and sang during countless nightclub appearances. "The notion that Dean Martin 'coasted' through his career is completely exaggerated." That was just the face he showed the world.

with Frank Sinatra

MEL TORME

The Velvet Fog

I had been chasing Mel Torme' for years. In 1984, in a Long Island town named Port Jefferson, along with cornetist Dick Sudhalter, singer and pianist Daryl Sherman and bassist supreme Jay Leonhart, Mel and I talked about his life in show business.

At the 1995 Long Island Jazz Festival Mel showed up all right and dished up a terrific show---and I mean a terrific show, and we did a pre-show interview, and due to the show's running over and Mel's firing up an appreciative crowd with encores, the interview was again, shortened. The tour had to catch a bus for the next gig.

Mel Torme first impressed me in the bright, happy MGM collegiate film Good News, with lovely June Allyson and Peter Lawford, who sang "Be a Ladies Man" with Mel, who also crooned through the title song, showing off his impressive singing talents for the first time on screen. In his book , the 1967 version of The Big Bands, George Simon noted in 1946 Artie Shaw began featuring some quality singing on his new label called Musicraft Records. "Back came the strings, and in came some exceptionally good singers, Kitty Kallen and a young Chicagoan and his vocal group, Mel Torme and the Meltones, who provided some brilliant singing on some Cole Porter tunes, "Get Out of Town" and "What is This Thing Called Love."

So, who was this actor/song writer/ arranger/ drummer/ innovative jazz singer , dancer, and musical director Mel Tormé?

Mel actually started as a child of four singing solo with the then world-famous Coon-Sanders Orchestra on a coast-to-coast radio show originating from the Blackhawk Restaurant in Chicago. "An important band, it was really like--well--Benny Goodman-- an amazingly popular big-name for the time," Mel said. "It was 1929. I loved radio - you see, for me, radio was more fascinating than my set of Lionel trains."

The first song Mel ever sang in public was "You're Drivin' Me

Crazy" with the Coon-Sanders Orchestra. Later he sang it with the Buddy Rogers band at the College Inn in the Hotel Sherman, which became a regular gig for Mel. "That song finally became a hit for me in 1947," Mel said.

Over the years Mel kinda sneaked up on the public. In 1949, for instance, Bing Crosby had a big hit with "Dear Hearts and Gentle People", my friend Frankie Laine sold big with "Mule Train," and Mel scored high with "Careless Hands". But, "Careless Hands" was not as big or as nationally accepted as the recordings of the more established Crosby and Laine. These guys

a youthful Mel Tormé

were scoring hit after hit, year after year, but Mel was a comparatively new voice, although he had an earlier hit with a very smooth rendition of Rogers and Hart's "Blue Moon," a recording which earned him the sobriquet "The Velvet Fog", but in late 1996, in perhaps one of Mel's last interviews before he fell ill he was asked: "I heard you didn't like being called 'The Velvet Fog.'"

Chuckling, Mel said, "Freddie Robbins (Robbins Nest disc jockey) gave me that back in 1947. It stuck like glue, so I kinda came to grips with it. I don't mind it now because a lot of older people come up to me and say, 'Gee, I grew up with you and we loved your records and, of course, you are 'The Velvet Fog' to us.' So, I suddenly took a look at myself and I thought - why am I being so abrasive? It's not terrible- and it is descriptive - - it's not how I sing now, I mean I am no more 'The Velvet Fog' now than Frank Sinatra. I used to sing in that creamy, soft way, and so I have gotten to the point now where my license plates on my car say 'Le Phog,' he laughs heartily.

At one time Capitol Records thought that Mel would replace Frank Sinatra after Frank's career began nose-diving at the dawn of the rock and roll era. But Mel was a jazz singer and not accustomed to being instructed what to sing and how to sing it, so it didn't work out. Instead, he moved on to record albums with fellow arranger Marty Paich, particularly on a 1960 album Mel Torme' Swings Shubert Alley.

Here's the Torme' story: Mel was first a drummer: "I was a drum-and-bugle corps kid in grammar school. I loved Chick Webb and, obviously, Gene Krupa," Mel told Fred Hall, "and finally, Buddy Rich. Those are the people who motivated me as a young man." Then, an actor: "I was a child radio actor, probably one of the five busiest child actors in America, from 1933 to 1941." Mel did Mary Noble, Backstage Wife; Captain Midnight; Little Orphan Annie; and even Jack Armstrong radio shows. Next, a songwriter and vocal group arranger very influenced by the fact that Frank Sinatra broke away from Tommy Dorsey's orchestra and went on his own as a solo vocalist. "I could see the writing on the wall," he said, "and since I was a singer, I just followed the path of least resistance. And look what's happened to me. I mean, my God, look at me: I've become a singer!"

Quintessential musician: Besides drums, he plays a four string guitar and piano. As a songwriter, "A Lament to Love," his first song written at age fourteen, was eventually recorded by Harry James. Mel was still in high school.

Author: In addition to writing non-fiction articles about gun-collecting, motion pictures, World War I aviation, and sports cars, Mel has written both fiction and biographical books. Among them a semi-factual Western called Dollarhide (under the pseudonym Wesley Wyatt), which was later re-written for The Virginian television show; The Other Side of the Rainbow , about working the Judy Garland television show during a frenetic nine-month period; his own autobiographical It Wasn't All Velvet; a portrait of his good friend, big band drummer Buddy Rich, Trapps, The Drum Wonder, done as a last wish by Buddy to Mel, and more recently, My Singing Teachers, reflections on a lifetime of listening and learning to all the greats who influenced his life. Whew! Mel worked very hard.

Influences: His earliest days were captured by the imagination of Duke Ellington. The Ellington touch was home base. "You gotta understand," Mel said, "I was a Duke Ellington idolater. I mean, there are not words. I can't describe what I felt for Duke Ellington ----on a personal as well as a professional plane. "Mel was also struck by Bing Crosby and Ella Fitzgerald, "those two vocalists more than everyone else - moved me -put their hands in the small of my back and said...'Go!' Nobody comes close to Ella - I miss her. Bing - well - he was the singer of the century, the man who started all of us." As arranger & musical director: Let's talk about the Mel-Tones.; "It only lasted four years," Mel noted, "but we did a lot in that time. Aside from recording with Artie Shaw, we sang everything, everywhere. If anybody wanted to hear singing, we'd be there to sing for them. It was during the War - - we went to the Hollywood Canteen and sang there endlessly - also traveled to many camps all over the map." Mel's Mel-Tones performed brilliantly on "White Christmas," "What is This Thing Called Love," with Artie Shaw, "Day by Day," with Bing Crosby (who was a Mel Torme' admirer), and "Am I Blue," among others.

As a (jazz) vocalist : "When I recorded 'Again,' 'Blue Moon' was on the back side. After 'Again' ran its course, 'Blue Moon's' success was astonishing to me - I was knocked out by it - Pete Rugolo (the arranger) was a big help." With the event of the "Lulu's Back in Town" recording, Mel Torme left the crooning business: "I was kinda a crooner before that - now I sounded like an instrument. I went to Bethlehem Records and first put out 'Lulu,' and the audience said, 'Hey this guy can sing jazz.'"

Mel wrapped up his life's philosophy: "I'm proud of achieving, more than anything. When you stand in front of a great symphony orchestra - like the Boston Pops - and they're playing the notes I put down on paper, it's the closest thing to being God-like. I think, 'those people are playing my music.' As for retiring--if you rest, you rust. When I look around and find it's not fun anymore, then I'll quit. But, right now I'm having too much fun singing."

At this writing, Mel Torme' was marking time in his living room. Struck down by a stroke in August of 1996, while in the studio doing a tribute to Ella for a CD, Mel had to quit performing. By Christmas a respiratory infection set in, but doctors said his long-term outlook was good. He was definitely a fighter, receiving daily physical, occupational and speech therapy." I recall Mel's closing words of his autobiography: "Early on, it certainly wasn't all velvet. Now the fog has lifted."

But the Velvet Fog never lifted after that.

Mel and Beverly Beveridge sing to Bing

JOHNNY MATHIS

The Voice of Romance

It's true, like Frankie Laine, Johnny Mathis never sang with the bands, but, like Frankie Laine, he came upon the scene too late for the Big Bands and, like Frank, Perry Como, and Tony Bennett, wow...how he could sing. Take his interpretation of just these four songs alone: "Chances Are," "A Certain Smile," "Wonderful, Wonderful," and "It's Not for Me to Say" and you have a singing career solidly constructed through Johnny's incomparable phrasing and articulation, not to mention a brilliant microphone technique reminiscent of the early singing innovators Crosby and Como.

On a warm January day in 1998, Johnny Mathis and I sat around his great indoor pool in the Hollywood Hills in Los Angeles, California, in a clearly Southwestern garnished room filled with exotic palms, totems, and cactuses growing in large baskets, among rattan chairs and soft, wide couches, under a high, concaved, box-framed glass ceiling, his home for over 30 years.

"Welcome to my home, Richard, I hope you love it here as much as I do!" Johnny had just returned from a three-day engagement in Clearwater, Florida. We had been trying to get together for a few months.

No secret, Billboard charts have established Johnny as a world-class romantic singer who has prevailed over 45 years. By some accounts, Johnny Mathis is second only to Frank Sinatra as the most consistently charted albums artist. His Greatest Hits spent 490 weeks - count them: nine-and-a- half consistent years on the charts.

Johnny Royce Mathis owes a lot to his dad, Clem Mathis, who fostered his son's career from the time he was a small boy living with his large family in a San Francisco basement apartment. "I learned an appreciation of music from my father who taught me my first songs. He had worked in vaudeville back in the 1920s, and always encouraged me and my sisters and brothers to sing."

When Johnny was only 13, his father, realizing his son's exceptional singing ability, took him to see a Bay area voice teacher, Connie Fox, who taught him vocal scales and exercises, voice production, and some operatic skills. "I paid for these lessons by working around Miss Fox's home doing odd jobs, and what little time we had together was very precious and very special. Each day I would take the streetcar from George Washington High School in San Francisco, down to the terminal and then took a train across the Bay and studied with her. We concentrated mainly on voice production. I tried to take more theory, harmony, and piano, but I had so much going on with my athletics. Connie told me that if I learned to produce my tones properly (precise use of diaphragm and vocal chords, and accurate breathing techniques) that I'd probably sing as long as I wanted to. If I ever had an advantage, it was that I learned to sing correctly right from the start so I didn't get sick all the time. Over the years, I probably only canceled two or three performances."

Johnny was very active in school with Student Body President activities as well. Like any kid, he found time to do everything.

Music was always very special to young Johnny. He knew that someday he would get involved more seriously, "And, I knew the athletics thing was almost played out because I knew I had gone as far as I could." Unlike his hero, Nat "King" Cole, the whole singing experience did not come natural to Mathis. "The sound that I have did come naturally, I mean God gives us these little gifts, but Nat, Sarah, and Ella --people like that -- they never studied voice in their lives."

Johnny admits he never tried to be different; "I actually tried to copy all the other singers. Nat Cole was my big hero and I think the best singer of all of them. I listened to his music over and over again. Then I listened to Billy Eckstine and Sammy Davis, and then I took all the girl singers like Ella, Peggy Lee, and Lena, of course, and I tried to emulate the high, soft singing that they did. The women have a very flexible sound. I have the advantage of having a big register so I could sing a lot of high and middle range and low notes."

"You mean --like in Maria - the closing notes of that song?" I said.

"Exactly -- that's amazing that you picked that up...that night after night, year after year, I can still sing that delicate, little high note."

Originally desiring to become an English and physical education teacher, John Royce Mathis enrolled at San Francisco State College. He

became "the best all-around athlete to come out of the Bay area,î according to local newspaper reports. He set a high jump record only 2 inches
short of the Olympic record of the time. Two of his best friends, Bill Russell and Casey Jones, went on to play with the Boston Celtics.

One Sunday afternoon, while singing weekends at the Blackhawk
night club, Johnny was spotted by the club's co-owner Helen Noga, who
promptly took charge of Johnny's career and who asked Columbia Jazz
A & R man George Avakian, who was in the area on vacation, to come to
hear Johnny sing at Ann Dee's 440 Club, where she had just booked him.

After listening, Avakian quickly sent this now famous telegram to
his record company: "Have found phenomenal 19-year old boy who could
go all the way. Send blank contracts."

Although he was invited to participate in the 1956 Olympic trials in
Berkeley, California as part of the USA team, his dad encouraged him to
forsake it for a recording career. "Good decision, don't you think?" Johnny
said.

I guess you would have to say Johnny Mathis is mostly a romantic ballad singer, although he manages to make Christmas carols sound
magical, the way they should be interpreted. Nevertheless, he was
booked into jazz oriented New York's Blue Angel, Basin Street, and the
Village Vanguard. Then, fortunately, Johnny was placed under the management of Columbia's Mitch Miller, who told him to avoid jazz and record
pop records. Miller's magic was at work once again. He found "Wonderful, Wonderful" and "It's Not for Me to Say" for the young balladeer.

"The first time I heard my recording of "Wonderful, Wonderful"
on the radio, I knew I would become a singer for the rest of my life. I
had made the recording about a year before and they took a long time
to release it. I had played it myself on my own phonograph, but it wasn't
magical until I heard it played on the radio."

"Were you surprised by the phenomenal success of that recording?"

"I was flabbergasted. To this day I am still in awe. I cannot believe
that I've had this career, because I did not plan anything.

"About five or six people in my life -- that had to be there -- if they
weren't I don't think that I would be doing what I am doing today. First, My
Dad, who introduced me to music, then Helen Noga who discovered me
and pushed me. George Avakian, who brought me to Columbia Records,
and then there was Mitch Miller, who took over my recording career and
taught me literally everything that I know to this day about how to make
a record." Johnny maintained that Miller was brilliant, not in an easy way,
but more aggressively. Johnny was young, ready and willing to accept --
and he needed the strong, positive Miller guidance.

When Johnny chooses a song for a recording, he sets priorities: "The first thing I hear, which is probably what most people hear, is a

melody. If it has a pretty melody, I love it. And then, of course, I have to have some literate words to sing. When I go hunting for songs, I usually hunt by composers."

Those two songs were followed by "Chances Are," a monumental hit of its own, and the most requested song at his concerts right up to today. It was Johnny's first Number 1 hit. Another great tune "The Twelfth of Never" made it big in 1957. No one who was a teen at the time will forget those recordings. Johnny's rapid vibrato imparted a sentimental, bittersweet quality to that type of love song.

By 1960, he was voted number one male singer for the year, although he was up against rock performers Elvis Presley and Ricky Nelson. Johnny does a great job, too, on Cole Porter's "Begin the Beguine," Erroll Garner's composition "Misty," and Henry Mancini's own "Moon River."

In 1978, Deniece Williams and Johnny recorded a duet album that included the single "Too Much, Too Little, Too Late" that reached number one in 1978, and with his friend Dionne Warwick, recorded "Friends In Love" that made the Top 40 in 1982. Johnny has also duetted with Gladys Knight, Jane Oliver, his hero's daughter, Natalie Cole, and Nana Mouskouri. When you add it all up, it must be realized that Johnny Ma-

with Tony Bennett

this' incredible commercial recording success ranks third, just behind Frank Sinatra and Elvis Presley and ahead of the Beatles and the Rolling Stones. Like so many other vocalists of the 1950s, '60s, and '70s, Las Vegas became headquarters to many a Mathis headliner concert over the years. Additionally, Johnny went on to perform internationally from Japan to England and back to the White House, where he sang in a Jerome Kern tribute for the President in 1994.

"I've always been proud of my two Grammy nominations, for "Misty" in 1960 and my album salute to the great Duke Ellington in 1992." A fellow Society of Singers member, Johnny has given generously to help other singers in need. Since 1962, he has managed over 50 Tonight Show performances. "I think that may be a record, too." he said.

Unlike some singers, Johnny Mathis never sings when he is at home. I couldn't even coax him to utter one note. "I get so tired of hearing the sound of my voice," he said, "that's why I love to sing duets. I grew up singing in a lot of choirs and quartets in school. That's what I really like."

The whole thing with Johnny's success at concerts is preparation. "I make sure that I can sing everything that I have to sing on stage. That gives me the confidence I need. There's no one in the world who had less confidence than I did- - I didn't like the way I looked or acted or sang, I was shy and wasn't in command."

Johnny Mathis keeps going strong. What's his secret? I believe it's his consistency to purpose, uncompromising professionalism, great organization, and lots and lots of hard work. "The type of people who like my music are, right across the board, average people who like all kinds of music. They're not musical snobs. It's amazing, I go all over the world to places like Brazil, Germany and France, and it's the same everywhere I go. People that I care to spend any time with seem to like my music."

Johnny Mathis really takes good care of himself these days. He watches his diet and quit drinking alcohol some time ago. He works out five times a week, and the whole process has actually strengthened his voice. "At this point in my life I am really excited to see just how long I can sing at a level that I'm comfortable with. I think I'll be the first one to know when I no longer sound good. Then I'll quit. I'm very careful. I stretch out my performances, and do no more than three days in a row and then I come home for two to three weeks and rest up, play golf, and visit with my friends, like this visit with you."

For up and coming singers, Johnny advises them to get to know their craft and to be very good at what they want to do, if they want success.

Well, Johnny Mathis is still out there singing, and he is proud of what he has done over the years, especially those first recordings that set up his life's work.

Johnny Mathis and Andy Williams

JOE WILLIAMS

Every Day He Sang the Blues

Joe with his boss - Count Basis

Catching up to venerable blues vocalist Joe Williams was not an easy routine even in the 1990's. Fresh from a couple of gigs at New York's famed Blue Note jazz club with the Count Basie Orchestra where he had put on an absolutely remarkable show of both old and new favorites to standing ovations, Joe, resting at home between tours, became victim to my jingling his memory bank divulging the history of his bounteous career. I allowed him no rest as he slumped deeply into an easy chair, unlike the over six foot frame we were used to seeing when he's standing on stage with those large eyes and flashing teeth.

Born in Cordele, Georgia, Joe was blessed with a dedicated mother who, under difficult conditions, took him to Chicago and kept him in school.

"Life was very hard and I worked at any job I could find," he recalled thoughtfully, "I was a man-child in the streets. I worked at selling newspapers, carrying ice, anything -- and I finished three years of high school, which was difficult in those days." His mother interested him in music, although he wanted to be a baseball player, but, he said, "I drifted into playing the piano and listening to the strongly dramatic--very rhythmic urban blues." His other teacher was the radio. He listened carefully to Duke Ellington when broadcasting from the Cotton Club. He was also impressed by the powerful Paul Robeson and Lawrence Tibbett, two great operatic voices of the 1930s.

His absolute influence? "That'll be Joe Turner. I never sang the blues before until I heard Turner and decided that's how it's supposed to be. That, for me, was the difference. Turner was a great body standing like a statue out there and just belting out one after another."

The Great African Prince Sings!

Joe Turner was the great robust blues singer who earlier played the Kansas City circuit accompanied by Pete Johnson's piano. He would sometimes sing all night. In 1941 Turner was signed by Duke Ellington who found him fascinating. "He turns every song into a great blues song," Ellington said. Joe also credited Ethel Waters and Herb Jeffries as strong musical influences.

Joe Williams' (formerly Joseph Goreed) big band credentials began at age 16 with Johnny Long's band. (That's when his mother and aunt chose the name Williams as Joe would go around and ask local bandleaders on the south side of Chicago to let him sing with their band). Next was work with Erskine Tate and Jimmie Noone's (in Chicago,) sometimes performing with all three at the same time. Then he performed with Coleman Hawkins, Lionel Hampton (where he was paid eleven dollars a night to start) and finally toured with Andy Kirk's big band in 1946.

"I was with Hampton four months or so, but I never recorded with him because of the recording ban. That's when I first met Frank Sinatra. He was with Dorsey at the Paramount. Dorsey backed his singers better than any band. I learned from that meeting." Joe's legendary tenure with Count William Basie existed from 1954 to early 1961. It's where Joe established his name, expanded his repertoire, and, it is acknowledged, helped increase the fame of the Basie band. That great locomotive band was the perfect showcase for his range and versatility. When people think about Joe Williams, it's almost always about that association with Basie. Joe's definitive recording "Everyday I Have the Blues" was the superior one recorded with Basie in 1955. It became his theme song. On that same album Joe included "Going to Chicago" and "Alright, Okay, You Win," two of his long-standing classics.

After Basie, Joe performed in front of Harry "Sweets" Edison's quintet for a while and has freelanced ever since. He has collaborated with jazz pianist George Shearing on an album and completed two with trumpeter Thad Jones and jazz drummer Mel Lewis. Joe has returned to Basie time and again, even with then ghost- bandleader Frank Foster in 1992. In 1984 Joe appeared in Boston at Symphony Hall with Sarah Vaughan, backed by the masterful pianist Norman Simmons and a blue-ribbon trio.

"You have performed with just about every great jazz singer and even some non-jazz singers," I noted.

"Oh, Yeah! Ella --- Ella---and Lena, and Dinah, and Sarah - - Dizzy (Gillespie), Carmen (McRae), everybody, and that means Marlena Shaw, Diane Schuur, Diane Reeves, and Cleo Laine, too."

Over the years Joe Williams has shown himself to be at home with all forms of rhythms: blues ballads; romantic standards; bright, up-tempo things, and soulful blues. The range is part of the Williams mystique. With a pillowy voice and regal presence, he exudes confidence, being now the elder statesman of blues singing.

"In 1994 - after wanting to do an album of spirituals for some time, I recorded the album Feel The Spirit - you know, stuff like Go Down Moses and The Lord's Prayer. I had to do that, Richard. And I'm glad I did.

Joe and I talked more about our friend Count Basie. I interviewed Bill and Catherine Basie back in 1982. Bill, his valet, and I helped him change from street clothes to concert cloth. Bill, after suffering a heart attack in 1976 and a victim of severe arthritis, needed help at this point in his life, even to simply dressing himself.

We agreed that Bill Basie was a gentle, very nice man. "His band members loved him too," Joe said, "He gets out of the way and let's them play. He lets the guys play so they have pride in what they do because they are doing it, "Joe went on, "How do you conduct feelings? That's the reason they have sounded so good for all that time. If there were problems within the band, we would always straighten it out without involving Basie. We were artists that tried to act like artists. The musicians were all proud men who believed in getting the music right."

When Count Basie celebrated his 80th birthday in 1983 at a Greenwich Village, New York, night club, Joe blew out the cake candles. Basie called him his Number One son. Joe Williams and Bill Basie never shook hands when they greeted one another- they vigorously hugged every time. While with Basie, Joe was voted best blues singer five times in the Downbeat Magazine reader's poll.

"He spent a lot of time kidding me," Joe said, "but in that kidding there was always a lesson. When I come out to sing, I change and emotionalize and begin to feel the audience out there, and my songs come across more personalized-more sensitive- more dramatic - and I love it." he said. I choose my own songs and do them exactly the way I feel them at the time."

"Joe," I pointed out, "you are considered the last of the jazz/blues singers of the Big Band Era. How do you think history will record your place in jazz singing?"

"I have no idea. I am a singer, and I sing. I sing only songs that I feel I can do well. Be it Billy Joel's stuff (he recorded "Just the Way You Are") or Cole Porter. I don't sing today for that reason…being memorialized." He smiles and hunches his shoulders from the easy chair.

Joe had some advice for up and coming singers: "They have to find their own way. They have to put in the time, the hardships, the experiences. They have to approach something new-something different. You can't imitate the great distinctive voices. When a group of singers tries to sound alike because of a current popular sound, it doesn't work. I remember when everyone was chasing Bing Crosby. There was (Russ) Columbo, Perry Como, Dean Martin, Pat Boone, and so many others. They found their own way eventually. It got them started. But they had to find their own way in the end." Joe never copied his predecessor Jimmy Rushing, although he often sang with him, because the distinctive sound of Rushing was so unique. "I wouldn't have attempted to approach what he was doing. Like Louis Armstrong and Billie (Holiday) - that distinctive sound is what you don't get involved in at all," he said. "It's true that the old songs were best. As Norman Simmons wisely says, 'when singers perform today nobody falls in love.' It's different now."

Joe Williams album Nothing But the Blues for which he won the Grammy in 1985 found him in prime form performing with jazzmasters Eddie Vinson, tenor Red Holloway, organist Brother Jack McDuff, Ray Brown, and other All Stars.

"You seem to get better with each successive album," I said, "They say you have created a more interesting singer in yourself in your later years."

"I hope so because you should get better as you go."

The summer of 1991 found Joe Williams being honored by the Society of Singers in Las Vegas. Henry Mancini, Greg Morris, Keely Smith, Della Reese, Robert Goulet, Billy Eckstine, Nancy Wilson, Al Hibbler, and Marsha Warfield were there among many others saluting his lifetime of success as a great singer of the blues. His lovely wife of 40 years, Jillean, was among the faithful. A remarkable pleasant person, Jillean is English, raised in Surrey, a great fan of Winston Churchill, and faithful to the Queen. Although Joe and Jillean live in Las Vegas, Joe never sings there. "I wouldn't work any of the main rooms there unless they dealt me the full treatment," he said.

It was in July of 1996 at the Dakota Bar in St. Paul when Joe launched into the great favorites "Dimples," "CC Rider," "I Got It Bad and That Ain't Good," "Tenderly," and "Satin Doll." "I don't remember feeling that good. I think every pore in my body was open that night, Richard. I am 78 years old now but I feel like forty. It was one of my best." They say the audience was swaying and hooting uproariously, enjoying every moment. He sings so clearly with such fine diction. The name of Joe Williams will always be synonymous with impeccable and excellent jazz singing. I was fortunate to be a friend.

HERB JEFFRIES

He Arrived by Way of Flamingo

Talking to Herb Jeffries is like talking to a long-time friend. Herb is out there working every day of his life and hard to catch up with. "I get up and open my eyes and I'm happy and I am healthy and grateful that there is something for me to do out there everyday," he said to me one early Monday morning from his beautiful home in the California desert where he likes to carefully observe hummingbirds and similar thrills of nature. "I am trying to write my memoirs," he said," but I find it hard to sit down for any length of time to write, Richard. I am a nature kind of guy and am more suited to the outdoors."

Herb Jeffries first association with the Big Bands was with Erskine Tate, followed by Earl Hines, Sidney Bechet, and Blanche Calloway, before becoming a member and now the only remaining survivor of the great Duke Ellington Orchestra of 1941- 1943. Some of the legendary instrumental soloists of that band were Ben Webster, Jimmy Blanton, Harry Carney, Juan Tizol, Lawrence Brown, Cootie Williams, Barney Bigard, Johnny Hodges, and Rex Stewart. What a lineup!

Herb was happy to talk about his stellar singing career: "Singing with America's greatest bandleader and showman was a great stroke of luck for me. I had been making a series of Western movies in Hollywood during the 1930's and was appearing in a film called The Bronze Buckaroo in 1940. It was being shown at the Apollo Theater where Ellington was appearing on stage. He introduced me to the audience as The Bronze Buckaroo, and it stuck. I did some songs with him, and he hired me on the spot that night. I was making movies, but I knew I'd rather sing with

Ellington, so I gave up movies for a while. Historically, down the road a hundred years or so, it may someday be compared to having played alongside Mozart or Beethoven - yesterdays great composers. I believe Ellington will go down as one of America's great composers. Music was everything to him. He was in love with music, more than anything in the world."

In those days, Herb could imitate any known singer and often would imitate Bing Crosby at rehearsals, "Both Swee' Pea (Billy Stray-horn) and the Duke heard me one night and said, 'Hey, keep that voice - that's the one we want you to use,' they called out to me. Of course, I eventually came into my own and dropped all those voices that weren't my own. But, I also have to tell you that Bing Crosby was my strongest influence. I can still notice the sound of Bing even in my work today."

While Herb was with Ellington, songwriters Ted Grouya and Ed Anderson wrote an interesting, but un-Ellington kind of tune titled "Flamingo." "When the boys brought the song to Duke one day, he was kinda busy, so he asked me to listen to it and see if I liked it. I did. Duke asked me to pass it over to Swee'Pea to arrange. Duke then gave the song a test - like he always did with new songs- right in the theater where we were performing. When the people really showed they liked it, he figured it would sell, so he recorded it."

While in Miami, Herb was so fascinated with the song "Flamingo" that he obtained permission to go to nearby Hialeah to study flamingos in their natural habitat in order to get a feel for interpreting the song. Herb is a warm, emotional singer, always injecting strong feelings into his performances: "You know, Richard, I have always been a bird lover and have owned some exotic birds. Flamingos are very graceful, and, like a flamingo, I would like to fly - you know, like all kids dream of flying - I just want to raise my arms up and fly like a flamingo." Herb's enthusiasm and strong baritone voice sounds like a man half his age.

"Flamingo" is one of the era's most memorable recordings and certainly Herb Jeffries most durable contribution to the Ellington legacy. Tony Martin and others have also recorded it, but "Flamingo" belongs to Herb Jeffries.

Herb Jeffries recording of "Basin Street Blues" is another of his incredible recordings. "I recorded that one with Buddy Baker in 1946 - I was a more mature - more independent singer - by that time. It was on Exclusive Records. I was a junior partner with independent producer Leon Renee'. I also recorded "When the Swallows Come Back to Capistrano" which became a hit for me."

And the subject of the intricacy of the song "Lush Life" came up. "I recorded that song as Nat (Cole) also did, and I enjoyed it. You, know," he said, "Swee'Pea wrote that song - music and lyrics - when he was only 17 years old. Isn't that amazing? I love that song. It is a mature piece of material. Just stop and listen to it and you will realize what a philosopher Swee' Pea was."

Herb told me that he remains busy doing concerts almost everywhere. When he does jazz or western concerts he reminds his audience that the two musics are interrelated, "Both musics were born in America - Jazz and Western. Neither were borrowed from Europe. Rock has been an important spice to music. There are so many different cultures here - and the musics are merging, that's for sure...but very slowly."

Herb Jeffries last album was entitled The Bronze Buckaroo Rides Again, issued by Warner Brothers. "I signed with Warner some years ago, Richard, doing country western and jazz. I've been making records and doing appearances. The audiences remain large. A three day festival draws 50,000 people."

Of the 14 selections, which covers 60 years, you can hear his work from the cowboy films of the thirties, tracks with both Earl Hines and Sidney Bechet, four Ellington numbers including the great "Flamingo" and "Jump for Joy" and live selections from his early appearances at the Apollo.

"Sixty-seven years, Herb," I said, "that's a long time. But what about the '60s, '70s and '80s? Where were you?"

"In Paris," he smiled, "where I had a night club called the Flamingo for ten years." Herb had realized his shifting popularity to Europe in 1950, so he emigrated to France, along with a handful of other jazz expatriates.

Back in the United States Herb Jeffries opened at the Mocambo in Los Angeles, and also worked Ciro's and other night clubs in the area. He moved to Hawaii, living there throughout the seventies where he also toured the clubs and even owned his own nightspot for a while. The eighties found him back in California doing clubwork and taking time to write his memoirs which he titled Echoes of Eternity, a sort of autobiography composed of prose and poetry yet to be published. I will be ninety-six in September (2007) and I play three rounds of golf every week, do dozens of charitable shows, and with my wife, Regina, help run our theatrical production business, and I've been a vegetarian for 58 years.

Herb Jeffries is an articulate voice for his music, his inspiring lifestyle, and for the musical hero of his life, the great Duke Ellington. My long conversations with Herb Jeffries enriched me, generating images of an age gone by filled with great music performed by celebrated musicians and singers. He is one of the distinguished voices.

"Most people arrive on this planet by stork, Richard. I arrived by Flamingo."

Herb Jeffries remains on the scene even today, 2008. "I'm a vegetarian Richard, and I don't eat fish, either. Mercury, you know."

AL MARTINO

SPANISH EYES
Music by BERT KAEMPFERT
Lyrics by CHARLES SINGLETON and EDDIE SNYDER

KEYS
04540
Recorded by AL MARTINO on CAPITOL RECORDS
Roosevelt Music Co., Inc.
75¢

HE HAS BUT ONE HEART

Al Martino and I go back to 1998 when we talked about his wondrous career as a class "A" singer of all the great ballads.

Al, formerly Alfred Cino, croons those great tunes "Here in My Heart," "I Love You More and More Each Day," "Mary In the Morning," and his signature classic, the million seller and overwhelming international favorite, "Spanish Eyes," that melts many hearts.

Al's Italian immigrant dad was a brick layer and builder of postwar homes. Al first worked with him in the construction of the homes. An older friend, the legendary Mario Lanza, encouraged Al to pursue his own career as a singer.

"As an impressionable youngster I got started the same way so many others did, I listened and was influenced by other singers on the radio. There was Al Jolson, Tony Martin, Sinatra, Perry Como, Frankie Laine - and so I bought their records and began to sing along with them. Of course, you haven't developed your own style yet - it doesn't appear until years later."

Talking to Al Martino that day from his Beverly Hills home, we touched on the development of his singing style: "I began to vocalize first with a piano, then with a trio at local clubs around Philadelphia, and then I became a winner on an Arthur Godfrey's Talent Scouts show, and before you knew it, I was making records."

Luckily for Al, he found a backer right away in Bill Borrelli, who had heard him on the talent show. "He liked the way I sang and thought I would be the perfect singer to record a song he was working on called 'Here in My Heart,' Al recalled, "So with two other financial backers, Busillo and Smith, we formed the recording company BBS Records, perhaps the very first independent record label, just to produce my first recording." It was, of course, the first time that very popular song was ever sung or recorded. And, like a miracle, it went straight to number one on the charts.

"We had no idea it would score that well, even though I liked the song very much from the beginning, and it was actually written just for me."

Monty Kelly, an arranger and friend of Al Martino, worked diligently with him, locating and rehearsing quality studio musicians, directing the orchestra in the careful arrangement of this recording. "When you want to make a record, you simply hire an orchestra. That's the usual pattern. You don't have to have your own established orchestra to make a record, "Al explained.

Al brought the newly-produced recording to Capitol Records: "I drove to California in my Father's 1952 Ford taking the record with the BBS label - it took me three days to get there - and tried to sell it to Capitol. I had but five days to seal the deal, as I had made an agreement in Philadelphia that if I didn't sell the record to Capitol within five days, it would revert back to another manufacturer owned by Dave Miller. I had to forfeit all my royalties if Capitol didn't buy it. That was the gamble. As bad luck would have it, they didn't. So I gave it to Mr. Miller. It became a hit, as we all now know, and, of course, I received no royalties."

"Nothing at all?" I asked.

"Not one penny."

Another very memorable Al Martino vignette: "In the early sixties I heard an instrumental melody on the radio called 'Moon Over Naples,' which was written by German orchestra leader and composer Bert Kaempfert. It had been released in America, and I had a copy of it, but I didn't know there were lyrics written to it. Then somebody wrote a lyric, I heard it on the radio, and I didn't like it at all. So I called the publisher and said, 'If you dump that record that's out there right now, I'll give you an exclusive on a new and much better lyric.' I had alternate lyrics written for the song by Ted Snider and Larry McCousick."

That event happened in 1965. It became Al Martino's biggest hit and one of the most popular records of all time. The song: "Spanish Eyes."

As Al's career took hold, he did very well singing in and for the movies. He performed "Hush, Hush, Sweet Charlotte" for the Bette Davis film of the same name, which led to the coveted role of Johnny Fontane in the 1972 award-winning film The Godfather. The tune was an Italian piece entitled "O Marenariello" ("I Have But One Heart,") written by Johnny Farrow. It was perfectly suited for Al. He also recorded the film's poignant theme "Speak Softly, Love."

"Phyllis McGuire of the McGuire sisters called me to say she read the book. She knew about my life more than any other performer so she thought I was perfect for the part. I was, like other singers who sang in nightclubs, by organized crime in the beginning. So I had my own story that paralleled the character of Johnny Fontane. The director, Francis Ford

Coppola didn't want me in the film for some obscure reason, so I had to reach some pretty important people over his head to remain in the film. I didn't enjoy working on a film knowing the director didn't want me, and that's why I turned down the next Godfather film."

"It's not always easy selecting a song you want to record. For me, the best way to hear a song is to get a good demo of it...especially from the composer. He usually will send you a lead sheet set for the piano, but that's not good enough. You have to have the writer's interpretation, because he wrote it. Johnny Symbol wrote 'Mary In the Morning' and sent me a demo of him singing it while he played the guitar. So I hired him to play at the recording session."

That song is one of Al Martino's most popular and the one he still receives so many requests for at concerts. Like so many American vocalists, Al Martino's recordings fare better in Europe. "People in Europe are true music lovers. Here, they mostly think of just one thing - rock and roll, or rap, or anything dished up and pushed upon the public by Top 40 radio. In Europe, especially the adults, they appreciate our kind of music and promote and play it consistently over the rock stuff."

Al lived in England from 1953 to 1959 where he enjoyed a great popularity as a performer. While trying to get a hold of him for updated material for this book, I found he was performing in Germany, where he frequently tours. From Germany he flies back to his home in California and back again to the East coast where he did a one night, annual show, at Westbury Music Fair, (North Fork Theater) where I finally caught up with him.

About possible retirement: "I believe in being productive. That's why I will never retire. It's not a question of how long I can go. I think one should always be productive. Retirement is out of the question because it means you are unproductive. What am I trying to prove? This! If a person wants to be productive - survive - he has no alternative. He has to keep going. I think I have reached that point now. I'm supposed to be productive, and I am. I love performing on the road. I love to record. I also love to ski. It's what you want to do. It's called living. I like to work and live."

On August 8, 2004, on Public Television, Al Martino personally appeared during a pledge week promotion wherein they presented a one hour concert he made during the 1970s in Edmonton, Canada, performing his almost entire book of songs. Al talked nostalgically about his good fortune as a singer and went on to lip-synch his new album's featured tune "Come Share the Wine," which, has gone on to add to his vast repertoire of fine songs.

GUY MITCHELL

A Crying Heart

What an exhilarating experience reminiscing about Guy Mitchell with Guy Mitchell at his Las Vegas home. Fresh from appearances in Nashville, Guy's enthusiasm is not unlike his peppy originals "My Truly, Truly Fair" and "The Roving Kind," some of the delightful songs I enjoyed so much as a young man, songs that established Guy as a singing star back in the early fifties. Those top-selling recordings were produced under the tutelage of Columbia Records master A & R (Artists and Repertoire) man, Mitch Miller. Miller had first offered the songs "The Roving Kind" and "My Heart Cries for You" to Frank Sinatra, who, although experiencing a serious career reversal at the time, turned Miller down cold: "So I called Guy Mitchell, and he recorded both sides, which became instant hits," Miller said. Miller also coined Guy Mitchell's adopted name, lending his own full first name to Guy for his new surname. Guy's 1956 blockbuster, "Singing the Blues," arranged by Ray Conniff, was number one for 26 weeks and became the biggest selling record between the '50s and '70s.

A few weeks ago, while visiting with Jerry Vale, he explained that it was Guy Mitchell who introduced him to Mitch Miller in 1950. Guy said: "I was singing in a club on Long Island and Jerry was the house singer. I said to my manager, 'Hey, there's a kid out there singing, and he's singing better than me.' So I asked Jerry to come to my dressing room and told him that he was very good - and he said, 'Thank you very much, Mr. Mitchell.' and I told him I'm not a Mr and that just Guy would be okay. So I took his number down and got hold of Mitch and the rest is history."

That introduction and eventual association with Mitch Miller established Jerry Vale as a singing star along with the impressive stable of performers who recorded at Columbia records, including Tony Bennett, Rosemary Clooney, Frankie Laine, and Johnny Ray. Although once a classical music (oboe) performer, Mitch Miller was an under-appreciated star-maker who was criticized by many, but produced an amazing quantity of popular records that sold extremely well and were adored by most of the public, if not the critics, thereby creating more singing stars than any other record producer of his time. All of Miller's protégés advanced to even greater success, graduating into their own solo careers. "We were all unknown quantities, Richard. Miller made us. He took a chance on us."

In his book Lucky Old Son, Frankie Laine noted, "We ended up enjoying a long string of successes together, and from the start Mitch demonstrated a talent for setting off voices in original, if not downright quirky, musical settings. Who else would've put a harpsichord on a Rosemary Clooney record, or backed Guy Mitchell with swooping French horns?"

"No matter when I perform, Richard, the people want to hear the old hits, like "Belle," ("Belle, Belle, My Liberty Belle" "Sparrow ("Sparrow in the Treetop"), "Heart," ("My Heart Cries for You") , "Roving" ("One of the Roving Kind "), and "Pittsburgh" ("Pittsburgh, Pennsylvania ") - you know what I mean. So I still sing them - and they give you standing ovations. And you can't do a medley -- they want the whole song as you originally did it the first time. It's an osmosis between you and the audience. They even start singing with you after the first few bars. They know all the words, Richard."

Guy Mitchell honestly appreciates and respects his audience. "Rich, in your first book, the Trumpet book (The Best Damn Trumpet Player) you said Woody Herman would've given up if he had to play stuff he did twenty years before. I don't have that luxury."

For his work at Columbia, Guy earned a spot in the Columbia Records Hall of Fame, was honored with a star on the Hollywood Walk of Fame, and won Billboard Magazine's Triple Crown Award for an artist who hit the #1 spot, sold best in stores, and was most played on jukeboxes, all simultaneously. Only a few have achieved that position.

"But, listen, Richard, I also played with the Big Bands. I sang with Harry James at a special concert, and spent two weeks playing with Tommy and Jimmy Dorsey when they made up to keep the bands together." Guy also toured briefly with Stan Kenton and Lionel Hampton: "I was supposed to be the headliner, Rich, but when Hamp played his great theme 'Flying Home,' I said to him afterwards, 'You are the headliner.'"

Formerly Albert Cernick, Guy Mitchell was born in Detroit on February 27, 1927. His Yugoslavian born parents moved from Colorado and then to LA in 1938. As a kid, Guy auditioned for the movies while singing on radio station KFWB in Hollywood, but the family moved on to San Francisco and Guy settled down to life as an apprentice saddle-maker and part-time rancher.

Singing the Blues

"My singing career started at three, they tell me, at Yugoslav weddings. In high school I would ride in rodeos, but, when I didn't win any money riding bulls and bucking horses, I would sing for some bucks in the barn. I only did that to make my way home so I could get back to school by Monday morning.

"I really didn't want to be a singer, but I could sing well and I really dug Al Jolson, Perry Como, Sinatra and Crosby. But, if I had to decide, one or the other, it'd be horses and rodeos and ranchin'. In the Navy I ended up singing with the Navy band. Ray Anthony had a band on another ship next to us - and I wound up singing with his Navy band. When I got out, I went back to the saddle shop and rodeoing. But, I also liked music, so I auditioned for western singer Dude Martin's radio show--you know--country - - pop stuff. They kept asking me to sing more songs and I went on the air. It didn't hit me though until I was on the air - and guys at the rodeo heard me and said I sounded terrific--- and the advice that I'd get to buy a ranch a lot quicker by singing for good money than rodeoing. Then, I heard (pianist-bandleader) Carmen Cavallaro's singer got sick at the Mark Hopkins (hotel in San Francisco) and they needed a singer right away." Guy figured that ranch he desired would be attained sooner singing with a name band like Cavallaro, so he hustled up to MCA (Music Corporation of America, who managed many performers), and volunteered to sing even without the presence of a piano.

"I said, I don't need a piano. What do you want to hear?" Guy sang "Pretend" Nat Cole's then popular recording." They liked it. So we went over to the Mark Hopkins and there was a line of guys on each side waiting to audition. I really couldn't wait on this line - I wasn't being pigheaded, mind ya,- I had to get back to the rodeo, so I said to myself - 'this settles it, I'm going back to the rodeo.' But this MCA guy let me up first with Cavallaro, and I sang "Mam'selle", and got the job. I couldn't believe it! Guy made his first recording with Carmen Cavallaro on Decca.

Recalling an unusual adventure during Guy's first appearance at the Copacabana Nightclub in New York evoked some humorous memories: "I turned down doing the Copa a couple of times, but I finally agreed to do it -- because you have to do the Copa just once-- even though to me it was a snake-pit -- really was. But I went and did it anyway. The first night, Richard, became a hit because - right in the middle of all these pop songs - like 'Roving' and 'Truly Fair,' and maybe some standards like 'Body and Soul' ...and maybe an Italian song...'I Have But One Heart,' but right in the middle I threw in a country medley--and would you believe-- at the sophisticated - supposedly -- Copa--they went nuts! I even had to sing it upstairs (in the lounge) for the staff. Isn't that somethin' else?"

Like Bing always did, Guy Mitchell also sang all day long: "Throughout the day I sing all kinds of music, Richard. I'm a singer, and so I always sing."

"Why I went broke in the cattle business, Richard? Guess you have to feed them!"

Guy Mitchell retired from the singing business for health and personal reasons throughout the '60s and '70s. He returned to raising cattle and quarter horses on a ranch in Idaho. In-between Guy suffered from a rare condition known as leucoplakia (of the throat), and was cured, he says, by the power of prayer. "It's funny, the fringe benefit of the illness was I sing like I did in my twenties - like 'Truly Fair' - I sing those songs in the same key as I did then. That's got to be a miracle." Guy said.

By the late 1970s Guy ventured back. "They came looking for me at the ranch. They were doing a tribute to Arthur Godfrey and Mitch Miller, with all the old crew, and this guy (John Quincy Adams with PBS in New York), believe it or not, came all the way from New York City to find me- - and they talked me into going to New York for this tribute. I thought I was too scared to come back." But, he did. And he went on and on singing all over the world. His 1980's release of 'Always on My Mind' and' Wind Beneath My Wings' continue to sell today along with re-issues of his early recordings.

My lifelong affection for Guy Mitchell and his music was a thirst never quenched until today when the years were bridged and punctuated on a common ground, a gregarious get-together that was a total pleasure for me, a fan and writer. I had a lot to thank Guy Mitchell for, and I did!

Russ Columbo

A Career Cut Short

Bing Crosby once spoke about his rival Russ Columbo, the "Prisoner of Love" recording star: "I worked with Russ in 1930 at the Cocoanut Grove. We were in the Gus Arnheim band together. He played violin (and accordion) and sang. I just sang. I am sure if Russ had lived (longer), he would have been a big, big star. A talented, fine musician, he was a most attractive and appealing fellow." His similar crooning is sometimes mistaken for Bing's. Appearances at the Cocoanut Grove catapulted both Crosby and Columbo's careers.

In 1931, Ruggiero de Rudolpho Columbo formed his own band and became a sensation with a very silky, ballad style of singing, suggesting him as a Bing Crosby rival. One of the songs that heralded him was his own composition "You Call It Madness" (but, I call it love). Columbo toured the U.S. and Europe singing "Prisoner of Love," "Paradise," "Auf Wiedersehen," and "Too Beautiful for Words," among others. Columbo made a few films: Moulin Rouge, Wake Up and Dream, The Street Girl, and Broadway Through a Keyhole. He also recorded with Jimmie Grier's orchestra. His exciting, promising career came to a sudden end in a bizarre accident. On September 2, 1934, a photographer friend was showing him an old pair of dueling pistols and struck a match to one of them that, unbeknown to anyone, turned out to be loaded. Russ Columbo was hit in the head by a ricocheting bullet and died on the way to the hospital.

PROUD OF HIS ROOTS

When Julius La Rosa and I got together during the summer of 1997, we discovered we lived but a few blocks from one another during the mid 1940's in Brooklyn, New York. You could find me glued to my Admiral phonograph play-ing mostly Bing while Julie was dreaming of singing like Frank Sinatra.

"In Grover Cleve-land High School I was the vocalist with the school dance band. We sang mostly dance charts. Then I heard Sinatra. Before him a singer was just an adjunct to a band - always sing-ing in tempo, never paying much attention to the lyrics. He taught me that songs are really little poems. He was the first to put a comma here, a hyphen there, three dots here, and a period there. What he was doing was telling the story as he interpreted it. Before that, a singer sang (Julie sings) "I love you truly" but Frank sang (Julie sings again) ' love you-- tru -- ly, ' giving the words meaning---interpreting the song the way the composer intended. Ask any singer my age and they will tell you that Sinatra was their major influence."

Julie, as he likes to be called, joined the Navy after high school and wound up in Pensacola, Florida, aboard a ship as an electronics technician. Arthur Godfrey , the great CBS radio personality, was there earning his Navy "Wings" which meant he had to qualify by landing and taking off from an aircraft carrier six times. "Someone - to this day I don't know who it was- - a kid in my division - got word to him to catch their shipmate at the enlisted men's club. He did, and heard me sing 'The Song Is You' and 'Don't Take Your Love from Me' and after the show he said to me, "When you get out of the Navy - look me up - I've got a job for you.'"

Julie followed through on exactly November 19, 1951, and began singing on Godfrey's radio show. "I had no show-business experience. The six months I spent on the radio show gave me a chance to get comfortable before I was to join his television program. And, God bless (bandleader) Archie Bleyer. He was a major influence early-on. He saw I was just a kid, so he took me under his wing."

Archie Bleyer made a professional singer out of an inexperienced Julius La Rosa. A conservative gentleman, Bleyer was actually an excellent leader of men. A foremost writer of stock arrangements before the Big Band Era, Bleyer arranged and conducted an orchestra at Earl Carroll's Club in Hollywood during the 1930's.

"My first hit was unexpected. The song 'Anywhere I Wander' had been recorded by Tony Ben-

nett, Mel Torme' - and others - remember - in those days everyone would record the same song - but nobody had a hit with it. I liked the song (it came from the film Hans Christian Andersen) and sang it on the Godfrey radio and Wednesday night television shows a number of times. We got a lot of mail asking where can I buy the record?' I wasn't recording at the time. That was when Archie decided to start Cadence Records."

The first Cadence record was "Anywhere I Wander?" I guessed easily. It became a big hit for Julie.

"Yes," Julie said, "and the record catalog number was 1230 - a number I'll never forget for two reasons - 1-2-30 is both my birthday and the catalog number of my first recording."

Another big hit for Julie at the time was the serendipitous and charming "Eh, Cumpari," a Sicilian folk song similar in structure to "Old

McDonald Had a Farm" with instruments instead of animals. "Eh, Cump- ari "means - well - you get married and you ask a friend to be best man - you are cumpari. It's a very close relationship between two people. A friend has a child - you are asked to be Godfather - we are now cumpari," Julie explained, "I had a lot of fun recording that song. Everyone loves it. It's infectious like Rosemary Clooney's 'Come-on-a-My House.' It is a Sicilian song I sang as a kid."

Proud of his Italian roots, Julius La Rosa nevertheless told me a very amusing story about his trip to Italy: "I was visiting my uncle in Palermo, Sicily, and asked to see where my father was born. He took me to an area of the city comparable to what we call Hell's Kitchen, on the West side of Manhattan. When I got back to the hotel I sent him a tele- gram: 'Dad, saw where you were born. Glad you moved.'" Julie's dad was the quintessential radio repair man. He opened and closed a number of shops during his life - eternally searching for that better, more lucrative location. "He was known as Charlie, the Radio Man," Julie said.

Julie recounted the most infamous event of his life, his on-the-air firing by his somewhat tyrannical boss, Arthur Godfrey. "Well, I broke a rule. I hired a manager. You couldn't have a manager when you worked on the Godfrey show. Godfrey called William Paley, CBS Chairman, and told him my new manager, Tommy Rockwell of General Artists, informed him that in the future all dealings with Julius La Rosa had to go through his office. I've been told Paley said to him, 'You hired him on the air - so fire him on the air', and Godfrey did while millions were watching. It was October 4, 1953.

After singing his song "Manhattan," Godfrey summarily executed him: "That was Julie's swan song with us. He goes out on his own now, as his own star, to be seen own his own show. Wish him Godspeed, as I do." Godfrey declared.

"Did you say anything to Godfrey afterwards?"

"Yes. After the show I thanked him for giving me my break. It was all cordial, no rancor. In an interview many years later, Godfrey said: "The only SOB that ever said thank you, was that kid, Julie."

Julie lives in New York, North above Manhattan, and remains ac- tive singing wherever people want to listen. We keep in touch.

Mighty Mighty Man Gone too Soon

Whenever I hear the Three Penny Opera classic "Mack the Knife" I think of Bobby Darin and the great rendition that established him. (Not that's there is anything wrong with Louis Armstrong's version). The same goes for the tunes "Clementine" and "Beyond the Sea." It also seems that all Darin's recordings were performed upbeat, utilizing many types of rhythms. Maybe Bobby knew his life would be cut short and so he tried to get as much of music and life in as possible. In the seventeen years he recorded, he sure packed in every genre of product available to him in the business.

Born in 1936 and sadly gone in 1973, Bobby Darin was a confident force in music like very few before or after him. Influenced mostly by Frank Sinatra, he began as a rock and roller, drummer and piano player, and worked up into the great music standards by way of pop country, gospel, swing, and jazz. Regardless of style, Bobby Darin tried everything - a one of a kind performer.

Bobby performed at the Copacabana, recorded an album with the great composer/lyricist Johnny Mercer, backed by legendary Billy May, and performed mightily on television and in films.

Born on May 14,1936, Bobby was a prime product of the Bronx, New York, but, unfortunately contracted dreaded rheumatic fever as a little kid, an illness that damaged his heart and was the eventual cause of his passing in December, 1973.

Bobby was obsessed with making an early name for himself in

show business. After graduating high school and attending a year of college, he became a demo writer and singer at the Brill Building in New York, the heart and soul of Tin Pan Alley, where songwriters, song pluggers, arrangers and publishers gathered to offer their wares, in written and recorded music, to all the world.

Bobby Darin's first hits, both that he wrote himself, were with Atco Records with the release of "Splish Splash" (written with Jean Murray in 1958) and "Dream Lover" in1959. This success followed up with an album entitled "That's All," a sturdy compilation of standards performed in the unmis-   takable Darin style and featured what was to become his biggest hit, "Mack the Knife." Well, he won two Grammy's as both Record of the Year and was cited as Best New Artist, and he never looked back. He was like the little engine that would, could - and did.

Bobby was but twenty-three when he was invited to important career boosting engagements in musically teeming Las Vegas and at the famed Copacabana in New York, where all the great performers of his day were sooner or later engaged. Besides singing in his act, Bobby also performed remarkable impressions and played piano. He successfully welded together swing with rhythm and blues, with rock in-between.

A prolific actor, composer, and vocalist, Bobby Darin did it all, and in record time. He appeared in no less than thirteen films, had his own television variety program (1972 and '73), composed a startling number of songs, some for motion pictures and others for popular recordings. He led Las Vegas star Wayne Newton to success when he suggested to him the song "Danke Schoen." You see - Bobby, always grateful, gave something back.

First married to actress Sandra Dee, his costar in Come September , with whom he had a son, Dodd Darin, and then a second marriage to Andrea Yaeger. Bobby Darin passed in December 1973 when he was only thirty-seven years old. But, what a career he created in such a short time. In 1990 he was posthumously inducted into the Rock and Roll Hall of Fame and into the Songwriters Hall of Fame in 1999, and in that same year his prolific and exciting life and career were documented on Public Television.

BUDDY GRECO

AN EVENING WITH

BUDDY GRECO

The Green Room

AT THE CAFE ROYAL

Benny Goodman's Protégé - Still Playing and Singing

Another successful classical, musical product of Philadelphia is jazz piano playing-vocalist Buddy Greco, who began working at fifteen in his own trio in 1941. He named them Three Shades of Rhythm . Buddy's dad had freelanced as an opera performance critic all while managing his own popular record shop, as well as hosting his own radio show on WPEN, Philadelphia. Buddy loved to listen to the records of the Big Bands at his dad's shop, specifically the Benny Goodman swing band. Buddy studied classi- cal piano at the famous Philadelphia Settlement House. While playing in a trio in 1948 at Philadelphia's Club 13, Buddy was scouted by Benny Goodman's band manager, leading to Buddy's playing in the band by the end of that year.

Playing piano, arranging, and singing in that great Goodman organization, was a dream come true for the young musician. His ultra-hip interpretations of classy songs fit in nicely with the ever-expanding Goodman band.

During the following few years Buddy recorded dozens of sides with Benny and would sometimes lead the band while on overseas engagements.

When Benny Goodman first hired Buddy in 1948, Buddy was riding a rocket with his own trio's recording of Carmen Lombardo's "Ooh!

Look-a -There, Ain't She Pretty?" with Buddy on the vocal.

"I received only thirty-two dollars for that recording," he said. However, Buddy didn't feel so bad after learning the Andrews Sisters received only fifty-dollars for their blockbuster recording of "Bie Mir Bist du Shoen" and had to split it three ways.

"After the record 'O-o-h Looka There..' was released, a lot of leaders wanted me to join their band, but I was never interested. But when Benny called, I responded. I had always admired him and I wanted to learn my profession the best way possible. So, I gave up a lot of bucks to go with Benny. For some obscure reason Benny took a liking to me. He also knew I had won a scholarship to Curtis Institute when I was fourteen and I think that impressed him.

The first thing Benny had Buddy play at his audition for the band was a serious classical piece:

"He just threw it in front of me like nothing. And I played it, and that afternoon he took me to meet the great Igor Stravinsky. And, Benny knew I had perfect pitch."

When Buddy became comfortable with the band, he would invoke some mischievous musical nonsense now and then: "As a tease, sometimes I would change the key on the introduction to certain songs, and he wouldn't be able to catch it right away, so he'd come in on the original key, then look over his glasses and give me the famous Benny Goodman 'ray.' He must have fired me ten times during the year and a half I was with him, then promptly hired me back with a raise each time."

Buddy's overall relationship with the unusual personality of Goodman combined with his own mercurial self was generally good. "Sometimes he would invite me to stay with his wife and kids at their apartment in New York. He would also send money to my parents, which wasn't typical of him. Who would do such a thing? To me Benny was always kind and generous and I loved him for that."

During his time with Goodman, Buddy Greco introduced specially arranged bebop and modern jazz material into the band's book. During an engagement at the Hollywood Palladium Buddy had to take over directing the orchestra when Benny suddenly took ill with a bad back and had to leave the podium, signaling Buddy to take the stand and lead the band.

Buddy traveled to London with Benny to perform with a London based orchestra because the British Musicians Union would not permit the entire band to come over to play. The band, fronted by Goodman, with Buddy as piano player, received rave reviews, even though pickup musicians were rounded up to form a musically valid jazz band. These musicians knew the Goodman book and just how to play it.

A year later, Benny Goodman disbanded, complaining that "The music was different for him and he would rather play the early stuff." Buddy said, "overall and after working it a bit, Benny thought the bop material was wrong for the future of his kind of music, and decided he was through with it."

In the early fifties, Buddy began writing tunes for other singers, like Rosemary Clooney, and performed on his own radio show. When I was with NBC Guest Relations in the early fifties, I remember Buddy working on the Jerry Lester late night forerunner of the Tonight Show, called Broadway Open House, with vocalist David Street and musical director Milton De Lugg. 1967 found Buddy's show as the summer replacement for Jackie Gleason's TV show. Buddy shared the show, costarring brilliant drummer Buddy Rich. It was named the "Away We Go!" series and featured many fine musicians and comedians.

Buddy with Jerry Vale

To many, Buddy Greco is acknowledged as a Frank Sinatra style vocalist, performing all the classic tunes of the great composers in the 'bel canto' style, adding his own endings and vocal charm to performances.

The 1970s found Buddy living in Europe for a while, performing prolifically in appearances throughout Europe and down under the Equator in Australia.

This singer's singer has made 65 albums with so many diverse performers and in many genre's stretching from bop through country, including big band and ballads too. He has recorded 100 singles. He has played piano with the great London Symphony Orchestra and recorded with all the great, all-star musicians. The London recordings are his favorite, as he played, arranged and directed the orchestra. In 1955 Buddy recorded with vocalist compatriots Alan Dale and Johnny Desmond on Coral, and was featured on television programs starring singer Andy Williams, comedian-dancer Donald O'Connor and pianist, composer, and host Steve Allen.

Buddy's last notable work was performing at revered Carnegie Hall for a tribute to his friend, pianist and vocalist, the wonderful Nat "King" Cole.

Recently Buddy and I have been talking about writing his biography. Keep tuned.

Vic Damone

Still Breaking Hearts

Vito Rocco Farinola, known to all as Vic Damone - the guy who Sinatra claimed, ..."had the best set of pipes in the business," celebrated 50 years in the singing business in 1997 and performed at a sold-out one-man Carnegie Hall concert on January 24, 1998. Afterwards, his publicist Rob Wilcox told me the show was a terrific success.

Vic worked as an usher at the New York Paramount Theater when he was a kid and became influenced by Frank Sinatra. Vic's voice, although clear as a bell, was similar to Sinatra's style and voice tone in his early period, especially on his 1946 radio air-checks "You Go To My Head" and "All Through the Day," Sinatra style songs Vic performed on station WHN.

"Most songs have been recorded by Frank Sinatra," Vic said, "but you have to try to give them a new interpretation." Vic cheerfully admits the emulation was deliberate at the time, "I tried to mimic him. My training, my learning process was watching performers onstage. I decided that if I could sound like Frank, maybe I did have a chance."

For me, Vic Damone's most appealing recording was "You're Breaking My Heart," which will always be his song as Tony Bennett's is "I Left My Heart in San Francisco." Vic, of course, did not come up with the Big Bands, but he appeared in a movie, The Strip, with the great Louis Armstrong, Jack Teagarden, and Earl Hines. In the 1955 film Hit the Deck,

Vic sang Vincent Youmans' wonderful song "Sometimes I'm Happy," and my friend, arranger/conductor Frank De Vol directed Vic singing "An Affair To Remember," the title song from the 1957 hit movie.

Vic sometimes avoids those old tunes in his current work, but always does Lerner and Loewe's classic "On The Street Where You Live," from Lerner and Loewe's My Fair Lady," for my money the definitive recording of that song. Vic toured with Bob Hope's USO troupe at Chu Lai, Vietnam in 1966.

Vic kinda retired for a while then appeared back on the scene in the early eighties, mostly because of a renaissance he enjoyed in England. It seems a DJ, BBC's David Jacobs, gave Vic a lot of play, especially on his 1961 album The Pleasure of Her Company . Vic toured the British Isles to standing room audiences during the eighties. "When he walked on stage, before he sung a note, he received a standing ovation everytime, everywhere," said Denis Brown of The Dick Haymes Society in a recent society newsletter. In 1996, twenty-five of Vic's Mercury Recordings was reissued under the title, The Mercury Years.

Vic Damone appeared onstage as Sky Masterson at Westbury Music Fair in a revival of the 1940's Broadway musical Guys and Dolls. Over the years he has performed regularly at Michael's Pub and Rainbow and Stars in New York, and in important venues in Las Vegas and Atlantic City.

Some people say Vic Damone hates show business, "But, I'm never tired of singing," he says emphatically. Luckily, Reader's Digest had issued The Legendary Vic Damone quality CD with 30 new and 30 old recordings.

Vic sings with snapping fingers, bobbing his head and tilting his shoulders, savoring each syllable, singing in a rich, conversational baritone that's still robust and romantic. A true Italian troubadour.

Vic's "Farewell Performance" on February 10, 2001 at the Kravit's Center in West Palm Beach, Florida, backed by a 60 piece orchestra, was a night to remember.

Vic lives in Florida now with his caring wife Rena Rowan-Damone, a former designer at Jones, New York, and who heads philanthropic foundations to help various charities.

a very young Vic Damone

EDDIE FISHER

Grossinger's Kid Singer Goes Hollywood

with Elizabeth Taylor

I met Eddie Fisher only once. While in the Army, he was gracious to appear on the very first Dean Martin and Jerry Lewis muscular dystrophy telethon at New York's NBC television studio 6B. My job was to admit the talent and document their appearances. Eddie, who was dressed in uniform and accompanied by Army personnel, talked to me while I was waiting to usher him on stage. He was very thin and very young - I was thin and even younger.

One of seven children, Edwin Fisher was brought up in Philadelphia in relative poverty. Although the family name was either Tisch or Fisch -Eddie was not sure which - the name Fisher was already adopted by his tyrannical father before Eddie was born in 1928. "We were certainly very poor. But I was lucky. I was born with a voice. Who knows why? Nobody else in the family was musical at all." Eddie said.

Eddie sang "Santa Claus is Coming to Town" at a school concert. He won first prize. He went on to sing in school, churches, and synagogues. "I wanted to become a cantor and sing in the temple," he said. The richness of that music had a profound effect on the young singer.

Eddie went through the usual growing pains most singers have experienced on the way up. Al Jolson, Bing Crosby, Jerry Vale - almost everyone. When Eddie received a single ticket to see Perry Como's radio show, Perry asked the audience if anyone wanted to sing. "I found myself jumping out of my seat. He called me up on stage and I sang his own song "Prisoner of Love." The audience loved it---then Perry said, 'Well, I guess I'll have to sharpen up my barber tools,' with a smile, of course."

Eddie, by his own admission, was more of a belter than a crooner but, he admired both Frank Sinatra and Bing Crosby, the great crooners of his young life. The first break came when Buddy Morrow was forming his own orchestra and was looking for a band singer. Lester Sacks, who was with Frank Sinatra's publishing company, auditioned Eddie. Satisfied with what he heard, Lester, brother of Columbia head Manie Sacks, awarded Eddie the job which was opening at the Lincoln Hotel in New York. "I was paid seventy-five bucks a week, and was I excited, "Eddie said.

Eddie was seventeen and scared. Buddy Morrow (who now fronts the Tommy Dorsey Orchestra) fired him after just three days because Eddie could not keep time or read music. Luckily, Charlie Ventura was in the audience on his last night and hired him to sing with his band at the Boston Post Lodge, a dance hall in Larchmont, New York. Unhappy with Ventura, Eddie received another break, an audition at the famous Copacabana in New York as an opening act for then popular comedian Joe E. Lewis beginning in the fall. What a break - - and for $125.00 a week. But, first he had to spend the Summer singing with Eddie Ashman's band in the Terrace Room at Grossinger's upstate New York Catskill Mountain resort. The gig at the Copa turned out to be that of a disappointing production singer - never singing alone - just doing silly Copa songs with chorus girls.

After some slow breaks, Eddie Fisher was finally 'discovered' by popular vaudeville and then major radio star Eddie Cantor the following summer while singing at Grossingers. He toured with Cantor, who really liked the 21 year old, and Eddie idolized Cantor as one of his life's heroes. "Cantor paid me five-hundred dollars a week, which was a lot of money for someone who had been living on Coke and crackers, and he gave me clothes and an expensive wristwatch."

Thanks to Eddie Cantor, when he arrived in Hollywood, Eddie met the royalty of radio: Jack Benny, Bob Hope, George Burns, and Edgar Bergen, but, his really first success came as an opening act for Danny Thomas where he brought down the roof at Bill Miller's Riviera in Fort Lee, New Jersey. Eddie sang "Thinking of You" and RCA moved quickly to capitalize on Eddie's recording. With help from orchestra leader and arranger Hugo Winterhalter, Eddie recorded "Turn Back the Hands of Time" and "Bring Back the Thrill."

"It was 1950 and Eddie Fisher had finally made the big-time," Eddie said.

The world opened up. Eddie was in demand everywhere: the La Vie en Rose Club, the Paramount (with the Mills Brothers), Ed Sullivan's televised Toast of the Town variety show, Martin Block's Make-Believe

Ballroom at radio station WNEW, and with disc jockey Brad Phillips, all in New York. In Philadelphia it was the important Dick Clark Show, and in LA Johnny Grant's famous show. Eddie Fisher was a fast-rising star at twenty-two.

Eddie Fisher's singing style arrived with his hit "Oh! My Pa-Pa" that always sounds vital and fresh. He delivers it with belief and heart." I knew it would be a success," Eddie told me, "although it was pure smaltz, it somehow touched everyone, including my own parents, who at the time, thought I sang it just for them."

Edwin Jack Fisher became a private in the United States Army. Out in 1953, Eddie had his own Coca Cola, Coke Time TV show televised from the very same studio 6B., which lasted for three very successful years.

Consider the songs: "I Need You Now" and "Anytime" as well as "Wish You Were Here" and "Downhearted" were hits for the successful troubadour. Those songs suited him perfect.

with Debbie Reynolds

Even More Guy Singers

Vic Damone, Sammy Davis Jr., Jerry Vale and Jack Jones

LOUIS ARMSTRONG: Played then Sang. I guess you can say that Louis sang as well as he played. Did he play first, or sing first? No matter, he always sang. The legend of Louis dropping a songsheet and continuing on, thereby inventing what's called 'scat-singing' seems to be true, since I have read about it over and over. This was supposed to happen when he was performing with the Hot Five on a song called "Heebie Jeebies."

Some purists were very unhappy when Louis sang more than he played later on in his career. He was considered by many as being an artistic derelict. His singing emanated from his early cornet playing. Although his voice was untrained, he achieved vocals through shouting, but improved along the way arriving to his totally distinctive, instantly recognizable timbre. In some singer's recordings you have to stop and reflect, since so many singers of the era sounded somewhat the same, because emerging singers emulated one another, especially those that preceded them. But Louis' voice is unmistakable.

Songs like "St. James Infirmary" and "Basin Street Blues" are some early notable performances, yet nobody copied him. How could they without risking exposure as flagrant imitators. Louis grunted and gasped and distorted notes but always came back on track after straying way off. Billie Holiday did that too! "It's A Wonderful World" sung by Louis is the trademark recording that so easily identifies him in today's world.

The unmistakable sound of Louis Armstrong's great trumpet and gravelly voice is truly one of America's treasures.

CAB CALLOWAY: THE HI-DE-HI-DE-HO MAN

Louis Armstrong and Billie Holiday

After nixing an offer to play basketball with the Harlem Globetrotters, Cab Calloway hustled his way through the Roaring Twenties and right into The Cotton Club where he made his indelible mark. "We played in the Cotton Club whenever Duke had a 'gig' some-where else," he said in his autobiography. When he sang in a white zoot suit, his presence on stage was electric. He'd sing, "Hi-de-hi-de-ho," and the audience answered, "Wah-de-do-de-way-do-ho," that started acciden-tally when Cab forgot the words while on a radio show and began scatting the lyrics. Calloway made his fans forget the Great Depression with his singing, stomping and dancing.

"In the simplest terms," Cab said, "we were raising hell in those days. We were in and out of the movies, making records, smashing atten-dance records everywhere, and doing national radio shows. Lord, were we riding high., beginning with Jolson's The Singing Kid . We did about ten films."

Tall and slender with hair waving from side to side, he punched out songs like "Minnie the Moocher," who became a household name. "Since 1931, when I wrote Minnie, I've written more than a hundred tunes, some of them alone, often out of my own loneliness, and a few of them with others. I don't need to add that none of them has ever been as important to me as Minnie , though I have had fun with many of them." Calloway worked and played with Louis Armstrong, Lena Horne, Duke Ellington, Al Jolson, Dizzy Gillespie and Bill "Bojangles" Robinson. Cab Calloway knew how to entertain and make people happy.

In 1937, when the Cotton Club closed, Cab Calloway took his band on the road for an extended tour. Records were broken at the New York Paramount, the Meadowbrook supper club in Cedar Grove, New Jersey, and the Cocoanut Grove and Zanzibar Club in Manhattan.

In 1967, at the age of sixty, Cab performed a Broadway show opposite Pearl Bailey in Hello, Dolly!

Some of Cab's jive talk that appears in his constantly updated Hipsters Dictionary, and words like apple (the big town), canary (girl vocalist), cat (musician in a swing band), Armstrong's (upper register, high trumpet notes), "gimme some skin" (shake hands), the Man (the law), are lasting colloquialisms we have absorbed over the years. Cab Calloway was one of the great singing bandleaders who helped shaped the Big Band Era.

Cab Calloway

In the 1950's, when I worked at NBC, I knew a song writer named J. Fred Coots who wrote "Santa Claus is Coming to Town", "You Go to My Head," and "For All We Know." Fred and I would talk for hours about his role writing songs (with Benny Davis) for Cab Calloway and the Cotton Club Parade shows. "We were so busy we hardly had time to breathe," he once told me, "Cab was an honest-to-goodness super entertainer. It was a joy to write songs after the tradition of Harold Arlen and Ted Koehler (both collaborated on "Stormy Weather" for the Cotton Club). Cab loved good music, fast horses, a game of cards and a bottle of whiskey, a few close friends, but most of all, life itself. Working with him was the most exciting time of my life."

Sadly for us, on November 18, 1994, an 86 year old Cab passed away.

JIMMY RUSHING - Mr. Five by Five

This great Basie Band blues-singing soloist was a most distinctive individual. His generous body and his powerful voice were standards of the 1930's Basie organization. Born James Andrew Rushing in 1902, both his parents were musicians His father was a trumpet player in a brass band, and his mother a church singer, so James studied music theory in Douglas High School in Oklahoma City and Wilberforce University in Ohio. His Uncle Wesley taught him how to sing the blues. Migrating to the West Coast, he played parties with Jelly Roll Morton and was a singing waiter in night clubs. In 1925 he toured with the great Walter Page's

Blue Devils, making his first records in 1928 and 1929.

Rushing's prolific career spanned Bennie Moten's and Basie's great locomotive band that was working the Reno Club in Kansas City. "Jimmy's enthusiasm and optimism kept our boys going even when the going got rough on those tough days on the road," Basie told me back in the 1980's during an interview. The recording "Boogie-Woogie" (also called "I May Be Wrong") became long-standing Rushing-Basie standards.

Back in those days there were no microphones. "You had to have a good pair of lungs to be heard," Jimmy said.

In 1950, when Basie broke up his first band, Jimmy tried retiring, but

Jimmy Rushing

couldn't take the quiet life: "The first time a band came through town I'd be finished. It happened and I told my wife we were packing our bags and going back to New York." In his own band he recorded "Goin' To Chicago" (a Joe Williams favorite) in an album Jimmy Rushing Sings The Blues, accompanying himself on piano. His players were Walter Page, Jo Jones,and Buddy Tate, all Basie sidemen. Jimmy reunited with Count Basie in 1957 with Lester Young and Jo Jones at the Newport Jazz Festival, the tracks of the festival released later on Verve recordings. In 1962, he recorded with Earl Hines Band and my friend Budd Johnson on "Gee Baby, Ain't I Good to You" and "Who Was It Sang That Song." Jimmy Rushing admired most the singers Ethel Waters, Perry Como, Bing Crosby, and Louis Armstrong, "You see," he said, "I love music and I love singing it." We lost Jimmy Rushing in 1972. Joe Williams has valiantly carried the torch for that kind of blues singing ever since. Both Basie and Budd Johnson told me they very much admired the work of Jimmy Rushing.

FATS WALLER-Lived Hard-Died Young

Most everybody loved Thomas Fats Waller, whose songs were mostly cheerful and definitely unforgettable, effervescent and energetic. Born Thomas Wright Waller on May 21, 1904 in New York City, he began as a piano player for the Fletcher Henderson Orchestra when he was only twenty-three, although he started playing professionally at the age of fifteen even though his father, a clergyman, tried to stop him.

A black musician in a white-dominated industry, his was a story of

Fats Waller

hard struggles of a once serious piano stylist. I recall Red Norvo telling me that while married to Mildred Bailey and living in Forest Hills on Long Island, Fats Waller used to go over to their house along with people like blues singer Bessie Smith, vocalist Lee Wiley, and bandleader Bunny Berigan, "and play and sing and eat like crazy. We were all good friends. Fats was well-known then, "he said. Actually Fats Waller was one of the few outstanding jazz musicians to achieve wide commercial fame during his lifetime. He obscured his great musical talents under a guise of a singing comedian. From 1934 on he recorded dozens of records with his own band, mixed with both slapstick and charm.

Waller was influenced by James P. Johnson, who found the stride school of jazz piano.

Waller wrote lots of great songs: "Ain't Misbehavin'," "I've Got a Feeling I'm Falling," "Honeysuckle Rose," "What Did I Do To Be So Black and Blue" and "Squeeze Me" (his first success), are just a few, most of which he personally recorded and sang publicly, employing his own original brand of ingenious clowning. His son, Maurice Waller, collaborated with Anthony Calabrese on his biography, Fats Waller, in 1977.

EDDY HOWARD
To Each His Own, He Found His Own

Eddy was another musician/singer bandleader, recording songs like "It's All in the Game," "Old Fashioned Love," "Can't We Talk it Over," and "When My Dreamboat Comes Home." His orchestra started in 1942. Eddie was the boy singer. He had a way with a song and a way with an audience. He earlier recorded his theme song "Careless" which he wrote with Dick Jurgens' band that turned out to be one of his most popular recordings. Eddy played both guitar and trombone. His best-known recording was, of course, "To Each His Own." In 1962-63, beyond the demise of the Big Band Era, Eddy Howard returned to gigs on Catalina Island, off the coast of California, performing with a small group during the summertime until his accidentally premature death in 1963 at his home in Palm Springs, California.

BOB CARROLL
Singing Gentlemen, Fine Actor

A resident of Port Washington, New York, when he passed away in 1995, Bob Carroll began his singing career with the Charlie Barnet band at the time Lena Horne was Barnet's girl singer. His marvelous baritone voice was also heard in the bands of Jimmy Dorsey and Glenn Miller (Army Air Force Band). Some said he was a Crosby imitator. If he was, he did it better than anyone, according to Will Friedwald in his book" Jazz Singing." Then, as an accomplished actor, his best known role was his portrayal of Tevye in the national tour of Fiddler on the Roof in the '70s. Bob also appeared on television with Steve Allen, Jackie Gleason, and Johnny Carson. His Broadway credits were Fiorello (as Mayor LaGuardia), La Cage aux Folles, and Shenandoah. Bob appeared frequently with the Los Angeles Philharmonic as baritone soloist.

When I spoke to Bob's wife Nadine she spoke of his other achievements over a long and successful career. "Bob appeared in concert with his good friend Skitch Henderson and the New York Pops at Carnegie Hall. Bob was semi-retired in his last years," she added, "and made so many benefit performances for the Actors Home in New Jersey and frequently volunteered at St. Francis Hospital in Roslyn. New York.

JOHNNY MERCER
A Man Bursting with Talent, Was Also a Singer

Johnny with Margaret Whiting

My friend, Song Star Margaret Whiting once said that prolific songwriter Johnny Mercer was a man bursting with talent and always looking for a place to channel his energies. "Johnny, once an out-of-work actor, passed a sign outside a theater that said LYRICS WANTED. He went in and found both his profession and his wife, Ginger, who was a dancer in the chorus," she said. Mercer went to Hollywood, worked with Hoagy Carmichael on "Lazybones," returned to New York, worked with Paul Whiteman and later, on the radio with Benny Goodman, where he wrote a song a week.

With Glenn Wallich he formed Capitol Records. Their second release was Ella Mae Morse and Freddie Slack's band doing "Cow-Cow Boogie" which sold 25,000 copies in the first week. Capitol was responsible for advancing the singing careers of Nat Cole, Jo Stafford, Peggy Lee and Margaret Whiting. But Johnny was also a singer. Among his recordings are his own "Mr. Meadowlark" (with Bing Crosby), "Personality," "Candy," (the latter two written by others), and his "Ac-Cent-Tchu-Ate the Positive," "G.I.Jive," "Glow Worm," "On the Atchison, Topeka, and the Santa Fe," and a lot of other songs written by himself and others.

Johnny Mercer's southern drawl and warm, good-natured style made him a natural, singing on radio in the 1940's. I loved him best when he sang his own compositions.

"He once told me, 'Grow up, kid,'" Margaret recalled. After all, Margaret knew him well and was a protégé. "It was the best advice I ever received." Margaret Whiting loved Johnny Mercer, her mentor, her hero. For me he was a great songwriter, and a not-so-bad singer. Dedicated to musical excellence, Johnny Mercer's policy reflected his approach to all his work, whether writing or singing.

VAUGHN MONROE
He Was Racing With the Moon

I remember huddling in doorways of narrow-front record shops along New York's Forty-second street during the winter of 1948 , where outside were mounted harsh-sounding speakers blaring Vaughn Monroe's wonderful recordings of "Ballerina" and "Ghost Riders in the Sky." One of those days I looked up and there was a figure of Vaughn Monroe beaming high above the marquee' outside the Strand Theater, which showcased his name in lights. Inside, when the movie ended, the house lights came up, and Vaughn's formidable great band broke out with his theme "Racing with the Moon," as the great stage rose up from the orchestra pit.

Born in 1911 in Akron, Ohio, Vaughn played in the school band and won the State Trumpet Championship at 14 years old. This allowed him to go to Milwaukee and play under the direction of famed band conductor and composer John Philip Sousa, inspiring Vaughn to become a bandleader. He first recorded his voice with Larry Funk's band singing "Rain" and "Too Beautiful for Words."

After efforts in other bands, Vaughn organized his own band, and my friend, the prestigious band booker of the agency named after him, Willard Alexander, booked him, bringing him to the attention of RCA, where he recorded for years and wound up as their spokesman. His first important gig was playing the New York Paramount, voclaizing his theme "Racing with the Moon" for the first time, which he wrote with arranger John Watson. Adding a string section to the band, he toured nationwide, eventually opening a large dinner theater/restaurant

in Framingham, Mass. He sang on his own show, The Camel Caravan, and appeared in western movies. Vaughn continued to record even after he disbanded his orchestra in 1953. Remember "Sound-Off," "There, I've Said It Again," both immense hits.

BUDDY CLARK
Oh, Those Doris
Day Duets

Buddy Clark's duets "Love Somebody" and "Baby It's Cold Outside" with Song Star Doris Day are his two most important hits besides his solo rendition of Jack Lawrence's "Linda."

Born Samuel Goldberg, Buddy started with Gus Arnheim's orchestra, then hooked up with Nat Brandwynne's band in the early thirties. He emigrated into Wayne King's band, later becoming a featured vocalist with Freddy Martin's orchestra. He recorded prolifically with all these groups from 1932 and into the forties. On his one recording with Benny Goodman, Buddy recorded a duet with Helen Ward on a song called "Not Bad." On a trip back to Hollywood from San Francisco after watching a ball game, he died when the plane crashed. He was thirty-eight. I particularly enjoy his rendition of "Peg of My Heart," that illustrates his appealing crooning style. Like Russ Columbo, we'll never know how far he would have gone, had he lived longer.

JOHNNY JOHNSTON
Handsome is as Handsome Does
I always liked Johnny Johnston. A vocalist with the Richard Himber band, Johnny is best remembered as an independent soloist, introducing the famous wartime songs "That Old Black Magic," "I Don't Want to Walk Without You" and "Laura." With Capitol Records he turned out some very good numbers, "Easy to Love," "Dearly Beloved," and "Spring Will Be a Little Late this Year." He was good looking enough to be selected by Paramount Studios and later MGM for a few movies: Star Spangled Rhythm, Sweater Girl, and You Can't Ration Love with Paramount and the successful This Time for Keeps in 1947 for MGM.

John was a very romantic baritone. In 1951 he appeared in A Tree Grows in Brooklyn, a musical, singing "I'll Buy You a Star," a show stopper if you ever heard one. In those days Johnny would take you aside to proudly show pictures of his little girl Patty Kate, his daughter with actress/singer Kathryn Grayson. If you can find the Capitol CD Great Gentlemen of Song, you can hear some of Johnny Johnston's best vocals. Johnny passed from us in January 1996 at the age of eighty.

ANDY WILLIAMS
A National (Singing) Treasure
Hailing from Wall Lake, Iowa, Andy Williams has had a long run after separating from The Williams Brothers (with Kay Thompson) and joined with Steve Allen's TV show. "Andy always chose good material," said his boss. Andy was actually one of the choir boys in Going My

Andy Williams

Way when Bing sailed into "Swinging on a Star." With a string of great hits behind him: "Born Free," "Moon River," the definitive version, and "A Summer Place," "The Village of St. Bernadette," which I love. Andy now does most of his performing in Branson, Missouri, where he owns a theater named Moon River and where the Lennon Sisters and dozens of popular performers hang out.

JACK JONES
A Song in the Air

Allan Jones was a great, popular light classical singer back in the 1930's, appearing in a couple of Marx Brothers films A Night At the Opera and A Day at the Races, as well as in an operetta entitled The Firefly with Jeanette McDonald. His great song was "The Donkey Serenade." Allan's son is Jack Jones, whose mom was actress Irene Hervey.

Jack Jones is a chip off the old block, starting, like so many others, imitating the then most acceptable sound of Frank Sinatra. However, his engaging style and pleasant voice led him to success during the 1960's, when he recorded "Lollipops and Roses" and "Call Me Irresponsible." Between 1962 and 1968, Jack had twenty successful recordings on the charts. His biggest hits were" Wives and Lovers" in 1963 and "The Race Is On" in 1965.

Jack Jones' two 1960's albums, The Impossible Dream and Dear Heart, were reissued in 1985 on MCA Records. Jack won two Grammys, one in 1962 and the other in 1964. Jack has also toured with Bob Hope's Christmas USO troupe in the 1960's. They played at Tan Son Nhut, Vietnam during the Christmas holidays in 1965.

STEVE LAWRENCE
A Musical Permanent Bond

Steve Lawrence first found success on Steve Allen's original Tonight Show on NBC television in New York. It's also where Steve first met another young singer, Eydie Gorme'. After some time on Steve's show, they married in 1957 in Las Vegas at the El Rancho where they were the opening act for Joe E. Lewis. Like a lot of his contemporaries, Steve sounds a lot like Frank Sinatra sometimes. Once, when I heard him on New York's WQEW, I swore it was Sinatra. Then his own recognizable sounds came through later in the recording. However, Steve's recordings "Portrait of My Love" and "Go Away, Little Girl" are distinctly his own.

Born Sidney Leibowitz in Brooklyn, New York, in 1935, Steve also became a Broadway performer. He appeared in Ervin Drake's What Makes Sammy Run? in 1964. "I spent two years of my life in that show.

Doing Broadway was very important to me. I auditioned for the part three times - and they finally gave me the job."

Steve recorded "I Gotta Be Me," "I recorded it first, before Sammy Davis did. Eydie and I told Sammy to record it too, because we felt he would do it even better. He did. Sammy's is the best version."

In 1991, Steve and Eydie toured with Frank Sinatra during his Diamond Jubilee Tour. Steve always sings 'More,' one of his signature tunes, during his tours. The couple duets on songs like 'Baby It's Cold Outside' and 'Our Love is Here to Stay,' trading off songs, singing counterpoint and finishing each other's vocal punch lines.

For thirty-five years Steve and Eydie have traveled the world, and at Westbury Music Fair, now known as the Capitol One Theater, like many other venues, they are almost always sold out soon after the promotional announcement. Not many can accomplish that, even in 2007.

DON CORNELL
Big Voice, Big Heart

It was always hard to tell who had the most enthusiasm in the Cornell family, Don or Iris. That enterprising couple had worked very hard to insure that a new generation, as well as reminding the previous one, got to hear the man with the big voice, long-respected Big Band vocalist, Don Cornell.

Don and I got together only once, but it was a day-long rehearsal and meeting backstage at Westbury Music Fair during a Don Cornell-Jerry Vale joint concert performance in 2002. He was still the handsome, engaging performer then, dressed in tux and ready to take on the audience of over 3000 fans.

"He still sings in the same key as when he was young," a bubbly Iris said. "After losing my first wife edith to cancer after 36 years of marriage, I was dejected and had no desire to perform. Iris changed all that for me in 1978, when we were married," Don was saying, "she's been managing things successfully for over 20 years now. I consider myself twice blessed."

In concert, when Don sang "The Wind Beneath My Wings," it's clearly dedicated to Iris, "....singing it as if only she were in the room," wrote Anthony DeFlorio III , in a review earlier when Don appeared at Resorts International in Atlantic City.

My recollection of Don's hit "It Isn't Fair," recorded with the Sammy Kaye orchestra in 1950, convinced me of his ability to put over a song and make it a hit, as he clearly accomplished with this great 1933 Richard Himber song.

Stepping back a bit, Don first began to sing in local clubs in the

Bronx, New York, playing guitar and singing with the Mickey Alpert band at the Edison Hotel in New York City in the 1930s.

"I also played and sang with the McFarland Twins, the sax playing brothers who had their own band, and with Lennie Hayton's orchestra." Don sang with Loring "Red" Nichols and His Five Pennies, too. His singing *teachers* were Bing Crosby and Russ Columbo: "We all looked up to Bing as the singer who started it all. My first record date was with the Bobby Hayes' band vocalizing "Trust in Me," later a big hit for Eddie Fisher."

Don was born of immigrant parents on Mott Street and moved to the Bronx. "We had no radio, so we entertained ourselves. My father played the mandolin. Mom sang in the church choir, so on Sunday we had a family sing-a-long which included my four brothers. Music was instilled in us as in so many other Italians."

He acquired the name of *Don Cornell* very simply. "It was difficult to sell a name like Lou Varlaro in show business in those days, especially since Italy's dictator Mussolini had joined the Axis Countries with Hitler during the second World War. Every time they called out my name there would be some boo's from the audience." So, one night I was standing in the wings, and Sammy Kaye called out, 'Now,

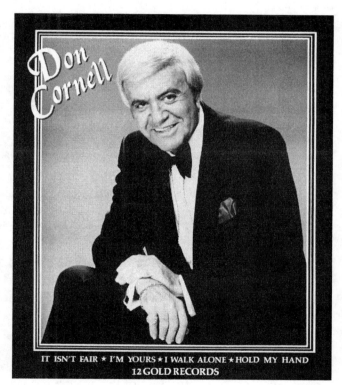

IT ISN'T FAIR ★ I'M YOURS ★ I WALK ALONE ★ HOLD MY HAND
12 GOLD RECORDS

here's Don Cornell,' and I'm looking around thinking, 'who the hell is that?' And, Richard, that is how it all started." Don spoke like he sang - clear and strong. Don broke into the big time beginning in 1950 with the Sammy Kaye, *Swing and Sway* backed recordings "It Isn't Fair," "Daddy," "Harbor Lights," "Serenade of the Bells," and one of my Don Cornell favorites, "Stage Door Canteen."

"With Sammy," Don recalled, "we had an itinerary that ran from January to January, with only one week off for Christmas." Don left Kaye to perform military service with the Army Air Corp., then later rejoined the band.

The tune "Heart of My Heart" recorded with fellow vocalists Johnny Desmond and Alan Dale was always a big request song for Don at concerts. Don has a Gold Record for each year from 1950 through 1962. "The first, 'It Isn't Fair,' is the most requested, followed by the Coral recording 'I'm Yours,' Don said, "and we engage a full orchestra so we are able to retain the original chart s when I do these requests. The fans always expect to hear the original versions."

"Hold My Hand," another big Cornell hit, one that became a # 1 hit in England and remained on the charts for 21 weeks, was featured in the 1954 movie *Susan Slept Here. It* received an Academy Award nomination, unfortunately to be eclipsed by a luckier entry "Three Coins in the Fountain."

Don excels on many great recordings: "I'll Walk Alone," "That Old Feeling," "Most of All," "The Bible Tells Me So," (by Roy Rogers and Dale Evans) "Play Some Music for Broken Hearts," "When I was a Child," "Most of All," and "Love is a Many Splendored Thing." Don's classic baritone has remained in demand for all the ensuing years and right through 2003, something he never expected.

"I have always believed a song tells a story. It must be interpreted through feelings," Don said during our meeting, "the message must be conveyed by the singer to the listener. That's how it's done."
Don usually closed his concerts with a tune called "Old Man Time:" That song was given to me by my dear friend Jimmy Durante. My first job after leaving Sammy (Kaye) in 1950 was at Palumbo's in Philadelphia, where all the big names performed. I was on the bill with Durante. On about the third day he called me into his dressing room and said, 'I have a song for you. I want you to take it and put it away and don't sing it for forty years. You're too young to understand it now.' If you check the lyrics, you can understand what he was trying to tell me."

"He gives you youth and he steals it away, He gives you nice pretty hair and turns it gray."

Now, with Don's passing, his recordings becomes a legacy. Don Cornell was probably the last of the reigning crooners who began as a boy singer with the Big Bands of the 1930s and 1940s. And, imagine, he was still singing in the year 2003.

On Monday, February 23, 2004 Don Cornell passed from us at Adventura Hospital from advanced emphysema and diabetes. Don was a lifelong smoker who just wouldn't quit. I remember his last appearance with Jerry Vale on May 19, 2002. On stage he sat upon a stool and held the mike stand. His voice was no different than the early Don Cornell, but his legs would not hold him for the required hour. Back in the dressing room, along with his assistant Zora, his wife Iris, Jerry Vale, myself, and

Jerry's manager Larry Spellman, we wondered where Don disappeared for a minute or two. He was in the dressing room having a cigarette. Everyone chided him, but he just smiled weakly.

Iris Cornell intends to carry on Don's great legacy of music, which, she says "... we will have forever and ever."

PAT BOONE
No More Mr. Nice Guy?

A descendant of Daniel Boone, Charles Eugene Boone first saw light in Jacksonville, Florida, 70 years ago. His parents wanted a daughter they were going to name Patricia, thus they called their son, Pat. So, okay, he never sang with the bands, but he sure sang his head off for all the following years. He mean-

Pat Boone

dered into the singing business via Ted Mack's Original Amateur Hour (The American Idol of its day) and Arthur Godfrey's Talent Scouts. "Two Hearts, Two Kisses," "One Love" was his first hit in 1954. "Ain't That a Shame" was second. We all know the tremendous success of "Love Letters in the Sand" that remained on the charts for 34 weeks. Add "Moody River," "April Love," and "Friendly Persuasion" - well, you know what I mean. ***Pat also holds the all-time Billboard Magazine record of 200 consecutive weeks on the charts with more than one song.***

Pat Boone is a friendly, spiritual guy with an ideal family and 15 grandchildren. Being neighbors, Rosemary Clooney's son Gabriel married Pat's daughter, Debbie (who also had a tremendous hit with 'You Light Up My Life'). A few years ago Pat was not wearing his white bucks but had traded them in for a heavy metal outfit and was singing Ozzy Osbourne's "Crazy Train." (He was only kidding, of course).

Today, Pat is active with the Society of Singers out in L.A. and is an effective conservative motivational speaker. Pat and I exchange notes every now and then!

JIMMY ROSELLI
A True Italian Troubadour

One song alone would certify the above fact. "When Your Old Wedding Ring was New." That recording changed Jimmy's life. The long hard hours of playing small clubs and receiving low pay were finally paying off, wrote Anthony De Florio III in an article written in 1996. "When he gets out in front of the spotlight, he gives his all - every minute with every song."

It was on December 26, 1925 when Jimmy found first light in Hoboken, New Jersey. He lost his mother the next day, and Grandfather "Papa Roselli raised him, instilling much love and an

Jimmy Roselli and his wife Donna

appreciation of music in the young man. He began singing in church choirs and later at the Gay Nineties Room at the local Meyers Hotel. Jimmy was a first-prize winner at a Major Bowes Amateur Hour show, the same place where Frank Sinatra got his first break.

The Second World War summoned Jimmy for a stint in Army. His need to sing even then was fulfilled on radio from Linz, Austria, while traveling with the 42nd Rainbow Division Band. After being discharged in 1946, Jimmy took singing lessons and went on to perform throughout the east coast where he became a great favorite, thanks in part to assistance from the great Jimmy Durante in 1954. The lovable, popular Durante, a singer in his own right, encouraged him and solicited the management of the famed Latin Quarter nightclub in New York City to raise his salary and extend his engagement. Jimmy went on to play all the big clubs in and around New York, including a major appearance at the Copacabana in 1964 (with a response so fantastic that the management extended his four-week engagement to a five-year contract), Palumbo's in Philadelphia, and later at Carnegie Hall.

"Mala Femmina" (as arranged by Ralph Burns)," Pal of My Cradle Days," "This Heart of Mine," and "Come Into My Heart" are some of Jimmy Roselli's best recordings that still endear him to millions. Today, Jimmy is retired in Florida.

ROBERTO TIRADO
Popular Weatherman Turned Singer

Once upon a time on Long Island, a veteran television anchor weatherman named Roberto Tirado developed a great following and ap-

Cover Art and Photography of Alicia Tirado - M. Grudens

peared at community charity events as a singer. Yes, a singer! Then, during an appearance at The Tilles Center, Long Island's Carnegie Hall, entertainer Steve Allen caught Roberto's performance and inquired: "Was that you who created the screaming I just heard backstage? Well, it was a pleasure to hear you sing so well."

That did it! With that kind of encouragement, Roberto's singing career surfaced and he promptly recorded a great CD titled Pris-

oner of Love. This writer, actor, producer, and Emmy-winning weatherman, can really sing. Sounding a little bit like Tony Bennett and Dick Haymes on one single track alone, Roberto also rises to dramatic heights with the selections "Begin the Beguine" and Cole Porter's great standard "Night and Day." And, a credit to his Spanish heritage, Roberto sings "Besame Mucho," reflecting his feel and intense passion for lyrics. Roberto is currently working out an album of his favorite love ballads to be entitled STAR*DUST to compli-

Roberto Tirado - Photo M. Grudens

ment this very book, with yours truly as director and producer and Wayne Sabella as Musical Director.

REMO CAPRA
A Rediscovery

Now, here is a crooner, born in Bari, Italy, who is still making music, despite the fact that record producers are not currently issuing our kind of music on CDs. Remo Capra, a successful construction engineer who by day would supervise rock blastings for the construction of some of the most prestigious buildings in New York City over many years, has performed with the great Louis Armstrong back in the fifties at Basin Street in New York when such jazz luminaries as trombonist Trummy Young, drummer Barrett Deems, and bassist Arvell Shaw played with the Armstrong All-Stars, and also sang with the original Tommy Dorsey band.

Remo Capra with Fans at the Italian Crooners Luncheon - 2005 - Photo M. Grudens

"I met Tommy Dorsey in New York and he introduced me to Tino Barzie, who eventually became my manager. Tommy heard me sing and invited me to sing with his orchestra on weekends. I loved singing and made records with Columbia, but my heart was divided, so I could not give up my engineering, which I also loved to do. If I made people happy by singing, that is fine. It is all possible if you like what you are doing. Besides, I like to be busy."

In 2001 coinciding with the publishing of his book Bridge Over Niger, and in coordination with Barnes & Noble, Sony released the albums "Just Say I Love Her" and "Say We Are Still Together," composed of the great standards crooned with a true Italian flavor, sandy but elegantly lilting voice; "I've Got You Under My Skin,"(recorded live at the Blue Note), "What Now My Love,"(recorded in 1973 with Neal Hefti), "Passing By," (recorded in 1956 with Tommy Dorsey), and a good number of standards with conductor Frank DeVol recorded with Columbia in New York.

This is an enviable list of recordings and all done very nicely by a gentle and accomplished crooner who believes in the lyrics, as he sings them passionately and according to the lyrical requirement.

Remo once worked with composer Irving Berlin, later obtaining

permission to translate Berlin's song "How Deep is the Ocean" into Italian lyrics with nice results and easy to listen to. You can find it on his album Best American Love Songs in Italian and English along with "As Time Goes By" and "The More I See You" with full orchestra and strings.

This man, who would not give up his career as an engineer, really captures the essence of all the great songs he has crooned over the years and right up into this new century.

BIG BAND SINGERS

...and their Big Band Affiliations

Here is a list of male big band singers and their big band affiliations. (Courtesy of Vince Danca's 1984 Complete Jazz Calendar) before the 1942 recording ban that silenced all instrumentalists but allowed singers to record with vocal backgrounds only. By the time the ban had ended, singers reached new popularity and the big bands would never be the same again.

A

Bob Allen
  Tommy Dorsey
  Hal Kemp
Paul Allen
  Frankie Carle
Stuart Allen
  Richard Himber
Terry Allen
  Will Bradley
  Red Norvo
  Larry Clinton
  Claude Thornhill
David Allyn
  Jack Teagarden
  Boyd Raeburn
Dorsey Anderson
  Tony Pastor
  Jan Savitt

Harry Babbit
  Kay Kyser
Harry Barris
  Gus Arnheim

  Paul Whiteman
Gene Barry
  Teddy Powell
Paul Barry
  Lennie Hayton
Tex Beneke
  Glenn Miller
Lee Bennett
  Jan Garber
Ruble Blakely
  Lionel Hampton
Jimmy Blair
  Teddy Powell
Merwyn Bogue (Ishkabib-
ble)
  Kay Kyser
Bon Bon (George Tunnell)
  Jan Savitt
Al Bowlly
  Ray Noble
George Brandon
  Sammy Kaye
Phil Brito
  Al Donohue
  Eddy Duchin
  Jan Savitt
Don Brown
  Tommy Tucker

Jimmy Brown
  Sammy Kaye
  Blue Barron
Russ Brown
  Jan Garber
Clyde Burke
  Raymond Scott
  Casa Loma
  Blue Barron
  Sammy Kaye

C

Paul Carley
  Reggie Childs
Russ Carlyle
  Blue Barron
Art Carney
  Horace Heidt
Bob Carroll
  Tony Pastor
  Charlie Barnet
  Henry King
  Jimmy Dorsey
  Ted Fio Rita
  Glenn Miller (USAAF)
Jimmy Castle
  Chuck Foster
  Kay Kyser
  Dick Jurgens
Ronnie Chase
  Les Brown
  Joe Haymes
Charles Chester
  Shep Fields
Harry Cool
  Dick Jurgens
Perry Como
  Ted Weems
  Freddie Carlone
Jerry Cooper
  Eddy Duchin
Don Cornell
  Sammy Kaye

McFarland Twins
Larry Cotton
  Horace Heidt
  Jimmy Grier
Bing Crosby
  Gus Arnheim
  Paul Whiteman
Bob Crosby
  Anson Weeks
  Dorsey Brothers
Maury Cross
  Sammy Kaye
Ken Curtis
  Tommy Dorsey
  Shep Fields

D

Alan Dale
  George Paxton
Don D'Arcy
  Sonny Dunham
  Art Mooney
  Boyd Raeburn
Bill Darnell
  Edgar Hayes
  Bob Chester
  Red Nichols
Johnny Davis
  Fred Waring
Dennis Day
  Claude Thornhill
Ronnie Deauville
  Ray Anthony
Denny Dennis
  Tommy Dorsey
  Ambrose
Hal Derwin
  Shep Fields
  Artie Shaw
Johnny Desmond
  Gene Krupa
  Bob Crosby
  Glenn Miller (USAAF)

Alan De Witt
  Tiny Hill
  Jan Savitt
  Tommy Dorsey/Glenn
Miller

Buddy De Vito
  Harry James
Larry Douglas
  Carmen Cavallaro
Mike Douglas (Dowd)
  Bill Carlsen
  Kay Kyser
Morton Downey
  Paul Whiteman
Howard Dulany
  Frank Dailey
  Gene Krupa

E

Ray Eberle
  Gene Krupa
  Glenn Miller
Bob Eberly
  Dorsey Brothers
  Jimmy Dorsey
  Wayne King
Billy Eckstine
  Earl Hines
Skinnay Ennis
  Hal Kemp

F

Peter Famularo
  Sammy Kaye
Elmer Feldkemp
  Freddy Martin
  Bert Lown
Manuel Fernandez
  Enric Madriguera
Alan Foster
  Bob Chester
  Sammy Kaye

Art Mooney
Stuart Foster
  Ina Ray Hutton
  Bobby Sherwood
  Tommy Dorsey
Walter Fuller
  Earl Hines
Jack Fulton
  Paul Whiteman

G

Kenny Gardner
  Guy Lombardo
Buddy Gately
  Tommy Dorsey
Parker Gibbs
  Ted Weems
Bobby Goday
  Shep Fields
  Hank Biagini
Charlie Goodwin
  Horace Heidt
Cliff Grass
  Gray Gordon
  Guy Lombardo
Carl Grayson
  Henry Busse
  Spike Jones
Buddy Greco
  Benny Goodman
Merv Griffin
  Freddy Martin
Parnell Grina
  Lawrence Welk
Dan Grissom
  Jimmie Lunceford

H

Bob Hannon
  Henry Busse
  Buddy Rogers
  Harry Sosnik

Paul Whiteman
Dick Harding
   Claude Thornhill
Paul Harmon
   Johnny Long
Leroy Harris
   Earl Hines
Jack Haskell
   Les Brown
Sherman Hayes
   Del Courtney
Bob Haymes
   Bob Chester
   Carl Hoff
   Orrin Tucker
Dick Haymes
   Carl Hoff
   Harry James
   Freddy Martin
   Benny Goodman
   Tommy Dorsey
Fritz Heilbron
   Jan Garber
Ray Henricks
   Benny Goodman
Woody Herman
   Tom Gerun
   Isham Jones
Al Hibbler
   Jay McShann
   Duke Ellington
Bob Houston
   Johnny Long
   Vincent Lopez
   Glenn Miller (USAAF)
Eddy Howard
   George Olsen
   Dick Jurgens
Gene Howard
   Stan Kenton
   Bob Chester
   Teddy Powell
Buddy Hughes
   Gene Krupa

Jimmy Dorsey
Lazy Bill Huggins
   Enoch Light
Pee Wee Hunt
   Casa Loma
Jack Hunter
   Elliot Lawrence

I

Red Ingle
   Spike Jones
   Ted Weems

J

Herb Jeffries
   Earl Hines
   Duke Ellington
Bob Jenny
   Claude Thornhill
Bill Johnson
   Bert Block
Jay Johnson
   Stan Kenton
   Bobby Sherwood
Johnny Johnston
   Richard Himber

K

Ray Kellogg
   Sonny Dunham
Ronnie Kemper
   Dick Jurgens
   Horace Heidt

L

Dave Lambert
   Charlie Barnet
   Johnny Long
   Gene Krupa
Snooky Lanson
   Ray Noble

Harlan Lattimore
  Don Redman
Bill Lawrence
  Jimmy Dorsey
Billy Leach
  Art Kassel
Ford Leary
  Larry Clinton
Jack Leonard
  Bert Block
  Tommy Dorsey
Tommy Leonetti
  Tony Pastor
  Charlie Spivak
  Shorty Sherock
Frankie Lester
  Hal McIntyre
  Buddy Morrow
Bill Lockwood
  Sam Donahue
Carmen Lombardo
  Guy Lombardo
Lebert Lombardo
  Guy Lombardo
Art Lund
  Jimmy Joy
  Benny Goodman

M

Artie Malvin
  Ray McKinley
Gordon MacRae
  Horace Heidt
Muzzy Marcellino
  Ted Fio Rito
Dean Martin,
  Sammy Watkins
Joe Martin
  Isham Jones
  Del Courtney
  Joe Reichman
  Jan Savitt
Tony Martin

Ray Noble
Tom Gerun
Anson Weeks
Bob Crosby
Glenn Miller
Ray McKinley
John McAfee
  Eddy Duchin
  Tony Pastor
  Harry James
  Johnny Hamp
Bob McCoy
  Horace Heidt
Red McKenzie
  Paul Whiteman
  Red Nichols
Johnny Mercer
  Paul Whiteman
  Benny Goodman
  Frankie Trumbauer
Tommy Mercer
  Ray Anthony
  Buddy Morrow
  Charlie Spivak
Dick Merrick
  George Paxton
  Jerry Wald
  McFarland Twins
Marty McKenna
  Sammy Kaye
Jimmy Mitchelle
  Erskine Hawkins
Vaughn Monroe
  Larry Funk
  Jack Marshard
Skip Morr
  Henry Busse
  Lou Breese
Joe Mooney
  Buddy Rogers
  Sauter Finegan
  Frank Dailey
Buddy Moreno
  Dick Jergens

Griff Williams
Ray Morton
  Ruby Newman
Herb Muse
  Les Brown

N

Joey Nash
  Richard Himber
Skip Nelson
  Chico Marx
  Glenn Miller
  Bob Strong
  Casa Loma
  Teddy Powell
Al Nobel
  Hal McIntyre
  Carl Hoff
Leighton Noble
  Orville Knapp
Donald Novis
  Gus Arnheim
  Anson Weeks
  Jimmie Grier
Jimmy Palmer
  Bobby Byrne
Skeeter Palmer
  Joe Haymes
Tony Pastor
  Irving Aaronson
  Artie Shaw
Jerry Perkins
  Mal Hallett
  Jan Savitt
Harry Prime
  Randy Brooks
  Ralph Flanagan
Frank Prince
  Ben Bernie
Arthus Prysock
  Buddy Johnson

R

Carl Ravazza
  Tom Coakley
  Anson Weeks
Chuck Richards
  Fletcher Henderson
  Chick Webb
Lee Richardson
  Luis Russell
Al Rinker
  Gus Arnheim
  Paul Whiteman
Don Rodney
  Carmen Cavallaro
Clyde Rogers
  Freddy Martin
  Joe Haymes
  Hank Biagini
Andy Russell
  Alvino Rey
Henry Russell
  Horace Heidt
  George Olsen
Jimmy Rushing
  Benny Moten
  Count Basie
Tommy Ryan
  Chuck Foster
  Sammy Kaye

S

Tony Sacco
  Enric Madriguera
  Eddie Paul
Kenny Sargent
  Casa Loma
Jimmy Saunders
  Harry James
  Charlie Spivak
Bill Schallen
  Alvino Rey
  Van Alexander

Sony Schuyler
George Hall
Vincent Lopez
Abe Lyman
Terry Shand
Freddy Martin
Lew Sherwood
Eddy Duchin
Frank Sinatra
Harold Arden
Harry James
Tommy Dorsey
Frank Sinatra, Jr.
Tommy Dorsey
(Ghost-Donohue)
Larry Southern
Will Bradley
Gary Stevens
Tex Beneke
Charlie Spivak
Buddy Stewart
Gene Krupa
Charlie Barnet
Claude Thornhill
Larry Stewart
Ray Noble
Leo Reisman
Phil Stewart
Wayne King
Bill Stoker
Kay Kyser
Freddy Martin
Jack Shilkret
Butch Stone
Van Alexander
Les Brown
Larry Clinton
Eddie Stone
Freddy Martin
Isham Jones
Al Stuart
Bob Chester
Joe Sudy
Henry King

Joe Reichman

T

Ziggy Talent
Vaughn Monroe
Elmo Tanner
Ted Weems
Larry Taylor
Charlie Barnet
Eddy Duchin
Ruby Newman
Tommy Taylor
Teddy Powell
Benny Goodman
Mitchell Ayres
Pha Terrell
Andy Kirk
Pinky Tomlin
Hal Kemp
Mel Torme
Chico Marx
Claude Trenier
Jimmie Lunceford

U

Billy Usher
Randy Brooks
Miguelito Valdes
Xavier Cugat
Jimmy Valentine
Will Bradley
Harry Von Zell
Charlie Barnet

W

Stuart Wade
Bobby Byrne
Freddy Martin
Teddy Walters
Jimmy Dorsey
Earle Warren

Count Basie
Country Washburn
    Ted Weems
Dick Webster
    Jimmie Grier
Buddy Welcome
    Mal Hallett
    Jan Savitt
Henry Wells
    Andy Kirk
    Jimmie Lunceford
Cliff Weston
    Joe Haymes
    Tommy Dorsey
Dick Wharton
    Bunny Berigan
    Henry Busse
Gene Williams
    Johnny Long
    Claude Thornhill
Joe Williams
    Lionel Hampton
    Count Basie
Charles Wilson
    Sammy Kaye
Stanley Worth
    Eddy Duchin
    Vincent Lopez
Arthur Wright
    Sammy Kaye
    Kay Kyser
    Leo Reichman
    Buddy Rogers

Clark Yokum
    Tommy Dorsey
    Mal Hallett
Ralph Young
    Les Brown
    Shep Fields

The Ladies Who Sang With The Bands

Words and Music by Lee Hale

There were Big Bands and small bands and combos and such;
Back in the forties, we loved them so much
There were sections of brass and reeds and rhythm,
And one more ingredient that always went with 'em
In front of the band facing swingers and squares,
The Ladies Who Sang With The Bands,
Sitting all night on those hard folding chairs,
The Ladies Who Sang With The Bands
They went on the road playing ballrooms and dives,
Going through hell with those orchestra wives;
But how they could floor us, with one little chorus:
The Ladies Who Sang With The Bands.
Their records made hist'ry and money galore;
And oh, those recordings were grand;
But somehow there weren't any royalties for
The Ladies Who Sang With The Bands.
Sitting and Smiling, they'd wait to go on;
Wondering when they could go to the john.
Regrets they had none of,
I wish I'd been one of
The Ladies Who Sang With, just one of the gang with,
The Ladies Who Sang With The Bands

Bea Wain

Edythe Wright

Martha Tilton

Kay Starr

Helen Forrest

Mildred Bailey

Helen O'Connell

Peggy Lee

The Early Vocalists
Bessie Smith to Mildred Bailey to Ella Fitzgerald

In the beginning God made Heaven and Earth and then, in a wild, extraordinary moment, added the powerful vocal influences of Ma "Gertrude" Rainey, Bessie Smith, Mildred Bailey, Ethel Waters, Billie Holiday, Ella Fitzgerald, and Dinah Washington. What a magnificent cornucopia of great jazz voices.

MA RAINEY AND BESSIE SMITH

Bessie Smith

In 1923 Ma "Gertrude" Rainey, an absolute original was the undisputed top blues singer. A genuine diva, she was known in those pioneer days as the Mother of the Blues, who shouted and moaned the laments of her life's condition. They say that one day she came to the town of Chattanooga, Tennessee, heard Bessie Smith and took her in tow as a member of her famous traveling blues troupe. Legend has it that Ma Rainey literally kidnapped Bessie at the age of twelve, forcing the girl to go with her show, teaching her how to sing the blues, Ma Rainey style; but that was denied later by those who really knew. Actually, they got along fine, but Bessie never learned much about singing from Rainey's troupe. She was a natural singer and her own person who learned all aspects of her craft. She could Charleston and do funny turns, then send an audience into a trance with her shy, but earthy blues. Rainey was more like a mother than a teacher to Bessie Smith. Remember, too, history will bear out there was just no blues predecessor to Ma Rainey.

Historically, for unknown reasons, female blues singers followed male blues singers. "Bessie Smith, had she lived a full life, would have been right there on top with the rest of us in the Swing Era," Lionel Hampton said during our interview about the great female singers. "She was known as the 'Empress Of The Blues.'" With a raucous and loud voice, a complete command of a lyric and the ability to bring first-hand emotion to a song, there was misery in what she did, but some say she just had to bring it all out in her music.

The post World War I period brought the blues north. By the early 1920's, Bessie Smith was a recording and performing giant, two hundred pounds of human emotion packed behind her vibrant, powerful voice. She made over 150 records and was so successful that her record sales literally saved Columbia Records from bankruptcy, even though they had voices of Eddie Cantor and Al Jolson in their stable. Her record sales surpassed a stupendous 10 million in a time when there were relatively few phonographs and little available money for the average person to purchase them. Along the way she earned a great deal of money, at one time making two thousand dollars a week, but, just as easily, lost it all. She gave it away or spent it on liquor, or lost it to men predators.

There was magic in her voice. Some say her songs represented the common man in his sorrow and sometimes terrible condition. The main themes of her songs were love, sex, and misery. The recordings "Sorrowful Blues" and "Rocking Chair Blues" were promoted heavily by Columbia. Magazine and newspaper ads in 1924 read: "Having a phonograph without these records is like having ham without eggs."

Louis Armstrong recorded with Bessie when he was only twenty-four years old and fresh from King Oliver's Creole Jazz Band in Chicago. He joined Fletcher Henderson's orchestra and, with Bessie, he had met his match: He later said: "She thrilled me always. She had music in her soul." That recording date, January 14, 1925, although not important at the time, would, for critics and scholars, stand as a memorable date in jazz history. The session started with W.C.Handy's endlessly recorded "St. Louis Blues," and became the definitive recording. The selections on the rest of the session, "Reckless Blues," "Cold in Hand Blues," and "Sobbin' Hearted Blues," all became classics, attesting to her greatness.

By the 1930's good blues singers' popularity began diminishing, falling behind the proliferating jazz singers who were out working the scene. Bessie saw the day when Ethel Waters' more sophisticated torch singing pushed her off the boards. Bessie went down---still trouping. Her untimely death at the age of forty-one in a September, 1937 automobile accident virtually coincided with the renaissance of traditional jazz that began in the late thirties. By 1938 Columbia released the first Bessie Smith reissues, a new generation of blues women began to record, and Bessie was already becoming a legend. If she had lived, just imagine her singing with the great locomotive band of Count Basie. It would have been something to hear.

ETHEL WATERS

Ethel Waters lived several musical lives. She started out in black vaudeville as a long-legged dancer and singer known as Sweet Mama Stringbean. One of the first black singers to be accepted on the same level with white singers, Ethel Waters was first to demonstrate the many possibilities for jazz singing in good commercial tunes. As an example, she made the first recording of the immensely popular Dinah, later performed by many other notables including Bing Crosby. Although her style was different from Bessie Smith's, Ethel had an enormous personality and talent, but it was difficult for her to compete with Bessie Smith the star.

In 1932 and '33, Ethel Waters recorded with Duke Ellington, along with a group of other well-established singers like the Mills Brothers, performing selections from all-black revues, including the Blackbirds of 1933. Her rendition of "I Can't Give You Anything But Love," recorded with Ellington in 1932, is the definitive version, eclipsing that of Aida Ward's in 1928. Ethel also recorded with Bennie Carter and Teddy Wilson earning respectability even as a Bessie Smith-type blues singer. When beginning her stage appearances, she devised a cute opening where someone off stage would ask, "Are you Ethel Waters?" and she'd answer, "Well, I ain't Bessie Smith." It would excite the audience and then she would break out with a heartbreaking blues number.

Ethel Waters was also a remarkable lady of the theater. From early childhood she envisioned herself a great actress. Her later celebrity as an actress eclipsed her importance as an accomplished singer of the blues. Along with Bessie and Louis, she shone as a distinctive singer of her time. She considered Ma Rainey and Bessie Smith and other blues singers as shouters. Her acceptance by the public was due to an advised change in her repertoire. Stepping away from Smith-like songs, she adopted songs other than blues. Although she never could read music, she would say, "My music is all queer little things that come into my head. All queer things that I hum."

This led to engagements at the Cotton Club in Harlem and the Plantation Club on Broadway, to recording sessions with Jimmy and Tommy Dorsey, Benny Goodman and many more, and finally to the movies notably As Thousands Cheer in 1933 and Cabin In The Sky in 1940, where she sang her unexpected success "Taking A Chance On Love," thereby achieving success as both singer and actress. Her rendition of "I Can't Give You Anything But Love" with the Duke Ellington orchestra in 1932 is the most enduring version on record. On the second chorus of this recording, she almost sounds like a man, the voice lowdown and bluesy.

Ethel Waters, a blues singer, jazz singer, actress, and riveting personality, could swing in the jazz idiom of the times. In the book The Real Jazz, author Hugues Panassie wraps it up accordingly: "Her voice, although a miracle of smoothness, is nonetheless firm and penetrating, clear and supple, swinging, caressing, cynical, with myriad's of little touches and inflections....since 1930 she had been influenced to some degree by Louis Armstrong. As a matter of fact, Ethel Waters' influence on female jazz singers is almost as great as that of Louis Armstrong." Later, Ethel Waters became a star of the religious world when she traveled and preached with the Reverend Billy Graham's troupe.

MILDRED BAILEY

Mildred Bailey was an immensely successful singer of the newly established Swing Era with her particular mastery of phrasing. Part Couer d'Alene Indian, she was xylophonist (not vibes) Red Norvo's wife and later sang with his band. She credited her Indian heritage for the unusual

quality of her high-pitched tone, which balanced her warm lower range.

After running away from home because her father remarried after her Mother died, Mildred originally got in the music business in Seattle, Washington. "She had a job demonstrating sheet music in a ten cents- a -

Mr. & Mrs. Swing - Mildren Bailey with Red Norvo

copy music store. She played piano and sang each song for customers," Eighty-nine year old Red Norvo told me during a conversation I had with him, "She had an excellent memory. Before a recording date she would go over a song once or twice with me at home and simply memorized it. She always recorded in one take."

In the 1930's Mildred had her own NBC radio show on Monday, Wednesday, and Friday nights for 15 minutes. "That's where I first met her - I was backing her," Red said.

Mildred Bailey and Red Norvo were known as Mr. and Mrs. Swing, a sobriquet levied on them by George Simon in Metronome Magazine. With Norvo and pianist-bandleader Teddy Wilson of Benny Goodman Quartet fame, Mildred waxed some great recordings. Her recordings of "Melancholy Baby," "A Lull In My Life," and "Russian Lullaby" (a little known tune but a favorite with jazz performers) are the best examples of her superiority in the genre. "Rockin'Chair," Hoagy Carmichael's classic, became a hit and was always identified as Mildred's own. "She used it as a theme song," Red said. It was a variation of the blues, although some-what closer to the new swing patterns.

"Hoagy used to hang around on the movie set of King of Jazz, Paul Whiteman' (with Bing Crosby) landmark film. He wanted Mildred to introduce the song because he thought she could sing it better than any-one else," Red said. Mildred became known as the "Rockin' Chair Lady". "Her recording of 'Lazy Bones' - you know, Johnny Mercer's tune - he was her friend and she always did his tunes - and "More Than You Know," were her best recordings as far as I'm concerned."

Mildred Bailey remains as one of the finest jazz vocalists of the Big Band Era. "She possessed a clear voice and excellent diction (a' la Frank Sinatra) and vocalized with conviction and warmth. "Her diction was so exceptional," Red reiterated. Again, like the later Sinatra, she con-sciously surrounded herself with the best musicians available.

Red Norvo and others too, have said that with her recording of "Rockin Chair," Mildred Bailey became the very first girl singer of the Big Bands. Credit for this goes to the uncanny ability and foresight of Bruns-wick Records A & R man Jack Kapp, who later formed Decca with his brother Dave, worked with Bing Crosby, and was responsible for the suc-cess of the Andrews Sisters, Rosemary Clooney, Tony Bennett, and other great vocalists. Mildred was Al Rinker's sister. Al was one of Bing Cros-by's original singing partners in the Rhythm Boys singing group along with Harry Barris It was Mildred who encouraged the three friends to come to Hollywood. The rest,of course, is history. Many years later Mildred ap-peared with Bing Crosby on his landmark radio show in L.A. in 1950 and together they sang "I've Got The World On A String," just like they did in the earlier Paul Whiteman days.

Mildred died in 1951 in a Poughkeepsie, New York hospital, not far from her upstate New York, farm. She had retired in 1949. Mildred Bailey, although mostly unknown to the modern world, was the catalyst for many singers including Frank Sinatra. Tony Bennett told me in no uncertain terms that it was Mildred Bailey who influenced his singing career the most as did Frankie Laine. "Bing told me many times that he learned to sing from Mildred," Red proudly declared. In his autobiography Call Me Lucky, Bing said, "I was lucky in knowing the great jazz and blues singer Mildred Bailey so early in life. She taught me so much about singing and about interpreting popular songs."

And, there is this little-known story: "She was responsible for discovering Billie Holiday along with John Hammond," Red recalled, "They were up on the second floor of the Apollo (Theater in New York) where the white people sat, when Billie appeared on stage in an amateur show, and Mildred excitedly said ' That girl can sing!' and ran downstairs to find out her name."

Take a moment one quiet day and put Mildred Bailey's records on the turntable and simply listen.

BILLIE HOLIDAY

When it comes to improvisation, it's a rule that the singer must keep the song recognizable. The lyrics can stray off the melody line but must arrive back on track by the end of a phrase. Billie Holiday was the master of this kind of singing. If Bessie Smith's example ennobled a tradition, Billie was the singer whose life spelled out that tradition. "It's not a matter of what you do, but how you do it," Fats Waller once declared.

Billie Holiday's recording of "What A Little Moonlight Can Do" with Teddy Wilson clearly demonstrates this musical necessity. Here a plain song takes on jazz expressions of major proportions.

Billie's best recordings, I believe, were made with pianist and bandleader Teddy Wilson.

"She made the most beautiful records with her friend Lester Young, when she recorded with me back in the thirties," Teddy Wilson personally told me back in 1982. Lester Young's tenor sax suited Billie Holiday perfectly. Her voice was also her instrument. Like Bing Crosby, Billie skillfully took advantage of the advent of the microphone, using her supple, sensitive voice to embrace it, delivering a song in a totally different way than when not using the microphone. Remember that Billie was not a blues singer, as 95% of her recordings were not blues by any account.

In later years Billie's voice became a mere shadow of her greater days. The voice and spirit was worn and sounded old. Her stressed life of drugs and abuse, heaped upon her mostly by others, ended in an early death at forty-four. There was no doubt as to Billie Holiday's credentials as a major , influential jazz voice of the 20th century. Almost every vocalist who followed, male and female, acknowledge their debt to the quintessential jazz singer Billie Holiday. In February 1997 Tony Bennett, at 70 years recorded an album entitled: Tony Bennett: On Holiday, a tribute recording where the magic of modern electronics permits Tony to sing a duet with Billie - "God Bless The Child." He's earned the right.

ELLA FITZGERALD

After Holiday there was a host of female singers performing on the swing circuit. You can never say too much about the success that was Ella Jane Fitzgerald. So much has been written about Ella who was really a contemporary of Billie Holiday and also rates as one of the best voices of the Jazz Age and the Big Band Era. Growing up, she absorbed the sounds of Connee Boswell and

Happy Birthday Ella! - L-R: Steve Rossi, William B. Williams, Sarah Vaughan, Bill Dana, Dorothy Killgallon, Johnny Ray, Harold Arlen, Fran Warren and Ella

her Sisters, Bing Crosby, and Louis Armstrong. Her big hit with the Chick Webb band that led her to the big time was "A Tisket, A-Tasket," which she co-wrote with bandleader Van Alexander. It was a late 1930's swinging, pouty version of an otherwise dull song and an auspicious beginning for the talented teenager. Shortly after her mother died, Chick Webb actually rescued Ella from a fate in an orphanage by adopting her as his own daughter. Ella was a somewhat gawky, rather unruly - scarcely chic-bandstand singer. But it was her voice that appealed to Webb.

In the forties, Ella scored with "How High The Moon" and George Gershwin's "Lady Be Good," both durable Big Band Era favorites and a prelude to her scat vocals, leading jazz straight into bebop by the late 1940's. She was the prototypical swing singer. "She uses the blues structure when she improvises: she can hum a blues languidly or drive it joyously through fast tempo and melody changes," said Stuart Nicholson in his biography of Ella. Her story is strikingly opposite Billie's. Although both were initially handicapped by poverty and race, the difference was temperament and personal strength. There was no alcohol, addiction, or degradation. Ella Fitzgerald was constantly amazed at her fame. A somewhat nervous performer, she was never at home with interviews or publicity even up to the end. I know about that very well. I once had an opportunity to interview Ella, but, as luck would have it, a terrible snow storm prevented me from traveling the twenty-five miles to the theater that appointed evening. I never got a second chance. And believe me, I tried.

The Songbook albums produced by her manager and producer since the 1950's, Norman Granz, were great individual albums and definitive interpretations of songwriters George Gershwin (the best of them-it contains the best version of "Of Thee I Sing" ever done), Jerome Kern, Cole Porter, Harold Arlen, and Irving Berlin. They are considered lasting treasures of American music. They are all so exceptional. William B. Williams, then legendary host of New York's WNEW's, Make Believe Ball-

Ella with Dizzy looking on

room for many years, called Ella the "First Lady of Song," or sometimes just plain Ella. As Leonard Feather astutely observed in his 1972 book, From Satchmo to Miles: "Ella Fitzgerald is one of the most flexible, beautiful, and widely appreciated voices of this century."

Her thirteen Grammy Awards started with the 1958 Best Vocal

Performance, Ella Fitzgerald Sings The Irving Berlin Songbook, to the 1990 Best Jazz Vocal Performance for All That Jazz. She has been honored with honorary doctorates at both Yale and Dartmouth Universities. Accepting the Yale award, she said with characteristic modesty, "Not bad for someone who only studied music to get that half-credit in high school." In 1979 she received a Kennedy Center Honors Award.

During her final days, her old friend Bea Wain, a wonderful Song Star herself with those treasured recordings "Deep Purple" and "My Reverie" recorded with Larry Clinton, went driving around town together with Ella and her chauffeur.

"It was April 25 and Ella's 78th birthday. Our mutual friend Joyce Garro and I were at her home celebrating her special day. We were laughing , singing and eating birthday cake. We reminisced about our past, beginning in the latter part of 1937 when I was singing with Larry Clinton and she was with Chick Webb. Although she was ill, Ella usually went for a ride in her big beautiful car every day. On this day she invited me to come along. She sat in the front with her driver and I was in the rear with her nurse. The radio was tuned to one of the jazz stations and, of course, we were listening to Ella coming over the air. She sang along with herself and clapped her hands in time. She called out the names of some of the musicians and remembered them really well. I have to say that the ride with Ella on her last birthday was a tremendous thrill. I loved her so much and I miss her so...."

A tribute was held at Carnegie Hall on Tuesday, July 9, 1996 to celebrate the life and career of Ella Fitzgerald. Margaret Whiting, Bobby Short, John Pizzarelli, Harry "Sweets" Edison, Lionel Hampton, Ruth Brown, Herb Ellis, Jack Jones, Diana Krall, and Chris Conner were there contributing through song. It was voiced by Jonathan Schwartz, the excellent disc jockey of New York's (at the time) radio station WQEW, the most listened to radio station playing standards in the United States. It was intended to be a testimonial to a living legend, but wound up as a fitting eulogy to the excellence of Song Star Ella Fitzgerald.

DORIS DAY

Doris sent this photo in 2007

One hot summer day in 1948, when I was sixteen and living in Brooklyn, New York, I ducked into my neighborhood movie theater to seek relief from rising temperatures and to see Romance on the High Seas. In the cool darkness, a young band singer turned actress vocalized the movie's romantic ballad "It's Magic." I became enamored by both song and song star, pretty and fresh-looking Doris Day, the postwar girl next door.

Eight years earlier, while Benny Goodman was reorganizing his old band and Lionel Hampton was starting a new band, this young seventeen year- old ex-dancer from Cincinnati, formerly Doris Kappelhoff, whose idols were Betty Grable and Ginger Rogers, began a band-singing career with little-known Barney Rapp in Cincinnati. He promptly switched her name to Doris Day , having once heard her singing "Day After Day" on local, amateur radio.

"I thought Doris Day sounded so phony!" Doris explained, "he said he thought it sounded just perfect, and my mother liked it; I really never did. It didn't sound real. Isn't that funny?"

Doris had turned to singing after her dancing career was sidelined by a shattered leg incurred in an auto-train accident. "To encourage me in music, the doctor gave me a ukulele, but it didn't mean much. When I was dancing I also sang in a personality class. We would pick a song that we liked and sing a chorus and then we would make up a dance to perform in front of the other kids." Doris said that her father had a wonderful voice, "He had perfect pitch. He taught piano, violin, and theory and even directed a choir."

Ella Fitzgerald was a definite influence in Doris' life: "The one voice I listened to above others belonged to Ella. Her voice fascinated me, so I'd sing along with her, trying to catch the subtle way she sang the words."

One of Doris' early Big Band affiliations was with Bing's brother Bob Crosby. In 1986 while I was with Bob Hope backstage at Westbury Music Fair, Les Brown told me he first went to see Doris while she was performing with Crosby at the Edison Hotel in New York. In his boyish manner, he offered her a job and signed her up, "Like many others at that time, she was unhappy in the Crosby organization, so she readily accepted. I simply asked her if she wanted to join up with my band."

"I was so happy to join up with Les, isn't that funny? He just had to ask me. But I stayed for only one year."

"I ran a tight ship," Les said, "The band was clean with no drinking, drugs or hard language while working. Doris' first recording was the ditty 'Beau Night in Hotchkiss Corners.' Doris was so young that her mother enlisted the help of my trusted trombonist, Si Zentner, who took her to work and brought her home every night."

"I was very lucky working with Les," Doris said. "The boys were so great. They softened things up for me when everything could have disillusioned and soured me." The Les Brown Band Of Renown became known inside the business as The Milkshake Band. And, according to Les: "If ever there was a milkshake girl, it was Doris."

"Then I left the band to get married and Les was furious. He was so mad. And it turned out to be a terrible mistake," Doris said, "So I took a job in Cincinnati at WLW, a really huge station. My old singing coach knew the manager and got me a job on a show called Moon River at midnight, for goodness sake. I sang three love songs each night. One night Les and the boys heard me in their rented car - they were on tour and were traveling through the area. Les said...' Hey, that's Dodo singing. We've got to get her back in the band'. They found where I lived and haunted me until I agreed to go back. But I had my son, Terry, but my mother agreed to travel with us and help take care of him. And that's how it happened! I went back with Les."

The more memorable "My Dreams are Getting Better all the Time" and Doris' biggest big-band hit, "Sentimental Journey" which consistently appears on the Top Ten all-time list of songs of that era when polls were retaken, were recorded in 1944 after she rejoined the band.

"Nobody was especially impressed when we first played that tune," Doris recalled, "But after we played it on a couple of broadcasts, the mail started pouring in. Before that I don't think we'd even planned to record it. But of course we did-right away - and you know the rest.

"We had so much fun in our band bus when we were on tour. The guys were so funny," Doris revealed. "We just laughed all the time. We were a family. We laughed and we cried - I'll always have those memories."

Doris left the Les Brown band again in 1946 and worked the night club circuit for a while, including dueting a couple of winsome recordings in 1947 with soft-crooner Buddy Clark: "Love Somebody" and "Confess." And how about their version of "Baby, It's Cold Outside."

Down on her luck, having a tough time trying to make ends meet while living in a trailer in Hollywood and supporting her new baby, Doris was helped by Manie Sacks, a well-liked NBC vice-president (I later worked under Manie myself a few years later), who helped arrange a night club job for her. She landed a contract at the Little Club in New York even though it lasted but a few months. She was soon back in Hollywood trying to rear-range her life.

Doris' start in motion pictures was accidental: "Acting in films had never so much as crossed my mind. I was a singer and all my talents were motivated toward that."

Fortunately, and unknown to Doris, movie director Michael Curtiz was frantically searching for a lead actress/singer for a musical that was ready for filming, Romance on the High Seas. The score, including the song "It's Magic," written by Sammy Cahn and Jule Styne for Judy Garland whose deal with the studio fell through, was just perfect for Doris' style and personality. The songwriters were able to convince Doris to sing at a party at Jule Styne's house: "Jule told me he and Sammy just wrote a score for a movie and wanted to know if I was interested in playing the leading role. I gasped and said that I thought they would want an experienced singer and Sammy said, 'I'm not so sure.'" This led to a screen test the next morn-ing. The test was frenetic and hectic, but Doris wound up with the part. As Curtiz opined in his thick Hungarian accent, "I sometimes like girl who is not actress. Is less pretend and more heart." "It's Magic" became a #1 top seller for months.

In-between films with Warner, Doris traveled with Bob Hope's USO troupe in 1948. "Doris is one of the great singers," said Bob during our last interview, "she really puts over a song. She has a good sense of timing, like Bing Crosby. She has that quality that lights up the house. When she sings a ballad, she can really get to you."

While with Warner Bros. she appeared in a series of mostly minor backstage type musicals with various co-stars - Ronald Reagan, Gene Nelson, Jack Carson, Gordon MacRae, and Gene Kelly. It was with Kirk Douglas (her voice juxtaposing Harry James' expressive trumpet) where I feel she touch downed a significant mark in her singing and film career in the 1949 film Young Man with a Horn, a movie based on the life of legend-ary jazz cornetist Bix Beiderbecke. It was so well done. It produced an abundant album of great songs: "With a Song in My Heart" lighting the way and Harry James' crying trumpet playing background and release. In 1952, a film "I'll See You in My Dreams" with Danny Thomas, covering lightly the career of song lyricist Gus Kahn, was also a high musical spot in Doris' film career.

Doris recorded the bouncy "A Guy is a Guy" that year and, with Frankie Laine, a South African duet called "Sugarbush." In 1953 she captured "gold" with her big hit film, the rambunctious, two-fisted Calamity Jane costarring he-man singer Howard Keel, she served up the exhilarating

"Deadwood Stage" and the 1954 Oscar winning ballad, "Secret Love." The film Young at Heart in 1955 with her earlier radio show Hit Parade partner, Frank Sinatra, and "I'll Never Stop Loving You," from the film Love Me or Leave Me, a chronicle of earlier vocalist Ruth Etting with Jimmy Cagney, gave her a worthy dramatic opportunity. "Que Sera, Sera!" (Whatever will be, will be) which aptly describes Doris' personal attitude toward life, sparkled as an Oscar winning song from the movie The Man Who

1964 with Alfred Hitchcock - *The Man Who Knew Too Much*

Knew Too Much , filmed mostly in Marrakech and London, directed by Alfred Hitchcock and costarring Jimmy Stewart. "I just never expected that song to become a hit," Doris said. It is the song best identified with Doris by later fans just as "Sentimental Journey" is the favorite with earlier admirers.

"Wow, what an experience making that movie," she further explained. "It was uncomfortable. In Marrakech it was over 100 degrees every day, and you roasted. Then in London it was freezing, so I caught pleurisy and had to stay in bed for a week. The traveling was difficult. But Jimmy Stewart was my darling friend and I appreciated appearing with him and working for Mr. Hitchcock."

The Pajama Game in 1957 with Broadway tenor John Raitt was one of her best musical endeavors and a big commercial hit for the studio. Her last musical film, Jumbo, in 1962 did not fare as well, but that is subjective, isn't it? Doris' last top forty hit recording was" Everybody Loves a Lover."

Doris' movie career covered 20 years and 39 films ---lasting until 1968. Of course, the popular comedies Pillow Talk with Rock Hudson, That Touch of Mink with Cary Grant, Teacher's Pet with Clark Gable, Please Don't Eat the Daisies with David Niven, and It Happened to Jane with Jack Lemmon are fondly remembered by Doris Day movie fans.

There have been some dark days in the life of Doris Day, including several early brief marriages and later, serious financial problems. Upon her husband Marty Melcher's passing, it was discovered her life savings had been grossly mishandled, depriving her of all her money and assets. This unfortunate condition left Doris in serious debt which took years to resolve and recover.

During the period of 1968 to 1972 it was The Doris Day Show on

Les Brown with Doris Day

television. At first she reluctantly honored contracts set up by her late husband. The show started off with poor scripts and venues. Eventually she turned the show around, hiring new producers and scriptwriters who worked out a new format, somewhat emulating the comedy movies accomplished with Rock Hudson, like Pillow Talk.

Doris Day's life thrives on eleven acres in lush Carmel, California, where she keeps all her "babies." Those "babies" are all her pets. "My life is so full-thanks to all my beautiful pets," she says. Her motto is "Thanks for Caring" a message from her Doris Day Animal Foundation, a nonprofit organization dedicated to aiding abused animals. One of its priorities is to help solve the pet overpopulation crises through spaying and neutering companion animals.

"It's the four-leggers that make everything work, make everything worthwhile and everything beautiful," and, she added "...my public image of America's la-di-da happy-go-lucky virgin, carefree and brimming with happiness was more make-believe than any part I ever played in any movie.

When I last heard from Doris, she helped me with the book Jukebox Saturday Night where we devoted a chapter to her favorite man - Les Brown.

"I live now," she said when I asked about her future, "I don't live in the future. I don't live in the past, I live right now. Right now everything is just lovely." She told me she really means it!

In memory of her son Terry Melcher, and to honor professional veterinarians, Doris has designated the Doris Day Animal Foundation to contribute a $75,000 grant to establish an endowed veterinary scholarship in shelter medicine at the University of California, Davis School of Veterinary Medicine.

Recapture the Feeling

Shortly after the June 1996, release of the first book in this series, The Best Damn Trumpet Player, I sent a signed copy with a letter soliciting comments to Big Band vocalist Connie Haines and promptly received an absolutely stunning handwritten reply by return mail.

Dear Richard:

Thanks for this great book. Reading about all my good friends and my best friend, Helen O'Connell, made me very happy. But, I'm so disappointed you did not interview me too, since I have so many personal memories of Satchmo and Harry James as we worked together throughout the years.

But, God is Good - I've continued to have a full-time career and I recorded my best album in 1988, that is still selling well. Last November I performed for three weeks in a fabulous show saluting the end of World War II, saluting the USO and all my work with Bing Crosby, Bob Hope, and Frank Sinatra at Trump's Taj Mahal in Atlantic City. My life's work was shown on dual screens during the 1 1/2 hour concert. I am flying all over the country for various State Governors with this inspiring show.

Then I'm sailing for Russia on a cruise tour. It's all so exciting. C'mon let's get another book going. Richard, get back to me.

God Bless, Connie.

Let's drift back a few decades into one of America's old southern cities, Savannah, Georgia, where a beautiful baby, Yvonne Marie Ja Mais, was born to aristocratic parents. Known since for most of her life as Connie Haines, a sobriquet assigned to her by ex-boss bandleader Harry

James when she was but fifteen. Yvonne always knew she one day would be a famous singer.

Characteristically, from very early in her life, Connie Haines always begins each day with a prayer,

Father God,
I place my hand in Yours today.
Here is my life. Show me the way.

Connie's first public appearance was at age four in the Baby Saucy Show in Savannah, and at five she was already Florida State Charleston Champion. After rapid success in those formative years, dancing and singing reached deep into her blood. She loved to perform. Aunts and uncles enthusiastically encouraged her, and her loving mother moved her carefully along. It was the jazz age of Al Jolson, Sophie Tucker, Ed Wynn, and Eddie Cantor. Then success at an amateur contest led to an NBC contract as the Little Princess of the Air. Later, after a bout with scarlet fever, Connie began singing in Miami, Florida, as a vocalist with Howard Lally's orchestra. When auditioning for representation by the William Morris Agency in the old Brill Building in New York City, band leader Harry James happened to be present and heard Connie sing "I Cried For You" and "I Can't Give You Anything But Love." He called some two hours later and offered the fifteen year old a job with the band. She started that very night at forty dollars a week, opening at the old Benjamin Franklin Hotel in Philadelphia. "I remember I wore a white taffeta gown," Connie said.

"Yvonne Marie Antoinette Ja Mais is quite a name, but it won't fit on the marquee'," Harry James considered carefully. "No, you look like a Connie to me. Haines! Connie Haines! It goes with James." he was quite sure, and the young lady nodded okay. Listening to the radio expecting to hear her daughter Yvonne sing with the James band, her mother almost called the police until she heard her voice and realized the singer introduced as Connie Haines was, in fact, her own little Yvonne Marie.

"We went on the road in a band bus. After several nights of sleeping on a bus, it was a strange feeling to check into a Main Street hotel; be able to hang up your clothes; to wash your hands when you wanted to, not when the bus driver told you to; and to lie on a bed that wasn't moving in a normal sleeping position. But it was an exhilarating experience. Then a wonderful guy named Frank Sinatra joined us."

Harry James tried to change Frank Sinatra's name too, but, according to Connie, a confident Frank said typically: "You want the voice, you take the name."

"Frank was lots of fun on the bus trips. He was always in good spirits. He pitched in, always doing his share and more," Connie confided. The recording Connie made with Harry, "Comes Love, Nothing Can

Be Done," is my absolute Connie Haines favorite. She sounds so young, so cute, so bubbly, energetic and charming. I also favor "Don't Worry 'Bout Me," typically pleasant Haines material to listen to over and over.

"You know, Richard, I don't sound that way anymore. That was fifty years ago. I made that record singing to cold padded walls. A microphone was stuck in my face. All I could feel was panic. But it became a hit record. It was not until I joined Tommy Dorsey months later that I finally began to feel relaxed when recording. I really loved my audiences. They were my friends. I preferred singing to them live."

Frank and Connie eventually joined Tommy Dorsey's band, as James' organization was faltering financially at the time. He eventually came back into the fray, however, after the success of "You Made Me Love You," a song Harry greatly admired after hearing a very young Judy Garland sing her heart out to a Clark Gable photo in a sentimental MGM movie, and after heavy promotion by Martin Block on the New York radio station WNEW on his show, the Make Believe Ballroom. Connie's version of that tune became a hit for her later on.

"Frank and I developed a little feud when we were with Dorsey," Connie revealed to me, "and he would not sing at the same mike with me. He would not even look at me. So I would pick a young man or two in the front row," she continued, "and direct my sing- ing at him on songs like "Snoo- tie Little Cutie," or "Oh! Look at Me Now," or

with Tommy Dorsey

"Let's Get Away from It All," and that would make Frank even madder. But we finally stopped teasing one another, then kissed and made up on New Year's eve night in 1941.

On those recordings, Connie said, she would get ten dollars and Frank twenty-five, even though they sold millions of records. "That's the agreement we had. We were unknown kids and he (Tommy Dorsey) was training us." Dorsey's was considered the star-maker band.

Connie was so young with Dorsey that to perform one-nighters her mother had to give Dorsey guardianship, accomplished before a judge, in order for her to travel interstate on a bus with all those men in the band.

Tommy Dorsey also featured The Pied Pipers, a singing group comprised of three young men and beautiful Jo Stafford. They performed immortal songs like "I'll Never Smile Again" and others backing up Connie and Frank. "What Is This Thing Called Love" and "Will You Still Be Mine"

with Jane Russell (L), Beryl Davis (Top) and Rhonda Fleming (R)

were hits for Connie, the latter written especially for her by Matt Dennis and Tom Adair.

Her favorite Sinatra duets remain "Oh! Look at Me Now" and "Let's Get Away from It All," arranged by Sy Oliver. "I use those arrangements right to this day," she said.

Connie admits being influenced by Billie Holiday, Mildred Bailey, and Kate Smith. While convalescing with childhood rheumatic fever, she studiously observed the sound of Kate Smith on the radio, always desiring to emulate those powerful phrases, continuing it right up to today.

Connie told me the famous story of how her dress once caught fire back stage while performing with Tommy Dorsey at New York's old Madison Square Garden:

"While I was backstage getting ready to sing, someone threw a cigarette from one of the tier seats. It caught in my net dress and ignited. I was enveloped in flames. Frank Sinatra quickly flipped his jacket off and slammed it at me. It knocked me to the floor. I did not know what hit me.

The coat and the fall snuffed out the flames. My long hair was scorched and the back of my dress was burned off. Tommy kept vamping while I was on fire. He wasn't aware of what was happening. Back up on my feet, I heard my cue and ran on stage. I moved up to the mike and let go right on the beat."

Tommy's mouth dropped when he realized what had happened as they noticed the burnt dress with the sides flying. Connie feels that her early rooted, lifelong training enabled her to go on with the show.

The Tommy Dorsey band tour wound up in Hollywood. Their first movie for MGM, Ship Ahoy , also starred dancer Eleanor Powell. But, exhausted by the long tour, Connie elected to quit the band but remained in Hollywood for four years as the Song Star of the Abbott and Costello Radio Show, performing in theaters from coast to coast during the summer hiatus.

Connie soon became the star of an easy, half-hour variety radio show, Your Blind Date, involving servicemen audience participation and listeners as well. It was Hollywood's answer to New York's Stage Door Canteen.

At that time, songwriter Johnny Mercer formed a new record company named Capitol, and Connie cut the record "He Wears a Pair of Silver Wings," conducted by Gordon Jenkins. It was her first solo recording after her band associations. She soon became a cover girl, gracing Variety, Billboard, Downbeat, and Life magazines.

Connie subsequently made movies at MGM. There was The Duchess of Idaho with Van Johnson & Esther Williams and ten additional films. She recorded countless sides, played in night spots, and even made guest appearances on Bob Hope and Bing Crosby's radio shows. She sang in the Billy Graham Youth For Christ movement, too. She was clearly in her element- expression in entertainment and dedication and personal involvement in what she believed. Real fun was church participation and singing to our servicemen.

Later, she starred in the summer stock productions West Side Story, Showboat and Come Blow Your Horn, and then with Mickey Rooney, replacing an ailing Judy Garland on a national theater tour. "Judy was the greatest talent of all time, to step into her shoes and take her place on stage, I would've gladly sung without being paid," Connie acknowledged.

"I had my own television show for years with Frankie Laine, all throughout the fifties, and then we traveled for years all over the country performing in theaters everywhere as Mister and Miss Rhythm," Connie proudly said. She loved Frankie Laine. Who didn't?

Over the years Connie has appeared with so many stars and on so many shows that it would be impossible to list them all in this chronicle. But meritorious to mention are performances with jazz pioneer Louis Armstrong and no less than five command performances for four Presidents: Eisenhower, Kennedy, Johnson, and Ronald Reagan twice. It was at the 50th anniversary of Pearl Harbor when she appeared with the elder President Bush.

Her best friends today are those with whom she shares her life-long religious life. Actress Rhonda Fleming, British singer Beryl Davis, actress and vocalist Jane Russell. "We teamed up singing gospel songs in 1954 for Decca Records. Our first recording "Do Lord" was a million seller. There were twenty-six other hits we sang while touring half-way round the world in concert until 1984. We grew up together in the church; we got married all at the same time and had wedding showers and prayed for babies....and now we've got 'umpteen grand kids." She used to fly out to the coast from her Florida home to do one-nighters just to see her friends.

Along the way, Connie received the Courage Award in 1988 from President Ronald Reagan at a White House ceremony for the American Cancer Society.

Connie's lifetime mission was to tell her story about beating cancer, imparting inspiration to those around her, influencing others to pursue treatment where many of them were reluctant to seek medical assistance. "I'm living proof that you can be victorious over that disease," she said.

Glenn Miller's Larry O'Brien, Connie and Richard - at the 2003 Book Signing Luncheon in Stony Brook, NY

On October 1, 1996, Connie called me after spending three weeks in the hospital for, as she says, "a bunch of problems," and to recount her recent appearance in Atlanta, Georgia, her home state, where she was received by the Governor and countless fans--more than she could believe. "They shouted out to me, and it made me feel no pain," she announced with her usual, uplifting spirit.

In early December, Connie returned to the hospital to wrap up the balance of her med problems. "When I get out, "she promised, "I will write you a foreword for the Song Stars book."

"Sure!" I returned, "You'll have to stay home for six weeks...no traveling...no performing....I've got you grounded." (But I was thrilled.)

"And," she added, "I'll find some time to locate those photos of Louis Armstrong and myself...and also the photos with Jane (Russell) and Beryl (Davis) for the book."

"That would be great!" replied grateful me.

"Comes love," she added, "nothing can be done."

A short time later, Connie and I put together her biography and called it Snootie Little Cutie - The Connie Haines Story.

Connie with Ella Fitzgerald

Helen Forrest

Helen Forrest with Harry James

Voice of the Big Bands

Once upon a Big Band time, Helen Fogel, a very young girl from Atlantic City, New Jersey, sang her heart out regularly on New York radio station WNEW for very little pay. In those days some radio shows were labeled "sustaining," meaning the show had no sponsor and, consequently, low pay for performers. But they aired anyway. Helen wasn't worried because the exposure eventually led to a salaried CBS Network job vocalizing alongside trumpeter Bunny Berigan . Fortunately, bandleader Artie Shaw heard her one night at the Madrillon Club in Washington, D.C. and promptly contacted Helen to ask her to sing with his band. Although Billie Holiday was the current featured singer with the Shaw band, she was weary of the racist treatment received on the road despite the best efforts of the concerned bandleader and decided to quit. Billie, the only black performer in the all-white Shaw band, had to endure degrading racial indignities quite common in those days.

Recalling her friend Billie Holiday, Helen said: "Billie was just wonderful to me. Always trying to help, she used to tell Artie to let me sing some of her songs. She was really a great, caring person." During the following year or so, 21-year-old Helen recorded 38 singles with Shaw at RCA's New York studios. It was 1939 and the Big Band Era now in full swing.

Helen Fogel, now known to all as Helen Forrest, was appearing professionally and being recognized as the best singer Shaw ever had. Helen learned to dramatize a song: "I try to sing so a guy can picture soft lights and his girl," Helen told a Look Magazine interviewer back in 1944. Her voice always evoked excitement and emotion.

Helen skipped over to Benny Goodman's band after Artie Shaw suddenly disbanded his organization in late 1939 by suddenly walking off the bandstand at a hotel where he was performing. Joe Graydon, Helen's friend and personal manager for over 45 years, explained that it was because Artie was apparently unable to endure the pressure fame had brought him, "and he thoroughly disliked his audiences." Joe added, "He summoned the band to his room and told them that he was through and offered the band to Helen or (valued sideman) Tony Pastor."

Later, Shaw explained that he considered the whole music business a "racket" and moved to Mexico. But in less than a year, he was back and busier than ever.

Helen had no problem finding work: "Benny said I was his singer." Helen told me, "I didn't even have to audition. ...but I had to take a pay cut from $ 175.00 a week to $ 85.00. I took it because I wanted to work with Benny's band even though Benny once said I couldn't sing. Benny really didn't care much about singers anyway."

Helen sang some distinctive, early Eddie Sauter quality arrangements including "Darn That Dream," her first and perhaps best Goodman recording. "The Man I Love," another Sauter arrangement, highlighted by Helen's special vocalizing techniques, is further proof of her ability to deliver fresh melodic textures unexpectedly. In August of 1941, Helen suddenly quit the Goodman band "to avoid having a nervous breakdown," she said, paving the way for sultry Peggy Lee. In 1940 Helen recorded "Ghost of a Chance" with Lionel Hampton and the Nat "King" Cole trio.

Helen had always admired the way Harry James played the trumpet, "so I thought I'd fit in perfectly with the band. I contacted Harry on a hunch. Peewee Monte, Harry's manager, had me come over to sing at a rehearsal, and after that Harry asked the guys in the band to take a vote and they decided they wanted me. So Harry agreed."

In retrospect, my all time personal favorite Forrest recording of that period turned out to be Harry Warren's "I Had the Craziest Dream" from the Betty Grable, John Payne film Springtime in the Rockies, in which Helen appeared as the vocalist with Betty's soon to be real-life husband, trumpet-playing Harry James' Orchestra. But, unknown to many, the making of that movie adversely affected Helen Forrest's relationship with James, as they were lovers and approaching marriage until Betty Grable entered the scene. For my money, that celluloid clip still stands as one of the best musical Big Band moments portrayed on film. That latter fact was mutually agreed upon during an interview with Harry James in early1983 when we recalled that recording's special moment: "I think it was one of my best mo-

ments, too," Harry said.

It was during her tenure with Harry James that Helen recorded her best-known standards just as Billboard began publishing charts: "I've Heard That Song Before," an incredible 13 weeks as the number-one song on the list, "I Don't Want to Walk Without You," "Skylark," "Mr. Five by Five and others, all great wartime favorites. In the film Shine On Harvest Moon, she sang the haunting "Time Waits for No One." Listen carefully, as Helen infuses the song with rich sentimental messages.

It seems that Harry James' band provided extraordinary support for Helen's talents, and his arrangers enhanced those performances by interjecting nontraditional violins and capitalizing on her unique presence. Now not just a girl band singer accompanying a dance number, Helen developed definitive patterns of delivery that were more individually expressive than most vocalists of her time. She favored the orchestral settings that best fit her crying kind of style. Arrangements were built around Harry's horn and Helen's voice. Remember Helen's heartbreaking rendition of "I Cried for You" in the film Bathing Beauty with Harry? What a delivery.

Then Helen teamed up with song stylist Dick Haymes, recognized internationally as one of the best male baritones of all time. Together, they produced six top-ten duets: "Long Ago and Far Away," "It Had to Be You," "Together," "I'll Buy That Dream," and "Oh! What It Seemed to Be." Each of those singles sold over one million copies.

Beyond the Big Band Era, Helen earned a solid reputation in the supper-clubs, and there was heavy radio work in the '50's including her regular show with Dick Haymes. Additionally, Capitol Records revived some of her old hits in an entirely new album. While with Capitol she joined up with James once again in an album entitled Harry James in Hi-Fi. One of the selections was "I'm Beginning to See the Light," a song previously recorded by Kitty Kallen.

In 1954 Helen was singing with a trio instead of a big band at a club in Long Beach, California. "To tell the truth," she said, "I didn't go for the idea of a trio backing because it meant I couldn't use my library of big band arrangements. But Bob Braman and the boys do such a great job that now I'm more than happy."

Whenever Helen played the small clubs, she was always surprised at the big welcome she received. "I am always surprised as well as thrilled, and not only for myself but for others, because it's a sign of better things ahead for musicians and singers, as well."

In 1964 Helen toured throughout the United States (especially Las Vegas), Australia, and Britain with Frank Sinatra, Jr. and the Tommy Dorsey Orchestra. In the late Sixties she was reunited once again with James on an album entitled 20 Pieces of Harry James, revealing that her singing techniques and ability to tear at the heartstrings was just as effective as ever.

In the late Seventies, Helen teamed with Dick Haymes, Harry James, Hildegarde, The Pied Pipers, and the Inkspots in a nostalgic revue fittingly The Big Broadcast of 1944. Helen headlined with Dick Haymes in the Fabulous Forties at the Parker Playhouse in November of 1978 and electrified the audience with her vocal skills. She projected a warm, gracious personality - a pairing of talent and charm. All this activity worked out very well, but within four months the untimely death of Dick Haymes in March of 1980 really affected Helen.

They had been very close, having starred together on the very highly rated Autolite weekly radio show from 1944 until 1948 with Gordon Jenkins and his orchestra and the 4 Hits and a Miss singing group Thursday nights first on NBC and then on CBS. "Dick was terrific fun. He would make me laugh so hard and often that the laugh became famous," Helen said in her autobiography. "Dick thought the laughs and unexpected lines he threw at me livened up the show."

"Dick was one of the greatest singers of our era," Helen said, "and was the finest gentleman I've ever known and a dear friend." Helen spent many hours at Dick Haymes' bedside just before he died. "It still hurts me to talk about him."

Helen's stroke in 1980 left Helen terrified she'd be paralyzed. For a while she couldn't walk or talk. "But I'm very lucky," she said. "I recovered. I didn't even need vocal therapy to get my voice back."

In 1983, on the Stash label, Helen performed in a jazz setting with some fine musicians including pianist-composer Hank Jones and premier bassist George Duvivier, mostly reviving a handful of her old hits produced under the title of Sunny Side of the Street. Audiophile records released a batch of her radio transcriptions from the 1950's with accompaniment by either Carmen Dragon or The Ray Bloch Orchestra. At that time it was Wendell Echols of Jazzbeat who labeled her the Queen of the Big Band Singers in his review of this very good CD release. Helen's latest albums are on the Hindsight Label with Carmen Dragon's orchestra.

Joe Graydon told me that because of Helen's tenure with James, Goodman and Shaw, she has often been referred to as "The Voice of the Big Bands." "Another title which stuck with her was "One take Helen," he said, "because her first recording take was always great. Don Kennedy, host of Big Band Jump, a nationally syndicated radio show, and editor of the Big Band Jump Newsletter, has uncompromisingly selected Helen Forrest as the finest Big Band girl singer of the era. "Her vocals soared without losing feeling; they retained a crispness without sacrificing the emotional effect....and what are vocals for if not to affect the emotions of the listener," he went even further, "it's certainly true that the best artists of all kinds are the ones whose technique is not evident....who make it seem easy."

Helen Forrest made it seem easy.

FRAN WARREN

Fran Warren Sings

Hurrah for gutsy Fran Warren, the hip Bronxite kid who grew up a few subway stops from the 1940s hot Harlem jazz spots, who was initially inspired by the legendary Billie Holiday and urged on by musical friend and her sponsor, Billy Eckstine, and wound up girl singer in the sensational Charlie Barnet band when she was just short of eighteen. Her illustrious career has moved ahead enthusiastically. In 1994 Fran played out a lengthy Hawaiian gig, and without taking a breath, got herself set for a Northeast club tour which included Boston, Philadelphia and even New Jersey. Her benefit work throughout 1995 with the Society Of Singers in L.A. just adds to her long list.

My first encounter with Fran Warren was backstage in old Glen Cove, on Long Island's Gold Coast, where she appeared for the first time as Mame at the Northstage dinner-theater, a then newly -renovated proscenium stage which was converted over from a 1927 vaudeville house. There she laid them in the aisles with her heartwarming rendition of "If He Walked Into My Life Today."

You no doubt will remember Fran as the magical teen-age vocalist for Claude Thornhill's band when she recorded one of the Big Band Era's most enduring classics "Sunday Kind Of Love." It's remains the song that most identifies her.

"I received only fifty dollars to record that song, but I built my whole career around it." Fran said. When she performed that charming ever-green at places like Michael's Pub in Manhattan, it always brought down the house and dampened a few cheek.

This girl has done everything and more having performed in Pajama Game, played Adelaide in Guys And Dolls, Nellie Forbush in South Pacific, Sharon in Finian's Rainbow, Lorelei in Gentleman Prefer Blondes, Dolly in Once More With Feeling, Linda in Flower Drum Song, and even in a revival of The Big Broadcast with Harry James. She was always a sellout at jazz club engagements in Manhattan. Overall, Fran has recorded 700 singles and over 20 albums in almost 50 years of singing.

Back in 1943 she was known in the neighborhood by her given name, Fay Wolfe. A sixteen year old hopeful, one day she ventured out quite alone and scared to legendary 52nd Street, then the Mecca of jazz, to see and hear

a singer named Frances Fay and a chance meeting with young singer, Billy Eckstine, who invited her to a club across the street to hear Billie Holiday. Billie learned she was an aspiring singer and invited her to sing by personally leading her to the bandstand, saying, "Sing it pretty." The song was Gershwin's "Embraceable You" and Fran sang her heart out. Remaining until 2: A.M., it was Billy Eckstine who took her home to worried parents who had expected her back much earlier. Some months later it was a concerned Billy Eckstine who telephoned her to tell her to use the sobriquet Fran Warren for her career name.

"Where did you get such a name?" she asked , "Well, there's a bootleg wine called 'Warren's Sweet Wine', it's a good name, kid, and it looks good on you, so don't argue with me----use it!" And she did. "It just worked better than Fay Wolfe." Billy told me this story many years later.

When she was able to audition for girl singer in Duke Ellington's famous orchestra, the Duke dutifully took her aside and told her, "Listen, honey. You can't sing with this band."

Puzzled, Fran asked, "Don't I sing good enough?" and the Duke replied empathetically, "Yes, you do. But, listen to me. When you become eighteen and when Charlie Barnet's Band comes to New York--you go see him and tell him I sent you. That's the band you should be singing with."

"So, I took his advice, and auditioned for Barnet --and Kay (Starr) was just leaving--so he hired me. We opened at the Apollo a few days later and it was wonderful. It was the real beginning for me and I knew I was in the business to stay."

After Big Band experience, Fran turned to the musical stage: So there we were in a little town, in a little theater, in a little dressing-room, talking Big Band music. It was mostly about the collection of scattered voices and players who made up the Big Band Era and about fellow performers she had known and works alongside, but who mostly pass each other like ships in the night, the latter observed by both Woody Herman and Harry James.

Fran Warren possesses a conspicuous bravura quality, so evident in her performances, especially when she sings such songs as "Over The Rainbow" and "Hello Young Lovers." That night it was "Mame" followed by a recording date and a television show?

Meeting Fran Warren was a wonderful, refreshing experience. Retired now, Fran still lives in the same apartment in New York City for over 40 years that she did when she began her return to New York after her first success. Fran recently retired from her work with the Society of Singers in New York, due to illness. Our prayers at this date are with her.

BERYL DAVIS
Glenn's Last Vocalist

To Richard
Thanks for the Memories"
I'll be seeing
you!
Love
Beryl Davis

On November 2, 1944, a communiqué from Lieutenant General Jimmy Doolittle at Eighth Air Force Headquarters outlined invitational travel orders to a pretty young British singer as an authority for providing entertainment at Air Force installations in England. The excited young lady was London born Beryl Davis. Beryl was the only British civilian ever attached to the 8th Air Force.

In 1999 Beryl Davis and I had first sat down to talk about her friend, Big Band vocalist Connie Haines, for Connie's forthcoming autobiography Snootie Little Cutie. Connie, Beryl, and actresses Rhonda Fleming and Jane Russell are very close friends. Today, from her Palm Springs, California home, Beryl and I once again got together to talk about her own illustrious singing career that had spanned over 50 years and was still a work in progress.

This is her story:

"My father was a bandleader, and we lived in the center of London. I started my career as a dancer. I would sing one chorus and dance two, then I gradually sang two chorus' and danced one, and then finally left out the dancing part altogether. I was just three, and became the girl vocalist when I was merely eight."

This auspicious beginning was performed in notable music halls all over England, Ireland, Scotland, and Wales, as Beryl's dad, at the time, was an orchestra pit leader, and she, on cue, would hop up on stage and sing a rousing chorus of "Constantinople," collect a box of chocolates and then run offstage to smiles and applause.

Her guitarist father had inherited the popular , Stan Kenton-style,

Oscar Rabin dance band when ill-health forced Rabin to delegate more of the band leader work to him. And, like their American counterparts, the new Harry Davis orchestra fulfilled endless one-nighters. Beryl traveled with the band much like Doris Day with Les Brown and her friend Connie Haines with Harry James then Tommy Dorsey.

"All the American singers were my musical heroes, Richard. I listened to the Big Bands all the time because it was the only way I could learn the songs, particularly when the war came. We were really isolated, and perhaps would get just one record a month , and everybody would run to the music store to find a new song. We did all the Glenn Miller, Benny Goodman, and Tommy Dorsey stuff. I would listen on my little wind-up phonograph to Ella Fitzgerald, Helen O'Connell, Helen Forrest, Maxine Sullivan, and someone who would become my lifelong friend, Connie Haines. I tried very hard to emulate Ella the most, trying to learn that special, clear Ella sound."

Beryl's career blossomed throughout the war and she became England's prominent vocalist.

"From my father's band, I freelanced with all the important British bands. I sang with Mantovani, Syd Lawrence, and Ted Heath, all the great bands of England, and wherever I was needed. When they wanted a vocalist, they simply called me. I was a very quick learner. Before the war came I was in Paris singing with Stephane Grappelli and Django Reinhardt, and when we arrived back in England to go on tour, England declared war. I continued on tour with Stephane in a small group that included (pianist) George Shearing, and it was a wonderful time of my life Richard, musically speaking."

In the early days of the war, Beryl was one of the group's resident players at famous Hatchett's Restaurant, featuring the hot jazz violin of Stephane Grappelli, Arthur Young at the piano, and "Chappie" D'Amato and Belgian gypsy Django Reinhardt playing swing guitar.

The little group toured all the theaters with the bombs regularly falling all around them. "We just learned to handle the pressure. I was working the entire time and there I am running from door to door in an air raid. I would have to be down at the BBC, who had me under contract, at odd hours of the night, over there on Portland Place to do a broadcast to the Armed Forces or the BBC World Service. Bombs would be dropping, and you just did your best to dodge them. Well, if you didn't dodge them, well, that was that, you know."

Beryl was not terrified, as you would expect her to be under such circumstances. For her and other brave Britons, the daily bombings became a way of life. She would find herself in the bomb shelters or subway entertaining people who were nervous and could not sleep."

Then Glenn Miller came to town. "I was very excited about that, because, for me, that was the creme-de-la-creme of bands. Glenn wanted to be part of the overseas entertainment force --- and he had (vocalist) Johnny Desmond and the Crew Chiefs (singing group with Artie Malvin, Lynn Allison, Ray McKinley, Gene Steck, Murray Kane, and Steve Steck); and I was invited to join because I had an American style, and an American sound, accent, and knew all those Miller charts. Glenn was quiet, elegant and very much a leader."

Beryl Davis became the number one favorite girl singer of American Forces overseas. The very last show that Beryl performed with the Glenn Miller Band was at the Queensbury Club, on Lower Regent Street in the heart of London, on December 12, 1944. She sang the haunting war song "I'll Be Seeing You." Today, Beryl signs off with "I'll Be Seeing You" every time as a salutation after signature.

With Tommy Dorsey

"As he left, he patted me on the shoulder, and he said, 'Good show, kid.'I'll be seeing yuh.' That was the last time that I saw him."

After Glenn Miller was lost on that fateful plane trip over the English Channel, Beryl decided to expand her career and emigrate to America.

"I always wanted to go to America -- for the music - and for no other reason. I wanted to meet Nat King Cole, Frank Sinatra, Helen Forrest, Benny Goodman, - ever since I was a little girl, I wanted to meet them in person. I love my home country, but all of the music I loved came from America. So I had to go there to see things first hand. "Beryl by this time was singing regularly with the BBC doing ten shows a week.

America took to Big Band singer Beryl Davis, and Beryl Davis took well to America.

"I was booked into the Commodore Hotel. I woke up on my first day in New York and looked down the Avenue of Americas and saw so many people and taxis. I ran out the door and walked around the city for hours, just absorbing everything. Growing up in London, I had the impression it was a huge city; when I went back, I realized how small it really was."

Bob Hope heard her recording of "I'll Be Seeing You," and, through my old friend, band booker supreme Willard Alexander, brought her to Hollywood to debut on his radio show. Chosen by Frank Sinatra himself to be his partner for one year on Your Hit Parade radio show, Beryl replaced

Bing, Beryl and Bob

Doris Day, who went to Hollywood for her first movie Romance on the High Seas.

"Frank was very kind and supportive, and always a perfect gentlemen. He always included me, as after each show we would go out to dinner." Beryl's singing reputation expanded, leading to featured engagements with the Benny Goodman, Vaughn Monroe and David Rose orchestras.

In California, Beryl met and married Peter Potter, a popular Hollywood disc jockey. They had three children and remained married for seventeen years living in their Taluca Lake home.

"One of the most exciting times of my life was when I joined with my new friends, Connie Haines, Jane Russell, and Rhonda Fleming, and recorded "Do, Lord," a record that went gold. We were all members of the same church, the Hollywood Presbyterian Church, which you can read about in depth in Connie Haines' new autobiography Snootie Little Cutie, due out this fall."

CONNIE HAINES
I asked Connie Haines about "Do,Lord's" success.

"How did Jane, Beryl, and I get together as a singing group? It happened back in 1954 at Beryl's St. Stephen Episcopal Church. I agreed to sing at a fund-raising event there. Della Russell was there to sing with her husband (singer) Andy Russell. Jane Russell was also there. In the basement, we dressed and practiced before the event. 'Connie, what am I going to do, just stand there with egg on my face?' Jane complained. We can all sing an old church spiritual, called "Do, Lord," I told her.

"Beryl was from London and never heard of the song. But we worked on it, rehearsed and perfected it in no time, and we sang it for the church group and later picked up another friend, Rhonda Fleming, when Della had to leave, and recorded it for our Four Girls tour."

The girls sold a million records and performed the song on the Bob Hope, Red Skelton and Ed Sullivan shows, and on shows featuring Milton Berle, Abbott and Costello, Arthur Murray and Hedda Hopper. They went on to record a dozen more uplifting spiritual songs. The royalties from "Do, Lord" were divided up and donated to the girls' separate church or charity.

Beryl continued on , singing with Mel Torme, the Gene Krupa Orchestra, Kay Kyser's Band, and, over the years, on many salutes to Glenn Miller.

Beryl was married to drummer Buck Stapleton, ironically a member of the Glenn Miller Air Force Band,and a later Promotions Manager for Capitol Records. They had been married for thirty-four years until she lost Buck a few years ago. Earlier, they had lost the Taluca Lake home in an earthquake and went to live in a Palm Springs condo.

Beryl is still a dynamic performer in the Big Band world of today. Her rendition of "I'll Be Seeing You" has become her vocal trademark and is always dedicated to the memory of Major Glenn Miller.

"I'm honored to still be working part of the music scene. Sure, it's not the good old days anymore, but I notice that young musicians are taking a good look at the charts of the Big Bands, and I want to work with those kids and pass along the Big Band legacy. One of the things that makes me doubly happy is that I'm not just an observer. I'm still part of the scene."

Beryl Davis was performing on cruise ships, singing her heart out with Tommy Dorsey's Bill Tole and Les Brown's premier clarinetist Abe Most, while sailing from Florida to Acapulco in shows appropriately called The Glenn Miller Hit Parade.

Beryl has virtually retired from singing these days after performing annually for many years at Glenn Miller reunions at England's Twinwood Airfield & Control Tower Arena where Glenn Miller took off for France and never returned.

For absolute joy find and play Beryl with Stephane Grappelli singing "Star Eyes."

JO STAFFORD

The Stafford Sisters' Lead Singer Goes Solo

When Jo Stafford's recordings "You Belong to Me," "Long Ago and Far Away," "My Darling, My Darling," "I'll Be Seeing You," "You'll Never Know," "There Are Such Things," and "Embraceable You" stop selling, the Earth will surely stop spinning.

Jo Stafford and her songs are at the very root of America's musical legacy. To the G.I.'s of World War II, she was G.I.Jo because of her association with those stirring, ever-familiar strains our servicemen, known as G.I.'s clung to during those desperate wartime days. It has been said that when men go to war they need a connection to home. Jo Stafford surely reminded them of home. Her voice evoked calm and reassurance when it was needed most. Jo seemed to be the clean cut---not the pin-up type, but the wholesome high school sweetheart. Her recordings touched them in barracks, field kitchens and hospitals. When she sang "I'll Be Seeing You" or "There Are Such Things," memories began and comfort was felt.

Jo Stafford started with a singing group composed of her own two sisters and herself. "We were known as the Stafford Sisters," she explained. "By the age of ten, I was reading music and could play piano pretty good." Sisters Pauline and Christine were older and first performed as a duet on Long Beach, California, radio station KFOX with their own show. "I was able to join up with them upon graduation from high school," she added.

"It was the very natural thing to do," she said, "and we had quite a successful run of it." The trio worked the southern California radio circuit and backed up Hollywood movie musicals. Earlier, Jo had received several years of classical voice training, with an eye to some day becoming an opera singer. That never materialized. "I simply had to go to work after high school."

Then, in 1938, Jo joined up with a group of seven men singers, calling themselves The Pied Pipers. "I graduated to the Pipers and we worked on the movie Alexander's Ragtime Band (an Irving Berlin musical starring Alice Faye, Tyrone Power, and Don Ameche). The Pipers were literally created on the set between takes when we started to sing together. We would sit on the studio floor and work out parts of a song."

The Pipers joined up with the Tommy Dorsey aggregation in 1938, but after a while Tommy realized he could not afford to pay all eight, so he let them go. When the group reduced itself to four members (Chuck Lowrey, Clark Yocum, John Huddleston, and Jo), Tommy re-hired them in December of 1939 and added a skinny kid named Frank Sinatra and a young Connie Haines as the regular band singers. They went on to record a batch of very successful hits: "There Are Such Things," "Street of Dreams," "Oh, Look at Me Now (with Connie Haines) and the biggest hit of all, the one that established vocal groups forever "I'll Never Smile Again."

Jo Stafford remembered Frank Sinatra when he first joined the band and the Pipers, "As he came up to the mike, I just thought, Hmmm--kinda thin. But by the end of eight bars I was thinking, 'This is the greatest sound I've ever heard.' But he had more. Call it talent. You knew he couldn't do a number badly."

Jo was the Pied Pipers' lead singer and a regularly featured soloist with Dorsey, but, "I always considered myself, first and foremost, the distaff member of the Pied Pipers." Jo was considered an especially cool, self-assured person with great musical control and a sly equally cool sense of humor. She soon began singing solo ballads. It was Connie Haines who sang the cutesy, upbeat numbers. Connie told me that Tommy Dorsey called Jo "....the mellow trombone voice of the band."

In 1943, utilizing her talents and armed with techniques learned from Tommy Dorsey' s trombone playing, the endearing Jo Stafford left the Pipers, and, at the request of her friend, Dorsey junkie and prolific composer- songwriter Johnny Mercer, began recording for the newly formed Capitol Records out in California.

Just when Jo Stafford and the Pipers began with Dorsey, her future husband, arranger Paul Weston, had left the band to oversee the musical career of Dinah Shore, write music charts for the Bob Crosby Band, and also to work for Paramount Pictures on Hope and Crosby road films. He had written two big songs that Sinatra and Jo recorded, "I

Should Care" and "Day by Day."

Paul Weston was Johnny Mercer's first musical director at Capitol and was the influence and arranger of many of Jo's hits such as "Whispering Hope" and "My Darling, My Darling," duets with baritone Gordon MacRae and "Candy" in 1945 with John and the Pipers, "Long Ago and Far Away" and "I Love You."

After twelve years of working together at Capitol, and subsequently at Columbia, where she recorded the hits "You Belong to Me," "Shrimp Boats" (written by Paul), "Make Love to Me," and "Jambalaya" (written by Hank Williams, Sr.), "Paul and I produced albums of parodied, off-keyed music under the pseudonym Jonathan and Darlene Edwards, just for the fun of it, which included drummer Jack Sperling (who had to quit because he couldn't stop laughing) . It was sort of a musical joke, where Paul played piano and I would sing, well, with too many beats to the bar and with wrong chords, perhaps characterized as a slightly inebriated duet--all for fun. We never thought it could catch on." A handful of albums were sustained and actually sold well, and the strange duet remarkably developed a loyal following Jo and Paul Weston spent the summer of 1961 in London doing a set of television shows. They became as equally endeared to the British population as they had to their fans in their own country.

It is safe to say, and by her own admission, that Jo Stafford never enjoyed performing before an audience and never craved stardom. She much preferred the recording studio and was immensely successful in the process. During the period of her reign, 1939 through the middle-sixties, Jo Stafford was always in the top five when it came to popularity polls and almost always the number one girl vocalist. When her record sales with Columbia reached twenty-five million in 1954, they presented her with a Diamond Award.

From Jo Stafford's first solo recording, "Little Man With A Candy Cigar," to her parodies as Darlene Edwards, she has proved that a successful career and a successful home life can be achieved if it is desired. Now, Jo Stafford, with Paul gone, spends her life in her comfortable Century City, California home. Her son has his own recording company and her daughter is a singer in her own right.

Jo was delighted to discover that her recording of "You Belong to Me" made the 60 year all-time listeners list of favorite songs polled in 1997 by New York's radio WQEW.

A New Era in Jazz Singing Begins

I had the privilege of holding many conversations with Anita O'Day in her later years and learned a lot about her first hand.

When former dancer Anita O'Day joined the Gene Krupa Band in 1941, an entirely new era in jazz vocalizing was officially launched. This girl had a definite personality and set a style of band singing that dominated the 1940's.

She was a wild chick, all right," her new boss recalled, "but, boy, how she could sing." Unlike the feminine, cute, little-girl presence, Anita scored as a hip jazz musician. Even her clothes were different, looking more like the musicians attire, than girl singer tresses and ribbons. It was take-me-as-I am-or-get-out-of-my-way style.

Drummer Gene promptly teamed Anita up with another new, talented acquisition, a small guy nick-named Little Jazz, electrifying trumpeter Roy Eldridge. Roy had an already established reputation in jazz improvisation, so between them a creative new swinging musical style fully blossomed. The co-mingling of instrument and voice-instrument worked well. The band flourished with "Let Me Off Uptown" (her best performance with Krupa for my money), "Georgia On My Mind," "Green Eyes" and "Murder, He Says," where, as Roy said, "Anita sounds like a jazz horn." Anita herself declares her unusual, husky voice was the result of a tonsillectomy that went partially wrong. It forced her to sing in short phrases. They recorded many exciting sides together, but the alliance of vocalist and soloist didn't last very long. The relationship broke down between them and a feud actually developed. Fortunately, those innovative recordings still hold up very well today. Thanks to Anita O'Day, it was Krupa's best years as a bandleader.

Critics of the time said Anita had more in common with Billie Holiday than Billie's contemporary counterpart Ella Fitzgerald. Teddy Wilson told me that at one time he couldn't tell Billie from Anita on certain songs. Anita delivered those long-held feathery notes, bending an occasional tone like Billie, so that the combined effect was a gathering of unmistakable, rhythmic jazz material never quite heard that way. For sure a composite of Billie and Ella with shades of Bessie. And, why not! They were the obvious influences of Anita's early musical experiences.

A jazz singer, by definition, works in an instrumental manner, improvising just like a musician does on his instrument. In the case of Anita O' Day, she has always been able to do just that: altering the tune as the song progresses, creating interesting melody lines-- short of "scatting." That's what Billie did!

Evidently, a jazz singer's voice is much like a musician's instrument. The voice improvises while it provides vocals and sounds, like "scat" singing in the style of Ella, Armstrong, early Crosby, or super-scat Mel Torme. When Anita turned her efforts to ballads, she offered a very different voice and interpretation. She could be sensitive and subdued, unlike her usual hip, swinging style. Words were unimportant-interpretation was paramount. For Anita it was expression in a new abstract mode.

In the spring of 1944, Anita linked up with band leader Stan Kenton, commencing the band's swingingest history. She motivated the band with her direct, swinging singing style. The masterful tenor sax of Stan Getz and the arrangements of Dave Matthews (who also played tenor sax) moved the band with infectious numbers, including Anita's impeccable 1944 version of "And Her Tears Flowed Like Wine" (my personal O'Day favorite - so much a definitive jazz classic) recorded that May. Anita stayed with the band for just a short time.

This new school of singing ushered in by Anita O'Day had its roots in early jazz vocalizing and its torch was passed on to the singers who immediately followed. It was June Christy in 1945 who followed Anita in the Stan Kenton organization and continued the style.

Anita sang briefly for Benny Goodman in 1943 and joined in another association in October, 1959, when Benny put together a group fronted by xylophonist Red Norvo and hired Anita to sing for the group. The tour covered much of Europe and lasted one month. According to Anita, Benny continually upstaged her, as he was known to do to his vocalists.

"Benny didn't want anyone to stand out above him or his orchestra," she said, "and a few days into the tour, he cut me down to just two numbers." Goodman was accused by others of blatantly attempting to monopolize the spotlight during performances.

The Man I Love, recorded in 1954, is where Anita O'Day shows her stuff--- stretching notes, bending them back, re-creating melody as she moves along and spontaneously reconstructing melodies while in musical flight. She "scat" the lyrics like the be-bopper she was becoming.

In 1956, Anita O'Day recorded "Honeysuckle Rose" and "The Nightingale Sang In Berkeley Square." Oh!, how I love that recording of "Nightingale." The huskiness in her voice is deep and prominent, the mood

Anita, Helen O'Connell, Bob Crosby, Ronald Reagan, and Jack Leonard

elegant and even sexy. Her voice is the equivalent of a low group of harmonious instruments rising and increasing with the fullness of the piece as demanded, as though carefully measured instruments were subjoined and then taken away. It's downright beautiful to hear over and over again. Anita is performing it again - right now - for me, while I write about her unique career. In the 1982 version of the Jazz Book, author Joachim Berendt declared Anita O'Day to be "the greatest white female jazz vocalist, "with, if I may add, musical assurance of virtuoso caliber and great improvisational capacity.

During the 1970's Anita played regularly at Ye Little Club in Beverly Hills and occasionally returned to engagements at Reno Sweeney's showcase in New York City. Anita was also part entrepreneur, selling record albums at the gate at retail prices instead of marketing them through normal distribution channels. Of course, it kept the albums from garnishing the deserved attention by critics and distributors it would have ordinarily received.

In March of 1980, Anita hooked up with a Mel Torme' show at Carnegie Hall called Mel Torme' and Friends that also featured Woody Herman and his Herd, saxophonist Jerry Mulligan, and pianists Teddy Wilson, Bill Evans and George Shearing. As Mel punctuated in his book It Wasn't All Velvet, "What friends!"

In her biography Hard Times, High Times, Anita told her life story with no punches pulled. She tells it pretty much the way she sings and performs. Everyone realizes that you always know what you get from Anita O'Day. Frankie Laine proves the point in his biographical book That Lucky Old Son: "In 1935, before I left the Arcadia Ballroom (Elizabeth, New Jersey), I became acquainted with a precocious little girl in the marathon dancing contest who was already developing into a mature vocalist at the age of 14. She would follow me around like a little puppy after every song I sang and pepper me with questions: 'Why did you pick that tune? Why did you phrase like that? How come....how come....how come?' Of course, when they found out she was underage they pulled her right off the floor, but her brief stint in the contest marked the beginning of my association with a lady who became one of our great jazz stylists, Anita O'Day."

Anita went on the quest for learning her craft during those early years, sitting in at various musicians' haunts in Chicago until someone would hire her to sing. She had just changed her name to O'Day from Colton before Gene Krupa caught her one night during a club date. He listened to her sing but one song and hired her.

In 1994 Anita performed at the Sportsman Lodge in Studio City,

California for the Society of Singers, Ladies Who Sang with the Bands benefit. The song was "Let Me Off Uptown" with the band trumpet player doing the Roy Eldridge part.

Jack Ellsworth reminded me of a set of Cole Porter lyrics once sang by Anita O'Day on a Verve recording of "You're The Top" that punctuates the quality of our unique Song Star, Anita O'Day:

Lionel, Anita and Louis

You're the bop, you're like
Sarah singin'
You're the bop, you're like Yardbird swingin'
You're the minus gong, you're the greatest song
that Eckstine ever sung,
You're a Moscow mule, you're so cool
You're Lester Young
You're the high in a Downbeat tally,
You're the guy who owns Tin Pan Alley
You're Tatum's left hand, a Goodman swing band,
A Lena Horne who won't stop
But if baby I'm the bottom, you're the bop!

ROSEMARY CLOONEY

America's Singing Sweetheart

In 1977 Song Star Rosemary Clooney wrote her autobiography This For Remembrance in collaboration with author Raymond Strait. Her friend and fellow thespian, Bing Crosby, composed the foreword and said, "Looking back over our long relationship, I have to smile. I'm reminded of all the good times Rosemary and I had together, the fun we had working with the musicians; the kidding, the needling, the ribbing, the laughs-in pictures, radio and television. She's a great singer, and a great lady."

No one could have said it better. Bing and Rosemary Clooney got along just fine and accomplished some terrific recording, radio, television and film sessions together. In Bing's film, White Christmas, with co-stars Vera Ellen and Danny Kaye, Rosemary vocalized on two solid selections, "Count Your Blessings", a definitive Clooney sound, and the best selling song of all time, Irving Berlin's "White Christmas,"in a duet with Bing.

As Rosemary described it: "Over the years Bing and I have done the whole entertainment circle together. We were always around each other and became great friends. But, one day I sat down and said to myself, "What the hell am I doing singing here with Bing Crosby?" For her the realization was monumental.

Well, we'll have to turn back a bit to the middle of World War II and the saga of the pretty and lively singing Clooney Sisters, Rosemary and Betty, to discover how that miracle eventually materialized. Long before that book, before life's difficulties, before the five wonderful children, Miguel, Maria, Rafael, Monsita, and Gabriel; and long before she had to fight her way back to a renewed, meaningful life, Rosemary Clooney began her interesting journey on a road to becoming a much-loved, world-class Song Star.

As World War II kicked into high gear and defense plants were cooking 24 hours a day, Cincinnati's Keith Albee Theater played host to many of the touring Big Bands. Betty and Rosemary, now living with their maternal grandparents, were treated to tickets. They all loved to hear the Big Band sounds performed live in their own town. At the big drug store on Fountain Square, they played the jukebox to the expressive sounds of the Harry James band with Helen Forrest delivering "I've Heard That Song Before" and Kitty Kallen emotionalizing for the hopeful return of their loved ones singing "Kiss me once and kiss me twice, and kiss me once again, "It's Been A Long, Long, Time."

Bing Tells Rosie to Count Her Blessings

With a three-song repertoire, the girls auditioned for a job with WLW, a Cincinnati radio station, and copped a twenty- dollar-a-week (for each girl) job. They moved in with their Aunt Jean in the city close to the studio, slept on the couch while simultaneously attending Our Lady Of Mercy Academy, saving more money Rosemary said, "...then when I was making $20,000 a week in later years." In a local band fronted by a trumpet-playing friend the girls became bona fide Big Band singers. They were billed as the Clooney Sisters. They soon joined up with Doris Day's old big band affiliation, the popular Barney Rapp Band, who played bigger club dates in the area. Next stop, a stint with former Artie Shaw sideman, bandleader Tony Pastor, who had just started up.

The butterflies were starting; they were in the big-time now. Rosemary was eighteen and Betty just fifteen. They looked great in their twin dresses. It's simply amazing how early in life most of the Song Stars began their professional careers. Billie Holiday, Ella Fitzgerald, Connie Haines, Kitty Kallen, Doris Day, Helen O'Connell, Fran Warren, and some others were all teen-agers. They literally grew up on the bandstand and spent a good portion of their lives sleeping in band buses, and motels and hotels.

The Steel Pier in Atlantic City was their first Pastor engagement, and it was also their first look at an ocean. "We were so excited, we never slept." Rosemary said, "We studied our lead sheets and rehearsed and rehearsed. It was make-it-or-break-it time for us." The chaperone was their Uncle George steadfastly assigned to them by their grandmother. One-night stands that followed were held at college proms, barn dances, subscription dances, hotel ballrooms, dance pavilions, and theaters.

"After each show, we would climb aboard our chartered bus and sleep until we arrived at the next place where we did another show," Rosemary remembered. During that time, the girls took their first plane trip. They were headed for the Hollywood Palladium.

When Rosemary got off the plane, she fell instantly in love with California's soft air and warm climate and would come to love California for the remainder of her life.

During that period, after recording an album with Tony Pastor, Rosemary received a great review from Downbeat Magazine, which said: "Rosemary Clooney has an extraordinarily good voice, perhaps the nearest thing to Ella Fitzgerald's we've ever heard." Rosie literally flipped out.

"After that review everything changed." And according to Tony Pastor in George Simon's book The Big Band Era: "They were smart kids," he said, "they had good ears and some corny arrangements of their own. But Ralph Flanagan, (later to lead a Glenn Miller style band) who was writing for us, gave them some good new arrangements, and they did just fine."

I remember one particular movie short (pre-MTV) with Tony and Rosemary dueting on a cute little song entitled "Movie Tonight." A great Clooney performance with shades of Helen Forrest and Anita O'Day from within this very new Song Star. Tony moved her right along, and Rosemary carried her share off very well. The camera loved her bright face and eager smile.

"After three or so years of band bus traveling," Rosemary noted, "Betty decided to quit and I remained with Tony as a single. And Uncle George went home with her."

That's when Rosemary developed her easy and friendly singing manner. Her first solo recording in 1946 was "I'm Sorry I Didn't Say I'm Sorry When I Made You Cry Last Night"- whew, what a long title. It was noticed by radio disc jockeys everywhere as something special, but Rosemary explained: "I was so scared that I couldn't sing above a whisper. They seemed to like that sound which I created through my own fear," she said, smiling inwardly. Rosemary never sounded quite like that again.

Teaming up with personal manager Joe Shribman, who managed Tony Pastor, Rosemary launched a career on her own. Tony Bennett enlightened me about it somewhat when he and I talked about some of the singers of his time: "Her big break came on a show you may remember called Jan Murray's Songs For Sale in 1950. Rosemary won hands down- I came in second- on Arthur Godfrey's Talent Scouts which won her a "gig" on Jan Murray's show, Songs For Sale. She was simply great!" This led to more engagements and the popularization of an earlier Columbia recording, a resplendent version of "Beautiful Brown Eyes." In 1951, song pioneer Mitch Miller, the visionary A & R man at Columbia Records, and the man responsible for the success of many singers including Tony Bennett, Frankie Laine, and Guy Mitchell, convinced Rosemary to record a bouncy number with the unusual name of "Come On-a My House," an adaptation by William Saroyan and Ross Bagdasarian of an old Armenian folk song.

"I didn't want to do such a unromantic, silly number," Rosemary said, "I was a ballad singer, and I hated that song. I thought it was a cheap way to get attention. But he insisted and threatened to fire me if I didn't show up at the studio. Well, it turned out he was right." In a few weeks the song became a national best-selling record. "Who else could have put a harpsichord on a Clooney record or backed Guy Mitchell with swooping French horns ("My Truly, Truly Fair")?" Frankie Laine said when we talked about Miller's influence on singing careers.

"That's true," cited Rosemary, "Mitch could bring people together. He was a hit-maker. A lot of us started together. Tony Bennett, Frankie Laine, Guy Mitchell at Columbia. Patti Page at Mercury, Doris Day and Dinah Shore also at Columbia. Mitch was there making sure everything sounded right."

Her subsequent recordings kept topping the music charts: the moving song she loved so much, "Hey There!" mine and WNEW disc jockey William B. Williams' favorite Clooney recording from Richard Adler and Jerry Ross' Broadway show Pajama Game; the lighthearted "Botcha Me;" "This Old House;" and the perky "Mambo Italiana." With husband Jose Ferrer, she recorded the selections "A Bunch Of Bananas" and "Woman" and with world-famous actress and friend, Marlene Dietrich, "Dot's Nice - Don - na Fight", a cute little ditty. Hank Williams' "Half As Much" is also a commendable Clooney specialty as is one of her best and most successful recordings, "Tenderly," which appears over and over again on Top Ten lists of great recordings of the era including the 1996 WQEW top tunes of the last 60 years.

While working on the Tallulah Bankhead Sunday radio show, I remember Rosemary at a rehearsal in the Center Theater, across the street from the NBC studios on West 49th Street (the theater is now gone). The Big Show was the last great resistance of radio to the new monster called television. It was underwritten by then mega-sponsors Reynolds Metals, Anacin, and Chesterfield Cigarettes with Tallulah as Mistress of Ceremonies. The greatest talent of the times appeared on that show. It was where President Harry Truman's daughter, Margaret, appeared for the first time as a professional vocalist. It was on that day, April 13, 1952, that Rosemary met her future friend, Blue Angel and Golden Earrings motion picture icon Marlene Dietrich. She enthusiastically complimented Rosemary's singing and offering encouragement, suggesting they remain in touch with one another. They did and became good friends.

Under contract to Paramount, given full opportunity to display both her verve and voice, a successful, young and peppy Rosemary Clooney began a movie career. First, The Stars are Singing, then Here Comes The Girls with my friend Bob Hope, singer Tony Martin, and Arlene Dahl. This refreshing and attractive Song Star followed up with Red Garters, Deep In My Heart, and in 1954, White Christmas-for my money a most memorable Rosemary Clooney movie. She was at her best in voice and looks and even learned to execute some remarkable dancing routines.

Released from Paramount and now free as a bird, television beckoned the former big band singer and movie star. It was regular appearances on The Steve Allen Show, Perry Como's show, Ed Sullivan's Toast Of The Town, and a special with master -arranger and special friend, Nelson Riddle and his Orchestra.

Her own show, The Rosemary Clooney Show, debuted in May, 1956, over KKTV in L.A., quickly networking to New York in only a few months. A gracious hostess with that appealing husky throat, Rosemary's musical pleasantries handily carried the TV torch.

"I tried to strive for intimacy by playing not to a studio audience but to just one or two people looking in," she explained to me one night in Huntington, New York's Heckscher Park back in 1984 just before an outdoor performance.

In 1956, Rosemary scored with Duke Ellington as a jazz singer, no less.

Characterized with jazz surroundings and the effects of Johnny Hodges' sax, Cat Anderson's trumpet, and the trumpets of Clark Terry and Ray Nance she sang "Grievin'," a beautiful jazz recording written and arranged by Billy Strayhorn. In my opinion, it's one of Rosemary's best recordings ever. Try to find a copy of it. You'll love it. It's a different Rosie.

Some twenty-five years later, it would be more jazz for Rosemary Clooney with jazz stars Warren Vache and Scott Hamilton. At that time, John Oddo who also supervised Tom Postilio's first album, What Matters

Most, arranged all her work.

Rosemary has, of course, recorded endless singles, many children's records along the way, and albums- lots of albums. Some with Bing Crosby, Les Brown, her good friend Buddy Cole and his Trio, Tony Bennett, Woody Herman, Scott Hamilton, and Nelson Riddle, mostly on RCA. On the Concord label, it's been recordings of mostly small group jazz albums in tributes to the great song writers. During the late '70's and early '80's it was the "4 girls 4" tour with Margaret Whiting, Helen O'Connell, and Kay Starr.

In September, 1996, Rosemary appeared on Carnegie Hall's hallowed stage in a fitting commemorative tribute to the master arranger, Nelson Riddle, with John Oddo directing the music under the auspices of the Concord Jazz Festival.

Rosemary Clooney's life in those days was a happy time. She shared grandchildren with legendary Pat Boone, who has been Rosemary's neighbor for many years. Neighborhood kid Gabriel Ferrer married childhood sweetheart Debbie Boone. Pat, his wife Shirley, and Rosemary enjoyed the bounty that is called family.

In late December, 1996, Rosemary Clooney toured, wrapping up at the Sands Hotel and Casino in Atlantic City, New Jersey, in a show she called Rosemary Clooney's White Christmas. She sounded better and better and still was able to get home for Christmas with that family she loved so much. Rosemary's nephew, George Clooney keeps the Clooney name going these days after we lost Rosemary in June, 2002. She was one of America's Sweethearts.

with Frank Sinatra, Dean Martin and Kathryn and Bing Crosby

Helen O'Connell

Every Singer's Friend

In the early 1950's I went to work for NBC News in New York and wound up gathering news for The Today Show. In 1956 Big Band singer Helen O'Connell joined that same, now classic, morning show as co-host to the show's pioneer host, Dave Garroway. That's the one entity Helen and I held in common until our paths crossed head- on one evening in 1984. This time, Helen, backstage in a crisp between-shows housecoat, stood replying to trivial questions I pursued about her still lively ca-reer, while I held a tape-recorder in one hand and a group of 3 x 5 cards in the other. We finally found ourselves face-to-face with music the only common denominator.

"I guess the high point of my musical career was when Bob Eberly and I sang those great duets for Jimmy Dorsey," she said with that famous, cute, mischievious grin, while sipping some hot tea.." People loved those recordings ...and they still ask me about them."

Standing on the sidelines at this meeting held in an

anteroom to her Westbury Music Fair dressing room, friend and fellow performer Frankie Laine joined the conversation reminding Helen and I that it was during a chance breakfast meeting with Jimmy Dorsey's secretary, Nita Moore, on a New York Street that Frank learned from Nita about Jimmy's search for a girl singer.

with Richard Grudens - 1984

"It happened that I saw Helen the night before at the Village Barn down on Eighth Street (he takes Helen's hand in his ---) singing with Larry Funk and his band, so I told Nita about her and Jimmy went to see her perform and that's how he hired her," he recalled , glancing at Helen who was nodding her head up and down in approval.

"It couldn't have happened better for me. That was the beginning of my being known at all. That was my favorite band and Bob Eberly was my favorite singer, but," she leans over and plants a smooch on Frank's bearded cheek, "I love Frank, too!"

At the beginning of Helen's career, an issue of Downbeat Magazine called her a cross between Ella Fitzgerald and Mildred Bailey, a really odd combination for sure. Bob Eberly once told me in a telephone conversation that Helen squeaked her voice cutely on the recording of Green Eyes when she sang, and emphasized the phrase "those cute and limpid, green eyes" because "she just couldn't reach the high notes," implying a limited vocal range. Helen denied it completely: ".....it was just my preferred way of accenting the phrase." The popularity of those duet recordings earned her top spot in the Metronome poll of 1940.

Helen O'Connell came to light on May 23, 1920, in Lima, Ohio.

She first sang by the very delicate age of 13. "My father died and I had to help support our family, so I left home at sixteen," she recalled, "but I did sing professionally when I was thirteen with the Austin Wylie Orchestra back in Cleveland."

Helen considers the second recording she ever made, All of Me, her favorite, "..and I also think George Gershwin's Embraceable You was one of my best, too." They both define her singing skills quite clearly.

"What about, Jim? I asked, referring to her hit single Jim Never Sends Me Pretty Flowers.

"Oh, yeah, I know. I guess I love that one, too!" Lots of people do too!

It's amazing how Helen hadn't changed much from the 1950's to the

1980's. She retained that perky, youthful appearance throughout the industrious, grueling years of the Big Band Era right up to now: "We'd work all day in a theater sometimes doing five shows, then we'd go to someplace like the Cafe' Rouge (a nightclub in New York's Hotel Pennsylvania) and do a few more shows. I was lucky if I ever saw another girl singer that I knew or a musician somewhere along the line, unless we went to 52nd Street (the New York City jazz nightclubs center of the time) for a rare night out. We were all very busy and the years passed quickly, and here we are."

It's curious that Helen O'Connell is perhaps the best-known singer and one of the best-loved performers of the Big Band Era, probably because of the recordings Green Eyes and Tangerine alone. It's curious to note that that group of famous duets, including Amapola and Yours, were created quite accidentally: The Jimmy Dorsey Orchestra was allotted just three minutes at the close of a formatted weekly radio show, so arranger Tutti Camaratta devised a unique formula that featured all the stars of the series. Bob Eberly sang the first chorus of a song as a ballad, then the tempo was to pick up so the entire band would play part of the selection, then the tempo was to slow down and Helen came in for a semi-wailing finale. The formula worked so well that Dorsey used it on subsequent recordings, and Green Eyes alone sold 90,000 copies in a few days, which was a record in a time when 25,000 copies was equal to a million seller today.

After doing three movies with Jimmy Dorsey, they offered Helen a movie contract. She was to do a Bing Crosby, Fred Astaire picture (probably Blue Skies or Holiday Inn). When they realized she could not and would not dance, it ended before it began. Of course, Helen had actually taught dancing at one time, but she was more interested at this time in getting married and bringing up a family than in the fame and fortune earned through making movies. She did marry and had four girls with first husband Cliff Smith.

"Later, when I went back to work I had more offers to do movies, but I began working with Frank De Vol at the Palladium and then went on the road with singer Vic Damone for some very good money."

Further statistics reveal Helen as hostess for CBS's Top Tunes show in 1953; star of her own NBC show in the late fifties; interviewer for NBC's Here's Hollywood, and hostess for the Miss Universe Pageant for nine years. Fellow vocalists Margaret Whiting, Rosemary Clooney and Kay Starr toured with Helen for a spell in an act they called Four Girls Four that terminated when the girls apparently got on one-another's nerves and the length and effort of touring became tiring. Helen has appeared on and off with the orchestras of Woody Herman, Glenn Miller and Artie Shaw. Her commercials (she was once the spokesperson for Polaroid), personal appearances and recordings are too many to list.

In 1991, Helen and composer-conductor Frank DeVol tied the knot. As both active participant and board member Helen spent endless time with the Society of Singers, an L.A. based charitable association that assists down-and-out singers and other musical performers. She spent lots and lots of quality time with her grandchildren,too.

During 1992, Helen was kept pretty busy headlining eight Jimmy Dorsey concerts including some cruise ship adventures. An August, 1993, Big Band show at Valley Forge Music Fair in Pennsylvania, the sister showcase to Westbury Music Fair where we held our interview, was the last known professional performance of Helen O'Connell.

During an interview with the Big Band Jump Newsletter, Helen was once asked : "What question do people most often ask you?"

Among some other things this warm, caring, and lovable vocalist of the Big Band Era said: "People often ask me about the Big Band Era and all the other wonderful performers, but I can't answer that. I know I was continuously working. I tell the people, if I'd known the Big Band Era was going to be so important, I'd have paid more attention to it."

HELEN O'CONNELL

This accomplished lady may have been recognized for her great recordings, but again, loving babies were very much more important to her than a celebrity life in music. "My real kicks in life are just being around my little, tiny grandchildren," she said ever so warmly.

Why, in 1990 Helen even had a great-grandchild by the name of Gentry Allen! She enjoyed the remaining three precious years of her life with those beloved babes. Fortunately for us, the music featuring Helen O'Connell goes on through her evergreen recordings. Her philosophy about the art of singing summed up like this: "Those who are successful don't need any advice from me. Those who are just starting out must be willing to pay their dues. I don't mean work for peanuts-get all you can, but don't turn your nose up at getting learning experience. Sing whenever you can. You just have to keep trying until somebody (important in show business) hears you and hands you a break, a start.   I think you have to know something about your trade once you get there."

Helen O'Connell lost her battle with cancer in 1993.

LENA HORNE

Song Star with a Message

In October, 1944, Lena Horne became the first black person to appear on the cover of a popular movie magazine. Her great ambition had been to use a God-given talent and hard-won success to win respect. Lena Horne always envisioned a better heritage for her people. That meant financial, economic, and cultural advantages. Her lifetime hero was opera singer and entertainer Paul Robeson.

My friend William B. Williams worshipped Lena Horne. He would always talk about her and regularly played her recordings on his show The Make Believe Ballroom, a popular radio show on New York's WNEW during the '60's, '70's, and '80's. He drawled huskily when announcing a recording "Lena," -- and everyone knew exactly whom he meant. When she appeared in a one-woman Broadway show during the early 1980's, he consistently promoted it on the show. She was also a regular in-person guest.

Lena Horne surfaces from a great family that dates back to 1777 in the state of Maryland. Over one hundred years later Cora and Edwin Horn (the e added later) moved to New York City in 1896. They settled in the area West of Seventh Avenue in an area known as

San Juan Hill near the Grand Opera House on Eighth Avenue. During the Twenties you might have seen jazz artist Jelly Roll Morton, or even Scott Joplin himself, headline there.

Their two small sons, Errol, and Teddy who married Edna, a black "princess" a freckled, green-eyed minx. She had known Teddy all his life. Lena Mary Calhoun Horne was born to that union on June 30, 1917, in a small Jewish lying-in hospital. It was the year Scott Joplin died and the year The New York Times first used the word jazz . (Lt. Errol Horne went to France in 1918 and perished from influenza.)

Lena began her illustrious career in 1919, becoming a cover girl at the age of two-and-a-half, starring in the October, 1919 issue of the NAACP Branch Bulletin. Her father Teddy left his Brooklyn home and went west in the summer of 1920, leaving his family alone on Chauncey Street where they had lived with his parents. Marriage and family stability was not his life's interest.

After a somewhat difficult life of being shunted from city to city, Lena sometimes stayed with her mother and sometimes with her grandmother. It was Miami, then Jacksonville, and back to Brooklyn again. Then, Ohio, to be left with a middle-class doctor's family, sharing a top floor room with a maiden aunt, and then on to Macon, Georgia, to be left with two old women. She finally migrated to Fort Valley, near Macon, with her Uncle Frank Horne. Lena grew to love Fort Valley, but was truly a Horne of Chauncey Street, Brooklyn, where she was sure of whom she was.

It was in the Junior Guild of Brooklyn's annual charity show where Lena landed her first starring role. She had the biggest part and sang all the best songs: "Night and Day" and "I've Got the World on a String." As a result her photograph appeared in the local papers with nothing but bravo reviews. Then Edna, her mother, had a secret plan. She knew the dance captain at the Cotton Club in Harlem, and, although Lena was only seventeen, she was able to get her a spot in the show's New Revue. Duke Ellington, Cab Calloway, and the great Louis Armstrong were featured performers. Anyone who was anyone went to the Cotton Club: actors George Raft and Greta Garbo, violin genius Jascha Heifetz, Britain's Lord Mountbatten, baseball's Babe Ruth, and entertainer Eddie Cantor, who once said that if he were elected President he'd hold the Inaugural Ball at the Cotton Club.

She became the pet of the Cotton Club, "protected" by the Dutch Schultz mob who owned Harlem, Lena earned twenty-five dollars a week. She became everybody's kid sister and once sang in place of Aida Ward, a Cotton Club star who had a sore throat. Lena sang "As Long As I Live" in place of the ailing Aida. Lena was beginning to be noticed. Her father even came to see her, although he was black and not allowed to sit among the strictly white audience. He was so well- regarded by the Cotton Club owners that they permitted him to watch from a special section. Lena was awestruck by the Cotton Club, the wealth of the patrons, and the notoriety of its owners. The nightclub was a large horseshoe-shaped room with tables on two levels and booths against all the walls. Mexican and Chinese food was always served, except for fried chicken after hours.

Her second break came in the fall of 1934 when Broadway producer Laurence Schwab, who noticed her in the Cotton Club chorus line, cast her as a quadroon as part of a voodoo ballet in a show called Dance with Your Gods.

After Gods closed, Lena viewed the club in a more realistic light. "I saw that twenty-five of us were herded into one tiny, crowded, windowless dressing room in which we had barely enough space to sit down. It stunk from ashtrays, newspapers, make-up, fan magazines, cartons of stale chop suey and the reek of perfume and cigarette smoke. I longed for a breath of fresh air and some place I could stretch my aching limbs and go to sleep." But Lena was otherwise grateful for the job.

After that show, her mother Edna badgered the Cotton Club management for a better show spot for her daughter, but was refused. So, She joined Noble Sissle's sweet band, a favorite of the black middle-class and older whites. They went on the road, her mother traveling right along. Sissle helped improve Lena's act. He taught her to properly phrase a song and perfected her diction, confirming his well-known dedication to imparting poise and polish in a vocalist Sissle was very happy with Lena whom he renamed Helene Horne. Together, they were a class act.

In 1936 Sissle's orchestra was the first black band to play at the famous Ritz-Carlton in Boston. Lena sang the winsome "Blue Moon" and developed a following, mostly students from nearby Harvard University.

John Hammond noticed Lena. He, of course, was the angel responsible for the promotion of Benny Goodman, Count Basie, and Billie Holiday, to name a few, and the catalyst behind the 1938 Benny Goodman

Concert that brought respectability to jazz music.

At this time the very pretty Lena was introduced to twenty-eight year old Louis Jones of Pittsburgh. Lena was charmed by his good manners and favorable position in life and decided to marry him. She settled down and became pregnant with her daughter Gail.

Lena went to Hollywood to make a film she never got paid for, returned to New York, and was cast in the short-lived Blackbirds of 1939 on Broadway to great revues. Then Lena received a break. Bandleader Charlie Barnet was appearing in the Bronx and his girl singer took sick: "Wow! Who are you?" were Charlie's first encouraging words to Lena Horne when she applied for the job. As Big Band crooner Bob Carroll tells it: "We were working at the Windsor Theater in the Bronx (N.Y.) and something had happened to the girl we were using. Somebody remembered this pretty girl who was working in a movie house, and they sent for her. It was Lena. I remember she had long, straggly hair, and her dress wasn't especially attractive. She ran down a few tunes in the basement of the theater, and then, without any arrangements, she did the next show - not only did it, but stopped it cold. She was just great." Lena was accepted, touring on the road once again as the girl singer in a big band.

Traumatic racial incidents befell the young star: Most hotels had a "No Blacks Allowed" policy and sometimes Charlie threatened to pull the whole band out. At times it worked. At college dances, Charlie would be told that Lena was unacceptable, so she got the night off. Other times she could sing, but not sit on the bandstand. On Southern tours, Lena was given vacation with pay. Once, while waiting, she recorded with bandleader Artie Shaw who had heard her sing "Good for Nothing Joe." The record "Don't Take Your Love from Me" was waxed. In frustration Lena quit Barnet and moved back to her beloved Chauncey Street home. The marriage to Louis was virtually over even though her second child, Teddy, was born after a short reconciliation that never lasted.

John Hammond was instrumental in getting Lena a job in Cafe' Society, one of New York's most notable clubs, where he was chief talent scout. It was an unsegregated nightclub that helped launch the careers of Josh White, Zero Mostel, Billie Holiday, Hazel Scott, and Judy Holiday.

Lena first met Billie Holiday backstage at Kelly's Stable. They immediately took a liking to one another. They conferred and compared. Lena opened at Cafe' Society with the fine Teddy Wilson band and sang Billie's "Fine and Mello" and George Gershwin's beautiful "Summertime." Which was performed so well that critics noticed and bestowed praises in their columns and on the radio.

That launched Lena's career. Then a Carnegie Hall show with Teddy Wilson, Count Basie, Bunny Berigan, and Hazel Scott, among others, boosted her even higher.

It was on to California to work the opening of a new club, the Trocadero, fashioned after the Cotton Club. Lena was invited to attend a performance by Duke Ellington, who was appearing in a show called Jump for Joy in Los Angeles. There she met Ellington sidekick, composer and pianist Billy Strayhorn, who became her lifelong friend, sister and soul mate. Billy re-arranged Lena's entire repertoire, shaping her into a major attraction at local clubs. Duke Ellington thought Lena a delicate beauty. The Hollywood crowd loved her. There were admirers Cole Porter, Marlene Dietrich, John Barrymore, and Roger Edens, chief of musicals at MGM who attended those shows. Lena soon found herself a member of the MGM "stable of stars."

Lena went to work at the Mocambo on the Sunset Strip and was a smash. Humble and elegant, Lena prevailed as an artist of stature. Soon it was the definitive songs "Honeysuckle Rose" and "Brazilian Boogie" in movies directed by Vincente Minnelli that endeared her to the public. Starring in the 1942 movie Cabin in the Sky with Ethel Waters and Eddie "Rochester" Anderson , also directed by Minnelli, Lena was the darling of the technical crew. Despite that, the film, that also starred Duke Ellington, Eddie "Rochester" Anderson, and Bill "Bojangles" Robinson, established a new kind of image for black women in the movies. It opened in New York at the Capitol Theater. Duke Ellington and Lena appeared on stage as live show attractions. The show and movie were a smash.

Lena returned with an engagement at the Savoy Plaza Persian Room, being the first black entertainer to play the room. Ironically, she had her own room to rest and change in but could not stay overnight. She took that in stride and was an absolute success. Someone said she would need Madison Square Garden for her next stand. Time, Newsweek and Life held features on Lena all in the same week in January, 1943.

Lena unselfishly worked the USO and Hollywood Canteens to en- tertain and serve coffee and doughnuts to lonely servicemen. "It made me happy to contribute something to our fighting men," she said.Back in Holly- wood, Lena first met her husband-to-be, studio conductor Lennie Hayton ,at lunch in the studio commissary. "At first we didn't get along," she said, "but we quickly became a twosome. Lennie would write special arrangements ---he suited me musically---he stretched me musically, we dug each other... were always in tune with one another." Lennie directed music at MGM. He was formerly pianist-arranger for Paul Whiteman's King of Jazz Orchestra. He arranged music for legendary jazz cornetist Bix Biederbecke, trumpeter Bunny Berigan, trombonist Jack Teagarden, the Dorsey Brothers, and Bing Crosby, who were all members of the orchestra. Lennie and Lena worked together on the 1946 Jerome Kern musical film Till the Clouds Roll By in which Lena sang "Why Was I Born" and fellow performer Frank Sinatra sang "Old Man River."

Lennie and Lena decided to get married. It would isolate her from the world. It was illegal for whites and blacks to marry in California in 1946, ...and," she said, "Hollywood society began to cold-shoulder us." So the couple went east. It was hotels and more hotels in New York City. They traveled to Europe, the war being over, and viewed war-torn London. Lena appeared with Ted Heath's big band at the London Casino. As one of the first American performers to play postwar London, Lena was a great success. England was very familiar with her Big Band performances and movies. In Paris, it was appearances at the Club des Champs-Elysees, near the Arc de Triomphe. Lena befriended Edith Piaf and actors Simone Signoret and Piaf protege' Yves Montand. Lennie and Lena secretly married in Paris and then sailed home.

Lennie continued his work as MGM musical director on a batch of new movies: Good News, The Barkleys of Broadway , and Words and Music (in which Lena appeared), while Lena was invited to sing at Harry S. Truman's Presidential Inauguration. In 1950 they revealed their marriage to the press, and thus the world, and sailed once again to Europe. Lena performed at the Palladium as the Korean War broke out. She toured the English Isles. For the rest of the decade, the couple would be regular European summer residents.

Lena's appeared on television with her friends Ed Sullivan, Perry Como, Steve Allen, and Tex and Jinx. Lena appeared on Broadway once again, this time in a 1957 musical Jamaica, as its star. The consensus was: "Lena plus music equals a BIG winner."
Lena remained the queen of the nightclubs long after Jamaica folded.

with Bandleader Noble Sissle - 1935

Lena's 1981 hit Broadway show Lena Horne: The Lady and Her Music, the show William B. Williams helped promote on his WNEW radio show, was the best of the season. It ran 14 months to sellout crowds. Reviews were absolutely superlative. She had been rediscovered. "I was a different Lena...at last a free Lena," she said to me.

Lena has won just about every award possible including the coveted Kennedy Center Honors along with comedian Danny Kaye, composer Gian Carlo Mennotti) playwright Arthur Miller, and classical violinist Isaac Stern.

For smooth listening, get a copy of Lena's We'll Be Together Again and An Evening with Lena 1993 and 94 albums on CD. You will play them forever and ever.

At the Society of Singers tribute to Lena Horne in late June, 1997, at Avery Fisher Hall, Lincoln Center, New York, it was a great party for a great star. It was also a celebration of Lena's 80th birthday.

Kitty Kallen

Little Things Still Mean a Lot

Okay, devoted Big Band culture buffs, can you identify the young lady named Katherine who sang with the Jan Savitt Band on KYW-CBS radio in Philadelphia at the adolescent age of 14 and continued on to vocalize as the "Girl" with jazz trombonist Jack Teagarden's Orchestra, "Sixteen Men and a Girl," in 1939?

This very same young lady was featured with Jimmy Dorsey on the recording favorites "They're Either Too Young or Too Old" and "Besame Mucho" (it means Kiss Me Much) , a duet with vocalist Bob Eberly, and, by the time she reached 18, sparkled effortlessly under trumpet playing Harry James' tutelage with a cluster of # 1 hits that became standards before she reached the age of twenty.

It's pretty Katherine "Kitty" Kallen.

Strangely enough, some people need to be reminded of Kitty Kallen's sensational performances with the Big Bands. She holds the distinction of being the only girl singer who was featured with four of the most famous Big Bands: Artie Shaw, Harry James, and both Dorseys - Tommy and Jimmy. Not that Jack Teagarden's band was a lightweight; that would make it five. People seem to be more familiar with those very popular singles Kitty originated beyond the Big Band days: those terrific hits "Little Things Mean a Lot" that lovely song suited her perfectly) and "In the Chapel in the Moonlight in 1954;" "If I Give My Heart to You" in 1959, and the immensely popular RCA recording "My Coloring Book" in 1962 that again won her the acclaim she richly deserved.

Although blockbusters all, I personally prefer those early Big Band gems and the rhythmically advanced swinging style she delivered during her tenure with those bands. For me, maybe it's simply a matter of musical choices.

If you want to talk to Kitty Kallen during the winter, you'll have to wait until she returns from her six-months-a-year hangout in Mexico (she adores the Indian culture as well as the climate), her most favorite place other than her permanent Hudson River-style home in Northern New Jersey.

While talking with Kitty at her New Jersey home in a beautifully decorated room with a magnificent grand piano, she admitted being nervous when first replacing Helen Forrest. "There I was, following another Helen. First it was Helen O'Connell who I followed in Jimmy Dorsey's band, and now Helen Forrest in Harry James' band. Well, I mentioned to Harry that I was a little bit nervous, but he managed to make me feel so comfortable I soon forgot my butterflies. He told me not to worry, that I'd do just fine, and....I did!"

Kitty got along extremely well with Harry James: "Harry was a very good teacher and a great boss. I had the honor of working with him every single night. He was the most talented musician I ever worked with. He was gifted and modest. Harry loved what he was doing, and you knew when you were on the bandstand that he liked what you were doing. You didn't have to prove anything to Harry. He appreciated your work. And I never, ever heard Harry rehearse or warm up for a show," she went on to say, "Jack Teagarden and Jimmy Dorsey always practiced scales to warm up for a show; Harry never did that. Don't you think that was amazing? And he never talked shop in the off hours. It was one of the greatest periods of my life."

On the Astor roof, May 22, 1943, the first year after she joined up, Kitty Kallen sang her first song with Harry James. It turned out to be one of the Swing Era's definitive jazz standards, "I'm Beginning to See the Light."

That long-standing evergreen was followed by the bouncy" Waiting for the Train to Come In" and the great wartime hit- ---Kiss me once and kiss me twice, and kiss me once again...... "It's Been a Long, Long Time." How I love her rendition of that wonderful tune. Notably, "I'll Buy That Dream," "I Guess I'll Hang Out My Tears to Dry," and the still-popular" Candy" paraded right behind while she sung her heart out with the Harry James' band.

"Working for the Big Bands was a matter of discipline and hard work," Kitty ardently explained over a cup of tea, "You'd receive a song sheet in the morning and had to learn it and then perform it that very same evening. You rehearsed it all day until you got it right. The song "11:60 P.M." was the toughest song I ever sang. I think I do 16 bars before taking a breath. The guys in the band would take bets. 'Is she going to take a breath, or isn't she?'

"I didn't enjoy singing that song, even though Harry wrote it. Now that most of these songs have been re-issued on digital CD's, the quality is unbelievable. When I hear it, no kidding, I feel like I am back sitting on the bandstand." Kitty was saying, "and I have a confession to make. I really never listened to myself. But, after listening to these new re-recordings, I think I was not too bad." Kitty has that rare vocal quality that wills you to listen to the words of a song, a straightforward purity of melody.

Kitty left the Harry James' band at the suggestion of James, who envisioned the inevitable industry change whereupon vocalists would become more important properties than the bands themselves, inadvertently forecasting the era of the great vocalists which, in retrospect, evolved as the bands gradually disbanded. "He said to me, 'Listen, Sinatra's out there; Peggy Lee and Perry Como are out there. They're all out there, and I think you are ready.' Then he added, ' Try it'. And I did. He was right!"

Kitty was one of the most sought after supper club singers when she first met publicist Budd Granoff in 1947 at the Copacabana Nightclub in New York City. They were married one year later. Budd chose all Kitty's' songs, including 1954's biggest hit record, # 1 on the charts for an impressive twenty-six weeks, "Little Things Mean a Lot."

But, then Kitty Kallen actually lost her voice along the otherwise smooth road. Three long frightening years later, with help from husband Buddy and recording Artists & Repertoire man Mitch Miller, Kitty bravely broke what seemed like a curse to her . In 1959 she recorded "If I Give My Heart to You" and was back on the road to success. Her "My Coloring Book" has been recorded by many artists since, but Kitty clearly "owns" it Kitty Kallen was married for over 48 years to Buddy, who was a music publisher and very successful television syndicator. Sadly, Budd Granoff

passed away on April 28, 1996. The loss had hit Kitty, her only son Jonathan, a United Nations attorney, and her three grandchildren very hard. Since then, little things still mean a lot for Kitty Kallen.

Connie, Kitty and Helen

Cordially, Kay Starr

KAY STARR
NATIVE AMERICAN
"YOU CAN FEEL
THE MEMORIES START-
ING"

On the drive to the (Harry) Chapin Rainbow Stage in Huntington's Heckscher Park to meet Kathryn La Verne Starks, a.k.a. Kay Starr, I stuffed a re-issued Glenn Miller album which included the little-known numbers "Baby Me," and "Love With A Capital You" in the car tape deck and let play them over and over, listening carefully to those very sweet Miller evergreens and the light and fluffy female delivery. Both featured Kay Starr on the vocal. She was just a mere fifteen then and had recorded these two sides for the Miller band because their regular girl singer, Marion Hutton, was ill. It wasn't the "Wheel Of Fortune" Kay Starr you would easily recognize, it was the pre-Charlie Barnet- who-would-change- her voice - forever - era - Kay Starr, but it was definitely the best female vocalizing ever heard on a Miller recording, although there were only a few recognizable traces of the legendary vocalist we all know so well.

When Marion returned the next week, "mom and I packed our bags and got back home to Memphis with just three cents in our pocket."

She was nine years old when she first sang on a Dallas, Texas radio station. "It was on WRR at the Melba Theater in Dallas."

"And for no pay." I documented, prying easily.

"Right----no pay!"(girlish laughter)

"A fifteen minute show for five days a week."

"Yes, then much later when I was fourteen, I went with Joe Venuti and was with him every summer ' til I was sixteen...then briefly with Glenn Miller where I made those two recordings." I told her of my musical homework during my trip to the theater.

"Your voice was so different. I learned somewhere that you had (voice) trouble when you were with Charlie Barnet."

At Heckscher Park, Hungtington, NY

"I did, after singing for three years with Charlie, and you're singing over George Serabo's arrangements, you can bet that it affected my throat. It actually ruined my voice temporarily.......a lot of people said that it made me sound different.... the keys didn't change, so....I don't know."

"Well, maybe it was just a change over the teen-age sound."

"It could be, but you know it took me a year to recover and I started with piano and they let me add bass after many weeks then drums with no sticks, just brushes, for more weeks and it took me all that time before I was able to sing with a full-blown band again. I had to learn everything all over again like having to walk from a crawl." She was thinking it over, not having talked about it much lately, she said.

"So the loud Barnet band was indirectly responsible."

"Partially. I think that ignorance is bliss. Charlie would say, 'So your throat's bad. So what...sing anyway." ...and I listened to him like an idiot."

"I sang over, around and under colds the whole time I was with Barnet, but then I finally developed a sort of pneumonia and was on the verge of (throat) polyps, and I'm sort of a frontier woman, I don't get sick easily or stay sick very long and it was not my nature to faint, but I did for the first and only time in my life. Even on those Miller recordings you just mentioned, I wanted to make those records so badly that I sang above my key...again...Marion sang one-and-a-half octaves higher than I.....but I did it anyway, it made no difference."

Was she nervous at that tender age? "No, I was excited. I was so young."

Some say that after all that throat trouble she developed a huskier, throaty voice, which is really her trademark, the sound that unmistakably identifies her.

"Well, maybe...." She gives in a little.... "maybe I just grew up."

While with Joe Venuti and the Camel Caravan show, Kay left to get back to Tech High in Memphis. "I thought Joe was trying to get rid of me, so I cried. It was a panic." But Joe finally got her to understand that he really liked her and that she had to finish school then she would be able to go to Detroit and then to New York with the band to do a radio show.

Next, it was work with Bing's brother, Bob Crosby. As his vocalist, she was approached by the Camel Cigarettes people to star in a weekly radio show, but the deal fell through. "The ad agency wanted a bigger name." she said.

Of all the familiar, successful songs she recorded with Capitol during her career , including "Side-By-Side," "Bonaparte's Retreat," "Angry, " and her golden "Wheel Of Fortune," she names the latter as her favorite and claims never to get tired of singing it. "When I think I'm wearied of it, and I wonder, Oh, maybe people are tired of it. But what happens is, every time I start to sing it, somebody reaches over and touches somebody next to them, or they just smile, and you can just feel the memories starting, you know, and you can't deny that's what it's all about.

"It was like the marriage between Tony Bennett and "I Left My Heart In San Francisco" and Frankie Laine with "I Believe.""

"Yes, and the people love it the best. And, don't forget, it bought me my house and determined my future."

"Wheel of Fortune" has sold over 5 million records and was just beginning to sell in Russia.

In the seventies Kay took her act to Lake Tahoe and Las Vegas, working about 25-30 weeks a year at places mostly of her own choosing and singing a repertoire of her own choice.

"You once said that a good singer is a singer who tells a story to music. Do you stand by that statement today?"

"Well, actually what I said was, a singer is no more than an actor or actress set to music, because you are only as good as the story you tell and people like to hear things they can identify with, and that's the story."

Kay Starr started out in country, being from Oklahoma and composed of 3/4 Cherokee and 1/4 Irish blood, it was a natural progression.

"I was a child of the depression and we didn't have any money to buy records, we didn't have a record player, so whoever was big on radio, I listened to. I lived in Texas---that's country music territory."

In the eighties it was a nationwide tour with Four Girls Four (Margaret Whiting, Helen O'Connell, Rosemary Clooney, and at one time, Rosemarie), and a big comeback at Manhattan's Freddie's Supper Club which was so widely praised. In 1991, she, Connie Haines and Margaret Whiting climbed back on the Florida circuit with 3 Girls 3 and also went to Texas with the Mills Brothers all while recovering from foot surgery.

Kay is active in the wonderful organization so many of us support, the Los Angeles based Society Of Singers, which helps singers get some tender, loving care, especially when in need, (I'm also a member without doing much but lending a little support) . She also works to help her fellow Native Americans as a member of the board of the Los Angeles Indian Center. Kay Starr never had long to dream about those goals, she won fortune and fame a long time ago, and she's still telling her stories to music. Today, I received Kay's annual Christmas card No. 25, that's how long we've been talking Christmas and Big Band music.

SARAH VAUGHAN

THE ORIGINAL DIVINE ONE
Sassy Sings

I first heard Sarah Lois Vaughan sing in the flesh while conversing backstage with Tony Bennett at Westbury Music Fair: "Isn't it wonderful to do an interview with Sarah singing in the background. I feel so inspired when I listen to her!" he said. While I talked to Tony, it was clear that Sarah was very much with us spiritually, while actually only a few hundred feet away, live on stage, singing to a packed house.

About an hour later Sarah Vaughan and I sat face-to-face on a soft leather couch in her dressing room between shows.

We talked awhile about her early association with the revolutionary band of jazz innovators, Dizzy Gillespie, Budd Johnson, Charlie Parker, and Billy Eckstine, when they played together in the Earl (Fatha) Hines Band. After all, it was Billy who discovered Sarah while he was singing with Earl, and he convinced Earl to hire her. Dizzy and Sarah worked up some great duets with Sarah on piano (- --Yes, piano! She was taught piano and organ from the age of seven years.) but, most unfortunately were never recorded because the recording ban was in effect at that time due to striking musicians. There is however, one existing recording of Dizzy and Sarah with her on the piano.

Nevertheless, Sarah states much of her musical development occurred during that alliance. Billy formed his own band in 1944, leaving the Earl to play more conservative material, taking along Sarah, Budd, and

Dizzy. It was the beginning of the new and exciting sounds of Be-Bop. (Billy also hired a budding star by the name of Miles Davis who was just starting out). The band was on a be-bop kick and blossomed with the help of this generally timid young performer from Newark, New Jersey (Sarah was 20) who sang with so much innovation and feeling.

"I listen to the musicians, the horn players, more than anything. That's where I get my stuff. I steal a lot. I'm a big thief. I just do it different so I don't get caught. My hands are my heart." Some have tried to cast jazz singer Sarah as a blues singer, which she was not. Sarah once told music writer Gene Lees, ".....I am not and never have been a blues singer," But, Gene adds in his book, Singers and the Song , "she is also a gospel singer. There is a great deal of church in her work." Sarah brings emotion to the surface by coloring the sounds in her almost supernaturally controlled throat, not in the usual way of imitating speech patterns in the reading of a lyric.

For instance, there's Sarah's timeless renditions of "Don't Blame Me" "Body & Soul," "I Should Care," and "I Cried For You." (Sarah's first break came with her performance of "Body & Soul" sung at an amateur contest in Harlem's famed Apollo Theater where Billy Eckstine first heard her.) In other, more socially tolerant times Sarah might have been a candidate for grand opera. She had the complete command of the harmonic materials of songs.

Over her career, Sarah Vaughan, who won the Downbeat polls of 1973 and 1975, has sung in over 60 countries in every place from intimate night clubs to stadiums with over 100,000 in attendance. She has performed with the Boston Pops, the San Francisco Symphony, and the Los Angeles Philharmonic. She has recorded endless singles and albums, although for a five year period in the late sixties, she had no recording contract but continued to tour internationally.

Somewhat direct when asked, Sarah admired her peers: "If the material is good, if the melody is good, and if the person singing it catches my ear, then it's good music that I can like. If an artist knocks me out---I listen. I can't stand screaming voices when you can't hear the lyrics."

You felt very good in the presence of Sarah---you really do. Her genuine sincerity shone through the warmth of each expression and the marvelously clear, vibrant voice. Sarah's voice was actually three voices: soprano, alto, and baritone, and she mixed them excellently when and where she needed to and had such consummate control of vibrato, especially true in her later years.

Everyone called Sarah by a different nickname. William B. Williams of New York's WNEW simply called her Sass: Billy Eckstine extends it to Sassy Her sobriquet is really The Divine One. Her business card says "The Divine One." Some call her Divine Sarah and still others, The Great Sarah.

After Sarah Vaughan passed on from cancer in 1990 at the age of 66, there was a tribute at Carnegie Hall. Bill Cosby emceed and Dizzy played and Roberta Flack sang Sarah's own "Tenderly." There was much emotion backstage, but what really gave the night it's release of grief were the comments of Billy Eckstine. "She was my little sister, my baby." Billy said with a catch in his voice. "...and I loved her very much."

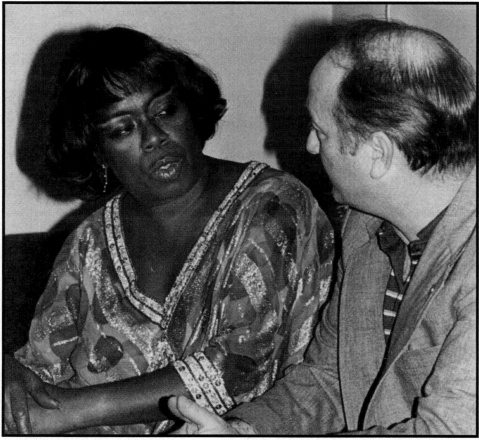

Sarah and Richard at Westbury Music Fair

PEGGY LEE
A Lyrics Drama

"Well, I've never been able to define a jazz singer," Peggy Lee said, " but I can tell when I hear one." Then she leaned back and added : " I believe it's a composite thing of good taste and understanding harmonic structures. It doesn't necessarily mean that they have to "scat" sing at all."

Peg thinks that it's good phrasing and good material that qualifies a capable jazz singer. "That means the voice has to maybe jump a couple of measures- if needed- to re-establish where you started out - always knowing where 'one' is."

Sultry singer Peggy Lee, formerly Norma Deloris Ekstrom, instituted the important part of her career when, after slipping into Helen Forrest's shoes with the Benny Goodman band in 1941, she recorded her sulky, ,jazzy rendition of "Why Don't You Do Right?" in 1942. That recording made her an international star.

Peg really started her professional career quite modestly at the age of fourteen. It was an unheralded debut on local radio station WDAY in Jamestown, North Dakota. It was there that program director Ken Kennedy christened her Peggy Lee. She eventually landed a job with the popular novelty band of Will Osborne, the slide-trombonist, vocalist, and drummer leader who composed the swing era hit "Pompton Turnpike."

In a cocktail lounge at Chicago's Ambassador Hotel shortly before Helen Forrest quit, Benny heard Peggy sing and promptly hired her. After twenty months with Goodman, that molded her into one of the most famous female vocalists of the time, Peg and her guitarist husband, former Goodman sideman Dave Barbour, quit the band in 1943 and went on to record a batch of great hits they wrote on their own in the years following, while Peg impersonated a retired, professionally inactive, simple housewife. "Dave would come home," she said, "the dinner wasn't ready - but the songs I worked on all day was."

These are the numbers I most identify with when it comes to Peggy Lee's hits: "It's a Good Day," "I Don't Know Enough About You," and a

deft little ditty they composed in 1948 while vacationing in Mexico, "Manana." Aside from teaming with her husband, Peggy has written over 500 songs with various collaborators including Broadway's Cy Coleman who penned "Witchcraft"and many other Broadway tunes; producer and leader Quincy Jones; orchestra leader and composer Victor Young ("Emily" and "The Shadow of Your Smile" composer), and composer Johnny Mandel. She was careful not to mark them with slang or things that might date the piece so they would not be overtaken by time. "I guess that's an instinct. It's not just good luck to keep a song's standard quality," she noted.

When singing, Peg's voice sort of whispers confidential resonant passion even on the most fragile numbers. Hard songs become dreamy; harsh songs translate into soft songs. Novelty songs become ballads. Some have called her the "Actress of Song." It was Duke Ellington , however, who christened her the "Queen of Song."

In those days, Peggy had always entertained her fellow celebrities and just anyone she knew who wasn't in the business at her lavish home on Kim Ridge Road in Beverly Hills. It was through these parties that Duke Ellington and Peggy got to know one another and became very warm friends. They had always admired one another. Peg had written the lyric for Duke's theme melody for the film Anatomy Of A Murder, "Gone Fishin'." Peg threw a special dinner party for the occasion in the Duke's honor. Charlie Barnet and Frank Sinatra were invited, as was Cary Grant. That party deepened their friendship. At a later gala tribute held at Madison Square Garden and sponsored by the NAACP, so the story goes, Peggy showed up with Quincy Jones to support the Duke. While Peggy was on stage performing, Duke, who was backstage talking with Louis Armstrong, turned to him and said, "Louis, now we really have royalty on that stage. She's the 'Queen.'"

Some critics have suggested Peg emulated the styling of Billie Holiday, but that was impossible. "We had no radio where we lived in North Dakota," she said, "we didn't even have electricity. When I finally heard

Count Basie coming out of Kansas City, I didn't think of it as swing or jazz or anything. It just sounded like good music to me. I can't say I emulated any special singer, until I first heard Maxine Sullivan. She communicated so well - I liked her simplicity." Nat King Cole, however, said that when Peg sang "Sometimes I Feel Like a Motherless Child," she sounded just like Billie Holiday, but Peg just shrugged it off.

Peg always got very involved in her music, favoring best the theme song she wrote for the 1950 movie Johnny Guitar. Her favorite album was The Man I Love, recorded in 1957 and orchestrated by musical genius Nelson Riddle, and actually conducted by Sinatra himself . One selection, "The Folks Who Live On The Hill," a quiet, prayerlike piece recorded earlier by Bing Crosby, is a typical reverie style Lee rendition.

When Peggy recorded her swirling, stampeding Decca version of Richard Rodgers' evergreen waltz "Lover," he was quoted as lamenting, "Oh, my poor little waltz, my little waltz. What happened to my little waltz?" Later, being the very kind and amiable figure he was known to be, he approached Peg: "You can always sing anything of mine." Peg felt that comment from the great composer was quite a compliment.

In a change of pace, Peg's "Is That All There Is?" is a life-weary mystical selection written by rock writers Jerry Leiber & Fred Stoller that sticks in your mind and may even keep you awake at night. "Though the song wasn't written for me, it just happened that the lyric paraphrases my life, "Peg said. "I've been through everything including the death experience, but I believe the song is positive. Of course, we all know there is more." Few know that Peggy Lee's very early life was that of an abused child at the hand of a cruel stepmother. The abuse that lasted until she was seventeen had an odd effect in that Peggy became a mild, non-violent person, which countermands the expected future life of an abused person. She came to hate violence of every kind.

Peg's movie credits include the 1955 Lady Is a Tramp where she did four separate voices and sang three individual songs; Pete Kelly's Blues, a 1956 film with Jack Webb which earned her an Oscar nomination as a fading nightclub singer, and the 1952 Danny Thomas re-make of The Jazz Singer . As a Bing Crosby specialist, I recall a Bing Crosby movie in which Peg appeared. It was a so-so film, the 1950 Mr. Music, but, in a peppy party scene, Peg and Bing warble several bubbly choruses of the song "Life Is So Peculiar." Although her role was a short cameo, the two entertainers became good friends and singing partners. Peg sang regularly on Bing's radio show. "Before I met Bing, I had always secretly loved the Rodgers and Hart song 'Down By The River,'" Peg explained, "that he sang years before in (the 1935 film) Mississippi, and I told him how I felt about it. One night, when I went to dinner with him to a little place in San Francisco, he actually sang it for me. He somehow convinced the piano player to play it and then sang it for me personally. Can you imagine that? It was a memorable evening. There was always a certain security for me in just thinking about Bing."

It was unfortunate that Peg's own career in films never took off. She certainly could act. It was her one career disappointment. When singing, as I have noted before, she portrayed many characterizations. Part singer, part actor, she lived each song according to the character in the lyric. Peggy had, of course, appeared on countless television shows including the one in which a young Frank Sinatra made his debut performance on Bob Hope's second ever TV show.

Peggy Lee was really in a class with counterpart Frank Sinatra. Although she too began her career with the Big Bands, Peg continued her lifelong career as an individual artist choosing her own songs, backup musicians, tailored format, and a very classy wardrobe. Peg has emerged an accomplished and respected, world-class entertainer.

"I learned more about music from the men I worked with in the bands, "she says, "than I've learned anywhere else. They taught me discipline and the value of rehearsing and how to train. Even if the interpretation of a particular song wasn't exactly what we wanted, we had to make the best of it."

P.S. I almost forgot to mention Peg's stellar version of "Golden Earrings" from the Ray Milland, Marlene Dietrich film of the same name. It's on my personal all-time top ten list.

FRANCES LANGFORD

Mother Langford
Lands a Giant Tuna

In 1993 I sent Frances Langford a letter along with a copy of an article I did for World War II Magazine about her old boss Bob Hope and their wartime travels with the USO. Everyone knows that Frances, whom Bob dubbed "Mother Langford" on those trips because of the concerned motherly nurturing to some of the troupers, was one of the original entertainers engaged by Bob to help entertain our servicemen during the dark days of that terrible war. Frances responded from her Florida residence with a kind reply inviting me to interview her. That was in 1995. Frances' only contact with her contemporaries those days was limited to periodical conversations with Bob Hope and limited benefit appearances. After exchanging some words about mutual friends Connie Haines and Kitty Kallen, we reminisced about the life and career of Frances Langford.

Born in Lakeland, Florida, in 1914, Frances studied opera at Southern College, but tonsillitis altered her vocal capacity from soprano to contralto.

"I was very surprised at the change in my own voice," she said, "it was like listening to someone else."

Band singer and radio star Rudy Vallee heard her sing in New Orleans in 1935 and hired her to appear on his radio show Rudy Vallee and His Connecticut Yankees. She practiced her singing skills on Rudy's show for over a year.

A role in the unsuccessful New York stage play, Here Goes the Bride in 1933 was devastating to her career. However, at Cole Porter's birthday party held atop the Waldorf Astoria in New York, Frances sang "Night and Day," which was then Cole's newest song. This was before Fred Astaire and Ginger Rogers put the song to work in the movies, and long before Frank

Sinatra recorded the definitive version.

"Johnny Green was the orchestra leader. Cole asked me to sing his

song "Night and Day" at his party. I rehearsed it briefly and then sang it....I believe...the first public performance of the song. Many important show business people were there including movie producer Walter Wanger. That night he invited me out to Hollywood for a screen test. I soon did my first picture for him."

with Bob Hope, Tony Romano and Jerry Colonna

This led to a part in Every Night at Eight with George Raft and the movie Collegiate, both in 1935. They were followed by Broadway Melody of 1936, and Hollywood Hotel in 1937 with Benny Goodman and his orchestra who was very hot at this point); Too Many Girls in 1940, and Hit Parade of 1941. In 1939 Frances was chosen as The All-American Girl.

A radio role was created for her on Hollywood Hotel , an hour-long popular weekly variety show with Hollywood actor Dick Powell as Master-of-Ceremonies. The program featured a twenty-minute dramatic production with Hollywood stars, introduced by celebrated gossip columnist Louella Parsons.

Within a few years, Frances Langford had shared the mike with just about every important vocalist of the time: Louis Armstrong "Pennies from Heaven"-also with Bing), Rudy Vallee, Tony Martin, Bob Hope, and Bing Crosby "Gypsy Love Song" which illustrates the sweet capable voice that was early Frances working with Bing's rich baritone. Frances also worked her pipes with the Jimmy Dorsey, Benny Goodman, Skinnay Ennis, Stan Kenton, and the Les Brown Bands. "That's pretty good credentials, isn't it Richard?" "Are you kidding?" said I.

Remember James Cagney's wonderful 1942 film Yankee Doodle Dandy? Well, it was Frances Langford who vocalized the thrilling version of George M. Cohan's song "Over There." That's my overall favorite Frances Langford performance. She belted and delivered it with an enthusiasm unlike anyone else.

"Jimmy (Cagney) called me and wanted me to do those (George M.) Cohan numbers because he said I would do them better than anyone else. I was very pleased. It was a big and wonderful film....and it's lasted so long. I see it on television every now and then."

During her travels with Bob Hope, she performed personally for, and was befriended by, General Jimmy Doolittle, George Patton, and Dwight

Eisenhower while overseas on those USO tours. General Eisenhower decorated Frances with a special citation for unselfishly entertaining our troops under wartime conditions.

There was a charming story about Frances' first experience singing to Naval personnel at the San Diego, California Naval Base. "It seems they had to cut the song "You Go to My Head," realizing a little late that the word head was the Navy word for toilet," she told me to giggles.

Servicemen, especially overseas, always enjoyed Frances Langford, generally the first American girl seen by them in months. When she would sing a sentimental ballad, some of them would actually shed tears. Seeing a very pretty all-American girl from home and listening to familiar songs they associated with their own sweethearts brought back visions of home that jokes alone could not achieve, even when delivered by a great comic like Bob Hope.

As Bob Hope recounted to me during one of our interviews: "...I'll always love the ones with heart and courage who went with me on USO tours during the war, like Frances Langford. I couldn't have done it without her and the others," a great acknowledgment of her talents and character, indeed! Frances traversed the entire war zone with Bob during all those courageous trips.

By 1945, the war over, Frances starred on her own radio show back home, so she had to quit the tours. Frances was inadvertently responsible for Bob Hope's long association with Les Brown and his Orchestra. It seems that in 1948 Bob was searching for a replacement for Frances, who had been with him on his radio show for years, and someone brought him records of Les Brown and his singer Doris Day. Doris never joined the show, but Bob was so enamored by the sounds of Les Brown that he signed them.

In 1952, I was working the Martin & Lewis telethon at the NBC studios in New York. That's where I first met Frances Langford. My job was to cue her onstage at just the right time. We shared a sandwich at noon and talked about, what else, those USO tours. She appeared onstage exactly at 1:19 AM right after comedians Phil Silvers and Jerry Lester.

In 1953 Frances Langford appeared briefly in the movie The Glenn Miller Story which starred June Allyson and Jimmy Stewart. She played along with performers Louis Armstrong, Gene Krupa, bandleader Ben Pollack, and Glenn's regular singing group The Modernaires, all playing themselves. Frances sang a great rendition the first gold record ever, Chattanogga Choo-Choo with Glenn and the Modernaires near the end of the movie.

In 1959, Frances and Ralph Evinrude married, and Bob was able to convince Ralph to allow Frances to perform once again with Bob and his traveling Christmas USO troupe consisting of the old World War II cast. bases, bringing home to servicemen at lonely outposts during Christmastime.

Then, there's the saga of the Bickerson's, the long-running, outrageous weekly radio show aired in the mid-fifties and ran into the '70's. Don Ameche was John and Frances Langford played Blanche. They screamed fiercely at one another every week over the radio. Blanche would accuse

John; John would fight back; then Blanche would cry, and John would repent. It was the marriage experience portrayed at its worst. The hilarious show lasted for a number of years.

"They even made two albums of the show and they sold pretty good," Frances said.

On the Hollywood Palace, a television variety show, Frances appeared with her friend Bing Crosby, along with old pal Don Ameche in April of 1967. 1991 had her appearing with a long list of other stars on a television show called Stars and Stripes, depicting Hollywood and World War II American movie classics. Tony Randall narrated while Maxene Andrews of the Andrews Sisters, Dorothy Lamour, Eddie Bracken, Bob Hope, and Bing Crosby performed in clips covering performances at military camps and their selling of war bonds.

"What are you doing for fun these days?"

"Well, you won't believe it..." she was filled with pride, "I am a deep-sea fisherman."

"A what?" I shot back to this petite, retired Florida citizen.

"My biggest catch was a 750 pound blue-fin tuna."

"HOLY SMOKES......how do you do that? How does anyone do that?"

"I've always been a fisherman...for years. I just know how to do it. You have to know how," she re-assured me. "We have a 110 foot boat, the Santa Clare. We have taken the boat to Europe and fish all the way. "Her husband was, at the time, Mr. Stuart, former Secretary of the Air Force under Roosevelt during World War II and then a Tulsa, Oklahoma attorney.

singing with Benny Goodman

"You know, I don't see anybody much anymore, I'm away from all that...you know ..living in Florida. I don't go to those parties like I used to."

Not too many of us will forget the face and voice of the lovely Frances Langford, all-American girl whom we lost in 2007.

LYNN ROBERTS

THE LAST of the BIG BAND SINGERS

I consider lovely Lynn Roberts to be the last and one of the best of the Big Band Era and beyond vocalists.

"I believe I was the only lady band singer who sang with both Tommy and Jimmy Dorsey, Harry James, and Benny Goodman - and not for just short periods," Lynn said. She and I were reminiscing about her association with those remarkable Big Bands. While other vocalists were well out on their own, Lynn, young and enthusiastic, was headlining the last years of those formidable touring bands.

Born in Brooklyn, New York, but raised in Elmhurst, Queens, Leonore Theresa Raisig, like many other Song Stars, got off to an early start on the Horn and Hardart Children's Hour radio show in New York. "Then, before long I was appearing on Ted Steele's local afternoon television variety show. Irene Day, who was band leader Charlie Spivak's wife and former band singer for both Spivak and Gene Krupa, called me at the station after seeing the show and invited me to an audition along with many other hopefuls: 'My husband is looking for a female singer for our band. Would you be interested? I responded with a definite --Yes! 'Then go to Nola Studios later today,' she advised.

"So I did and later that night they called with good news. I got the job for sixty dollars a week, which was a lot of money then---I paid my own hotel bills and even sent money home to my mother. I was just 15 years old and I stayed on for one-and-a-half years."

"But like other singers Rosey Clooney and Doris Day, weren't you sort of young to tour from state to state with a group of male musicians on a bus?"

"Oh, sure! That's why my mother kept looking for a stay-in-New York kind of job for me. She discovered that Vincent Lopez, who was a steady attraction at the Taft Hotel in New York City, advertised for a band singer. Mom got me an audition and I got the job. Then, while I was there, (Tommy) Dorsey's road manager spotted me one night while he was having dinner at the Taft and called me over and asked me to go with Dorsey."

"And.......?"

"What? Are you kidding? I couldn't wait. I went traveling on a bus again."

"I remember a short film that I have on video tape in which you were performing with both Jimmy and Tommy Dorsey in 1955 and your trade-mark ponytail was flying all over the place while you vocalized on one of the Dorsey's biggest hits "Yes. Indeed!" Wasn't there an anecdote about that infamous ponytail?" In the film Lynn was swinging her hips, snapping her fingers, almost unable to contain herself , her bright blonde hair bouncing back-and-forth from shoulder to shoulder in an infectious rhythm, her head swaying from side to side.

"Yup! Tommy fired me after five years because I wouldn't cut it off. He said he didn't like it anymore. So we had a big fight."

"What did you do?"

"I left the band .....for eight months. But while I was singing in a club in Montreal, Tommy came in to see me one night. He was sitting at the bar, so after my song I went over to say hello. He promptly asked me to come back because he was going to appear at the Paramount with Frank Sinatra. So I said OK."

"Did you have to cut off the ponytail as part of the deal?"

"No, I didn't!" she said triumphantly to my expected grin.

Lynn considers the high point of her career to be that very performance at the New York Paramount Theater with Frank Sinatra and Tommy Dorsey in 1956. "It was the end of a great era," Lynn fondly reminisced, "shortly after Tommy and Jimmy were both gone."

"By the way," she said, "That video you have was from a movie short filmed in 1954 and it was called The Dorsey Brothers Encore. Actually I had been with Tommy when Jimmy joined up with him in 1953. It was known as the Last Fabulous Dorsey Brothers Band. As you know, Tommy died suddenly in 1956. He had a big meal and was in the throes of a terrible divorce and had taken some sleeping pills...he became sick and couldn't wake up... it was a nightmare. He was only 51 years old. Everyone was in shock."

"Yes, I remember that day. The entire music world was stunned. I recall Warren Covington telling me the story," I recalled to Lynn, "he said it was the band's day off from a lengthy gig at the Statler Hotel's Cafe Rouge' in New York."I asked Lynn about her duration with Harry James.

"Let's see! I started in 1978 and remained with him until he passed away in 1983." Harry had considered Lynn to be one of his best vocalists ever, according to Harry James expert Joe Pardee of the Harry James Appreciation Society. Joe was kind enough to present me with a personally narrated five tape gift highlighting Harry, his band personnel and his vocalists. Some of those recordings prove Lynn's worthiness as an impressive Big Band vocalist.

with Bob Eberly

"I remember watching you rehearse when I interviewed Harry in '82, but you were busy with the band out front and I had to get to Westbury Music Fair for another interview and was running late," I explained.

Lynn considers her personal best recording to be all her recordings, although she confesses to being overcritical of her work. "But, I think probably my favorite is the tribute album I did for Harry James." The MGM album, Harry, You Made Me Love You, was released in 1983, just after Harry's passing.

"But, between Tommy and Harry, wasn't there a time you worked with the Pied Pipers?"

"Oh, sure! In the Seventies Warren Covington owned and managed the Pipers and I was the lead singer for about five years. Sometimes Warren would sing the 'Sinatra' stuff, backed by the group like they did in the '40s with Tommy. I liked the way Warren sang and managed things. It was a great experience for me.

Lynn worked with Benny Goodman for ten years beginning in 1961. She sang with the band and toured Europe with the sextet too and is featured on the Benny Goodman Reader's Digest Album. On the sensitive subject of relationships with legendary Benny Goodman, many vocalists have complained about his riveting "Goodman Ray," where he would stare menacingly at players and singers when he disapproved of one thing or another. "I thought I knew how to handle Benny, and I did for a long while. But one day I got the 'ray'," she said, "I won't tell you why, but I will tell you I have probably the only letter of apology Benny ever wrote and it hangs prominently on my wall."

Lynn has appeared at Michael's Pub in New York, toured Israel with the Mel Lewis orchestra, and was featured at Osaka Symphony Hall in Japan in their very first jazz concert ever. The year 1993 found her as the highlight of a Palm Beach, Florida, tribute to Carnegie Hall. "Gigs" at Tavern on the Green and The Rainbow Room and other jazz venues have been regular events for her over the years.

The Palm Beach concert reviews encapsulated my own personal feelings about Lynn Roberts: One newspaper said, "...on stage she had no affectations and appeared to love what she was doing. Her voice shows no sign of age; it was crystal clear and beautifully controlled. Her charm and enthusiasm coupled with a great vocal style made her the absolute hit of the show. "Lynn has always been the hit of the show. Even New York critic Rex Reed, compliment miser, says, "......Lynn sings like an angel."

Tommy Dorsey Clips Her Curls

If you want to hear Lynn Roberts at her best, get her CD album, Lynn Roberts- The Men in My Life - devoted to songs made popular by both Harry James and the Dorseys, as well as some of the others.

Lynn sent me some wonderful photos includ- ing one rare snapshot with Tommy Dorsey pretending to "clip" her infamous pony- tail on a day off alongside a swimming pool in Las Vegas.

Today Lynn Roberts sings with the Gene Krupa Orchestra conducted by Michael Berkowitz. Reviewer Frank Roberts said: "Lynn is 71 but looks like 51 and sings like she is 31." How about that!

DINAH WASHINGTON

Dinah Washington and Lionel Hampton go back a long way. Here's the way the exuberant

"Hamp" told it to me: " A little girl named Ruth Lee Jones, who worked in the powder room of Garrett's Bar in Chicago where I was playing and sometimes worked for Walter Fuller's Quintet, came out and sang for me. I liked her and hired her on the spot. I instantly changed her name to Dinah Washington, but she didn't care what I called her so long as I gave her a job with my band. I don't know how I came up with that name, but she took it and became famous with it."

"Hamp" had a good eye for talent, having also discovered jazz singer Joe Williams on the very same day. Dinah remained with the band for about a year. Before that, she toured with the Sallie Martin Gospel Singers. Her gutsy style, unique phrasing, and feeling for the blues transcended category. Among the blues ladies during the interim of Bessie Smith to Aretha Franklin, Dinah Washington emerged fitfully from the world of rhythm-and-blues to successfully embrace a popular repertoire.

She began, as so many others have, as a gospel singer and offered a taste of what a trained gospel singer could do when shifting gears into jazz blues and more popular music. Her recording with Hampton, "Salty Papa Blues," is a blues classic. "Baby, Get Lost" and " Bitter Earth" were two of her best early hits. Her remarkably powerful mezzo-soprano voice was driven with sharp attacks and a fiery, swinging drive. On her recording of "That Ole Devil" you can hear distinct influences of Billie Holiday. Quincy Jones rates his album made with Dinah Washington, Swingin'

Miss D, as one of the best albums he ever made. " Dinah Washington was fantastic, the greatest person I've ever worked for," said Fred Norman, Tommy Dorsey and Charlie Spivak trombonist and arranger, " She amazed me at one of our first sessions by recording a number in one take. 'That's it!', she said 'I know,' said I. "

A lot of people thought Dinah Washington was sort of a rough character, but it wasn't true. Once when she had a record date in Detroit where she also owned a restaurant, she would spend weeks supervising and handling the cash at the restaurant, not thinking about music at all. When one of the musicians finally got up the nerve to approach and ask her about

working out the sounds required for an upcoming date, she replied : " Oh, don't worry about that, Sonny. You go back to New York, and I'll pick the tunes." She dutifully went back to the cash register.

A string of hits on the Mercury label were: " What a Diff'rence A Day Makes," " It Could Happen To You," "Our Love Is Here To Stay," and " For All We Know." These are the gems for which Dinah will be most remembered. You can still hear them playing somewhere everyday. She made a good song mean something. The terse, sardonic quality, the personal meaning she gave to every lyric, and the gutsy timbre are all strikingly in evidence with every performance. My favorite recordings, consumated in 1961, were "Unfor-gettable" and "September In The Rain." Dinah made many albums includ-ing The Bessie Smith Songbook, a tribute to some one she both admired and emulated. In 1963 an unfortunate mixture of alcohol and pills put an early end to the life of Song Star Dinah Washington.

Ina Ray Hutton - Bandleader

Jo Stafford and Paul Weston married in 1952. It wasn't unusual that singers and musicians married. Doris Day married Les Brown sax player George Weidner; Peggy Lee married Goodman guitarist Dave Barbour; Frances Wayne married Woody Herman trumpeter Neal Hefti; June Christy married Stan Kenton tenor saxist Bob Cooper; June Hutton (who replaced Jo in the Pipers) married Axel Stordahl (Tommy Dorsey and Frank Sinatra arranger), and Kitty Kallen's first marriage was to Jack Teagarden's clarinet player. Some singers married their bosses: Harriet Hilliard to Ozzie Nelson,

Neal Hefti and Frances Wayne

Paul Weston and Jo Stafford

Georgia Carroll to Kay Kyser, Dorothy Collins to Raymond Scott, Ann Richards to Stan Kenton, and Betty Grable married Harry James.

Peggy Lee and Dave Barbour

Ivie Anderson, Duke Ellington's classic performer on the original 1932 recording "It Don't Mean a Thing if It Ain't Got That Swing" and "Mood Indigo," died too young and is still missed. Ivie was the Duke's best fitting to-the-orchestra -style singer. When she sang "Stormy Weather" at the London Palladium, some of the audience broke down and cried. Favorite Ellington recordings with Ivie include "When My Sugar Walks Down the Street" and a silly song, "Love Is Like a Cigarette." She joined Ellington's band at just the right time, 1931, at the peak of his career, and became the band's first regular singer.

Ivie Anderson learned her craft while living in a convent. The vaudeville circuit was her venue for many years and included the Cotton Clubs in New York and L.A. She had the distinction of being the first black vocalist to sing with a white band. The band was the Anson Weeks Orchestra, a two-beat style band, featured for years at the Mark Hopkins Hotel in San Francisco. Ivie was just the right vocalist, interpreting the Duke's sensitive tunes. Everyone agrees--critics and musicans alike- that, although Ellington had a succession of female vocalists during the ensuing years, Ivie was the most sensitive and most talented of them all. "... Every girl singer we've had since Ivy had to prevail over her image," Duke Ellington said in his 1973 biography, Music Is My Mistress, "She was our good luck charm. We always broke performance records when Ivie was with the band.

Ivie left Duke Ellington in 1942 because of illness, but not before the great recording of "I Got It Bad and That Ain't Good" was waxed in 1941. She died at the age of forty-five from asthma. On a brighter note, Ivie Anderson was very successful with a Los Angeles restaurant called The Chicken Shack where she earned a comfortable living in her off years.

Pearl Bailey was born in Newport News, Virginia, in 1918 and her first band association was with the Cootie Williams Orchestra after she won a singing contest at the Apollo theater. She also sang with the bands of Noble Sissle, Edgar Hayes, and Cab Calloway in various nightclubs in Washington D.C., Baltimore, and New York. A definite jazz singer, but more a Broadway show singer, Pearl was especially acclaimed for her appearance in the all-black version of Hello Dolly. She married jazz drummer Louis Bellson and performed in many Las Vegas shows. Pearl sang in the movies Porgy and Bess, Carmen Jones, That Certain Feeling and All the Fine Young Cannibals. She had appeared many times with Bing Crosby on his various television shows. Her books, The Raw Pearl and Talking to Myself, classify her insights and experiences where, she says, ".....I offered up my life's experiences for all to examine." We lost Pearl in 1990 after years of ill health.

Pearl Bailey

Betty Carter, a stylist of extraordinary effort who goes strongly against the contemporary grain, has a cult following like Song Star Carmen McRae, but found it hard to appeal to larger audiences. In the 1970's she pulled everything together, closing out her Billie Holiday mode. Her individualistic representation of herself presents a calm but intense quality in her jazz phrasings. Betty was one of the really few singers who improvised with feeling. She drew her listeners into her songs. Backed by her own trio, she appeared in clubs, concerts and college

Betty Carter

dates in 1972. Some have nominated Betty Carter to "scat" knighthood, so to speak. She worked as hard at it as any sax player. People either love or hate Betty's style of jazz-scat-singing. Although some consider her the logical heir to Ella's work, Betty was strictly her own lady and represented jazz in the modern mode. Her "What A Little Moonlight Can Do" contain the best examples of her kind of "scatting."

Born **Lillie Mae Jones** in 1929, Betty honed her skills in church work. In 1947 she had the opportunity to sing with Charlie Parker's Quintet, her first contact with professionals. She joined up with Lionel Hampton: "I knew she was good, so I hired her as soon as I heard her sing at the audition," Hamp told me, "but we had our problems." Betty went on to appear with jazz star Miles Davis and toured with Sonny Rollins in Japan. She recorded with Ray Charles in the late Fifties. Betty fell victim to the '60's rock era, but prevailed later with recordings like "Spring Can Really Hang You Up the Most," performed with a trio, her best setting musically.

June Christy

June Christy, born in Springfield, Illinois, in 1925, June was the heir apparent to Anita O'Day who found June, whose real name was Shirley Luster, in 1945 performing at a Chicago nightclub called The Three Deuces. O'Day was weary of performing and traveling with the Stan Kenton band and told June she would be leaving the band and advised her to audition for the job. June sounds a lot like O'Day. She was pretty, blond, bright, friendly and very well liked by her fellow performers. Her recordings of "Tampico" and "Willow Weep for Me" in 1945 were great commercial successes.

She began it all at age thirteen singing with a local band then joined the Boyd Raeburn band in Chicago. After recovering from scarlet fever, she sang with Benny Strong's band and performed at the Three Dueces. While with Kenton, June married (and stayed married) to tenor sax player Bob Cooper who was a member of the band. In 1954 she made an album entitled Something Cool her best work for my money. Critics say the song Something Cool itself is owned lock, stock and barrel by June Christy alone. Other attempts to vocalize it have failed miserably. My favorite Christy recording is Benny Carter's 1958 version of "When Lights Are Low," arranged by her husband Bob. She is also accompanied by Bob playing with the Kenton band. It's typical cool, husky Christy.

June went into semi-retirement in the late '60's, after recording her last album at Capitol records, emerging occasionally for night club engagements in the Hollywood area. In 1972 she made a guest appearance with Kenton at the Newport Jazz Festival. Chris Connor followed June into the Kenton Band. The three girls' singing styles and sounds were very much alike, although Anita was the original, the peppiest, and the most innovative. Nevertheless, June Christy is a wonderful Song Star and deserves recognition here. She has always been a Big Band singer and felt uncomfortable in small combos. Stanton bassist Eddie Safranski, an old friend of mine from NBC studio days, once told me he preferred the voice of June Christy over any band singer he has known or worked with. A worthy tribute from a worthy musician.

Blossom Dearie, a Song Star with meritorious cocktail piano and song- writing skills, draws out all the expressive qualities of a song. She worked with Woody Herman, and her efforts with The Blue Stars vocal group in Paris were simply first-rate. I love the recording "It Amazes Me" recorded in 1959 and backed with Mundel Lowe's experienced guitar, Ray Brown's bass, and her own piano and vocalizing. Blossom is elegant, polite, and funny, too! She lights up the songs she sings. The little girl, squeaky quality denotes her singing personality. A composer, too, she wrote her hits "I Like You, You're Nice" and "Hey John." Blossom Dearie was first a pianist, sitting in with the likes of The Modern Jazz Quartet and others. Doubling on voice was a second career that came a little later. Blossom commands her own special audiences with a faithful following. Her singing has always been simply pleasant with an unvaried repertoire you could count on.

Blossom Dearie

Helen Humes sang with Harry James and Benny Goodman. Her best number was "Between the Devil and the Deep Blue Sea" with Basie in 1939. While with Count Basie's band in 1938, Jimmy Rushing was the blues singer, so she was usually assigned ballads too. The expressive shading in her delivery was usually thrown away when she sang the blues. Count Basie first discovered Helen Humes at the Cincinnati Cotton Club in 1937. She cut many sides with Basie including "Thursday," "Blame It on My Last Affair" and "Sing for Your Supper."

Helen Humes

She quit the harsh life of road tours in

Helen Humes

1941 and began her club appearances in New York City. She later settled in California then joined up with impresario Norman Granz for the Jazz at the Philharmonic series. In the '50's Helen recorded with many companies and contributed to movie sound tracks. It was with Basie again in a television film entitled Showtime at the Apollo, followed by tours to Australia with Red Norvo in the Sixties. Downbeat once rated her with Ella Fitzgerald and Mildred Bailey as one of the best singers of the Big Band Era.

Helen "retired" in 1967 taking work in a munitions factory in Louisville, Kentucky, because she felt agents were no longer interested in her. She emerged in 1973 when friends convinced her to revise her singing life. During her autumnal revival of the 1970's, she shifted from blues singer to ballad singer, proving her merit. Her personal favorite, "Every Now and Then," which she recorded in February 1975, accompanied by pianist Ellis Larkins and Buddy Tate's tenor sax, underlined her ability as a balladeer. Some say she sounded better at the age of sixty than when she was in her prime. She was still swinging in 1980, the year before her death, with tenor sax player Buddy Tate and his band.

Carmen McRae

Carmen McRae - a clipped, precise delivery, even more pronounced than Dinah Washington's, is Carmen McRae's trademark. There is no doubt of the respect she commanded in the jazz community. A piano playing vocalist, Carmen appeared with the bands of Benny Carter and Mercer Ellington during the 1940's. She was saw the light of day in Harlem, New York, and took formal piano lessons before winning a talent contest at the famed Apollo Theater. There she met Billie Holiday, who she described as her hero, and whom she said instilled encouragement into her and advised her to persevere if she wanted to be successful as a singer. A solo vocalist since then, Carmen continued to tour, especially in Japan during the 1960's and '70's. She sang with Benny Carter's big band in 1944 and went on to perform with Count Basie and Earl Hines. She completed more than 20 albums including "I Am Music" and "You Can't Hide Love." She played the clubs in L.A. and vicinity and made many recordings, including a great version of "Some Other Spring" in 1961. She is a veteran of many jazz festivals and is revered by a legion of fans, even now. In a recording done in Japan entitled Carmen Alone, she sang and played piano, illustrating her excellent repertoire. In the 1980's she performed on an RCA album Carmen Sings Monk. It was a great attempt to vocalize Monk's quirky melodies.

An asthma sufferer, she sometimes performed while sitting on a stool and was bedridden at the end of her life. Her last public performance was in 1991 at one of her favorite singing residences, New York's Blue Note club, where she became ill.

Carmen, one of the Big Band Era's premier vocalists and a distinct favorite among jazz musicians, died in Beverly Hills on November 10, 1994. Carmen McRae was considered part of the troika of female American jazz singers that included both Ella and Sarah.

Dinah Shore: When Fanny Rose Shore came to New York, she landed a non-paying job at New York radio station WNEW. The program

manager, sensing her talent, arranged an audition with Martin Block, legendary disc jockey of Make Believe Ballroom fame, and she sang the song Dinah. Block accidentally introduced her on the air as Dinah Shore, forgetting her first name. "I was so grateful," Dinah said later in an interview, "that I never corrected him." She sang on WNEW with another unknown youngster, Frank Sinatra. She became popular in the late

Dinah Shore with Count Basie

1930's, when she could be heard singing with the Chamber Music Society of Lower Basin Street and on the Eddie Cantor Show as a "regular." Dinah was one of Cantor's many successful proteges. She also once sang with the Leo Reisman Orchestra in 1939 and the enthusiastic Peter Dean "scat"-singing band around the same period.

Some of Dinah's best were: "Yes, My Darling Daughter," "Dear Hearts and Gentle People," and "Buttons and Bows" from the Bob Hope film Paleface. Dinah was not entirely a product of the Big Bands; she prevailed during the period from roughly 1947 to 1953, although she was once almost hired

Best Wishes
Dinah Shore

by Woody Herman-almost. Was he sorry later! Later, she was a featured star on her own long-running TV show where she would always close the show throwing a kiss at the camera with a memorable, lovable grunt... mm.m.m.m.m.muh!

Keely Smith

Keely Smith - Mostly identified as the singer who made it with her then husband, trumpet player and bandleader Louis Prima, on the 1958 blockbuster recording of "Old Black Magic," Keely Smith is still actively singing today. Frances Langford once told me she loves to listen to Keely, saying: "She has such a great singing voice---I love to listen to her." Louis and Keely played a lot of Las Vegas "gigs" in the '60's where they had a strong following. Keely Smith works very hard today for down-and-out singers as a member of the Advisory Council of the Society Of Singers in L.A. and she has recently released an album in 2008. How about that?

Maxine Sullivan was the Song Star vocalist known as the Loch Lomand girl after her 1937 noteworthy, Claude Thornhill recording of that song. The wonderful bell-like quality sound in her voice mixed with remarkable musical integrity is Maxine's trademark. Her 1937 version of Irving Berlin's "Blue Skies"- not exactly a folk song- brought a different feeling to jazz singing. Maxine played valve trombone and trumpet, too. In the Sixties, Maxine actually worked as a nurse, busy with community affairs in the Bronx, New York. In her 1967 comeback at a New York Town Hall, she prevailed. Next,

Maxine Sullivan

Maxine toured with the World's Greatest Jazzband from 1969 through 1975, including an appearance at the Newport, Rhode Island, Jazz Festival. Even at the age of 64, Maxine was still singing with that gentle swinging quality that established her originally.

"Liltin" Martha Tilton followed Helen Ward in the Benny Goodman band. She appeared in the famous 1938 Carnegie Hall Concert, showing up in an expensive pink tulle dress she bought at Lord & Taylor for the occasion. There she sang "Loch Lomand," a swing rendition of a Scottish song recorded previously by Maxine Sullivan that past summer. Martha previ-

Martha Tilton

Goodman's Martha Tilton

ously sang with Jimmy Dorsey. She projected a wholesome girl-next-door appearance and was very attractive . She stayed with Benny for two years. In 1939 she dominated all Benny Goodman recordings for RCA Victor with great numbers like "And the Angels Sing" (which she sang once again in 1994 at a Society Of Singers party in LA) and "Bei Mir Bist du Schoen" (accompanied by Ziggy Elman's great trumpet), among others. She appeared in the 1956 movie The Benny Goodman Story, personally selected by Benny himself, along with other veterans of the band, for the sound track.

Bea Wain is the Song Star whose wonderful rendition of two great songs, "Deep Purple" and "My Reverie," recorded with Larry Clinton's Orchestra, will live forever. Together with her husband, radio announcer supreme Andre' Baruch, they were known as Mr. & Mrs Music on New York's WMCA. Andre' was the original announcer on the Kate Smith and the Fred Waring Shows and Bea was in the chorus in both. "That's how we started together," said Bea, "That's how it happened. We began dating."

Bea started with the Kay Thompson singing group. "We were 13 girls and 3 boys. Most of the kids in the chorus did not read notes. We would learn songs by listening to Kay on the piano. She would play a chord.

Bea Wain

The low voices would watch her thumb. The middle voices would watch her middle finger. And the high voices would watch her pinkie. When she played we followed her fingers and we got a great spontaneous sound. I was very proud to be in that group."

Bea Wain represented a certain class with a very distinctive sound. When she vocalizes "You Go to My Head," or "My Heart Belongs to Daddy," you can grasp the feeling. I love her impeccable voice. I always imagined Bea Wain singing all her famous songs in a lavishly furnished, royally appointed drawing room somewhere in the grand Waldorf Astoria Hotel. Bea graduated to the Larry Clinton Band, whose own fame leans a lot on this terrific Song Star. In the late Thirties she sang on radio's Hit Parade with husband Andre' doing the announcing chores. Read the footnote on the Ella Fitzgerald segment of this book for a charming insight into the life of Ella as told by her friend Bea Wain.

Helen Ward with Benny Goodman

Helen Ward got her jump-start with the Benny Goodman Band just as the band took off during the ground-breaking 1934 Palomar Ballroom swing-fest. Helen was a New York girl singing with a New York voice and later broke her own ground with Eddy Duchin's and Will Osborne's Orchestras. My friend Willard Alexander, who represented Benny, helped hitch Helen to the high-flying Goodman Band. He knew her swinging rhythms worked well with Benny's new style. However, Helen never remained with one band, preferring the independent road. She was subsequently featured with the bands of Teddy Wilson, Harry James, Gene Krupa, and even Hal McIntyre, but never remained very long with any of them. Some consider her the archetypical band singer, widely imitated, closely followed by those who followed her. She was quick and snappy and employed an exuberbance that was contagious.

After some work in radio as a producer, Helen Ward joined with a Goodman comeback in the early '50's and performed again with Larry Clinton on some album work. Her 1953 rendition of "What a Little Moonlight Can Do" is a personal Helen Ward favorite.

Cassandra Wilson - One evening, surfing the internet, I ran across a comment on a jazz music message board, it read: "When you worship at the shrine of Cassandra Wilson, she is never regarded as the 'hottest thing out there,'" the note replying to a previous message, "She is the Supreme Highness of Jazz to come sit at the feet of Billie, Sarah, Ella, Betty, and Carmen." Vocalist, arranger, and composer Cassandra Wilson deserves mention here because she is one of the heirs of those Song Stars who started with the bands. There are no Big Bands today, as we knew them, to boost her career. Rock rhythms are her background, but she deals in the

Cassandra Wilson

other facets too. She tends to originate her repertoire, rather than follow the old stuff, and remains a Song Star of the future. However,her rendition of Billie Holiday's "I Wished on the Moon" is the closest Cassandra Wilson comes to the Big Band Era's legacy as far as I can tell.

Lee Wiley

Lee Wiley - hardly a jazz singer, but a genuine Song Star, Lee Wiley's personal phrasing and tone fit the musical demeanor that was Eddie Condon's 1930's and '40's band featured at his Greenwich Village, New York, nightspot. Her sophisticated style on Broadway songs moved them over into the jazz idiom. One of the most popular 1930's singers, she sang with devastating sex appeal and great instincts of what was best for her voice. Her late career recording of "West of the Moon" in 1956 is an example of that special skill. William B. Williams and Jonathon Schwartz of New York's WNEW radio played Wiley frequently during the Seventies and Eighties, especially the albums of the works of George Gershwin and Cole Porter that she recorded early in her career. Her influence was notably cornetist Bix Biederbecke, whom she emulated; but Billie Holiday emulated her, as did Peggy Lee. Her last public performance was at the Newport Jazz Festival in 1972 , re-uniting her with Eddie Condon. She died in 1975, a legend in her time.

Teresa Brewer, Margaret Whiting, Patti Page, Fran Warren - Back Row: McGuire Sisters

Bob Hope and Shirley Ross (Courtesy Paramount Pictures)

Some More Chicks

Vera Lynn, a most revered English vocalist with the Bert Ambrose Band in London especially during World War II, who sang those stirring songs that helped win the war, "We'll Meet Again," "The Last Time I Saw Paris," and "They'll Be Bluebirds Over the White Cliffs of Dover ."

Shirley Ross who forged her first mark with the Gus Arnheim band before recording "Thanks for the Memory" with Bob Hope from the movie The Big Broadcast of 1938. It became Bob's famous theme. And pretty **Frances Wayne**. How about her efforts with both Charlie Barnet and Woody Herman? Her personal best: "Happiness Is a Thing Called Joe."

Do you remember a perky **Eydie Gorme** who first starred with trombonist Tex Beneke in the late 1940's, drumming up all those original Glenn

Jo Ann Greer

Miller charts for the faithful? Catch her version of "If He Walked into My Life." And there was lovely **Louise Tobin** who warbled with Will Bradley and three neat singers, **Lucy Ann Polk**, **Jo Ann Greer** and **Eileen Wilson**, who also graced the early Les Brown bandstand.

Del Courtney's premier vocalist was **Dotty Dotson**, performing mostly at the Claremont Hotel in Berkeley, California. **Kay Weber's** duration with Bob Crosby's group was short but musically effective. Don't forget sexy Abbe Lane who kept the Rumba King Xavier Cugat's band popular with her dynamic vocals. **Lillian Clark Oliver**, one of the original Ray Charles Singers and once a Pied Piper, appeared on the Perry Como Show in the '50's and recorded with Count Basie, Tommy Dorsey, Louis Armstrong, the Norman Luboff Choir and the Ray Coniff singers. What a career! **Peg LaCentra**, Artie Shaw's first singer ever, dubbed the singing voices of actresses **Ida Lupino** and **Susan Hayward**. She also sang with Benny Goodman, and in 1939 she starred in The Peg LaCentra Show for NBC radio. Lest we forget, the Ray Charles Singers has featured many lady Song Stars over the years.

Edythe Wright sang some smoothies with Tommy Dorsey just before the Sinatra/Haines/Pied Pipers era. Eddie Duchin featured the DeMarco Sisters high atop the Waldorf-Astoria for a while before their prolific engagements in Las Vegas. One of my favorite people ever, Maria Ellington, devoted wife of Nat "King" Cole and mother of Natalie Cole, sang beautifully with the Duke during the band's heyday.

British born Mabel Mercer, her mother a music hall performer, was first a dancer. She sang those out-of-the-way type songs in a subdued manner usually only with a piano and mostly in small clubs. A singer's singer, Mabel influenced folks like Frank Sinatra, Lena Horne, and Nat "King" Cole, by their own admissions.

Future movie stars June Haver and Betty Grable got their start with Ted Fio Rito in the mid-Thirties. Betty made some sides with husband Harry James too. Do you remember Eugenie Baird's vocals with Glen Gray and his Casa Loma Orchestra? Lovely Ruth Robin graced the Phil Harris bandstand in the Thirties with her rhythmic phrasings. June Hutton was the popular girl singer with Ina Ray Hutton's blonde bombshell, all-girl band in the late Thirties. June also became a Pied Piper after Jo Stafford left the group and was on the recording of "Dream." The Skylarks made a melodic difference with Harry James' band while he worked in the movies.

Bandleader/Vocalist Ina Ray Hutton

Broadway star Vivian Blaine's first efforts animated Al Kavelin's New York City band in the Thirties by singing "Love Is Gone," and Dorothy Lamour began it all in Herbie Kay's band in 1934 singing at the Blackhawk Restaurant in Chicago before all those Hope/Crosby flicks. Ann Richards was a latter star of the Stan Kenton band in the late Forties.

The Barrie Sisters were the "Waltz King" Wayne King's magical vocalists in the thirties. Among many others, **Dolores Hawkins** and **Ginnie Powell** took turns vocalizing with the Gene Krupa and Boyd Raeburn bands.

Prolific maestro Kay Kyser and his "Kollege of Musical Knowledge" headlined **Ginny Simms** and **Georgia Carroll**. Ginny's CD release entitled There Goes That Song Again is a worthwhile tribute to this worthy Big Band Song Star. Guy Lombardo featured his sister **Rosemarie Lombardo** on the vocals, and Johnny Long sponsored **Julie Wilson** as his very fine girl singer. Benny also starred **Lisa Morrow** singing "Give Me the Simple Life"--so good, too!

Bouncy movie star **Betty Hutton** first sang with Vincent Lopez in New York and her sister **Marion Hutton** was a star with Glenn Miller in the Forties. I love her swinging version of "Ding , Dong, the Witch Is Dead." Marion joined Miller in 1938, and, except for a brief period in 1941 when she took time off to have a baby, she remained until September 1942. **Dorothy Claire** filled in for Marion during that period. Song stylist **Mindy Carson's** refrains started with Johnny Messner expressing the band's theme "Can't We Be Friends" before she went off on her own. **Pat Collins'** fine efforts with my old friend Moe Zudecoff (you know him as Buddy Morrow) and his original band, before he fronted Tommy Dorsey's ghost band, were first rate. Of course, **Harriet Hilliard** was bandleader Ozzie Nelson's swinging vocalist, future wife, radio/tv partner, and, later, mother of lightweight rock and roller legendary Ricky Nelson.

Besides **Dinah Shore** and **Lee Wiley**, **Anita Boyer** also contributed to Leo Reisman's Boston orchestra. Anita was also with Tommy D. Bandleader Buddy Rogers (married later to movie star **Mary Pickford**) showcased **Marilyn Maxwell** (known then as Marvel Maxwell) in the late Twenties in New York City.

Movie beauty and **Connie Haines'** singing buddy **Jane Russell** took her turn band singing with Kay Kyser as did Toni Arden with Al Trace. **Carolyn Grey**, a **Peggy Lee**-like singer sang with Gene Krupa and Woody Herman. Check out her Boogie Blues.. "scats" and all. Blues belter **Vicky Lee** did it all on "Baby Don't Love Me No More" with Lionel Hampton.

Nan Wynn did the honors with Raymond Scott, as did his wife-to-be **Dorothy Collins**, especially with the radio and television shows Your Hit Parade. Artie Shaw established many Song Stars in his band including **Anita Bradley**, **Bonnie Lake**, and **Georgia Gibbs**. **Ella Mae Morse's** wonderful, classic rendition of "Cow, Cow, Boogie" shored up the Freddie Slack Band for a long while. Song stylist **Jane Morgan** did some time with Dick Stabile and his band before her solo career took off. You will remember her version of "Fascination." **June Richmond** was with Cab Calloway on "Angels with Dirty Eyes" and with Jimmy Dorsey too.

Besides our Song Star **Kitty Kallen**, the Jack Teagarden orchestra supported vocalists **Linda Keene**, **Phyllis Lane** and **Sally Lang**, as well as **Jean Arnold**, shared the "mike" with **Jane Essex**, **Kay Doyle**, **Lillian Lane** and **Maxine Sullivan** in the band of Claude Thornhill.

Bandleader Orrin Tucker told me not too long ago that he discovered **Bonnie Baker** and was convinced she could be a singing star. "I brought her into the band and, early in 1939, while we were playing in the Cocoanut Grove in Los Angeles, we recorded "Oh, Johnny" for Columbia. In a few months she was one of the hottest singers in the nation, making our band a big national attraction. "Bonnie almost eclipsed the name of Orrin Tucker. He never would feature a singer after that experience. Tommy Tucker's band showcased **Amy Arnell** in his 1930's appearances mostly in the midwest. Film singer **Alice Faye** articulated her early efforts with Rudy Vallee's band in the Thirties. Surprise for most girl singer fans: The Anson Weeks orchestra highlighted none other than **Dale Evans**, future wife of the "King of the Cowboys" himself, Roy Rogers. She was a soulful singer. **Kay St.Germaine** and **June Knight** also participated in Weeks' group as did Tony Martin and Bob Crosby. Kay became the featured singer with Eddie Cantor on his radio show. Besides the **Lennon Sisters**, **Alice Lon**, **Lois Best** and **Jo Ann Hubbard**, as well as **Roberta Lynn**, also articulated their melodies throughout the years with bandleader Lawrence Welk and a mention for **Daryl Sherman** who has played piano with Dick Sudhalter's band. I interviewed her in the late Eighties and she was a definite, upcoming Song Star then. She's a big-time artist in New York these days - 2008.

June Valli started with Arthur Godfrey's Talent Scouts and performed with the bands of both Ralph Flanagan and Art Mooney. June was a summer replacement for Andy Williams and worked with Johnny Carson and my pal Bob Hope. She was the voice of "Chiquita Banana." **Peggy Clark** (one of the **Clark Sisters**) from North Dakota sang during the war at USO spots and then with Tommy Dorsey from 1943 to 1945. She also sang with the Skylarks in the Harry James band. **Sue Allen** Brown warbled with Benny Goodman and the Hit Parade orchestras and recorded with Henry Mancini, Mel Torme' and Les Baxter. As the renamed Sentimentalists, the **Clark Sisters** big hit was "Sunny Side of the Street" with Tommy Dorsey.

Helen Grayco worked with both the Spike Jones Band and Stan Kenton (at the Hollywood Palladium). She married Spike Jones. "Love and Marriage" and Teach Me Tonight were her best hits with RCA. It was **Mary Ann McCall** who sang with Tommy Dorsey in 1938, Woody Herman in 1939, and Charlie Barnet in 1940. She was a great jazz singer admired by jazzmen. **Gloria Wood** was a singer with Horace Heidt, Hal McIntyre, and Kay Kaiser. She was one of the Johnny Mann Singers and had a great hit with the "Woody Woodpecker Song." **Virginia Craig** Pruett was also a revered Song Star who sang with Bob Crosby, Billy May, Wilbur

Hatch and with the Hilo's, one of the best singing groups ever. And true Song Star **Gilda Maiken (Anderson)** ,one of the famous Skylarks and founders of the Society Of Singers, was a sensation on the **Dinah Shore** TV shows for years and sang with the bands of Herman, J. Dorsey, and James. **Paula Kelly** was

Paula Kelly

wonderful too, best remembered for her membership in the Modernaires singing group with Glenn Miller, although she started with Dick Stabile and later sang with Artie Shaw. **Ginny Mancini**, wife of the wonderful Henry Mancini,sang with Tex Beneke's band after the war, "...an experience I treasure," says Ginny. **Jeanne Hazard**, nee Taylor began with Jimmy Greer and **Jan Savitt** and recorded with Count Basie. Forget not **Lil Armstrong** who sang with husband Satchmo, but also ran her own band in 1937. Catch her "Bluer Than Blue."

Irene Day was a Krupa Song Star and then joined Charlie Spivak whom she eventually married. And remember that bandleader beautiful **Ina Ray Hutton** who also sang pretty good with her own band.

Harry James also featured **Gail Robbins**. Her interpretation of Gershwin's "I've Got a Crush on You" is just elegant. **Della Reese**, current TV angel, did it well with Erskine Hawkins in the early '50's. And, how could you forget **Dorothy Dandridge's** rendition of "Chattanooga Choo-Choo" in the film Sun Valley Serenade.

Any one of these Song Stars could make or break a band. Their joyful voices, filling the air with melodic expression backed by a multitude of talented musicians, prolific arrangers, and innovative band leaders, furnished us with the musical nutrition we needed when we needed it most.

What about Nancy Wilson - the thrush from Columbus, who sang with Rusty Bryant's Band in the 50's?

I hope I haven't left any one out.

THE CANARIES

The Girl Vocalists and their Bands

A listing of 215 Big Band female singers coming to you over the airwaves from a supper club, a ballroom, or a metropolitan hotel. If you didn't know the band, you sure recognized your favorite canary.

"Good Evening, ladies and gentlemen. The coast-to-coast network of the Columbia Broadcasting System presents for your listening and dancing pleasure, from the beautiful Hotel Astor Roof, high atop New York's glamorous Great White Way, the music of Tommy Dorsey and his Sentimental Gentlemen of Swing. To start things off Tommy and his trombone join the boys in the band, along with Frank Sinatra and the Pied Pipers, to invite you for a stroll - 'On the Street of Dreams.' "

A

Dorothy Allen
   Shep Fields
Ivy Anderson
   Duke Ellington
Amy Arnell
   Tommy Tucker

B

Mildred Bailey
   Paul Whiteman
   Red Norvo
Pearl Bailey
   Cootie Williams
Eugenie Baird
   Tony Pastor
   Glen Gray
   Art Mooney
Wee Bonnie Baker
   Orrin Tucker
Penny Banks

   Red Nichols
Betty Benson
   Ray Herbeck
Gracie Barrie
   Dick Stabile
   Abe Lyman
Lois Best
   Lawrence Welk
Rose Blaine
   Abe Lyman
Janet Blair (Lafferty)
   Hal Kemp
Meredith Blake
   Jack Teagarden
Betty Bonne
   Frankie Carle
   Les Brown
Anita Boyer
   Artie Shaw
   Tommy Dorsey
   Jerry Wald
   Leo Reisman
Jean Bowles

Woody Herman
Anita Bradley
   Artie Shaw
Betty Bradley
   Bob Chester
   Gray Gordon
Ruth Bradley
   Bunny Berigan
Dorothy Brandon
   Chuck Foster
Betty Brewer
   Tommy Dorsey
Dolores Brown
   Erskine Hawkins
Wini Brown
   Lionel Hampton
Betty Brownell
   Henry Busse
Bernice Byers
   Harry James
Pauline Byrne
   Artie Shaw
   David Rose

C

Edith Caldwell
   Leighton Noble
   Orville Knapp
Rosemary Calvin
   George Paxton
Kay Carlton
   Henry Jerome
Carmene (Calhoun)
   Skinnay Ennis
Lily Ann Carol
   Louis Prima
   Charlie Ventura
Thelma Carpenter
   Count Basie
   Teddy Wilson
Georgia Carroll
   Kay Kyser
June Christy

Stan Kenton
Savannah Churchill
   Benny Carter
Betty Claire
   Claude Thornhill
Dorothy Claire
   Bobby Byrne
   Sonny Durham
   Glenn Miller
   Bob Crosby
Harriet Clark
   Sonny Durham
Betty Clooney
   Tony Pastor
   Pupi Campo
Rosemary Clooney
   Tony Pastor
Dorothy Collins
   Raymond Scott
Frances Colwell
   Dean Hudson
Chris Connor
   Claude Thornhill
   Stan Kenton
Elisse Cooper
   Eddie DeLange
   Tony Pastor
   Jan Savitt

D

Carlotta Dale
   Jan Savitt
   Will Bradley
Dorothy Dandridge
   Jimmie Lunceford
Jeanne D'Arcy
   Johnny Messner
Ramona (Davies)
   Paul Whiteman
Kay Davis
   Duke Ellington
Dolly Dawn
   George Hall

Doris Day
    Barney Rapp
    Bob Crosby
    Les Brown
Irene Day
    Charlie Spivak
    Gene Krupa
Gloria DeHaven
    Bob Crosby
    Jan Savitt
Jayne Dover
    Van Alexander
    Bunny Berigan
    Joe Haymes
Mary Dugan
    Larry Clinton
Patti Dugan
    Johnny Long
Marilyn Duke
    Vaughn Monroe
Dorothy Dunn
    Kay Kyser
Marianne Dunn
    Will Osborne
    Charlie Ventura

Joan Edwards
    Paul Whiteman
Jean Eldridge
    Duke Ellington
    Teddy Wilson
Marie Ellington
    Duke Ellington
Judy Ellington
    Charlie Barnet
Betty Engles
    McFarland Twins
Dale Evans
    Anson Weeks
Dottie Evans
    Carl Hoff

F

Ella Fitzgerald
    Chick Webb
Nancy Flake
    Frank Dailey
    Red Norvo
Helen Forrest
    Benny Goodman
    Harry James
    Artie Shaw
Kay Foster
    Benny Goodman
    Georgie Auld
    Tony Pastor
Connie Francis
    Tommy Dorsey
Marion Francis
    Frankie Masters

G

Lynn Gardner
    Will Bradley
Ruth Gaylor
    Hal McIntyre
    Hudson-DeLaange
    Bunny Berigan
    Mitchell Ayres
Georgia Gibbs
    Frank Trumbauer
    Hudson-DeLange
    Artie Shaw
Julie Gibson
    Jimmie Grier
Patricia Gilmore
    Enric Madriguera
Eydie Gorme
    Tex Beneke
Betty Grable
    Ted Fio Rita
Dolores Gray
    Richard Himber
Maxine Gray

Hal Kemp
Carolyn Grey
   Woody Herman
Jo Anne Greer
   Les Brown
   Dick Stabile

H

Connie Haines
   Howard Lally
   Harry James
   Tommy Dorsey
Sally Ann Harris
   Art Kassel
   Raymond Scott
Virginia Hayes
   Ben Cutler
Rita Hayworth (Cansino)
   Xavier Cugat
Harriet Hilliard (Nelson)
   Ozzie Nelson
Claire (Shanty) Hogan
   Johnny Bothwell
   Jimmy Dorsey
Louanne Hogan
   Terry Shand
Billie Holiday
   Count Basie
   Artie Shaw
Lena Horne
   Noble Sissle
   Charlie Barnet
Marjorie Hughes
(Ede Carle)
   Frankie Carle
   Paul Martin
Helen Humes
   Count Basie
Frances Hunt
   Lou Bring
   Benny Goodman
   Ben Pollack
Betty Hutton

Vincent Lopez
Marion Hutton
   Glenn Miller

I

Trudy Irwin
   Kay Kyser

J

Ida James
   Erskine Hawkins
   Earl Jones
Ella Johnson
   Buddy Johnson
Vickie Joyce
   Jimmy Dorsey

K

Kitty Kallen
   Jack Teagarden
   Artie Shaw
   Harry James
   Jimmy Dorsey

Carol Kay
   Woody Herman
   Russ Morgan
Sharri Kaye
   Woody Herman
Dee Keating
   Al Donohue
   Ray Anthony
Linda Keene
   Red Norvo
   Lennie Hayton
   Tony Pastor
   Jack Teagarden
Paula Kelly
   Dick Stabile
   Chico Marx
   Artie Shaw

Glenn Miller
Al Donahue
Phyllis Kenny
Jerry Blaine
Shep Fields
Yvonne King
Alvino Rey
Horace Heidt
Jerry Kruger
Gene Krupa

L

Peg La Centra
Artie Shaw
Benny Goodman
Bonnie Lake
Artie Shaw
Jack Denny
Dorothy Lamour
Herbie Kaye
Abbe Lane
Xavier Cugat
Kitty Lane
Bob Chester
Charlie Barnet
Bunny Berigan
Lillian Lane
Claude Thornhill
Jerry Wald
Muriel Lane
Bob Crosby
Woody Herman
Priscilla Lane
Fred Waring
Rosemary Lane
Fred Waring
Helen Lee
Orrin Tucker
Mary Lee
Ted Weems
Peggy Lee
Benny Goodman
Lee Leighton

Jimmy Dorsey
Kay Little
Tony Pastor
Georgie Auld
Shirley Lloyd
Ozzie Nelson
Rose Marie Lombardo
Guy Lombardo
Marcy Lutes
Ray McKinley
Imogene Lynn
Ray McKinley
Artie Shaw
Freddy Slack
Phyllis Lynn
Franke Carle

M

Mary Ann McCall
Woody Herman
Charlie Barnet
Tommy Reynolds
Margaret McCrae
Benny Goodman
Marion Mann
Bob Crosby
Peggy Mann
Enoch Light
Larry Clinton
Teddy Powell
Ben Pollack
Scottee Marsh
Orrin Tuckeer
Dolores Martell
Tony Pastor
Lea Matthews
Woody Herman
Virginia Maxey
Jimmy Dorsey
Ziggy Elman
Tony Pastor
Marvel(Marilyn) Maxwell
Ted Weems

Vi Mele
    Jimmy Dorsey
    Henry Busse
Mary Ann Mercer
    Mitchell Ayres
Dolly Mitchell
    Paul Whiteman
    Kay Kyser
    Stan Kenton
Sue Mitchell
    Woody Herman
Adelaide Moffet
    Enric Madriguera
    Jack Jenney
Liza Morrow
    George Paxton
    Benny Goodman
    Freddy Slack
Ella Mae Morse
    Freddy Slack
    Jimmy Dorsey
Phyllis Myles
    Frankie masters

N

Patricia Norman
    Eddy Duchin
Betty Norton
    Carl Hoff
    Hal McIntyre
    George Paxton

O

Helen O'Connell
    Larry Funk
    Jimmy Dorsey
Anita O'Day
    Gene Krupa
    Stan Kenton
Dolores (Dodie) O'Neil
    Artie Shaw
    Bob Chester

Jack Teagarden

P

Rosalind Patton
    Elliot Lawrence
Madelaine Perry
    Earl Hines
Evelyn Poe
    Bob Zurke
Lucy Ann Polk
    Kay Kyser
    Tommy Dorsey
Ginnie Powell
    Harry James
    Boyd Raeburn
    Jerry Wald
Patti Poweres
    Tony Pastor
    Georgie Auld

R

Leah Ray
    Phil Harris
Nancy Reed
    Skitch Henderson
Gail Reese
    Glenn Miller
    Bunny Berigan
Dottie Reid
    Muggsy Spanier
    Buddy Rich
    George Paxton
Ann Richards
    Stan Kenton
Lynne Richards
    Andy Kirk
    Jimmy Dorsey
June Richmond
    Andy Kirk
    Jimmy Dorsey
Ruth Robin

Phil Harris
Doris Robbins
  Ben Pollack
Gale Robbins
  Art Jarrett
June Robbins
  Eddy Duchin
Lynn Roberts
  Tommy Dorsey
  Charlie Spivack
  Harry James
Betty Roche
  Duke Ellington
  Savoy Ssultans
Billie Rogers
  Woody Herman
  Jerry Wald
Lina Romay
  Xavier Cugat

§

Miriam Shaw
  Les Brown
  Richard Phillips
Lynne Sherman
  Sonny Burke
  Count Basie
Joya Sherrill
  Duke Ellington
Dinah Shore
  Ben Bernie
  Leo Reisman
Ethel Shutta
  George Olsen
Ginny Simms
  Tom Gerun
  Kay Kyser
Keely Smith
  Louis Prima
Helen Southern
  Larry Clinton
Jo Stafford
  Tommy Dorsey

Judy Starr
  Hal Kemp
Kay Starr
  Glenn Miller
  Charlie Barnet
  Joe Venuti
Kay St. Germaine
  Anson Weeks
Frances Stevens
  Jack Denny
  Red Nichols
Roseanne Stevens
  Ozzie Nelson
Maxine Sullivan
  Claude Thornhill
  John Kirby
  Teddy Wilson
  Jimmie Lunceford
  Benny Carter
Kay Swingle
  Ted Fio Rito

T

JoAnn Talley
  Bob Strong
Irene Taylor
  Seger Ellis
Siser Rosetta Tharpe
  Lucky Millinder
Liz Tilton
  Ken Baker
  Buddy Rogers
  Jan Garber
  Bob Crosby
  Ray Noble
Martha Tilton
  Benny Goodman
  Jimmy Dorsey
Louise Tobin
  Benny Goodman
  Bobby Hackett
  Will Bradley
  Jack Jenny

Ruthie Vale
    Dean Hudson
Betty Van
    Benny Goodman
    Vido Musso
Gloria Van
    Hal McIntyre
Sarah Vaughan
    Earl Hiines
    Billy Eckstine

Bea Wain
    Gene Kardos
    Artie Shaw
    Larry Clinton
Jayne Walton
    Lawrence Welk
    Del Courtney
Helen Ward
    Benny Goodman
    Harry James
    Bob Crosby
    Gene Krupa
    Freddy Martin
Fran Warren
    Art Mooney
    Claude Thornhill
    Charlie Barnet
Dinah Washington
    Lionel Hampton
Frances Wayne
    Sam Donohue
    Woody Herman
    Neal Hefti
Martha Wayne (Stewart)
    Claude Thornhill
Kay Weber
    Jimmy Dorsey
    Dorsey Brothers

Bob Crosby
Loyce Whiteman
    Gus Arnheim
Jayne Whitney
    Johnny Hamp
Lee Wiley
    Leo Reisman
    Jess Stacy
Eileen Wilson
    Les Brown
    Will Osborne
Gloria Wood
    Kay Kysere
Edythe Wright
    Tommy Dorsey
Nan Wynn
    Emery Deutsch
    Hal Kemp
    Raymond Scott
    Hudson-DeLange

Helen Young
    Johnny Long

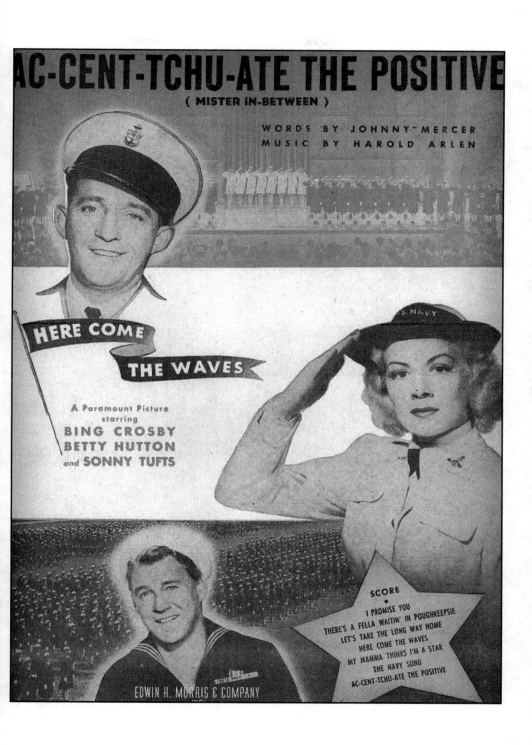

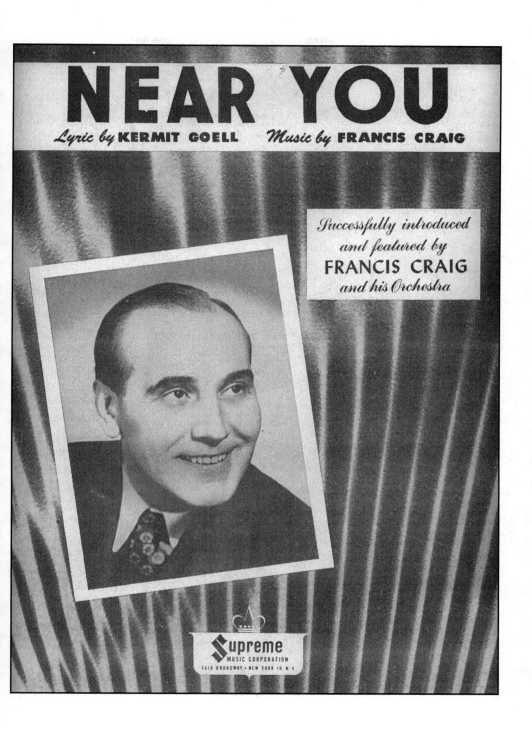

THE SINGING GROUPS

Of The Big Band Era and Beyond

The Southern born Brox Sisters were Kathlyn, Dagmar and Lorraine who were very popular in the first Music Box Revue at the New York Theater that ran from 1921 to 1924, then appeared all over the U.S. in various productions, and in the London version of the same show in 1923. They appeared in the film The King of Jazz in 1930 with the Paul Whiteman Orchestra and Bing Crosby.

The Boswell Sisters - Connee, Martha and Vet

Connee Boswell (lead singer of the Boswell Sisters), who shored up the bands of both Dorseys, Red Nichols, and Don Redman, too, was also the arranger for the singing Boswells. She was Bing Crosby's favorite female partner on the Kraft Music Hall and an early role model for Ella Fitzgerald on "scat" singing. A brave girl confined to a wheelchair most of her career due to an early bout with polio, Connee excelled on piano, sax and trombone, too.

The three Boswell Sisters, Connee (earlier Connie), Martha, and Vet (for Helvetia), who sang earlier as a pre -Andrews Sisters group, were far ahead of their time. They arrived on the music scene in 1925, became nationally prominent in 1931 and were quickly acclaimed . Her family members were her mentors as they all sang together in quartets. The sisters could play many instruments and performed earlier as an instrumental group then graduated to vocalizing, after experimenting with their creative, special sounds. They worked so long and hard together developing their vocal capacity that they became always instantly in tune with one another. After her sisters left the act, Connee continued as a single, setting early styles of jazz-oriented "scat" singing. Her best recordings were "They Can't Take That Away from Me" "The Loveliness of You," "That Old Feeling," "Bob White,"(with Bing Crosby) and "Stormy Weather." Connee passed away on October 12, 1976, at the age of 69. I'm thankful the Andrews Sisters came along and continued the great tradition of the excellent Boswells, aren't you?

The Andrews Sisters

Patty, Maxene, & LaVerne -IT'S APPLE BLOSSOM TIME

I have always been in love with the Andrews Sisters. Ever since I first heard Patty, Maxene, & LaVerne vocalize Bie Mir Bist Du Schoen

, it was the beginning of my long-running affection for them. The three gals from Minneapolis were my personal entertainers. Their recordings punctuated my life at many meaningful milestones. For me, and for millions of others, during World War II and later into the fifties, they were the definitive female strains of the era.

When the girls recorded the favorite, "Rumors Are Flying" and Patty did that doubling-up-jive patter with such melodic perfection, "Whatta-ya-do-do-do that keeps 'em buzzing..." I couldn't wait until the record was over so I could play over and over again.

When I initiated my search for Patty Andrews in 1984, I had almost given up until I obtained the telephone number of her manager, Wally Weschler. So I placed the call and a woman with a familiar ring to her voice answered with a sweet, "Hello, who is this?"

"Hi", said I, and I identified myself, "is this the office of Wally Weschler?"

"Why, Yes!"

"Well, I'm actually looking for Patty Andrews."

"It's me! It's Patty!" was the bubbling reply.

"Patty Andrews?" I repeated in disbelief and relief.

"Yeah!" she shouted.

Well, it was just too easy. Wally turned out to be husband, manager, and musical director.

By her own description, Patty is a very happy and busy singer living in a beautiful, Tudor-style house near Encino, California. During the eighties she regularly worked the California concert circuit with band leaders Tex Beneke, Larry Elgart, and the Harry James Orchestra at places like the Hollywood Palladium. Her concerts consisted of new and refreshing popular songs, but she always finished off a concert with some of the earlier Andrews Sisters evergreens.

After some small chatter, Patty and I settled down to talk about the Andrews Sisters. When they were only teenagers attending dancing school, they began mimicking the then-popular Boswell Sisters, who dominated the late twenties until they broke up in 1936, with Connie continuing on as a soloist. They, like Patty, the youngest, Maxene, a few years older, and LaVerne, the oldest, were actual sisters.

The girls entered the Kiddy Reviews during the summer months on the Orpheum Theater Circuit in Minneapolis. Larry Rich, one of the headliners in the vaudeville show, invited the girls to become a permanent part of his show touring the country on the R.K.O.(Radio-Keith-Orpheum) circuit. They would perform 4 to 5 shows a day sandwiched between movie showings. Not having their own charts or any special arranger, they copied the Boswell arrangements.

"When you are young, there is always someone you look up to," she said, "so we did what they did and it helped launch our career. We would sing things like "Shuffle Off To Buffalo," and "When I Take My Sugar To Tea," and "I Found a Million Dollar Baby in a Five and Ten Cents Store."

The girls enthusiasm and devotion to the Boswell's kept them going and eventually brought them to their own accomplished, personal style. Patty

Patty Andrews - sent to me on her 90th Birthday - 2008

sang the lead and solo parts, Maxene the high harmony, and LaVerne took the third part.

"We would work all day until we perfected new songs in our own new, bouncier style. It was then we realized we had something special to offer."

The girls never took singing lessons: "It wasn't until many years later---after problems with laryngitis---that I finally had to take (singing) lessons to learn how to breathe properly in order to prevent damage to my vocal chords.Patty explained.

"Then one day upon reaching St. Paul, Leon Belasco, a big band leader, heard of us, came to see the show and offered us more money. We were making thirty dollars a week and he would raise it to fifty if we would join up with him," Patty said, "So just like (Frank) Sinatra left Harry James to join Tommy Dorsey to make enough money to live on---we joined Belasco. But," she added, "the band broke up when we got to New York and the only job we could get was singing on the radio twice a week with Billy Swanson's band at the Hotel Edison."

The Andrews Girls

This was to be the girls first big break. Dave Kapp, Vice President of Decca Records, heard them while traveling crosstown in a cab and went directly to the hotel where he found Patty sitting in the lobby during a break. He handed her his card and invited her to show up the next day at Decca.

"It was the beginning of an association that lasted seventeen years." She noted proudly. It was Jack Kapp, however, who was the creative genius behind Decca.

"He was young and aggressive and like a father to us girls. He was Dave's older brother and President of the company. He got us to record with Bing Crosby and later to make movies with the Ritz Brothers, Abbott and Costello, Bob Hope, and Bing.

Their first big recording was taken from an old Yiddish folk song with English words added by Sammy Cahn and Saul Chaplin. "Bie Mir Bist Du Schoen" became a commercial success.

"It's funny," she added, "We only got fifty dollars - me and my sisters-and our mom and dad ---for recording that song," laughing as she reminisced. But we later wrote a better contract with Decca." However, that recording became the catalyst in their career.

Soon they released a constant barrage of wonderful recordings that were rhythmic, bouncy, and gutsy - - - not to exclude that '40's expression---jivey. They swept the country with "Joseph, Joseph," and "Oh, Ma Ma (He wants to Marry Me)," in 1938 and "Hold Tight," "Billy Boy," "Beer Barrel Polka," "Well, All Right," and their first recordings with Bing, "Ciribiribin," "Oh! Johnny, Oh!," and "South America Take It Away" in 1939.

In those takes, Bing took the solo and the girls the choruses: "We loved recording with Bing. It was always so exciting. He always would do a little something unexpected, like the time he sneaked in that line at the end of 'Pistol Packin' Momma' - 'Lay that thing down before it goes off and hurts someone.' He broke us up. We were a compliment to each other," she mused. "Bing would always record at eight in the morning," she revealed, "I guess he used to vocalize in the car on the way to the studio---and he always wore his golf clothes. He claimed his voice had a husky quality in the morning."

In 1940 the hits were, "Hit The Road," "Beat Me Daddy Eight to the Bar," the definitive "I'll Be with You in Apple Blossom Time," and another one of those favorites "Ferry Boat Serenade" .. (you know....."I love to ride the ferry, where people are so merry. There's a man that plays the concert-ina, On the moonlight upper deck-or-ina.") And how about "Boogie Woogie, Bugle Boy (from Company 'B')" from the Abbott and Costello film Buck Privates which all added most agreeably to their musical sky-rocket. All their songs and arrangements during this period were selected by Dave Kapp,their A & R (Artists and Repertoire) man.

"He was even able to choose our movie songs. That's how songs like 'Aurora,' 'Yes, My Darling Daughter,' and 'Daddy (I Want A Diamond Ring)' became ours."

Kapp had the the girls record with Al Jolson, Dick Haymes, Bob Crosby, Woody Herman, Carmen Miranda, Jimmy Dorsey, and even Danny Kaye. The song "Any Bonds Today" which they recorded during the war helped greatly with the sale of Defense Bonds. The girls also sang regularly at Armed Forces Camps, U.S.O.'s, and Stage Door Canteens which were sort of night clubs where armed forces personnel could go cost-free and meet movie stars and other famous celebrities when on liberty or leave.

In 1942 came the memorable, "Don't Sit Under the Apple Tree," the bouncy, "Pennsylvania Polka," and one of the most stirring World War II songs ever recorded, "When Johnny Comes Marching Home." Then came their super-selling recording "Rum & Coca Cola." It sold over seven million copies, a great feat in the wartime forties considering the shortage of shellac, the raw-material that produced the 78's. It was a song recorded only because there was 15 minutes of radio time left to use up and it was "...just stuck in," Patty recalled.

The demand for that recording was so great that both RCA and

Columbia Records gave up their shellac allotment in order to allow Decca to meet the demand.

On a later album with Gordon Jenkins and his orchestra, Patty was soloist on "I Want to Be Loved," and she absolutely excelled with "It Never Entered My Mind." Here is Patty Andrews at her phonetic and melodic best. It is performed so perfectly. Patty was indeed the leader of the girls and all the sounds must be channeled through the leader. The Andrews Sisters succeeded because of Patty's leadership and solos.

The girls performed at the London Palladium in 1950,then broke up a few years later. But, in-between, they performed on their own radio program and made many motion pictures: Stage Door Canteen ,The Road To Utopia (with Bing & Bob) In The Navy, Buck Privates, Argentine Nights, and Follow The Boys.

Maxene passed on October 22, 1995, and LaVerne in 1967.

We're fortunate to have the recordings of the Andrews Sisters, which will probably be used by female group singers as a measure of their own abilities for many years to come.

Shortly after my first Andrews Sisters interview was published in Long Island P.M. Magazine, Patty called me to offer thanks and told me she would use the printed article to help promote her act. That was in 1985. Patty Andrews is now officially retired, although you can find her with friends at California Big Band reunions now and then. We have remained friends over all these years. I sent Patty birthday flowers on her 90th in early February, 2008.

The Pied Pipers

The Original Pied Pipers with Tommy Dorsey

Of course, the Pipers were around even before Jo Stafford joined the once all-male singing group back in the California movie studio days. The original members were John Huddleston, Chuck Lowry, Hal Hopper, Woody Newbury, Whit Whittinghill, Bud Hervey, and John Tait. It became an octet with the addition of Jo Stafford.

The group came to the attention of the public while performing on the Raleigh-Kool radio show in 1938, when Tommy Dorsey hired the group to sing with his band. Because he could not afford to pay eight singers, Tommy let them go after the show. When the group re-emerged as a quartet - three guys and a gal, Tommy reconsidered and rehired them. The group was now composed of Jo Stafford, Chuck Lowry, Clark Yocum, and John Huddleston.

While with Tommy Dorsey, the Pipers sometimes backed singers Connie Haines, Frank Sinatra, and later Dick Haymes, especially on specialty songs and recordings. Frank would always do his best to work harmonically with the group. Jo was a very cool and calm singer, but always considered herself simply the distaff member although she sang lead. Their

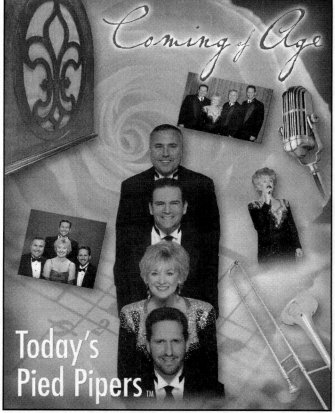

Top to Botton Kevin Kennard, Don Lucas, Nancy Knorr and Chris Sanders

first and biggest hit "I'll Never Smile Again," was written by Ruth Lowe who, while mourning the loss of her husband, was inspired to compose the song. "Oh! Look At Me Now" was another big hit, written by pianist Joe Bushkin and included my friend Connie Haines and Frank Sinatra.

During that time the Pipers and Dorsey made the movies Ship Ahoy and DuBarry Was Lady for MGM with Frank Sinatra, Jo Stafford, Buddy Rich and Ziggy Elman as stars. The Pipers remained with Dorsey for two years: 1940 to 1942.

The Pipers began working with Johnny Mercer, becoming the first artists to sign with his newly-formed Capitol Records. That recording and now Piper theme song Dream won the first Gold Record for Capitol and the Pipers and was featured on their Chesterfield Music Shop radio show.

They performed with Frank Sinatra on the Lucky Strike program Your Hit Parade. In 1944 June Hutton, bandleader Ina Ray Hutton's younger sister and wife of arranger Axel Stordahl, replaced Jo Stafford who left to go on her own at the urging of Johnny Mercer who wanted her to record solo for Capitol. She had just married Capitol arranger and leader Paul Weston.

Warren Covington: The Pipers with June, who remained for four years, appeared in the film Make Mine Music in 1946. When Tommy Dorsey suddenly died in his sleep on November 26, 1956, Willard Alexander, head of the booking agency, called upon me to front the Tommy Dorsey Band which I did until 1962. At that time the Pipers were simply composed of various studio singers.

In the Seventies, because of my association with Tommy Dorsey's great band, I was asked to organize a "salute" to Tommy and include a vocal group like the Pipers. Researching ownership of the Pied Pipers, I learned that no one had retained rights so I was able to obtain ownership through properly registering copyrights and trademarks. The smooth sounds of the Pied Pipers were alive once again.

At one time Lillian Clark Oliver, one of the Clark Sisters and Sy Oliver's wife, performed with the Pipers for a while, as did lead singer Lynn Roberts, Tommy's former soloist."

During the Eighties and right up to today, the Pipers still play "gigs" at showcases everywhere with Big Tribute Bands like Tommy Dorsey (under Buddy Morrow's direction. Of course, personnel in the Pipers has revolved throughout the years. The group today is composed of singers Nancy Knorr, Chris Sanders, Don Lucas, and Kevin Kennard. Some of their best performances have been" I'll Never Smile Again," "Sunny Side of the Street," "At Last," "Dream," "There Are Such Things," "Street of Dreams," and "Oh, Look at Me Now," all perennial favorites and all done in the original arrangements. The Pipers still have millions of fans. They wrote the book on singing groups. Their timeless songs and the nostalgia evoked by those memories keep the Pied Pipers music going and going.

Nancy Knorr, a Song Star in her own right with her own unique style, has been a classical musician, playing viola with the St.Louis Philharmonic Orchestra and in many chamber groups. As a vocalist Nancy has performed over the years with the Tommy Dorsey Orchestra, Les Brown's Band of Renown, Tex Beneke's band, as well as the Warren Covington and Jimmy Dorsey bands. As Pied Piper proprietor and lead singer, Nancy continues to tour and also solos with the Pipers, to recreate the elegance and sound of America's greatest music.

The Ink Spots

Bill Kenny, Orville "Happy" Jones, Charlie Fuqua, and Ivory "Deek" Watson were the original Ink Spots, one of the best singing quartets during the Big Band Era . Throughout the forties they produced the numbers "We Three," "I Don't Want to Set the World On Fire," "I'm Making Believe," and, with Ella, Fitzgerald "Cow-Cow-Boogie" and "Into Each Life Some Rain Must Fall." I liked the Ink Spots performing "If I Didn't Care" - didn't you? Al Rivers, a later Ink Spot from 1949 to 1958, recorded all the famous numbers and even started another Ink Spots in 1985.

The Ink Spots

The "Mods" Modernaires

When Glenn Miller was adding more musicians to his band he extended it even further, experimenting with a singing group known as the Modernaires, whose spokesman was Hal Dickenson.

The Modernaires

"The first time we did anything with Glenn was recording the theme for WNEW disc jockey Martin Block. It was entitled "It's Make Believe Ballroom Time," and was re-corded on October 11, 1940. And, that's where Glenn first got the idea that he wanted to have a quartet singing with his band. And, just a few recording sessions later, we became an official part of the Glenn Miller organization for good."

On Christmas day of 1940, the Moder-naires stepped into New York's Pennsylvania Hotel, located the beautiful Cafe Rouge, and sat down there in their raggedy clothes. Observing the band in rehearsal, they were awe stricken by the hearty, twangy vocals of Tex Beneke, and were mesmerized by the musical excellence of the number one band in the world, a band who had just won the coveted "Billboard" listeners poll.

"The fact that we were going to appear with the band was almost breathtaking. Glenn bought us dinner. If we'd have known that in advance, we would have had something more expensive to eat. We officially joined with the band in 1941. At the first session we performed a Jimmy Van Heusen song, 'You stepped out of a dream.'"

The Modernaires were a group of four musical guys with diverse backgrounds from Buffalo, New York. Hal Dickenson was the lead singer and a Presbyterian; Ralph Brewster, a Christian Scientist who played trumpet; Chuck Goldstein was a Jew, and Bill Conway was a Catholic, who also played guitar. None of them read music. They sang and played, as they say, strictly by ear.

Chuck Goldstein: "Hal was the lead singer, but could only sing the melody. I could sing both upper and lower harmony. Bill would sit with his guitar and we would learn our songs working together in our own special harmony. And we made pretty good money, getting a hundred and twenty-five bucks each, plus bonus'"

The "Mods" had been working with Paul "Pops" Whiteman, who graciously allowed them to tear up their contract in order for them to join up with Glenn. Glenn felt the presence of a vocal group would attract customers around the bandstand enabling people to stand eye-to-eye with both players and vocalists.

Aside from the great hits "Chattanooga Choo Choo," "Don't Sit Under the Apple Tree" and "Kalamazoo," the Mods introduced with Glenn Miller, they also produced the beautiful ballad "Perfidia," with Dorothy Claire, "You Stepped Out of a Dream," with Ray Eberle, "Sweeter Than the Sweetest," with Paula Kelly, "Booglie Wooglie Piggy," also with Paula Kelly and Tex Beneke, as well as "I Know Why," one of Glenn's greatest hits, also with Paula Kelly. Of course, the hits came through the years until the disbanding of Glenn's civilian band in September of 1942.

Billy May arranged specifically for the Modernaires from time to time.

"When the Mods wanted to do something other than backing up the featured singers, they came up with 'Sweeter Than The Sweetest,' so I made a special arrangement for them. Chuck Goldstein and Hal Dickinson and I were never really happy with that arrangement, but Glenn was in a hurry to get it to the recording studio. I think it could have been even better. With Glenn, you know, the band was always very well rehearsed and everything was marked. There was no need to conduct the band because it always was so well rehearsed. So with great arrangements and strong rehearsals, the band didn't need anyone standing up there waving a baton."

Today's Modernaires are known as the Moonlight Serenaders.. Julia Rich is the lone female singer with the Mods today combined with playing members of the band doubling up as vocalists. You could close your eyes and appreciate each interpretation of the original charts with full orchestral backing, transporting you back a few years evoking the sounds of the original Modernaires.

The Mills Brothers

With Dan Clemson

On April 29, 1998, Donald Mills celebrated his 83rd birthday and his 74th year as an entertainer. For the past three years he had served as patriarch of the Mills family in America. In February, 1998 The Mills Brothers were honored with a Grammy Lifetime Achievement Award. What a deserved, uplifting honor for this amazing man and his wonderful brothers!

The Mills Brothers

In January of 1998, I received an encouraging word from Donald Mills' son, John: "I have received your request to interview my father with regards to your book. He will be happy to talk to you next week. Best Wishes." John H. Mills,II. This was a break and a privilege for me since Donald Mills had avoided personal interviews in the last few years.

Donald Mills was then the sole survivor of the renowned all-male singing group, The Mills Brothers. He continued to pursue his lifelong odyssey as a singer. The Society for the Preservation and Promotion of The Mills Brothers Musical History is the personal passion of founder and editor of Remembering the Mills Brothers Newsletter, Dan Clemson. Dan has written much about this first black troupe to break through racial barriers who had gained a mass following in the USA, reaching plateaus never thought possible by any vocal group in their time.

According to Dan Clemson: "The parents of the four Mills Brothers, John Charles, Herbert Bowles, Harry Flood and Donald Friedlich, were gifted singers. John Mills Sr. sang and managed the Four Knights of Harmony, a traveling barbershop quartet, and Eathel Harrington Mills performed in light opera. The boys sang for pennies in front of their dad's barbershop when the youngest was seven and the oldest twelve. The influences were certainly there for them, as well as the vocal training acquired from their parents, and the hands-on experience they received as church choir members."

The Four Boys and a Kazoo (a popular tinny, musical toy) started their career at the Mays Opera House in Piqua, Ohio, an event that would alter their musical style and catapult them to fame as a quartet. Stage fright before a large audience and the fact that young John had forgotten the all-important kazoo, the desperate trouper cupped his hands over his mouth and to the surprise of everyone produced sounds far better than that of the tinny kazoo, causing a sensation. What a revelation- what a sound! What an idea!

By now, the boys, John-bass, Herbert- tenor, Harry - baritone, and Donald- lead---added realistic imitations of various musical instruments to their barbershop harmonies. Mastery of the sounds of first, second ,and third trumpet, combined with the accompaniment of a $ 6.25 mail-order guitar played by John, would soon earn them the title of the "human orchestra."

The boys, now with matured voices, impressed programmers at radio station WLW, Cincinnati, and were hired. Within a year, they left and with the help of Duke Ellington and Seger Ellis (the Mills long-time manager), made their way to New York City in 1929, auditioned for CBS radio, and signed a three-year contract with a young, fledging radio executive named William S. Paley. They went from $ 140.00 a week to $3,250.00 thanks to their radio show and a 14 week engagement at the Palace Theater, where they shared the bill with Bing Crosby, establishing one of the fastest climbs in show business.

Their first recording with Brunswick, "Tiger Rag" and "Nobody's Sweetheart," reached the top of the charts, becoming the first million-selling record ever by a vocal group. Their unique sound caught the attention of the movie studios, and in 1932 they appeared with Bing Crosby in his first starring film, The Big Broadcast, singing "Hold That Tiger." The film also featured a now legendary cast of greats: George Burns and Gracie Allen, Kate Smith, Cab Calloway, The Boswell Sisters, and The Street Singer-- Arthur Tracy. It was the first of their 14 feature film appearances: "We did a lot of cartoons too, you know, the bouncing ball films where we sang the lyrics and everybody in the audience sang along," Donald explained, "It was wonderful going from cartoon to The Mills Brothers."

The boys vocalized their way through Twenty Million Sweethearts in 1934, Broadway Gondolier in 1935 (with Gary Cooper), Reveille with Beverly in 1943, and When You're Smiling in 1950. Interesting sidelight:

Brunswick printed a disclaimer on every Mills Brothers recording: "No musical instruments or mechanical devices used on this recording other than the guitar," because their special sounds were often mistaken for the real thing.

"Shine," with Bing, reached number one in January 1932, the first of a string of Top 10 tunes that year." 'Good-bye Blues,' our theme from the start, was finally recorded in 1932," said Don, "The flipside was "Rockin Chair" with Harry doing a talking bass bridge and me repeating the lyrics on the afterbeat." In 1933, the Mills and Bing Crosby recorded "My Honey's Lovin' Arms" on January 26th. The musical sounds reproduced by those wonderful guys are astounding. It is my preferred Mills Brothers/Bing Crosby recording, also featuring Bunny Berigan on trumpet, Tommy Dorsey on trombone, and Eddie Lang on guitar at the beginning and close of the record. What a collection of talent on one recording.

The Mills Brothers performed with many big bands: "Diga Diga Do" with the great Duke Ellington, "Doin the Low-Down" with the wild Cab Calloway, "In the Shade of the Old Apple Tree" with jazz master Louis Armstrong, "we exhibited our drive and even dared to emulate instruments." Don recalled.

"In 1934, we played London's Palladium and were even invited to appear before King George V and Queen Mary, the first Command Performance ever by black artists. I guess we were the Beatles of the 1930s. Harry later loved to tell our audiences that anecdote."

After the death of young John from a lung ailment, the boy's father took his place, literally saving the group from disbanding. He remained rhythmic bass for the next twenty years. The Mills Brothers' career spanned the world, and in 1942 they unearthed an old, unknown song called "Paper Doll."

"When we first heard the song, we didn't like it. So, we worked on it, came up with a new concept and recorded it," Donald remembered, "It was a turning point for us." The recording remained number one for 30 weeks, including 12 weeks on Your Hit Parade radio program.

Other great hits during this period include "Up a Lazy River," "You Always Hurt the One You Love," "Till Then" and with new lyrics by Johnny Mercer, "Glow-Worm." When their father retired in 1956, they carried on as a trio, continuing on the club circuit and recording sessions. On Dot Records, they recorded "Get a Job" and "Cab Driver" in 1968.

And, according to Dan Clemson: "By 1981, the boys disbanded after 56 fruitful years. Harry passed away in 1982 and Herbert in 1989. Don and his son, John Hutchinson II, continued on after a brief respite, becoming the fourth generation of Mills family performers. The duo's soundshave always featured a repertory of old Mills Brothers favorites, and are strikingly similar to that of the former trio. But, they would never add a non-family member."

"We considered that way back in 1936 when our brother passed away," Don added, "We tried different guys and it never worked. So, we decided against it, and our father ended up joining us. There are natural harmonies in family groups, a special blend. There are only two of us now, but young John and I are accorded the same standing ovations that the full group received throughout the decades. We flip-flop the harmony parts, just as we used to do, and take turns singing lead."

Henry Miller, then president of General Artists Corporation, has been faithfully booking Mills engagements all over the world for over 50 years. "It's remarkable how the two men achieve the same harmony and beat the original group had, "he told me recently.

So, how do they do it? "The simplicity of the songs that we sing makes the audience tap their feet and clap their hands," said Don, "Lyrics you can understand, melodies that are melodic, does it just fine." Of course, you have to add the inimitable Mills' skills.

No one knows how long Donald will continue to sing: "It's been a long, long road. I thought I would be retired by now. But, I enjoy singing; this is my life," Don said to me then. "And I have my son to work with, so everything's going to be just fine."

"The Mills Brothers were the genesis of modern-day black harmony singing," continued Dan Clemson, "They were preceded by a handful of black groups in the style of the traditional camp meeting shouts. The Mills raised the black vocal group from one of novelty status to a commercially accepted form. This singularly unique family fed the dreams of younger black artists and showed them they could reach for the stars..... and touch them. The later accession of Motown groups proves that to be true.

The Lennon Sisters
Jimmy Durante's "Goils"

The first question I posed to the lovely Lennon Sisters, after four solid kisses planted one by one on their cheeks followed by a variety of giggles, was "Did Jimmy Durante really call you 'my goils?'" I asked them one summer's night backstage at a performance.

"Oh! yes," replied Kathy. "He loved us and we loved him. We appeared with him on our joint television show in 1969."

I had just stepped into their dressing room after completing an interview with Nashville music legend Eddie Arnold. Eddie's manager, Jerry Purcell, unexpectedly invited us to meet the other act in the show, the precocious, now grown-up Lennon Sisters- Janet, Kathy, Diane, and Peggy. While I began the inquisition , my photographer Camille Smith did the camera clicking. "Where are you girls going these days....what's happening? It seems a long time since we've heard from you."

The Lennon Sisters

Dianne
Kathy
Peggy
Janet

"Well...we travel ...maybe four or five times a year --when it's beneficial money-wise for us to all go together." They all talked at once. "We have to support our stageman and drummer too. We usually back up people like Andy Williams and Eddy (Arnold) in places like Vegas and sometimes we travel as our own single act. We try to bring along some of the kids and husbands if we can...but at different times. We limit it to three or four trips a year....the most." The girls always sang those catchy, jaunty, specialty tunes they have been famous for.

"In what kinds of situations?"

"Places like this....theaters in the round...or at state fairs. We'll be moving on to Atlantic City right after this." This was 1986 and the four girls never looked lovelier or acted more enthusiastic, like kids on a carousel, each trying to grab the ring. The familiar faces with those infectious smiles made it an absolute joy to be with them.

"The youngest one is Janet, right?" They stood together with kimonos draped over their bodies, expecting to go onstage in about forty-five minutes. We had interrupted "make-up" time.

"That's me," answered Janet from behind. Janet was the most famous face of the Lennons.

"Is it true...at least that's what I have heard...that you quit (Lawrence) Welk because he would not give you a raise after a long time on a very low salary?" I presumptuously inquired to get things started.

"Basically, yes," answered Kathy, "We began with him--being four girls in one family...and he paid us scale. But we were there a long time at group scale and felt we deserved solo scale," they argued, "but, when we got married and were raising children and so on....what we took home...simply wasn't enough for the time we were spending away which was a full five days a week."

The girls had been with Welk for almost 12 years.

Welk had reasoned that they were gaining fame and attention appearing on his world-famous television show and that was to be considered a sort of payment. Welk was known to pay all his performers only scale. The girls took home only $ 100.00 each. He believed they could make fabulous sums at appearances at state fairs on their own time with the publicity they received from being on his show. The girls began in 1955 on Welk's Christmas Show and surprised the experts by drawing 30 million viewers almost every week.

"Oh, sure! It was a wonderful showcase for what it was, but we had gotten to the point where we needed to grow and so we ended up going on the road," said Kathy, who seemed to be general spokeswoman for the group.

"Leaving the Welk show came at a time when we wanted to grow musically and didn't want to be treated as little girls," piped up Janet, "and so this allowed us to leave town these four times a year and make----- FIFTY---times more money than to stay and do the Welk show. It worked out much better for us financially."

"Was Welk upset about it?" I asked. It was widely reported that he was.

"I don't know...we were with him for twelve-and-a half years. We loved him very much, and he us. He raised us. We were just little kids. There are no hard feelings. We had to make a change and maybe he didn't understand," they replied over camera directives and clicks.

The Lennons' sentimental ballads and sweet songs executed in close harmony was a welcome contrast for viewers and listeners compared to the rock and roll being promoted to the public at that time.

"There are so many people we meet that played with our paper dolls and colored in our coloring books and now they're all the same age as we are and they are now parents like us. We grew up right alongside our fans, "Peggy was saying.

Camille dutifully posed the girls standing around a kneeling me," This is going to be the best picture of my life, "I said...to more giggles, then, "O.K., girls. For the record I would like each one to state their name and age and how many children you have."

"All right...I'll start......I'm Peggy, and I'm married to Dick Cathheart and we have six children." Dick was a trumpet player in the Welk organization and was currently freelancing. "Married nineteen years next week."

"I'm Diane and married to Dick Gass and have three children, two girls eighteen and nineteen and a boy seventeen who plays in a rock band."

"Okay! I'm Janet and married to John Bahler--second marriage--(the first to ABC page Lee Bernhardi and had three children) and have five children and am raising them all."

"Oh, God!" I muttered, "little Janet, an American institution is married with teenage children."

The girls infectious laughter brightened the room.

"I'm last...I'll finish off. I'm Kathy and married to Jim Derhris who is a chiropractor and we have no children and we've just been married one year. This is my second marriage. (The first was to Mahlon Clark, another Welk musician who also played with Ray McKinley's band.)

Back in those days the top programs were the Ed Sullivan Show on Sunday and Lawrence Welk's on Saturday nights. That was it for musical variety shows. Everybody knew where to find the Lennons.

"Now, when you go home and the show is over and all the lights are gone, what do you do?"

"We do what every other housewife does. We scrub floors and take care of our children and husbands," said Kathy. "We all live in L.A. and see each other almost every day. One of us teaches school. At the time there was not one pool or grandiose house among the four, even though they really could have afforded it."

"We spend our evenings watching television and enjoying our families," boasted Janet.

"We love our homes and family, and we also love our careers." said Diane," and all of our sons play in rock bands and perform at school."

"Do you all get along as sisters?" I treaded carefully with that one.

"Yes," said Diane, "We really do! We have seven other brothers and sisters, so we have a large family."

May You Always

Words and Music by
LARRY MARKES and DICK CHARLES

Recorded by
THE McGUIRE SISTERS
on Coral Records

HECHT-LANCASTER & BUZZELL, INC.
Sole Selling Agent: Keys-Hansen, Inc. • 119 West 57th Street • New York 19, N.Y.

"When you are preparing for a tour, how do you get it all together?"

"When we put in new material, we learn the music, we learn the dancing. We rehearse and rehearse, but only the new stuff, otherwise we know our regular parts and need minimum rehearsing. Once it's up 'here,'" Janet said pointing to the brain behind her forehead, "we never have to rehearse it again."

The girls' appearance was a happy, upbeat, uptempo show with lots of close harmony. "We get to do old songs, new songs, production numbers with four costume changes, and thoroughly enjoyable vignettes."

"The audiences are incredible," the girls declared almost in unison, forever talking over one another, "there are always standing ovations every night."

"It's always a good, warm crowd," Janet Lennon reassured me.

The Lennons enjoyed that, and so did we.

The McGuire Sisters

Christine, Dorothy and Phyllis have done this and been there in a wonderful 46 year career that took them from Middletown, Ohio to five White House appearances. After some church work they won a spot on Arthur Godfrey's Talent Scouts where they remained for six years that led to a full career on top TV shows and performances from Las Vegas to the Waldorf Astoria. Some of their top recordings were "Sincerely," "Goodnight Sweetheart, Goodnight," "Sugartime," "May You Always," and "Picnic." The McQuire Sisters were the natural followers of the Andrews Sisters and were popular in the 1950's and '60s. The three girls are alive and well.

The King Sisters

Donna, Yvonne, Louise, and Alyce King gained prominence during the Big Band Era with dozens of hits: "In the Mood," "Rose O'Day," "Jersey Bounce," "Milkman, Keep Those Bottles Quiet," "Saturday Night is the Loneliest Night of the Week,"and "Six Lessons from Madame La Zonga." The girls were from Salt Lake City and were regulars on Kay Kyser's radio shows then joined a new band formed by Luise's husband, legendary guitarist Alvino Rey. The made the "Hut Sut Song" and "I'll Get By" hits for the band.

Alvino and the King Sisters: Yvonne, Donna, Louise and Alyce

The King Family show ran from the 1960's until 1969 as the girls eased into retirement.

The Hi-Lo's

It was 24 year old Gene Puerling who founded the Hi-Lo's in 1953. This quartet of fine singers had no category. They sang pop, jazz, barbershop, calypso, and musician theater as well during the 50's and 60's. Their unusual arrangements set them apart from all other male groups. Members Bob Strassen (replaced by Don Shelton in 1959), Clark Burroughs, and Bob Morse excelled on "June in January," "Fools Rush In," "Whatever Lola Wants," with their incredible vocal range. They recorded a great album with Rosemary Clooney: Ring Around Rosie.

The Ames Brothers

The four Ames Brothers began it all in Malden, Mass in a nonprofessional but musical family. The boys Gene, Vic, Joe and Eddie were brought up on classical music by their parents who were Russian Jewish immigrants from the Ukraine who read Shakespeare and semi-classics to their nine children.

The Ames Brothers

They performed touring Army and Navy bases and were offered a job in Boston and the Fox and Hounds nightclub under the name the Armory Brothers and built a popularity. They got work with Art Mooney's orchestra and were "discovered" by Milt Gabler of Decca Records who had them cut a few sides just before the recording ban. When the ban was lifted they were the first artists to record for Coral Records. They shortened the name to Ames when they recorded the sensational single "Rag Mop" with "Sentimental Me" on the other side.

They became regulars on the Arthur Godfrey and Ed Sullivan shows. The boys recorded the popular "Undecided" with Les Brown's band.

The DeCastro Sisters

In 1945 the DeCastro family moved to the United States from Cuba and became portages of famed movie star Carmen Miranda and formed a singing trio in Miami, Florida. Peggy, Cherie and Babette De Castro's style emulated the Andrews Sisters, but with a slight difference, an added Latin flavor. Their biggest hit is "Teach Me Tonight" in 1954.

The Fontane Sisters

The Fontane Sisters, who backed Perry Como all the way, were Bea. Geri and Margi Rosse, originally all from New Milford, New Jersey.

They first performed with their guitarist brother, Frank, who was killed in the war. They joined with Perry Como on his radio show 1945-1948 and continued on Perry's television show thru the 1950s aand on many subseqent recordings.You may add the Dinning Sisters, the Four Aces, Kirby Stone Four, Four Lads, Mel Torme's Meltones (See Torme chapter), The Merry Macs, and Tommy Dorsey's Sentimentalists.

The Fontane Sisters

Honorable Mentions

Some other groups were The Four Aces ("Love is a Many Splendored Thing") The Four Lads ("Moments to Remember)," The Lettermen, The Four Freshmen, and the lone Roy Kral (half of the Jackie (Cain) and Roy team), contributing their versions of the songs of the era. And how about the Kirby Stone Four, the Merry Macs, and Tommy Dorsey's Sentimentalists.

The Four Aces

You will recall the popular singing group 6 Hits and a Miss: Bill Seckler, Tony Paris, Marvin Bailey, Lee Gotch, Vincent Degen, and Mac McLean are the 6 Hits who performed for Capitol Records and on Bob Hope's show and backed Dick Haymes on some Decca discs.

Fred Waring and his Pennsylvanians featured the voices of the harmonious Lane Sisters (Rosemary, Priscilla, and Lola). The Chordettes sang "Mr. Sandman" recorded with Archie Bleyer.

theme song of
SIX HITS AND A MISS
featured on Bob Hope's Program

PART FOUR

Big Band Associates

The Broadcasters

BIG BAND ASSOCIATES

JOHN HAMMOND was the quintessential jazz fan. He loved jazz and blues. He was born wealthy and used his own money to produce records and encourage musicians and vocalists. In the thirties, John worked for Columbia Records and produced recordings with Fletcher Henderson, Billie Holiday, Bessie Smith, and later Benny Goodman. Benny married John's sister, Alice. Besides shaping the careers of artists like Holiday, Basie, and Goodman, he also later uncovered the talents of Pete Seeger, Aretha Franklin, Bob Dylan, and Bruce Springsteen.

John Hammond

John Hammond was important to jazz, and thus to popular music. He traveled endlessly to sell the world Big Band music.

MITCH MILLER

Frankie Laine and I talked about Mitch Miller in late 1998.

"At Mercury, Mitch became the new kid on the block. He was a classical guy, and I figured 'What's a guy like him going to do for me?' I soon found out he was smart and eager for advice, and a great storyteller. Mitch demonstrated a talent for setting off voices in original, if not downright quirky, musical settings. Who else would've put a harpsichord on a Rosemary Clooney record, or backed Guy Mitchell with swooping French horns?

After working with one another and getting to understand our mutual needs, Mitch came up with a song that he considered a combination of "Old Man River" and "Black

Jove–
Mitch
Miller

and Blue." We took it over to my piano accompanist and friend Carl Fischer's house and listened to it. The title was 'That Lucky Old Sun.' It was a change of pace for me, but it was a fantastic song and I decided it would be a good way to begin our association. The rest, as they say, is history."

When he moved to Columbia as A& R man, Mitch selected the song "Singing the Blues" for Guy Mitchell, "Cold, Cold Heart" for Tony Bennett, "Half as Much" and "Come On-a-My House" for Rosemary Clooney, "Cry" and "Just Cryin' in the Rain" for Johnnie Ray, "Two Purple Shadows" for Jerry Vale, and "American Beauty Rose" for Frank Sinatra. Not a bad list of hits. Mitch and Frank Sinatra did not get along very well, so Guy Mitchell wound up with hits that otherwise would've been Sinatra's.

Mitch Miller's own hit recordings with his Mitch Miller and the Gang begun in 1950 with his adaptation of the Israeli folk song "Tzena, Tzena, Tzena" with a choral background, became his signature. Songs like "The Yellow Rose of Texas" and "The Children's Marching Song" from the film The Inn of The Sixth Happiness, were great Miller successes.

Over the last few years Mitch Miller spends his time mainly directing George Gershwin works in symphony halls. An endeavor bringing him back to his early classical roots.

WILLARD ALEXANDER
BIG BAND SALESMAN

In 1934, young Willard Alexander, a bright 'band booker' who was working for MCA (Music Corporation Of America) representing and promoting such popular sweet bands as Wayne King, Sammy Kaye, Horace Heidt, Guy Lombardo, and Eddy Duchin, crossed over to work for the equally large and aggressive talent agency, William Morris, up until then a mostly vaudeville and nightclub star agency. There he initiated a big band department and developed a creative and efficient group handling such veterans as Duke Ellington, Paul Whiteman, and Count Basie, and bravely took on numerous new and untried avant -garde musical organizations like those of Dizzy Gillespie, Billy Eckstine, and Charlie Spivak. He brought them to the attention of the public through strategic bookings in theaters, pavilions and night clubs all over the United States.

He eventually formed his own, now legendary, Willard Alexander Agency

Inc. of Madison Avenue (New York) and with satellite offices in Chicago, Beverly Hills, and London, England, he represented the cream of the music industry.

I have concluded that Willard Alexander, known to be a tough business man, was really a very gentle and self-effacing man; a man with vision , and clearly a gentleman of the golden era, that he must somehow be held responsible for the success of many key players of the Big Band Era.

One night in 1983 I ran into Willard Alexander backstage at Westbury Music Fair on Long Island where he had booked The Glenn Miller Orchestra with Larry O'Brien as the current leader. We found ourselves on a park-style bench in the hallway listening to Dizzy Gillespie relate funny stories, as he was always inclined to do at gatherings, and began our own intimate conversation.

"I guess you've been through this sort of thing a thousand times." I said referring to the gathering in the hall just before showtime, the noise almost drowning out our exchange of words.

"Well, quite a few over a period of many years....I guess that's true. But, I always like to attend the opening night of a band run. It's something I've always done." Willard had a bandage on his nose, having just returned from his doctor, the result of a minor operation earlier in the day. With the anesthesia wearing off, he was beginning to feel a bit uncomfortable and was being constantly interrupted by well-wishers who somehow knew of his condition:

"Willard, I hope you don't mind me asking all these old and obvious questions."

"Oh, No! I'm always glad to talk about this wonderful business."

"How long have you been doing all this?"

"Well, I was an agent in business in Philadelphia even when I was in college at the University of Pennsylvania where I was a junior. I majored in music, studied music, and followed musicians. But then I joined MCA which was a growing agency in 1934 and, of course, it became the largest agency in the business. I was there for 6 years. Then I resigned and founded the band department for the William Morris Agency and then I soon opened my own agency which I still have today...which is representation of many big bands."

It was actually a panacea of the Big Bands including Benny Goodman, Count Basie, Buddy Rich, Glenn Miller, Duke Ellington, Jimmy Dorsey, Tommy Dorsey, Artie Shaw, and even Vaughn Monroe.

"Of course you know John Hammond well, but do you still get together with him on talent hunts like the old days?"

"Sure, we get together occasionally, but he's not feeling too well these days." He said. Actually it was Hammond who urged Willard to fly out to Kansas City with him where they discovered Count Basie, who

Hammond had heard on the radio while riding in a taxi.

Willard explained that Hammond was a wealthy young man who just liked music so much that he supported it and was always bringing new faces he thought were good and promoted them wherever and whenever he could. Billie Holiday and Benny Goodman were also discovered by Hammond. He introduced Willard to Benny, and after hearing Benny play, Willard booked him immediately on the Let's Dance radio program in 1935.

"He never was an agent or booker, he just got a kick out of it." Willard said. "You know Benny married Hammond's sister and they had two girls."

I liked Willard Alexander. He was really from the old school. A perfect gentleman from an earlier time, he wore a characteristic pin-striped, three-piece suit with a white oxford button-down shirt and a polka-dot tie. It was Willard who represented Benny Goodman at the time of the landmark 1938 Carnegie Hall Jazz Concert.

"Willard, that had to be quite a feat, you know, to get a popular jazz band to play one of the world's finest theaters where heretofore only serious classical music was performed."

The corridor noise was becoming so deafening that Willard began to shout his answers into my ears: "BELIEVE IT OR NOT, IT WAS VERY EASY TO MAKE BOOKINGS FOR THE JAZZ BANDS AT THAT TIME ALMOST ANYWHERE, THEY WERE BECOMING IN GREAT DEMAND AT ALL THE PAVILIONS."

"HOW DID YOU KNOW THE WORLD WAS READY FOR BENNY GOODMAN?"

"WELL, WE THOUGHT BENNY'S NAME WAS KNOWN WELL ENOUGH TO TRY IT. IT WAS A GUY NAMED WYNN NATHANSON, A PUBLIC RELATIONS MAN WHO WAS WORKING WITH BENNY ON THE CAMEL CARAVAN SHOW, WHO RECOMMENDED WE DO A CONCERT AT CARNEGIE HALL, BELIEVING THE WORLD WAS READY FOR BENNY'S KIND OF STUFF. YOU KNOW....IN THOSE DAYS THERE WERE VERY FEW CONCERT HALLS---NO AVERY FISHER OR LINCOLN CENTER....:"

Then a hallway lull as several of the participants dispersed. Willard and I got up and ambled our way into a dressing room located a few feet across the corridor where Camille Smith, my photographer, took a few photos.

"How did you work it all out?" I asked him as we reclaimed a leather couch where I had interviewed Billy Eckstine and Dizzy Gillespie earlier in the evening.

"Well, we all had something to do with it. We selected the services of Sol Hurok (the World-famous impresario). I did the actual booking and Hurok did the publicity...you know, getting out the word that modern jazz would be played at Carnegie Hall for the first time. It was the first Jazz concert Hurok had ever done. But his named carried weight in the field."

"And you were sure it would work?"

"Oh! Yes! When you get as big and as hot and confident as Goodman was in those days, why not? We felt we had a winner..and we were right. Filling 2,800 seats was no great thing for a concert hall. We were sure it would work. You know, it was a new approach...the beginning of great new things for the Big Bands."

"Would you say it was one of the great accomplishments of your life?"

"Well," he smiled thoughtfully, "I had a lot to do with it, not all to do with it, and Mr. Hurok had a lot to do with it...I kinda brought them together with Nathanson, but Benny was the key player because he could have done any concert anywhere at the time and I'm sure it would have succeeded. We certainly couldn't have done any better or been more successful. I guess I can say it was an important part of my career...Benny's too...and Hurok's..and even Nathanson's."

Willard wrote me in 1983 and requested a few of copies of the photos we took together that night: "Frankly," he wrote, "these are the best photos I've had in years. In the meantime, let's get together and have lunch soon. Thanks again."

"Absolutely," I wrote, "let's get together and talk more music and history. I was really quite honored in your presence and thank you for talking to us and posing. Jazz owes a lot to you for your efforts, no one can ever deny that."

Willard passed on very shortly thereafter. He was 76. Another giant was gone.

SALLY BENNETT - Magic Moments with the Big Bands

Sally Bennett was an amazing, enthusiastic lady. In her time she had talked with and entertained, and been photographed with, more celebrities than Oprah Winfrey.

A composer, musician, playwright, model, actress, poet, radio and TV personality, and author of the book Sugar & Spice, "A composite of most of the lyrics I've written...over 100 songs," she said. Sally, who was born in Pennsylvania, has hosted President Eisenhower's Inaugural Ball, walked the White House Rose Garden with President and Mrs. Johnson., and had been a companion of the young Grace Kelly and Jackie Kennedy. Most of Sally Bennett's life has been overflowing with what she had called "magic moments." So much, that she actually composed the song "Magic Moments "to celebrate them. The song was recorded by Buddy De Franco's Glenn Miller Orchestra in London, England, and was featured at Tricia Nixon Cox's wedding and at Nelson Rockefeller's grandiose

Harry James, Sally Bennett and Pee Wee Monte

party for Henry Kissinger. Many of those "moments" have been spent promoting the Big Bands. In fact, Sally was the founder of the Big Band Hall of Fame which first, officially opened their doors at the Palm Beach, Florida Community College on March 22, 1999. It was a fitting tribute for the Big Bands, and everyone was there. Now, the Big Band Hall of Fame and Museum has been re-located in Yesteryear Village at the South Florida Fair.

Sally came from a long line of classical musicians, but always wanted to sing with big name bands and write their songs. Her musical circle of friends included Frank Sinatra, Sammy Kaye, Guy Lombardo, and Tommy Dorsey, drawn from her days as an Atlanta, Georgia, disc jockey on radio station WBGS, and those in Cleveland, Ohio in 1966. "A few years later, my show in Cleveland was canceled when I refused to play rock n' roll. Our Big Band music is still sorely needed today. "

Back in 1967, bandleader Sammy Kaye honored Sally with an hour concert featuring all her original songs - both words and music. The idea was to launch a crusade to revive interest in the Big Bands, which eventually led to the founding of the Big Band Hall of Fame. That first ball was held at the Sheraton Cleveland Ballroom and became an annual event, featuring the bands of Glenn Miller, Guy Lombardo and Harry James.

"She's done a wonderful job with it," said director Bob Kasha, who also secured the bands that played at the Big Band's early balls, and now manages the new Xavier Cugat band. "It's been a long labor of love for her."

Sally had very strong feelings for the museum:

"To not commemorate this era of music is like hiding a Picasso or a Rembrandt in a cellar," she told me during a long and pleasant conversation we had one day. She had consistently and actively promoted her ideas to help keep Big Band music alive. Through the years she organized many annual Big Band balls which eventually evolved into charity events to support her dream museum.

Sally began collecting items when she interviewed Big Band people during the 1950s in Atlanta. "When I interviewed these people, I would kid them, 'Give me something to remember you by," she said. "Liberace took his tie off that very minute and gave it to me."

The museum's aim was three-fold: to honor big-band composers, vocalists and musicians. For 16 years the museum has existed only as money-raising events at which many Hall-of-Famers have been inducted. She had gathered an extensive collection of Big Band artifacts for the museum, including copies of my first three books and much memorabilia collected while she was conducting radio and television interviews of Big Band personalities.

Among them are many rare photos, bandleaders Russ Morgan's trombone, Billy Butterfield's and Harry James' trumpets, Glenn Miller's bandstand jacket, a mirrored ball that hung over the famed Aragon Ballroom in Chicago, an autographed baton from bandleader Guy Lombardo, and an Xavier Cugat Orchestra bandstand.

In 1995, The Big Band Hall of Fame charity, which was held at the famous Breaker's in Palm Beach, inducted bandleader Jack Morgan, and composer Claire Rothrock Graham who composed "Old Cape Cod" with music by the Russ Morgan Orchestra, conducted by his son, Jack.

In 1996 the Hall of Fame held a special tribute to Sammy Kaye for his assistance, belief, and dedication to establishing the first Big Band Hall of Fame. Sally was presented with The Music of Your Life Award in the same year by mutual friend Al Ham, President and Founder of Music of Your Life which syndicates Big Band musical formats to radio stations throughout the country.

Only Frank Sinatra, Tony Bennett, Rosemary Clooney and Dinah Shore have previously received it.

In 1997, the Big Band Hall of Fame Ball featured the Glenn Miller Orchestra, directed by Larry O'Brien, and honored music man, vocalist Don Cornell. Over the years, especially in the formative stages, Sally Bennett had enlisted many famous names of the 20th Century to help her along with her project: Dinah Shore, Count Basie, Bob Hope, Alan Jay Lerner, Guy Lombardo, Douglas Fairbanks, Jr., Ray McKinley, Pat Boone, Robert Merrill, Roberta Peters, Richard Tucker, Tammy Grimes, Buddy De Franco, Jonah Jones, Buddy Rogers, George Hamilton, Alan J. Lerner, Joni James, Frances Langford, Hoagy Carmichael, Mitchell Parrish, Mitch Miller, Bob Crosby, Bob Crosby, Mike Douglas, Nelson Riddle, George Hamilton, George Murphy, Marla Trump, Joe Franklin, Arthur Godfrey, Harry James, former Vice President Hubert Humphrey.

In 2001 Sally and I put together her biography and named it "Magic Moments."

Today, with Sally Bennett gone, her husband Paul and bandleader Ben Grisafi lead the charge for the growth and world recognition of the Sally Bennett Big Band Hall of Fame and Museum with Ben as Musical Director and Trustee and leader of the Big Band Hall of Fame Orchestra.

JACK LEBO - Big Band Report

When cartoonist/writer Jack Lebo walked into the Bristol Pilot office with an armful of cartoons. He was impressed. Lebo began producing his editorial cartoons a week later, and has been at it ever since. Lebo was born and raised in Philadelphia. His first published cartoon appeared in the Philadelphia Evening Bulletin when he was twelve. Over the years, his editorial cartoons appeared throughout the country in various publications, garnering 10 awards from the Freedoms Foundation at Valley Forge.

Jack Lebo with Louis Prima

During the Korean conflict, Jack joined the U.S. Air Force and served for 25 years, as cartoonist, writer, newspaper editor, broadcaster and in Air Force public relations and was sent to interview show business celebrities, including Bob Hope, Jerry Lewis, Jimmy Durante, John Wayne, and dozens more.

After retirement Lebo became Chief of Media Relations at McGuire Air Force Base in New Jersey. After ten years he has been freelancing, drawing editorial cartoons and writing entertainment columns.

Jack now writes a column entitled Big Band

Jack Interviews Band Leader Orrin Tucker

Report, covering the world of Big Bands, musicians and vocalists for half a dozen national and overseas publications. The Lebo's, Jeanne and Jack, reside in Levittown, PA.

In the winter of 1948 Jack Lebo found himself stranded on a street corner in a developing snow blizzard. Looking ahead for a bus, one came along all right, it was the Band Bus of Gene Krupa who stopped and invited him aboard.

"It was bandleader Krupa himself. The bus was on its way to a local gig in Philadelphia. Aboard was Roy Eldridge and Anita O'Day and the entire orchestra."

Jack had a great interview wit Krupa who also directed the bus to take Jack to his nearby home.

"A few days later, I received a now treasured signed photo inscribed, "'To Jack-Most sincerely to a swell guy - Glad it was the Krupa bus that gave you a lucky lift."

MUSIC OF YOUR LIFE
Al Ham And The Music Of Your Life

You can travel from city to city and on many AM radio stations you

are likely to hear The Music of Your Life, a syndicated radio disc jockey show whose format plays the standards and the Big Bands and other music of yesteryear.

It was started by a musician, composer, and arranger, turned business man Al Ham in 1977 on radio station WDJC in Bridgeport, Connecticut. Al had played bass for Artie Shaw when he was merely seventeen. He arranged for Tony Pastor while the Clooney Sisters, Rosemary and Betty, were singers with the band. When Tex Beneke reformed the Glenn Miller Orchestra after World War II, Al sat in with his bass. Later, he worked for Henry Mancini as an arranger.

Al Ham

While with Columbia records, Al produced an unknown Johnny Mathis recording "Wonderful, Wonderful," the song that catapulted Mathis to fame and fortune. "When I first heard it on the radio, one year after I recorded it, I knew singing would be my life's work. I was in awe, believe me," Johnny told me a few seasons ago, "and I still am."

Al's unique singing group The Hillside Singers, recorded the tremendous hit "I'd Like to Teach the World to Sing." Al has composed and arranged many commercials for radio and has received an Academy Award Nomination for an adaptation and scoring of the Warner Brothers film Stop the World-I Want to Get Off, and received a Grammy award for his production of James Whitmore's Give 'Em Hell, Harry.

Afraid America was losing the music exposure battle to rock & roll, Al Ham rallied to the cause by introducing his Music of Your Life formula to radio stations everywhere. He may well have saved our kind of music, even spawning imitators, which was all right with him.

"Here," Al said, "Bing Crosby will sing for you, Ray Anthony will play for you, and the Mills Brothers will harmonize for you, so stay tuned."

JOHN TUMPAK

Out on the West coast there is a fellow who writes up stories and interviews of practically all the participating Big Bands, musicians, vocalists, and arrangers associated with this book. His name is John Tumpak, and he has been a source of information and verification for many of my books. He writes for Dancing USA, L.A. Jazz Scene, Big Band Academy of America, Joslin's Jazz Journal, and other publications, and covers everyone from Bix Beiderbecke to Benny Goodman to The Andrews Sisters, and even about the 90th birthday of Butch Stone of the Les Brown band, and not only in short vignettes, but in full detail and with accuracy. When he writes about the Hollywood Palladium, he names the streets and cross streets where it is located. John's columns are usually dominated with his unique, personal style and are derived from interviews of his subjects, some of which he has established personal friendships. John covers the music scene very well both writing and lecturing. It keeps the L.A. Jazz Lamp burning.

John Tumpak

Thanks, John.

Sidebar

by John Tumpak

Jo Stafford – An American Musical Icon

Who do you think is the number one ranked female vocalist of the 1940 to 1954 pre-rock era? The answer is Jo Stafford, one of the most admired song stylists in the history of American popular music. Singing either solo, as lead singer for the Pied Pipers, or in duet with both Frankie Laine and Gordon MacRae, and under several pseudonyms, she recorded an incredible 110 top Forty hits during her storied career. Her body of work includes the Broadway show tune, folk, jazz, novelty, pop, and religious genres. In addition to her recording success, she appeared on radio and television, in the movies, and was dubbed GI Jo by servicemen thanks to the sentimental ballads she sang during World War II. Jo Stafford is truly an American musical icon.

In 1916 her father, Grover Cleveland Stafford, moved to California from Gainsboro, Tennessee to seek his fortune. He settled in Coalinga, a small town in the San Joaquin Valley southwest of Fresno, to work for the Southern Pacific railroad. After a few months with the railroad, he was hired by the Shell Oil Company to work as a roughneck. He would spend the rest of his working life with Shell, eventually becoming a foreman with his own company car supervising a dozen rigs.

Stafford returned to Gainsboro in September 1917 to bring his wife, Anna York, a distant relative of World War I hero Sergeant Alvin York, to Coalinga. On November 12 1917 Jo Elizabeth Stafford was born in Coalinga in a company-owned house on a site called lease 35. She was the third of what would be four Stafford sisters. Other than the fact that Anna played the five-string banjo, there was no history of any notable music accomplishment in her parent's families.

Jo Stafford commented on her start in singing during a recent interview at her home in Los Angeles' Century City area: "I had two older sisters, Chris and Pauline. They were eleven and fourteen years older than I. We were a spread out family; my younger sister was seven years younger than I am. My oldest sister, Chris, always told me that I started singing back in Coalinga before I can even remember."

In 1921 the Stafford family permanently moved to Long Beach, California when the nearby Signal Hill oil field opened. It was in Long Beach where Jo Stafford formally studied opera while she was at Polytechnic high: "I did classical singing as a coloratura soprano. I remember singing the aria "Caro nome" from Verdi's Rigoletto at the Long Beach Terrace Theater while I was still in high school. Unfortunately, talent scouts weren't scouring for sopranos, so I had to go to work when I graduated in 1935."

Work meant joining her older sisters who were already singing as the Stafford Sisters on their own KHJ radio show in Hollywood. The trio also regularly performed on the station's David Brockman's California Melodies and KNX's The Crockett Family of Kentucky shows. The Crockett Family was on nightly during the week and featured a special barn dance show on Saturdays. They were a pure country group that provided Stafford her initial introduction to the world of country music. The sisters rounded out their whirlwind schedule by singing background music for films at several movie studios.

After three years of apprenticeship doing radio and film work around Hollywood, Stafford unknowingly started on the road to musical fame and fortune in 1938 when one of the Big Band Era's most famous musical groups, the Pied Pipers, was serendipitously formed. She talked about how it all came about on Don Kennedy's Big Band Jump radio show in 1999: "I was on what we used to call a cattle call at 20th Century Fox for a musical that starred Alice Faye and Don Ameche called Alexander's Ragtime Band. Just about every singer in Southern California was on it; there was a huge singing chorus. That's when I met a quartet called the Four Esquires and a trio called The Rhythm Kings. All seven of them were young men. We started fooling around on the set *continued*

THE BROADCASTERS

and Their Big Band Radio Themes

JOE FRANKLIN
Record Selector for the Big Bands on WNEW

Joe Franklin and Richard at the Al Jolson Festival - M. Grudens Photo

Back when Joe Franklin was seventeen, he worked as the music librarian and record picker for New York's legendary "Make Believe Ballroom" disc jockey Martin Block on radio station WNEW. That was back in the 1940s. Now, in 2005, some 60 odd years later, Joe has become an icon of his own.

He started in television in 1950 and is credited with pioneering the talk show format that has translated into a prolific art form spawning shows like the Tonight Show, Dick Cavett, David Letterman, Conan O'Brien, and the Today Show with all its counterparts. His show, simply called the Joe Franklin Show, was the longest running show in television when it dropped the curtain in 1990. It ran for 43 consecutive years.

But, by now, the Tonight Show has broken his record, but there were many more hosts. Joe was always alone as host. The Guinness Book of Records claims that Franklin holds the record for hosting 31,015 shows, and has been credited with helping to establish the careers of a number of popular show business personalities along the way.

"I did more than 28,000 episodes, interviewing everybody and anybody, which someone told me works out to about two episodes a day for over forty years."

"Anyone in show business was welcome to appear on my show. Sammy Davis, Jr., Bill Cosby, Barry Manilow, Barbra Streisand, and even Woody Allen got their jump-start on my show. My Bing Crosby's interview, with his wife, Kathryn, is still the interview to beat. In Richard Grudens book Bing Crosby-Crooner of the Century the entire interview is printed exactly as we aired it.

In 2002, International Al Jolson Society member Brian Decker interviewed Joe Franklin about their mutual idol, Al Jolson:

"When I was picking records for the great Martin Block on the Make Believe Ballroom show Jolson came in and Martin asked me to bring in a Jolson record, so I brought in Jolson's 1912 recording of "Movin' Man, Don't Take My Baby Grand," and Martin played it while Jolson looked back and told me to: 'Break that record, Franklin,' while the record was playing on the air.

"I enjoyed and prefer the earlier Jolson voice. People say that Jolson's voice was different when he made The Jolson Story. And it was! So was Crosby's voice different over six different decades, and you can say Sinatra had six different voices, too. Jolson's voice became deeper, raspier, just different in 1946, after he had his left lung removed in 1945. That made the difference.

William B. Williams - "Hello World!"

"I enjoyed Jolson's earlier material, like "Hello Central, Give Me No Man's Land," which still gives people goose-pimples when they hear it. And I enjoy "On the Road to Calais," another of the Brunswick recordings. "Mother of Mine (I Still Have You.)" is another favorite. But, when he did "Alexander's Ragtime Band" with Bing, that, along with his duets with Patty, Maxine, and Laverne, the wonderful Andrews Sisters, were all great recordings that will live on.

"I think I have played the recordings of every known singer who has even sang a song." Joe says. And he probably interviewed every one of them at one time or another. Joe Franklin is still active today in broadcasting and always will be.

ART FORD

Art Ford's Milkman's Matinee on WNEW. Art Ford also managed daytime and evening shows. Ford ran the show from 1942 until 1954 when he shifted to the daytime schedule. Bob Jones emceed the Milkman's Matinee during the fifties using the same theme.

Art Ford

When the world should all be sleeping
And a melody comes creeping
Everything's okay
At the Milkman's Matinee

When you hear a band a swinging
And you hear somebody singing
It's no cabaret
It's the Milkman's Matinee

That's the time the sandman hasn't got a chance
Oh, no! It's clear.
Cupid waits and looks around for new romance
While the Milkman syncopates

Down the Milky Way each mornin"
Dance your cares away 'til dawnin'
Everything's grade "A"
And as a last resort he drops a quart
LOOK OUT
It's the Milkman's Matinee

MARTIN BLOCK AND AL JARVIS

The Make Believe Ballroom radio disc jockey show was conceived in 1934 and hosted in Los Angeles by pioneer Al Jarvis, who also coined the term "disc Jockey." The show was duplicated by others including Martin Block on New York's WNEW. The show continued on with host Jerry Marshall. William B. Williams took over the mike in 1963, hosting the show until his passing in 1986. The theme of the WNEW version was a Glenn Miller recording "Make Believe Ballroom Time." Martin Block broadcast from an actual ballroom studio complete with chandelier, red velvet chair and black linoleum on the floor.

At one point, in a legal suit, orchestra leaders Fred Waring, Sam-

Al Jarvis

Martin Block

my Kaye, and Paul Whiteman sued WNEW to prevent them from playing records on the air, but lost the case in a landmark decision. At that time record labels carried the warning: Not Licensed for Radio Broadcast. The purpose was to prevent records from undermining performers contracts, which usually called for exclusive services. WNEW's victory opened the door for all radio stations to fill the air with recorded music. So, we all owe a deep debt to WNEW Radio. On December 2, 1992, WNEW left the airwaves. The station was losing money. It was succeeded by WQEW, from the original WQXR, and remained on the air for a short while.

Make Believe Ballroom Time
Harold Green, Mickey Stoner & Martin Block

It's Make Believe Ballroom Time
Put all your cares away
All the bands are here
To bring good cheer your way

It's Make Believe Ballroom Time
And free to everyone
There's no time to fret
Your dial is set for fun

Just close your eyes and visualize
In your solitude
Your favorite bands are on the stand
And Mr. Miller puts you "In the Mood"

It's Make Believe Ballroom Time
The hour of sweet romance
Here's the Make Believe Ballroom
Come-on children, let's dance
Le-et's Da - nce

PETER POTTER

Peter Potter was one of the first radio record showmen to create a solid niche for himself in the field beginning at KNX radio in 1934. . He had abandoned his ambition to become a movie actor after some thirty-eight minor film roles.

He later made the transition to television with Saturday Night Dance Party and Jukebox Jury. Peter never liked the term disc jockey, but after searching for a new way to reinvent or describe the term, he finally gave up and made the best of it.

CHUCK CECIL

Cecil's radio show, The Swinging Years began in Los Angeles in 1956 over KKJZ 88.1, Long Beach, California. After serving in the Navy in World War II, Chuck found various work in radio and after learning all he could he turned to work as a disc jockey with his The Swinging Years show on KFI during a time when Big Band recordings were being reissued. He talked the station management into giving his show a try. It clicked from the start. Twenty-two years later he

Chuck Cecil

moved to KGIL in San Fernando, California, and ten years later, in 1987, moved to Los Angeles on National Public Radio KPCC in Pasadena.

Jazz writer John Tumpak: "In 1996 the current formula of The Swinging Years consisted of four hours of programming each week. In addition to swing music, Cecil added a feature The Vintage Years, a twelve minute segment that combined historical notes with the top hits of a given year. The Hall of Fame feature of the show was a fifteen minute interview with a Big Band personality. The show concluded with Bandstand Jamboree, airing actual live remote broadcast performances from places like Frank Dailey's Meadowbrook in New Jersey or the famed Glen Island Casino in New Rochelle, New York."

Cecil's collection of more that 40,000 tracks on 4000 LPs, 10,000 tracks on 5,000-78s and over 300 hours of taped interviews with the greats of the Big Band Era supports this veteran programming specialist and his Big Band Era radio shows.

AL "JAZZBEAUX" COLLINS
The Purple Grotto - WNEW

In 1997 I spent some time with Al Jazzbeaux Collins, not your ordinary disc jockey. Shortly after time as a successful jock at KDIL in Salt Lake City Collins began his fame at WNEW after an interview with station manager Bernice Judis by putting together an impromptu show in the studio, using the device of music behind his talking. This intrigued Judis and was hired.

Al "Jazzbeaux" Collins

The studio he was assigned to was purple. His opening was "This is Jazzbeaux and I'm in the Purple Grotto," with Nat Cole singing underneath. He had a fictitious owl named Harrison, a long-tailed, purple Tasmanian owl, he talked about throughout his show.

Jazzbeaux would also do a live show at the nearby Embers nightclub where piano greats Teddy Wilson, Art Tatum and others would perform nightly. He would tell his listeners that he and Harrison would get on the subway to go to the Embers. He would put on a six minute record, and by the time it started he was downstairs in a waiting taxi. It sounded like he was opening a door, and there he was in the night club.

When Art Ford left Al ended up with the all night show The Milkman's Matinee.

Jazzbeaux left WNEW, gigged at NBC for a while and then back to WNEW where the great artists like Count Basie and Duke Ellington would show up in the studio. Later on, Jazzbeaux sought and found easy work in San Francisco at KSFO doing the same show.

Jazzbeaux once played Art Mooney's "I'm Looking Over a Four Leaf Clover" over 50 times although he gave it different titles each time but had to lock the door of the studio to stop from being fired.

Al "Jazzbeaux" was one of the most popular and extraordinary disc jockeys.

JACK ELLSWORTH
Memories in Melody from WALK to WLIM to WALK

Jack was an institution at WALK radio on Long Island and endured for thirty years with his Memories in Melody Big Band show until Top Forty format took over.
Then he, his wife Dot and newscaster George Drake established WLIM nearby and dispensed the same kind of music. Years later Jack sold the station and was invited back to WALK where he is still running the same show every morning from 10-12 at the age of 85. Dot still manages the show from behind the wings. Jack was a favorite of Frank Sinatra who favored him with "spots" for his Sunday morning show Songs by Sinatra that he has been running for over 50

Jack Ellsworth - M. Grudens Photo - 2007

years. I've been interviewed on Jack's show many times as each of my books were published and I have brought in performers Jerry Vale, Connie Haines, and Carmel Quinn for surprise interviews. Jack graciously promotes all my books. Recently, The Big Band Hall of Fame in Palm Beach, Florida, has designated Jack Ellsworth Big Band Ambassador for his contributions to the ultimate proliferation of Big Band music.

Frank Sinatra: "Jack, we've traveled many musical miles together, my friend. I am delighted to send cheers and bravos to you on 50 marvelous years of championing our kind of music. As I raise a glass of bubbly, I thank you for your generous support of my career--you're a good man."

FRED HALL

Fred's *Swing Thing* radio show Interviews and two books, *Dialogues in Swing* and *More Dialogues in Swing*, are well known. Fred was a veteran broadcaster whose syndicated radio Swing Thing was heard nationally and in Europe. He was a former network newsman and owned his own radio stations. He has produced jazz and Big Band concerts and records and knew just about all the Big Band leaders and vocalists and they were the subjects of his books.

Fred was a freelancer taking assignments from Mutual and ABC radio over thirty years and developed an interview technique composed of empathy and advance research and earned deserved respect from his subjects. Like me, Fred enjoyed talking with his heroes and started his career with an interview with Helen Forrest, probably the best singer of the Big Band Era. His interviews present an impression of each star performer first as a human being, second as a performer.

Fred Hall

Fred Hall: "The music business is a small industry and I always found that cross-connecting was important: Mel Torme talks about Artie Shaw and Shaw speaks about George Shearing and so on. It's important to promote the mutual-admiration society that interconnects musicians and singers and arrangers, composers and leaders. After all, each is necessary to the other."

FREDDIE ROBBINS
ROBBIN'S NEST

Fred Robbins started as a disc jockey and went on to become a television host and celebrity interviewer. Fred began his career in Baltimore. In 1942 he landed a job on WHN radio in New York with his snappy patter drawn from a previous radio show, the 1280 Club Jazz Show. On his show he would say slangy things like, "Hiya cat, wipe your feet on the mat. Let's slap on the fat and dish out some scat."

Robbins became the disc jockey of Robbins Nest radio show on New York's WINS, WABC and WNEW. He later became a film producer for behind-the-scenes features on movie making for CBS and wound up on CNN as an interviewer and wrote profiles of celebrities for many magazines.

SYMPHONY SID

Freddie Robbins - 1948

Sid Torin earned his name Symphony Sid from working at a New York Lower East Side record store called the Symphony Record store. He started as a disc jockey at WBNX in the Bronx. Sid worked many stations in New York and was known for his "hipster' lingo and knowledge about jazz and developed a loyal following. The song, "Jumpin' with Symphony Sid" was written by the great Lester Young with lyrics by King Pleasure. Sid would broadcast from legendary 52nd street jazz clubs The Three Deuces, Royal Roost, Bop City and Birdland.

Sid wound up in Boston and started playing rhythm and blues material and even Gospel music. He returned to New York to play jazz once again until he retired to Florida in the 1960s.

DICK WHITTINGHILL

At first Dick Whittinghill tried acting, then singing as an original member of the Pied Pipers with Tommy Dorsey, then went into radio broadcasting and began a successful 30 year career on radio. Dick was the most popular radio personality in the Los Angeles area. On his show on KMPC from 6 to 10 am daily he coined the phrase "Did You Whittinghill This Morning?" which became the title of his 1976 best selling autobiography. My good friend Tess Russell, Dick's girl friday, was a great help to me in providing contacts for interviews on my first few books. Her husband George is in the management office for the one and only Johnny Mathis, which led to my first Mathis interview for my book, The Music Men.

Dick used his on air exposure to help Vietnam War vets to obtain jobs, and also raised hundreds of thousands of dollars for THE Long Beach Memorial Hospital. You can see Dick Whittinghill in reruns of many Dragnet and Perry Mason TV shows.

JONATHAN SCHWARTZ

Jonathan Schwartz, the son of famed songwriter Arthur Schwartz,

Jonathan Schwartz

who wrote the classic "Dancing in the Dark" and other standards, is one of the best disc jockeys that ever used a microphone. Jonathan worked at New York's WNEW-FM from 1967 to 1976 after great efforts at WNEW-AM and its successor-heir station WQEW that carried on the WNEW music after it closed down.

Jonathan is also a singer in his own right as well as an author. Known and respected for his expertise on Frank Sinatra's musical career, even Sinatra himself was impressed. Today, Jonathan serves as a programming director for XMs High Standard music channel, and his Sunday show offers a mix of music and conversation and interviews on WNYC and XM Satellite Radio.

RICH CONATY

Dick Conaty is a champion of the music of the 1920s and 1930s, music that can be heard on his The Big Broadcast radio program emanating from Fordham University on station WFUV.

Rich Conaty

His interest in such music began when he heard a broadcast from Hofstra University in Hempstead, New York when he was living in nearby Queens. He loved the music of the Boswell Sisters, who predated the Andrews Sisters, and over the years was able to interview the Boswells, Cab Calloway, and other stars of the era.

Anyway, he attended classes at Fordham and joined the radio staff and hosted a show called "In the Mood," after Glenn Miller's successful recording of the 1940s. After a while he renamed it "The Big Broadcast" and has been on the air with his show for over 30 years.

Rich has been collecting 78s for all that time and would travel to almost anywhere to retrieve offers to play on his 8 PM to Midnight show. Store stock 78s that have never been played are the prizes he tries to find. They are not worn out and can sound even better than their CD counterparts. On the show Rich will have tributes to songwriters of that period and play their songs by varied artists. You can hear Eddie Cantor and Al Jolson, Bix Beiderbecke, Eddie Lang and Bunny Berigan, as well as Bing and the Rhythm Boys. So, if you live in the New York area and you see Rich Conaty driving his 1950 Nash Ambassador with a trunk full of 78 recordings, wave, then tune in to WFUV.

"The Big Broadcast was a pretty unusual show, content-wise, thirty years ago. It's almost unique today," Rich says, "I haven't heard any other program that blends classic jazz with pop vocals and dance bands of the same period."

AL MONROE

"In my early youth I contracted asthma. My physician father kept me from outside activities so I wound up on my window sill watching my friends play stickball and touch football. Fortunately, my portable radio kept me company and introduced me to The Make Believe Ballroom radio show where I cultivated a keen interest in what the disc jockeys were playing, that is, the music of the Big Bands, their musicians and vocalists.

Al Monroe

"WNEW's famed jocks Martin Block, William B. Williams, Ted Brown, Jerry Marshall, and Jim Lowe led the charge for what has become the great American Songbook.

"Now, I am one of those disc jockeys as host of my own radio show On the Bandstand over WNTI 91.9 FM Hackettstown, New Jersey, every Sunday morning.

"I present to my listeners the great music of that period that still brings joy and happiness to millions, despite the fact that rock and roll material dominate the airwaves. Songs written by Irving Berlin, George Gershwin, Jerome Kern, Cole Porter, Richard Rodgers, Harold Arlen, Sammy Cahn, Ervin Drake, and Jack Lawrence, with interpretations by Artie Shaw, Harry James, the Dorsey brothers, Count Basie, Duke Ellington, Les Brown, and Benny Goodman, and all the relatively lesser- known bandleaders, performers and singers.

My Sunday programs will sometime commemorate America's holidays and memorials. On Valentine's Day I present a special tribute to the ladies. On July 4th you will hear great vocalists perform patriotic songs by George M. Cohan or Irving Berlin that may be sung by Frank Sinatra or Perry Como, and certainly Bing Crosby and Doris Day. And so on.

It is my deepest prayer that I may be able to continue presenting our great American musical performers On the Bandstand for a long time to come. Tune in, won't you?

CHRIS VALENTI
The Big Band Broadcast

For the love of the music of the Big Band Era and its obvious absence on mainstream radio, Chris Valenti inaugurated his long-running

Chris Valenti

show The Big Band Broadcast over Long Island radio, first over WBAU in 1991, then on WHPC in 1996. The show consisted not only of the music of the big bands and their vocalists and musical stars, but he set up a request line for any listener to call in their favorites, live over the air, and they were allowed to add their personal reminiscences, all adding up to a unique type of programming.

Chris added to the flavor of he show with on-air live interviews with the stars from Frankie Carle to Doris Day. Besides the usual commercial recordings, Chris added "air checks" of such stars as Harry James with Helen Forrest radio shows among many others.

"The music I focus upon is primarily from the period of World War II, stretching back to the early 1930s. The big stations will play 'In the Mood' and other big pieces, but we play the stuff they haven't heard in over 40 years, like the 'B' sides of the great recordings.

And, as if he hadn't enough to do, Chris Valenti just completed a book about baseball entitled "Innings In Time" that you can find on Amazon.

DON KENNEDY
Big Band Jump

When Don Kennedy was a kid, his older brothers played in a family band that would rehearse in the family living room. At thirteen with much musical background, Don built a studio in the basement and broadcast big band music using an antenna attached to a pear tree in the backyard. Today, he is doing just about the same thing, except his 2 hour Big Band Jump radio program reaches two hundred stations nationwide.

Big Band Jump is not just music, it includes interviews with musicians and bandleaders and vocalists who produced the music on the recordings he plays on his show.

I got involved with Don when I offered some of my interviews, including those appearing in this book, for use in his Big Band Jump Newsletter. Don was happy to feature some of them. A typical issue features

Don Kennedy, Max Wirz (Swiss Radio)

an interview of Artie Shaw, letters from readers, a trivia quiz, a feature on The Valencia Ballroom with photos, book and record reviews, upcoming radio show program titles, and opportunities to purchase books and records that are featured in each issue.

On the air since 1986, Big Band Jump carries the music to small radio stations throughout the country to big band music-starved fans. The address is Box 52252, Atlanta, GA 30355, the place where you can join Big Band Jump.

P.S. The Don Kennedy Show is Don's local, similar program.

RON DELLA CHIESA
Keeps The Good Music Alive

by Frank E. Dee

Ron Della Chiesa ... truly an iconoclast musicologist of radio not only of the New England airwaves, but where ever he appears in person. Without doubt, Ron carries the message in keeping the good music and the nostalgic songs we all love, alive. Ron's success comes from his hard work from his earliest beginnings in radio, which has led him to a valid musical place in life supported by the accumulation of the many wonderful listeners who have come to love this man.

In keeping the legends of the Big Bands, pop singers and the classics alive,

Martin Block brings together the leading jazz musicians of the day for a live session in the WNEW studios - L-R: Tommy Dorsey, Jack Jenney, Bunny Berigan and Roy Eldridge

Ron goes all out to continue his journey to pay homage to the super stars of an nostalgic era who sang or played good songs in great bands. For sure... We could all enjoy and understand those lyrics because the words were so meaningful.

If you're from New England, or visiting the hub area and your looking for a good fabulous dancing party to kick up those heels to some terrific music supplied by one of the best musicians of our time, you'll love Al Vega, and you'll love the Strictly Sinatra and Music America dances hosted by Ron Della Chiesa.

You can also hear Ron Della Chiesa's Sinatra and Music America shows on GMMY RADIO each morning from 7:30 A.M. to 8:30 A.M. [PST]... GMMY Radio visits the senior centers and senior mobile parks carrying the message of the good music format that Ron Della Chiesa offers. You may be surprised to know that seniors living in the senior mobile parks in California are now getting to know Ron Della Chiesa, via GMMY Radio computer.

I firmly believe the day will come when Computer Radio will one day will be installed in every car, broadcasting worldwide where ever you drive in whatever state or country you may be living, you will be able to hear shows such as Ron Della Chiesa.

Most Obediently Yours
Frank E. Dee
Its A Slice Of Heaven...Broadcasting Worldwide
www.gmmy.com/GMMYRADIO.htm

Where Do You Go Today To Hear The Big Bands Live In Person

Milt Bernhart

But, first:
A NOTE FROM PREMIER TROMBONIST MILT BERNHART

Written when he was President of the Big Band Academy of America in 1999, and long after he played that sensational trombone solo on Frank Sinatra's recording of Cole Porter's "I've Got You Under My Skin."

"I've felt for as long as I can remember that music recordings have an important role to play--- pleasure, education, promotional, all of that and more.

But records can't come close to the real live thing. If you are too young to have heard Duke Ellington and His Famous Orchestra then...you never will! But you say you've heard recent releases, and what do I mean? It's not the same!

That's just what I mean....it's not the same! The playing on the record may be fabulous, but the player was playing to a microphone, not an audience in most cases, and that makes a big difference in my humble opinion. The microphone hears all, but couldn't care less. It's more than a rumor that the best music ever - was not recorded. Is that bad?

And if you were there, you may have even tried to describe what you heard to someone who wasn't there. Didn't work, did it?

You just had to be there! Please understand.

Like life itself, you go with the bumps. It's worth it.

And besides...for all of us, both performers and listeners, there's more good music just up ahead. Don't you hear the orchestra warming up, and the excited buzz of the audience as they find their seats.? Anticipation is in the air. Music is about to claim us. Are you ready?

Thank you, God!

In the United States there were, and still remain, hundreds of places to see and hear the touring Big Bands, from Performing Arts Centers that have been converted from old obsolete movie houses, to outdoor concerts in the parks, in high schools and colleges north to south, east to west, dotted throughout the entire country.

THE GREAT BALLROOMS

One of the first hotels to host a dance band was the St. Francis Hotel in the heart of San Francisco, way back in 1913 when it hired Art Hickman's small band to play in its prestigious Rose Room. In 1915, a visitor, famed theatrical producer Florenz Ziegfeld heard them play and brought the eight-piece band, which consisted of piano, trumpet, drums, violin, trombone, two banjos, and bass,to New York to play in the Ziegfeld Follies revues and other nearby venues, perhaps initiating the dance band craze at the dawn of the Big Band Era. The Hickman band later showcased a string and sax section and is believed to be the first dance band to employ the use of saxophones.

THE PALOMAR BALLROOM

Built in 1925 the Palomar, the most famous and largest ballroom on the West Coast was where, in 1935, Benny Goodman almost single-handedly ushered in the Big Band Swing Era. Imagine, its dance floor could accommodate four thousand couples. Admission was forty cents for men and twenty-five cents for ladies. Opening night at the Palomar, formerly the El Patio Ballroom, drew twenty thousand including many screen notables and other celebrities. The building had a large mezzanine, a balcony and a seventy-five hundred square foot outdoor patio. It was simply magnificent.

All the Big Bands were featured at the Palomar led by the bands of Tommy Dorsey, Glenn Miller, Artie Shaw, Glen Gray, Kay Kyser. Radio KFLJ broadcast nightly from the Palomar and was heard over networks carrying the nations most popular music of The Big Bands, their vocalists and featured musicians from coast-to-coast.

Soon after the Palomar was remodeled to include modern air conditioning and other amenities, fire destroyed the ballroom in late 1939 and never rebuilt.

THE MEADOWBROOK

On Pompton (Turnpike) Avenue in Cedar Grove, New Jersey lies an important venue of the Big Band Era, Frank Dailey's Meadowbrook, where just about all the bands had played. Unlike most ballrooms of the times The Meadowbrook remains intact, although it is a shadow of its former self.

The Meadowbrook (In Two Stages)

The Meadowbrook was like a large motel with second story porches and awnings over the large windows on the first floor, and shutters flanking the side windows. It was painted white with a grassy knoll rising in front with center steps that led to the entrance.

Tommy Dorsey's Orchestra played "I'm Getting Sentimental Over You" there, and Glenn Miller's masterpiece "Moonlight Serenade" was frequently performed in this popular showcase. Frank Dailey, who lived nearby, opened the Meadowbrook in 1930 hoping to showcase his own band The Meadowbrook Syncopators.

"In the late evening of Tuesday, March 12, 1940, if you were listening to NBC radio, you would have heard Glen Gray's orchestra playing its theme, "Smoke Rings," "according to Bill Buchanan, who once wrote an article about the Meadowbrook for the Montclair, New Jersey, Times. "During that period, the major networks featured late night Big Band broadcasts from many nightclubs, hotels, and ballrooms throughout the country. Billy May's arrangement of "Pompton Turnpike" played at the Meadowbrook put the hoofers in the fast lane with its tempo, and the growling trumpet was that of Billy himself.

"Across the radio dial you could also tune in to the Big Bands from the Raymore Ballroom in Boston, the Mayfair Restaurant at the Van Cleve Hotel in Dayton, Ohio, and the Rustic Cabin in Englewood, New Jersey, where Frank Sinatra was discovered by Harry James who was listening to these very broadcasts on his car radio when he first heard him.

"These late night radio programs were passports to fame for the bands, because young people would hear the broadcasts from distant places, and when the band arrived in their own city, fans lined up to greet them.

"The Meadowbrook complex on Route 23 in Cedar Grove, has long been shuttered, and surrounding shrubbery has reclaimed the once sparkling landscape. But if you meander up the steps and listen carefully at the entrance door, you may still be able hear the music from another time played by the Big Bands you always loved."

The Sunnybrook Ballroom

"In those days there were no tables or chairs in the entire ballroom," according to Jim Wardrop, author of Let's Head for the Brook! - The Story of the Sunnybrook Ballroom, "No liquor was ever served - just soft drinks and soda fountain treats. The dress code required a jacket and tie for guys, and nice dresses for the girls. Zoot suits (over exaggerated clothes) were often seen on the jitterbugs and gators around the bandstand. The age of admission was eighteen. A ticket cost seventy-five cents for the big-fee name bands. Dances were held from 8:30 PM to 2:30 a.m. with forty-five minute sets of music."

As with most ballrooms, especially during the Depression years, groups of teens filled a car and headed for a place like the Brook.

"The Brook had been a 67 year fixture, consisting of a large swimming pool, picnic area, ballroom and restaurant," according to Big Band music aficionado Carl Harner, a long time resident of nearby Boyertown, Pa., who remembers the Brook. "Over the years I have been surprised at the number of people I meet all over the Philadelphia area who used to go there. It was an amazing place in its heyday."

"In cold weather everyone's hat, coat, and boots were thrown on huge piles in the corners of the ballroom," Wardrop writes, "crowds jammed the Brook eager to strut their stuff on the large Norwegian maple floor."

All the name bands played the Brook at one time or another. Hal Kemp was a frequent visitor. Charlie Spivak played more New Year's gigs than anyone. Frank Sinatra, Connie Haines, and the Pied Pipers first introduced "Sunny Side of the Street " with Tommy Dorsey right there on the Sunnybrook stage. When Connie Haines and I worked on revising her biography in late 1998, a glance at an entry in her private diary of 1940 read, "Saturday, April 20 - We played Pottstown's Sunnybrook tonight. I went over really well. The kids liked me. But, the bus ride back made me sort of sick, though."

On his last civilian tour in 1942, before he formed the Army Air Force Band, Glenn Miller played the Brook on February 28th and drew 7,200 fans. "The room was so crowded most of the kids stood in place all evening as there was no room to dance."

THE TUNE TOWN BALLROOM

"I remember back in 1937 very well," says Vince Rowe, a former big city music writer. The scene was a small midwestern community completely devoid of live entertainment. My thirst for this new music came from radio broadcasts and records. Then I traveled to St. Louis where the real thing existed: The Tune Town Ballroom."

Vince had made plans to see the great Chick Webb at Tune Town. He knew his style and all the personnel of the band. "That wondrous dance emporium that I'd heard so much about (you may remember the Count Basie recording "Tune Town Shuffle" in honor of this popular danceland location), was filled with dancers-jivers and jitterbugs elbowing and jostling for a few feet of swing space. I went right to the bandstand, and there in full flower with instruments blaring was the great thirteen piece Webb orchestra."

Chick Webb was there, a man of the hour: "Chick, the littlest big man there ever was - the leader and number-one drummer, was leading his beautiful band. It was exciting and thrilling to stand there and watch these great musicians play "Stompin' at the Savoy," "Don't Be That Way," "If Dreams Come True," and "Organ Grinder's Swing.""

Almost unnoticed was a young girl sitting shyly on a straight-backed chair to the right of her leader: "She didn't attract much attention until she got up to sing. When that happened, all dancing stopped and everybody crowded around to hear this young talent perform. And was she so good singing her own wonderful song, that nutty novelty nursery rhyme "A-Tisket, A-Tasket " (written with my old friend, bandleader Van Alexander) that she had lost her yellow basket," Vince recalled, "It was none other that our later 'First Lady of Song,' Ella Fitzgerald, when she was just nineteen."

On that big band summer night in 1937, Vince Rowe and hundreds of others got a thrill and a memory at the Tune Town Ballroom in St. Louis, Missouri, that has lasted a lifetime.

THE STARLITE BALLROOM

In Hersey, Pennsylvania, the Starlite Ballroom was a legendary venue, catering to dancers who came by trolley from Harrisburg and Lebanon beginning way back in 1917.

In the early days and into the '40s, men who wanted to gain entrance to the Starlite had to wear neckties and coats and the women, dresses only. If you forgot your tie it would cost you a quarter to a house tie rental. Top bands played the Starlite, but it is said that Lawrence Welk failed to draw enough patrons to make a profit.

The Starlite was centered in an area among trees and park like settings alongside a lake. "Cool breezes kept the dancers from being steeped in sweat while dancing. With a whopping 23,000 sq. ft dance floor and thousands of yards of fabric draped from the ceiling to help create a

The Starlite Ballroom, Hershey PA, 1940

luxurious atmosphere, the Starlite Ballroom enjoyed success right up to the 1970's. That stately old pavilion closed it doors in 1977 forever.

THE VALENCIA BALLROOM

In 1939 the Valencia Ballroom of York, Pennsylvania, celebrated its tenth year of presenting some of the greatest attractions of the Big Band Era like Kay Kyser, Tommy Dorsey, Casa Loma, Horace Heidt, Sammy

Kaye and most of the other prevalent bands of the time. Although York was rural, people would travel as much as two hundred miles to attend dances there. By 1959, the Valencia's rule was over, a church taking its place through the '80s. The building is still there perhaps echoing the beautiful sounds of the Big Bands it hosted over more than twenty years.

THE GRAYSTONE

When ballroom dancing swept America, the Graystone Ballroom in Detroit. once owned by bandleader Jean Goldkette, with its great central chandelier with mirrors that reflected sparkling light , and its domed ceiling that was covered with colored fabrics, became the place to be seen during the 1920s until the end of the second World war.

"The mezzanine around the entire ballroom is canopied and replete with inviting chairs and divans where guests may rest or lounge while enjoying the music and a full view of the dancers below," boasted

the management in ads. Many of the Big Bands played engagements in this fine ballroom. Eight thousand people a week patronized the Graystone Ballroom in its heyday. "In 1930 we opened at the Graystone Ballroom. Charley Horvath and Charley Stanton were in charge and they said there were only two great dance bands in the country, Gene Goldkette's Victor band and us-the Fletcher Henderson band," according to cornetist Rex Stewart , whose greatest glory was his eleven years with Duke Ellington, "We had men like Buster Bailey, Don Redman, and Russell Smith working with us then."

THE GLEN ISLAND CASINO

When Graham Pass of BBC radio inquired about the existence of the famed Glen Island Casino, which he wanted to visit in April, 1999 while on a Big Band visit to New York. A simple inquiry revealed that this great romantic spot that showcased the Big Bands of the 1930's and '40s was gone, replaced by the Glen Island Country Club, its original building totally redesigned with not a trace of the old look left.

The Glen Island Casino was located on Long Island Sound in New Rochelle, New York. The softly lit main ballroom, graced with very high French - styled windows that overlooked the Sound was on the second floor. The natural wood walls enhanced its beauty. The structure was perched majestically among stately trees that proliferated the island. There were tables on the small balconies off the second floor dining room.

Glen Island Casino

Fortunately, the beautiful rendezvous was managed by two romantics, Eugene Flohr and Karl Brandon with Fritz Dittrich as maitre d'hôte.

About 10 o'clock the kids with a jitterbug upbringing started to do their thing dancing to the heart of the best bands in the business, many who got their start at the place.

Glenn Miller opened there in May of 1939, followed by Glen Gray's Casa Loma Orchestra. Glenn Miller's shows were produced as live radio

GLEN ISLAND 1941

shows. The Glen Island Casino represented glamour and prestige, where only the best and most popular bands were featured.

MORE DANCE BAND BALLROOMS

The Savoy and Grand Terrace Cafe' in Chicago, the Benjamin Franklin Hotel in Philadelphia, and in New York it was the Arcadia, Roseland (both Manhattan and Brooklyn versions),the Cafe Rouge' in the Pennsylvania Hotel, all very popular in the '20s,'30s and '40s, especially with Glenn Miller's Orchestra.

The Biltmore Hotel and Cocoanut Grove in Los Angeles, the Mark Hopkins and Palace Hotels in San Francisco, the Taft, Lincoln, Commodore, and New Yorker Hotels in New York, also booked notable dance bands as did the Marine Ballroom of Atlantic City's Steel Pier in New Jersey and The Rainbow Room, high up on Rockefeller Center's 65th floor, where Ray Noble's Orchestra with vocalist Al Bowlly prevailed for so many years, and where Glenn Miller discovered his special "sound".

Savoy Ballroom flyers.

When the Trianon and Aragon Ballroom's first opened in Chicago, many other towns and cities tagged their newly-opened ballrooms by the same names. Most bands played popular dance music, although jazz-oriented groups began executing a new style they called swing. The prestigious Ritz Carlton Roof in Boston was a favorite gig for Duke Ellington, as the Hippodrome in Baltimore was for Glenn Miller in his early days.

During the 1920s, Roseland, a very popular ballroom located at 51st Street and Broadway in New York City employed two rotating bands as a standard policy. Sam Lanin, a former member of John Philip Sousa's world-famous military band, directed the first Roseland band. Alumni of Lanin's various bands went on to become leaders of a number of groups formed during the Big Band Era. Jean Goldkette's Orchestra played Roseland, too, and in the off-season toured New England ballrooms.

Three Unsung Songwriters of Tin Pan Alley
Who Made The Big Bands Come True

I Like New York In June,
How About You?
I Like a Gershwin tune
How about you?

Once during an interview, composer Harold Arlen said, "A good lyric is the composer's best friend." According to Arlen, a close bond between composer and lyricist is essential to the success of a song. Normally, a song is created when the usual thirty-two bar melody is written, and lyrics (words), are added and then arranged for interpretation by a musician, a group of musicians (band or orchestra), or a vocalist or group

EVERY LITTLE MOMENT

LYRIC BY
DOROTHY FIELDS
MUSIC BY
JIMMY McHUGH

Featured by
WILL OSBORNE
and his Orchestra

ROBBINS MUSIC CORPORATION
799 SEVENTH AVENUE - NEW YORK

of vocalists. To become a song, a composition must include words. Reversing that role, a song may be defined as poetry set to music. A question may be: What came first, the chicken or the egg? The lyric or the melody? To which George Gershwin once glibly replied, "it's the contract."

A notable composer is distinctive in melodic line and construction. A distinguished lyricist is able to formulate words for already written music, which is extremely difficult to accomplish, by any stretch of the imagination. Is it easier to write music to words, or words to music?

During the course of my career, I've known three songwriters. When I co-managed the NBC radio and television Ticket Division in New York back in the 1950's, I became a friend to songwriter J. Fred Coots who had written the legendary, perennial song "Santa Claus is Coming to Town" and the standards "You Go to My Head," and "For All We Know." I exchanged available broadcast tickets, which he gave to his friends for personal use, in exchange for personally inscribed song sheets. We always wound up talking about music and how his life consisted of an unending effort to plug his songs and help maintain them in public use in order to earn royalties, by which he lived.

A songwriter named Joe Howard, who also wrote tunes for entertainer Beatrice Kay (mostly about the Gay Nineties), would keep me company on some days. He was down and out, and aging, so what available broadcast tickets I could spare he would give to friends in an effort to restore his validity in a world that seemed to have forgotten him. (Late in 1952, comedian Milton Berle, known then as Mr. Television, honored Joe Howard on his Texaco Star Theater television show).

During the same period I spent many a lunch hour with a young piano-player who fronted an instrumental trio who performed gigs at local New York Hotels, as well as on Steve Allen's daytime, pre-Tonight Show television program Date in Manhattan. His now familiar name is Cy Coleman. In one of the unused third floor radio studios, I would sit alongside Cy on his piano bench while he practiced with his trio. I would woefully sing along. Stan Kenton sideman, and then NBC studio musician Eddie Safranski played bass. We became lunch-time buddies. I often attended those Cy Coleman gigs at the Park Lane Hotel on weekend evenings with my friends. Cy was experimenting writing songs even then. "Witchcraft, "The Best is Yet to Come," and "The Colors of My Life" remain some of his best.

In my last three books, The Best Damn Trumpet Player, The Song Stars, and The Music Men, I wrote about many of the musicians, vocalists, and arrangers of the Big Band Era and beyond. None of these books could have been written unless somebody first wrote the songs these musicians were to play, the vocalists sang, and the arrangers orchestrated.

Although not known as songwriters, some of the subjects of those books also composed music or wrote lyrics at one point or another in their career: Mel Tormé "The Christmas Song," Peggy Lee "Manana," Paul Weston "I Should Care,"
Ella Fitzgerald with Van Alexander - "A Tisket, A Tasket," Lee Hale "The Ladies Who Sang with the Bands," Frankie Laine "We'll Be Together Again," Al Jolson "My Mammy," Bing Crosby "Where The Blue of the Night," Duke Ellington "Sophisticated Lady," Larry Elgart the theme of "American Bandstand," "Bandstand Boogie."

Today, Tin Pan Alley is essentially The Brill Building and immediate vicinity in New York City, the singular place where music publishing offices were located and where songwriters and song plugger's congregated. The fourteen

BE FAIR

Words and Music by MACK WOLFSON, JACK WOLF FINE and EDWARD R. WHITE

Recorded by
DON CORNELL

W & B MUSIC PUB. CORP.   1619 Broadway, New York 19, N.Y.

story Brill is located on the Northwest corner of Forty-ninth Street and Broadway, once having housed the Zanzibar nightclub and Dempsey's Restaurant. Jack, the great heavyweight champion, used to sit at a table next to the window so passerby's could see him and be lured to enter the place. Two blocks north, at 51st Street was 1650 Broadway, home of Irving Berlin Music Publishing and the second "Tin Pan Alley." I understand that Ervin Drake wrote the Frank Sinatra standard "It Was a Very Good Year" in the office of publisher Artie Mogul at 1650 Broadway.

Ervin tells the fabled story of two music publishers. "Way back, two such firms were Mills Music, headed by Irving and Jack Mills, brothers. Their reputation was not the best. Across town in Radio City, was the home of Edward B. Marks Music and they had a like reputation. The joke among old-time songwriters was that when it came to pay royalties to writers, Marks paid off in mills (1/10th of a cent) and Mills paid off in marks. (In Germany the mark had fallen to an all time low.)

The original Tin Pan Alley first centered around West 28th Street in New York City at the turn-of-the century and up to World War I, where many of the music hall singers and vaudevillian actors once lived. Their many song-publishing offices, like the old Jerome Remick Company, employed piano players to demonstrate newly published songs for vaudeville performers who may have been searching for new musical material and for the general public at large. One of these pianists who worked as song-pluggers for the Max Dreyfus firm, Chappell Music was young George Gershwin. But Dreyfus soon learned he had a young genius on his hands and signed him up as a composer, like Jerome Kern and Richard Rodgers. They all started with Dreyfus.

The location later moved uptown to Forty-Sixth Street, between Broadway and Sixth Avenue, and when sound of radio dominated the music business, Tin Pan Alley re-located into lush office suites beneath the shadow of NBC's Rockefeller Center, extending up to Fifty-second Street where CBS radio was located.

The designation Tin Pan Alley , actually a sobriquet for the sheet-music publishing industry, was adopted from the tinkling, sometimes out-of-tune pianos being intensely exercised, sounding to a passerby like tin pans being drummed upon as groups of songwriters simultaneously demonstrated their craft at the offices of various publishers through sometimes open windows. Tin Pan Alley was the place where sheet music was written, demonstrated, packaged, and vigorously peddled. Remember, with no radio or television, sheet music had to thrive and survive on the strength of song sheet demonstrators playing a new tune in those storefront offices of publishers who also relied upon the illustrated sheet music covers that artfully portrayed the allegory of a tune, sometimes featuring photos of a popular musician or vocalist who had successfully performed it on stage or on recordings. To create a hit song, the axiom of the time was, "You got to say "I Love You" in thirty-two bars," and "keep the title short and memorable."

The participants called themselves Alleymen. The Alleymen, faced with radio companies refusal to pay songwriters for airing songs, and restaurants blatantly playing songs without compensating their authors, organized ASCAP , the American Society of Composers Authors and Publishers, which still solidly and securely represent the song writing community in all aspects.

Some composers collaborated with a single lyricist or maybe just a few, and some with many. Irving Berlin and Cole Porter were noted to write both the

music and lyrics to almost all their compositions. Richard Rodgers collaborated first with Lorenz (Larry) Hart and later with Oscar Hammerstein II. Composer Harry Warren, noted mostly for songs composed for Hollywood musicals, collaborated with lyricists Al Dubin, Mack Gordon, Ralph Blane, Arthur Freed, Ira Gershwin, Leo Robin, Billy Rose, and others. Like Warren, Harold Arlen acquired many additional lyricists when he first split with Tin Pan Alley and Broadway and went to California to work for the movies. After all, being work for hire, composers were not always able to select their lyricists. Lyricist Ted Koehler was Harold Arlen's early, principal collaborator especially during their two shows-a-year job at Harlem, New York's famous Cotton Club. Along the way Arlen linked up with E.Y. "Yip" Harburg (who wrote the lyrics for Arlen's Wizard of Oz music); Johnny Mercer, Leo Robin, Ralph Blane, Dorothy Fields, Ira Gershwin, and even author Truman Capote, back on Broadway for their show House of Flowers.

Although most of us are more familiar with the names of Irving Berlin, Richard Rodgers, Cole Porter, or George Gershwin, it must be realized that the names of Harold Arlen and some others surely belong among this unique group of musical geniuses. No one can say why the name of Harold Arlen, who composed the great standards "Come Rain or Come Shine," "Over the Rainbow," "That Old Black Magic," "Stormy Weather," and my favorite Arlen piece "My Shining Hour," among many others seems to be relatively unknown compared to his counterparts. It may be argued that Arlen had perhaps too many collaborators, thus his name became somewhat diluted. This was due partially to the lyricist selection process when he composed for the Hollywood studios, known then as the "composer's haven."

Ervin Drake, Jack Lawrence, and George David Weiss are three sensitive poets who wrote many beautiful songs during the Big Band Era and beyond. These tunesmith's names may probably be a bit unfamiliar to you, but here they are. Let me introduce you to: Ervin Drake

Recently, I was telling Ervin Drake that Frankie Laine proclaimed to me that his best and most favorite recording was Ervin's Drake's "I Believe," a song written in 1948 for the TV musical series "USO Canteen," starring vocalist Jane Froman. It was introduced on Thanksgiving Day 1952, and sung one month later on her nationally broadcast Christmas Show. However, Frankie, who performs the definitive version, recorded it in 1953, and it carried on "The Hit Parade" for a solid 23 weeks.

"Shortly after writing it I showed it to Mitch Miller when he was in charge at Columbia, and Mitch said, 'This is for Frankie Laine!' He just knew."

Ervin Drake and I were talking songs on one sultry August afternoon in 1998. Ervin is a trim, robust octogenarian, who has a bell-clear voice like that of a radio announcer and an enthusiasm for music, his own songs included, which, he sometime likes to sing himself. He is a good singer.

In early '98, a CD by teen-age country song star LeAnn Rimes, featuring his song "I Believe," remained number-one on the Billboard charts for over 10 weeks. And a few months later, Barbra Streisand recorded an album featuring that inspi-rational composition, selling over three million copies. The song's universal appeal has made it a worldwide hit.

Richard and Ervin Drake - 2005, M. Grudens Photo

Barbra Streisand recorded "I Believe" twice, in two different albums, both going over a million. Later she recorded Drakes' "One God," as well.

FRANKIE LAINE

"I first heard "I Believe" when Mitch Miller came out to see me in California. He sang four bars of Ervin Drake's song for me (and he is a terrible singer), but even his voice made sense of it. The lyrics were a simple but moving declaration of faith, and seldom had words touched me so deeply. It was almost more of a prayer than a song. In my life I've often turned to Him for comfort and guidance. He's always come through, so the song didn't only speak to me, it spoke for me."

I Believe for every drop of rain that falls,
A flower grows,
I believe that somewhere in the darkest night,
A candle glows.
I believe for everyone who goes astray,
Someone will come to show the way.
I Believe, I Believe
I believe above the storm the smallest prayer,
Will still be heard,
I believe that someone in the great somewhere, hears every word.
Every time I hear a newborn baby cry,

Or touch a leaf,
Or see the sky,
Then I know why,
I believe!

Ironically, Ervin Drake originally studied drawing, painting, and lithography at the College of The City of New York, but music and lyrics captivated his interest.

"But, Richard, while at school, I contributed songs and some sketches to school productions, and even sold a couple of songs to a publisher. I also helped my dad in the wholesale furniture business. But, I used to cheat on my dad by sort of moonlighting in a place we call Tin Pan Alley, where I tried to sell my songs. It was the place where song publishers convened their business. All the songwriters gathered there."

A songwriter-lyricist, Ervin Drake is also a prolific TV producer, writer, and composer. From 1948 to 1962 he was involved with some 700 telecasts, most of them weekly programs, involving , among others, Steve and Eydie, Yves Montand, Gene Kelly, Carol Haney, Jayne Mansfield, and Johnny Carson.

Ervin Drake finally sold his first tune "I Like It" for three-hundred dollars in 1941. "An impressive amount for the times," he recalled. His song "Good Morning Heartache," with music by Irene Higginbotham and Dan Fisher, was originally turned down by music publishers as being non-commercial, until recordings by Billie Holiday, Joe Williams, Ella Fitzgerald, and Tony Bennett - along with winning an ASCAP (American Society of Composers, Authors, and Publishers) Award, proved otherwise.

Ervin's first success was called "Tico-Tico," earned by composing words for a popular Brazilian melody by Zeqfuinha Abreu that was featured in the Walt Disney film Saludos Amigos in 1942. A year later my friend PattyAndrews sang it with her sisters, Maxene and Laverne, with Xavier Cugat's Orchestra performed it in the film Bathing Beauty. Ervin wrote words and music to another hit "Rickety Rickshaw Man," recorded by Eddie Howard in 1945. It became a million-seller.

Ervin's contribution of lyrics to "Perdido," an instrumental piece composed by valve trombonist Juan Tizol, a member of the great 1944 Duke Ellington Band, converted that song into a solid classic. "I was honored to be linked with Tizol and consider him one of my best collaborators." Ervin said.

JUAN TIZOL

"We were traveling," Tizol recalled in 1978 for Time-Life Records, "and I was sitting in a railroad coach tapping the window and the melody came to me. I thought that's pretty good and I better write it down before I forget it. I gave it to the Duke that evening and he liked it."

"I was in Washington with the band," Ervin continued, "and one night Juan was playing an interesting tune and I asked him - 'What is that?' and he said, "Perdido". I said, 'You think it needs words?', and he said, 'If you come up with the right ones--sure!' So I wrote the words to his nifty tune."

I reminded Ervin of June Christy's solid version of that song recorded a little later with Stan Kenton's band, as the best version I have heard. "Yes, but don't forget Cleo Laine, who also did it beautifully - - and Sarah Vaughan... and how about Ella's," he recalled. "They are all good!"

Along the way, Ervin composed: "Castle Rock" (Frank Sinatra swings gracefully with it!); both words and music for "It Was a Very Good Year," composed for the use of the Kingston Trio during the 1950s, and, of course, one of Frank Sinatra's most important signature recordings after he discovered the song in 1965 when he heard the Kingston Trio performing it on radio

while driving in his car one evening, and included it on his album September of My Years; "Across the Wide Missouri" (for Hollywood's film of the same name,) "A Room Without Windows" from What Makes Sammy Run, (Steve Lawrence excels on this one), and one of my personal favorite's "Come To the Mardi Gras" -- recorded by Freddy Martin's Orchestra.

"I became very excited when I first heard Frank Sinatra's recording

IT WAS A VERY GOOD YEAR

Words And Music By **ERVIN DRAKE**

Recorded by **FRANK SINATRA** on Reprise Records

KEYS
R 04515

REEDLANDS MUSIC CORP

75¢

Ervin Drake's Masterpiece

of "It Was a Very Good Year." I was in London where publisher David Platz first told me about it. He played it for me over the phone. I listened and then asked to hear it again. I loved it. When I got back home, the first thing I did was to buy the LP and played it thirty times the first day. I was ecstatic. To this day I get a real charge whenever that recording is played.

"Frank Sinatra and I became friends because of that song," Ervin said, "It brought him a Grammy. Over the years he would call me at least twice a year -'Hi! Ervin,' He would say. 'How are you, Ervin?' and, 'do you need anything?' Frank was always caring and concerned about his friends and people who have helped him."

Ervin's tune "The Father of Girls" has also brought him acclaim, having been recorded by Paul Anka, Pat Boone, Jerry Vale, Perry Como, and Mike Douglas - all of them fathers of girls.

We talked about songwriters being present at a great recording of their song. "You're rarely there at recordings, Richard. I could tell you about the few times in my life when I have actually been there."

One of those events was when Billie Holiday recorded his song "Good Morning Heartache" in New York's Decca Recording Studio: "I was in the room. I didn't even have the guts to say 'How do you do?' or even utter my name. I was too intimidated - being just twenty-six and very scared and excited," he recalled . "I remember all the details about the date and what Billie did right after first singing it -- where she demanded a drink ---from a bottle wrapped in a paper bag --- and got it --- then continued to drink from it throughout the session, much to the dismay of arranger Sy Oliver, who was also conducting."

Like many other composers, besides his contributions to the Big Band Era, Ervin has worked the Great White Way: "I composed both words and music for Budd Shulberg's play What Makes Sammy Run? which starred a young Steve Lawrence, as well as Sally Ann Howes and Robert Alda-- Alan's dad. It had the longest run in the history of the Adelphi-54th Street Theater."

The standard song "A Room without Windows" was from that show and was recorded by Steve Lawrence, Sammy Davis, Jr., and Buddy Greco.

"You know, Richard, I actually went back to school after all those years to study composition at Julliard in 1963 and took lessons in composition and orchestration from the great classicist Tibor Serly, Bela Bartok's principal pupil." From 1965 to '68, Ervin extended his studies, perfecting orchestration, and piano techniques.

Like many noted artists in entertainment, Ervin has received his share of accolades. "Good Morning Heartache" won the ASCAP Award. "I Believe "has won The Christopher Award, and there is the Grammy nomination for the score of What Makes Sammy Run, and an Honorary Doctorate in Music from the prestigious Five Towns Music College in Dix Hills, New York, where my friend, Dr. Stanley Cohen, is President.

On November 9, 1998 Ervin Drake was honored at Five Towns College in a retrospective of his works. As honored guests, bandleader Ben Grisafi and I happily witnessed actor and vocalist John Gabriel 'performance of "Good Morning Heartache," "It Was a Very Good Year," "A Room Without Windows" and "Father of Girls." In a surprisingly strong and rich voice, Ervin vocalized his songs "The Rickety Rickshaw Man," "Al Di La" and "Come To The Mardi Gras." An absolutely wonderful four-man a cappella group called the Future Four performed the best choral version of "I Believe" that I have ever heard. The college's Festival Chorus vocal group performed a thrilling version of "Across the Wide Missouri" and closed with a fulfilling reprise of "I Believe."

Later that month, Ervin participated in Hofstra University's Frank Sinatra seminar, The Man and His Music. And, in London, on October 4th that year, at the historic Drury Lane Theatre, Ervin Drake proudly performed his song "It Was a Very Good Year" in a stirring Frank Sinatra tribute to benefit the Princess Diana Charities.

It was his shining hour.

JACK LAWRENCE

Today I talked with the man who wrote the lyrics to the song "All or Nothing At All," Frank Sinatra's first solo hit recording; Rosemary Clooney's blockbuster hit "Tenderly;" Don Cornell's comeback success

"Hold My Hand;" words and music to Buddy Clark's charming perfor-mance of "Linda; "Harry James' signature solo "Sleepy Lagoon;" Dinah Shore's "Yes, My Darling Daughter;" and both words and music to the Ink Spots' famous theme "If I Didn't Care." What a pleasant conversation it was:

"I really owe Rosemary," Jack Lawrence was telling me at his West Redding, Connecticut home. "' Tenderly' was an important song for Rosy, and her success with it became important to me."

Rosemary Clooney was honored in the fall of 1998 by the Soci-ety of Singers in L.A., and Jack was there to honor her." "I also took a full-page ad in the journal to let her know just how I feel," Jack said. My friend Lee Hale, author of the book Backstage with the Dean Martin Show produced the video of the party and sent me a copy of the Clooney party. Rosemary sang his song "Tenderly," very tenderly.

Jack was also very friendly with bandleader Harry James back in the forties when Frank Sinatra was James' vocalist. "I showed him "All Or Nothing At All." They both loved the song; so they recorded it. "Jack said, "The original recording label read "All Or Nothing At All" HARRY JAMES AND HIS ORCHESTRA in large print--then in very small letters underneath - Vocal by Frank Sinatra. The record bombed. When Frank later auditioned for Tommy Dorsey, he sang "All Or Nothing At All," and that earned him the job with Dorsey. After leaving Tommy, going out on his own, and starring at the Paramount as a single, the musicians went on strike. Columbia couldn't take advantage of this great prize they had in Sinatra, trying to make a capella recordings with singing groups. But it didn't work. Lou Levy, who had published "All Or Nothing At All," reminded Columbia to pull the earlier recording of the song, and re-release it with Frank Sinatra's name on top. Now, with Frank hot, it will probably do well. It was Frank's first record success on his own."

Jack is still a vital, busy man in his eighties who never retired and doesn't intend to: "I work when it strikes me and I rest otherwise. Many of my friends are gone, but I've been fortunate, being in good health, I'm still around to put some words on paper and hope they turn out pretty good."

Jack Lawrence started picking out tunes back in the East New York section Brooklyn, New York, when he was just a lad of twelve.

"My first big hit was "Play Fiddle, Play" which was featured in a 1933 movie they still show on television once-in-a-while Dinner At Eight, with John Barrymore, Marie Dressler, and Wallace Beery."

It was quite a thrill for the twenty-year-old songwriter: "Richard, that song opened the doors for me in the music business. I became very friendly with Jack Kapp of Decca Records, and Decca had what they called an R & B Label that featured all the black bands of the time, so I got to know Andy Kirk and his Clouds of Joy, and the Mills Brothers--- and Ella. "This unique access enabled Jack to bring his songs up to Decca and they would record them even before they were formally published.

"I wrote the melody "What's Your Story, Morning Glory?" for Mary Lou Williams," he sings it out loud for me, "and others for Andy Kirk, too." Jack has written both words and music for some songs, having collaborated on others with composers Burton Lane, Hoagy Carmichael, and Victor Young, although he prefers writing his own complete songs.

Jack loves to tell the story about the origin of his legendary song "Linda:"

"I wrote that song for a three-year-old little girl named Linda Eastman. Her father, Lee Eastman, was an attorney for some big bandleaders and some writers, like me. I was visiting Lee at his Scarsdale (New York) home. His wife Louise, and another daughter Laura both had songs written after their name, as did their son Johnny, but, Linda did not. So he asked me to write a song for Linda. So I did. Linda was not a popular name at the time, so I found it hard to get it published. Of course, it was later recorded by Buddy Clark and it became a number one hit."

There is an interesting epilogue to this story. Married, Linda turns out to be Linda McCartney. When Linda suddenly passed away in 1998, Jack was invited to New York's Riverside Church by her husband, former Beatle Paul McCartney: "It was a very touching ceremony, and the last speaker was Paul. He said, 'When Linda was forty-five, I wanted to surprise her, so I got together a Big Band, and made a recording of me singing Jack Lawrence's song, 'Linda.' 'Oh, she loved it,' he went on, 'and I think we end on a high note tonight, so I'm going to play that recording.'

"And when he was finished, he started walking up the aisle, and when he saw me, he stopped for a moment and he hugged me, saying, 'Thanks, Jack.'"

To Jack's overflowing cornucopia, you can add "Poor People of Paris," "No One But You," "Beyond The Sea," "Sunrise Serenade," and "With the Wind and the Rain in My Hair." How happy has he made you over the years?

GEORGE DAVID WEISS

Another one of our remarkable songwriters is Califon, New Jersey resident George David Weiss. Look over this treasury of pure evergreens: The Ames Brothers' "Can Anyone Explain," Patti Page successes "Confess" and "Cross Over the Bridge," Gordon Jenkins' "I Don't See Me In Your Eyes Anymore," Sammy Davis' hits "Mr. Wonderful" and "Too Close for Comfort," The Andrews Sisters popular recording of "Rumors Are Flying," and that special song performed by Louis Armstrong "What A Wonderful World."

"I wrote that song especially for Louis at his personal request," said this former arranger for both Stan Kenton and Vincent Lopez, whose extensive musical education at the Julliard Conservatory of Music in New York has sure paid him off handsomely.

Back in high school - 1948 - I remember Frank Sinatra's recording of Weiss' "Oh! What It Seemed To Be" being played at the weekly dance in the gym, and the dancers floating to Frank's version of that seemingly perfect love song - so poignant - in the right place for young romantics. Frank made perfect use of his phrasing techniques on this beautiful song.

My first book The Best Damn Trumpet Player, described Weiss' song "Rumors Are Flying" in a chapter about the Andrews Sisters: "When they recorded my favorite "Rumors Are Flying," and Patty did that doubling-up-jive patter with such melodic perfection, Whatta-ya-do-do-do that keeps 'em buzzing... I couldn't wait until the record was over so I could lift the recording arm and play it again and again.

And, how about Kay Starr's great version of Weiss' marvelous tune "Wheel of Fortune," a song that Kay told me she never gets tired of singing: George David Weiss' compositions have helped make stars of people like Frank Sinatra, Sammy Davis Jr, Kay Starr, and The Andrews Sisters. "Yes, that's true," he said, "but it's funny - no one has ever heard of me," as we both laughed. When he composed "What a Wonderful World" for Louis Armstrong at the request of Teresa Brewer's record producer husband, Bob Thiele, the record bombed, as they say. It took a revival of Louis' recording featured in the film Good Morning ,Vietnam with Robin Williams to at last turn that song into a million-seller.

George David Weiss cooperated closely with Jack Rael in producing two important first songs for Patti Page - "Confess" and "Cross Over the Bridge," which were originally two-part songs. Jack Rael was Patti's manager for 50 years. When he first discovered her, and began searching for something special to showcase her talents, he invoked an "overdubbing" process first on the song "Confess," which produced that famous echoing sound that sounded like a group singing different harmonic parts when it was actually one person.

Well, that's the short story of three wonderful poets of Tin Pan Alley; Ervin Drake, Jack Lawrence, and George David Weiss. Can you count how many hours you may have spent enjoying, maybe singing along with, or even dancing to their splendid lush, lyrical words and music?

BILL CHALLIS
The Most Important Jazz
Arranger of the Big Band Era

BILL CHALLIS
AND HIS ORCHESTRA - 1936

The Band includes Artie Shaw, Charles Margulis, Manny Klein, Jack Jenny, Will Bradley, Larry Binyon, Frank Chase, Harry Bluestone, Frank Signorelli, Artie Bernstein, Dick McDonough, Chauncey Morehouse, others.

CCD-71

Back in the Spring of 1978 I spent an appreciative afternoon at the Massapequa, Long Island, home of jazz giant Bill Challis. Bill, soft-spoken with a gentle nature, liked to fuss in his garden set on the creek that adjoins his modest home.

His name may be unfamiliar to most of you, but, make no mistake, Bill Challis' work had a profound effect on the music world when he arranged for the innovative orchestra's of Fletcher Henderson, Jean Goldkette, Paul Whiteman, Artie Shaw, Casa Loma, and specifically for artists Bing Crosby, Bix Beiderbecke (Challis transcribed "In a Mist" and thereby saved it for posterity) and many of the early jazz musicians who shaped the sounds of jazz impressionism, the revolutionary music of 80 years ago that grew into the Twentieth Century's best and most popular music. Harmonically and rhythmically, his charts were favored by musicians.

While with Jean Goldkette's orchestra of the 1920s, Challis initiated the screaming jazz and peppy gaiety of the Charleston sounds and "whispering cymbals." His interpretation of "Dardenella," one of the most famous jazz tunes of the era, was one of the most influential arrangements of jazz in the popular strain. His work gave birth to a rise of jazz in popular music that still exists today.

Bing Crosby, lead singer of the Whiteman Orchestra, and one of the Rhythm Boys with Al Rinker and Harry Barris, wrote in his biography Call Me Lucky ".....and the arrangers, fellers like Ferde Grofe, Bill Challis, Lennie Hayton, Victor Young, Glenn Miller, and Jack Teagarden- all of them - how lucky I was to be a part of that great era."

Bill Challis was the specialist who guided Bix Beiderbecke, the young genius cornet player, by drawing out his qualities. Bix's beauty and depth of tone was enhanced by Challis' arrangements - as no one else possessed the ability to push the beat and somehow cause the band to swing along. Only Red Nichols and (later) Harry James ever came close to Bix's ability and skill of instrument use.

Bill's landmark chart "I'm Comin' Virginia" recorded in April 1927 by the Whiteman orchestra, includes Loring "Red" Nichols on cornet; Jimmy Dorsey on alto sax & clarinet; Eddie Lang on guitar; Harry Barris - Vocal, is one of jazz's great recordings. Noted beats, use of cymbals in the particular jazz arrangement included Vic Berton's invention of a pedal, known as the Charleston Pedal, for quality tone changes on kettle drums.

Bill's arrangements, some of which used countermelody in ensemble in a way that was used by future bands of the 1930s and 1940s, revolutionized popular music and the influence is so far-reaching that it defies interpretation because its branches and spinoffs of its use in so many fragmentation's would almost be impossible to trace. But its roots are firmly and recognizably planted in music history.

Bill retired to his original home on a lake near Wilkes-Barre, Pennsylvania living in equal harmony with nature just as he did in his music.

In Gene Lees' wonderful book Waiting for Dizzy, there is a charmingly written chapter covering the illustrious career of my friend Bill Challis which you will enjoy reading.

The Sinatra Effect—The Importance of the Arrangers
Richard Grudzinski
Professor
Berklee College of Music
Boston, MA

In an earlier book by Richard Grudens' The Music Men I had written a technical explanation of what an arranger does:"Arranging is the art (and craft) of adapting a musical composition to a specific instrumental and/or vocal combination," but that doesn't tell the entire story.

One could compare the arranger to an architect who designs the home or office to a clients specifications, while retaining the personality of the client in mind. In this case, a singer is the client for whom the musical arranger creates the structure of the music specifically for the singer.

Or you may compare it to the role of the set designer, or cinematographer for a movie, or a painter who places the portrait of the person in its proper setting. It's the arranger who provides the ocean of background colors, through which the singer navigates. The arranger knows the singers' range, timbre, personality, as well as the colors of the orchestra, and how to paint the appropriate canvas, which will become the final piece.

A song is a short story, usually a two to four minute tale of love, or other expression. It's the arrangers' job to provide just the right setting for the story, as told by the singer. Frank Sinata was lucky enough to have some of the best arrangers in the business provide that setting for him. His two most important arrangers were Billy May and Nelson Riddle, two

Riddle and Sinatra at Work

of the finest music arrangers. Like Frank, both were veterans of the big bands. All these guys could swing!

Of the two arrangers, Nelson Riddle was most important, having been instrumental in restructuring Franks' fledgling career in the early 1950's. When Frank signed with Capitol Records, it was Nelson who provided great swinging arrangements for Sinatra's dance numbers, and wonderfully sweet string arrangements for his ballads. The Sinatra- Riddle collaboration was a marriage made in Hollywood Heaven.

With the release of "I've Got the World on a String," Frank was back. It became his first hit with Capitol and the first of many great future recording collaborations with Riddle. Just listen to that track! It begins with Frank singing over a warm, subdued sax pad. Then, just at the right moment, the brass section enters with a big hit. The arrangement then slips into high gear, with plenty of brass pops, and mellow trombone and sax pads underneath Frank's marvelous baritone. In fact, Nelson once compared Frank's voice to a cello...dark, yet smooth and wrote for it accordingly.

Riddle, a veteran of the big bands, was also a student of the great composers/orchestrators (another word for arranger) Maurice Ravel and Claude Debussy. These two Frenchmen have influenced more jazz and pop musicians than all others in the history of music. Nelson was particularly intrigued by Ravel's mastery of the orchestra, and Debussy's use of gentle colors (particularly flutes) in his work. Ravel, in particular, is noted as the master of orchestration...the art of writing for the orchestra. To get an idea of Ravel's mastery of the orchestra, first listen to his orchestration of Moussorgsky's "Pictures at an Exhibition". This was originally written and performed on piano. If you listen to the orchestra version, and then the solo piano version you will experience Ravel's mastery. It is stunning! The way that Ravel could add just the right colors to this piece established Ravel as one of the greatest orchestrators of all time.

Then listen to "La Mer," by Debussy, and you will see how these two influenced not only Nelson Riddle, but also Duke Ellington, George Gershwin, pianist Bill Evans, and the great jazz arranger Gil Evans. And those are just a few of the masters influenced by these two giants of the orchestra.

Now, listen carefully to the strings and flutes on the recording of "All the Way". This was Nelson at his most lyrical and romantic. Then the brass enters with a little interlude, just before the final phrase. And the ending is just like the ending to a symphony. In "Young at Heart"we can hear how he used the strings and flutes in a kind of call-and-response with Frank. The trombones provide the cushy pad on the bottom while the harp and celeste (a bell-like keyboard instrument) add that sugar, or ear candy on top like the frosting on a cake. The sound is lush and evocative, but not corny as Nelson had a sophisticated sense of harmony, which he got from Ravel and Debussy.

One of Nelson's great strengths was his writing with the lyric in mind, as well as the music and, of course, consideration for the singer. He knew just how to highlight the words, which suited Frank very well, as he was perhaps the greatest at delivering a lyric. Frank never sang a song, he told a story, and interpreted the lyric and made you believe the story as if he had lived the lyrics himself.

The swing arrangements used a particular formula: the strings would provide a kind of a floating cushion, while the brass punctuated the space between the lyric and the rhythm section just swung. Listen to the interplay between the strings and the muted brass in "Nice and Easy" and you'll get the picture. Nelson knew just when the song should reach its climax, which is normally about 80% through the tune. At the end he brings in the flutes (one of his signature features) to bring the tune to a beautiful conclusion. Paul Horn, the noted flutist, remembered Nelson Riddle: "The flute has always been used in film scoring with a symphony orchestra, but for a pop arranger to use wood winds (including flute, oboe, clarinet) the way he did, was unique. And the flute played a major part. He was really a painter of sound. He used the colors of musical instruments as a painter would use colors on a canvas and the flute was one of the primary colors."

One of the best Billy May arrangements written for Frank was "Come Fly with Me" used to great effect in the movie Catch Me if You Can when Leonard DiCapprio's character eludes the FBI by distracting their attention by strolling through a group of great looking, female airline attendants. That entire scene seems to evoke the period perfectly.

Billy was famous for his great use of brass and slurping saxes. The sax sound was achieved by featuring the altos in unison a third higher than the tenors, also in unison (playing the same notes), and scooping up into the written notes, as if slurping a soda through a straw. And they played it with a mellow sound. You can hear this towards the close of the tune. It has that vintage dance band sound. Yet, Billy's sense of harmony was equally as hip as Nelson's as they possessed many of the same influences. In fact, they often ghosted for one another, a common practice where one arranger would mimic another by emulating his style—which is why it's often difficult to tell them apart.

There are arrangements written by one guy while the other received the credit, usually done for political or practical reasons. If one arranger got too busy, he would call in another to assist. The ghost would write in the style of the "original" and thus get the job done.

While Nelson studied arranging with Bill Finegan (who wrote arrangements for Tommy Dorsey and Glenn Miller), and while living and working in Hollywood, later studied counterpoint (the craft of writing one musical line against another) with noted composer Mario Castelnuovo-

Tedesco.

Billy learned on his own without the benefit of professional instruction. It was said that he studied solfeggio (the art of sight singing), looking at notes on a piece of sheet music and singing the notes without playing them on an instrument. It's noteworthy that both men were accomplished brass musicians.

Arrangers perfect their style by constantly studying the instruments of the orchestra, harmony and counterpoint, and writing, writing, and writing even more. And, it doesn't hurt if they played in one of the great dance bands as Billy and Nelson each did. Not only were Nelson and Billy veterans of the dance bands, but also many of the players who performed on their recording sessions were veterans of those same bands. They all knew and played alongside one another and were familiar with the arrangements of those writers during their tenure with those great bands. They achieved that swinging, hip, sophisticated sound because they had lived it since the late 30's.

Nelson Riddle with Nat King Cole at Capital Records

For both of them, it all came together with Frank Sinatra during the period of the early 1950s to the mid 1960s, until the period of rock and roll began to take over with a new, musical sensibility.

With rock and roll and the musical styles that followed, we witness the blurring of the role of the producer, engineer and arranger. During Billy and Nelson's day, they wrote the music, the engineers captured the sound on tape and the producer rode shotgun over the entire process, in particular the budget. The producer would oversee the entire project. In any event, some one has to make those creative decisions: to use strings and saxes and brass, or synthesizers and electric guitars. Whether you call them arrangers or the producers, they put the music together; they create the setting for the singer. It might be done at the mixing board, or on a computer, or written down on music paper as in the days of Sinatra, Riddle and May—the process is the same—only the methods are different. It's still musical arranging.

While musical styles change, and the role of the producer, engineer and arranger blur, we may never see the likes of Nelson Riddle, Billy May, and the other great arrangers of their day again. They were masters of their art, they made it happen because they only had to do one thing— write great musical arrangements.

Editor Notes:

I enjoyed the way legendary arranger Frank De Vol, who arranged Nat Cole's masterpiece "Nature Boy," illustrated it for me a few years ago while talking to him from his California home: "You get a letter from your mother. You see it and read it, and you actually see your mother, not just the words she wrote on paper, but the person you know and love. You picture her perfectly. When I see a melody on a piece of sheet music, I can read it the same way and I can sing it and know what it sounds like without title or words appearing. I know what it sounds like in my mind. Whether it be sad, funny, slow or fast - what it should be, and I can see it clearly. A musician does not have to do that - he just reads the part written for his instrument. An arranger sees and understands all parts and pieces. He takes music and makes it different. He must know how to write for six men, or 17 men, or 100 men, and what will be played and how it will be played, and exactly what it will sound like - much like a painter knows how to create a painting."

Frank DeVol first played lead sax and arranged for popular bandleader Horace Heidt in the 1930's: "Me, Alvino Rey and the four King Sisters were not satisfied with Heidt's material and so we all left to form the Alvino Rey Band where I quit the sax and did all the band's arrangements." In later years, Frank arranged at Columbia Records for Tony Bennett, Doris Day, Peggy Lee, Frankie Laine, and Ella Fitzgerald. He has arranged charts for scores of movies including Cat Ballou, Guess Who's Coming to Dinner, and Hush, Hush, Sweet Charlotte. Married to Song Star Helen O'Connell for six years before she passed on.

Individuality is also affected here, otherwise all bands and singers would wind up sounding pretty much the same. Some classic cases are: Glenn Miller, who worked so long and so hard to find that "special sound" for which he searched so long. When Glenn directed clarinetist

Johnny Mince to play the trumpet part with his clarinet when the trumpet player didn't show up for work one night, Glenn's quest ended. By arranging to have the clarinet play on top-playing a double with the tenor below-Glenn Miller's long sought after special intonation finally arrived. Of course, Glenn had arrangers like Bill Finegan and Jerry Gray who were responsible for arranging Glenn's biggest hits. "On the ballads I listen to the words first. That gives me an idea of how to structure the chart," Bill Finegan once said.

Not long ago I remember Kay Starr telling me that George Siravo's very brassy, resounding orchestrations for the stomping sounds of the Charlie Barnet band almost destroyed her vocal chords as she vainly tried

Pete Rugulo

to sing above it. Positive for Barnet; trouble for Starr. Kay had to learn to sing all over again because the band's power forced her to sing loudly, ultimately preventing her from singing. "It actually ruined my voice temporarily...it took me over a year to recover." Kay Starr's voice changed after that episode. On the positive side, it was Siravo who wrote the magnificent arrangement of "It's Magic" for Doris Day, "Who Can I Turn To?" for Tony Bennett, and "When Your Old Wedding Ring Was New" for Jimmy Roselli. He also arranged for Frank Sinatra, Glenn Miller, Gene Krupa, and Charlie Barnet. George Siravo is one of the unsung heroes of the Big Band Era. He and Frank Sinatra worked in tandem for years, and he often "ghosted" for Axel Stordahl at Columbia, turning out some magnificent charts.

Talk about enormously successful arrangements. Tutti Camaratta, arranger for Jimmy Dorsey, constricted to three minutes at the end of a radio show, devised a unique formula that featured all the stars of the show. He had boy singer Bob Eberly sing the first chorus of a song as a ballad, then the tempo was to pick up so the entire Dorsey band would play part of the selection, then the tempo was to slow down and Helen O'Connell came in for a semi-wailing finale. We all know the success of "Green Eyes," "Amapola," and "Tangerine" - beautifully arranged by Tutti.

Pete Rugulo, a modernist, progressive, and innovative arranger who studied the careers of Igor Stravinsky (Russian composer of revolutionary musical impact in the modern school) and Darius Milhaud (a French composer who developed polytonality- a simultaneous use of different keys) wrote 90% of Stan Kenton's charts. "In the day when even

Benny Goodman and Basie played single harmonies in 4/4 or even 3/4 waltz-time, I added all kinds of dissonance and incorporated some of Milhaud's ideas into jazz using 5/4 material which was never used before," Pete told me just yesterday. He began writing compositions, more like concert pieces, for the Kenton tours. "Stan really liked them - he even had me rearrange 'Artistry in Rhythm,' his great theme." Pete also arranged Billy Strayhorn's "Lush Life" for Nat Cole. "Billy wasn't crazy about the piece. He had it tucked away for ten years. I kind of redid the verse a lot - I added a lot of bars and stuff. He liked it pretty plain, I think. But I liked it the new way and so did Nat." Pete Rugulo's version is absolutely the most important "Lush Life" ever accomplished on a recording. When speaking to Maria Cole recently, she heartily agreed and felt that Pete's arrangement best suited Nat's version of the Strayhorn masterpiece.

The arranger doesn't just write down notes for musicians to follow, he may actually coach the players and consult closely with the leader of a band. Billy Strayhorn is a fine example. Billy was a composer and arranger for Duke Ellington, who himself was an accomplished orchestrator. But the Duke wanted to expand the band's repertoire, so he hired Strayhorn, who developed into one of the best musical arrangers of the Big Band Era. Billy would utilize the special skills of individual musicians and build the arrangements around their best features, thereby showcasing each player. A great Strayhorn arrangement example was the brilliant "Flamingo" that was recorded by Herb Jeffries. I love that recording.

In discussing the subject with master arranger Billy May, he declares arranging as: "When someone like Irving Berlin writes a song, they usually write just the piano part. If a vocalist is added, they can simply work it out. But, an arranger takes that song and does the background of say an instrumental version, keeping in mind perhaps the addition of a vocalist - figures the key and the vocalists range, and, depending on the mix of instruments you employ, arranges it accordingly. Now, a guy like Sinatra, besides being a great singer , is really a better musician --with fine musical taste --than people give him credit for. He will sit with you for hours and work out what he wants. Does he want to do a ballad with strings, or does he want to work with a dance band sound?"

Billy May is one of the most prolific arrangers of the Age. He has worked with singers like Nat King Cole, who recorded over 60 to 70 sides on The Billy May Sessions albums, and on Peggy Lee's album Pretty Eyes, as well as Frankie Laine's work at Columbia, on Billy Eckstine's Roulette album, Vic Damone's Strange Enchantment album, Ella Fitzgerald's various albums, and Frank Sinatra's recordings. They all owe a lot to his arranging skills. Billy's exceptional introduction to Glenn Miller's "Serenade In Blue" is my favorite.

"With all those singers and bands, it's always a meeting of the minds. You work together to produce the sounds you both want to

Gordon Jenkins

achieve." Billy began very young playing a tuba in high school, but ended up playing the trumpet: "I became intrigued with the makeup of orchestrations and began making arrangements by the time I was fourteen. I could always tell what the music would sound like in my head. I would utilize the band instruments available in a given band to reach the best effect.

"When I first worked in Hollywood, I would arrange works around the ability of the excellent players who were employed in the established studio bands, so it became easy to get them to accomplish what was needed for a given project." Billy began arranging for Ozzie Nelson's first radio shows; he wrote arrangements for the powerhouse Charlie Barnet band, setting the band's style, and for John Scott Trotter's Orchestra on Bing's famous radio show, including his work with Bing on Decca records. He wrote and played in Glenn Miller's band with fellow arrangers Bill Finegan and Jerry Gray. His own Billy May 1951-53 band wound down (the Big Band Era was over by then) when stationary (no traveling) Hollywood work became available. "I've been here ever since, "he said.

Arranger Gordon Jenkins wrote for Isham Jones, Judy Garland, Nat "King Cole, Dick Haymes, Helen Forrest, and Frank Sinatra, wrote the song "Goodbye" and composed "Manhattan Tower." Read the book "Goodbye" for Jenkins bio written by his son, Bruce. A fine book.

Bing Crosby's favorite arranger, John Scott Trotter, first worked for Hal Kemp; Henry Mancini of "Moon River" fame was Tex Beneke's musical writer; Pete Rugolo emanated from Stan Kenton; Edgar Sampson - also a composer ("Don't Be That Way" and "Stompin' at the Savoy") wrote for Chick Webb; Neal Hefti worked for Basie and, with Ralph Burns, played and arranged for Woody Herman (Woody once told me he never arranged, but that he was a good editor). Axel Stordahl, Paul Weston, and Sy Oliver all were established Tommy Dorsey arrangers who went on to arrange for many future bands and singers, and Bobby Haggart wrote arrangements for the Bob Crosby Band with the help of Matty Matlock and Deane Kincaide. Bob Crosby called Haggart "the undiscovered George Gershwin of our day." Bob is the author of the song "What's New?" among others. And, as noted, Frank De Vol began his arranging career with Horace Heidt.

Gordon Jenkins - 1944 - at home San Fernando Valley, CA

The bandleaders appreciated the arrangers: "Fletcher. He was the arranger," said ace drummer and band leader Gene Krupa, "and my first band back in the thirties was the best I ever had - with Fletcher Henderson." "Fletcher was one of the great orchestrators of the era," Benny Goodman told me back in 1984, "his arrangements were fascinating - you always hear something different each time you hear a number."

Mel Torme', an arranger himself, said: "My early role models cling to me with a kind of musical static electricity: Fletcher and (Eddie) Sauter , Jerry Gray. Duke himself. And the latter-day saints: Jerry Mulligan and Gil Evans, Marty Paich, Neal Hefti and Ralph Burns, and so many more."

"While I was at Columbia (Records)," said my mentor Frankie Laine, whose appreciation of quality arranging is evident in his work, "I had the chance to work with some of the greatest arranging talents in the business: Paul Weston, Percy Faith, Frank DeVol and others, who helped build my career through their great arrangements."

THE TOP TEN

BY TOP TEN - POLL TAKEN IN 2008

VAN ALEXANDER

Bandleader, Musician, Songwriter (A Tisket-A Tasket)

1. Begin the Beguine - Artie Shaw
2. Sing, Sing, Sing -Benny Goodman
3. 'Taint What You Do - Jimmie Lunceford
4. Sentimental Journey - Les Brown, Doris Day
5. Cherokee - Charlie Barnet
6. I Can't Get Started - Bunny Berigan
7. It's a Wonderful World - Armstrong
8. A Tisket - A Tasket - Ella Fitzgerald
9. One O'Clock Jump - Count Basie
10. And the Angels Sing - Benny Goodman

ERVIN DRAKE

Songwriter, "I Believe," "It Was a Very Good Year," "Al Di La."

1. Perdido - Duke Ellington
2. East St. Louis Toodle-oo - Duke Ellington
3. Never Go Lament - Duke Ellington
4. And the Angels Sing - Benny Goodman
5. Sing, Sing, Sing - Benny Goodman
6. Castle Rock - Harry James/Frank Sinatra
7. All or Nothing At All - Harry James/Frank Sinatra
8. Begin the Beguine - Artie Shaw
9. Frenesi - Artie Shaw
10. Don't Be That Way - Benny Goodman

TONY "B" BABINO

Entertainer and band vocalist, Al Jolson Tribute Artist

1. In the Mood - Glenn Miller
2. Let's Get Away from It All - Tommy Dorsey/Sinatra/Connie Haines/ Pipers
3. Sing, Sing, Sing - Benny Goodman
4. Moonlight Serenade - Glenn Miller
5. Green Eyes - Jimmy Dorsey/Bob Eberly/Helen O"Connell
6. Swinging On a Star - Bing Crosby
7. Chattanooga Choo Choo - Glenn Miller/Ten Beneke
8. Begin the Beguine - Artie Shaw
9. I'll Be with You in Apple Blossom Time - Andrews Sisters
10. Sentimental Journey - Les Brown/Doris Day

ANTHONY DI FLORIO III

Writer/Music Critic and Philosopher

1. You Made Me Love You - Harry James
2. Begin the Beguine - Artie Shaw
3. In the Mood - Glenn Miller
4. I Can't Get Started - Bunny Berigan
5. Begin the Beguine - Artie Shaw
6. All or Nothing at All - Harry James/Frank Sinatra
7. I'll Never Smile Again - Tommy Dorsey/Frank Sinatra/Pied Pipers
8. Woodchoppers Ball - Woody Herman
9. Cherokee - Charlie Barnet
10. Duke Ellington - Take the "A" Train

JOHN PRIMERANO

Songwriter, Singer, Pianist

1. In the Mood - Glenn Miller
2. Moonlight Serenade - Glenn Miller
3. Chattanooga Choo Choo - Glenn Miller/Tex Beneke
4. Woodchopper's Ball - Woody Herman

5. Sing, Sing, Sing. - Benny   Goodman
6. String of Pearls - Glenn Miller
7. Oh, Look at Me Now - Tommy Dorsey, Connie Haines, Pied Pipers
8. I'll Never Smile Again - Tommy Dorsey/Frank Sinatra/Pied Pipers
9. Elmer's Tune - Glenn Miller/Modernaires
10. One O'Clock Jump - William Count Basie

JACK LEBO

Writer, Critic, Broadcaster

1. Moonlight Serenade – Glenn Miller
2. Begin the Beguine – Artie Shaw
3. One O'Clock Jump – Count Basie
4. Cherokee – Charlie Barnet
5. Sunnyside of the Street – Tommy Dorsey
6. No Name Jive – Glen Gray
7. 720 In The Books – Jan Savitt
8. Woodchoppers Ball – Woody Herman
9. Let's Go Home – Charlie Spivak
10. Jersey Bounce – Benny Goodman

ANN JILLIAN

Actress, Vocalist, Writer, Lecturer

Hi Richard,

Here are the choices I made for my favorite Big Band tunes.

There is nothing as great as hearing the lush sounds of a Big Band. Whether it's a love song, lively swing, instrumental, or torch, the Big Band sound can evoke an immediate emotional response. Over the years I've been privileged to be able to sing some of these outstanding songs on various variety programs I appeared on. I sang some on the Broadway stage in Sugar Babies. Bob Hope allowed me to recreate some Big Band songs with lavish production numbers as did the major networks for whom I worked. Sammy Cahn gave me the opportunity to sing some of his own songs on stage, and I chose some "chestnuts" myself for my own musical act.

While my son thinks I'm kind of ancient (he's not too far from right) he really wasn't around when some of these memorable songs were performed. Still, I was just so happy to be able to perform them when I did. So, here's my list of favorites with a load of sentimentality behind my choices.

1. I've Got Rhythm
2. I'll Be Seeing You
3. Until The Real Thing Comes Along
4. Body And Soul
5. It Don't Mean a Thing if it Ain't Got That Swing
6. More Than You Know
7. Young at Heart
8. My Ship
9. I Only Miss Him When I Think Of Him
10. Second Time Around

ANDY MURCIA
Artist Management, Producer, Author

Richard,

Because I'm older than Ann Jillian, here are some big band tunes from the era you requested that might make sense for you list:

1. In The Mood - Glenn Miller
2. Chattanooga Choo-Choo - Glenn Miller/Tex Beneke
3. A String of Pearls - Glenn Miller
4. Little Brown Jug - Glenn Miller
5. I've Got a Gal in Kalamazoo - Glenn Miller/Tex Beneke/Modernaires
6. Tuxedo Junction - Glenn Miller
7. Pennsylvania 6-5000 - Glenn Miller/Ensemble
8. Moonlight Serenade - Glenn Miller
9. Stompin' At The Savoy - Benny Goodman
10. Satin Doll - Duke Ellington

AL MONROE
New Jersey Radio Personality for Big Bands and Vocalists

Officer - Society of Singers.

1. Moonlight Serenade - Glenn Miller
2. In the Mood - Glenn Miller
3. Begin the Beguine - Artie Shaw
4. Sentimental Journey - Les Brown/Doris Day
5. I'll Never Smile Again - Tommy Dorsey/Frank Sinatra
6. I Can't Get Started - Bunny Berigan
7. And the Angels Sing - Benny Goodman/Martha Tiltin
8. Tangerine - Jimmy Dorsey/Bob Eberly/Helen O'Connell
9. Deep Purple - Larry Clinton/Bea Wain
10. It Isn't Fair - Sammy Kaye/Don Cornell

MIKE KAPTANIS
Crosby Expert, Writer, Collector Music 1926-42.

1. South Rampart Street Parade - Bob Crosby
2. Sing, Sing, Sing - Benny Goodman
3. Indian Love Call - Artie Shaw
4. Lover Man - Billie Holiday
5. The Eel - Bud Freeman
6. He Ain't Got Rhythm - Jimmie Rushing
7. Sweet Leilani - Bing Crosby
8. Here Lies Love - Bing Crosby
9. Tank Town Bump - J.R. Morton
10. Tight Like This - Louis Armstrong

CONNIE HAINES

1. Let's Get Away From It All - Me w/ Tommy Dorsey
2. White Christmas - Bing Crosby
3. Sentimental Journey - Doris Day and Les Brown
4. Moonlight Serenade - Glenn Miller
5. Sunnyside of the Street - Tommy Dorsey
6. Begin the Beguine - Artie Shaw
7. Chattanooga Choo Choo - Glenn MIller
8. You Made Me Love You - Harry James
9. Snootie Little Cutie - Me, Frank and The Pied Pipers
10. Do Lord - Jane Russell, Rhonda Fleming, Beryl Davis and Me.

JERRY VALE

1. Prisoner of Love - Perry Como
2. Moonlight Serenade - Glenn Miller
3. It Isn't Fair - Don Cornell
4. Jezebel - Frankie Laine
5. Wanted - Perry Como
6. Laura - Frank Sinatra
7. Nancy with the Laughing Face - Frank Sinatra
8. Two Purple Shadows - Jerry Vale
9. Angelina - Louis Prima
10. My Way - Frank Sinatra

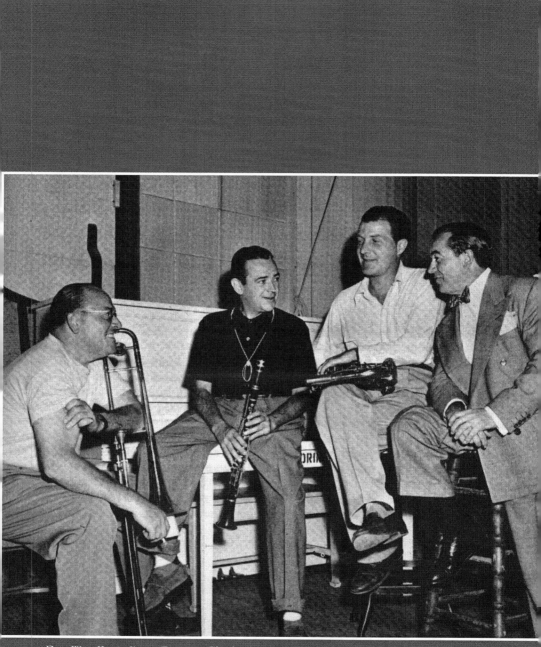

Pee Wee Hunt, Jimmy Dorsey, Charlie Barnet, Jan Garber

BEN GRISAFI'S BIG BAND
HALL OF FAME ORCHESTRA - Alumni's Hideaway

In a never-ending search for musicians who have scattered themselves throughout Big Band oblivion, except those who live in and around Los Angeles, California, where so many have settled down to a life of either casual retirement or taking gigs as studio musicians to augment the music of Hollywood, I have, at last, found a pot of gold at the end of the Big Band rainbow ---right here in the East.

Here, a major group of alumni musicians are still playing their instruments smack in the middle of composer, arranger, and saxophonist Ben Grisafi's Big Band Hall of Fame Orchestra.

When Ben Grisafi had his band on Long Island just a few years ago I found Chuck Genduso, the trumpet player who blew beautifully with Harry James, Tommy Dorsey, and Ray McKinley, and Dan Repole, a great trombonist who honed his notes with Guy Lombardo, and also produced for Tommy Tucker, and Les and Larry Elgart - Larry being Best

Man at his Atlantic City wedding.

Pete Chively was once modernist Stan Kenton's, and Billy May's bassist; Ed Matson tinkled piano smoothly for trumpeter Billy Butterfield's band, and Al Miller rolled his drumsticks for Xavier Cugat and played with Buddy Rich and Louis Bellson's band; Bobby

Nelson blew tenor sax with Louis Prima, Lee Castle's Jimmy Dorsey Ghost Band, and Tommy Dorsey's orchestra. Featured alto sax player Chacey Dean wailed with Charlie Barnet, upbeat Stan Kenton, and the much tamer Mitchell Ayres. Tom Alfano employed his lead alto with Les and Larry Elgart and Johnny Long's band. Tito Puente's jazz oriented band had Schep Pullman managing baritone sax chores for nine years. Charlie Henry worked with the Johnny Long and Ralph Flanagan bands, and Jack Carman performed on trombone in the swinging bands of Buddy Rich, Boyd Raeburn, and Georgie Auld. Trumpeter Mike Lewis has performed with the bands of Tex Beneke and Harry James and backed music luminaries Tony Bennett, Sammy Davis Jr., Mel Torme, Andy Williams, Gladys Knight, and Sarah Vaughan, as well as Joe Williams and Vic Damone. Vocalist Denise Richards performed with the Dorsey Brothers and Glenn Miller Orchestras. Whew!

Now that's a Big Band full of veteran players. It's no wonder Ben Grisafi's two CD's, Talk of the Town and But Beautiful are selling well everywhere. And, as you listen, you will think about Les Brown and Larry Elgart playing Grisafi charts.

Younger musicians, who com-

Ben Grisafi on the Beach in Aruba - 1997
Yvette Grisafi Collection

plete the band's roster hold great respect for the seasoned alumni, and, in contrast, the alumni members are amazed with the fine, talented players who comprise today's music scene. There are very few non-school bands of this size available for young, upcoming musicians who prefer playing the band's '40s style music.

For validity, Ben Grisafi has played tenor sax with Billy Butterfield, Randy Brooks, and Cab Calloway and led a band opening at Carnegie Hall for our mutual friend, vocalist Jerry Vale, with his arrangement of "My Buddy." He has appeared with vocalists Al Martino, Julius La Rosa, and Margaret Whiting. WALK and other New York radio stations dubbed "But Beautiful" as the best compact disc of 2000. With the timbre of the Les Brown and Larry Elgart band, Ben effects all the arrangements, and he has since arranged over forty selections for his next CD.

Ben Grisafi and I first met at a luncheon a few years ago at the old Three Village Inn in Stony Brook, Long Island. Upon learning of Ben's activities through vocalist Roberto Tirado (Ben backed and arranged Roberto's own CD Prisoner of Love album), who was profiled in my book The Music Men, I invited Ben to meet Max Wirz, a European disc jockey and author from Switzerland who was visiting me and whose radio shows, Showtime and Light and Breezy, dominated Swiss Big Band American style radio, reaching into France and adjoining countries. Ben and I hit it off as old friends, and, later, joined songwriter Ervin Drake, actor, vocalist John Gabriel, and myself in a tribute to Ervin at Suffolk County's Five Towns College at the invitation of College President Dr. Stanley Cohen. Ervin Drake composed Frank Sinatra's "It Was a Very Good Year" and Frankie Laine's "I Believe."

"I began taking sax lessons at thirteen," said Ben. "I kept it from my parents because they could not afford to pay for it. I got a job setting bowling pins at nearby Benson Lanes. Lessons were one dollar and the instrument rental was also one dollar. Because of my very young age, I had to practice more to qualify for playing in the local band. When my teacher, Carl Pinto, recommended advance studies, I subwayed to Manhattan to study under another fine teacher, Louis Arsine."

Lafayette High School music studies provided excellent musical training for Ben Grisafi. Upon graduating, he began playing in local bands. "I began going to Nola Studios in Manhattan where many big bands rehearsed and recorded. I recall Gene Krupa rehearsing with sidemen Gerry Mulligan and Charlie Ventura. I trekked to see live bands play at the famous Metropole on Broadway. On famous 52nd Street, between 5th and 6th Avenue, I could hear the sound of developing jazz and bebop reaching the street from the Onyx Club or The Three Deuces where Coleman Hawkins, Ben Webster, or Georgie Auld would be playing."

By the age of seventeen, Ben played with Randy Brooks and Billy Butterfield, whose solo on Artie Shaw's "Stardust" recording is classic.

Ben was drafted into the Korean conflict and was placed in the Army Band, playing out his time in service clubs and in parades and uniformed dance parties.

Upon discharge, Ben Grisafi married and became a jeweler, finding work at New York's Diamond Center, but continued playing gigs weekends on the then very lean music scene. With other jeweler musicians, Ben helped form a band, naming it the Gem Tones, playing steady weekends at places like the Picture Lounge on Long Island.

"One summer I sat in a band in the Catskills, fronted by drummer, and later record promoter and director Pete Bennett. I was excited about my first professional arrangements, "Ferryboat Cha Cha" and "Woodpecker Cha Cha," which were recorded on the Cupid label. I also performed in rock and roll shows with stars like Bobby Rydell, Fats Domino, and the Supremes.

In 1993, Ben met an important person that changed his direction;

"Bob Rosen became the one major force in my life. A record producer, Bob had engaged important jazz players like (pianists) Billy Taylor and Marty Napoleon. His vast recording experience guided me through the myriad levels of recording, studio mixing, evaluating, and editing. He spent many hours teaching me and has become a dear friend and confidant. Without Bob Rosen, there would be no Ben Grisafi band, recordings, or arrangements for you to hear."

Ben with Paul Bennett

Ben, and the music world lost Bob Rosen in 2006.

In 1993, Ben organized a 40th reunion with the original Dixie Division dance band of his early fifties Army days. He surprised them with an eighteen piece impromptu band, arranging a dozen songs including "Dixie" and "Back Home in Indiana," where the group was last stationed before disbanding. Members arrived from everywhere, urging and encouraging Ben to continue with the band after the party had ended.

"I began running dances, which were musically successful, but not financially. Slowly, bookings grew and I continued writing arrangements at a rapid pace. I did not want to copy other's arrangements. In 1995 my first CD Talk of the Town was released, followed by But Beautiful, with my wife Yvette gracing the cover and the terrific Denise Richards performing the vocals on both, with all original arrangements." The band had backed vocalist Roberto Tirado, on his CD entitled Prisoner of Love. Roberto was a well-known New York area television personality and a very fine singer.

Radio station WALK and Jack Ellsworth engaged Ben Grisafi's Alumni Big Band for Jack's 50th Anniversary as a disc jockey and 75th birthday. Jack has always been impressed with Ben's band, citing his work over the air and in his weekly newspaper column.

In 2002 Ben and Yvette Grisafi moved lock, stock and sax to Palm Beach Gardens, Florida where he became associated with Sally Bennett's Big Band Hall of Fame.

Sally Bennett, who was the founder of the Big Band Hall of Fame, had recently passed away. Hoping to keep the Hall of Fame intact, her husband Paul was searching for someone with valid Big Band credentials to head the Hall of Fame. I introduced Ben to Paul Bennett, Sally's husband and after a few get-together sessions, Ben now proudly leads the Big Band Hall of Fame Orchestra, and has become an active Trustee and champion of Big Band music throughout the world.

Mike Ficco

Mike Ficco and the Long Island Jazz Orchestra

Mike Ficco's musicians, unlike other performing Big Bands specializes in the original arrangements of the big band and swing orchestras of the 1930s & '40s. Whether in a cabaret or concert setting, you can count on hearing the music of Miller, Basie, Shaw or Ellington. Every member of the orchestra is a conservatory trained artist who loves to play and derives satisfaction from the love and joy of the music itself.

Formed by Mike Ficco, the orchestra is recognized as one of the most exciting and versatile 16 piece jazz big bands in the East. As Mike says, "You have to hear them live to believe it." That utterance has always been the universal cry from musicians. You have to be there! Sure, there are the recordings when the band played to a microphone, but, then there is the band that plays to an audience. What a difference.

There's Mike on sax with Rich Fornaro, James Miceli, Joel Camp, and Steve Costenbader. On trumpet you'll find Barry Schwalb, Barry White, Kevin Cordone and Mark Opaz. Trombonists Rod Borrie, Ken Mahoney, Kevin Delargy, Bill Cordone play with Rhythmists Jimmy Guarnieri-drums, Neal Ralph-keyboard and Adam Mazzaferro on bass. The vocals are handled by Frank Russo's Sinatra stylings.

The Spitfire Band from Canada
by Riverwalk Jazz

The Toronto based Spitfire Band is a dance band formed in 1981 as a studio orchestra by singer Jackie Rae, with trumpeter Mickey Erbe as music director and arranger, and trombonist Laurie Bower as vocal arranger.

With the success of its first LPs, The Spitfire Band and Flight II it began to perform publicly in 1982, making its debut in St Catharines, Ontario,Canada, and giving the first of many concerts at Ontario Place. Rae has served as featured vocalist and master of ceremonies, and Erbe as bandleader. After a Christmas album that year, Home for the Holidays it had LPs issued in 1983-5 by Columbia, A Sentimental Journey, and later Swings Down Broadway, Swinging the Movies. A compilation, The Make Believe Ballroom was issued in 1990.

Initially the band's repertoire comprised Erbe's updates of swing-era classics "Marie," "Tuxedo Junction," "In the Mood," "Pennsylvania 6-5000," "I'll Never Smile Again," but came on record to include movie and Broadway themes, and other pop material. Personnel is not listed on the band's LPs but has included musicians from Toronto's jazz and studio circles - :, trumpeters Arnie Chycoski, John MacLeod, and Dave Woods, saxophonists Bob D'Angelis, Steve Lederer, and Jack Zaza, and trombonists Bower and Bob Livingston.

Pat Longo And His Hollywood Jazz Band

Out on the coast is the exciting band of Pat Longo. A sax player who played with Harry James, whose help allowed Pat to form his own orchestra in 1978.

His first recording "Chain Reaction" propelled his all-star aggregation into clubs, ballrooms and concert venues around the country. His first album was Extreme Heat. Pat has performed with a stash of greats that include Tony Bennett, Frank Sinatra, Jr., Sarah Vaughan, Rod Stewart, and dozens more.

Mike Vax Jazz Orchestra And Big Band

Mike directs, crazy as it may seem, both orchestras. Emanating from Oakland, California, his orchestra (formerly the New Oakland Jazz) is made up of a gaggle of big band alumni from such as Stan Kenton, Woody Herman, Buddy Rich, Duke Ellington, Tommy and Jimmy Dorsey, Glenn Miller, Cab Calloway, Ray McKinley, and Tex Beneke, adding up to some of the finest musicians on the West coast - San Francisco Bay area.

The Big Band features much Kenton material and includes alumni from the 1952-78 Stan Kenton band. They perform not only the old, nostalgic Kenton book, but newly written material in the Kenton style, but they do not try to be the Stan Kenton Band.

Their "Friends of Big Band Jazz" helps support our friend Al "Jazzbeaux" Collins Memorial Scholarship Fund with proceeds from sales of its CDs. The goals here is to perform meaningful music, and talk about the importance of the jazz heritage in America and to bring jazz to the younger generation.

Mike Vax, a product of Oakland, has been leading a band since he was in college and was first trumpet and road manager of the Stan Kenton Orchestra and co-leader when Kenton was recovering from surgery. He once led the Dukes of Dixieland in New Orleans and has produced and directed music for over 25 jazz festivals over the years.

Vince Giordano & the Nighthawks

Vince Giordano began his lifes trip into the world of music at the age of five. The discovery of a slew of 78-rpm-period records in his grandmother's attic, ranging form grand opera to Joe "King" Oliver, ignited the flame. He soon learned tuba, string bass, and bass saxophone. By the age of 15, he was a working musician.

His love of the vintage music of the 20's and 30's led him to explore other facets of this music. He began to read books about jazz. He also began a self-initiated apprenticeship with the legendary William Challis (arranger for the Paul Whiteman Band and the Jean Goldkette

Vince Giordano

Orchestra in the 20's) that lasted four years. This gave Vince the education he sought: a thorough grounding with first-hand experience in the sounds of the great Jazz Age era from Challis and the other older musicians he met and played with.

Vince continued to expand his musical abilities and was soon fully established as a freelance musician in New York, playing in Broadway pit bands as well as recording sessions and traditional jazz bands. He began collecting original jazz charts, and he soon established Vince Giordano's Nighthawks--a band dedicated to playing the golden era of jazz repertory.

Vince's attention to the authenticity of transcribing arrangements from old recordings, his insistence on precision, and his love of re-creating the music transformed his Nighthawks into the most sought-after jazz band in New York City. Vince Giordano's Nighthawks have been booked for black-tie galas at the Metropolitan Museum of Art, the New York Public Library, the New York City Ballet, the Waldorf Astoria, and for private parties for many prominent New Yorkers, as well as the Rainbow Room, the Carlyle Hotel, "21," and the Copacabana.

Vince has been invited to perform at the Smithsonian, Carnegie Hall, the JVC Jazz Festival, Lincoln Center, and the Breda Jazz Festival in Holland. Described by one critic as a "poet of the jazz repertory frozen by time... the authenticity of the music coupled with his first-hand knowledge of the original material provides him with insights, experiences, and an integrity that is unique to the musical world."

Also a big-band historian and collector, Giordano has more than 30,000 scores in his collection, most of which were found on cross-country trips spent poking around in musicians' basements.

The Swingtime Big Band of Jerry Costanza

The Swing time Big Band of Jerry Costanza, sax player, vocalist and leader, with Mike Carubia as musical director, and ace pianist and arranger Wayne Sabella, and a very dedicated group of musicians on Long Island has been around since 1979. Mike has taught theory at Ward Melville High School and played with almost every living legend from Tony Bennett to Jerry Vale- and on over 25 Broadway shows from Les Mis-

Swingtime Big Band of Jerry Costanza

erables to Saturday Night Fever and has written and recorded over 100 original pieces of music. Jerry Costanza is an accomplished vocalist, beginning it all with his father's band when he traveled with the band as the band's "roadie" but only on the condition that his father would let him sing with the band. Lately, Jerry has joined forces with Steve Shaiman and the Swingtime Big Band validated with producer and arrangers Andy Farber and Mike Carubia to round out a great musical organization.

Active Tribute Bands

The following orchestras in the United States still have active tour schedules:

In the year 2007-2008 The Canadian Spitfire Band, The Harry James Orchestra, The Les Elgart Orchestra, The Hal McIntyre Orchestra, The Nelson Riddle Orchestra, The Cab Calloway Orchestra, The Tommy Dorsey Orchestra, The Terry Myers Orchestra, Les Brown's Band of Renown, Tony Corbiscello Big Band, Vince Giordano & the Nighthawks, Mike Carubia Big Band, Jack Morgan and the Russ Morgan Orchestra, The Sammy Kaye Orchestra with Roger Thorpe, The Jimmy Dorsey Orchestra with Bill Tole, The Jan Garber Orchestra with Howard Schneider, Bobby Layne & His Orchestra, Hunter Fuerste and his American Vintage Orchestra, The Dick Jurgens Orchestra, The New Gene Krupa Orchestra, The Count Basie Orchestra, The Tom Daugherty Orchestra, Don Scaletta and the Jazz Project - Salutes Stan Kenton, The Woody Herman Orchestra directed by Frank Tiberi, The Artie Shaw Orchestra directed by Dick Johnson, The Blue Moon Big Band, Rob Leonard leader, and the Ben Grisafi Big Band Hall of Fame Orchestra, Mike Ficco Long Island Big Band and the marvelous Glenn Miller Orchestra directed by Larry O'Brien who plays all the original Miller charts including a stirring "Danny Boy" solo that's truly music to your ears.

In England, the most notable venues are Pontin's Holiday Centre on London Road in Suffolk, U.K., and Potters Leisure Resort, on the Coast Road in Hopton-on-Sea, Norfolk, U.K., where in the Summer of 2007 Big Band festivals were held with The Pasadena Roof Orchestra, The John Miller Orchestra, The Official Glenn Miller Orchestra directed by Ray McVay, the Syd Lawrence Orchestra, directed by Chris Dean, the Len Phillips Big Band, and the Joe Loss Big Band directed by Todd Miller.

Another popular showplace is the famed London Palladium where, after 60 years the Big Bands have returned.

USA "Ambassador" Award Certificates
Recipients

Richard Grudens	Long Island, NY	Writer, Author of multi big band related books
The Olney Big Band	Olney, MD	Big Band
Don Kennedy	Atlanta, GA	Writer, DJ Publisher Big Band Jump
Jack Lebo	Levittown, PA	Writer, columnist for American Rag etc.
Roget Pontbriand	Palm Beach, FL	Professor Palm Beach Atlantic University
Palm Beach Atlantic Jazz Ensemble	Palm Beach, FL	Big Band
Jack Ellsworth	Long Island, NY	Disk Jockey
Russ Dorsey & Les Elgart Orchestra	Texas	Big Band
Swingtime Big Band	Long Island, NY	Big Band
Bob Scherago	Golden Age of Radio	Disc Jockey, "One Night Stand"
Dick Bertel	Golden Age of Radio	Disc Jockey, "One Night Stand"
Arnold Dean	Golden Age of Radio	Disc Jockey, "One Night Stand"
Don Jones	Apple Valley, CA	Publisher Ragtime USA
Big Band Hall of Fame Orchestra	West Palm Beach, FL	Directed by Ben Grisafi
Paul Cohen Big Band	Tamarac, FL	Big Band
Robert Robbins	Pennsylvania	Writer, USA Secretary Big Band International
David Bernhart	Burbank, CA	Big Band Academy of America
Ken Poston	Long Beach, CA	Los Angeles Jazz Institute
Robert C. Florence	Thousand Oaks, CA	Limited Edition
Brian L. Pastor Big Band	Philadelphia, PA	Big Band
J. Stewart Jackson	Denver, Co	Woody Herman Big Band
Donald L. Pentleton	West Newton, MA	Hal McIntyre Orchestra
Michael N. Vax	Pittsburg, CA	Jazz Orchestra

International "Ambassador" Award Certificates
Recipients

Dai Kimoto Swing Kids	Switzerland	Big Band
Thilo Wolf Big Band	Germany	Big Band
Dani Felber	Switzerland	Big Band
Hazy Osterwald	Switzerland	Diietikon-Big Band Festival
Pepe Lienhard	Switzerland	Big Band
Billy Gorlt	Switzerland	Big Band
Walter Henne	Germany	Disc Jockey
Gerhard Klussmeier	Germany	Disc Jockey
HAMBURGER Lokalradio	Switzerland	Radio Station
Kurt Mettler	Switzerland	Radio Eviva DJ
Max Wirz	Switzerland	Disc Jockey
Hugo Strasser	Germany	SWR Big Band
Paul Kuhn	Germany	SWR Big Band
Max Greger	Switzerland	SWR Big Band
Will Salden	Europe	GMO Europe (Glenn Miller)
Jonny Cooper	South Africa	GMO South Africa (Glenn Miller)
Kurt Brogli	Switzerland	Big Band
Rene Gubelman	Switzerland	Big Band Festival Organizer
Big Band Festival	Switzerland	Swing in Dietkon
Bill Ashton	Great Britain	Director National Youth Jazz Orchestra
Roy Belcher	Great Britain	Founder of Big Band International Magazine
Malcolm Laycock	Great Britain	Disc Jockey and writer for BBI
Diane Lusher	Great Britain	Widow of Don Lusher & Leader of the Ted Heath Band
Tony Mundell	Great Britain	President & Publisher of Big Band International
John Ruddick	Great Britain	Director of Midland Youth Orchestra
Sheila Tracy	Great Britain	Author & Radio Personality

NEWER FELLAS

"Hey, you must be one of the Newer Fellers"
Bing to Frank in the film High Society

Tony B. Babino
A Singing Storm Who Keeps Going Strong

Tony B. might just be the classic trailblazing, high-energy vocalist

of the new age of popular music. His qualifications match those of all the singers of past generations, in a time identified as before and during the Big Band Era, and beyond. Those were the days when the great Al Jolson and the prolific crooner Bing Crosby had established the era of the vocalists and cleared the way for followers Frank Sinatra, Perry Como, Jerry Vale, Don Cornell, Eddie Fisher, Johnny Mathis, Vic Damone, Al Martino, Tony Bennett, and a handful of others who tossed their vocal skills into the arena to compete for the Gold Ring.   Tony B. and his counterparts are a distinct extension of those remarkable careers. Are those days about to resurface? Is the world ready for good music again? It will, if Tony B. has his way. He's trying to bring it all back.

In his quest for excellence in performing Tony B. has carefully surrounded himself with qualified people in his arena, from personal manager Robert Rosenblatt, who has provided unwavering support in matters both legal and career; to arranger and premier piano accompanist Richie Iacona, whose arrangements, as Tony B. states: "...breathes new life into classic standards, but give my own original compositions the edge they need to stand on their own within the genre.'"

The friendship of song star Connie Haines, who sang shoulder- to -shoulder with Frank Sinatra in the bands of Harry James and Tommy Dorsey for three years as they grew up together in the Big Bands, has bolstered Tony B.'s career to an even higher plateau, having performed with Connie in Florida before ten thousand enthusiastic fans: "From the moment I met Connie, she took me under her wing and made me feel like family. She is a wonderful and beautiful person, and her talent is second to none. That lady can swing, baby! When we'd perform in Atlantic City night after night she'd invite me up on stage, not only to perform, but to share the spotlight. There aren't too many performers in this business who would extend an opportunity like that to someone new."

Tony B. began singing at a very young age after first being impressed by Bobby Darin's knockout recording of "Mack the Knife." Previously, he worshipped heroes Al Jolson, Frank Sinatra, Tony Bennett and Paul McCartney. Tony B.'s impressions of Al Jolson are simply unbelievable and matched to perfection.

Tony B.'s counterparts today are versed in the sounds of Michael Buble", Peter Cincotti, Harry Connick, Jr., John Primerano, and John Pizzerelli. Tony's power and production are overpowering and contain a punch that knocks you

Tony and Richard at the Al Jolson Conference - 2005 - M. Grudens Photo

out. He is a Sinatra, a Darin, a Bennett, and a Jolson, if you will, all in one.

Tony and I first met when I hosted a book signing and luncheon for Big Band vocalist Connie Haines a few years earlier upon completing Connie's biography "Snootie Little Cutie."

After lunch, Tony and Connie spontaneously launched a performance from their Stars and Stripes Revue show. Then Tony launched into an impromptu a capella version of Jolson, singing "When the Red, Red, Robin Comes Bob Bob Bobbin' Along." Well, the power and phrasing, as well as the distinctly accurate performance was amazing. He mesmerized the crowd that had gathered around him.

"I became interested in Al Jolson when I was just a kid. I was watching the Million Dollar Movie on our local Channel 9. One day The Jolson Story came on, and from that moment, even though I was just a kid, I wanted to locate all the Jolson music that I could to listen to. I thought he was phenomenal. I was transfixed on Jolson and his music for life."

Up to now, Tony B. has performed at important venues such as Atlantic City, on cruise ships, Las Vegas, and the Florida circuit. His mounting credits to date span numerous personal performances, recordings, and total involvement in his trade. His recording of the Harold Arlen classic "Come Rain or Come

Tony B. with Connie Haines

Shine" was selected by Arlen's son, Sam, and his wife Joan, to be featured on a Harold Arlen Songbook album, sharing tracks with Tony Bennett, Faith Hill, Eric Clapton, Jane Monheit and Natalie Cole.

Swingin' Around is Tony B.'s great CD with Richie Iacona playing a real quality piano and conducting the orchestra. Tony seems very much at home with Richie's piano close by, especially on "Watch What Happens," "Till There was You," and "Almost Like Being in Love," all three the best

of Tony B. It's an album worthy of comparing to Sinatra sometimes, and Darin other times. Both are ingrained in Tony's psyche.

Jane Monheit
A New Class of Singer

Watching Jane Monheit close-up singing her wonderfully different arrangements of familiar songs is an exhilarating experience. She flips her hair and delves deep into "Over the Rainbow," and you know you are listening to someone special

Jane Monheit

singing something special.

A product of the south shore of Long Island, Jane Monheit is a jazz singer with a voice that burst forth from her fledgling beginning in 2001. She has since performed in London and Tokyo as well as everywhere else. Her husband, Rick Montalbano, is the trio's drummer who backs her so well. "Moon River" is a favorite of her fans and she can move along with a bossa nova beat as well as anyone.

Michael Bublé
Songs by Sinatra

Michael Bublé (pronounced boo-blay) is a new guy on the block from British Columbia with Italian grandparents, naturally, who encouraged

Michael Bublé

his singing, Michael's voice is sometimes a dead ringer for Sinatra, and sometimes for Darin, although his voice is youthful sounding having not completely matured. I first noticed Michael when I heard and saw him singing while watching television ice skating events in early 2004.

Michael performed in the 2004 Super Bowl extravaganza along with Celine Dion and Shania Twain. Michael has the flair and penchant for becoming a full-blown star and seems to be a hard working and enthusiastic performer trying to make his way up the ladder.

"My grandfather was my best friend when I was growing up. He encouraged me to sing. He wanted me to learn the songs he loved so much, music that has passed over my generation. Then I knew I wanted to become a singer and I knew this was the music that I wanted to sing."

When Michael sang "Mack the Knife" at the wedding of Prime Minister Brian Mulroney's daughter, he was noticed by producer David Foster of Warner Records who signed him with Reprise Records. Michael's rendition of "Moondance," "Come Fly with Me," "The Way You Look Tonight," and "How Can You Mend a Broken Heart" is proof enough of his star capabilities. His self titled thirteen selection CD is an indication that a star may be born as we listen.

Fortunately, Michael is a long way from his working days at Chuck E. Cheese, and at work in a liquor store, and light commercial fishing with his dad.

Peter Cincotti
Newer Than New

Peter Cincotti is just 23 year old. He sings like Sinatra.Or Buble'. Or Connick. Some say he is destined for the big-time. When still very young he was exposed to jazz singer Ella Fitzgerald and big band leader and composer Duke Ellington. He began studying piano when he was three and started his vocals at fifteen.

Although he says he tries to stay away from songs beyond his years, he will eventually sing the appropriate standards, or, if they come his way, fresh and new songs that may become great songs. Piano wise, he follows his major influences Bill Evans and Oscar Peterson. He is graduating to the piano stylings of Nat "King" Cole, another worthy influence.

Peter Cincotti

Because he is so young, it's virtually impossible for him to sing mature songs like "April in Paris," or "September of My Years," or even Ervin Drake's "It Was a Very Good Year," But he has great expectations and, as we all know, the years go by quickly.

Peter Cincotti considers himself more a piano player than a singer. He prefers working in a trio setting. But his voice is rich and lush and will be an important adjunct to his career.

Peter's album On the Moon, with classic standards like "I Love Paris" and the South Pacific classic, one of my favorite Rodgers and Hammerstein songs, "Bali Ha'i," in a fresh, unusual version. It resonates throughout.

Peter appeared in the Bobby Darin bio that starred Kevin Spacey as Darin. The film is entitled Beyond the Sea. You can also find him on the Tonight Show now and then.

Julia Rich
Big Band Vocalist

Julia Rich's first performance with the Glenn Miller Orchestra was in 1985,at the Opryland Hotel in Nashville, Tennessee. Julia, a preacher's daughter from Nashville, has since become the featured female vocalist for the orchestra. Over the last almost 20 years, she has been touring through

Julia Rich

every state in the union, the Canadian Provinces, Spain, South America and even Japan. As an aspiring singer was much encouraged by her mother and father, Reverend Fred, and June Blankenship. She literally grew up singing in church choirs and at revivals conducted by her dad.

With a Bachelor of Music degree, she picked up harmony singing from the Methodist hymnal and a fondness for the voice of Judy Garland. For her, voice lessons were helpful, and with a feeling for jazz, she turned to the sounds of the great Sarah Vaughan and legendary Billie Holiday, but the best instructions received turned out to be listening to premier vocalist Ella Fitzgerald on a pair of headphones. The direct, intense concentration directed Ella's spirited voice permanently into Julia's psyche. Feeling a divine spark, Julia became uplifted by Ella's phrasing principles.

Today, Julia Rich enjoys performing in the many beautiful, old theaters, opera houses, and high School auditoriums throughout the country, full of friendly people who enjoy good music. It constantly encourages and inspires her. Watching couples that have danced together for 50 years and listening to them muse about what the music meant to them early in their lives together enriches her feelings for the great music the Glenn Miller Orchestra perpetuates. While singing with the orchestra, Julia has been fortunate to have performed with The Mills Brothers, Rosemary Clooney, Jerry Vale, Connie Haines, and other great voices that preceded her own career. Julia has received invaluable inspiration and encouragement from Dr. Paul Tanner, of the original civilian Glenn Miller Orchestra, and Irene Wolf, Glenn's sister, who was a cherished friend.

From time to time, Julia sings with a small group and sometimes just a piano or guitar, making music with many worthy musicians over the years. Larry O'Brien considers Julia Rich to be one of the best Glenn Miller Orchestra vocalists ever. Along the way, Julia Rich has recorded two albums for Cardinal Records: "I'll Take Romance," and "The Way You Make Me Feel."

Tom Postilio
Revisited

When Tom Postilio appeared in my first book, The Best Damn Trumpet Player, he was billed as the New Kid on the Bandstand-Sinatra Style. Tom Postilio is his real name, by the way. Tom was twenty-five at the time and we lunched in a cozy bistro named Sophie's in St. James, New York.

Tom had already been performing at the fabled Village Gate, at Eighty-Eight's, and the prestigious Rainbow Room high up the ladder in Rockefeller Center. During the Summer of 1995, Tom toured ten months with the world-famous Glenn Miller Orchestra and my good friend, Larry O'Brien, the band's director, who, by the way, is still the leader. His debut album struck a familiar chord with the great standards, but with a new voice, and poignant moments of brilliance.

"I couldn't imagine doing anything else. When I am on stage I feel at home. I love what I do." Where have we heard that before? From Frank...from Tony Bennett? Of course!

Tom first fell in love with "our kind of music" when he was thirteen and had discovered his dad's archived Frank Sinatra albums.

"My interest grew out of a love for Frank Sinatra, whose music I love and when I began to sing, people actually began to compare me to him."

Soon, Tom realized he could not build a career on sounding like Sinatra, so he began developing his own style, as others, who emulated Sinatra, had done before him. Before performing, Tom warms up by singing in the shower:

Tom took three years of voice to learn the right way to vocalize. When he has the time, he opts for musical checkups. The eight month tour with the Glenn Miller Orchestra helped Tom strengthen song production in his earlier years. Concerts were held in small VFW Halls as well as the gigantic Hollywood Bowl with 18,000 in attendance.

"I was a little scared there, Richard, but now I go on more relaxed in my regular gigs like Vegas and Atlantic City. One of the natural hazards of the business is getting a little nervous before performances. They say it happens to everyone. You do pick up that extra energy - I go through jumping jacks to get the blood flowing."

Tom once met Sinatra:

"I really didn't 'meet' him. It was that I shook his hand for two seconds. But, it was kind of a weird, incredible feeling...like touching God! It was at Carnegie Hall in 1987. I couldn't believe his hand was so small......I don't know, it seemed unusual." "I love the word 'crooner'. It's so evocative of that era with its great music and all the people who are my heroes. Sometimes I even think I don't belong in this age; that I should have been around 40-50 years ago when pop music was music and not just noise as it is today."

John Primerano

John Primerano is a one -of -a -kind troubadour. He is in his late 40s, and plays and sings the entire book of the Golden Age of Music, including the works of Cole Porter, Richard Rodgers, Sammy Cahn, George and Ira Gershwin, Irving Berlin, Harold Arlen, Harry Warren, and dozens of composers. John has even written a

few tunes of his own, and, he has put them both on a single CD. They are both promising songs fit for a Sinatra, Bennett, or Roselli, but for now sung by John himself.

John is a soft spoken keyboard wizard who has virtually memorized practically every known song and never plays with the aid of sheet music that most piano players need when performing. John makes a living playing and singing in clubs mostly around the greater Philadelphia area. His voice evokes sounds of Roselli, Dick Haymes and sometimes Sinatra, himself.

My wife, Madeline, and I sat down with John Primerano at the famed Stonybrook Three Village Inn one afternoon in July, 2005. He came up to meet us from his home in Philadelphia for this interview and recounted snippets of his career which began when he was just a kid.

A few weeks later John joined us once again for an appearance at a luncheon sponsored by radio station WALK- Long Island, and hosted by Italia Mia personality, gracious and popular Luisa Potenza, whose radio show airs on Sunday's from eleven to one.

John played his heart out to an appreciative audience, especially when he played and sang a popular Italian medley that began with "Oh, Marie" and concluded with "Al Di La." I've never known any artist who could play and sing at the same time so effectively, except perhaps Nat "King" Cole, Bobby Short, or lately, Michael Feinstein, currently on the New York scene. I remember Nat's wife, Maria Cole, telling me how difficult playing and singing simultaneously was for her husband who perfected the art sitting askew on a piano bench turned away from the keyboard and never glancing back while playing those difficult jazz accompaniments. John adds further excitement to his piano with rippling arpeggios and amazing keyboard magic, never looking down as his melodies poured forth great music and those fingers serpentined back and forth over those black and white ivories.

Born and raised in Philadelphia, John began piano lessons when he was eight and worked professionally as a piano accompanist for U.S.O. groups when he was just fifteen. He studied music, earning a degree in composition at Temple University's School of Music. Playing for a variety of singers over the years has forced John to become proficient in transposing songs to convenient or alternate keys on the spot.

John Primerano - Italian Crooner's Luncheon - May 2005 - M. Grudens Photo

"Sometimes a singer would have the sheet, but could not sing in the arranged key, and other times they would have no sheet music at all, but I was able to accommodate them in either case."

John began working the South Jersey seashore resort areas and spent ten years performing at venues from Atlantic City's Resorts International to important venues in Cape May, and every place in-between.

"I have never made a dollar any other way than playing piano and singing my songs - although I've done a few acting jobs when film companies would come to the Philly area. "I am kind of fortunate that I have a steady following. Some folks come to see me from as far away as Yonkers, above Manhattan, Allentown, and even further. Philadelphia is, for me, a strong base of operation, where I have developed my vast repertoire."

With John's two great songs, "Saloon Song" and "Maybe Some-day" gathering national attention, he feels he may now have an chance to move up the ladder, perhaps to garner new engagements. "Maybe Some-day" was featured on "Dick Robinson's American Standards by the Sea, a nationally syndicated program. The song is a sort of sentimental sample of a time when popular music is what people listened to and enjoyed without the frenetic backgrounds and harsh lyrics of today.

"When I write a song, I usually have a particular performer in mind whom I would like to record the piece. It was Tony Bennett in mind when I wrote 'Saloon Song.'

John's influences were Frank Sinatra, Bobby Darin, and Tony Bennett. The composers he admires are pianist Peter Nero, Henry Mancini and songwriter Burt Bacharach.

The world of today needs more saloon singers like John Primerano. He has the depth and the maturity of musical experience and the talent and the drive to complete his dream.

"No matter where I am playing, I imagine that I am on stage at a great Academy of Music, or at Carnegie Hall. I always thought the best compliment someone could bestow on a performer was that he always performed as a professional in his work. And that's how I have always tried to live my life."

John's latest CD entry into the Big Band style of music is his new offering, "Somewhere South of Heaven," which you can find on Amazon.com, where it is doing just fine. It includes his own "Maybe Someday," Saloon Song," the title song "Somewhere South of Heaven," and Ervin Drake's "Al Di La," and the standards "Again,"It Had to Be You," and Harry Warren's "I Only Have Eyes for You." Good stuff, all.

Lou Lanza
Newly Established Guy on the Block From Philly

Philadelphia has already digested and documented the music of Lou Lanza, and my counterpart, music critic and author Anthony DiFlorio III, was able to pinpoint his exact location for me: Fairless Hills, Pennsylvania, in a neat, new twin-style house with his wife Maria, two cats, Scat and Bijou, and a well-tuned piano.

Lou Lanza (not a stage name) is not related to Mario Lanza, whose name was not really Lanza, anyway. Articulate and intelligent, Lou will be thirty-eight in July. Singing Sinatra, Torme, and maybe a little Feinstein, Lou Lanza will sometimes evoke the sounds of John Birks Gillespie himself. His two albums, Corner Pocket and The Road Not Taken, are both trips down memory lane and glances into the future. Who else do you know who can smooth over Rodgers and Hart's "My Funny Valentine" to

Lou Lanza

his dad's and uncle's unusual arrangement with crying violin and viola; beautifully scat through Dave Frishberg and Bob Dorough's" I'm Hip," and bop over "A Night In Tunisia", emulating three different singers doing three different gigs? And, when you're sure you know him, he turns around and deals a little Rap, too!

Ideas come alive when you talk with Lou Lanza. We sat down on this beautiful day in January of 2007 to talk music. He is very serious about his career.

"I learned from Sinatra," Lou began, "especially his early Dorsey days and the later Columbia stuff. I sang along with Sinatra each day, trying to learn the craft." Sid Mark, a well-known disc jockey on WWDB in Philly, who has played Sinatra recordings over his fifty-year career with shows named Friday with Frank or Saturday Sounds with Sinatra, influenced the young Lanza. Lou wanted first to be a baseball player and was once scouted by the Philadelphia Phillies. "I was a pretty good center fielder and had a great ability to generate bat power into the gaps." But, singing his own songs took over his life. Lou's family is all musical. His dad, Louis Lanza Jr. was a violinist with the Philadelphia Orchestra, his Uncle, Joseph Lanza, played the viola, and his son, Joseph Lanza Jr., is concertmaster of the London Ontario Orchestra in Canada. His mom, Joan Trombetta-Lanza, was a classical singer and organist, and her brother Vince was a musical arranger and director.

Lou Lanza really sings for his supper. During the day he does weddings, masses, and funerals, and at night does gigs around Philly, and, of course, performs nationally, including a gig at New York's elegant Tavern -On-The Green, his debut in the Big Apple, and at the Los Angeles Cine' Grill in the Hollywood Hotel.

Lou was fortunate to be taught his craft by the famous voice teacher, the late Carlo Menotti, who also coached Tony Bennett, Frankie Avalon, Liza Minelli, Laura Branigan and others. "He believed that you had to take care of your voice - but not to baby your voice --- your vocal chords," Lou explained, "and that you had to train as though you were training for a voice marathon, pacing yourself, getting stronger, lasting longer, perhaps for the days you have to do three--four -- or maybe up to six shows a day."

Lou puts his piano to work allowing him to learn both music and lyrics through practice at home. "If I have to rework a vocal, even though I am isolated from musicians, I am able to continue after rehearsal sessions. I can perfect passages or pace myself. Being able to play as well as sing is a definite advantage."

Lou Lanza confesses to singing all day as Bing Crosby once did. "I love singing, so I sing. It helps my voice strength to sing, so I sing. That's what I do. When I performed in off -Broadway version shows like West Side Story, Grease, or The Fantasticks, I sang all day to keep my voice strong and practiced. You get better with practice, that's for sure. I wish I had two more hours in the day, to get to some of the other songs I'm not quite ready to do yet in public," he said with a yearning.

Lou has proven himself and continues to persevere. With the help of composers Harold Arlen, George Gershwin, Lorenz Hart and Richard Rodgers, Johnny Mercer, Neal Hefti, and even Dizzy Gillespie, not to mention the select musicians and arrangers, Lou Lanza is definitely still carrying the torch into the future from his vantage point in Philly.

Singer, actor, walking musical encyclopedia, Lou Lanza is definitely on the right road. It's the talent of vocalists like Lanza that keeps the music going.

Diana Krall
Jazz's Vocal Future is Bound for Glory

There is a young, smart, and lovely jazz pianist-vocalist on the scene who plays a superlative piano and sings like a fine instrument. She's no longer new, but she is still a wonderful performer at the peak of her life's career. She is Diana Krall (Crawl-not Crall).

If you surf the internet music forums, you inevitably wander into the music message areas where you will find exchange boards on jazz trumpeters, pianists, vocalists, sax players, and drummers. Here you merge into ongoing arguments about who is the best among them, past or present. The name Diana Krall appears regularly in those forums along-

Diana Krall

side more well-known, established performers . Internet subscribers rate her up there with Abbey Lincoln, Betty Carter, Shirley Horn, Cassandra Wilson, and Dinah Washington. Participants keep urging their peers to check out this breezy, wispy voiced pianist-song star. Some comments were: "She sounds a lot like Carmen McRae," or "She's another Ella- reborn." Diana doesn't

belt out a song but will take some chances in phrasing, expressing her repertoire coolly. Her piano swings graciously. Then, a casual glance at Diana's album photo shows an extremely pretty forty year old. Her long blonde tresses suggest a glamorous movie star, not a jazz singer. Diana's family was always involved in the love of music in one way or another. Her uncle sang a lot like Bing Crosby, and her father played stride piano, emulating the strains of the great Fats Waller. "We sang all kinds of stuff, old pop tunes, Fats Waller songs - everything. My grandmother's favorite was" Hard Hearted Hannah," Diana proudly said, "and Dad has every recording Fats Waller ever made. He has an incredible collection of music, including the old cylinders - so I heard of lot of music from the time when recording began." She admits being influenced by Claude Thornhill, the bandleader who recorded "Sunday Kind of Love" with Fran Warren: and Jean Goldkette, prolific bandleader of the Thirties whose band members included Glenn Miller; Joe Venuti; pioneer arranger Bill Challis, a distinct Diana Krall influence; Charlie Spivak; and Artie Shaw.

Dave McKenna and, most importantly, Nat "King" Cole were later influences. Cole's trio instrument arrangement of piano, bass and guitar -- minus drums- fascinated her. Diana is also seriously interested in the works of Nina Simone, Shirley Horn, and Roberta Flack.

So, this young, vivacious lady piano player and jazz vocalist left her Nanaimo, British Columbia, home to seek her fortune in the world of jazz. After having studied classical piano since the age of four, performing with the high school jazz band, and actually performing three nights a week at a local restaurant, she felt ready for further training and, with a music scholarship in her pocket, signed up with Boston's Berklee College of Music (the largest private music college in the U.S., whose patron saint is Duke Ellington). She stayed on for 18 months studying piano with emphasis on jazz in the style of Nat "King" Cole. So her association with the Big Bands of the past was very much alive in her heart. With the strong influences of those Big Bands imbued in her character, musical views and training, Diana Krall was now getting ready to take on the world.

Back home she met drummer Jeff Hamilton and bassist John Clayton, opening the floodgates of opportunity. The meetings led to further study with pianist Jimmy Rowles, a veteran of Benny Goodman; Tommy Dorsey; and Bob Crosby, in California. She also learned a lot of bass lines from elegant pianist Dave McKenna, long associated with trumpeter Bobby Hackett. "I have always loved Dave since high school and I've got all his records."

Back in Toronto, she finished her training with multi-instrumentalist Don Thompson, formerly active in L.A. with the likes of Charlie Parker and Boyd Raeburn's Orchestra. "Don gave me lessons while I was in high school and it was great to be back with him," she said. During this period Diana polished her singing skills as well.

The early Nineties found Diana performing in Europe with Ray Brown on a "gig" in Geneva, Switzerland; for a week in Paris; and in the 1995 North Sea Festival in Holland. Bassist Ray Brown admittedly is her "godfather." The great veteran of Oscar Peterson's group is her personal friend. Diana certainly hangs out in excellent company with the cream of jazz.

In August of 1996, Diana appeared in her New York cabaret debut in the 90 seat Oak Room at New York's Algonquin Hotel, a famous venue for current music greats. It led the Wall Street Journal to declare "Diana Krall is bound for glory."

Once when Diana was appearing at a small hotel lounge, customers would ask, "Where's the piano player?" She'd reply," I am the piano player."

Her appearance in Carnegie Hall in a tribute to saxophonist Benny Carter was a personal smash. She sang Carter's classic tune "Fresh Out of Love."

Diana revels in the rich tradition that is jazz: "My idea of a fun evening," she says, "is to sit around with my records of Billie Holiday, Ella Fitzgerald, Sarah Vaughan, and pianists like Bill Evans and Art Tatum, and put them on the turntable one after another."

In 1998, I wrote: "Call me in a few years and remind me of my intuitive prediction that Diana Krall will indeed take her place among the finest song stars who ever graced a bandstand or faced a microphone."

And, there are more:

There are a handful of modern singing stars of note who have found a niche in the music of the Big Band Era over the last few years. Among them are **Laura Fygi, Steve Tyrell, Madeleine Peyroux,** and **Stacey Kent.**

Listening to Steve Tyrell you might say he is not a wide range, productive voice, but the word is charming like the voices of Fred Astaire or Bob Hope, or other non-singers who really sang well. His song selections are "I've Got a Crush on You,"

"The Simple Life," and other Sinatra selects. He is sold out everywhere. A former producer, songwriter, music supervisor and performer, he has won Emmy's and has been nominated for Academy and Gold Globe Awards. Mainly, he sings the American Song Book of the Big Band Era.

A now favorite singer, Stacey Kent is Big Band Era Jazz. The theme is usually romance in the style of Ella and Billie and Nat

Madeleine Peyroux

"King" Cole, which qualifies her for mention in this book. Billboard likes her, as does England's valid Jazz Rag. Her best is her album Breakfast on the Morning Tram, an album. She sings "You're the Top" top notch.

Madeleine Peyroux is definitely a song star singing "Smile," "Everybody's Talkin'," and "Once in a While." These are tunes she keeps going in a very Billie Holiday style. She is considered a born artist. She comes from Georgia but lived in Paris. Her recordings push boundaries but the feeling is 1930s Ella or Billie, and, you guessed it, Piaf.

Laura Fygi sings all the American composers from Cole Porter to Kurt Weill, and even Glenn Miller and George Gershwin in adaptations you might not expect. But they remain jazzy, although they are all evergreens we all know.

And, finally, **Norah Jones**, daughter of Ravi Shankar, sings soft jazz. Her first album old a million and won her a Grammy Award for Best New Artist. Her idols are Willie Nelson, Billie Holiday and pianist, Bill Evans.

Norah plays piano and sings much like Nat "King" Cole. She is currently winning hands down Grammy's including Record of the Year and other vocal awards that total ten. Her recording collaborations with Ray Charles, Dolly Parton and various artists proves she's up-and-coming, and apparently staying - and she is less than 30.

Norah Jones

BIG BANDS *International*

The Magazine for Big Band Fans!

www.bigbandsinternational.org

No. 118   February 2007

Congratulations!

CHRIS DEAN and the SYD LAWRENCE ORCHESTRA,

voted for the ninth consecutive year, by the readers of

BIG BANDS INTERNATIONAL as their

FAVOURITE BAND for 2006

RAY McVAY and the GLENN MILLER ORCHESTRA
were voted second place, and

PAUL LACEY'S BACK TO BASIE ORCHESTRA
awarded third place.

Plus inside this colour issue:

All our usual features for your reading pleasure...

Don't miss our review of
40 years of the Syd Lawrence Orchestra in our next issue.

plus much, much more . . .

An Appreciation Of Glenn Miller's Music And Beyond

Herb Miller and Big Bands International Founder Roy Belcher

By Europe's and England's Best Bandleaders
Compiled by Max Wirz

For coverage of the European appreciation of the Glenn Miller Orchestra and other dominating Big Bands, we have enlisted our dear friend Max Wirz to comb through Glenn's European counterparts, old and new, and bring to us their own developments. Max met with and interviewed Europe and England's current and official Glenn Miller Orchestra leaders, Europe's Will Salden, and England's Ray McVay and, John Miller, Glenn's nephew, and a host of other great orchestra leaders.

Max filed his first installment after sitting down with Wil Salden immediately following a one-night stand for Continental Europe's only licensed Glenn Miller Orchestra at the International Dixieland and Blues Festival at ALBISGÜETLI in Zurich.

Max interviewed Britain's Ray McVay aboard the Queen Elizabeth II as it crossed the Atlantic with Ray performing Glenn Miller music aboard the great cruise ship. Max caught up with Ray in New York, the day following a book content meeting with Max, his wife Nelly and my wife, Madeline at the historic Three Village Inn. Aside from his interviews with Wil Salden and Ray McVay, he talked with Hazy Osterwald, Bryan Pendleton, Billy Gorlt, Andy Prior, John Miller (Herb Miller's son and Glenn's nephew) Peanuts Hucko, Thilo Wolf, Oski Brunnschwiler, Pepe Lienhard, Paul Kuhn, and other leaders.

JOHN MILLER
Herb Miller's Son, Nephew To Glenn

At Pontin's (Big Band) Holiday Center in Pakefield, on the wind-blown Eastern coast of England, John Miller spells out his connection to Glenn Miller:

"There were three brothers, and a sister: Deane, Glenn, with two n's, my father, Herb, and Irene, all gone now. I am Herb Miller's son, making me Glenn Miller's nephew. The Herb Miller Orchestra was formed by my father twenty-eight years ago, in 1980. He ran it until 1987, when he passed on to someplace better, I hope. Rather than see the orchestra fall, I took over and have been running things since. After over twenty years, everyone thought it was time the name be changed, and so it was then billed as John Miller and his Orchestra."

John Miller - Nephew to Glenn, Directing the Orchestra of his father Herb Miller

Originally, John's father worked in the states and when he was asked to come to England to form a big band, he agreed, taking John along. By 1995, the band performed about 130 dates per year. In 1995 the band toured with Peanuts Hucko, of the original band, along with his wife, the former Mrs. Harry James, vocalist Louise Tobin. Peanuts earlier fronted the Glenn Miller Orchestra in the United States from January through September of 1974.

Max brought up the subject to John about the validity of the movie The Glenn Miller Story, always a contention among original participants and fans.

"There were a lot of true things in the movie and, of course, a lot of inaccurate Hollywood items. One true thing: Helen would always say, 'Oh, Glenn! Honestly!' It was her favorite saying, and June Allyson repeated that often in the film. However, Glenn was a very positive guy, nothing like the Jimmy Stewart personality. Stewart handled the slide on the trombone very faithfully, close to what he would have to do, had he been actually playing. Paul Tanner coached him.

"Glenn knew exactly what he was doing. He did call Helen after a year and said, 'Come to New York, I am going to marry you.' Not, what do you think?, or should we? When Helen said that she was engaged to the son of the hardware store owner, a very lucrative family with money, Glenn simply said: 'Have him drive you to the station!' And, he did. Glenn knew exactly what he was doing. He didn't know how to lose."

Currently, John Miller is doing everything connected with music. A friend, popular bandleader Andy Prior and John have been performing together on special events. The full sized band is still touring England performing basically Glenn Miller, because, as John says: "It's Miller, because I am a Miller."

Although John is an accomplished trombone player, he readily leaves the playing to those in the band he feels are better. Unlike the 130 shows per year accomplished in 1995, the band now performs about 75 shows per year with the John Miller Orchestra.

John, the Miller name evokes magic among fans attending shows, but the name doesn't work, unless, as John says, "No matter whose nephew you are, it means little unless you deliver, and give them something of your own. Just being a nephew is not enough. Gathering good musicians to play is very important for the band. John is a good front man, much like his uncle Glenn once was, and the players say he is tops with them.

John Miller took over the complete running of The John Miller Orchestra in 2004, that includes signing of checks on the 40 -50 jobs they do each year. "Running a band this size is like having 17 illegitimate children to support, but the musicians do the job in the end."

Their big jobs are the open air concerts and the biggest is the Glenn Miller Festival of Jazz, Jive and Swing held at the Glenn Miller Museum at Twinwood, the airfield in Bedford, England, from which Glenn took his last flight.

Now, in 2007, here is John Miller playing music in the Miller mood in Shanghai, China. Yes, Shanghai!

Max Wirz: "John Miller and his gang perform at Potters at Hopton on Sea twice a year, and I were wondering if the audience is still the same, or even younger.

John: The age seems to be under 40. And we have been playing a few University balls and they are always a hit because it is the only experience they will ever have with a big band in full flight."

Recently, just after Shanghai, the band performed in Dunstable and got a good write-up saying "John's got that old black magic, too! His laid- back charm is a huge winner and the great arrangements of all the Miller favorites were present and in great form."

John Miller's Great China Gig - October 2007

It all started about 5 months ago. Plenty of time. Wrong. It took virtually all of that. Nothing was certain until the last eight or nine days and it was like living in a filing cabinet.

October 18 - 10:00am Leave the house after spending the previous 48 hours packing gear to accommodate restricted 20 K one bag limit that the Band was allocated.

12:00 arrive Heathrow, check in gear and musicians at 1:00

4:00pm take off for 5:00hr lay over in Paris. Buy the guys dinner in the cheapest place I could find. (What do you expect, I'm a bandleader.)

11:15 Take off for shanghai

October 19 - 4:15 pm Arrive in China. Great, we're here. Wrong. Coach ride,1-1/2 hour.

6:00pm Off load men and material-scrum for rooms. Pull rank/Me first. (Bandleader) - Find something to eat-hit the sack.

October 20 -Up with the larks, down to the river for an hour, group lunch.

1:00 Leave for theater for setup with Bob Howard so he can sort out his drums. The drums were interesting. Real antiques. The translator said they were the drums that Gene Krupa learned on.

5:00 Band arrives for sound check and light refreshments before show.

7:15 Show time —Wrong. All the sheets said different times and the tickets said 7:30. Well what can you expect when everything has been translated from Chinese into French then in to English and back again.

I had to fight to extend set times to 45 min. and 1 hour (including encore) After all we had been through, no way was I going to settle for two 371/2 minute sets.

With so little time, we nailed them hard with In The Mood and hit the ground running. A little bit of "Moonlight Serenade" and then a trip on the "Chattanooga Choo Choo." Red is considered a lucky color in China, and Fiona Paige, in her slinky red thing, thrilled the World starting with the advice that they should "Straighten Up and Fly Right." Fiona has been wowing audiences with the Band for twenty years, this year. (She joined the Band when she was 6). A pleasure to work with, great to have around and a fantastic asset. Despite having to cut numbers left and right to meet the time constraints, I managed to get Fiona singing half a doz. more culminating with "Old Black Magic." Lord 'O Mercy that woman can peddle a song. The Chinese ate her up. I do believe that by the end of the night, they would have voted for adoption.

I can't really say why "Tuxedo Junction" goes over so well because with the guys wandering all over the place, musically it is a joke. With a non-English speaking audience I always have concerns which seem to work themselves out in the end and not matter. Maybe this jumping in their laps is part of a physical communication that our Orchestra does so well and makes us truly an international entertainment machine.

We played lots of the standards, you've got to with a name like Miller, but one can't help injecting ones self into everything. It's sort of Miller plus Miller. We close the first half with "Two O'Clock Jump" and the extended trombone "free for all" goes down well in any language.

Bobby Cutting opened the second half Ray Anthony's theme "Man with the Horn." Always an audience stunner that leaves their mouths open. There's always a heartbeat pause before the applause starts.

We've got more features now. Uncle Glenn, to my knowledge, never had a bass solo. I looked back at our bass man Roy Babbington and realized what an opportunity resided there. Roy is world class.

I have always been fascinated with his tuning/testing/warm up routine. Amazing stuff. I got out Glenn's "Blue Skies" which has a a few bars of bass figure at the beginning. I told Roy to play anything he wanted in any key and, when he was ready, to play the bass intro and the Band would come in. At letter M in the arrangement the bass figure is repeated. The Band cuts and Roy is off again and then brings the Band back in with the little melody. I didn't mention it to the guys until we were on stage and quickly told them what to do. I can't stand these arduous rehearsals. Worked like a charm and it was touching to see the Band applauding when it was over. It's now a standard part of the show.

The Chinese liked it too.

It's standard to hire drums and bass on jobs you fly to and the drums are NEVER up to spec. China was no different. Despite the ancient kit, Bob Howard pulled off a memorable solo that will have them tapping their feet for years.

We closed with "In the Mood" again. It is the only closer there is to a Miller concert. There was a dance club called Shanghai Swings that I met at the interval and I called them out and up onto the stage. They were a surprise to all and really helped to polish off the evening with a flash.

I won't bore you with the subsequent travel details. Enough to say we left the hotel at 5:30 am, laid over in Amsterdam for two hours and got home at 8:00pm Sunday the 21st.

It was hard to keep my jaw off the floor when the guys came to me and said what a great time they had had. As it turns out, I think most of them would have done the job for 50 Quid. Why can't I find out these things sooner. (Cheap Band leader, it's a prerequisite to the job.)

Would "I" do it again? In a heartbeat. Just give me my "A" team. The trick is never to work things out to an hourly wage. That's a heart breaker, that is.

Max: Everyone was satisfied, although there were no translations of announcements, but the music transcends language. It had to be interesting to see "In the Mood" or "Moonlight Serenade" looks written in Chinese. John promised to send Chinese program by mail. 'Have fun, John said.' "On John Miller's possibility of a return engagement in China: "I will go anywhere anytime. Shanghai will have us back, we killed them and put smiles on their faces."

Epilogue: "Well, I remain the last blood relative to Glenn Miller active in show business. It's not surprising that Glenn's music is still popular today. It was designed for people. It is good solid music. You'll find everything in Miller music that you find in Bach, Beethoven, Ravel, and Strauss. It's happy music and it should appeal today as it did sixty-eight years ago. I think it will never be forgotten."

Wil Salden

Wil Salden and Max Wirz

WIL SALDEN And His Glenn Miller Orchestra Of Europe

Today, Europe's Glenn Miller Orchestra, directed by Wil Salden of Holland, performs everywhere in Europe. This friendly Dutchman was born on June 14, 1950 in Obbicht, Holland. He studied piano, led his own bands, and played piano for the radio and TV

Wil Salden and the Glenn Miller Orchestra of Europe

orchestra of Hilversum, which he later conducted.

I talked with Wil....yes, only one "l" in Wil - prior to the concert at the 7th International Festival of Light Music in Winterthur.

The Glenn Miller Orchestra, with offices in Hammersbach, Germany, gathers musicians from Germany and Holland, and does a lot of traveling throughout the year in Europe with 180 concert dates between Stockholm, Sweden, and Sicily, Italy.

"I was always inspired by the Big Band swing music of the thirties and forties. Back in 1978 and 1979 I began planning to play Glenn Miller music on a regular basis. That was not so simple. Of course, you could find arrangements of 'Moonlight Serenade' or 'In the Mood,' but these were not originals and did not sound the way Miller should sound. I did some Miller-style arranging myself, but I got in contact the Glenn Miller Foundation in the USA. So, since

Jutta Schmidt and Kurt

1990 we legally represent the Glenn Miller Foundation."

Like Glenn Miller and other bands of the Big Band Era, this band travels by bus. One day it's a small town near Salzburg, Austria, and the following day they arrive in Winterthur, Switzerland. In two days later they are playing Berlin. One hundred eighty performances is quite a load and there is no life for the musicians - no time for family or little things. Of the 180 shows, only 20 are dances.

"We choose from a vast repertoire. The people like the original Miller standards, so we give them five to ten every performance. We also play Glenn's arranged works of Franz Lehar, and the people are thrilled."

Wil Salden plays mostly concerts, "because Big Bands have become too expensive for ballroom organizers, but we do have a dance repertoire. Sometimes we change the selection sequence, just to sound different."

In every concert Salden plays familiar titles by other orchestras like those of Benny Goodman and Tommy Dorsey. One night, to 650 people, the band played Goodman's "Sing, Sing, Sing" and Dorsey's "Marie."

Among the band's vocalists, a vocal group called the Moonlight Serenaders re-create vocal renditions of the Crew Chiefs, the Modernaires, and the wonderful Andrews Sisters, who sang a lot with the Glenn Miller band.

Like their American counterparts, Wil Salden's orchestra playing Glenn Miller music is consistently sold out year after year doing 200 and more concerts a year in Germany, Holland, Switzerland, Luxembourg and Denmark.

Business manager Jutta Schmidt plans the tour so that as little time as possible is spent on the touring bus for the comfort of the musicians.

"Aboard the bus is spry, energetic, sax player Wiebe Schuurmans, who is 78 who easily keeps up with the younger musicians. He will continue to make music with us for many years," said Wil.

Miett Molnar, Marisske Hekkenberg and a new singer, Roos Jonker, alternately tour with the band.

"We will prevail despite some difficult times lately, but we are the authentic Glenn Miller sound and the people understand and appreciate that fact, which gives us the edge. And, we do the songs the 'Modernaires' did. We are the sound people want to hear."

Jutta Schmidt: "There are many bands out there that play 'Glenn Miller' music, but we have the original charts with the exact orchestration, and as Wil said, we will keep our quality and continued success."

RAY MCVAY
England's Glenn Miller Orchestra

Ray McVay and the Glenn Miller Orchestra of England

Sitting with Ray McVay in state room 2085, Max chatted with him about his unique musical ties to Glenn Miller:

"When I was about twelve, my dad would take me to the local record store on Saturday's where it was a tradition that he would buy at least one new record. My dad and brother were musicians. We looked at all the new records that had come in, like Benny Goodman, Harry James, and Glenn Miller. When I heard Harry James' 'Trumpet Blues' I thought that it was absolutely brilliant, gorgeous. Well, we listened to all the great bands then. Along the way I heard Glenn Miller's 'In the Mood.' I thought that was also fantastic. Then, dad played something softer, 'Moonlight Serenade.' Oh! My God! That was great and it sort of got me switched on to Glenn Miller.

As time progressed I received music lessons on the clarinet and saxophone. By the time I was 18, I began playing in different semipro local bands. My dad helped placed me in other bands, as well, so I could get as much experience as possible.

"Living in Gourock, Scotland, where I grew up, an hour's drive from Glasgow, Glenn Miller and his Orchestra and a lot of American troops came in during World War II. You see, I was attached to Glenn Miller from the very beginning. By eighteen I got tired busking with local bands, where you could not make any money. I told my dad I was going to London to try my luck. He was apprehensive, but blessed me going.

"In London, I played with various groups and wound up in a rock and roll band, becoming musical director with Larry Parnes, who imported American singers, but not necessarily their musicians.

"But, I had to get back to the big bands and Miller type music. An organization in England called Mecca Dancing, with every big city with a Mecca Ballroom, where everybody was dancing at that time. I auditioned for them with my band, and later he hired us to play at the Lyceum Ball-room on the Strand in London. This was my big challenge. I worked there for three and a half years and then over to the Hammersmith Palais, a really famous dancer's ballroom, and remained for four years. During the Lyceum tenure, we worked on a BBC television show, Come Dancing, doing twelve shows annually for twelve years running. It involved Glenn Miller style material in waltzes, fox trots, quicksteps, all of them. For me, playing Glenn Miller was great, as I loved his stuff and the public loved it, as well."

Ray McVay wanted to do a tribute to Glenn, even though it had been done by Lawrence and others. He wanted to bring in former Miller musicians, like Willie Schwartz, Billy May, Zeke Zarchy and Jimmy Priddy. But, Willie was too busy, as was May.

"In the Spring of 1986, however, Willie, Jimmy and Zeke came over and joined our tour. When we did 'Moonlight Serenade' with Willie on clarinet, you could hear a pin drop. It was absolutely immaculate. When the orchestra fin-ished playing the audience stood up, applauded and applauded."

"We were also a success in Japan and did the tour four times a year. When we signed up with David Mackay to become the official Glenn Miller Orchestra, we stopped the Japanese tour in deference to Larry O'Brien's U.S. Glenn Miller

Ray McVay and Max Wirz

Orchestra who had been serving that market. Glenn's music is powerful."

Ray McVay's musicians perform about 120 dates per year, about one every third day. "You know, Max, the cruise dates are nice as we remain in one place for six days and nights. No unpacking, a deserved rest for the band. At home, we perform at jazz festivals and castle con-certs throughout Scotland and Ireland. We even go to Spain and South America.

"Recruiting musicians is never a problem for Ray McVay. Most of the players have been with the band for years, so when one does leave, the spot is easily filled by another eager musician.

"When we play 'Moonlight Serenade' with five saxes, it sounds okay. You add the lead clarinet and it becomes magic. When we play this almost hymn-like song, we can see people becoming sentimental, even crying, because this song brings back memories and still receives the strongest and longest applause.

"It's Glenn's own composition. And, at the end of this song, at the end of the concert, when the audience stands up and applauds, I always say, 'I wish Glenn could still be around and see that people still enjoy his immortal 'Moonlight Serenade.'"

Aside from the wonderful stories of Wil Salden, John Miller, and Ray McVay, the European and English counterparts to Larry O'Brien's own Glenn Miller Orchestra, there remains a number of popular musicians who have been influenced, or maybe just touched, by the magic of Glenn Miller's music at one time or another in their professional careers.

BRYAN PENDLETON

In April of 2003, Max sat down with Bryan Pendleton, band leader, piano player, and arranger of big band music, at the Easter Weekend Big Band Bash at the Sand Bay Holiday Village, Weston-Super-Mare near Bristol, England.

Brian explains the loneliness of a long distance piano player. "In the old days, working piano bars and hotel lobby's you sit in a corner of the room playing your heart out and nobody is listening. But, it had its creative moments too."

After working big bands in the 1950s, it became obvious to Bryan that the big bands were folding and dance halls became discos. However, earlier, when he was a teenager, he had heard Glenn Miller's music on 78's he owned. The Glenn Miller Story film became the landmark, as hearing that music brought it to his attention, punctuating the difference from the sound of all the other bands.

"We bought arrangements from music stores, but they were bland, written for simple, straight forward music making. With encouragement from the sounds of leaders like Ted Heath, I listened to everything they played and learned, but in my own arrangements I added some salt and pepper to it. Every band sounds different than others. Glenn Miller's music with four instead of five saxophones and the clarinet lead was completely different.

"Miller wanted it mellow and sweet, so he came to the logical conclusion, that if he substituted an instrument that is pitched in the same key as a lead trumpet, he might get it. It was pretty obvious that the clarinet could do it. And, history tells that it fit perfectly. I tend to believe that it is the real reason for the clarinet lead."

From 1967, Bryan played with the Syd Lawrence band, that featured much Miller music, playing piano and arranging remaining for many years. Today, he plays with the Andy Prior organization. When he writes charts for Prior, he won't be asked to put in some Miller trademarks. Andy likes the period of Billy May, Ray Anthony, Basie, and Nelson Riddle. Billy May's material, for Bryan, is somewhere between Glenn Miller and the 1940s period brought forward into the 60s and beyond.

HAZY OSTERWALD

Max Wirz and legendary Hazy Osterwald have become old friends. At the Hotel Grand National in Lucerne, Switzerland, the two had once got together, and recently at Hazy's apartment in Lucerne.

Max Wirz and Hazy Osterwald

"Years before Glenn Miller brought his orchestra to England, we were listening to his U.S. civilian orchestra. He was a phenomena, overshadowing everything we had heard by other American bands.

"In 1942, I was in boot camp in the Swiss Army, and on Sunday's I went to the Congress House in Zurich, where Teddy Stauffer and his Original Teddies performed. I remember very well how they did 'Chattanooga Choo Choo.'

"When we all gathered around to hear the Glenn Miller Christmas show from Paris, you can imagine how sad we were to learn that he had perished just a few days earlier."

For Hazy Osterwald,

Eleonor Osterwald

Hazy Osterwald's First Band - 1944 with Kitty Ramon - Vocalist

Glenn's music was easy to listen to, and after hearing a tune, you could sing or hum it for hours, as many people confirm. Hazy would adapt Glenn's music for his own orchestra.

"The dancers asked for 'In the Mood,' 'Tuxedo Junction,' and 'Moonlight Serenade,' and would not let us go unless we also played 'Adios.' It was not easy to adapt the arrangements that was written for a seventeen piece band to even our sextet or slightly larger group. But, we did it, and the people loved us for it."

For Hazy Osterwald, Europe's great musical icon, who is now eighty-five years old and still working, Glenn's music was a true phenomenon, a one- in-a-million success that has lasted. Whenever he is a guest with a big band, there are Glenn Miller melodies included in his repertoire.

Besides Glenn Miller, Hazy Osterwald admired Louis Armstrong and Harry James as well in his younger days when he, himself played a trumpet. You can add Duke Ellington, Benny Goodman, and Artie Shaw to the mix of musicians he admired.

"It was more of the same in 2004, during Glenn's centenary. When we do these songs with small bands, however, it is difficult to sound Miller-like, but I performed some songs on vibes, with the sextet, and as a guest with the full size Dani Felber Big Band.

"The public is always the judge...and to find out what the public likes may take dozens of attempts and years to accomplish. As Glenn Miller or even Artie Shaw could have told you, there's no easy way to success," said Max Wirz.

DANI FELBER

For the record Max had encountered Dani when he was a teenager, playing cornet at a birthday party. This young man at the age of 35 has since then toured Europe with his own combo Jazz Dependents, playing more than 200 concerts, then graduating to his own big band in 2000, despite friendly advice not to do it. The band is composed of professional musicians mostly fresh from accredited jazz schools and directed by Dani, an extraordinary and dedicated leader at the dawn of a long and rewarding career.

Dani Felber

"I was about nine when my mother gave me a tape of Glenn Miller playing all the famous charts like, 'Chattanooga Choo Choo,' and 'In the Mood,' all those beautiful masterpieces. I became a fan right away and listened to the tape over and over. Then I saw The Glenn Miller Story and set a goal for

Dani Felber and Hazy

myself to copy this man and to some day stand on stage in front of my own band. Today, years later, I have my own Big Band, work with musicians on and with my own arrangements, looking, not unlike Glenn, for my own sound. I am happy to say, I have come a long way." Dani had received music lessons in local brass societies, play-ing marches and orchestral arrangements, having no idea of jazz or big band music until he received that tape cas-sette. Listening to those tapes compelled Dani to try his luck with a band like Glenn did at first.

"Glenn Miller had his clarinet led saxophone sec-tion and his trombone section. Then there were composers and arrangers, men like Miller

James Last on Bass, Hugo Strasser - Clarinet, Hazy Osterwald - Trumpet, Max Greger - Tenor Saxophone, Paul Kuhn - Piano and Vocal

who had conceptions on how their music had to sound."

These days Dani is involved with Europa Park Rust, a Disney style amusement park near Rust, Germany.

Dani: "We do various things, perhaps entertain with dinner music or dancing music at affairs and providing background for guest acts.

Felber has his Big Band, including 22 musicians, a classic big band that plays swing to bebop, and even waltzes,and a wide range of melodies and rhythms to suit the occasion. "The Party Band is recruited from the Big Band and the Jazz Quartet with bass piano, drums,and myself on trumpet and flugelhorn, and we appear in hotels and jazz clubs, and even have a band singer on the bandstand.

For a corporate event the band may use the swing book by Basie, Goodman or Dorsey, depending on the audience. And, now, Dani Felber receives requests to compose special songs. His "Berlin Tanzt" was contracted for the Bundespresseball in Berlin in front of Germany's President Horst Kohler. "This was very exciting for us."

And, in addition, the band regularly accompanies guest artists for concerts and recording sessions.

Recently, in an open dance in the grand hall of Zurich Main Station, that is larger than Grand Central Station, the band performed for 5000 happy faces who attended free because the sponsor is MIGROS, a Swiss grocery chain. Encores went on till 3 in the morning.

Dani Felber also plays some trombone, saxophone, mostly for use in composing and arranging, as he needs to know the range of instruments to limit demands on his musicians. "And, of course, I play piano, which provides the basis for composing and arranging my work.

Max: Dani receives many invitations to do guest appearances, but declines because he is so busy with his own organization and also conducts seminars and work shops on swing which are attended by young

Dani Felber Big Band

amateur and professional musicians, as well as established leaders and directors of local brass marching bands.

The life of music is full for Dani Felber. He is strict with his musicians as Glenn Miller once was with his band. "It takes precision and dedication for any popular song, for which I have written an arrangement to meet the demands of young dancers. Anyone who disagrees is in the wrong band."

It is important for Dani Felber to play his music for audiences and not for musicians themselves. You cannot drift away from music the people want to hear and dance to, or you may completely fail and drift away.

Max: Dani's growing success with his three band formations is proof he is doing the right thing the right way. His aim is to continue on that road to create and present quality music which will be light on the ears of a wide, appreciative public.

"Dani: "Swing will go on forever. Glenn Miller's music and other swing standards will be heard two, three hundred years from today. My wife Claudia is busy marketing our new CD Sweet Breeze to get more exposure through radio and TV. We are all working very hard to keep things going for the band. I am already composing and arranging for a followup Big Band CD." Keep listening.

HUGO STRASSER

Hugo Strasser, clarinet player and orchestra leader, grew up and studied music in Munich, Germany, when World War II broke out. Like Paul Kuhn, Bert Kaempfert, Max Greger, were leaders of dance bands, which in the '50s, '60s, and '70s appeared regularly on German radio and television stations, and toured throughout the country performing concerts and dances.

"In 1944 in Munich, I was 22 years old. Jazz and American music was forbidden in Germany. But, we secretly listened to this new music over 'sender' from France and England. Around that time I heard recordings of Glenn Miller and his civilian orchestra as well as his Army band and it fascinated me.

Swing Legends: Hugo Strasser, Paul Kuhn, Dani Felber and Max Greger

"Then, in 1944, Hugo Strasser had no idea, that in less than two years, he would be actually playing that music. When the war was over he got the chance to become acquainted with American soldiers and was soon performing in their service clubs. He remembered how perplexed the GIs were that they knew their music and were able to play it.

"The Glenn Miller sound was foremost, the saxophone section and how he put the clarinet in the lead. And then those trombones with their doo-wha, doo-wha. For us this was fascinating and we played with indescribable enthusiasm. Imagine, Max, we had survived a terrible war, and then suddenly we were allowed to play music, which was previously forbidden. It was like swinging on a cloud. It was the beginning of music as a profession for many of us."

Of course, Hugo Strasser played the music of many other big bands that were popular at the time, but Glenn Miller's music was the most influential. Hugo's pianists played like Duke Ellington, and their trumpet player emulated Harry James, and so forth.

"We graduated from there, and in 1948, we were hired by hotels and night clubs, a mixed audience of GIs and local citizens. Radio discovered us and so did television. We moved along step-by-step, adapted and perfecting our music style.

Another thrill was felt by Hugo Strasser who, with Ray Anthony, wrote a composition, "Lonely Trumpet" recorded by Ray Anthony. Although he received no monetary compensation, he didn't mind. It was important to Hugo that an American star was playing his composition.

"During 2004, we continued doing concerts in large and small cities of Germany. In each we had a Miller section with 'In the Mood', 'American Patrol,' and 'Moonlight Serenade.' We had to play these, no matter how often we have played them before. The highlight of each concert was the playing of 'In the Mood,' a song that will remain popular through this century, I am fully convinced.

Today, Hugo Strasser is one third of The Swing Legends with Paul Kuhn and Max Greger, touring relentlessly with the SWR Big Band, having the time of their lives in a long time career in swing music.

PEPE LIENHARD

Pepe Lienhard has been a musician and band leader since his teens. His fourteen piece show and pop orchestra and his seventeen piece swing band are known all over Europe. Along with vocalist Udo Jurgens, who has sold 70 million albums worldwide, Pepe Lienhard's band performed with Udo in dozens of concert halls all over Europe during 2004.

"The Glenn Miller Orchestra was the first big band which I recognized as such. 'Moonlight Serenade, ' heard on Swiss Radio, was my first experience with that sound. That was the mid fifties, when I was about ten."

When Pepe heard the Miller tunes "Tuxedo Junction," and "In the Mood," he was electrified, especially after being exposed to rock and roll for a while. He was fascinated with the clarinet lead as many other musicians before him. When he viewed Sun Valley Serenade and Orchestra Wives, he noticed the superb stage presence, and swung right along with the music.

"It was great entertainment, too. These frolicking, swinging tunes made the kids kick up their heels and those soft ballads were balm for the lonely and homesick. It has not been easy to motivate young musicians to play Miller songs. Their enthusiasm grew only as we got down to the details and fine tuning. Musicians tend to underestimate the Miller music, because it sounds so simple

Pepe Lienhard

and seems easy to play. Anyone can play Miller pieces, but to play things like 'Moonlight Serenade' so that it really sounds like an original Miller, requires a whole lot of skill and discipline."

Pepe Lienhard wasn't over-influenced by Glenn's music, but, he knew that as a bandleader you could not ignore the Miller charts. However, when the Swiss Army Band, under his direction, plays Miller tunes, and with Sammi Zund and his fellow singers swing into their Modernaires routine, they always receive the strongest and longest applause everywhere, and for every audience.

"In 2004 we had two projects that featured Glenn Miller music, involving concert tours through Switzerland and Germany. The seventeen piece Pepe Lienhard Orchestra performed at a special Glenn Miller Gala Show."

In 1995 Pepe Lienhard was commissioned to form the Swinging Swiss Army Big Band, a Swiss edition of a Glenn Miller-style Orchestra.

"I was thrilled to accept the job of forming and leading a Big Band again. So we set up auditions to test volunteers from many military marching bands. We wanted modern sounds, but not rock, and I was flabbergasted by the talent of the young players. Some were twenty and most younger than thirty. We had great fun. During Army Days in Frauenfeld, Switzerland, more than 100,000 visitors were treated to the band's concerts where the favorites Glenn Miller, Benny Goodman, and the Dorsey's charts commanded the most applause."

Pepe is a dinosaur of sorts who keeps coming back at every chance. He feels swing must go on. "My heart and the hearts of my band members very much favor our kind of music. Eventually it will have to be First Lieutenant Gilbert Tinner and other young European bandleaders who, together with us older fellows, keep bringing back the great music of the Big Band Era, and who will find ways to add their own licks to present new melodies in the Big Band format."

The best proof was the Zuri Fascht (Festival of Zurich) where SRO crowds, including grandpa's and grandma's, danced to "Moonlight Serenade," "Tuxedo Junction" and "In the Mood" for three days through rain and shine.

It is now 2007 and Lienhard leads three basic bands using three trumpets, two sax's, one trombone, a rhythm group and singers. "One, we entertain at private and corporate affairs. If Udo Jurgens(singer) tours with us, we add four strings."

Their Big Band is a classic band that plays all the standards that were composed during the Big Band Era. The third is the Swiss Army Band playing the music of the same period, and adding four singers. The band plays mostly in Europe, both far and wide and local. The band has also played for Europe's version of Dancing with the Stars television show.

The band does 100-150 concerts a year but no longer with the old stars who have left the scene, although young American singer Michael Buble performed as a guest on the TV show. The Swiss Army band performs mostly at government functions where the musicians serve out their military service.

PAUL KUHN

Germany's, seventy-eight year old, Paul Kuhn, profiled in the book Jukebox Saturday Night, is a much revered bandleader and entertainer.

Still active throughout Germany, his musical ensemble have played over one hundred concerts in 2003 and 2004 alone.

He feels he owes a lot to Glenn Miller.

"The very first recording I heard was by the Glenn Miller Orchestra. It was a kind of music that was totally unfamiliar to me, but it made a very big impression. So, I became a big band fan - and still am today.

"The Miller Army Air Corps band came to England during the war. I had heard a previous recording of 'Anvil Chorus', not recorded in the typical Miller sound, but I had a hankering for operatic melodies and thought it was special and different, although it was 'jazzed up' and in the opinion of the time, played in an unworthy way. We would listen to those BBC broadcasts with the American Band of the Expeditionary Forces with Glenn Miller and Ilse Weinberger. We also heard Artie Malvin and the Crew Chiefs, Bing Crosby, Johnny Desmond, Dinah Shore, Ray McKinley, and Irene Manning. Officials were directing their programs at the youth of Germany. The singers sang German texts phonetically-Diese Musik hat mich einfach umgehauen! The music knocked me over."

Paul knew that if someday he ever was allowed to play this kind of music, he would become a jazz musician, thanks to Glenn Miller. His colleagues Hugo Strasser, Max Greger, and Hazy Osterwald had similar feelings when they first heard Glenn. Paul fully appreciated the sound created by Glenn, and considered it a fabulous invention on the basis of his success.

In early 2004, Paul Kuhn and his group performed enriched Glenn Miller programs, which had been pre- sold out in palaces like the Friedrichstadt in Berlin with 2,300 seats. The performances there were sold out five consecutive evenings.

"In the 50s, 60s, and 70s, when we did our TV shows, or when we played at dances with the Paul Kuhn Orchestra and the Ute Mann Singers, we played so much Miller, that all of us had more than enough of it. Each of us must have played 'In the Mood' two thousand times in our careers. But the audience never tires of it and promoters and record companies insisted on the Glenn Miller sound."

For Paul Kuhn, with Glenn Miller musical material implanted in his brain for so long, he feels he can not help it when Glenn Miller material absorbs into new things and new arrangements.

These days Paul Kuhn has joined together with Max Gregor and Hugo Strasser to join the SWR Big Band("Sudwestdeutscher Rundfunk") and the band plays pieces so they call us three "The Swing Legends." These concerts have been successful in Southern Germany. "We are now in our eighth year and there is no end in sight. Good proof that beautiful Big Band sounds are not dead. We don't always play swing music, but we always play music that swings."

In 2008 Paul Kuhn has turned eighty: "...and if the good Lord pleases, I'll take a sabbatical from the Swing Legends and go on tour with the trio. That will be music which will keep the audience 'swinging and smiling'...to use Max Wirz's sign off line." (He chuckles!)

BILLY GORLT

At Billy and Irene Gorlt's home, after a perfect dinner, Max Wirz and Billy Gorlt exchanged Glenn Miller conversations."After obtaining my wings in glider school, I was transferred to a heavy mortar unit North of Frankfurt. Then, on my 18th birthday, I was taken prisoner by advancing American units, and wound up in a camp in France a few days later.

Billy Gorlt and Max Wirz

I was on detail to help transport wounded American soldiers and one of them had a Hohner accordion tied to his stretcher. I played it and learned American songs, becoming pretty popular."

Billy received lessons from a fellow POW, who was a musician before the war. He played in the POW band that performed at the officers Club. He got interested in the clarinet and saxophone. Still a POW in 1947, Billy played in a big band managed by a U.S. Sergeant, but staffed by POWs. By this time he became a good sight reader on clarinet and saxophone.

"We played printed arrangements of popular U.S. swing music charts received through Special Services. Oh, Max, those beautiful songs: 'In the Mood,' 'Moonlight Serenade,' and all the Dorsey and Harry James, Count Basie, and more charts..all the great music of the Swing Era. My self taught skills became a great advantage and earned me a spot in a club that performed seven nights a week."

When freed, Billy joined a circus band and eventually secured a job and continued to play for the American military right up to 1967, from 1960, under his own name with his own quartet. Looking back, Billy remembered hearing the strains of "Moonlight Serenade" and "In the Mood."

"It was a smooth and beautiful melody. It was a big band with that wonderful sound everyone talked about. We were all surprised at the simplicity of the melodies and beat. It was overwhelming, simply overwhelming. I thought, if they have such good music, they must be good people."

When Billy got to listen to Glenn's music, he noticed how carefully Glenn Miller had selected the music, melodies and rhythms. He would go from one different song to another, different in tempo, different in instrumentation and in sound.

"For me, Glenn was a good organizer of his material, and he knew what people wanted to hear and gave it to them. His perfection in music is what impressed me so. The arrangements wrote catchy introductions for each song. He was a stickler, a perfectionist."

Viewing the Glenn Miller Story film gave Billy Gorlt the idea to wear U.S. uniforms on stage. The audience went wild when they played "Tuxedo Junction" at the Prinzregenten Theater in Munich, Germany. It was like scenes from the movie, when Glenn played in hangars to GI audiences back in England in 1944.

"In 2004, in memory of Glenn Miller, we performed special program in the Stadthalle of Germering that Spring. There were five tunes for a vocal group who sang like the Modernaires. We were sold out.

In 2007 the Billy Gorlt combo and Big Band was presented in full at the Stadthalle (Town Hall) in Germering performing Benny Goodman's Carnegie Hall Concert of January 16, 1938, and to be authentic, Gorlt copied every title from the original recordings.

Billy Gorlt was recently presented the award "Ambassadors of Big Band Music" by Ben Grisafi and Paul Bennett of the Big Band Hall of Fame in West Palm Beach, Florida, in front of 750 people. Max Wirz made the presentation on stage during the Munich, Germany premiere Benny Goodman concert.

Billy Gorlt: "Big Band music will become some kind of Light Classics like the music of Strauss, Lehar and other musical composers. Big Band music will run on forever."

Andy Prior

ANDY PRIOR

Andy Prior's first connection to Glenn Miller was listening to Glenn's trombone section's boo-ba, boo-ba, boo-ba, and for him, that was enough influence. Andy was but six years old.

"I also remember the album cover sleeve with Glenn and his rimless glasses, because my dad wore them, too."

The effect was that Andy wanted to be a leader like Glenn, and he wanted to sing like Frank Sinatra or Mel Torme. For him, the Glenn Miller band was the one name in music that has created more employment for musicians than any other big band.

"Yet it's not the easiest of music to play correctly, but whenever we strike up a Miller song, the audience peps up. I think Syd Lawrence orchestrated new material in the Miller way, coming close to the original sound. Today, Chris Dean is using some of the AEF material as he fronts Syd's orchestra. But, it's 'In the Mood,' 'Tuxedo Junction,' and 'Moonlight Serenade' that the people want to hear, always."

Andy Prior has toured with The Magic of Sinatra tour throughout England with his own band, went to America in 2002 to front the Billy May Orchestra ghost band at the Stardust Hotel in Las Vegas, playing Billy's charts, then back to Las Vegas to perform with Ray Anthony's band. "While I was there, we had a reunion with Ray,

Max Wirz and Andy Prior

Johnny Best, Paul Tanner, and Billy May. It was a great experience."

FREDDY STAFF

In England, Freddy Staff, trumpet player and leader of his own orchestra and the Manhattan Swing Orchestra as well, encountered Glenn Miller music for the first time during World War II.

"I was about 13 years old. The Glenn Miller band was here and we heard it over the AFN radio broadcasts. After the war I got a Miller record, 'Moonlight Serenade. I was playing the bugle in the Boy Scouts."

At fifteen, Freddy entered a Harry James contest and won first prize, ten Shillings.

As a teenager he played in a local band, then in 1946 he played with the Royal Air Force band, until 1949. Upon his discharge, he attended the College of Music to receive teacher's qualification. Freddy played in the orchestra on the cruise ship, Queen Mary, making 12 trips to New York. When in New York, he took twelve trumpet lessons from noted instructor Benny Baker.

"I try to play like Harry James. I was initially impressed with Harry when he played in the film Two Girls and a Sailor. Boy, that was trumpet playing. I was dumb struck. I was playing trombone, so I switched back to trumpet. I began to emulate Harry's style. He was a 'pop' star. I would look in the mirror and imitate the way he blew. He did not puff his cheeks out and he kept his lips close together. But, that was in films. In reality, he puffed his cheeks out, too.'

Getting back to Glenn's music, Max, searched Freddy's memory:

"I think it was the sound, that saxophone sound with the clarinet lead, not the brass. It was so simple to score, it's close harmony, you've got the clarinet on top. It's so effective, and a marvelous trade mark for Miller fans. The success of 'Moonlight Serenade' proves it. The public wants a dance, so Miller is essential. Lately, I have started to do a Miller Medley, a few titles strung together. Our version of "American Patrol" is with a little bit of the famous Marine Hymn added. I like doing Glenn Miller, but people know me and we do a bit of our own material, and they accept it."

WIEBE SCHUURMANS

Wiebe Schuurmans is seventy-eight, plays clarinet and saxophone in the Glenn Miller Orchestra, directed by Wil Salden, and sings as a member of the Moonlight Serenaders, the new Modernaires, and has been with Wil's band since 1991.

At sixteen, after World War II, while Wiebe's father worked in a dairy, he played soprano saxophone. When he was at work, Wiebe secretly learned to play that instrument.

Wiebe Schuurmans with Max Wirz

"After the war, I joined an orchestra that had three accordions, one alto sax, and drums. My father did not like that. He wanted me to fulfill myself in a proper occupation. But later, when he saw and heard me play in the Radio Orchestra, he became very proud and happy.

"The musicians in the Radio Orchestra played swing music. During the war we heard American swing music over the BBC, but, listening to such music was 'verboten' (forbidden). Then, in 1945, during victory parties, we had dancers hopping with 'In the Mood,' 'My Guys Come Back,' and the difficult for us to do, 'Moonlight Serenade'."

For Wiebe, the influential music of Glenn Miller was mixed with the music of many American bands. From his early days, Wiebe Schuurmans played in many bands throughout Holland and Europe. He played clarinet in the Miller Sextet, and the Flamingo Quintet (a kind of Shearing band where the guitar is substituted by clarinet).

Wiebe was offered a job with the Dutch Metropole Radio Orchestra and grabbed it, and started playing baritone saxophone remaining with it until 1991. While with the sixty piece symphonic orchestra, that included a big band, he also helped out Wil Salden a few times. When he retired from the Radio Orchestra, he joined his now good friend, Wil Salden, for keeps. At seventy-eight, Wiebe manages to play over 200 one nighter's each year.

"I love it. The Glenn Miller Orchestra is well known throughout

Europe, playing the music people want to hear. The band is well managed and we travel in a comfortable bus and stay at good hotels. We all love it. The concerts are two hours and sometimes even longer. Sometimes it gets tiring, but, all in all, it's wonderful."

Wiebe: "Every concert is a new concert. Sometimes the folks are cool and hard to warm up. It's a challenge. Together with Wil, the girl singer and two other musicians, I am a member of the Moonlight Serenaders, doing the Miller songs. I get a chance, too, to play solos, and while on center stage, I seek eye to eye contact with someone in the audience and clown around a little.

"I think is it fantastic how Glenn's music continues to succeed. It is astounding how many people come to our concerts, year after year, and, as they grow older they bring their children and grandchildren to hear our Glenn Miller music."

In April, 2007, Wibe Schuurmans performed with the Wil Salden orchestra in a concert in Zurich at the Schutzenhaus Albisguetli both playing sax and clarinet and singing with the Moonlight Serenaders.

STEVE KING

Steve King, trumpet player with his own big band, met Max at Sand Bay Holiday Village near Bristol, England, on April 20, 2003.

"We mostly play contemporary music at our concerts, like the music of Bob Florence and Tom Cubis, but when we are at dance dates we play Glenn Miller music. The dancers will sometimes sit out a dance or two, and, when they ask for Miller tunes, naturally 'In the Mood,' 'Moonlight Serenade,' ' American Patrol', 'Serenade in Blue,' and 'Adios'-we do them and they love us for it."

Steve King plays swing music with his big band at Pontin's Pakefield and Potter's in Hopton-on-Sea, on the East Coast of England. He recalls the influence Glenn's music had on his later work. Now in his 36th year and with his own band, Steve explains his early encounter with Glenn's music:

"It was in the mid-seventies when I got into playing trumpet and wanted to play in a big band. Everyone related to the Glenn Miller sound and we trumpet players were especially intrigued by the trumpet solos. I listened to records of the original Miller band and, encouraged by this great music, went to listen to English big bands, like the Syd Lawrence Orchestra. I learned a lot from listening to these two great orchestras."

THILO WOLF

Thilo Wolf, pianist, drummer, composer, arranger, big band leader, was born in 1967. When he was but twelve, his father was a friend of

Klaus Wunderlich, the famous organist who played the Hammond, and would bring over American recordings of Glenn Miller and other artists when he would visit him.

Thilo Wolf

"As I recall very clearly, I thought 'Don't Sit Under the Apple Tree' was a real swinging number. Those records and the records of Max Greger and his Orchestra, was my first contact with the big bands.

"I played some of those themes on the piano and learned them by heart. Then I saw The Glenn Miller Story on TV and liked it very much. But, what impressed more was the dance scenes in the first Miller film, Sun Valley Serenade. That's when the Miller virus got me.

"And the Miller sax section with clarinet lead brought an unmistakable element. The fantastic arrangements, created by a number of innovative arrangers, were unique. Take 'Little Brown Jug.' Such a simple melody and wonderful arrangement. The secret probably does not lie in any one of those details but rather in the combination of them all."

Thilo plays Glenn Miller from available standard arrangements. He will take Glenn Miller material, but interpret it in his own way:

"Jazz is melody, harmony and rhythm. You can vary the melody only a little, but you can use various rhythms to obtain variety. However, I would never dream to rewrite 'Moonlight Serenade,' a piece that is perfect. Miller melodies put every crowd 'In the Mood.' When I was sixteen, we played Basie and Neil Hefti. We discussed whether Miller should be played at all. It was our youthful inexperience to almost taboo Miller, not wanting to play the old stuff which had been played a hundred, thousand times . We did not want to play easy tunes. But, today I know that it is very difficult to play these easy Miller songs so that they sound like Miller. And we have learned to respect that there were, and have been, millions of listeners who simply adored and still adore this music."

Now 40, here is Thilo Wolf, a national entertainment figure of great stature, and a host to great musicians and bandleaders such as Germany's Max Greger, Hugo Strasser, and Horst Jankowski, and America's Ray Anthony, and just two hours prior he and his Quartet performed a benefit concert in a lean-to, in near freezing weather at the Christkindle's Markt on the Waagplatz in Furth.

It was on the day of St.Nikolaus, and Thilo Wolf and I are sitting in his comfortable apartment talking about our kind of music.

"I see Big Bands sprouting up all over the place like dandelions in my back yard. There may be a music teacher, a marching band conductor, or a professional musician who likes swing music and goes out and recruits 16 to 18 young people, like the members in Andy Prior's band, and performs the charts of a Miller, Dorsey, or Basie band and make the crowds go wild.

Is it happening all over again? Andy Prior of England is certainly a great example of such a success. Andy occupies a unique place in Big Band music. He wants to replace nostalgia with a new beginning.

Thilo Wolf: "Let me explain, Max. What is expected of a big band? Your generation grew up with the music of the late 30' and 40's and almost automatically accept this as your

Thilo Wolf Big Band

standard. However, times have progressed, big band music has developed in different directions, it provides a wide spectrum of repertoires. To play Glenn Miller, when it is to sound like Glenn Miller is a challenging undertaking that is not easily achieved. However when it is simply "copied", it is dead. That goes for music by Goodman, the Dorsey's, Ellington, Shaw, you name them. My perception of music includes playing the original charts with utmost precision, to make the music sound 'original' or on the other hand and this is most important for me, add my own touch. Therefore I take on known themes, but rewrite and rearrange them in such a way that fits the talents and capabilities of my band. Thus the music appears alive and fresh. The musicians enjoy and love it. By doing this I keep the 'old'"audience, but attract also a new, somewhat younger audience. The success of our concerts and TV appearances is proof that this concept works."

Max: And as I am transcribing my conversation with Thilo Wolf some weeks after my visit to Fürth, I can add congratulations that the Big Band Hall of Fame in West Palm Beach, Florida has recognized him and The Thilo Wolf Big Band as "Ambassadors of Big Band Music".

EUROPEAN HONORABLE MENTIONS

European Honorable Mentions cover a list of Big Band associated individuals such as musician Gerhard Klussmeier, Jazz Program Director of Hamburger Lokalradio and author of books on Jazz who, as a freelance producer of jazz programs, was instrumental in creating a now well-established Jazz Society "Swinging Hamburg," a society for the support and promotion of traditional jazz from Ragtime to Mainstream.

Gerhard: "I am positive that Big Band sounds will prevail. We have lots of examples for this. The sound of the bands, their fascinating, swinging and melodic melodies pulsating in time with human hearts will continue to create joy and happiness."

Roland Wohlhueter, bandleader, teacher, musician, who plays trumpet and valve trombone, piano and sings, plays with the Landeslehrer Big Band (State Music Teachers Big Band). A musician since he was but eight, he has always played or conducted in a band or marching band. "I believe that our European Big Bands are equal to American bands in all respects. The SWR Big Band with the Swing Legends must be mentioned as they tour the country together keeping their own legend alive. Swing music has a renaissance. The signs are everywhere. There is an abundance of talented and well educated young musicians who are interested and willing to uphold the Big Band tradition, but they must be constantly led to it."

Dai Kimoto

Dai Kimoto is the director of The Swing Kids of Switzerland.

We are happy and honored to have you travel all the way from Switzerland to honor us with your wonderful music. Our Society wants to applaud your efforts to interest young students in the music of Glenn Miller and the Big Bands. Your concerts were exciting and we enjoyed having all of you visit the Glenn Miller Festival. The Glenn Miller Birthplace Society sincerely thanks you for coming and we wish you continued success.

Glenn Miller Birthplace Society *Marvin Negley*
Marvin Negley, President

Swing Kids

A trumpet player in the style of Louis Armstrong, Harry James and Bix Beiderbecke, began playing his music on Tokyo television. He married a Swiss gal and together they formed a family band, which served as the basis for his work with young musicians which he still does today. Dai has performed in the Pepe Leinhard Orchestra and the Jazz Heritage band of Vince Benedetti.

Swing Kids

His Swing Kids group has become very successful including a two week twelve concert tour of Japan in 2005. Two weeks in America to the Glenn Miller Festival and a concert at Berklee School of Music in Boston. 2008 will take them to Brazil and Argentina.

Chris Smith

Robert Habermann is a soloist with the Chris Smith and the String of Pearls Orchestra. He sings like his hero, Frank Sinatra and has impressed his audiences. He has studied in New York with song stars Kay Starr and Margaret Whiting and appeared on Broadway. "My first love was Sinatra and my first album was This is Sinatra. I loved his warm resonance. He was the untouchable legend. My Sinatra show in London's Royal Festival Hall was a huge success."

Chris Smith had heard Robert and began using him in The String of Pearls Big Band and now works with him regularly. Robert has discovered the songs of Kern, Porter and Gershwin, and even Peter Allen, Le'grand, and Kander and Ebb. "I call myself a Jobbing Singer and work nearly every week. I think Big Band music will live as long as the bands like Chris Smith's are around. Thanks too to "U Tube" and all the albums.

Chris Smith has the early honor of touring with singers Matt Munro and the great Shirley Bassey when he joined up with Frank Weir's Orchestra. Tromboning with John Dankworth's Orchestra in 1963, Chris was discovered by Ted Heath and played with him until he was twenty-seven. He joined the orchestra of Jack Parnell and remained for 15 years. He led the trombone section in Madrid on Frank Sinatra's world tour The Ultimate Event.

Chris played on many BBC TV shows and performed with Oliver Reed, Mel Gibson, Elizabeth Taylor and other stars. As a trombonist, Chris is known throughout the music world. In creating and leading The String of Pearls band, he has brought the Big Band sound current, and fulfilled a long standing ambition.

Max Greger

We introduced you to Max Greger earlier as part of Germany's Swing Legends along with Paul Kuhn and Hugo Strasser. Max has always been a premier sax player and bandleader with myriad credits to his name including film and television. After VE Day he led a small band playing in a U.S. Army Service Club, eventually utilizing American Big Band charts. This followed an absolutely fulfilling career that spanned from the 1950s to the present being involved musically with German television on a great number of popular quiz and variety shows, right up to today.

In 1977, Max went on his own with the Max Greger Orchestra and made many recordings. "My fascination for Glenn Miller developed with the film Sun Valley Serenade, which I went to see 10 or 12 times."

For Max Greger the success of the many European and English bands are holding up the Big Band music began essentially with the influence of Glenn Miller and other American bands of renown. "We will have to wait and see who will be the women and men who will carry Big Band music forward into the future. Different ideas of how a Big Band should sound will appear on the scene. One thing is sure, Big Band music will stay on for generations and generations to come."

Albi Matter has been active in show business for over 38 years and has acted as road manager, produced and promoted converts and even managed a music club. Albi was also the producer of Wil Salden's Glenn Miller Orchestra concert on April 26, 2007 followed by an appearance the following night of the Swiss Army Big Band directed by Pepe Lienhard, each night to 700 guest patrons. It is people like Albi Matter whose efforts in booking the Big Bands of Europe are not unlike the great American legendary impresarios like Sol Hurok, who booked Benny Goodman into Carnegie Hall in 1938, a landmark concert if ever there was one.

Willy Schmid

Willy Schmid rose from child star status to singer, musician, all-around entertainer and featured sideman in the DRS Big Band (Big Band of Swiss National Radio). Brought up in a fully developed musical family. In 1939, Willy and his siblings became staff singers with Teddy Stauffer's Original Teddies, a very popular Swiss band. After the Teddies they performed with Arthur Beul, composer of many popular ditties and cowboy songs and recorded them behind the Walter Wild and Walter Baumgartner's orchestras.

In the fifties, the Schmid's rented a restaurant which they named Restaurant Kindli and formed a band where they both entertained and fed their patrons and fans. In 1954, they voyaged to America and performed aboard the cruise ship and ran into Phil Silvers who introduced them to his agent and, as a result, they performed at the Blue Angel club in New York for seventeen weeks and had their songs rearranged into swing by Don Costa. Their act was called The Smeed Trio. They performed all over from New York to Reno and Las Vegas sharing the stage with Liberace and The Ames

Brothers.

At Radio City Music Hall, Max Wirz attended the Swiss Echoes show starring The Smeed Trio and a cast of 35. The entire show consisted of some of Europe's greatest acts of 1959. They remained in the United States eight years before returning to Swit-

Kurt Mettler of Radio Eviva Switzerland, Willy Schmid - Clarinetist of The Smeed Trio and Max Wirz

zerland.

Willy formed his own swing orchestra after studying at the Conservatory of Zurich. After retaining an official American Musicians Union card, he was able to perform with his orchestra at places like the New York Plaza in the 90s when he returned to the U.S. Today, Willy Schmid plays for special events with his own orchestra including public appearances in Gstaad and Zurich.

Willy: "First I am a musician, pianist and clarinetist, then singer, then composer and arranger. I practice piano daily. I pick on heavy pieces by Bach or Debussy. I also practice clarinet. These practice sessions keep my

A Young Smeed Trio - Claire, Willy and Werner with Swiss Band Leader Teddy Stauffer

spirit and fingers fit. From time to time, I perform with friends in Swing and Jazz combos and we swing it up for our jazz friends.

Kurt Felix is a remarkable personality born in 1941 and raised in Switzerland. He began his career at age 20 as a freelance radio journalist for Swiss National Radio. His career blossomed eventually bringing to him the highest possible honors, including Germany's Bambi Entertainment Award.

Although retired for years, Kurt continues to support the cause of

Big Band music in his newspaper columns as well as appearances on talk shows in Switzerland and Germany, to which he is often accompanied by his charming wife, former singer, Paola.

Kurt Brogli

Kurt Brogli began his musical life very early- since kindergarten. He studied piano, trumpet, singing and conducting, winding up at the Zurich Music Conservatory. In his teaching, he became the Village Maestro, being responsible for forty music teachers and hundreds of students. He found his way into Swiss Radio and over the years became the producer of Swiss Folk and Band Music, where he remains today. With over 70 musicians in the Swiss Band (The Concert Band of Swiss International Airlines), that was recently named "Ambassadors of Big Band Music" by the Big Band Hall of Fame in West Palm Beach, Florida, along with its conductor, participates in Music Festivals and European Band Music Festivals and carries our kind of music forward, including the future establishment of a Big Band Festival in Dietikon, near Zurich.

Roal Pietra

Roal grew up on the Rhine between Switzerland and Germany and in 1944 played clarinet and then trumpet in the local marching band. He played Glenn Miller material is his first big band job and in 1976 formed a Big Band with Fredy Banninger, a trombone player, and Walter Weber, on clarinet and alto sax. The band still exists today. They perform about six concerts a year, including private and public engagements, according to Weber. The band consists of members old and young-that is-19-68. David Regan is an American musician who moved to Switzerland in 1991 and became the rehearsal leader of the RP Roal Pietra Big Band. David believes a renaissance is going on as we go to press. Classic arrangements are part of total picture. American swing and jazz has a permanent hold on the music loving citizens of Switzerland and the rest of Europe.

Jonny Cooper

We must pay tribute here to Jonny Cooper' Orchestra from Cape Town, South Africa whose organization plays music from Glenn Miller to all the Big Bands. It is a major musical force in South Africa. Formed in 1993 they have performed at many major events and have signed with Prestige-Elite records in London. The band recreates the music of Glenn Miller where tourists can enjoy the music no matter where they come from. The band moves its equipment from venue to venue by truck and coordinates with band members at airports and hotels as required. Sometimes, according to Jonny, they perform to enthusiastic crowds of over 5000 people. "It's amazing," he says. Jonny's orchestra plays the Miller book and some things of his own.

Bernhard "Schugi" Schoch

Bernhard Schoch is a fine musician involved in television and plays lead trumpet in the Zurich Jazz Orchestra and the Picason Salsa Band.

He has performed with people from Clark Terry to Natalie Cole. The Big Band Connection was founded in 2000 with 17 chairs, plays at festivals, cultural events and every other form of get-togethers. The band encourages "lindy-hop" dance music for the younger audiences and dance clubs. "We cover a wide range of music, from Basie to Goodman to Miller," Schugi said.

The Zurich Jazz Orchestra plays serious music with highly trained musicians, and the Big Band Connection is composed of mostly amateurs, but good ones, who have other professions but who loves the music.

"Enthusiastic musicians of every age find common grounds to share, respect and pay homage to the traditions of the past that upholds and preserves treasures of the Swing Era," says Schugi.

BIG BAND PUBLICATIONS

Bing, The International Crosby Circle
3 Osborne Close, Wilmslow, Cheshire SK9 2EE UK

Big Bands International Magazine
2000 Richard Drive, Broomall, PA 19008

Big Band Jump Newsletter
Box 52252, Atlanta, GA 30355

Downbeat Magazine
102 N. Haven Road, Elmhurst, IL 60126

Friends of Dick Haymes Society Newsletter
c/o Roger Dooner, 2951 Tyler Street N.E., Minn, MN 55418

In Tune International
Flat 9, Milchester House, 12 Stevely Road, Eastbourne, East Sussex BN 20 7 JX

International Association of Jazz Records Collectors
Sterling Heights, MIchigan

International Sinatra Society Magazine
Box 7176, Lakeland, Florida 33807

Jazz Rag
Subscriptions, PO Box 944, Birmingham. B16 8ut, England

Joslin's Jazz Journal
Box 213, Parsons, Kansas 67357

Memory Lane
Essex, England, SS9 3UH Since 1968

Dancing USA
10600 University Avenue, Minn. MN 55448

L.A. Jazz Scene, N. Hollywood, Ca 91607

The Mississippi Rag
9448 Lyndale, MN 55420

Sheet Music Magazine
12 Depot Plaza, Bedford Hills, NY 10507

Jolson Journal
419 Glenwood Drive, Douglassville, Pa. 19518

American Rag
20137 Skyline Ranch Drive, Apple Valley, CA 92038

The Glenn Miller Birthplace Society
122 West Garfield, Clarinda, Iowa 51632

IN TUNE
INTERNATIONAL

THE ONLY MONTHLY MAGAZINE IN THE WORLD FOR LOVERS OF THE GOLDEN AGE OF POPULAR MUSIC NOW IN OUR TWENTY FIRST YEAR!

RHONDA FLEMING INTERVIEW
SAUTER-FINEGAN - BRITISH HIT PARADE 1957
STATESIDE - CD REVIEWS AND MUCH MORE

No 195   **MAY 2008**

WHAT'S IN A NAME
Nom de Plume
(Pen Name)

Tony Bennett	Anthony Dominick Benedetto
Will Bradley	Wilbur Schwichtenberg
Pat Boone	Charles Eugene Boone
Betty Carter	Lillie Mae Jones
June Christy	Shirley Luster
Buddy Clark	Samuel Goldberg
Russ Columbo	Ruggiero de Rudolpho
Pierino Como	Perry Como
Don Cornell	Luigi Francesco Varlaro
Bing Crosby	Harry Lillis Crosby
Vic Damone	Vito Farinola
Dolly Dawn	Teresa Marie Stabile
Helen Forrest	Helen Fogel
Glen Gray	Glen Gray Knoblaugh
Connie Haines	Yvonne Marie Ja Mais
Billie Holiday	Eleanora Fagan
Al Jolson	Asa Yoelson
Frankie Laine	Francesco Paolo Lo Vecchio
Steve Lawrence	Sidney Liebowitz
Peggy Lee	Norma Deloris Ekstrom
Abbey Lincoln	Anna Mildred Woolridge
Tony Martin	Alvin Morris

Dean Martin	Dino Crocetti
Al Martino	Alfred Cino
Giselle McKenzie	Marie Le Fleche
Glenn Miller	Alton Miller
Red Norvo	Kenneth Norville
Anita O'Day	Anita Colton
Sy Oliver	Melvin James Oliver
Patti Page	Clara Ann Fowler
Alvino Rey	Calvin McBurney
Lynn Roberts	Leonore Theresa Raisig
Artie Shaw	Abraham Arthur Arshawsky
Dinah Shore	Fanny Rose Shore
Francis Albert Sinatra	Frank Sinatra
Muggsy Spanier	Francis Spanier
Jerry Vale	Genaro Vitaliano
Dinah Washington	Ruth Lee Jones
Andy Williams	Howard Andrew Williams
Joe Williams	Joseph Goreed

BIBLIOGRAPHY

BEST BOOKS OF THE BIG BANDS

Balliett, Whitney. *American Singers*. New York, New York: Oxford University Press. 1988

Barnet, Charlie, with Stanley Dance. *Those Swinging Years*. New York,New York: Da Capo Press.1992

Crow, Bill, *Jazz Anecdotes*. New York, New York: Oxford Press.

Danca, Vince. *The 1984 Complete Jazz Calendar*. Rockford, Illinois: 1983

Forrest, Helen. *I Had the Craziest Dream*. New York, New York: Coward, McCann & Geoghegan, Inc.

Friedwald, Will. *Jazz Singing*. New York, New York: Collier Books, Macmillan Publishing Company 1990

Grudens, Richard, *The Best Damn Trumpet Player*. Stonybrook, New York: Celebrity Profiles Publishing 1996

Grudens, Richard, *The Song Stars*. Stonybrook, New York: Celebrity Profiles Publishing. 1997

Grudens, Richard, *Jukebox Saturday Night*. Stonybrook, New York: Celebrity Profiles Publishing. 1998

Grudens, Richard, *Chattanooga Choo Choo*. Stonybrook, New York: Celebrity Profiles Publishing. 2004

Hall, Fred. *Dialogues in Swing*. Ventura, California: Pathfinder Publishing. 1989

Hall, Fred. *More Dialogues in Swing*. Ventura, California: Pathfinder Publishing. 1991

Haskins, Jim. *The Cotton Club*. New York, New York: Hippocrene Books. 1977

Jenkins, Bruce. *Goodbye: In Search of Gordon Jenkins*. Berkerley, California: Frog Ltd. 2005

Kennedy, Don, Hagan Williams, Hank Morgan, *Big Band Jump Newsletter*, Atlanta, Georgia: Crawford Houston Group Inc. 1989 through 2007

Lax, Roger & Smith, Frederick. *The Great Song Thesaurus*. New York, New York: Oxford University Press. 1984

Lee, William F., *American Big Bands*. Milwaukee, Wisconsin: Hal Leonard Corp. 2005

Lees, Gene. *Waiting for Dizzy*. New York, New York: Oxford University Press. 1991

Levinson, Peter J. *September in the Rain*, New York, New York: Billboard Books. 2991

Levinson, Peter, J. *Tommy Dorsey*. Cambridge, Mass: Da Capo Press 2005

Nightingale Gordon. *WNEW Where the Melody Lingers On*: New York, New York Nightingale Gordon, 1982

Rust, Brian. *The Complete Entertainment Discography* 1890-1942. New Rochelle, New York: Arlington House. 1973

Sanford, Herb. *Tommy and Jimmy -The Dorsey Years*. New Rochelle, New York: Arlington House. 1972

Shaw, Arnold. *The Street That Never Slept*. New York, New York. Coward, McCann & Geoghegan. 1971

Simon, George, *The Big Bands*. New York, New York: The MacMillan Company 1967

Studwell, William E., and Mark Baldin. *The Big Band Reader*. Binghampton, New York: The Haworth Press, Inc. 2000

Walker, Leo, *The Big Band Almanac*. Hollywood, California: Vinewood Enterprises. 1978

Walker, Leo, *The Wonderful Era of the Great Dance Bands* . Berkeley, California: Howell-North Books. 1964 : Republication Da Capo Press. New York, New York: 1990

ABOUT THE AUTHOR

Richard Grudens of St. James, New York, was initially influenced by Pulitzer Prize dramatist Robert Anderson; New York Herald Tribune columnist Will Cuppy; and detective/mystery novelist Dashiell Hammett, all whom he knew in his early years. Grudens worked his way up from studio page in NBC's studios in New York to news writer for radio news programs, the Bob and Ray Show and the Today Show.

Feature writing for Long Island PM Magazine (1980-86) led to his first book, The Best Damn Trumpet Player - Memories of the Big Band Era. He has written over 100 magazine articles on diverse subjects from interviews with legendary cowboy Gene Autry in Wild West Magazine in 1995 to a treatise on the Beach Boys in the California Highway Patrol Magazine, and countless articles on Bing Crosby, Bob Hope, including a major Hope cover article covering Hope's famous wartime USO tours published in World War II Magazine. He has written extensively about Henry Ford, VE Day, Motorcycle Helmet Safety, DNA History, among other subjects.

His other books include The Song Stars-1997, The Music Men-1998, Jukebox Saturday Night - 1999, Snootie Little Cutie - The Connie Haines Story- 2000, Jerry Vale - A Singer's Life-2001, The Spirit of Bob Hope-2002, Bing Crosby-Crooner of the Çentury - 2003 (which won the Benjamin Franklin Award for Biography-Publishers Marketing Association),and Chattanooga Choo Choo - The Life and Times of the World Famous Glenn Miller Orchestra-2004, The Italian Crooners Bed-side Companion in 2005 and When Jolson was King in 2006.

Commenting about the book Jukebox Saturday Night in 1999, Kathryn (Mrs. Bing) Crosby wrote: "Richard Grudens is the musical historian of our time. Without him, the magic would be lost forever. We all owe him a debt that we can never repay."

Richard Grudens, and his wife Madeline, reside in St. James, New York.

Acknowledgements

This book is filled with lots of information gathered from lists and information accumulated by myself and others. A book or bible of this scale can not be accomplished by any one person, no matter whose name appears as author.

First, my appreciation goes to the most gracious and talented Kathryn Crosby, and the true icon of music, the late Frankie Laine. Kathryn passionately circumvents the earth to tell the story of her wonderful husband, Bing Crosby, so the world will continue to remember his great career and contributions to the formation of almost all future vocalists of the Big Band Era and beyond. Bing led the way. Everyone else followed. Frankie Laine was one of a kind. An accomplished performer, recording artist and mentor, I will always be grateful to him and will never forget his unselfish contributions to my works and the wonderful recordings he gave the world. God bless him.

My personal appreciation and thanks go to legendary Patty Andrews, Jerry and Rita Vale, Connie Haines, Doris Day, Larry O'Brien, Margaret Whiting, Ann Jillian, Joe Franklin, Tony B. Babino, Max Wirz, and the late Les Brown, Artie Shaw and William B. Williams, whose consistent and direct assistance helped this book come to fruition.

Professionally, I acknowledge the help of counterparts Anthony DiFlorio III, Jack Ellsworth, Al Monroe, John Tumpak, Jack Lebo, the late Jerry Fletcher, Camille Smith, Joe Pardee, and Gus Young. Appreciation also goes to the great Ervin Drake, songwriter and producer, for his contribution.

Personally, I thank Ben Grisafi, my son Robert Grudens, long time friends Bob Incagliato and Jerry Castleman (both who doubled as Jerry Vale's chauffeur when needed), who also helped with Jerry Vale's and Kathryn Crosby's appearances.

And, to Madeline Grudens, my wonderful wife and companion. It is she who designs, formats, edits, provides photo magic, and shares in every aspect of the production of this project.

Thank you all.

We are grateful to:

Madeline Grudens

Robert Grudens

Ben Grisafi

Bob Incagliato

Jack Ellsworth

Max Wirz

Jerry Castleman

Al Monroe

Jack Lebo

Camille Smith

Order Online at:

www.RichardGrudens.com

You can also find us at www.Amazon.com

Additional Titles by Richard Grudens

Explore the Golden Age of Music when the Big Bands and their vocalists reigned on the radio and all the great stages of America.

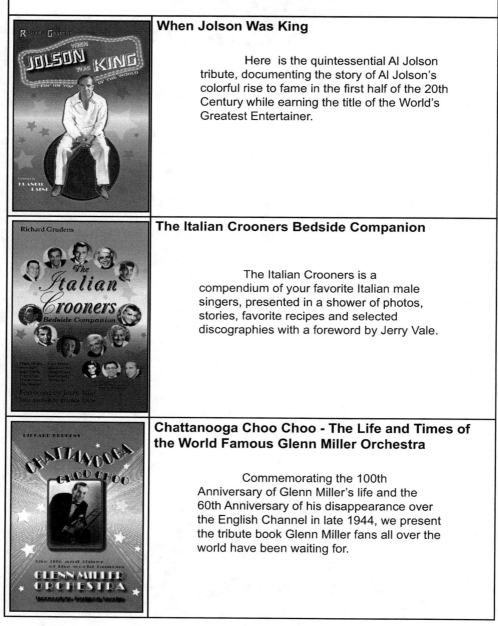

When Jolson Was King

Here is the quintessential Al Jolson tribute, documenting the story of Al Jolson's colorful rise to fame in the first half of the 20th Century while earning the title of the World's Greatest Entertainer.

The Italian Crooners Bedside Companion

The Italian Crooners is a compendium of your favorite Italian male singers, presented in a shower of photos, stories, favorite recipes and selected discographies with a foreword by Jerry Vale.

Chattanooga Choo Choo - The Life and Times of the World Famous Glenn Miller Orchestra

Commemorating the 100th Anniversary of Glenn Miller's life and the 60th Anniversary of his disappearance over the English Channel in late 1944, we present the tribute book Glenn Miller fans all over the world have been waiting for.

Bing Crosby - Crooner of the Century

Here is the quintessential Bing Crosby tribute, documenting the story of Crosby's colorful life, family, recordings, radio and television shows, and films; the amazing success story of a wondrous career that pioneered popular music spanning generations and inspiring countless followers.

The Spirit of Bob Hope:

Tracing Bob's charmed life from his early days in Cleveland to his worldwide fame earned in vaudeville, radio, television and films and his famous wartime travels for the USO unselfishly entertaining our troops. The best Bob Hope book with testimonials from his friends and a foreword by Jane Russell.

Jerry Vale - A Singer's Life

The wondrous story of Jerry's life as a kid from teeming Bronx streets of the 1940s to his legendary appearances in the great theatrical venues of America and his three triumphant Carnegie Hall concerts, with appearances at New York's Copacabana, whose magnificent voice has beautifully interpreted the 20th Century's most beautiful love songs.

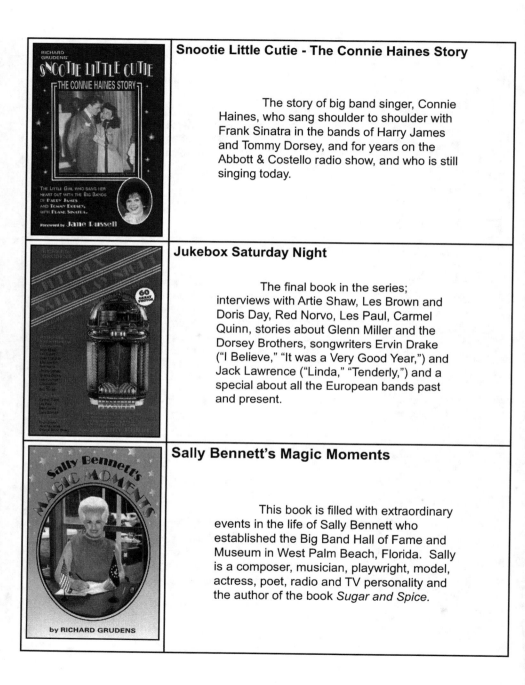

Snootie Little Cutie - The Connie Haines Story

The story of big band singer, Connie Haines, who sang shoulder to shoulder with Frank Sinatra in the bands of Harry James and Tommy Dorsey, and for years on the Abbott & Costello radio show, and who is still singing today.

Jukebox Saturday Night

The final book in the series; interviews with Artie Shaw, Les Brown and Doris Day, Red Norvo, Les Paul, Carmel Quinn, stories about Glenn Miller and the Dorsey Brothers, songwriters Ervin Drake ("I Believe," "It was a Very Good Year,") and Jack Lawrence ("Linda," "Tenderly,") and a special about all the European bands past and present.

Sally Bennett's Magic Moments

This book is filled with extraordinary events in the life of Sally Bennett who established the Big Band Hall of Fame and Museum in West Palm Beach, Florida. Sally is a composer, musician, playwright, model, actress, poet, radio and TV personality and the author of the book *Sugar and Spice.*

The Music Men

A Companion to "The Song Stars," about the great men singers with foreword by Bob Hope; interviews with Tony Martin, Don Cornell, Julius LaRosa, Jerry Vale, Joe Williams, Johnny Mathis, Al Martino, Guy Mitchell, Tex Beneke and others.

The Song Stars

A neat book about all the girl singers of the Big Band Era and beyond: Doris Day, Helen Forrest, Kitty Kallen, Rosemary Clooney, Jo Stafford, Connie Haines, Teresa Brewer, Patti Page and Helen O'Connell and many more.

The Best Damn Trumpet Player

Memories of the Big Band Era, interviews with Benny Goodman, Harry James, Woody Herman, Tony Bennett, Buddy Rich, Sarah Vaughan, Lionel Hampton, Frankie Laine, Patty Andrews and others.

Order Books On-line at:
www.RichardGrudens.com
Or Fax or Call Your Order in:
Celebrity Profiles Publishing
Div. Edison & Kellogg
Box 344, Stonybrook, New York 11790
Phone: (631) 862-8555 — Fax: (631) 862-0139
Email: celebpro4@aol.com

Title	Price	Qty:
The Best Damn Trumpet Player	$15.95	
The Song Stars	$17.95	
The Music Men	$17.95	
Jukebox Saturday Night	$17.95	
Magic Moments - The Sally Bennett Story	$17.95	
Snootie Little Cutie - The Connie Haines Story	$17.95	
Jerry Vale - A Singer's Life	$19.95	
The Spirit of Bob Hope - One Hundred Years - One Million Laughs	$19.95	
Bing Crosby - Crooner of the Century **Winner of the Benjamin Franklin Award 2004**	$19.95	
Chattanooga Choo Choo The Life and Times of the World Famous Glenn Miller Orchestra	$21.95	
The Italian Crooners Bedside Companion	$21.95	
When Jolson Was King	$25.00	
Star Dust - The Bible of the Big Bands	$35.00	
TOTALS		
SHIPPING IS FREE (Unless you require Priority Mail. Please include $4.00 for Priority Mail (2 days arrival time) for up to 2 books. Order will be shipped immediately. Add $5.00 Shipping Outside the U.S.		

Name:		
Address:		
City:	State:	Zip:
Country:		
FOR CREDIT CARDS, Please fill out below form completely:		
Credit Card #:		
Exp. Date:		
Signature:		
Card Type (Please Circle): Visa — Amex — Discover — Master Card		